Student Workbook for use with

Medical Assisting
Administrative and Clinical Procedures Including Anatomy and Physiology
Fourth Edition

Kathryn A. Booth RN, RMA (AMT), RPT, CPhT, MS
Total Care Programming, Inc.

Leesa G. Whicker, BA, CMA (AAMA)
Central Piedmont Community College

Terri D. Wyman, CPC, CMRS
Wing Memorial Hospital

Sandra Moaney-Wright, M.Ed.
Atlanta Medical Academy

Mc
Graw
Hill

Connect
Learn
Succeed™

Student Workbook for use with
MEDICAL ASSISTING: ADMINISTRATIVE AND CLINICAL PROCEDURES WITH ANATOMY
AND PHYSIOLOGY, FOURTH EDITION
Kathryn A. Booth, Leesa G. Whicker, Terri D. Wyman, and Sandra Moaney Wright

Published by McGraw-Hill, a business unit of The McGraw-Hill Companies, Inc., 1221 Avenue of the
Americas, New York, NY 10020. Copyright © 2011 by The McGraw-Hill Companies, Inc.

All rights reserved. Previous editions © 1999, 2005, and 2009.

1 2 3 4 5 6 7 8 9 0 WDQ/WDQ 1 0 9 8 7 6 5 4 3 2 1 0

ISBN 978-0-07-734009-4
MHID 0-07-734009-4

Contents

Procedures

v

Preface

The *Student Workbook* provides you with an opportunity to review and master the concepts and skills introduced in your student textbook, *Medical Assisting: Administrative and Clinical Procedures Including Anatomy and Physiology*, Fourth Edition. Chapter by chapter, the workbook provides the following:

Vocabulary Review, which tests your knowledge of key terms introduced in the chapter. Formats for these exercises include Matching, True or False, and Passage Completion.

Content Review, which tests your knowledge of key concepts introduced in the chapter. Formats for these exercises include Multiple Choice, Sentence Completion, and Short Answer.

Critical Thinking, which tests your understanding of key concepts introduced in the chapter. These questions require you to use higher-level thinking skills, such as comprehension, analysis, synthesis, and evaluation.

Applications, which provide opportunities to apply the concepts and skills introduced in the chapter. For example, using role play, you will perform such activities as developing a personal career plan and interviewing a medical specialist.

Case Studies, which provide opportunities to apply the concepts introduced in the chapter to lifelike situations you will encounter as a medical assistant. For example, you may be asked to decide how to respond to a patient who calls the doctor's office to say that she is having difficulty breathing or you may be requested to give information about the thyroid gland to a patient who has just been referred for thyroid testing.

Procedure Competency Checklists, which enable you to monitor your mastery of the steps in the procedure(s) introduced in a chapter, such as Preparing a Patient Medical Record/Chart and Performing a Surgical Scrub. Each procedure is correlated with the CAAHEP and ABHES competencies you will need to know to become a medical assistant. Answers to the material in the *Student Workbook* are found in the *Instructor's Resource Binder*.

Procedure Work Product Forms, are provided in a separate new section. These forms can be used when practicing and testing your skills. Make extra copies since you may use them more than once.

Application Activity Forms, are used to complete the application activities found in your student textbook. This new section helps tie together the learning between the textbook and workbook.

Ask your instructor for permission to check your work against these answers.

Together, your student textbook and the *Student Workbook* form a complete learning package. *Medical Assisting: Administrative and Clinical Procedures Including Anatomy and Physiology*, Fourth Edition will prepare you to enter the medical assisting field with the knowledge and skills necessary to become a useful resource to patients and a valued asset to employers and to the medical assisting profession.

Medical Assisting Reviewers

In addition, many people and organizations provided invaluable assistance in the process of illustrating the highly technical and detailed topics covered in the text. Their contributions helped ensure the accuracy, timelines, and authenticity of the illustrations in the book.

We would like to thank the following organizations for providing source materials and technical advice: the American Association of Medical Assistants, Chicago, Illinois; Becton Dickinson Microbiology Systems, Sparks, Maryland; Becton Dickinson Vacutainer® Systems, Franklin Lakes, New Jersey; Bibbero Systems, Petaluma, California; Burdick, Schaumberg, Illinois; the Corel Corporation, Ottawa, Ontario, Canada; Hamilton Media, Hamilton, New Jersey; Nassau Ear, Nose, and Throat, Princeton, New Jersey; Princeton Allergy and Asthma Associates, Princeton, New Jersey; Richmond International, Boca Raton, Florida; and Winfield Medical, San Diego, California.

We would like to express our appreciation to the following New Jersey physicians and medical facilities for allowing us to photograph a variety of procedures and procedural settings at their facilities: the Eric B. Chandler Medical Center, New Brunswick; Helene Fuld School of Nursing of New Jersey, Trenton; Mercer Medical Center, Trenton; Mercer County Vocational-Technical Health Occupations Center, Trenton; Plainfield Health Center, Plainfield; Princeton Allergy and Asthma Associates, Princeton; the Princeton Medical Group, Princeton; Robert Wood Johnson University Hospital, New Brunswick; Robert Wood Johnson University Hospital at Hamilton, Hamilton; St. Francis Medical Center, Trenton; St. Peters Medical Center, New Brunswick; Dr. Edward von der Schmidt, neurosurgeon, Princeton; Wound Care Center/Curative Network, New Brunswick.

We would also like to thank the following facilities and educational institutions for graciously allowing us to photograph procedures and other technical aspects related to the profession of medical assisting: Total Care Programming, Palm Coast, Florida; Wildwood Medical Clinic, Henrico, North Carolina; Central Piedmont Community College, Charlotte, North Carolina; Daytona Beach Community College, Daytona Beach, Florida; Roanoke Rapids Clinic, Roanoke Rapids, Virginia; and Everest University, Jacksonville, Florida.

Thanks also to Lynn Egler and Susan Findley for their assistance with various aspects of the project. A special thank you to Tiffany Heath for her content review.

Reviewers

Every area of the text was reviewed by practitioners and educators in the field. Their insights helped shape the direction of the book.

Medical Advisory Board

Gerry A. Brasin, AS, CMA (AAMA), CPC
Premier Education Group

Dr. Marina Klebanov, BDS, MSPH
Mandl College of Allied Health

Tabitha L Lyons, NCMA, AS
Corporate Program Manager–Medical Assisting
Anthem Education Group

Barry Newman, MD
PC Tech

Diane Peavy
Fortis Colleges

Adrienne Predko, M.A. Ed.
National Director of Education
MedVance Institute

Dr. Gary Zuckerman
Washington University School of Medicine

Connect Contributors

Dolly R. Horton, CMA(AAMA), BS, M.Ed.
Asheville Buncombe Technical Community College

Sepanta Jalali, M.D.
Columbus State

Merideth Sellars, M.S.
Columbus State Community College

Sherry Stanfield, RN, BSN, MSHPE
Miller-Motte Technical College

Nerissa Tucker, MHA, CPC
Kaplan University School of Health Sciences

Dr. Wendy Vermillion, DVM
Columbus State Community College

Mindy Wray, BS, CMA(AAMA), RMA
ECPI College of Technology

Byron Hamilton, BA, MA
Australian College of Advanced Education

Digital Symposium Attendees

Courtney M. Conrad, MBA, MPH, CMA
Robert Morris University Illinois

Bonnie J. Crist, BS, CMA, AAS (AAMA)
Harrison College

Patrick J. Debold
Vice President of Academic Affairs
Concorde Career Colleges, Inc.

Robert Delaney
Chair, Allied Health
Brookline College

Alice Macomber, RN, RMA, AHI, RPT, CPI, BXO
Keiser University, Port Saint Lucie Campus

Barry Newman, MD
PC Tech

Kathleen Olewinski, MS, RHIA, NHA, FACHE
Medical Assisting Program Director
Bryant & Stratton College - Milwaukee Market

Mickie Roy, LPN, CCMA
Delta College of Arts & Technology

Lisa M. Smith, B.S., RMA(AMT), BXMO
Medical Assisting Program & Externship Coordinator
Keiser University

Michael Weinand
Kaplan Higher Education

Dr. Barbara Worley, DPM, BS, RMA
Program Manager, Medical Assisting
King's College

Patti Zint, M.A., N.C.H.I.
Apollo College

Reviewers

Hooshiyar Ahmadi, MD, DC
Remington College

Diana Alagna, RN, RMA (AMT)
Branford Hall Career Institute

Yvonne Beth Alles, MBA
Davenport University

Ramona Atiles, LPN
Allied Health Program Chair
Career Institute of Health and Technology

Vanessa J. Austin, RMA (AMT), CAHI, BS
Clarian Health Sciences Education Center

Dr. Joseph H. Balatbat, MD
Sanford-Brown Institute

Katie Barton, BA, LPN
Savannah River College

Suzanne Bitters, RMA (AMT)-NCPT/ NCICS
Harris Business School

Alecia C. Blake, MD
Medical Careers Institute at ECPI College of Technology

Kathleen Bode, MS
Flint Hills Technical College

Cynthia Boles, CMA (AAMA)
Bradford School

Cindi Brassington, MS, CMA (AAMA)
Quinebaug Valley Community College

Robin K. Choate, LPN, CHI
Pennsylvania Institute of Technology

Stephen M. Coleman, NCMA
Central Florida Institute

Sheronda Cooper, BSD, BSN, MSFN, RMA (AMT), NRCPT(NAHP)
Director of Medical Assisting
Bradford School of Business

Janet H. Davis, BSN, MS, MBA, PhD
Robert Morris College

Linda Demain, LPN, BS, MS
Wichita Technical Institute

Carol Dew, MAT, CMA-AC (AAMA)
Baker College

CHAPTER 1

The Profession of Medical Assisting

REVIEW

Vocabulary Review

True or False

Decide whether each statement is true or false. In the space at the left, write T *for true or* F *for false. On the lines provided, rewrite the false statements to make them true.*

_____ 1. A practitioner is someone who practices a profession.

_____

_____ 2. The American Association of Medical Assistants works to raise standards of medical assisting to a professional level.

_____

_____ 3. You do not need to pass the American Medical Technologists certification examination to qualify as a Registered Medical Assistant (RMA).

_____

_____ 4. A Certified Medical Assistant [CMA (AAMA)] credential is automatically renewed.

_____

_____ 5. Accreditation is the process by which programs are officially authorized.

_____

_____ 6. Externships are voluntary in accredited schools.

_____

_____ 7. When a medical assistant is able to perform many duties in the office, the medical assistant is considered to be cross-trained.

_____

_____ 8. The Medical Assistant Occupational Analysis provides the basis for education and evaluation in the medical assistant field.

_____

Content Review

Multiple Choice

In the space provided, write the letter of the choice that best completes each statement or answers each question.

_____ 1. To receive certification or registration as a medical assistant, you must
   A. graduate from an approved program with a bachelor's degree in medical assisting.
   B. become a member of the American Association of Medical Assistants (AAMA) or American Medical Technologists (AMT).
   C. graduate from an approved medical assistant program and pass the AAMA or AMT examination.
   D. pass the AAMA or AMT examination.
   E. become a multiskilled professional.

_____ 2. Formal training programs in medical assisting
   A. are offered only at 2-year colleges.
   B. can be replaced by on-the-job training.
   C. must be approved by the AAMA or AMT.
   D. last 9 months to 2 years and award a certificate, diploma, or associate degree.

_____ 3. Being able to change your schedule and meet your employer's needs is considered
   A. self-motivation.
   B. flexibility.
   C. attitude.
   D. willingness to learn.
   E. being multiskilled.

_____ 4. The definition of diplomacy is
   A. taking a stand about your beliefs and morals.
   B. a positive attitude.
   C. holding yourself to high standards.
   D. being able to communicate without offending anyone.

_____ 5. A person with integrity
   A. maintains high standards.
   B. is honest and dependable.
   C. is reliable.
   D. is all of the above.

Sentence Completion

In the space provided, write the word or phrase that best completes each sentence.

6. Medical assisting is a(n) _____ allied health profession because practitioners can handle many different duties.

7. Using _____ means evaluating circumstances, solving problems, and taking action.

8. _____ is the ability to put yourself in someone else's shoes.

9. Effective _____ involves careful listening, observing, speaking, and writing.

10. Helping the receptionist prepare the next day's charts is an example of _____.

6. _____

7. _____

8. _____

9. _____

10. _____

11. It is important that a medical assistant's appearance reflects a _____.

12. Medical assistants should always conduct themselves in a _____.

13. Reporting a mistake to a physician is an example of _____.

14. Being able to understand both sides of any situation is an example of _____.

11. _____

12. _____

13. _____

14. _____

Short Answer

Write the answer to each question on the lines provided.

15. List three administrative duties performed by a medical assistant.

_____

_____

_____

16. List three clinical duties performed by a medical assistant.

_____

_____

_____

17. List three laboratory duties performed by a medical assistant.

_____

_____

_____

18. Describe ethical behavior for medical assistants.

_____

_____

_____

19. What is the scope of practice?

_____

_____

_____

20. List three areas of competence from the CAAHEP and/or ABHES list of competencies.

_____

_____

_____

21. To ensure HIPAA compliance, what is the best way to dispose of paper in the medical office?

_____

_____

_____

22. List three reasons why credentialing is important for a medical assistant's entry and advancement in the medical environment.

_____

_____

_____

23. Why is a good attitude important in a medical environment?

_____

_____

_____

24. What is tact?

_____

_____

_____

25. Why would body piercing affect your ability to obtain a job?

_____

_____

_____

26. Why is continuing education important for medical assistants?

_____

_____

_____

27. What is a managed care organization?

_____

_____

_____

28. What are three certification exams offered by the National Healthcare Association that medical assistants can take?

_____

_____

_____

Critical Thinking

Write the answer to each question on the lines provided.

1. Why is a medical assistant's willingness to work as a team member so important to a medical facility?

_____

_____

_____

2. How does self-motivation apply to your studies?

_____

_____

_____

3. Why would someone who does not pay attention to details be poorly suited for a career as a medical assistant?

_____

_____

_____

4. Why is your appearance so important in health care?

_____

_____

_____

5. How can you determine if your attitude is what is required of a medical assistant?

_____

_____

_____

6. Give one example of integrity in the medical office.

_____

_____

_____

APPLICATION

Follow the directions for the application.

1. **Appropriate Work Dress**

   Work with a partner to collect information on appropriate dress for work in a medical office.

   a. Collect and request a collection of uniform catalogs from the Internet. Here are two popular sites: www.Jascouniform.com and www.Allheart.com.

   b. Clip pictures of uniforms that you like and complete the "perfect" medical wardrobe.

   c. Research and find pictures of clothing and accessories that are not suitable for the medical profession.

   d. Make a collage of the two types of clothing—appropriate and inappropriate—and discuss with the class and instructor.

2. **Personal Qualifications of Medical Assistants**

   Make a list of the 17 personal qualifications of medical assistants and write a sentence or two describing how these qualifications enhance quality patient care and contribute to professional relationships with the allied health team in the medical facility. Facilitate a class discussion about your statements.

CASE STUDIES

Write your response to each case study on the lines provided.

Case 1

It is a very busy Monday and you only have one appointment slot open. One patient calls and complains of flulike symptoms and is feeling generally unwell. She would like an appointment today. A second patient calls complaining of vomiting and diarrhea and has been unable to eat for 24 hours. He would like to come in today but will wait until tomorrow. The third patient is a college student and forgot he needs a physical in order to be allowed to play basketball. He is in town for two days. An appointment today would fit in well with his schedule. Which patient should be given the appointment slot? If you cannot determine who should get the one available appointment, who should you consult regarding this decision?

_____

_____

_____

Case 2

Suppose you work as a medical assistant in a cardiologist's office. In your spare time, you read about new advances in heart medications. Even though only the doctor can prescribe medications, how might this knowledge help you in your job?

_____

_____

_____

Case 3

You are involved in a group interview. The medical assistant that you are interviewing is credentialed and has a lot of good experience. She seems pleasant, but you notice that she has a "Right to Life" tattoo on her forearm, a tongue ring, and facial piercings. How do you think your elderly patients and female patients will perceive her? How might the physician perceive her?

_____

_____

_____

Case 4

You are working with another medical assistant and you notice that she is recording vital statistics in the chart but is not actually taking measurements. What should you do? How does ethical behavior apply here?

_____

_____

_____

CHAPTER 2

Types of Medical Practice

REVIEW

Vocabulary Review

Matching

Match the key terms in the right column with the definitions in the left column by placing the letter of each correct answer in the space provided.

_____ 1. A physician who is a generalist and treats all types and ages of patients

_____ 2. A physician who diagnoses and treats diseases of the nervous system

_____ 3. A physician who specializes in the diagnosis and treatment of diseases of the heart and blood vessels

_____ 4. To assess immediate medical needs of a patient

_____ 5. A physician who specializes in treating patients with cancer

_____ 6. A physician who diagnoses and treats diseases and disorders of the muscles and bones

_____ 7. A physician who diagnoses and treats problems related to the internal organs

_____ 8. A physician who studies, diagnoses, and treats kidney disease

_____ 9. A physician who diagnoses and treats disorders of the gastrointestinal tract

_____ 10. A physician who diagnoses and treats disorders of the endocrine system

_____ 11. A physician who studies disease and the changes it produces in the cells, fluids, and processes of the entire body

_____ 12. A physician who diagnoses and treats diseases of the kidney, bladder, and urinary system

_____ 13. A physician who provides routine physical care of the female reproductive system

_____ 14. A physician who performs the reconstruction, correction, or improvement of body structures

_____ 15. A specialist who diagnoses and treats diseases and disorders with physical therapy

_____ 16. A physician who uses a "whole person" approach to health care

a. cardiologist
b. endocrinologist
c. family practitioner
d. gastroenterologist
e. gynecologist
f. internist
g. nephrologist
h. neurologist
i. oncologist
j. orthopedist
k. pathologist
l. physiatrist
m. plastic surgeon
n. triage
o. urologist
p. physician assistant
q. acupuncturist
r. massage therapist
s. chiropractor
t. doctor of osteopathy

_____ **17.** A specialist who treats patients who are ill or in pain without using drugs or surgery

_____ **18.** A specialist who uses pressure, kneading, stroking, vibration, and tapping to promote muscle and full-body relaxation

_____ **19.** A specialist who uses a Chinese theory based on beliefs of how the body works

_____ **20.** A health-care provider who practices medicine under the supervision of a physician

True or False

Decide whether each statement is true or false. In the space at the left, write T *for true or* F *for false. On the lines provided, rewrite the false statements to make them true.*

_____ **21.** An endocrinologist diagnoses and treats physical reactions to substances such as dust and pollen.

_____

_____ **22.** An otorhinolaryngologist diagnoses and treats illnesses of the ear, nose, and throat.

_____

_____ **23.** A neurologist uses medical instruments to correct deformities and treat external and internal injuries or disease.

_____

_____ **24.** A nephrologist uses medications to cause patients to lose sensation during surgery.

_____

_____ **25.** A doctor of osteopathy holds the title DO and focuses attention on the musculoskeletal system as it relates to the body as a whole.

_____

_____ **26.** A gynecologist specializes in the treatment of problems and diseases of older adults.

_____

_____ **27.** A gastroenterologist specializes in the diagnosis and treatment of diseases of the skin, hair, and nails.

_____

_____ **28.** A pediatrician diagnoses and treats childhood diseases.

_____

_____ **29.** A physiatrist specializes in taking and reading x-rays.

_____

_____ **30.** A typical treatment plan for a chiropractor involves exercise programs, manual treatments, and anti-inflammatory medications.

_____

_____ **31.** Massage therapists use techniques that increase circulation, remove waste products from injured tissues, and bring fresh blood and nutrients to areas of the body to speed healing.

_____

_____ **32.** Physician assistants are qualified to diagnose medical problems, order lab tests, and carry out treatment plans.

_____

Content Review

Multiple Choice

In the space provided, write the letter of the choice that best completes each statement or answers each question.

_____ 1. A physician who wishes to specialize in a particular branch of medicine
    A. must complete 1 additional year of residency in that specialty.
    B. must complete an additional 2 to 6 years of residency in that specialty.
    C. must complete a bachelor's degree in that specialty.
    D. may do so without any additional education.

_____ 2. Radiology is the branch of medical science that
    A. is a subspecialty of neurology.
    B. uses x-rays and radioactive substances to diagnose and treat disease.
    C. provides the scientific foundation for all medical practice.
    D. studies and records the electrical activity of the brain.
    E. introduces a small amount of radioactive substance into the body.

_____ 3. A professional who has studied the chemical and physical qualities of drugs and dispenses such medication to the public is a
    A. nurse practitioner.
    B. pharmacy technician.
    C. medical technologist.
    D. pharmacist.

_____ 4. Which of the following takes health histories, performs physical exams, conducts screening tests, and educates patients and families about disease prevention?
    A. Occupational therapist
    B. Associate degree nurse
    C. Independent nurse practitioner
    D. Licensed practical nurse
    E. Clinical laboratory technician

_____ 5. A health-care professional who works under the direction of a physician and manages medical emergencies that occur away from the medical setting is a(n)
    A. emergency medical technician.
    B. surgeon's assistant.
    C. radiation therapy technologist.
    D. pathologist's assistant.

Sentence Completion

In the space provided, write the word or phrase that best completes each sentence.

6. A physician who is a generalist and treats all types of patients is referred to as a(n) _____ by insurance companies.

7. Using therapy with electricity, heat, cold, ultrasound, massage, and exercise, a(n) _____ helps restore physical function and relieve pain following disease or injury.

8. _____ are allied health professionals trained to draw blood for diagnostic laboratory testing.

6. _____

7. _____

8. _____

9. A(n) _____ works with emotionally disturbed and mentally challenged patients and assists the psychiatric team.

10. A(n) _____ translates a physician's directions about patient treatments into comprehensive, typed records.

11. While transferring patients to the hospital, a(n) _____ records, documents, and radios the patient's condition to the physician, describing how the injury occurred.

12. One medical assistant specialty, that of the _____, involves assisting the pediatrician in administrative and clinical duties.

13. Working under the supervision of a physician and a respiratory therapist, a(n) _____ performs procedures such as artificial ventilation.

14. Working under the supervision of a medical technologist, a certified _____ performs routine procedures in bacteriology, chemistry, hematology, parasitology, serology, and urinalysis.

15. Membership in a(n) _____, such as the American Medical Technologists, enables one to get involved in relevant issues and activities.

16. A(n) _____ introduces a small amount of radioactive substance into the body and forms an image by detecting radiation as it leaves the body.

9. _____

10. _____

11. _____

12. _____

13. _____

14. _____

15. _____

16. _____

Short Answer

Write the answer to each question on the lines provided.

17. What is the purpose of a residency?

_____

_____

_____

18. When might a family practitioner send a patient to a specialist?

_____

_____

_____

19. What is the difference between a gynecologist and an obstetrician/gynecologist?

_____

_____

_____

20. What is the difference between an ophthalmologist and an optometrist?

_____

_____

_____

21. Discuss the differences in the training and job duties of an LPN and a medical assistant.

_____

_____

_____

22. What are three duties of a medical administrative assistant?

_____

_____

_____

23. In what types of settings can phlebotomists work?

_____

_____

_____

24. Explain the dfference between a licensed practical nurse (LPN) and a registered nurse (RN).

_____

_____

_____

25. What is osteopathic manipulative medicine?

_____

_____

_____

26. Describe the manual treatments and diagnostic testing that chiropractors use to treat patients.

_____

_____

_____

27. Describe the principles of acupuncture.

_____

_____

_____

28. Describe two conditions that a proctologist would treat.

_____

_____

_____

Critical Thinking

Write the answer to each question on the lines provided.

1. What are the benefits of learning about the medical specialties and subspecialties?

_____

_____

_____

2. What are the differences between medical assistants and physician assistants?

_____

_____

_____

3. Compare the education and qualifications of an MD and a DO, describing the differences in their training and approach to patient care.

_____

_____

_____

4. Discuss how a medical assistant may interact with other health-care professionals or specialists.

_____

_____

_____

5. Compare DOs and chiropractors. How are their practices different? How are they similar or the same?

_____

_____

_____

6. Why are patients referred to specialty physicians?

_____

_____

_____

APPLICATION

Follow the directions for each application.

1. Certification

Using the Internet, research the AMT, the AAMA, and the National Healthcare Association (NHA). Select two certifications that you would like to complete upon graduation. Request informational brochures and applications, and distribute them to the class.

2. Specialist Interview

As a follow-up to studying the various specialties, choose a medical specialist to interview and report on your findings.

a. Review the specialty careers described in the text. Select one.

b. Check the telephone book or other sources to find specialists in the area you chose. Write down the names and phone numbers of three to five specialists.

c. Call the offices of the specialists until you find a specialist who will grant you a 15- to 30-minute interview. Make an appointment for the interview.

d. Prepare a list of six to ten interview questions. Include questions that address the type and amount of education required, responsibilities and duties, and advantages and disadvantages of the specialty. Also include a question about what personal skills are required. Conclude by asking for advice that the specialist can offer someone interested in pursuing the specialty.

e. Dress professionally for the interview. Take your list of questions, a pen, and a pad to the interview.

f. Conduct the interview, keeping it within the time limit you promised. Thank the specialist for her time.

g. Send a thank-you note to the specialist within a week of the interview.

h. Share your findings with your classmates through a format of your choice: oral presentation, written report, or interview "question and answer" news article.

3. Medical Specialties

Research the Internet for specialties in which a medical assistant may be employed. Research the credentials needed and the experience required for the job. Then find a position within the specialty and research what duties are performed by the position and how you may gain those skills. Report your findings to the class.

CASE STUDIES

Write your response to each case study on the lines provided.

Case 1

You are currently working for an internist who treats a variety of skin conditions, such as acne, eczema, and hives. A patient presents with a small lesion that has not healed in several months. The physician requests that you submit a referral to a dermatologist. Why would this patient seek medical care from a dermatologist instead of being treated by the internist?

_____

_____

_____

Case 2

You are working in an OB/GYN practice. One of your patients confides in you that her husband is suffering from the sexual dysfunction impotence. She would like her husband to seek medical attention for his condition, but she does not know what type of medical specialty treats this condition. What type of specialist should the patient see?

_____

_____

_____

Case 3

You are working in a family practice office. A longtime patient makes an appointment for a diabetes follow-up. She weighs more than 500 pounds and is having difficulty controlling her diabetes as well as problems with general mobility. She asks you what options she has to lose the extra weight. What surgical options might be available to her? Will her insurance pay for weight-control surgery?

_____

_____

_____

Case 4

You are working as a lab assistant in a reference lab. You would like to work as a phlebotomist, but you need certification in phlebotomy as a requirement of the job. How would you research phlebotomy certification? Who should you contact?

_____

_____

_____

CHAPTER **3**

Legal and Ethical Issues in Medical Practice, Including HIPAA

REVIEW

Vocabulary Review

Passage Completion

Study the key terms in the box. Use your textbook to find definitions of terms you do not understand.

abandonment	durable power of attorney	law	negligence
agent		law of agency	subpoena
arbitration	electronic transaction record	liable	tort
bioethics	ethics	living will	treatment, payment, and operations (TPO)
breach of contract	felony	moral values	
civil law		malpractice claims	Uniform Donor Card
crime	Health Insurance Portability and Accountability Act (HIPAA)	Notice of Privacy Practices	use
disclosure			

In the space provided, complete the following passage, using some of the terms from the box. You may change the form of a term to fit the meaning of the sentence.

Medical workers must follow (1) _____ that govern the practice of medicine to prevent patients from filing (2) _____. Patients might charge (3) _____ if a medical worker does not perform an essential action or performs an improper one. A medical worker who stops care without providing an equally qualified substitute can be charged with (4) _____.

Doctors and their patients have an implied contract. A violation of that contract is a(n) (5) _____. If such a violation leads to harm, the violation is called a(n) (6) _____. Some lawsuits go to trial, whereas others are settled through (7) _____. If a case goes to trial, the people involved will receive a(an) (8) _____, requiring their presence in court.

1. _____

2. _____

3. _____

4. _____

5. _____

6. _____

7. _____

8. _____

According to the (9) _____, physicians are responsible, or (10) _____, for everything their employees do. A medical assistant is acting on the physician's behalf and is therefore a(n) (11) _____ of the physician.

Medical assistants often assist patients in completing a(n) (12) _____, which states what type of treatment the patient wishes or does not wish to receive if the patient becomes terminally ill or permanently comatose. The patient may assign a(n) (13) _____ to a person who will make medical decisions if the patient cannot. People who wish to donate one or more organs upon their death complete a legal document called a(n) (14) _____.

In addition to observing medical laws, medical workers must follow a code of (15) _____, which defines general principles of right and wrong. Medical workers may also have to deal with issues in (16) _____ when questions related to medical advances arise.

A(n) (17) _____ is an offense against the state. A(n) (18) _____ is defined as a rule of conduct. (19) _____ is considered a standard of behavior and the concept of right and wrong. (20) _____ serve as a basis for ethical conduct. Practicing medicine without a license is considered a(n) (21) _____. Crimes against the person are considered (22) _____.

HIPAA stands for (23) _____. Under HIPAA, (24) _____ limits the sharing of information within a covered entity, while (25) _____ restricts the sharing of information outside the entity holding the information. HIPAA will allow the provider to share patient information for (26) _____. The document under HIPAA that is the communication of patient rights is called (27) _____. The (28) _____ are the codes and formats used for the exchange of medical data under the HIPAA administrative simplification rule.

9. _____

10. _____

11. _____

12. _____

13. _____

14. _____

15. _____

16. _____

17. _____

18. _____

19. _____

20. _____

21. _____

22. _____

23. _____

24. _____

25. _____

26. _____

27. _____

28. _____

Content Review

Multiple Choice

In the space provided, write the letter of the choice that best completes each statement or answers each question.

_____ 1. The term *res ipsa loquitur* refers to cases in which
   A. the patient has a previously existing condition.
   B. the physician abandons the patient.
   C. the patient has already filed a lawsuit.
   D. the doctor's error was caused by faulty record keeping.
   E. the doctor's mistake is clear to everyone.

_____ 2. If a physician decides to terminate his care of a patient, the physician must
  A. tell the patient face-to-face.
  B. leave a message for the patient on the patient's answering machine.
  C. obtain the patient's consent.
  D. inform the patient's family.
  E. send the patient a certified letter.

_____ 3. Which of the following is *not* a legal procedure for medical assistants to perform?
  A. Maintaining licenses and accreditation
  B. Recruiting qualified medical assistants for the medical office
  C. Determining needs for documentation and reporting
  D. Diagnosing a condition

_____ 4. A physician's receptionist asks patients to sign in and list the reason for their visit. This receptionist is violating the patients' right to
  A. confidentiality.
  B. a second opinion.
  C. sue for malpractice.
  D. be seen by the physician in a timely manner.

_____ 5. While practicing within the context of an implied contract with a patient, the physician is obligated to do all of the following *except*
  A. use due care.
  B. provide complete information and instructions to the patient about diagnoses, options, and methods of treatment.
  C. promise the patient that he or she will recover completely.
  D. stay current regarding all technology and treatments available.

_____ 6. Crimes such as attempted burglary and disturbing the peace are examples of
  A. felonies.
  B. misdemeanors.
  C. civil law.
  D. intentional crimes.
  E. social crimes.

_____ 7. If a medical assistant gives a patient an injection after the patient refused the procedure, it could result in a charge of
  A. assault.
  B. battery.
  C. false imprisonment.
  D. *not applicable;* no charge would result because the physician ordered the procedure.

_____ 8. Preventing a patient from leaving the medical facility after administration of an allergy injection could be seen as
  A. an invasion of privacy.
  B. false imprisonment.
  C. an acceptable practice as long as it was documented in the chart.
  D. malpractice.

_____ **9.** If a patient can prove that she felt "reasonable apprehension of bodily harm," it can result in what type of charge?
    A. Defamation of character
    B. Battery
    C. Assault
    D. Negligence
    E. Slander

Sentence Completion

In the space provided, write the word or phrase that best completes each sentence.

10. Misfeasance refers to a lawful act that is done _____.

11. The four Ds of negligence are duty, derelict, _____, and damages.

12. The relationship between a doctor and a patient is called an implied _____.

13. Damaging a person's reputation by making public statements that are both false and malicious is considered _____.

14. Health-care practitioners who promise patients miracle cures or accept fees from patients while using mystical or spiritual powers to heal is considered _____.

15. A contract that is stated in written or spoken words is considered a(n) _____.

16. Torts that are committed without the intention to cause harm but are committed unreasonably or with a disregard for the consequences are _____.

17. A patient who rolls up her sleeve and offers her arm for an injection is entering into a(n) _____ contract.

18. A document that communicates patient rights under HIPAA is called _____.

10. _____

11. _____

12. _____

13. _____

14. _____

15. _____

16. _____

17. _____

18. _____

Short Answer

Write the answer to each question on the lines provided.

19. What is the difference between malfeasance and nonfeasance?

_____

_____

_____

20. List eight types of personal information that is considered individually identifiable health information under HIPAA.

_____

_____

_____

21. What types of protected health information are subject to the Privacy Rule under HIPAA?

_____

_____

_____

22. HIPAA allows the provider to share what type of patient health-care information with outside entities?

_____

_____

_____

23. List five recommendations under HIPAA to ensure chart security.

_____

_____

_____

_____

24. What are the civil penalties for HIPAA privacy violations?

_____

_____

_____

_____

25. What is authorization under HIPAA?

_____

_____

_____

26. HIPAA allows patient information to be disclosed without authorization in special circumstances. List five entities with whom or situations in which patient information can be disclosed without authorization.

_____

_____

_____

_____

27. Explain what a contract is.

_____

_____

_____

28. List and briefly define the four essential elements of a contract.

_____

_____

_____

29. List the four types of medical practice and provide an advantage of each.

_____

_____

_____

30. How can an office prevent lawsuits?

_____

_____

_____

31. What part of the medical record does the patient own and what part does the physician own?

_____

_____

_____

32. Describe the Federal False Claims Act.

_____

_____

_____

33. How can office equipment compromise confidential medical information?

_____

_____

_____

Critical Thinking

Write the answer to each question on the lines provided.

1. A medical assistant promises a terminally ill patient a cure. Whom can the patient sue, the doctor or the medical assistant? Explain.

_____

_____

_____

2. Do you think the number of bioethical issues will increase or decrease in the future? Why?

_____

_____

_____

3. A physician changes her schedule to be available from 9:00 A.M. until 3:00 P.M. Monday through Friday. Is the physician obligated to schedule evening appointments to accommodate her patients who work during her office hours?

_____

_____

_____

4. How can a medical assistant help prevent lawsuits?

_____

_____

_____

5. How can a medical office safeguard protected health information that is transmitted via fax machines, shared printers, and copiers?

_____

_____

_____

APPLICATION

Follow the directions for the application.

Writing a Letter of Withdrawal

Work with two partners. Take turns being a medical assistant, a doctor, and an evaluator. Assume that the doctor has asked the medical assistant to write a letter of withdrawal to a patient.

a. The doctor should explain to the medical assistant what the problem with the patient is and why he has decided to withdraw from the case. The medical assistant should take notes and ask questions as necessary.

b. The medical assistant should then write the letter for the doctor. She should make clear the doctor's reason for withdrawing from the case. She should also include the doctor's recommendation that the patient seek medical care from another doctor as soon as possible.

c. After the foregoing tasks have been completed, the evaluator should critique the letter, keeping in mind the following questions: Does the letter include the doctor's reason for withdrawing from the case? Does the letter include the doctor's recommendation that the patient seek medical care elsewhere? Is the letter free of spelling, punctuation, and grammatical errors? Does it follow a business letter format?

d. The medical assistant and the doctor should discuss the evaluator's comments, noting the strengths and weaknesses of the letter.

e. Exchange roles and repeat the procedure with another student as a doctor who wishes to terminate care of a patient for a different reason.

f. Exchange roles again so that each member of the team has the opportunity to role-play the medical assistant, the doctor, and the evaluator.

CASE STUDIES

Write your response to each case study on the lines provided.

Case 1

A patient has a sexually transmitted disease but does not want you or the doctor to contact any former sex partners. The doctor has asked you to handle this case. How much can you do to make sure these people are notified?

_____

_____

_____

Case 2

A doctor is about to leave on a special family vacation for two months. A new patient comes to the office with a collection of unusual symptoms that do not seem to be serious. The doctor tells the patient to make another appointment for after his return from vacation so that he can order some tests. What kind of lawsuit is the doctor risking? What should the doctor do instead?

_____

_____

_____

Case 3

You work in a large medical office with three other medical assistants. One of the other assistants discusses her patients with you during your lunch break together. What, if anything, has the medical assistant done wrong? What should you do about it?

_____

_____

_____

Case 4

As you walk through the waiting room, a crying woman stops you. Her 14-year-old daughter is in an examining room. The daughter insisted on coming to the doctor but would not tell her mother why. The mother is afraid her daughter is pregnant or has contracted a sexually transmitted disease. What should you say to the mother?

_____

_____

_____

CHAPTER **4**

Communication with Patients, Families, and Coworkers

REVIEW

Vocabulary Review

True or False

Decide whether each statement is true or false. In the space at the left, write T *for true or* F *for false. On the lines provided, rewrite the false statements to make them true.*

_____ **1.** Passive listening does not require a response.

_____

_____ **2.** Active listening involves two-way communication in which the listener gives feedback or asks questions.

_____

_____ **3.** Empathy is the process of feeling sorry for someone.

_____

_____ **4.** An aggressive person tries to impose his position on others or tries to manipulate them.

_____

_____ **5.** Rapport is a conflictive and argumentative relationship.

_____

_____ **6.** Conflict in the workplace arises when two or more coworkers have the same opinions or ideas.

_____

_____ **7.** An assertive person has low self-esteem.

_____

_____ **8.** Sitting in a chair with your arms crossed is described as having a closed posture.

_____

_____ **9.** Personal space is an area that is approximately 4 feet around a person.

_____

_____ **10.** Feedback is a verbal or nonverbal response from a patient that she understood what has been communicated.

_____

_____ **11.** The manner in which a person interacts with people is referred to as interpersonal skills.

_____

_____ **12.** Patients will see a medical assistant as standoffish and reserved when he portrays an open posture.

_____

Matching

Match the key terms in the right column with the definitions in the left column by placing the letter of each correct answer in the space provided.

_____ 13. "You appear tense today."

_____ 14. "Please, go on."

_____ 15. Allowing the patient time to think without pressure.

_____ 16. "I follow what you said."

_____ 17. "Hi, Mr. Smith. Florida sure agrees with you."

_____ 18. "Can I help you with your shoes, Mrs. Adams?"

_____ 19. "Is there something you would like to talk about?"

_____ 20. "So, you are here today because of your swollen ankles and dizziness?"

_____ 21. "Describe your level of pain on a scale from one to five, with five being the most severe."

_____ 22. "Tell me when you feel anxious."

_____ 23. "So what you are saying is that you feel the most pressure when you exercise?"

_____ 24. Patient states: "Do you think this is serious enough to discuss with the doctor?" Medical assistant replies: "Do you think it is?"

_____ 25. "Your granddaughter's first birthday sounded wonderful. Now tell me more about your headaches."

_____ 26. "You're visiting the doctor today regarding a cough. How long have you been coughing?"

a. acceptance
b. offering self
c. making observations
d. reflecting
e. clarifying
f. exploring
g. offering general leads
h. giving broad openings
i. mirroring
j. recognizing
k. silence
l. summarizing
m. encouraging communication
n. focusing

Content Review

Multiple Choice

In the space provided, write the letter of the choice that best completes each statement or answers each question.

_____ 1. Noise is anything that
   A. helps the patient give feedback.
   B. is a part of verbal communication.
   C. interferes with the communication process.
   D. is part of a communication circle.

_____ 2. Positive communication with patients may involve
   A. getting them to limit their questions to save time.
   B. being attentive and encouraging them to ask questions.
   C. telling patients who ask questions that their concerns are foolish.
   D. allowing them to act on angry or abusive feelings.

3. Which of the following is an example of negative communication?
    A. Maintaining eye contact
    B. Displaying open posture
    C. Listening carefully
    D. Asking questions
    E. Mumbling

4. Which of the following is *not* a communication skill?
    A. Active listening
    B. Anxiety
    C. Empathy
    D. Assertiveness

5. When interacting with patients of other cultures or ethnic groups,
    A. assume that they have the same attitude toward modern medicine that you have.
    B. never involve other family members.
    C. never try to speak their language.
    D. never allow yourself to make value judgments.
    E. assume that modesty is not essential.

6. Which of the following is not a deficiency need as defined by Abraham Maslow?
    A. Safety
    B. Love
    C. Esteem
    D. Physiological needs
    E. Empathy

7. The most effective manner in which to deal with an angry patient is to
    A. remind the patient that you are an educated medical assistant.
    B. defend the medical facility to the patient.
    C. walk away because a medical assistant should not put up with this behavior.
    D. demonstrate your sincerity and respect by remaining calm.
    E. All of the above.

8. According to Erikson, the life stage that exposes children to people other than their immediate family is
    A. Stage I.
    B. Stage V.
    C. Stage III.
    D. Stage IV.
    E. Stage II.

9. When a teenager begins to smoke at a young age because his peers are doing it, the child is most likely experiencing
    A. autonomy.
    B. ego identity.
    C. role confusion.
    D. inferiority.
    E. isolation.

Sentence Completion

In the space provided, write the word or phrase that best completes each sentence.

10. A communication circle involves a message, a source, and a(n) _____.

11. Being _____ when communicating with patients shows them that you, the doctors, and other staff members care about them and their feelings.

12. Your _____, which is the way you hold or move parts of your body, can send strong nonverbal messages.

13. If a patient leans back or turns her head away when you lean forward, you may be invading her _____.

14. The _____ syndrome refers to the anxiety that some patients feel in a doctor's office or other health-care setting.

15. Positive communication with superiors involves keeping them informed, asking questions, minimizing interruptions, and showing _____.

16. A(n) _____ manual is a key written communication tool that covers all office policies and clinical procedures in the medical office.

17. Explaining procedures to patients, expediting insurance referral requests, and creating a warm and reassuring environment are all examples of _____ in the physician office.

18. _____, a well-known behaviorist, developed a human behavior model that states that human beings are motivated by unsatisfied needs.

19. A condition that results from prolonged periods of stress without relief is called _____.

20. A world-renowned authority in death and dying, _____ developed a model of behavior that an individual will experience on learning of his condition. These behaviors are referred to as the stages of dying or the stages of grief.

10. _____

11. _____

12. _____

13. _____

14. _____

15. _____

16. _____

17. _____

18. _____

19. _____

20. _____

Short Answer

Write the answer to each question on the lines provided.

21. What are three other examples of negative communication?

_____

_____

_____

22. List the life stages per Erik Erikson and discuss the expected development traits of each.

_____

_____

_____

23. What is the difference between a stereotype and a generalization of different cultures?

_____

_____

24. What are three means of establishing good communication with a patient who is visually impaired?

_____

_____

25. What are three things you can do to improve communication with a hearing-impaired patient?

_____

_____

26. Describe three things you might do when dealing with very young patients.

_____

_____

27. What are three rules for establishing positive communication with coworkers?

_____

_____

28. Describe the importance of researching the community resources available in your area.

_____

_____

29. List Elisabeth Kübler-Ross's five stages of death and dying and briefly describe them.

_____

_____

_____

Critical Thnking

Write the answer to each question on the lines provided.

1. How does a person's nonverbal communication convey his true feelings even when his words say otherwise?

_____

_____

_____

2. Explain why learning developmental life span models can help you communicate with patients.

_____

_____

_____

3. Suppose a new medical office does not yet have a policy and procedures manual. What kinds of problems might arise?

_____

_____

_____

4. What therapeutic communication techniques can a medical assistant use when caring for an elderly patient? What defense mechanisms might elderly patients use?

_____

_____

_____

5. Explain how Elisabeth Kübler-Ross's model of the stages of death and dying can help both the families of terminally ill patients and the patients themselves.

_____

_____

_____

6. From the statements by the medical assistant in each scenario listed below, determine which statements are assertive and which are aggressive. Rewrite the aggressive statements to make them assertive.

A. A new patient to your office has begun taking antidepressants. When asking the patient about the new medication, you discover that the patient is only taking the medication when she feels anxious. You respond by saying, "Do you really expect to feel better when you are not following the physician's directions?"

_____

_____

_____

B. A patient has a billing question on a statement that he received recently. You respond, "Let me find the appropriate person to answer the question for you."

_____

_____

_____

C. A coworker uses a profane word by the reception window. You respond by telling her, "You're nasty."

_____

_____

_____

D. Your physician is in her office reviewing lab results when you burst in the room and say, "I have to talk to you now regarding my vacation."

_____

_____

_____

E. You are receiving your annual performance review by your supervisor and you don't agree on several of the improvement items. You respond by saying, "What do you know? You're not a clinical expert."

_____

_____

_____

F. A patient is yelling at you over the telephone and is using profanity with you. You respond by saying, "Please stop cursing at me and let's solve this problem together."

_____

_____

_____

APPLICATION

Follow the directions for the application.

1. **Policy and Procedures Manual: Writing Policies**

   A. Working in groups of three or four, write and develop policies for classroom etiquette, such as attendance, cell phone policy, dress code, homework, and testing policies. For each policy, write a consequence if the policy is violated.

   B. In the same groups, write and develop policies regarding laboratory procedures. Some examples include disposing of biohazardous waste procedures, removing contaminated gloves, and procedures for laboratory table disinfection. For each procedure, write the purpose of the procedure.

   C. Develop a policy and procedures manual using the following steps.

      1. Outline or plan for content, such as a table of contents

      2. Determine format of the documents

      3. Type separate documents for each policy and procedure

      4. State date each policy and procedure was adopted for the class

      5. Provide name of the writing team, class name, and instructor

   Present the policies as a team to the class.

2. Compile a list of community resources for the elderly. List at least 6–10. Format the list with the following components: organization's name, contact person, address, phone, e-mail address of contact person. Format using a *table style format.*

3. **Burnout Test**

   Unmanaged stress can often lead to job burnout in the profession of medical assisting. Answer the following questions *true* or *false* and check your score to see if you are likely to become a victim of burnout.

   _____ 1. I feel that the people I know who are in authority are no better than I am.

   _____ 2. Once I start a job I have no peace until I finish it.

_____ 3. I like to tell people exactly what I think.

_____ 4. Although many people are overly conscious of feelings, I like to deal only with the facts.

_____ 5. I worry about business and financial matters.

_____ 6. I often have anxiety about something or someone.

_____ 7. I sometimes become so preoccupied by a thought that I cannot get it out of my mind.

_____ 8. I find it difficult to go to bed or to sleep because of the thoughts that bother me.

_____ 9. I have periods in which I cannot sit or lie down; I need to be doing something.

_____ 10. My mind is often occupied by thoughts about what I have done wrong or not completed.

_____ 11. My concentration is not what it used to be.

_____ 12. My personal appearance is not what it used to be.

_____ 13. I feel irritated when I see another person's messy desk or cluttered room.

_____ 14. I am more comfortable in a neat, clean, and orderly room than in a messy one.

_____ 15. I cannot get through a day or a week without a schedule or a list of jobs to do.

_____ 16. I believe that the person who works the hardest and longest deserves to get ahead.

_____ 17. If my job/school/family responsibilities demand(s) more time, I will cut out pleasurable activities to see that they get done.

_____ 18. My conscience often bothers me about things I have done in the past.

_____ 19. There are things that I have done that would embarrass me greatly if they become public knowledge.

_____ 20. I feel uncomfortable unless I get the highest grade.

_____ 21. It is my view that many people become confused because they do not bother to find out all the facts.

_____ 22. I frequently feel angry without knowing what or who is bothering me.

_____ 23. I can't stand to have my checkbook or financial matters out of balance.

_____ 24. I think that talking about feelings to others is a waste of time.

_____ 25. There are times when I become preoccupied with washing my hands or keeping things clean.

_____ 26. I always like to be in control of myself and to know as much as possible about things happening around me.

_____ 27. I have few or no close friends with whom I share warm feelings openly.

_____ 28. I feel that the more you can know about future events, the better off you will be.

_____ 29. There are sins I have committed that I will never live down.

_____ 30. I always avoid being late to a meeting or an appointment.

_____ 31. I rarely give up until the job has been completely finished.

_____ 32. I often expect things out of myself that no one else would ask.

_____ 33. I sometimes worry about whether I was wrong or made a mistake.

_____ 34. I would like others to see me as not having any faults.

_____ 35. The groups and organizations I join have strict rules and regulations.

CASE STUDIES

Write your response to each case study on the lines provided.

Case 1

A young child is about to receive an injection. He is scared and tearful. You know the injection will hurt slightly, but you decide to put the child's mind at ease by telling him that it won't hurt a bit. Is this the best way to handle the situation? Explain.

_____

_____

_____

_____

Case 2

You are having a problem with a coworker. Both of you have the same job title and often work together to interview and prepare patients. This coworker cuts you off when you speak and contradicts you in front of patients. Her actions are affecting the way patients see you as a professional. How should you handle the situation?

_____

_____

_____

_____

Case 3

A male patient is waiting in the exam room to see the physician. He is seeing the physician for sexual dysfunction. You and several medical assistants are outside his room at the nurse's station and burst into laughter about a comment unrelated to the patient. A few minutes later, the patient leaves. What could have happened to cause the patient to leave? How could this have been avoided?

_____

_____

_____

_____

Case 4

A mother brings her 3-year-old into the pediatrician's office. The child is presenting with behavioral issues regarding potty training. The mother states that the child hides behind furniture instead of using the potty or alerting her of her need to use the bathroom. The mother stated that she has strict consequences when the child has an accident, such as timeouts when an accident occurs. In addition, the older sibling teases the child about accidents. According to Erikson, what is the life stage level for this child and a possible reason for this behavior?

_____

_____

_____

_____

CHAPTER 5

Using and Maintaining Office Equipment

REVIEW

Vocabulary Review

True or False

Decide whether each statement is true or false. In the space at the left, write T for true or F for false. On the lines provided, rewrite the false statements to make them true.

_____ 1. When leaving a message on an answering machine, it is important to leave a full and complete message so that anyone who picks up the message can fully understand the reason for the call.

_____

_____ 2. A telephone system can be configured so that all incoming calls ring on all the telephones in the office.

_____

_____ 3. Medical practices can now use the computer for Internet access and telephone communications.

_____

_____ 4. It is not generally necessary to turn off a cell phone when entering a medical practice.

_____

_____ 5. The improper or careless use of a patient's answering system or fax machine can be viewed as abusive behavior as determined by HIPAA law.

_____

_____ 6. An interactive pager (I-pager) is designed for one-way communication.

_____

_____ 7. Faxed material may include protected health information.

_____

_____ 8. When a copier jams, the first thing you should do is call technical support.

_____

_____ 9. Folding and inserting machines can only be used to fold paper in single folds.

_____

_____ 10. According to HIPAA law, when a medical practice sends documents to be shredded by a shredding company, they are no longer responsible for the confidentiality of the information.

_____

Matching

Match the key terms in the right column with the definitions in the left column by placing the letter of each correct answer in the space provided.

_____ **11.** Wireless technology

_____ **12.** A practice or behavior that is not indicative of sound medical or fiscal activity

_____ **13.** A small electrical device that gives a signal that someone is trying to reach the carrier

_____ **14.** Paging technology

_____ **15.** A device that scans documents for transmission

_____ **16.** A machine that consists of a meter and a mailing machine

_____ **17.** An alternative to the use of a switchboard and receptionist

_____ **18.** Transforming the spoken word into writing

_____ **19.** A feature of many copiers

_____ **20.** The cancellation of a check

A. A device assigned to a telephone number
B. Postage meter
C. Automated voice response
D. Collating
E. Abuse
F. Transcription
G. Beeper or pager
H. Cell phones
I. Fax machine
J. Voiding

Content Review

Multiple Choice

In the space provided, write the letter of the choice that best completes each statement or answers each question.

_____ **1.** An automated menu answering system
    A. answers calls and separates requests into categories.
    B. requires answering calls as they come in.
    C. does not notify the office when the caller presses the code for a patient emergency.
    D. is inappropriate for a medical office.

_____ **2.** Answering services
    A. are unreliable.
    B. are seldom used by medical practices.
    C. can have a direct connection to the doctor's office, answering calls after a certain number of rings.
    D. use mechanical voices rather than human voices.
    E. are only used in large cities.

_____ **3.** A word processor is helpful to the medical assistant because
    A. corrections can be made easily within a document.
    B. documents can be stored in memory.
    C. the creation of correspondence is a function of the medical assistant.
    D. All of the above.

_____ **4.** Which feature is *not* available on a photocopier?
    A. Enlarging and reducing the size of a document
    B. Collating
    C. Folding
    D. Stapling

_____ 5. Which statement is *not* true about fax machines?

    A. A fax machine uses a phone line.

    B. All fax machines require special thermal paper for printing.

    C. Faxes can be received 24 hours a day if the fax machine is turned on.

    D. When a fax has been successfully sent, most fax machines print a confirmation message.

_____ 6. What information can a medical assistant leave on a patient's telephone answering machine?

    A. The phone number and name of the medical practice calling

    B. Patient information

    C. Test results

    D. Prescription information

_____ 7. Interactive pagers

    A. are too expensive for widespread use.

    B. are difficult to learn how to use.

    C. have their own wireless Internet address.

    D. are critical to any medical practice.

    E. None of the above.

_____ 8. When the physician determines that a chart can be discarded, you should

    A. throw it in the trash.

    B. shred it.

    C. burn it.

    D. keep it for 7 years.

    E. store it in a confidential location.

_____ 9. The postage meter

    A. is a convenient and cost-efficient way to apply postage to office correspondence and packages.

    B. functions only when there is money in the postal account.

    C. automatically senses the weight of a letter or package.

    D. A and B only.

    E. None of the above.

_____ 10. A leasing agreement for large office equipment is

    A. always preferable to buying.

    B. advantageous when you do not have enough money to buy the equipment but you need the service it provides.

    C. always less expensive over the long term.

    D. never price negotiable.

Sentence Completion

In the space provided, write the word or phrase that best completes each sentence.

11. When the office is closed, many practices use a(n) _____, which will answer the phone, take messages, and communicate them to the doctor on call.

12. When a physician is out of the office, she may carry a(n) _____ so she can be reached if needed.

13. Some fax machines print on specially treated paper, called _____, which reacts to heat and electricity.

11. _____

12. _____

13. _____

14. A(n) _____ is a machine that applies postage to an envelope or package.

15. Medical assistants may be asked to _____ tape-recorded words into written text.

16. A(n) _____ imprints a check with the date, payee's name, and payment amount.

17. The only way to cancel an imprinted check is to _____ it.

18. If the price of the equipment or terms of the sale are not firm, there is room for _____, or bargaining for additional savings or more flexible terms.

19. A(n) _____ tells how a piece of equipment works, what its special features are, and how to troubleshoot problems.

20. Periodically, it will be necessary to conduct an equipment _____, which is a list of a business's equipment.

14. _____

15. _____

16. _____

17. _____

18. _____

19. _____

20. _____

Short Answer

Write the answer to each question on the lines provided.

21. Explain how an automated menu telephone system works.

_____

_____

_____

22. What are the benefits of faxing a document?

_____

_____

_____

23. Compare the advantages and disadvantages of an electronic typewriter and a word processor.

_____

_____

_____

24. How might you post packages without a postal scale?

_____

_____

_____

25. Why is using a check writer safer than handwriting a check?

_____

_____

_____

26. List the steps involved in purchasing office equipment.

_____

_____

_____

27. Describe the basic contents of equipment manuals.

_____

_____

_____

28. What does a maintenance contract cover?

_____

_____

_____

29. List three steps in troubleshooting a problem with a piece of equipment.

_____

_____

_____

30. List three pieces of information that many medical practices keep about individual pieces of equipment.

_____

_____

_____

Critical Thinking

Write the answer to each question on the lines provided.

1. How does the almost instantaneous communication of information afforded by today's office equipment influence patient treatment?

_____

_____

_____

2. Automated menus, voice mail, answering machines, and other office communication equipment reduce human contact between health-care workers and patients. What can you do to ensure that patients do not feel cut off by technology?

_____

_____

_____

3. How does office automation affect the staff in a medical office and the care they give patients?

_____

_____

_____

4. What could be a disadvantage of office automation?

_____

_____

_____

5. What might be the advantage of building a relationship with one or two suppliers of office equipment rather than with many?

_____

_____

_____

APPLICATION

Follow the directions for each application.

1. **Explaining How to Use Office Equipment**

   Work with two partners. One should take the role of a medical assistant who has worked in a medical practice for a while and knows how to operate all the office equipment. The second partner should take the role of a new medical assistant who is not familiar with the equipment. The third person should serve as an observer and evaluator.

   a. The observer should choose a piece of office equipment, such as a dictation-transcription machine. The experienced medical assistant should then give step-by-step directions on how to use the equipment. The new medical assistant should ask questions to clarify the directions.

   b. The evaluator should observe the training session while checking the directions given against those presented in the text.

   c. When the training session is complete, the evaluator should provide feedback by citing any omissions or errors in the instructions. All three partners should discuss the effectiveness of the session.

   d. Now exchange roles. The new evaluator should choose another piece of equipment to describe in another round of training.

   e. Exchange roles again so that each member of the team plays each role at least once. Repeat the activity until all partners achieve confidence in using each piece of equipment.

2. **Designing a Fax Cover Sheet**

   Design a cover sheet to accompany a confidential faxed transmittal from a medical practice.

   a. Decide on the type of medical practice. Create the names of the physicians and the address and phone number of the practice.

   b. On an 8½- by 11-inch sheet of paper, decide what information to include. Then design your cover sheet.

   c. Type the finished cover sheet. Check spelling, grammar, and punctuation.

   d. Compare your cover sheet with those of other students. Decide whether you have provided all necessary information. Discuss whether cover sheets should be typed or handwritten and why.

3. **Create an Equipment Inventory form**

   Design an equipment inventory form to list all the equipment in a typical medical practice.

   a. Decide on the type of medical practice. Create a form with the name of the practice centered at the top of the form.

b. The form should have columns for the following:

- The name of each piece of equipment

- The date purchased or leased

- An indication of whether each item was purchased or leased

- The price, if purchased

- The leasing arrangement, if leased

c. Use an 8½- by 11-inch sheet of paper and type the finished form.

d. Check spelling, grammar, and punctuation.

e. Compare your form with those of other students and determine the best format.

4. Perform equipment maintenance check on the photocopier in your office; document on the equipment maintenance log. (*The first check has already been completed for you.*)

Equipment Description	Shannon Photocopier	Model No. 123A9
Serial Number: 56AC90-001L		
Date	**Action/Comments**	**Initials**
9/17/XX	Machine checked	SM, CMA (AAMA)

CASE STUDIES

Write your response to each case study on the lines provided.

Case 1

You are the only one in the office. The physician calls and asks you to get a document over to the laboratory across the street. What can you do?

_____

_____

_____

Case 2

The office manager leaves you a note asking you to fax a document. You place the document in the sending tray of the machine and key in the phone number, but nothing happens. What do you do?

_____

_____

_____

Case 3

In researching a piece of equipment, you find two equally good options. One has a better price and one has a better maintenance agreement. How will you decide which to recommend?

_____

_____

_____

Case 4

You believe a word processor will help you work faster and more efficiently. Your coworkers say the office does not need a word processor. What should you do to convince them?

_____

_____

_____

CHAPTER 6

Using Computers in the Office

REVIEW

Vocabulary Review

Matching

Match the key terms in the right column with the definitions in the left column by placing the letter of each correct answer in the space provided.

_____	**1.** The physical components of a computer system	**a.** CD-ROM
_____	**2.** A blinking line on the computer screen showing where the next character that is keyed will appear	**b.** cursor
		c. database
		d. electronic mail
_____	**3.** A device that is used to input printed matter and convert it into a format that can be read by a computer	**e.** hard copy
		f. hardware
_____	**4.** The main circuit board that controls the other components in the computer system	**g.** ink-jet printer
		h. Internet
		i. motherboard
_____	**5.** A computer's temporary, programmable memory	**j.** multimedia
_____	**6.** A computer disk similar to an audio compact disc that stores huge amounts of data	**k.** multitasking
		l. random-access memory (RAM)
_____	**7.** Software that uses more than one medium—such as graphics, sound, and text—to convey information	**m.** scanner
		n. screen saver
_____	**8.** A printout of information from a computer	
_____	**9.** A type of machine that forms characters using a series of dots created by tiny drops of ink	
_____	**10.** A system that allows users to run two or more software programs simultaneously	
_____	**11.** A collection of records created and stored on a computer	
_____	**12.** A method of sending and receiving messages through a network	
_____	**13.** A global network of computers	
_____	**14.** A software package that automatically changes the computer monitor at short intervals or shows moving images to prevent burn-in	

True or False

Decide whether each statement is true or false. In the space at the left, write T for true or F for false. On the lines provided, rewrite the false statements to make them true.

_____ **15.** It is important to back up computer files and store them properly.

_____

_____ **16.** Telemedicine refers to the use of telecommunications to transmit video images of patient information.

_____

_____ **17.** CD-R technology enables the computer to comprehend and interpret spoken words.

_____

_____ **18.** Read-only memory (ROM) can be read by the computer, but you cannot make changes to it.

_____

_____ **19.** Random-access memory (RAM) provides speed to the computer. The more RAM, the faster the computer will perform.

_____

_____ **20.** To relieve the symptoms of carpal tunnel syndrome, hands while typing should be lowered below the waist.

_____

_____ **21.** The software is where information is stored permanently for later retrieval.

_____

_____ **22.** The central processing unit (CPU) is also called a microprocessor.

_____

_____ **23.** The blinking line or cube on the computer screen showing where the next character that is keyed will appear is called the pointing device.

_____

_____ **24.** A scanner is helpful in a medical office because patient reports from another doctor, a hospital, or another outside source can easily be entered into the computer.

_____

Content Review

Multiple Choice

In the space provided, write the letter of the choice that best completes each statement or answers each question.

_____ **1.** Another name for a laptop is a
  A. minicomputer.
  B. mainframe.
  C. notebook.
  D. microcomputer.

_____ 2. A subnotebook
    A. is also called a laptop.
    B. is not really a computer because it is too small to function fully.
    C. does not require software.
    D. is a miniature computer.
    E. is better than a palmtop.

_____ 3. The difference between hardware and software is
    A. none—there is no difference.
    B. hardware is portable and software is not.
    C. hardware means the physical parts of a computer system and software is the instructions within the computer system.
    D. software is portable and hardware is not.

_____ 4. The device that made today's computer possible is
    A. the abacus.
    B. the punch card.
    C. the vacuum tube.
    D. the micro chip.
    E. All of the above.

_____ 5. The keyboard is the most common input device. Other input devices include
    A. a mouse.
    B. earphones.
    C. software.
    D. speakers.
    E. file folders.

_____ 6. Which statement about ROM is *true*?
    A. It is permanent memory.
    B. It is the same as RAM.
    C. It is programmable.
    D. You can make changes to ROM.

_____ 7. The most common type of pointing device is a
    A. mouse.
    B. scanner.
    C. touch pad.
    D. keyboard.

_____ 8. A jump drive is
    A. a type of software.
    B. a way to provide portability to a large body of information.
    C. an internally attached drive.
    D. large and heavy.

_____ 9. A "multitasking" system means
    A. many different types of expenses are involved.
    B. the system has multiple uses.
    C. users can run two or more software programs simultaneously.
    D. None of the above.

_____ **10.** The term software means

    A. portable hardware.

    B. physical computer components.

    C. the input device.

    D. a set of instructions or program that tells the computer what to do.

_____ **11.** Which of the following is considered the most important piece of hardware in a computer system?

    A. RAM

    B. ROM

    C. The USB port

    D. The instruction set

    E. The CPU

_____ **12.** A zip drive is

    A. faster software.

    B. a high-capacity floppy disk drive.

    C. a type of mouse.

    D. the same as a jump drive.

_____ **13.** *Resolution* refers to

    A. color.

    B. the size of an image.

    C. the sound and clarity of a speaker system.

    D. the crispness of the images and is measured in dot pitch.

_____ **14.** The most common computer input device is a

    A. keyboard.

    B. cursor.

    C. modem.

    D. scanner.

_____ **15.** A database is

    A. a document.

    B. a collection of records created and stored on a computer.

    C. the software used by a computer.

    D. the hardware of a computer.

_____ **16.** E-mail etiquette is

    A. established when a practice creates a written e-mail policy spelling out the "dos" and "don'ts" concerning the use of the company's e-mail system.

    B. determined by each individual employee.

    C. not essential in a place of business.

    D. None of the above.

_____ **17.** A search engine is

    A. part of the computer.

    B. part of the software for a computer.

    C. a specialized website that connects with other websites for information.

    D. purchased annually.

_____ **18.** The first step in selecting new computer equipment is
      A. to set up a trial run of a new system for 30 days.
      B. to research into the needs of the office and the capabilities of the equipment.
      C. to remove the old system.
      D. to convert back to a manual system.

_____ **19.** A CD-R
      A. is another name for a CD-ROM.
      B. is the same as a CD.
      C. allows for information to be taken from a source and stored to a CD.
      D. is a type of modem.

_____ **20.** A computer password
      A. backs up computer files.
      B. can be shared by more than one employee performing the same functions.
      C. stores information.
      D. helps protect computer files.

Sentence Completion

In the space provided, write the word or phrase that best completes each sentence.

21. A _____ is a modem that operates over cable television lines to provide fast Internet access.

22. _____ is a measurement of how many instructions per second that the CPU can process.

23. Carpal tunnel syndrome is caused by _____ hand and finger motions.

24. The speed at which a computer can process information depends on the type and speed of its _____.

25. A _____ modem operates over telephone lines but uses a different frequency than the telephone frequency.

26. Word processing, database, and accounting software are examples of software that is written for a specific purpose, or _____.

27. _____ are high-resolution printers that use a technology similar to that of photocopiers.

28. Requiring a(n) _____ limits the computer users who can access files.

29. A _____ is a device used to input printed matter and convert it into a format that the computer can read.

30. _____ is a measurement of how much information can be sent or processed with one single instruction, and is calculated in bits or bytes.

31. A _____ is a computer that is very small and light. It cannot perform all the functions of a notebook computer but can be useful for people who need to have a computer available while they are out of the office.

32. To use a modem, you must have access to a _____.

21. _____

22. _____

23. _____

24. _____

25. _____

26. _____

27. _____

28. _____

29. _____

30. _____

31. _____

32. _____

33. Photocopiers can be configured with a _____ and can transmit the images of scanned documents to computers.

34. Users who access computer files can be identified with _____.

35. A _____ is a type of pointing device and is common on laptop and notebook computers.

33. _____

34. _____

35. _____

Short Answer

Write the answer to each question on the lines provided.

36. Compare a mouse and a trackball.

_____

_____

_____

37. Give one advantage and one disadvantage of a fax modem.

_____

_____

_____

38. Compare a diskette and a CD-ROM.

_____

_____

_____

39. What is the advantage of a dot matrix printer over a laser printer?

_____

_____

_____

40. Patient records are stored on the hard disk drive of a computer. What are three ways that you could give a copy of those records to a consulting physician?

_____

_____

_____

41. What are four kinds of medical information that you could find using the Internet?

_____

_____

_____

42. What are three sources of information you might turn to if you are having problems using a software program?

_____

_____

_____

43. How does a surge protector help maintain a computer system?

_____

_____

_____

44. What should you do to protect diskettes from damage?

_____

_____

_____

45. Based on what you have learned, write a list of general guidelines for purchasing a computer system for a medical practice.

_____

_____

_____

46. Describe the purpose of OCR software.

_____

_____

_____

47. Define and describe a virtual private network.

_____

_____

_____

Critical Thinking

Write the answer to each question on the lines provided.

1. If a medical office can afford only one computer, what kind should it purchase? Explain your answer.

_____

_____

_____

2. Why might it be useful to add a fax modem to a computer system even though the medical office already has a regular fax machine?

_____

_____

_____

3. Why might it be a good idea to take a computer course at an adult school or community college every few years?

_____

_____

_____

4. When buying a computer system, why is it a good idea to purchase all components from one vendor?

_____

_____

_____

5. How might a large medical office benefit from adding CD-R technology to its computer system?

_____

_____

_____

6. Why is it a good idea to use a screen saver designed to come on after only one minute of inactivity on a computer near a patient reception area?

_____

_____

_____

7. Describe a computer disaster recovery plan.

_____

_____

_____

APPLICATION

Follow the directions for the application.

Typing and Editing a Letter on the Computer

a. Open a new file on your word processing program and type the letter below, using the letterhead example of page 957.

November 4, 2011

Mr. Karl Cousin 24 Elm St.
Wilmington, NJ 12345

Dear Mr. Cousin:

I have been unable to reach you by phone, so I am writing to confirm your appointment for Wednesday, November 9, at 2:30 PM. If you will be unable to keep this appointment, please call us immediately at 555-7890 to cancel it or to change your appointment time. If we do not hear from you by Tuesday, November 8, at 2:30 PM, we will assume you will keep the appointment, and you will be charged for the visit.

Please remember that payment must be made at the time of your appointment unless you have made other arrangements with our office. Be sure to bring any pertinent insurance forms with you and give them to us. We appreciate your cooperation and look forward to seeing you at our office on November 9.

Sincerely,

Marty Miller
Office Manager

b. Print a hard copy of your letter. Then make these changes to the computer file:

1. In the inside address, add the patient's middle name: *James*.

2. Spell out the word *Street*.

3. In the second paragraph, delete these words: *and give them to us*.

4. Move the last sentence of the letter to the beginning of the second paragraph.

5. Save the letter under this file name: *confirm.apt*.

6. Print a hard copy of your revision of the letter.

c. Now open a new file and write another letter that a medical office might send to a patient, a newly hired staff person, or a laboratory, hospital, or consulting physician.

1. Print a hard copy of your first draft.

2. Exchange letters with a partner and suggest any changes that would improve his or her letter.

3. Use the computer function keys to improve your letter by adding, deleting, and moving information.

4. Print your final version.

CASE STUDIES

Write your response to each case study on the lines provided.

Case 1

The medical office where you work has just begun converting to a computer system. The doctors are concerned about the confidentiality of the files. What will you recommend?

_____

_____

_____

Case 2

A coworker is intimidated by the office's new word processing program. Nearly every day she hands you a letter she has handwritten and begs you to enter it on the computer and print it so she can send it out. You are getting behind in your own work as a result. How can you solve this problem and still maintain a positive relationship with your coworker?

_____

_____

_____

Case 3

You enjoy painting with watercolors, but lately you have had trouble opening the paint containers and controlling the brush. A few months ago your office converted to a computerized record-keeping system. Explain a possible connection and how you would address this problem.

_____

_____

_____

CHAPTER 7

Managing Correspondence and Mail

REVIEW

Vocabulary Review

Passage Completion

Study the key terms in the box. Use your textbook to find definitions of terms you do not understand.

annotate	courtesy title	letterhead
body	dateline	modified-block letter style
clarity	editing	proofreading
complimentary closing	full-block letter style	salutation
concise	identification line	simplified letter style

In the space provided, complete the following passage, using some of the terms from the box. You may change the form of a term to fit the meaning of the sentence.

Most business letters are written on (1) _____ paper, which identifies the business. The (2) _____, which is placed about three lines below the preprinted letterhead text, gives the day, month, and year. In the inside address, the receiver's name usually includes a(n) (3) _____, such as Dr. or Mrs. The receiver's name is repeated in the (4) _____. In the (5) _____, or block style, all lines are flush left. In the (6) _____, the dateline, complimentary closing, and other parts of the letter begin at about the center of the page. The (7) _____ omits the salutation and the complimentary closing.

1. _____
2. _____
3. _____
4. _____
5. _____
6. _____
7. _____

True or False

Decide whether each statement is true or false. In the space at the left, write T for true or F for false. On the lines provided, rewrite the false statements to make them true.

_____ 8. Tan Kraft envelopes are also called clasp envelopes.

_____

_____ 9. The standard setting for the margin in business correspondence is 2 inches.

_____

_____ **10.** You need to capitalize all the words in the closing of a business letter.

_____

_____ **11.** The USPS abbreviation PA stands for *Pennsylvania*.

_____

Content Review

Sentence Completion

In the space provided, write the word or phrase that best completes each statement.

1. The _____ is similar to full block but it differs in that the dateline, complimentary closing, signature block, and notations are aligned and begin at the center of the page or slightly to the right.

2. Two different styles of punctuation used in correspondence are _____ and _____.

3. The USPS abbreviation for Kansas is _____.

4. _____ include information such as the number of enclosures that are included with the letter and the names of other people who will be receiving copies of the letter.

5. _____ means thoroughly checking a document for errors.

6. The USPS uses electronic _____ to help speed mail processing.

7. The Web address for the U.S. Postal Service Web page is _____.

8. The USPS abbreviation for *center* is _____.

9. Most correspondence generated in a medical office, such as letters, postcards, and invoices, is sent by _____.

10. _____ is also called parcel post.

11. The first step in processing mail is _____ it.

12. To _____ means to underline or highlight key points of the letter or to write reminders, comments, or suggested actions in the margins or on self-adhesive notes.

13. Business letters written with the modified-block letter style with indented paragraphs are identical to the modified-block style except that the paragraphs are _____.

14. When writing a business letter, it is proper to include at least _____ in each paragraph.

15. "Enc" in a business letter means _____.

16. The space around the edges of a form or letter that is left blank is called the _____.

1. _____

2. _____

3. _____

4. _____

5. _____

6. _____

7. _____

8. _____

9. _____

10. _____

11. _____

12. _____

13. _____

14. _____

15. _____

16. _____

17. The _____ of a letter consists of single-spaced lines that are the content of a business letter.

18. _____, which can be printed from a computerized mailing list, can greatly speed the process of addressing envelopes for bulk mailings.

19. The most common envelope size used for correspondence is the _____.

20. _____ is the action the post office will take when a piece of mail does not reach its destination.

21. _____ written on the outside of a letter or package means that the letter or package should not be opened by anyone but the addressee.

22. _____ is the process that ensures that a document is accurate, clear, and complete; free of grammatical errors; organized logically; and written in an appropriate style.

17. _____

18. _____

19. _____

20. _____

21. _____

22. _____

Short Answer

Write the answer to each question on the lines provided.

23. What are some advantages of learning to manage correspondence for a medical office in a professional manner?

_____

_____

_____

24. List three types of envelopes commonly used in a medical office, and briefly describe their uses.

_____

_____

_____

25. What is the difference between a modified-block letter style and a simplified letter style?

_____

_____

26. Describe the voice of the sentence below. Then rewrite the sentence, changing the voice to make it more direct and concise.

The patient's blood sample was sent to you by our office on November 4, 2011.

_____

_____

_____

27. How do editing and proofreading differ?

_____

_____

_____

28. Why is an envelope with a typed address likely to be delivered more quickly than one with a handwritten address?

_____

_____

_____

29. Describe an accordion fold on a business letter, and explain why it is used.

_____

_____

_____

30. Describe a situation in which an item might be sent by fourth-class mail from a medical office.

_____

_____

_____

31. When processing incoming mail, why is it important to check the address on each letter or package?

_____

_____

_____

32. Describe the difference between certified and registered mail.

_____

_____

_____

Critical Thinking

Write the answer to each question on the lines provided.

1. As an assistant in a new medical practice, what correspondence supply would you order first? Explain your answer.

_____

_____

_____

2. Briefly describe two types of letters from a health-care professional in which the tone should be formal and two types in which the tone could be relaxed.

_____

_____

_____

3. Which of these errors could be considered most serious: a formatting error, a data error, or a mechanical error? Explain your answer.

_____

_____

_____

4. Why should a medical assistant take the time to learn and use the rules of spelling, punctuation, and capitalization?

_____

_____

_____

5. What are three problems that could occur if a medical assistant handled incoming mail in a disorganized way?

_____

_____

_____

APPLICATION

Follow the directions for each application.

1. Applying Basic Rules of Effective Writing

Read each of the following sentences for errors in spelling, word division, and capitalization and in the use of plurals, possessives, and numbers. If a sentence is incorrect, rewrite it correctly on the lines provided. Compare your corrections with those of a partner. Did you find the same errors? Did you miss any? Are there any writing rules that you need to study further?

a. The Patients left oricle showed evidence of a recent infarktion.

_____

_____

b. The abcess developed during the patients' recent trip to see his aunt.

_____

_____

c. The patient was given a perscription for a 10-day supply of ilosone, a form of erythromycin.

_____

_____

d. This 6-year-old patient reports falling from a slide at Ridge Street school this past tuesday.

_____

_____

_____

e. X-rays indicate hare-line fraktures of two cervical vertebra.

_____

_____

f. Vigorous work outdoors in hot tempratures apparantly aggravated pastor Henrys heart condition.

_____

_____

2. Handling Incoming Mail

Assume that you are a medical assistant whose duties include processing incoming mail. Some of the procedures that you follow are described below. For procedures that are correct, write *correct* on the lines provided. For procedures that are incorrect, write the correct procedures on the lines provided.

a. Collect everything from the office mailbox and process it a few items at a time throughout the day.

_____

_____

b. In the top-priority pile, place letters and packages sent by overnight mail delivery, special delivery, registered mail, or certified mail. To this pile, also add any newspapers or magazines.

_____

_____

c. After sorting the mail, open all the envelopes at once—except for those marked "personal" or "confidential"—and remove their contents, making sure to take everything out of each envelope.

_____

_____

d. Throw away the envelopes as soon as you have removed their contents.

_____

_____

e. Compare enclosure notations on each letter with the actual enclosures to make sure all items were included. Then make notes about missing items so that senders can be contacted.

_____

_____

f. Staple each letter to its enclosures so they cannot become separated.

_____

_____

g. Stamp any bills or statements with the date they are received.

_____

_____

3. Preparing a Business Letter

Read the following case study: You are a medical assistant working in a busy family practice office. One of the physicians (Dr. Casey Singleton) says to you. "Please prepare a letter to go to Mr. Ford. He is the attorney for Mrs. Smith. Just check her chart to get his address. Tell him that Mrs. Smith has not been coming to her scheduled appointments. Tell him that I can't help if she doesn't want my help!"

Instructions:

a. What questions might you have before you prepare this letter—use the lines below.

_____

_____

_____

_____

b. Type the letter, using the example letterhead on page 957, after you prepare the letter; use block style. The phone number for your medical facility is (605) 780-0098.

_____

_____

_____

_____

_____

_____

c. You have found the address of the attorney in the chart: Mr. William Ford/Ford, Wilkins, Ford Law Offices/135 Cinceros Ave./Ste. 3200/Plainfield, NJ 10987.

_____

_____

_____

4. Commonly Misspelled Words

Correct the spelling of the following words.

a. _____ abcess

b. _____ laynx

c. _____ chancrer

d. _____ nocomial

e. _____ defibillator

f. _____ parentral

g. _____ sphymomanometer

h. _____ Febuary

i. _____ comittee

j. _____ occassion

k. _____ truely

CASE STUDIES

Write your response to each case study on the lines provided.

Case 1

A new coworker asks you to proofread a business letter that he wrote. You notice that the letter contains numerous formatting and mechanical errors. You also suspect that there may be data errors in the letter. What should you do?

_____

_____

_____

Case 2

You have just finished preparing several letters for signing by Dr. Morris, a physician in your office. Most of the letters need to be sent out today, but he will be extremely busy with patients for the rest of the day. Dr. Fuchs, another physician in your office, has authorized you to sign her letters. Should you sign Dr. Morris's letters and send them out right away? Explain your answer.

_____

_____

_____

Case 3

While opening the office mail, you discover that a patient has enclosed a check for more than she owes. Should you take a moment from processing the mail to call the patient? Why or why not?

_____

_____

_____

Case 4

A patient has come to your office without an appointment because he has unexpectedly run out of a prescription heart medication. The physician's schedule is completely full, so you cannot give the patient an appointment. However, you know that samples of this drug are in the sample cabinet. The patient should not skip any doses of this medication. What should you do?

_____

_____

_____

CHAPTER 8

Managing Office Supplies

REVIEW

Vocabulary Review

True or False

Decide whether each statement is true or false. In the space at the left, write T for true or F for false. On the lines provided, rewrite the false statements to make them true.

_____ 1. A medical assistant should avoid storing boxes or supplies near a water heater, air-conditioning unit, heater, or stove.

_____

_____ 2. Paper cups are considered an administrative supply expense.

_____

_____ 3. The list of supplies the office uses regularly and the quantity in storage constitute the office inventory.

_____

_____ 4. The average medical practice spends between 10% and 15% of its annual gross income on administrative, clinical, and general supplies.

_____

_____ 5. A durable item is an item that is used indefinitely.

_____

_____ 6. When you receive a shipment or an order, it is important to check the invoice carefully against the original order and the packing slip.

_____

_____ 7. If an invoice says "Net 30," you have 30 days in which to pay the total amount of the invoice without penalty charges.

_____

_____ 8. When ordering by fax, it is always best to use the form provided by the vendor.

_____

_____ 9. A purchase order does not require an authorizing signature.

_____

_____ 10. A disbursement is a payment of funds.

_____

_____ **11.** Purchasing groups get the same prices as an individual ordering because the law requires equal pricing.

_____

_____ **12.** The unit price of an item is the price per item.

_____

_____ **13.** With most vendors, "rush orders" cost the same as orders delivered by standard shipping.

_____

_____ **14.** It is a good idea to take advantage of phone solicitations to help control costs of supplies.

_____

_____ **15.** The word "supplies" refers to expendable items or items that are used up and restocked.

_____

Passage Completion

Study the key terms in the box. Use your textbook to find definitions of terms you do not understand.

unit price	vital	disbursement
rush order	invoice	reorder reminder cards
clinical	Material Safety Data Sheet (MSDS)	inventory card or record page
administrative	computerized inventory system	

In the space provided, complete the following passage, using some of the terms from the box. You may change the form of a term to fit the meaning of the sentence.

In a medical office, a(n) (16) _____ for each item or category of items may be a 4 × 6 inch index card or a page in a loose-leaf binder. (17) _____ are usually brightly colored cards inserted directly into stock on the supply shelf to indicate when it is time to reorder. A(n) (18) _____ is the best choice for a large medical practice. To calculate an item's (19) _____, divide the total price of the package by the quantity, or the number of items. (20) _____ usually cost more than regularly scheduled orders and should be avoided when possible. The information supplied by the manufacturer describing the chemical breakdown of a product is called a(n) (21) _____. A payment of funds to a vendor is called a(n) (22) _____. Another name for a bill is a(n) (23) _____. Alcohol swabs are an example of a(n) (24) _____ supply. Insurance materials are an example of (25) _____ supplies. (26) _____ is a category of supplies that are essential to ensure the smooth running of the practice.

16. _____

17. _____

18. _____

19. _____

20. _____

21. _____

22. _____

23. _____

24. _____

25. _____

26. _____

Content Review

Multiple Choice

In the space provided, write the letter of the choice that best completes each statement or answers each question.

_____ 1. The best place to store the office holiday decorations is
   A. in a storage area away from heat and water.
   B. as close to the ceiling as possible because this item is used only once a year.
   C. by the furnace.
   D. near the water heater.
   E. in the patient bathroom.

_____ 2. Which group of items is considered general supplies?
   A. Lancets, tongue depressors, and sutures
   B. Lubricating jelly, alcohol swabs, and needles
   C. Paper cups, toilet paper, and liquid soap
   D. Copy paper, stamps, and pens
   E. File folders, insurance manuals, and forms

_____ 3. Paper administrative supplies should be stored
   A. in an upright position in the original shipping box to save space.
   B. lying flat in the original shipping box.
   C. lying flat after being taken out of the original shipping box.
   D. in an upright position after being taken out of the original shipping box.
   E. in a desk drawer only, after being removed from the original shipping box.

_____ 4. Unit prices are usually lower at larger quantities. Therefore, it makes sense to
   A. buy more items than you need and can store.
   B. buy items in bulk when the purchase can be stored and used within a reasonable amount of time.
   C. never buy items except in large quantities.
   D. not worry about comparative pricing because a small difference in price really doesn't matter.

_____ 5. You should order by "rush order"
   A. only as absolutely required.
   B. on Fridays to avoid the weekend.
   C. routinely.
   D. on Mondays to compensate for the weekend.

_____ 6. The Federal Trade Commission (FTC) requires supply companies to provide merchandise within how many days or to give you the option of canceling with a full refund?
   A. 90
   B. 60
   C. 180
   D. 30

_____ 7. A purchase requisition is
   A. a form that can only be used when faxing an order.
   B. another name for an invoice.
   C. another name for an MSDS sheet.
   D. only used when purchasing through a buying pool.
   E. a formal request from a staff member or doctor.

_____ **8.** Most durable items
    A. have a short shelf life.
    B. must be restocked often.
    C. are pieces of equipment that are used indefinitely.
    D. are made of paper for easy disposal.

_____ **9.** Holiday cards are an example of
    A. administrative supplies.
    B. general supplies.
    C. periodic supplies.
    D. noninventoried supplies.

_____ **10.** Which items must be stored separately from other products?
    A. Liquid soaps
    B. Poisons and acids
    C. Durable items
    D. Bulky items that require a lot of space

Sentence Completion

In the space provided, write the word or phrase that best completes each sentence.

11. Ordering online requires the use of _____ and _____.

12. OSHA stands for _____.

13. The oldest products should be stored on the _____ of the shelf.

14. New calendars and appointment books are examples of _____ supplies.

15. _____ must be stored out of site and in a locked cabinet.

16. If you make a cash disbursement, you should always obtain a _____.

17. The best way to deal with telephone solicitation is _____.

18. Another name for an invoice is a(n) _____.

19. The rules of good housekeeping and _____ apply to storage areas for clinical supplies.

20. _____ are groups of physicians who order supplies together to obtain a quantity discount.

11. _____

12. _____

13. _____

14. _____

15. _____

16. _____

17. _____

18. _____

19. _____

20. _____

Short Answer

Write the answer to each question on the lines provided.

21. Describe how to establish an online account for ordering supplies.

_____

_____

_____

22. What tasks are likely to be included in the medical assistant's responsibilities for maintaining supplies?

_____

_____

_____

23. List items that are important to include on an inventory card.

_____

_____

_____

24. Explain how inventory cards and colored adhesive flags can be used to track supplies that must be reordered.

_____

_____

_____

25. Explain the function of reorder reminder cards.

_____

_____

_____

26. Explain how to calculate a unit price.

_____

_____

_____

27. Briefly describe four categories of information you should obtain when investigating a vendor.

_____

_____

_____

28. What procedure should you follow when receiving a supply shipment?

_____

_____

_____

29. Who is inconvenienced when the supply of an important item runs out?

_____

_____

_____

30. Why is it wiser to order in bulk? Give an example.

_____

_____

_____

31. You notice that some items are always running out. What might you do to handle this situation?

_____

_____

_____

32. When preparing a check for a vendor, what information should be included on the front of the check?

_____

_____

_____

33. Why is it important to check an order carefully when it arrives?

_____

_____

_____

Critical Thinking

Write the answer to each question on the lines provided.

1. You have been put in charge of managing supplies for a large practice. You find that this responsibility takes most of your time. You would prefer to have more diverse duties. What might you do?

_____

_____

_____

2. The practice at which you work has been growing quickly. You think you may need to increase the quantity of certain items in the inventory, but you are not sure what quantity would be correct. What should you do?

_____

_____

_____

3. You have heard that ordering medical office supplies through a purchasing group may be less expensive than direct ordering from one office. How might you investigate purchasing groups in your area?

_____

_____

_____

4. A new vendor offers you prices that are far below what you are now paying. You can save the office a great deal of money, but the brands are unknown to you. How should you handle the situation?

_____

_____

_____

5. As you check a shipment of supplies, you discover that there is a greater quantity of one item than was ordered and that one ordered item is missing altogether. What should you do?

_____

_____

_____

APPLICATION

Follow the directions for each application.

1. Inventory Card or Page

You are setting up an inventory system for the office. Your first task is to design inventory pages to place in a binder. What information should you include for each item? List each category of needed information on the lines provided. Use a sheet of paper to design the inventory page.

_____

_____

_____

2. Unit Pricing

You are ordering 2-liter plastic bottles of saline solution for the office. Apex Medical Supply sells a ten-bottle package for $12.50. Acme Medical Supply sells the same brand and size in an eight-bottle package for $11.20. Which package is the better buy?

_____

_____

_____

CASE STUDIES

Write your response to each case study on the lines provided.

Case 1

As the person at your office in charge of ordering supplies, you take a call from an unknown vendor. He tells you that he has an overstock of your brand of photocopier toner. He wants to get rid of it, so he will let you have it for half the regular price. He instructs you to send a check to a box number he gives you; then he will ship the toner to you. What should you do? Why?

_____

_____

_____

Case 2

You have delegated the ordering of all supplies to another employee. Since this assignment, you have noticed that the cost of supplies has steadily increased. What factors could be causing this? What can you do to control the costs?

_____

_____

_____

Case 3

You receive a letter from a vendor threatening collection if an invoice that is now 6 months old is not paid immediately. You know that the invoice has been paid. How can you support your claim that your office has paid its bill?

_____

_____

_____

Case 4

As the new medical assistant at an office, you have been assigned the job of managing supplies. You review the supply-ordering system already in place. You research local supply vendors. Then you decide that the office would benefit by changing vendors for some of its clinical supplies. The doctor has been doing business with the present vendor for years and seems unwilling to change. Still, you ask for time to make a presentation to her and other members of the senior staff. What information should you present to make your case?

_____

_____

_____

CHAPTER 9

Maintaining Patient Records

REVIEW

Vocabulary Review

True or False

Decide whether each statement is true or false. In the space at the left, write T for true or F for false. On the lines provided, rewrite the false statements to make them true.

_____ 1. It is not necessary to document in the medical record when a patient in noncompliant.

_____

_____ 2. Patient records may be used to evaluate the quality of treatment a facility or doctor's office provides.

_____

_____ 3. Informed consent forms state that a patient has agreed to treatment.

_____

_____ 4. All written correspondence from the patient, a doctor's office, a laboratory, or an independent heath-care agency should be kept in the patient's chart.

_____

_____ 5. When creating the patient medical record, the first document to be placed in the chart is the Registration form.

_____

_____ 6. Transcription is the transforming of written notes into accurate spoken form.

_____

_____ 7. Problem-oriented medical records are a way to overcome the disadvantages of conventional medical charting.

_____

_____ 8. Objective data comes from the physician and from exams and test results.

_____

_____ 9. Electronic health records can be easily used in teleconferences.

_____

Content Review

Multiple Choice

In the space provided, write the letter of the choice that best completes each statement or answers each question.

_____ 1. When you are in doubt regarding who is authorized to sign a release of records form for a minor,
   A. always ask the oldest person.
   B. always ask the minor who is authorized.
   C. do not allow anyone to sign.
   D. you must ask a lawyer for guidance.
   E. you must always ask your superior.

_____ 2. When children reach this age, most states consider them adults with the right to privacy regarding all of their medical information.
   A. 18
   B. 19
   C. 20
   D. 21

_____ 3. Test results received from sources outside the practice are best organized in sections within what part of the medical chart?
   A. Laboratory and other test results
   B. A special section in the chart especially for outside source material
   C. The very front of the chart
   D. The very back of the chart

_____ 4. Which of the following elements of SOAP charting describes the data that comes directly from the patient?
   A. S
   B. O
   C. A
   D. P

_____ 5. Which of the following elements of SOAP charting describes the course of treatment to be followed?
   A. S
   B. O
   C. A
   D. P

_____ 6. What does the abbreviation PT mean?
   A. Partial
   B. Physical Therapy
   C. Patient
   D. Preoperative
   E. Professional Tone

_____ 7. The six Cs of charting include
   A. Conformity, Clarity, Cleanliness, Conciseness, Chronological order, and Confidentiality
   B. Conformity, Clarity, Completeness, Conciseness, Chronological order, and Creativity
   C. Client's words, Clarity, Completeness, Conciseness, Chronological order, and Confidentiality
   D. Client's words, Conformity, Cleanliness, Conciseness, Chronological order, and Confidentiality
   E. Client's words, Clarity, Conciseness, Conformity, Chronological order, and Confidentiality

_____ **8.** Conventional records are
   A. also called source-oriented records.
   B. also called POMR records.
   C. organized by problems of the patient.
   D. especially easy for tracking a specific ailment in a patient.

_____ **9.** The P in SOAP documentation stands for
   A. purpose.
   B. procedures.
   C. physical.
   D. plan.

_____ **10.** As a general rule, if information is not documented,
   A. it is not important.
   B. it is not useful.
   C. no one can prove that an event or procedure took place.
   D. it is illegal.

_____ **11.** The S in SOAP documentation stands for
   A. subjective.
   B. serious.
   C. sensitive.
   D. statistics.

_____ **12.** Original documentation
   A. is always selected instead of a copy to be given to the patient on request.
   B. cannot be faxed.
   C. legally belongs to the patient.
   D. legally belongs to the physician and belongs in the patient's medical chart.

_____ **13.** Completeness in charting means
   A. using the patient's exact words.
   B. dating all entries into a chart.
   C. not leaving out information.
   D. using precise descriptions and accepted medical terminology.

_____ **14.** The first form used in initiating a patient record is the
   A. informed consent form.
   B. doctor's diagnosis form.
   C. patient medical history form.
   D. patient registration form.

_____ **15.** The term *noncompliant* means that the patient
   A. does not understand.
   B. does not hear well.
   C. is not literate.
   D. does not follow medical advice and direction.

_____ **16.** If a physician who is dictating speaks with an accent and you find it difficult to understand the dictation, you should
- **A.** state you don't understand and stop.
- **B.** ask others in the office if they understand the physician and ask them to take dictation.
- **C.** record the dictation.
- **D.** do the best you can.
- **E.** ask the physician to speak more slowly than normal.

Sentence Completion

In the space provided, write the word or phrase that best completes each sentence.

17. The patient's past medical history, family medical history, and social and occupational history are included in a part of the chart called the _____.

18. It is important to date and _____ every entry you put in the patient chart so that it is easy to tell which items the medical assistant enters and which items other people enter.

19. When filling out patient charts, it is important to record patients' _____, not your interpretation of them.

20. To make chart data more concise, medical workers use standard medical abbreviations, such as "patient got _____" instead of "patient got out of bed."

21. All information in a patient's chart is _____, to protect the patient's privacy.

22. In a conventional, or source-oriented, record, all the patient's problems and treatments are recorded on the same form in _____ order.

23. In problem-oriented medical record keeping, each _____ is listed separately, making it easier for the physician to track a patient's progress.

24. When documenting problems, you must be careful to distinguish between signs, which are external factors that can be seen and measured, and symptoms, which are _____ that can be felt only by the patient.

25. Because the _____ of information in a patient's chart is important, check all information carefully before entering it.

26. The doctor's transcribed notes for the patient's chart should be initialed by the _____.

27. _____ provide physicians with easy access to patient information no matter where they are.

28. _____ charting describes a patient's condition by the use of four letters. The letters describe what the patient says, what the medical personnel see, an evaluation of the problem, and a directive for care.

29. _____ in medical records are not uncommon but must be changed immediately.

17. _____

18. _____

19. _____

20. _____

21. _____

22. _____

23. _____

24. _____

25. _____

26. _____

27. _____

28. _____

29. _____

30. _____ means "to leave out."

31. _____ is the age at which most states consider an individual to be an adult.

32. To maintain patient _____, never discuss a patient's records, forward them to another office, fax them, or show them to anyone but the physician unless you have the patient's written permission to do so.

33. A _____ contains a record of the patient's history, information from the initial interview with the patient, all findings and results from physical exams, and any tests, x-rays, and other procedures.

34. In the _____, patient information is arranged according to who supplied the data—the patient, the doctor, a specialist, or someone else.

35. _____ means in the order of the date in which it occurred.

36. _____ means to be brief and to the point.

30. _____

31. _____

32. _____

33. _____

34. _____

35. _____

36. _____

Short Answer

Write the answer to each question on the lines provided.

37. Explain the difference between patient signs and symptoms. List three examples of each.

_____

_____

_____

38. Describe why it is so important to use care when making corrections to medical charts.

_____

_____

_____

39. List four additions that a physician might want to make to a patient's chart.

_____

_____

_____

40. List five tips for fast and accurate transcription of a doctor's recorded dictation.

_____

_____

_____

41. Describe the SOAP approach to medical record documentation.

_____

_____

_____

42. List six common medical abbreviations that are difficult for you to remember.

_____

_____

_____

43. List six types of data contained in a patient's records.

_____

_____

_____

Critical Thinking

Write the answer to each question on the lines provided.

1. Why is it important to date every entry in the medical record?

_____

_____

_____

2. Do you think the advantages of electronic medical records outweigh the disadvantages? Explain.

_____

_____

_____

3. What could happen if a medical record was subpoenaed to a court of law and the record was incomplete?

_____

_____

_____

4. Why do medical records include notes of all telephone calls to and from a patient?

_____

_____

_____

5. How do the rules of privacy for the release of a 15-year-old patient's medical records differ from the rules that apply to an 18-year-old's records?

_____

_____

_____

APPLICATION

Follow the directions for the application.

1. Initiating a Patient Record

Work with two partners. Each of you should take turns being a medical assistant, a patient, and an observer/evaluator. Assume that this is the patient's first visit to the medical office.

a. Working together, create a model for a patient record. It must contain all the standard chart information, including forms for patient registration, patient medical history, and a physical exam. (You may use the forms shown in Figures 9-2 and 9-3 of the textbook as a guide.)

b. Have one partner play the role of the medical assistant and another partner play the role of a patient complaining of headaches. The third partner should act as the observer and evaluator. Have the medical assistant help the patient complete the patient registration form. Then have the medical assistant interview the patient and record the medical history, using standard abbreviations where appropriate, ending with a description of the patient's reason for the visit. The medical assistant should document any signs, symptoms, or other information the patient wishes to share.

c. Have the evaluator critique the interview and the documentation in the patient chart. The critique should take into account the accuracy of the documentation, the order in which the medical history was taken, and the history's completeness. The evaluator also should note the medical assistant's ability to follow the six Cs of charting, including the correct use of medical abbreviations.

d. The medical assistant, the patient, and the observer should discuss the observer's comments, noting the strengths and weaknesses of the interview and the quality of the documentation.

e. Exchange roles and repeat the exercise with a new patient. Allow the student playing the patient to choose a different medical problem.

f. Exchange roles again so that each member of the team has an opportunity to play the interviewer, the patient, and the observer once.

2. Correcting a Patient Record

a. Using the same patient information as in the model for a patient record created in Application 1, make a correction to three different parts of the record. Pay special attention to Procedure 9-3. Each team member should take turns making three corrections each.

b. Ask your instructor to review each correction and comment on your work. There should be no blacking out or the use of white correction fluid. All corrections should be clear and neat. All corrections should be dated and initialed. Make sure you indicate the reason you made the correction.

CASE STUDIES

Write your response to each case study on the lines provided.

Case 1

You accidentally throw out a sheet of a patient's medical chart. The trash has already been taken away, so there is no chance for you to get it back. You are new in the office, and you are afraid of losing your job if you tell the doctor what you have done. You remember the information that was on the sheet. You think you can easily rewrite it. What should you do?

_____

_____

_____

Case 2

The doctor you work for reads information about her patients into a tape recorder. You then must transcribe the information and enter it into patient charts. The doctor has a pronounced accent, and many of her words are difficult for you to understand. How should you handle the situation?

_____

_____

_____

Case 3

A former patient of the doctor you work for calls and asks you to send her medical records to her new doctor. She says it is important that the records get to her new doctor by this afternoon and asks you to fax them. Would you have a problem with this request? Why or why not?

_____

_____

_____

Case 4

Dr. Smith receives laboratory results from a test performed on Mr. Jones. He calls Mr. Jones at home on Monday, July 6, at 10:00 A.M. He gets no answer, but he leaves a message on Mr. Jones's answering machine asking him to call the office. By 10:00 A.M. the next morning, Dr. Smith has received no answer from Mr. Jones. He calls again and reaches Mrs. Jones and asks her to have her husband call the office. Mr. Jones calls the doctor's office at 2:30 that afternoon. Dr. Smith discusses the test results with Mr. Jones and asks him to make an appointment for the following week. Mr. Jones is connected with the receptionist. He makes an appointment for 11:00 A.M. on July 12. As a medical assistant, how would you record this series of events in Mr. Jones's chart? Use the charting form on page 919 to record events.

_____

_____

_____

CHAPTER 10

Managing the Office Medical Records

REVIEW

Vocabulary Review

Matching

Match the key terms in the right column with the definitions in the left column by placing the letter of each correct answer in the space provided.

_____ 1. Pullout drawers in which hanging file folders are hung

_____ 2. Horizontal filing cabinets

_____ 3. Reminder files

_____ 4. Frequently used files

_____ 5. Infrequently used files

_____ 6. Files that are no longer consulted

a. inactive files
b. vertical files
c. active files
d. tickler files
e. lateral files
f. closed files

True or False

Decide whether each statement is true or false. In the space at the left, write T for true or F for false. On the lines provided, rewrite the false statements to make them true.

_____ 7. If storage space is limited, there are a number of paperless options for storing files.

_____

_____ 8. No matter where you store files, you must consider the issue of safety as well as security.

_____

_____ 9. The rules of indexing state that all hyphenated names are always considered to be one name.

_____

_____ 10. HIPAA law requires that every covered entity have appropriate safeguards to ensure the protection of the patient's confidential health information.

_____

_____ 11. Physicians must keep all immunization records on file in the office for 2 years.

_____

_____ 12. In terminal digital filing, numbers are read from right to left.

_____

_____ 13. Horizontal file cabinets are also called lateral file cabinets.

_____

_____ **14.** A records management system refers to the way patient records are created, filed, and maintained.

_____

_____ **15.** Commercial records centers manage stored documents for medical practices.

_____

_____ **16.** When inserting documents into folders already in place in the drawer, lift the folders up and out of the drawer.

_____

_____ **17.** You should write the name of a patient on the tab of a file folder.

_____

_____ **18.** It is not important to use a file guide as a placeholder to indicate that a file has been taken out of the filing system.

_____

_____ **19.** The final step in the filing process is to store the files in the appropriate filing equipment.

_____

_____ **20.** In an alphabetic filing system, files are placed in alphabetic order according to the patients' last names.

_____

_____ **21.** Many legal consultants advise that doctors maintain patient records for at least 7 years to protect themselves against malpractice suits.

_____

_____ **22.** A file that has been cross-referenced has been placed in more than one location.

_____

_____ **23.** The American Medical Association, the American Hospital Association, and other groups generally suggest that doctors keep patient records for up to 10 years after a patient's final visit or contact.

_____

_____ **24.** *Indexing* is another term for naming a file.

_____

Content Review

Multiple Choice

In the space provided, write the letter of the choice that best completes each statement or answers each question.

_____ **1.** If you are unsure whether to cross-reference a file, the best policy is
   A. to not do it.
   B. to do it.
   C. to let someone else make the decision.
   D. to not put the file away. Set the file on your desk.
   E. to place the unlabeled file into the file cabinet or filing system.

_____ **2.** A numeric filing system
   A. is not used when patient confidentiality is especially important.
   B. organizes records according to the patient's last name.
   C. may include numbers that indicate where in the filing system a file can be found.
   D. is the only practical system for a large practice.

_____ **3.** Use color coding for files
   A. only when using a numeric filing system.
   B. to identify files belonging to specific categories of patients.
   C. only when you are using no other filing system.
   D. to reduce the risk of misplacing files.

_____ **4.** For tickler files to work effectively, they must be
   A. kept in file folders.
   B. kept in a file box.
   C. listed on a calendar.
   D. placed in the computer.
   E. checked frequently.

_____ **5.** The *first* step in locating a misplaced file is to
   A. look for the color of the misfiled chart.
   B. discuss it with the person in charge of the office.
   C. check the doctor's office to see if it is on her desk.
   D. check with the other employees.
   E. determine the last time you knew the file's location.

_____ **6.** The medical records for patients who have died should be placed in which type of file?
   A. Active
   B. Inactive
   C. Closed
   D. Reserved

_____ **7.** When files are organized in a variety of filing systems that place patient records one after the other in a pattern or an order, it is referred to as a
   A. sequential order.
   B. labeled order.
   C. tabbed order.
   D. standard order.

_____ **8.** A new patient is
   A. always an infant.
   B. a patient who has never been seen in the practice before.
   C. a patient who has never been seen in the practice before or has not been seen by a physician in the same specialty in the practice in 3 years.
   D. never a patient who transferred from another practice.

_____ **9.** To make the best use of a color filing system, you must
   A. use only bright colors.
   B. use no more than 4 colors.
   C. always color code a file based on the age of the patient.
   D. first identify the classifications that are important in your office.
   E. never combine a color-coding system with any other filing system.

_____ **10.** Filing guidelines
  A. help you file more efficiently.
  B. help you select a filing system.
  C. identify who is responsible for all filing.
  D. help you set up a tickler system.

_____ **11.** When selecting a commercial records center to assist with patient records, it is important to
  A. assess the monthly fee.
  B. assess the location.
  C. assess the system for retrieval and delivery of files.
  D. All of the above

_____ **12.** Who can take an original patient medical record out of the medical office?
  A. The office manager
  B. The medical assistant
  C. The nurse
  D. No one
  E. The patient

_____ **13.** The proper order for the steps of filing is
  A. sort, inspect, code, index, and store.
  B. store, inspect, index, code, and sort.
  C. inspect, index, code, sort, and store.
  D. index, inspect, code, sort, and store.

_____ **14.** Rotary circular files
  A. take up a lot of room and should only be used in a spacious office.
  B. can only be operated manually.
  C. are a good option when space is limited.
  D. can only be operated electronically.
  E. can be stored stacked on top of one another.

Sentence Completion

In the space provided, write the word or phrase that best completes each sentence.

15. Vertical files have a metal frame from which _____ are hung.

16. _____ can be skipped when filing patient records that have been previously filed.

17. To protect the confidentiality of patient records, always keep them in a(n) _____ area.

18. _____ are large envelope-style folders with tabs in which files can be stored temporarily.

19. When a record is filed in two or more places, it is _____.

20. If you need to keep some patient-related materials separate from the patient's medical record, you should create a(n) _____ file.

21. _____ is another term for naming a file.

22. When you put an identifying mark or phrase on a document to ensure that it is properly filed, you _____ it.

15. _____

16. _____

17. _____

18. _____

19. _____

20. _____

21. _____

22. _____

23. Placing files in a pattern or sequence is referred to as _____.

23. _____

Short Answer

Write the answer to each question on the lines provided.

24. Why is it important to completely remove a file from the drawer in order to file correctly?

_____

_____

_____

25. When small documents have wording on both sides of the paper, how should they be filed?

_____

_____

_____

26. What are two safety concerns when using filing equipment?

_____

_____

_____

27. What is the purpose of the tabs on file folders, and why are they positioned in different places on the folders?

_____

_____

_____

28. What is the purpose of the pockets on some out guides?

_____

_____

_____

29. You should choose file guides with a different tab position than your folders to help them stand out. How far apart should you position guides?

_____

_____

_____

30. Name the five steps in the filing process.

_____

_____

_____

31. List four formats in which inactive and closed files can be stored.

_____

_____

_____

32. Name and describe in detail the first step in filing.

_____

_____

_____

33. Why is it important to post a written copy of the practice retention policy near the filing area?

_____

_____

_____

34. Describe how supplemental files are different from primary medical records.

_____

_____

_____

35. Describe the "indexing" step in filing. What is included?

_____

_____

_____

36. Describe the steps to follow if a file is misplaced.

_____

_____

_____

Critical Thinking

Write the answer to each question on the lines provided.

1. Why is it important not to misplace patient files?

_____

_____

_____

2. What are some of the things that could possibly occur as a result of a medical file being lost?

_____

_____

_____

3. What filing system would you choose for a practice that has many patients who are celebrities? Explain.

_____

_____

_____

4. How can color-coded patient files be helpful in the care and treatment of patients who have illnesses such as diabetes or HIV?

_____

_____

_____

5. Who might be impacted when a medical file is mismanaged or lost?

_____

_____

_____

APPLICATION

Follow the directions for each application.

1. Creating a Patient Filing System

Work in groups of four students. Within your group, choose partners to work together.

a. With your partner, prepare a list of 15 hypothetical patients—complete with full names, ages, and primary ailments. Exchange patient lists with the other pair of students in your group.

b. With your partner, analyze the patient list you have been given. Determine what kind of filing system, alphabetic or numeric, is appropriate.

c. Organize the patients' names as you would for the filing system you have chosen. If you have chosen the alphabetic system, write each name on a different index card and organize the cards. If you have chosen the numeric system, create a master list that shows the numbers and the corresponding patient names.

d. Assume that your patient list is part of a much larger filing system that contains a similar mix of patients. Color-code your filing system. With your partner, decide what categories of information you need to identify through color-coding. Then assign colors to your patient list as appropriate.

e. After you have completed your filing system, meet with the other pair of students in your group and compare filing systems. How are they different? How are they alike? Each pair should evaluate the other pair's filing system for appropriateness and accuracy. Pairs should be able to justify their choices.

f. Form different groups of four students. Exchange your original patient list with a different pair of students and repeat steps **b** through **e**.

2. Setting Up a Tickler File

Work with two partners. Two of you are medical assistants in charge of setting up a tickler file. The third partner is an evaluator.

a. On the chalkboard, each student in the class should list one important date or activity that he needs to be reminded of weekly, monthly, or annually.

b. Working together, the two medical assistants should analyze the reminder information to be included in the tickler file. Decide how you will organize the tickler file. Will you use file folders, a wall chart, a calendar, a binder, or a computer file? Create the tickler file.

c. Have the evaluator critique the tickler file. Her critique should answer these questions: Has any information been overlooked, misplaced, or duplicated? Is the tickler file accurate? Will it help in the day-to-day workings of an office?

d. As a group, discuss the evaluator's comments, noting the strengths and weaknesses of the tickler file as well as its accuracy and completeness.

e. Exchange roles and repeat the activity, choosing a different way of organizing the tickler file.

f. Exchange roles again so that each member of the group has an opportunity to set up and evaluate a tickler file.

CASE STUDIES

Write your response to each case study on the lines provided.

Case 1

You are in charge of the patient filing system for an office with four doctors. The system seems efficient, except that there is no way of knowing who has removed a particular file. You have had to go on numerous searches for missing files only to find them on someone's desk. What change could you make to the system to reduce the need to search the office for missing files?

_____

_____

_____

Case 2

You have a new job. On your first day you learn that no one has filed in weeks. Medical records are stacked on the floor. No one in the office can find what they need and the physicians are complaining. You are told that there are at least two lost records. What do you do?

_____

_____

_____

Case 3

You have noticed that the patient files in your office contain medical records going back many years. It is becoming increasingly difficult to sort through all the documents and locate current medical information in a file. What can be done to solve this problem?

_____

_____

_____

Case 4

Your medical office stores all inactive medical records in cardboard boxes in an area next to the furnace and hot water heater. The boxes are stacked on top of each other in tightly packed rows. The boxes are numbered but it is not possible to read the numbering because there are so many boxes in the small room. The boxes are sitting directly on the floor and are stacked almost to the ceiling. What suggestions would you make to improve this situation?

_____

_____

_____

CHAPTER 11

Telephone Techniques

REVIEW

Vocabulary Review

Matching

Match the key terms in the right column with the definitions in the left column by placing the letter of each correct answer in the space provided.

_____ 1. screening a call

_____ 2. HIPAA

_____ 3. incoming calls

_____ 4. example of courtesy

_____ 5. enunciation

_____ 6. routing list

_____ 7. telephone answering system

_____ 8. documenting

_____ 9. automated telephone system

_____ 10. tone

a. speaking in a positive, respectful manner
b. calls made to the medical office
c. writing in the patient's chart
d. telecommunication
e. concerned with privacy and confidentiality
f. apologizing for delays or errors
g. specifies who is responsible for various types of calls and how the calls are to be handled
h. automated voicemail system
i. determining the need of the caller
j. clear and distinct speaking

Passage Completion

Study the key terms in the box. Use your textbook to find definitions of terms you do not understand.

enunciation	pitch	telephone triage
etiquette	pronunciation	

In the space provided, complete the following passage, using the terms from the box. You may change the form of a term to fit the meaning of the sentence.

The telephone is an important tool in today's medical practice. How you handle telephone calls will have an impact on the public image of the office. When speaking on the telephone, always use proper telephone (11) _____ to present a positive impression of the office. Make your voice pleasant and effective by varying your (12) _____. Remember not to mumble. Good (13) _____ will help the caller understand the important information you are trying to convey. Proper (14) _____ of the caller's name will help her feel welcome and important. In today's medical practice, the process of determining the level of urgency of each call and how it should be handled or routed is called (15) _____.

11. _____

12. _____

13. _____

14. _____

15. _____

Content Review

Multiple Choice

In the space provided, write the letter of the choice that best completes each statement or answers each question.

_____ 1. When checking for understanding during a call,
   A. watch for visual signals.
   B. ask the caller if there are any questions.
   C. repeat everything at least twice.
   D. ask the caller to explain the information to a third person.

_____ 2. The correct use of a telephone log includes
   A. keeping 3 copies of each phone message.
   B. keeping 2 copies of each phone message.
   C. using only a spiral-bound book.
   D. using only a message pad.
   E. giving the original message to the appropriate person and retaining a copy.

_____ 3. If a caller refuses to discuss his symptoms with anyone but the physician,
   A. schedule an appointment immediately.
   B. try to talk the patient into talking with you.
   C. have the doctor return the call.
   D. call the patient the next day to see whether he has changed his mind.

_____ 4. A fax machine
   A. should never be used to send a patient referral.
   B. is confidential.
   C. uses a phone line.
   D. is inappropriate for use in a medical practice.
   E. is a type of telephone routing system.

_____ 5. An automated telecommunications system
   A. is inappropriate for use in a medical practice.
   B. is used in many hospitals and ambulatory care settings.
   C. is more expensive than using a phone operator.
   D. requires that the caller know exactly who he wants to speak to.

_____ 6. What is the best way to deal with salespeople in a medical office?
   A. On the telephone, ask the salesperson to send information about new products and services.
   B. Do not speak to salespeople on the phone at all. Just hang up.
   C. Allow salespeople to meet with the doctor between patients based on how long they have had to wait.
   D. Medical assistants do not deal with salespeople in person or on the phone. That is the role of the doctor.

_____ 7. A patient calls and tells you he is having severe vomiting. What should you do?
   A. Make an appointment for the next day.
   B. Immediately put the call through to a doctor or handle the call according to the established office procedures for patients that need immediate medical help.
   C. Make an appointment for the patient within the next 3 days.
   D. Make an appointment for an annual physical exam.

_____ 8. If you are in doubt about whether a situation is a medical emergency,
   A. you should treat it like an emergency.
   B. you can ignore the situation if the patient tells you he does not want to see the doctor.
   C. you should ask the patient to sit down so he can be observed.
   D. you should rely on your intuition to do the right thing.

_____ 9. A medical assistant may release patient information to an outside caller
   A. only when requested to do so by the physician.
   B. only when that caller is a physician.
   C. only when that caller is an attorney.
   D. whenever it is requested.

_____ 10. Pronunciation is
   A. the high or low level of speech.
   B. the pitch of the voice.
   C. the tone of the voice.
   D. saying words correctly.
   E. speaking without any accent.

_____ 11. The best way to hold a telephone when you are using it is
   A. with one hand.
   B. with a telephone rest.
   C. propped on your shoulder so you have both hands free.
   D. propped on your shoulder, making sure you change shoulders every 3 minutes to avoid fatigue.
   E. Both A and B

_____ 12. Telephone triage
   A. is the screening and sorting of emergency incidents over the phone.
   B. is only done by RNs.
   C. is an automatic message that is easily programmed into an automatic router.
   D. means diagnosing the patient over the phone.

_____ 13. How do you properly respond to a patient who is asking for the results of a lab test?
   A. Tell the patient the results.
   B. Never tell the patient anything.
   C. Tell the patient the results only when the results are normal.
   D. Follow the policies of the medical office.

_____ **14.** If a patient remains dissatisfied after discussing a bill,

       A. document all comments and relay the information to the physician.

       B. tell the patient that you are sorry he is dissatisfied, but the bill stands as is.

       C. turn the patient's bill over to a collection agency.

       D. terminate the patient's care until the bill is paid.

_____ **15.** How should a medical assistant respond to patient complaints?

       A. Listen carefully but never admit mistakes.

       B. Defend the doctor and the policies of the practice.

       C. Be careful to only raise your voice when the patient raises his voice.

       D. Acknowledge the patient's anger.

       E. Do not allow the patient to talk down to you.

Sentence Completion

In the space provided, write the word or phrase that best completes each sentence.

16. The medical assistant handles calls that deal with _____ issues.

17. _____ is a medical emergency in which there is a drop in body temperature during prolonged exposure to cold.

18. If you will be discussing clinical matters over the telephone, it is a good idea to pull the _____.

19. Never release any patient information to an outside caller unless the _____ asks you to.

20. The medical assistant may be responsible for making routine _____ to verify that patients are following treatment instructions.

21. _____ is clear and distinct speaking.

22. Before ending a telephone call, it is good professional behavior to always _____ the important points of the conversation.

23. Keeping a _____ on the desk allows you to easily find frequently used telephone numbers.

24. When taking a telephone message, always record the date and _____ of the call.

25. _____ is a medical emergency in which the patient experiences paleness, feeling faint, and a weak, rapid pulse.

16. _____

17. _____

18. _____

19. _____

20. _____

21. _____

22. _____

23. _____

24. _____

25. _____

Short Answer

Write the answer to each question on the lines provided.

26. List the features of good communications skills.

_____

_____

_____

27. List three types of calls that a medical assistant would handle.

_____

_____

_____

28. List the steps to screen calls appropriately in the office.

_____

_____

_____

29. List three types of incoming calls.

_____

_____

_____

30. List at least 10 symptoms or conditions that would qualify as a medical emergency.

_____

_____

_____

31. What are five ways you can make your telephone voice effective?

_____

_____

_____

32. What is the typical procedure for putting a call on hold?

_____

_____

_____

33. How is telephone triage conducted?

_____

_____

_____

Critical Thinking

Write the answer to each question on the lines provided.

1. How can the telephone image you present have an impact on public perception of your medical office?

_____

_____

_____

2. Describe how you might handle a caller who is not a patient in the practice and who wants a prescription.

_____

_____

_____

3. Describe how a medical assistant might respond when a patient calls the office to discuss symptoms she is experiencing.

_____

_____

_____

4. If a patient calls with an emergency situation and can only stay on the telephone for 1 minute, what questions would be the most important to ask?

_____

_____

_____

5. Discuss what you should do if you do not know how to respond to a caller's question on the phone.

_____

_____

_____

6. The physician requests that you contact a patient and ask him to come in for an appointment, but the patient refuses to come in. What do you do?

_____

_____

_____

7. Discuss how you would respond to a patient who calls to request a prescription refill.

_____

_____

_____

8. Discuss guidelines for dealing with an angry caller.

_____

_____

_____

Name _____ Class _____ Date _____

APPLICATION

Follow the directions for each application.

1. Handling a Patient Call

Work with two partners. Have one partner play the role of an angry patient calling to complain about being billed for a procedure that never took place. Have the second partner act as a medical assistant handling the call. Have the third partner act as an observer and evaluator.

a. Role-play the telephone call. The medical assistant should listen carefully to the caller, taking notes about the details of the problem. The medical assistant also should be sure to ask all necessary questions.

b. The medical assistant should respond to the caller's complaint in a professional manner and explain the specific action that will be taken to address the issue.

c. Have the observer provide a critique of the medical assistant's handling of the call. The critique should evaluate the use of proper telephone etiquette, the proper routing of the call, and the assistant's telephone notes. Comments should include both positive feedback and suggestions for improvement.

d. Exchange roles and repeat the exercise. Allow the student playing the caller to choose another reason for the call.

e. Exchange roles again so that each member of the group has an opportunity to play the role of the medical assistant.

f. Discuss the strengths and weaknesses of each group member's telephone etiquette.

2. Taking Telephone Messages

Work with a partner to design the best possible telephone message pad or telephone log for a medical office.

a. Consider the various types of incoming calls that the medical practice receives. Review the different types of information that a person taking a message might need to obtain. Make a list of the types of calls and types of information. Think about the order in which the information is obtained. Decide how much space is needed for each entry.

b. Choose which you will design—a telephone message pad or telephone log. As you work with your partner to design it, consider these questions: What is the best size for the pad or log? How many messages will fit on one page? How will copies be made? What color will the pad or log be? Pay attention to the information that must be included, the space available for each message, and the layout of the page.

c. Test your telephone message pad or log. Have your partner role-play a patient calling a medical office. Use your message pad or log to take the message.

d. Then trade roles and repeat the role playing. Discuss the strengths and weaknesses of your message pad or log. Revise your design as needed.

e. Share your message pad or log with other pairs of students. Critique each other's designs. Discuss how the designs are different and how they are similar. Assess the strengths and weaknesses of each design. Offer suggestions for revisions.

f. Make final adjustments to the design of your telephone message pad or telephone log on the basis of your classmates' feedback.

CASE STUDIES

Write your response to each case study on the lines provided.

Case 1

You overhear another medical assistant speaking rudely to a patient. What should you do?

_____

_____

_____

Case 2

A salesperson is continually calling on the telephone at the busiest time of day, tying up the line that is used to take patient calls. How might you handle the situation?

_____

_____

_____

Case 3

In one morning, you receive calls from a patient with an emergency, an attorney, a physician from another medical office, and a salesperson. Describe how you would route each of these calls.

_____

_____

_____

Case 4

A patient calls and says that he thinks he is having a heart attack. What do you do?

_____

_____

_____

Case 5

Mrs. Rosetti calls the office and discusses a confidential medical problem with you. How should you handle this situation?

_____

_____

_____

Case 6

A physician calls and asks to speak to the physician in your practice. The physician is with a patient. What do you do?

_____

_____

_____

CHAPTER 12

Scheduling Appointments and Maintaining the Physician's Schedule

REVIEW

Vocabulary Review

Matching

Match the key terms in the right column with the definitions in the left column by placing the letter of each correct answer in the space provided.

_____ **1.** A type of scheduling in which patients arrive at their own convenience, with the understanding that they will be seen on a first-come, first-served basis.

_____ **2.** A type of scheduling that works best in large offi ces that have enough departments and personnel to provide services to several patients at the same time.

_____ **3.** A scheduling system in which several patients are given the same appointment time but are taken as they arrive so that the office schedule remains on track each hour even if patients are late.

_____ **4.** A type of scheduling in which a patient is booked months ahead of time.

_____ **5.** Using double-booking scheduling and clustering scheduling at the same time is an example of this type of technique.

_____ **6.** A patient who does not come to his appointment and does not call to cancel it.

_____ **7.** A term that describes a patient who has not been established at the medical practice.

_____ **8.** A term to describe a patient who is being sent to another physician for a second opinion.

_____ **9.** A term used to describe a patient who comes to see the doctor without an appointment.

_____ **10.** Another name for stream scheduling.

_____ **11.** Leaving large, unused gaps in the schedule.

_____ **12.** The appointment book is an example of this type of document.

_____ **13.** Contacting a patient to confirm an appointment.

_____ **14.** The basic format for an appointment book.

_____ **15.** An item that should be discussed with the physician during regularly scheduled meetings.

a. advanced scheduling
b. underbooking
c. matrix
d. referral
e. legal record
f. wave scheduling
g. modified-wave scheduling
h. time-specified scheduling
i. no-show
j. walk-in
k. open-hours scheduling
l. new patient
m. combination scheduling
n. tax schedule and payments
o. reminder notice or call

Content Review

Multiple Choice

In the space provided, write the letter of the choice that best completes each statement or answers each question.

_____ 1. A system used typically in emergency centers rather than in private practice is
   A. wave scheduling.
   B. double-booking.
   C. modified-wave scheduling
   D. cluster scheduling.
   E. open-hours scheduling.

_____ 2. What is the purpose of a matrix?
   A. It automatically informs patients of their appointments.
   B. It serves as a basic format for scheduling.
   C. It is used to obtain patient information.
   D. It indicates a referral.
   E. It reminds a medical assistant to call patients to confirm their appointments.

_____ 3. If a patient comes in unexpectedly with an emergency condition, it is vital that
   A. the nearest hospital be notified immediately.
   B. the patient be treated as quickly as the schedule will allow.
   C. a physician see that patient ahead of patients who may already be waiting.
   D. patients who have appointments at that time be given the chance to reschedule.
   E. the patient wait his turn.

_____ 4. A disadvantage of the open-hours scheduling system is that
   A. it assumes that two patients will actually be seen by the doctor within the scheduled period.
   B. it increases the possibility of inefficient down time for the doctor.
   C. patients become annoyed or angry when they realize their appointments are at the same time as other patients.
   D. it always means the patient will have a long wait.

_____ 5. What type of appointment scheduling system can be helpful if a patient calls and needs to be seen that day but no appointments are available?
   A. Stream
   B. Wave
   C. Modified-wave
   D. Cluster
   E. Double-booking

_____ 6. Which appointment scheduling system determines the number of patients to be seen each hour by dividing the hour by the length of the average visit?
   A. Double-booking
   B. Cluster
   C. Wave
   D. Advance
   E. Open-hours

_____ 7. The appropriate procedure to follow for a patient who misses an appointment is to
   A. document the no-show in the appointment book and in the patient's chart.
   B. notify the patient that she will be charged for the missed appointment and interest will be applied.
   C. refuse to reschedule an appointment for the patient.
   D. schedule another appointment for the patient but tell her she must call the day before or the appointment will be canceled.
   E. only reschedule the patient with the doctor's approval.

_____ 8. What should you do when a regular patient comes to the office without an appointment?
   A. Ask him how you can help him and notify the physician as needed.
   B. Ask him to leave and you will call him later.
   C. Take him directly to see the physician.
   D. Tell him he can't see the physician without an appointment.
   E. Tell him you can't make appointments for walk-ins.

_____ 9. Obtaining patient information for an appointment should include which of the following?
   A. Marital status
   B. Religion
   C. Age
   D. Occupation
   E. Purpose of the visit

_____ 10. If you are asked to take minutes at a medical meeting, you will need to
   A. create the agenda for the meeting as well.
   B. mail a notice to every person to notify them of the meeting.
   C. know how many people are expected at the meeting.
   D. prepare a report of what was discussed and decided at the meeting.
   E. call everyone and remind them of the date and time of the meeting.

_____ 11. What does the abbreviation CP stand for?
   A. Canceled procedure
   B. Complains politely
   C. Check progress
   D. Chest pain

_____ 12. Most minor medical problems, such as a sore throat, earache, or blood sugar check, usually require how many minutes?
   A. 10 to 15
   B. 15 to 20
   C. 20 to 30
   D. 30 to 45

_____ 13. The abbreviation Rx stands for?
   A. X-ray procedure
   B. Treatment
   C. Prescription
   D. Immunization

_____ **14.** Which of the following is the correct abbreviation for nausea and vomiting?

    A. N & V

    B. NV

    C. N/V

    D. N-V

_____ **15.** Appointments that are anticipated to require more time should be scheduled

    A. at the beginning of the hour.

    B. at the end of the hour.

    C. with another patient's 10-minute time slot.

    D. during a 10-minute time slot.

_____ **16.** The appointment book is a legal record and should be kept at least

    A. 1 year.

    B. 10 years.

    C. 5 years.

    D. 3 years.

Sentence Completion

In the space provided, write the word or phrase that best completes each sentence.

17. The abbreviation "NP" stands for _____.

18. To save time when entering information in the appointment book, you could use the standard abbreviation CPE to stand for _____.

19. A _____ is a way to remind patients to book an appointment in 6 months.

20. _____ scheduling systems can be programmed to lock out selected appointment slots, which can be saved for emergencies.

21. It is important to document a patient who is a no-show in the appointment book and in the _____.

22. To see a referral on relatively short notice is a matter of _____ to the referring physician.

23. Scheduling more patients than can reasonably be seen in the time allowed is called _____.

24. Appointments are often made outside the medical office for surgeries, consultations with other physicians, and various _____ tests.

25. In general, it is good practice to avoid scheduling diabetic patients for appointments at this time of day: _____.

26. Making travel arrangements for a physician may include securing airline reservations and requesting _____ of room reservations.

17. _____

18. _____

19. _____

20. _____

21. _____

22. _____

23. _____

24. _____

25. _____

26. _____

Short Answer

Write the answer to each question on the lines provided.

27. Why is it important to not throw away an old appointment book?

_____

_____

_____

28. How can having a list of standard procedures and the time required for each procedure help you be an efficient scheduler?

_____

_____

_____

29. What three pieces of information must you obtain to properly schedule a patient appointment?

_____

_____

_____

30. How does time-specified scheduling work?

_____

_____

_____

31. How would you select a scheduling appointment system for a medical practice?

_____

_____

_____

32. Give three examples of special scheduling situations that would require you to adjust the schedule for patient needs.

_____

_____

_____

33. Which takes more time and why: An established patient visit or a new patient visit?

_____

_____

_____

34. Why is it beneficial to involve the patient in scheduling his outside appointments?

_____

_____

_____

35. When using advanced scheduling, it is still advisable to leave a few appointment slots open each day. Why?

_____

_____

_____

36. What is an agenda?

_____

_____

_____

37. If a physician in your office refers a patient to another doctor, what is your fi rst step?

_____

_____

_____

38. Define locum tenens.

_____

_____

_____

39. What does the abbreviation NS stand for?

_____

_____

_____

40. What does the abbreviation GI stand for?

_____

_____

_____

Critical Thinking

Write the answer to each question on the lines provided.

1. Who is impacted when a patient is late for an appointment?

_____

_____

_____

2. Why might physicians prefer to schedule new patients first thing in the morning?

_____

_____

_____

3. Why is it important to document a no-show in the appointment book and the patient chart?

_____

_____

_____

4. What types of practices may require more than one locum tenens on call to cover during a physician's absence?

_____

_____

_____

5. What time of day should fasting patients be scheduled for appointments? Why?

_____

_____

_____

6. If the physician is running behind in the schedule for the day, how might you be able to help?

_____

_____

_____

7. List the information you need to book a patient's appointment.

_____

_____

_____

8. Describe the proper way to document a cancellation or a no-show in the appointment book.

_____

_____

_____

APPLICATION

Follow the directions for each application.

1. Scheduling Appointments

Schedule your classmates for appointments at a medical practice. Use the example in the documentation section on page 755.

a. Choose the type of specialty for the practice and the days and hours that the office will be open to see patients each week. Select a scheduling system for your office to use.

b. Determine five procedures (checkups, minor in-office surgeries, and so on) to be performed at the practice. Estimate the typical length of time for each procedure.

c. Schedule the students in your class for appointments, making sure that there is enough time for the procedures to be performed. For each appointment, record the patient's full name, home and work telephone numbers, purpose of visit, and estimated length of visit. Use abbreviations where helpful.

d. Evaluate the schedule for overbooking or underbooking. Share your schedule with another student and ask for comments. Revise the schedule as necessary.

2. Developing a Travel Itinerary

A physician in your practice is attending the American Medical Association's annual conference, to be held at the Hyatt Regency Hotel in Chicago. Develop a travel itinerary, using the sample itinerary found in Figure 12-2 in the textbook as a guide, that you can give to the physician and also keep a copy of in the office for reference.

a. Determine the dates of the conference and the dates of the physician's departure and return. Choose the airline that the physician will fly and note the flight times.

b. Record the itinerary in chronological order. Include telephone numbers and addresses of each location where the physician can be reached as well as the dates and times that the physician can be reached there.

c. Evaluate your itinerary. Are you able to contact the physician at every point during the trip? If not, is there additional information you can list on the itinerary?

d. Examine itineraries developed by your classmates. Is there something they included in their itineraries that you can add to yours?

e. With your classmates, discuss the value of having an itinerary.

3. Make an appointment for a patient. Use the example in the documentation section on page 755.

Patients:

Melody Webster wants to see Dr. Torrance on November 12 at 10:15 (regular office visit—generally 15 minutes in length)

Fern Santos (new patient) wants to see Dr. Hilbert (schedule her for at least 30 minutes—complete physical as a new patient—she can be scheduled either November 12 or 13)

Hope Maxwell needs a consultation on the 13th of November with Dr. Hilbert (consults are generally 30–45 minutes in length)

CASE STUDIES

Write your response to each case study on the lines provided.

Case 1

You are new in the office but you feel that the type of scheduling system used in the medical practice is not working well to meet the patient's needs. What could you do?

_____

_____

_____

Case 2

A female patient becomes upset when a man who just arrived at the office is taken to see the doctor immediately. The woman has been waiting for almost an hour and was supposed to be seen next. What should you do?

_____

_____

_____

Case 3

A medical assistant informs waiting patients that the physician will be delayed. She shares details about the emergency appendectomy the mayor's daughter needs, which will take at least an hour. She asks patients whether they prefer to wait, reschedule, or run errands and come back later. Has the medical assistant handled this situation appropriately? Explain.

_____

_____

_____

Case 4

You have been asked to create a cluster schedule for the office. In your own words, describe the steps you would take to set up this new system.

_____

_____

_____

CHAPTER 13

Patient Reception

REVIEW

Vocabulary Review

True or False

Decide whether each statement is true or false. In the space at the left, write T *for true or* F *for false. On the lines provided, rewrite the false statements to make them true.*

_____ **1.** The appearance of the reception area helps to create a patient's impression of the practice.

_____

_____ **2.** A bandage from a child's cut is infectious waste, but a used diaper is not.

_____

_____ **3.** The Americans with Disabilities Act protects people against discrimination because of their mental disability.

_____

_____ **4.** A contagious disease can be spread among patients waiting in a reception area.

_____

_____ **5.** People from different countries or cultures are considered to have special needs.

_____

_____ **6.** A color family is a group of colors that work well together.

_____

_____ **7.** Examples of specialty items in a reception area include chairs and sofas.

_____

_____ **8.** Patients should have clear, easy access from the parking lot to the medical office door as well as within the office.

_____

_____ **9.** A TTY is a device for hearing-impaired patients.

_____

_____ **10.** A bulletin board is appropriate in a medical practice.

_____

_____ **11.** Health magazines geared toward the general public are a good choice for reading material in a medical office.

_____

_____ **12.** It is not necessary to read pamphlets and brochures that are displayed in the reception areas as long as they are published by major publishing companies.

_____

_____ **13.** Some states have a relay service for patients with hearing impairments or those with speech disabilities.

_____

_____ **14.** No matter how tastefully it is decorated, the reception area will be unappealing if it is not clean.

_____

_____ **15.** The primary pastime in the patient reception area is watching television.

_____

_____ **16.** Stuffed animals are appropriate for pediatric reception areas because they are soft.

_____

Content Review

Multiple Choice

In the space provided, write the letter of the choice that best answers each question or completes each statement.

_____ **1.** The use of videos in a medical practice is
  A. always inappropriate.
  B. becoming a more common activity.
  C. appropriate only for children.
  D. appropriate only for adults for teaching purposes.

_____ **2.** The best toys for children in a reception area are
  A. toys intended for quiet play.
  B. toys that can be easily cleaned.
  C. toys that can be enjoyed while the child sits.
  D. All of the above.
  E. None of the above.

_____ **3.** A double door leading from the medical office to the outside of the building
  A. helps patients feel safe in the waiting area.
  B. discourages salespeople from entering.
  C. helps patients locate the office.
  D. minimizes drafts in the reception area.

_____ **4.** Which of the following items would be a good addition to a pediatrician's reception area?
  A. DVD player and children's DVDs
  B. Sponge ball and bat
  C. Stuffed animals
  D. Bottle of bubble-blowing liquid
  E. Bag of marbles

_____ **5.** Items on a reception bulletin board should be
  A. written in very large print.
  B. only related to government reports on food and drugs.
  C. changed daily.
  D. never contain information about drugs.
  E. tailored to patients' interests.

_____ **6.** Older patients may require furniture that is
  A. plastic.
  B. firm.
  C. brightly colored.
  D. extra soft to accommodate for their loss of muscle tissue.

_____ **7.** The correct amount of furniture in a reception area
  A. is enough furniture so that all patients and family members or friends who accompany the patient can sit comfortably, no matter how busy the office schedule is.
  B. is six chairs and one sofa.
  C. is 10 chairs and no sofas.
  D. depends on the size of the room and the number of windows and is usually six to eight chairs.
  E. is specified by OSHA safety regulations.

_____ **8.** The patient information packet includes
  A. magazine articles.
  B. billing and insurance processing policies.
  C. drug information.
  D. medical brochures.

_____ **9.** Pediatric reception areas
  A. are designed to meet the special size and needs of children.
  B. are required under federal law for all family practice offices.
  C. are different from traditional reception areas only in that all the furniture is smaller.
  D. are designed only for sick children.
  E. do not differ in any way from adult reception areas.

_____ **10.** A cleaning communications notebook is
  A. a means of communication between the office staff and the cleaning staff.
  B. a way to list special cleanup needs for the cleaning staff.
  C. a way to congratulate and thank the cleaning staff.
  D. All of the above.
  E. None of the above.

_____ **11.** A telecom teletype machine
  A. is required by federal law in medical practices.
  B. looks just like a regular telephone.
  C. looks like a laptop computer with a cradle for the receiver of a traditional telephone.
  D. is not capable of communicating with another telecom teletype machine.

_____ **12.** The Americans with Disabilities Act
  A. specifies that bars or rails are attached exactly 30 inches above the floor.
  B. does not address types of discrimination.
  C. maintains the rights of disabled people, including jobs.
  D. has no impact on the patient reception area of a medical practice.

Sentence Completion

In the space provided, write the word or phrase that best completes each sentence.

13. Many elderly patients feel colder because of _____.

14. Music in the reception area should reflect the interests of the _____.

15. The path patients must take to get from the parking area or street to the office and then back again is called the patient _____.

16. _____ is waste that can be dangerous to those who handle it or to the environment.

17. In a large medical office, the cleaning service is often supervised by a(n) _____.

18. One odor that can be prevented by displaying a sign in a patient reception area is _____.

19. OSHA requires the regular use of _____ as part of a cleaning schedule.

20. To protect patients and staff from being trapped by a fire, medical offices are legally required to install _____.

21. Reading materials in a patient reception area can be organized on tables or in a _____.

22. To protect all patients, but especially those who are immunocompromised, it is best to take _____ patients directly into the exam room.

13. _____

14. _____

15. _____

16. _____

17. _____

18. _____

19. _____

20. _____

21. _____

22. _____

Short Answer

Write the answer to each question on the lines provided.

23. Why are ramps important for a medical practice?

_____

_____

_____

24. What are five daily tasks involved in cleaning a reception area?

_____

_____

_____

25. Why should you take special care in cleaning up after a patient who has vomited or bled on the furniture in the reception area?

_____

_____

_____

26. How much furniture should there be in a patient reception area?

_____

_____

_____

27. How do you best clean a stain?

_____

_____

_____

28. Give two reasons why a medical office should have at least two exits.

_____

_____

_____

29. What are four types of appropriate reading material for the patient reception area?

_____

_____

_____

30. What is the best way to wash artificial flowers?

_____

_____

_____

31. List three ways you could make a reception area more comfortable for elderly patients.

_____

_____

_____

32. List four aspects of a reception area that can make a stay there seem longer than it actually is.

_____

_____

_____

33. How can you best determine the correct temperature for a medical office?

_____

_____

_____

34. List six guidelines for safety in the reception area.

_____

_____

_____

35. Define office access.

_____

_____

_____

36. List three warm colors.

_____

_____

_____

37. What are three factors to consider in determining the number of parking spaces a medical office needs?

_____

_____

_____

Critical Thinking

Write the answer to each question on the lines provided.

1. Why is it important to keep patients occupied and informed?

_____

_____

_____

2. Describe the best way to calculate how much seating should be in a physician's reception area.

_____

_____

_____

3. What kind of specialty items would you choose to add to the reception area of a geriatric practice?

_____

_____

_____

4. What type of music is best in a medical office and why?

_____

_____

_____

5. Why is it important to clean a patient reception area on a daily basis?

_____

_____

_____

APPLICATION

Follow the directions for each application.

Creating a Reception Area

Working with a partner, imagine that you have been asked to create a patient reception area for a small medical office. As you plan the area, keep the needs and comfort of the patients foremost in your minds.

a. With your partner, decide on the kind of practice for which you will be creating a reception area, such as a gerontology, orthopedic, or family practice. Then brainstorm a list of the characteristics, needs, and interests of the patients of this practice. Put the kind of practice and your list in writing.

b. Determine the size of the reception area. Base the size on the number of patients who will be using the reception area at one time. Make a diagram or floor plan of the area. If you wish, use graph paper and draw the area to scale. For example, you might decide that one square on the graph paper equals 2 feet in the reception area. Locate all doors and windows. Draw them to scale on the diagram.

c. Discuss the decor. Choose a color family, and select colors for the carpeting, furniture, walls, window treatments, and so on. Keep written notes of your selections.

d. Decide what furniture you will purchase and how it will be arranged. Keep in mind the needs of the kinds of patients who will use the reception area. Locate each piece of furniture on your diagram of the area, drawing each to scale.

e. Choose music, specific magazines and books, and special items for the reception area. Write down your choices.

f. Along with other pairs of students, share your diagram and written notes with the class. Join in a class discussion of the various reception area plans and how each area will meet the specific needs of the medical practice and its patients.

CASE STUDIES

Write your response to each case study on the lines provided.

Case 1

The physician is especially fond of tropical fish and wants to add a tropical fish aquarium to the office. You don't know how to correctly care for an aquarium of fish and fear it might be a hazard to young patients. What should you do?

_____

_____

_____

Case 2

One patient visits the medical office where you work at least once a week and brings her two preschoolers. At first, she asked you to keep an eye on them while she was in the exam room. Now she just leaves the children in the reception area, expecting you to babysit without being asked. You cannot stay in the reception area and watch her children. How can you handle this problem?

_____

_____

_____

Case 3

A pediatric practice has a small paved area just behind the office. Another medical assistant thinks the space could be used for a basketball court where children who are not sick could play while they wait for the doctor to see them or a sibling. Is this a good idea? Explain.

_____

_____

_____

Case 4

You are working in a large medical office along with two other medical assistants. You notice that you are the only one who routinely picks up and cleans the patient reception area. You feel others should be helping maintain this important area. What should you do?

_____

_____

_____

CHAPTER **14**

Patient Education

REVIEW

Vocabulary Review

Passage Completion

Study the key terms in the box. Use your textbook to find definitions of terms you do not understand.

consumer education	modeling	return demonstration	screening

In the space provided, complete the following passage, using the terms from the box. You may change the form of a term to fit the meaning of the sentence.

Patient education is a vital part of patient care. Preoperative teaching, for example, increases patients' knowledge about and participation in the surgical procedure. Through factual teaching and active demonstrations that include (1) _____, patients learn techniques that can enhance their recovery. The patient should repeat any demonstration, a practice that is called (2) _____. (3) _____ that is geared to the average person, in content and in language, helps increase awareness of the importance of good health. This kind of education includes encouraging patients to have regular (4) _____ tests for early diagnosis and treatment of certain diseases. Patients also benefit from learning about the medical office.

1. _____

2. _____

3. _____

4. _____

Content Review

Multiple Choice

In the space provided, write the letter of the choice that best completes each statement or answers each question.

_____ 1. Which of the following terms is used to describe an office's set of values and principles?
   A. Screening technique
   B. Benefits
   C. Confidentiality
   D. Philosophy
   E. Privacy rules

_____ 2. Which of the following topics would an educational newsletter most likely contain?
   A. Health-care tips
   B. A physician's credentials
   C. The payment policies of a medical office
   D. A community resource directory
   E. A list of the office's staff

_____ 3. The process of screening
   A. doesn't allow an early diagnosis.
   B. is free.
   C. differs according to patient age.
   D. is only advisable when symptoms are present.
   E. can't be done in a medical practice.

_____ 4. Some practices create simplified versions of their patient information packet for patients
   A. with hearing impairments.
   B. with visual impairments.
   C. who do not understand English.
   D. who will undergo surgical procedures.

_____ 5. When speaking to a patient who wears a hearing aid, it is best to
   A. filter out loud noises.
   B. raise your voice.
   C. speak at a normal level.
   D. speak very slowly.
   E. write down everything.

_____ 6. It is recommended that the water in the water heater be set at what temperature in order to prevent injury?
   A. 100°F
   B. 120°F
   C. 130°F
   D. 140°F

_____ 7. When developing a patient education plan, the first thing you must do is
   A. develop the plan.
   B. discuss the idea with the physician.
   C. perform the instruction.
   D. identify how intelligent the patient is.
   E. identify the patient's needs.

_____ 8. Which of these is the best definition of patient education?
   A. Patient education is the use of visual material to educate a patient.
   B. Patient education is the demonstration of a technique to a patient.
   C. Patient education is the use of verbal instruction to educate a patient.
   D. Any instructions—verbal, written, or demonstrative—that are given to patients are types of patient education.

_____ 9. Which statement about patient education is true?

    A. Patient education is always performed according to a well-defined plan.

    B. Patient education is only appropriate for intelligent people.

    C. Patient education takes many forms and includes a variety of techniques.

    D. Medical assistants are not generally involved in patient education.

    E. The physician is responsible for providing all patient education.

_____ 10. Many accidents happen because people fail to see potential risks. *Potential risks* means

    A. side effects.

    B. situations or things that can cause harm.

    C. preventive measures.

    D. situations or things that always cause harm.

_____ 11. *Preventive measures* means

    A. patient education.

    B. health-promoting behaviors.

    C. screening.

    D. anything that helps a patient avoid illness or injury.

_____ 12. The patient information packet should include

    A. the first bill or invoice.

    B. names of other medical practices that the practice is not associated with.

    C. medical brochures describing disease processes that relate to the patient's primary medical condition.

    D. a description of the practice and an introduction to the office.

    E. referrals to other physicians.

_____ 13. The patient confidentiality statement

    A. supplies a place for the patient to sign before any other practice information is released.

    B. is not commonly used in a pediatric practice.

    C. should state that no information from patient files will be released without signed authorization from the patient.

    D. is not usually part of the information packet.

_____ 14. The guidelines for healthful habits include adequate rest, which is defined as being how many hours of sleep each night?

    A. 7 to 8

    B. 8 to 9

    C. 5 to 6

    D. 10 or more hours

Sentence Completion

In the space provided, write the word or phrase that best completes each sentence.

15. Many accidents happen because people fail to see _____ and do not develop plans of action.

16. Health is a complex concept that involves the body, _____, emotions, and environment.

17. The first letter of the warning signs for cancer spell out the word _____.

15. _____

16. _____

17. _____

18. A patient information packet should identify office staff members according to their _____.

19. Elderly patients who have problems with memory should receive detailed _____ instructions.

20. Patients who will undergo a surgical procedure must first sign a(n) _____ form.

21. When you provide preoperative education, be aware that the fear and _____ of patients who are about to undergo a surgical procedure can adversely affect the learning process.

18. _____

19. _____

20. _____

21. _____

Short Answer

Write the answer to each question on the lines provided.

22. Why is patient education so important prior to surgery?

_____

_____

_____

23. List three ways to achieve good health.

_____

_____

_____

24. What is the general function of an occupational therapy assistant?

_____

_____

_____

25. What are three ways that a patient information packet can be helpful to patients? To a medical office?

_____

_____

_____

26. List five types of information that should appear in a patient information packet.

_____

_____

_____

27. When providing information to elderly patients, what are some important points to remember?

_____

_____

_____

28. Name some materials that are available for patient education in the public library.

_____

_____

_____

29. Identify and describe three types of preoperative teaching.

_____

_____

_____

30. Of the healthy habits listed in this chapter, which three do you consider the most important and why?

_____

_____

_____

31. List six practices that a medical assistant should use when educating patients with hearing problems.

_____

_____

_____

32. List three ways you can relieve a patient's anxiety.

_____

_____

_____

33. List five tips for preventing injury in the workplace.

_____

_____

_____

34. How might you explain to a patient the proper use of medications?

_____

_____

_____

35. List the eight steps to developing an education plan for a patient.

_____

_____

_____

36. Why is it important for a surgical patient to have someone drive her home after surgery?

_____

_____

_____

Critical Thinking

Write the answer to each question on the lines provided.

1. What are the advantages of developing a formal, written educational plan for a patient?

_____

_____

_____

2. How might your approach to educating children about healthful habits differ from your approach to teaching adult patients?

_____

_____

_____

3. What type of preoperative teaching plan do you think might be best for a patient who is blind?

_____

_____

_____

4. When educating patients with special needs, why is it important to be especially sensitive to their individual circumstances?

_____

_____

_____

5. What do you think is the most important tip for preventing injury in the workplace? Why?

_____

_____

_____

APPLICATION

Follow the directions for the application.

Preparing an Education Brochure

a. Use the Internet to choose a medical topic such as Leukemia or Sickle Cell Anemia.

b. Write at least 2–3 paragraphs about this particular medical topic and prepare in a brochure format.

c. You can also choose INSERT picture for your brochure.

Follow the instructions to prepare a brochure on your computer

1. On your computer, click **FILE, New**

2. On the left side of the screen you will see **TEMPLATES**; choose **on my computer**

3. Click on **Publications** and choose **Brochure**

4. You can then preview the brochure, and click **OK**

CASE STUDIES

Write your response to each case study on the lines provided.

Case 1

During a physical exam, a teenage patient admits to you that he lives "mainly on hamburgers and French fries," that he rarely exercises, and that he often gets fewer than 6 hours of sleep a night, except on weekends. "I'll worry about my health when I'm older," he tells you. What can you say to the patient to encourage him to adopt healthful habits now?

_____

_____

_____

Case 2

The physician you work for wants you to develop patient information that will fit on two sides of a 4- by 6-inch index card. There will be room for only the most important information. What should appear on the card?

_____

_____

_____

Case 3

The third level of disease prevention involves the rehabilitation and management of an existing illness. What might you say to a patient who thinks that rehabilitation is just a waste of time and money?

_____

_____

_____

Case 4

A patient calls with questions about her upcoming surgery. Her patient record reflects that the physician has already discussed the nature of the surgery with her. As a medical assistant, what are your responsibilities for ensuring that the patient is fully prepared for the surgery?

_____

_____

_____

CHAPTER 15

Health Insurance Billing Procedures

REVIEW

Vocabulary Review

Matching

Match the key terms in the right column with the definitions in the left column by placing the letter of each correct answer in the space provided.

_____ 1. A health benefit program designed for low-income, blind, or disabled patients; needy families; foster children; and children born with birth defects

_____ 2. Payments made by an insurance carrier to a policyholder

_____ 3. A fixed dollar amount that must be paid or "met" once a year before the third-party payer begins to cover medical expenses

_____ 4. The basic annual cost of health-care insurance paid by a policyholder

_____ 5. An organization the patient has a relationship with that agrees to carry the risk of paying for medical services

_____ 6. Authorization from a physician for a patient to receive additional services from another physician or medical facility

_____ 7. The oldest and most expensive type of health plan, it repays policyholders for costs of healthcare due to illness and accidents

_____ 8. A health-care benefit system for families of veterans with total, permanent, service-connected disabilities and for surviving spouses and children of veterans who died in the line of duty

_____ 9. A type of insurance, either provided by an employer for its employees or purchased privately by self-employed individuals, that is activated when the employee is injured.

_____ 10. An outside service that processes and transmits claims in the correct EDI format

_____ 11. The manager of the Medicare program

_____ 12. A form that accompanies payment by an insurer and that can include information about services not covered

_____ 13. The payment system used by Medicare

_____ 14. The PCP physician payment structure used by most HMOs

_____ 15. A plan that reimburses the patient's Part B deductible and coinsurance amounts after Medicare pays its portion

_____ 16. An effort by insurers to prevent duplication of payment for health care

a. deductible
b. capitation
c. CMS
d. CHAMPVA
e. third-party payer
f. coordination of benefits
g. remittance advice (RA)
h. fee-for-service
i. clearinghouse
j. Medigap
k. Medicaid
l. premium
m. disability insurance
n. referral
o. benefits
p. resource-based relative value scale

True or False

Decide whether each statement is true or false. In the space at the left, write T *for true or* F *for false. On the lines provided, rewrite the false statements to make them true.*

_____ 17. CHAMPVA covers the expenses of the dependents of veterans with total, permanent, service-connected disabilities.

_____

_____ 18. Some insurers require subscribers to pay a yearly deductible before charges are considered for payment.

_____

_____ 19. TRICARE is a Medicaid program.

_____

_____ 20. A managed care organization (MCO) sets up agreements with physicians as well as with enrolled policyholders.

_____

_____ 21. If a retired patient is covered by the plan of the spouse's employer and the spouse is still employed, Medicare coverage is primary.

_____

_____ 22. Exclusions are expenses covered by an insurance company.

_____

_____ 23. Medicare states that for services rendered from January 1 to September 30, claims must be filed by December 31 of the following year.

_____

_____ 24. Copayments are made to insurance companies.

_____

_____ 25. If an insurance carrier reviews a claim and determines that the diagnosis and the accompanying treatment plan are not compatible, the insurance carrier will not pay for the services rendered.

_____

_____ 26. The RBRVS system is the basis for the Medicare payment system.

_____

_____ 27. The procedure code gives the insurance carrier information regarding medical necessity.

_____

_____ 28. Preferred provider organizations (PPOs) never allow their members to receive care from providers outside the network.

_____

_____ 29. Simple errors often prevent the generation of a "clean" claim.

_____

_____ 30. A lifetime maximum benefit is established as a total dollar amount to be paid by an insurer.

_____

_____ **31.** When completing a CMS-1500 claim form for a TRICARE patient, section #4 should always be completed with the name of the patient.

_____

_____ **32.** Recipients of Medicare Part A and Part B can purchase Medigap insurance to cover gaps in health insurance coverage.

_____

_____ **33.** A taxonomy code is a 10-digit number that stands for a physician's medical specialty.

_____

Content Review

Multiple Choice

In the space provided, write the letter of the choice that best completes each statement or answers each question.

_____ **1.** Which of the following is a Medicare plan that charges a monthly premium and a small copayment for each office visit, but no deductible?
   A. Medicare managed care plan
   B. Medicare preferred provider organization plan
   C. Medicare private fee-for-service plan
   D. Original Medicare plan
   E. Medigap plan

_____ **2.** At the time of service, if required by the managed care plan, medical assistants collect
   A. deductibles.
   B. copayments.
   C. premiums.
   D. coinsurance.

_____ **3.** The nationally uniform relative value of a procedure is based on which of the following three things?
   A. The physician's specialty, the cost of living, and insurance rates
   B. The age of the patient, the diagnosis of the patient, and the geographic area of the practice
   C. The amount billed by the physician, the cost of the procedure, and the copayment of the patient
   D. The physician's work, the practice's overhead, and the cost of malpractice insurance
   E. The fee schedule of the physician, the geographic area of the practice, and the diagnosis of the patient

_____ **4.** Under the concept of the resource-based relative value scale (RBRVS) used by Medicare, the fee for a procedure is based on
   A. a formula based on using the relative value, the geographic adjustment factor, and a conversion factor.
   B. the generally accepted fee that a physician charges for difficult or complicated services.
   C. the average fee that a physician charges for a service or procedure.
   D. the 90th percentile of fees charged for a procedure by similar physicians in the same area.

_____ 5. Billing a patient for the difference between a higher usual fee and a lower allowed charge is called _____ and is not allowed by participating physicians.

    A. capitation

    B. assignment of benefits

    C. coordination of benefits

    D. third-party paying

    E. balance billing

_____ 6. Under Medicare Part B, patients are required to pay an annual

    A. deductible.

    B. copayment.

    C. coinsurance.

    D. claim submission charge for reimbursement.

_____ 7. Medicare Part A does not pay for

    A. inpatient expenses up to 90 days for each benefit period.

    B. medical care at home.

    C. outpatient hospital services.

    D. psychiatric hospitalization.

    E. respite care.

_____ 8. Patients enrolled in the Original Medicare Plan may purchase additional coverage under a

    A. Medicare Part A plan.

    B. coinsurance plan.

    C. Medigap plan.

    D. Medicare Advantage plan.

    E. fee-for-service.

Sentence Completion

In the space provided, write the word or phrase that best completes each sentence.

9. The largest federal health-care program is _____.

10. An insured's policy can also cover _____ of the subscriber, such as a spouse and children.

11. By law, physicians who participate in federally funded programs such as Medicare must accept the _____ charge as payment in full.

12. Patients sign a(n) _____ of benefits statement to permit providers to receive payments directly from third-party payers.

13. Physicians who enroll in managed care plans are called _____.

14. When filing a Medicaid claim, you should ask for and check the patient's Medicaid card to confirm the patient's _____.

15. Managed care plans pay physicians in one of two ways: by either contracted fees or a fixed prepayment called _____.

9. _____

10. _____

11. _____

12. _____

13. _____

14. _____

15. _____

Short Answer

Write the answer to each question on the lines provided.

16. List three of the basic steps in the claims process that are performed in a doctor's office.

_____

_____

_____

17. What does an eligible individual have to do to receive Medicare Part B?

_____

_____

18. Describe the process used to calculate what the practice must write off and what a patient owes when the provider is a Medicare participating physician.

_____

_____

_____

19. What does liability insurance cover?

_____

_____

20. Why must the X12 837 Health Care Claim be used for Medicare claims?

_____

_____

21. Describe a PPO. How does it operate?

_____

_____

22. List the five sections of data elements on the X12 837 Health Care Claim.

_____

_____

23. What is the purpose of the coordination of benefits clauses in insurance policies?

_____

_____

Critical Thinking

Write the answer to each question on the lines provided.

1. What could be the possible outcome of inaccurate medical billing?

_____

_____

_____

2. For a medical practice, what are some advantages and disadvantages of filing claims for patients rather than having patients pay their medical expenses and file their own claims?

_____

_____

_____

3. Why is it important to follow all claims security procedures when electronically submitting health claims?

_____

_____

_____

4. Technology known as the "smart card" has been developed to store a person's complete medical history. The information would be easy to access, update, and transmit. Do you foresee any problems with such a system?

_____

_____

_____

5. What aspect of a claim do you think is the most difficult to complete and why? How might you get help to complete this part?

_____

_____

_____

APPLICATION

Follow the directions for the application.

Developing Tools for Processing Claims

Work with a partner to analyze the information needed to calculate the practice and patient payments for a new medical practice. The practice will accept patients who have Medicare, Medicaid, workers' compensation insurance, managed care plans, and other types of insurance. The practice will use electronic claims processing.

  a. Begin by working with your partner to compile a list of items required for the claims processing steps in your medical office. Include the names of forms (such as the patient registration form); carrier rules (such as time limits); logs; and documents. If you cannot recall the exact name of a publication or form, write a brief description of the information it contains.

b. Review sections of Chapter 15 that describe claims processing for various health plans, such as Medicare, Medicaid, TRICARE and CHAMPVA, Blue Cross and Blue Shield, and PPOs. Add items to the list you began in step **a,** such as each plan's premium, deductible, coinsurance, and copayment.

c. Write a brief explanation of how each item is used in processing claims.

d. Identify and list sources of the items, if this information is given in the chapter. If possible, research websites for the information using a Web browser.

e. Organize the list by category of items or by type of insurance coverage or benefit on a chart or other type of graphic organizer.

f. Share your chart with other pairs in the class. Discuss various ways to organize these materials in a medical office.

g. In a full-class discussion, analyze the medical assistant's role in handling health-care claims in terms of the procedures and tools needed to comply with current requirements. Discuss ways to reduce the amount of paperwork involved in filing claims. Offer creative suggestions for streamlining or eliminating some steps in the process.

CASE STUDIES

Write your response to each case study on the lines provided.

Case 1

A new patient is completing your office's patient registration form. The patient tells you that she has insurance but does not have her card with her and does not know the effective date of coverage, the group plan number, or the identification number. Explain one or more ways to obtain the insurance information right away.

_____

_____

_____

Case 2

Your medical office receives a payment and a remittance advice (RA) from an insurer in response to a claim you filed for a patient. The RA notes that one of the services on the claim is not covered in the patient's plan. What steps will you take regarding the rejected portion of the claim?

_____

_____

_____

Case 3

A medical assistant coworker tells you that he doesn't see the point for all the security policies involved with submitting electronic claims. "After all," he says, "all the security we need is built into the system." How might you respond?

_____

_____

_____

CHAPTER 16

Medical Coding

REVIEW

Vocabulary Review

Matching

Match the key terms in the right column with the definitions in the left column by placing the letter of each correct answer in the space provided.

_____ 1. Codes used for healthy patients receiving routine services

_____ 2. CPT codes used to report the physician's exam of a patient to diagnose conditions and determine a course of treatment

_____ 3. A code that is used to report the services the physician provided for a patient, such as surgery

_____ 4. The sixth section of CPT codes

_____ 5. CPT codes used to report procedures done in addition to another procedure

_____ 6. The person with the ultimate responsibility for proper documentation and correct coding as well as compliance with regulations

_____ 7. A coding reference for patient diagnoses

_____ 8. A coding reference for medical services performed by physicians

_____ 9. A patient who has not received services from the physician within the last 3 years

_____ 10. A list of abbreviations, punctuation guides, symbols, typefaces, and instructional notes that provide guidelines for using a code set

_____ 11. A system developed by the Centers for Medicare and Medicaid Services (CMS) for use in coding services for Medicare patients

_____ 12. Acts that take advantage of others for personal gain

a. add-on code
b. physician
c. conventions
d. *Current Procedural Terminology* (CPT)
e. V codes
f. E/M code
g. fraud
h. Health Care Common Procedure Coding System (HCPCS)
i. *International Classification of Diseases, Ninth Revision, Clinical Modification* (ICD-9)
j. new patient
k. procedure code
l. Medicine — 90281–99602

True or False

Decide whether each statement is true or false. In the space at the left, write T for true or F for false. On the lines provided, rewrite the false statements to make them true.

_____ 13. To avoid the risk of fraud, medical offices have a compliance plan to uncover compliance problems and correct them.

_____

_____ 14. A diagnosis is a description of the patient's course of treatment.

_____

_____ **15.** The Alphabetic Index of the ICD-9 is used to verify a code selection after it has been looked up in the Tabular List.

_____

_____ **16.** An established patient has seen the physician within the previous three years before this visit.

_____

_____ **17.** In correct claims, each reported service is connected to a diagnosis that supports the procedure as necessary to investigate or treat the patient's condition.

_____

_____ **18.** During the global period, follow-up care related to the surgical procedure is included in the procedure payment from the insurance carrier.

_____

_____ **19.** In selecting a code from the ICD-9, you can safely ignore all cross-references.

_____

_____ **20.** A CPT modifier has three digits and a letter.

_____

_____ **21.** The Health Care Common Procedure Coding System was developed to code workers' compensation claims.

_____

_____ **22.** HIPAA calls for penalties for giving remuneration to anyone eligible for benefits under federal health-care programs.

_____

_____ **23.** Evaluation and management codes (E/M codes) are often considered the most important of all CPT codes because they can be used by all physicians in any medical specialty.

_____

Content Review

Multiple Choice

In the space provided, write the letter of the choice that best completes each statement or answers each question.

_____ **1.** ICD-9 and CPT coding reference books are updated
   A. annually.
   B. quarterly.
   C. monthly.
   D. every five years
   E. as needed.

_____ **2.** The most specific diagnosis code has
   A. three digits.
   B. four digits.
   C. five digits.
   D. five digits and a modifier.

_____ 3. Brackets–[ ]–are used around
   A. descriptions that do not affect the code.
   B. instructions.
   C. descriptions that do not affect the code.
   D. an incomplete term.
   E. synonyms, alternative wordings, or explanations.

_____ 4. Where in CPT would you look for guidelines on using each section?
   A. The preface
   B. The notes at the beginning of each section
   C. The appendixes
   D. The descriptions next to each code

_____ 5. The abbreviation NOS means
   A. no other symbol.
   B. not otherwise specified.
   C. not often seen.
   D. nearest order sequence.

_____ 6. Injections and immunizations require two codes: one for giving the injection and the second for
   A. the E/M.
   B. the substance.
   C. the V code.
   D. the global period.
   E. the evaluation.

_____ 7. In the Health Care Common Procedure Coding System (HCPCS), which codes duplicate the CPT?
   A. Level I
   B. Level II
   C. Category II
   D. Category III
   E. All of the above

_____ 8. CPT codes are made up of
   A. three digits.
   B. four digits.
   C. five digits.
   D. six digits.

Sentence Completion

In the space provided, write the word or phrase that best completes each sentence.

9. When choosing the diagnosis code for the health-care claim, the most specific code should be used by utilizing _____ digits when available.

10. To find the correct ICD-9-CM code, begin by looking up the main term in the _____.

11. _____ codes are used to track health-care performance measures, such as programs and counseling to avoid to-bacco use.

9. _____

10. _____

11. _____

12. A(n) _____ code for accidental poisoning is selected from the ICD-9 manual.

13. The period of time that is covered for follow-up care is called the _____.

14. The connection between the diagnostic and the procedural information is called the code _____.

15. The next revision of the diagnostic code set is called the ICD- _____ -CM.

16. When unbundling is done intentionally to receive more payment than is correct, the claim is likely to be considered _____.

17. The codes in the ICD-9 Tabular List are organized according to the source or _____ system.

12. _____

13. _____

14. _____

15. _____

16. _____

17. _____

Short Answer

Write the answer to each question on the lines provided.

18. List the six sections of the CPT coding reference.

_____

_____

_____

19. List the three indexes provided by the alphabetical index.

_____

_____

_____

20. List the five steps involved with selecting a correct ICD-9-CM code.

_____

_____

_____

21. List the three key factors that determine the level of an evaluation and management (E/M) service.

_____

_____

_____

22. List the five steps involved with selecting a correct CPT code.

_____

_____

_____

Critical Thinking

Write the answer to each question on the lines provided.

1. Why is accurate coding important?

_____

_____

_____

2. Why is billing for services that are not provided considered fraud? Why can't it be considered just a mistake or an error?

_____

_____

_____

3. Why are medical offices advised to keep the previous year's code books?

_____

_____

_____

4. What is the ultimate goal or desired outcome of medical coding?

_____

_____

_____

APPLICATION

Follow the directions for each application.

1. **Becoming Familiar with ICD-9-CM**

   Work with a partner. Use the most recent ICD-9-CM reference available to you.

   a. Using Appendix E of the ICD-9-CM, select four of the three-digit disease categories to study, such as iron deficiency anemias, chronic pulmonary heart disease, and diabetes mellitus.

   b. Study the entries for the selected category in the Tabular List. Make a note of the appearance of any conventions. If a *code also underlying condition* instruction is found, research the possible choice.

   c. Prepare a report of the codes that require fourth or fifth digits in each of the categories.

2. **Becoming Familiar with CPT**

   Work with a partner. Use the most recent CPT reference available to you.

   a. In the Surgery Section of the CPT, find the heading "Subsection Information" in the Surgery Guidelines

   b. Read the subsection notes for Removal of Skin Tags, Shaving of Lesions, Excision—Benign Lesions, and Excision—Malignant Lesions, analyzing the type of instructions provided.

   c. Prepare a comparison table of the instructions of the four subsection notes, covering these topics:

   • Definition of Method

   • Type of Anesthesia Covered

- Use of Lesion Size to Select Code
- Instructions on Modifiers

CASE STUDIES

Write your response to each case study on the lines provided.

Case 1

A patient with acute appendicitis with generalized peritonitis had an appendectomy that was performed using laparoscopy. What procedure code and diagnosis code would you report?

_____

_____

_____

Case 2

A 64-year-old male patient presented for his annual complete physical exam. A routine 12-lead electrocardiogram (ECG) and a general health panel laboratory test were also performed. What procedure codes and diagnosis code would you report on a health-care claim for this service?

_____

_____

_____

Case 3

A patient presented for evaluation after a fainting spell. The following tests were ordered by the physician: carbon dioxide, chloride, potassium, and sodium. The health-care claim that was submitted contained procedure codes for each test. You have not received any payment on this claim, although payments for other claims sent to the same carrier on that day have been received. What do you think accounts for the delay?

_____

_____

_____

Copyright © 2011 by The McGraw-Hill Companies, Inc.

CHAPTER **17**

Patient Billing and Collections

REVIEW

Vocabulary Review

Matching

Match the key terms in the right column with the definitions in the left column by placing the letter of each correct answer in the space provided.

_____ 1. An account with only one charge

_____ 2. An organization that manages delinquent accounts

_____ 3. A written description of the agreed terms of payment

_____ 4. An act that prohibits certain collection tactics, such as harassment

_____ 5. The process of classifying and reviewing past-due accounts by age from the first date of billing

_____ 6. An act that requires credit bureaus to supply correct and complete information to businesses for use in evaluating a person's application for credit, insurance, or a job

_____ 7. A law that sets a time limit on when a collection suit on a past-due account can legally be filed

_____ 8. An act that requires creditors to provide applicants with accurate and complete credit costs and terms

_____ 9. The court-decreed right to make decisions about a child's upbringing

_____ 10. According to this organization, it is appropriate to assess finance charges or late charges on past-due accounts if the patient is notified in advance

_____ 11. An account that is open to charges made occasionally

a. age analysis
b. Fair Credit Reporting Act
c. AMA
d. disclosure statement
e. legal custody
f. Truth in Lending Act
g. single-entry account
h. open-book account
i. statute of limitations
j. Fair Debt Collection Practices Act of 1977
k. collection agency

True or False

Decide whether each statement is true or false. In the space at the left, write T for true or F for false. On the lines provided, rewrite the false statements to make them true.

_____ 12. Immediate payment from patients brings income into the practice and saves the cost of preparing and mailing bills.

_____

_____ 13. Most physicians prefer to collect payments from patients at the end of each month.

_____

_____ **14.** The one major disadvantage to the use of credit cards in a medical practice is cost to the practice.

_____

_____ **15.** A billing cycle is a common billing system that requires that all the billing be done in the last week of every month.

_____

_____ **16.** The price list for a medical practice is called a charge slip.

_____

Content Review

Multiple Choice

In the space provided, write the letter of the choice that best completes each statement or answers each question.

_____ **1.** A superbill
   A. includes the charges for services rendered on that day.
   B. is given to the doctor after he sees the patient.
   C. is inappropriate if the patient has insurance.
   D. is mailed to the patient when the account is 30 days past due.
   E. is always completed electronically.

_____ **2.** A practice may buy accounts receivable insurance to protect the practice from
   A. welfare patients.
   B. employee theft.
   C. lost income because of nonpayment.
   D. malpractice.

_____ **3.** The Fair Debt Collection Practices Act of 1977
   A. allows you to call patients at any time to get payment.
   B. permits you to threaten to turn the account over to collections.
   C. permits you to harass the patient daily for payment.
   D. governs the methods that can be used to collect unpaid debts.

_____ **4.** Free treatment for hardship cases should be
   A. up to the receptionist to allow.
   B. expected by all patients in all cases.
   C. at the doctor's discretion.
   D. never permitted.
   E. based on the patient's financial statement.

_____ **5.** Acceptable form(s) of payment in a medical office is/are
   A. insurance.
   B. debit card.
   C. check.
   D. credit card.
   E. All of the above.

_____ **6.** A hardship case is defined as a person who is

    A. poor.

    B. underinsured.

    C. uninsured.

    D. All of the above.

_____ **7.** The purpose of an age analysis is to

    A. determine which accounts to turn over to collections.

    B. determine how much money is owed to the practice and how long it has been outstanding.

    C. classify and review past-due accounts.

    D. All of the above.

_____ **8.** Most practices begin the collection process with

    A. telephone calls, home visits, or letters.

    B. contracts or age analyses.

    C. credit checks, letters, or statements.

    D. credit checks or collection agencies.

    E. telephone calls, letters, or statements.

_____ **9.** Which of the following organizations offers certification for coding specialists?

    A. AMA

    B. AHIMA

    C. AAPC

    D. Both B and C

    E. Both A and C

Sentence Completion

In the space provided, write the word or phrase that best completes each sentence.

10. Money paid as punishment for intentionally breaking the law is referred to as _____.

11. The Truth in Lending Act covers bilateral credit agreements that involve more than _____ payments.

12. A _____ provides information about the credit worthiness of a person seeking credit.

13. This act prevents you from calling the patient before 8 AM or after 9 PM to request payment.

14. Health insurance for dependents of active-duty and retired military personnel is provided by _____.

15. When a physician treats other doctors for free, it is referred to as extending a _____.

16. A _____ is the average fee charged by all comparable doctors in the region.

17. A _____ is a price list for the medical practice.

10. _____

11. _____

12. _____

13. _____

14. _____

15. _____

16. _____

17. _____

Short Answer

Write the answer to each question on the lines provided.

18. Describe what cycle billing means.

_____

_____

_____

19. What is the purpose of using RVUs?

_____

_____

_____

20. When determining the responsibilities for minors, the parent who has legal custody can make what type of decisions?

_____

_____

_____

21. In an open-book account, does the time limit for collection begin when the account is initiated? Why or why not?

_____

_____

_____

22. How would you compute gross collection percentage?

_____

_____

_____

Critical Thinking

Write the answer to each question on the lines provided.

1. A patient is through seeing the doctor and he hands you his charge slip for services. You ask how he would like to pay. He hands you a credit card that the practice does not accept. What do you say?

_____

_____

_____

2. The physician has asked you to make some phone calls to request payment on delinquent accounts. What collection practices should you follow to avoid harassing behaviors or breaking the law?

_____

_____

_____

3. When handing a patient's account over to a collection agency, what information should you supply about the patient?

_____

_____

_____

4. Your medical practice is using a collection agency to collect past-due accounts. You receive a phone call from a patient who states that he has been contacted by the collection agency agent, who made threats to the patient. What do you do?

_____

_____

_____

5. Imagine that the doctor in your office is extending credit to a patient. What are the benefits of extending credit?

_____

_____

_____

APPLICATION

Follow the directions for each application.

Using the knowledge gained in the text, including Chapter 17, design a charge table or form that clearly defines each type of office care. Include such information as (a) is the patient a new patient, (b) is the patient an established patient, (c) was the appointment simply a consultation, (d) did the patient receive limited care, (e) did the patient receive comprehensive care, and so on. Define each type of care in detail so as to avoid any billing questions. A patient may come to you and argue that the type of care she received was "limited" and the physician checked "comprehensive" on the bill. You will need this form to show the patient exactly which services are given under each type of care.

CASE STUDIES

Write your response to each case study on the lines provided.

Case 1

A patient comes to you to pay for his office visit. He hands you the check and says he is in a hurry and cannot wait for a receipt. He leaves and you notice he has not signed the check. What do you do?

_____

_____

_____

Case 2

You are making collection calls. You call a patient and reach the patient's wife. You are told the patient is not there. The wife seems anxious to assist you and asks if she can help. What do you do?

_____

_____

_____

CHAPTER 18

Accounting for the Medical Office

REVIEW

Vocabulary Review

Matching

Match the key terms in the right column with the definitions in the left column by placing the letter of each correct answer in the space provided.

_____ 1. A chronological list of the charges to patients and the payments received from patients each day

_____ 2. The total amount of income earned before deductions

_____ 3. Money set aside to pay taxes to appropriate government agencies

_____ 4. A system that allows you to handle the practice's payroll without writing payroll checks manually

_____ 5. Federal Tax Deposit (FTD) coupon

_____ 6. Systematic recording of business transactions

_____ 7. The party who writes the check

_____ 8. Legally transferable from one person to another

_____ 9. Appears as a fraction on the upper edge of all printed checks

_____ 10. Shows the total owed to the practice

_____ 11. The original record of the doctor's services and the charge for those services

_____ 12. Lets you write each transaction once while recording it on four different bookkeeping forms

_____ 13. Business checks with stubs attached

_____ 14. A blank check that allows the depositor to withdraw funds from her account only

_____ 15. A (relatively) small amount of cash kept in the office to pay for small office expenses.

_____ 16. Employer's annual federal unemployment (FUTA) tax return

a. tax liability
b. ABA number
c. petty cash or revolving fund
d. charge slip
e. EFTS
f. Form 940
g. gross earning
h. Form 941
i. accounts receivable record
j. daily log
k. payer
l. bookkeeping
m. Form 8109
n. pegboard system
o. counter check
p. negotiable
q. voucher checks

True or False

Decide whether each statement is true or false. In the space at the left, write T *for true or* F *for false. On the lines provided, rewrite the false statements to make them true.*

_____ 17. Medical assistants should obtain information for the daily log from word of mouth from patients.

_____

_____ 18. Reconciliation means to compare the records of the medical practice with the records of the patient.

_____

_____ 19. To help with the practice's bookkeeping and banking, you need to understand basic accounting systems and have certain financial management skills.

_____

_____ 20. After accepting a check, you should set it carefully aside for the endorsement process, which should be done in a batch with other checks.

_____

_____ 21. All bookkeeping systems include records of income, charges (money owed to the practice), and disbursements (money paid out by the practice).

_____

_____ 22. To calculate net earning, you should subtract total deductions from gross earnings.

_____

_____ 23. A check would be nonnegotiable if it is signed.

_____

_____ 24. SUTA taxes are payable to the federal government.

_____

_____ 25. Information on a patient ledger card includes the patient's name, address, phone number(s), and the name of the person responsible for the charges (if different from the patient).

_____

_____ 26. Managing payroll does not fall within the medical assistant's scope of practice.

_____

_____ 27. FICA taxes fund Social Security and Medicare.

_____

Content Review

Multiple Choice

In the space provided, write the letter of the choice that best completes each statement or answers each question.

_____ 1. The purpose of the daily log is to
   A. provide a record of each patient seen.
   B. list appointments.
   C. reconcile all finances.
   D. None of the above.

_____ **2.** If the medical practice uses a payroll service,
  A. you don't have any responsibilities for payroll.
  B. you may supply time cards or payroll data to the service.
  C. you will still have to calculate the deductions.
  D. you will still have to write the checks.
  E. you will still have to mail the checks.

_____ **3.** The patient ledger card does not include the patient's
  A. name.
  B. insurance policy number.
  C. driver's license number.
  D. work number.

_____ **4.** For FICA tax, you should withhold from the employee's check
  A. half of the tax owed for the pay period.
  B. one-third of the tax owed for the pay period.
  C. one-quarter of the tax owed for the pay period.
  D. all of the tax owed for the pay period.

_____ **5.** In order to balance a daysheet or even a patient's ledger card, you will use this formula:
  A. Previous balance + Today's charges − (Payments + Adjustments) = Current balance
  B. Current balance + Today's charges − (Payments + Adjustments) = Previous balance
  C. Previous balance − Today's charges + (Payments − Adjustments) = Current balance
  D. Current balance − Today's charges + (Payments + Adjustments) = Previous balance

_____ **6.** Most bookkeeping software programs include
  A. grammar and spell-check features.
  B. built-in tax tables.
  C. electronic endorsements.
  D. built-in check codes.

_____ **7.** Federal unemployment tax is
  A. not paid by the practice.
  B. paid by the employee.
  C. not a deduction from employees' paychecks.
  D. not based on the employees, earnings.

_____ **8.** In which of the following denominations are travelers' checks printed?
  A. $5, $10, $20, $50, $100
  B. $5, $10, $20, $50
  C. $5, $10, $20, $50, $100, $500
  D. $10, $20, $50, $100
  E. $10, $20, $50, $100, $500

_____ **9.** The employee's payroll information sheet
  A. is maintained by the employee.
  B. does not include the employee's hourly wage rate.
  C. must maintain up-to-date, accurate payroll information about each employee.
  D. None of the above.

Sentence Completion

In the space provided, write the word or phrase that best completes each sentence.

10. An accounts payable record shows the amounts the practice owes to _____.

11. The _____ shows how much cash is available to cover expenses, invest, or take as profits.

12. Whereas assets are goods or properties that are part of the worth of a practice, liabilities are amounts owed by the practice to _____.

13. An EIN is _____.

14. A person who receives a check is known as a _____.

15. The ABA number on a printed check is a bank identification number that appears in the form of a fraction on the _____ of the check.

16. A medical assistant receives an additional $40 in her paycheck for a week in which she worked an extra hour every day. This makes her payroll type _____.

17. To replenish petty cash, you should write a check payable to _____.

10. _____

11. _____

12. _____

13. _____

14. _____

15. _____

16. _____

17. _____

Short Answer

Write the answer to each question on the lines provided.

18. Describe the importance of accuracy in bookkeeping and banking.

_____

_____

_____

19. What is the purpose of Form 941?

_____

_____

_____

20. What are some of the expenses recorded in the accounts payable records?

_____

_____

_____

21. Why is it advantageous to make frequent bank deposits?

_____

_____

_____

22. What should you do if you cannot read the handwriting on a check?

_____

_____

_____

23. What are four things you can find out by telephone banking?

_____

_____

_____

24. How do you start a petty cash fund?

_____

_____

_____

Critical Thinking

Write the answer to each question on the lines provided.

1. What is the purpose of a deposit slip?

_____

_____

_____

2. Why is it important to reconcile the monthly bank statement with your checkbook balance?

_____

_____

_____

3. Name some of the information listed on the patient ledger card and why each is important to keep up-to-date.

_____

_____

_____

4. Who is inconvenienced or harmed when there is a bookkeeping error?

_____

_____

_____

APPLICATION

Follow the directions for the application.

Using a disbursement journal (see example on page 925), create a record of office disbursements for a one-month period using the following information.

a. For the purposes of this exercise, use November 2012. Remember that you'll need a column for the date, payee, check number, and total amount plus each of the expenses listed here. You decide which check number to begin with.

b. Types of Expenses
- rent
- utilities
- postage
- lab/x-rays
- medical supplies
- office supplies
- wages
- insurance
- taxes
- travel
- miscellaneous

c. Monthly Expenses

Use this information to fill in your office disbursements ledger.
- 11/01 – Payment to La Jolla Property Management for rent, $1700.00.
- 11/01 – Payment to Anderson Janitorial for monthly office cleaning, $850.00.
- 11/01 – Office Depot for fax machine paper, $37.89.
- 11/01 – Pacific Telephone for monthly telephone services, $384.57.
- 11/01 – Pacific Gas Company for monthly gas and electric, $683.84.
- 11/01 – Cash for stamps at the post office, $32.00.
- 11/02 – Uni Lab for blood work, $55.00.
- 11/02 – Harris Medical Supply for general medical supplies, $75.00.
- 11/05 – Medi Quik X-Ray, $32.50.
- 11/06 – Staples Office Supply for general office supplies, $68.24.
- 11/12 – City Laundry (uniforms and towels), $125.00.
- 11/15 – Toni Guzzi (payroll), $76.08.
- 11/15 – Terry Smart (payroll), $89.84.
- 11/15 – Janet Garcia (payroll), $125.00.
- 11/15 – James Smith (payroll), $78.76.
- 11/17 – Toni Guzzi (reimbursement for travel expenses), $12.50.
- 11/20 – Stamps at post office from petty cash, $64.00.
- 11/23 – Medi Quik X-Ray, $35.87.
- 11/25 – World Wide Insurance, $189.00
- 11/30 – IRS, $537.00.

d. Be sure your amounts at the total of your record agree with the amounts in each of the accounts.

e. Please complete the transactions above to reconcile your bank statement for your facility. Use the reconciling bank statement form in the documentation section on page 977. The balance of the bank statement is $1326.00. The balance that is showing on your transaction journal is $1807.00.

Deposits:	3/23/xx - $ 57.00	**Checks outstanding:**	#234 - $115.00
	4/07/xx - 163.00		#239 - 78.00
	4/16/xx - 786.00		#243 - 18.00
			#247 - 236.00

f. Using the payroll register form on page 971, calculate and complete the rest of the employees' net pay for the month. The first employee has been completed for you.

CASE STUDIES

Write your response to each case study on the lines provided.

Case 1

You are a senior medical assistant in a physician's office in charge of all the bookkeeping and banking tasks. You decided to take a couple of days off and handed your duties off to a less experienced medical assistant. All she needed to do was make the Friday deposit at the bank, and you were supposed to call her on Friday to be sure it was done. You wake up in the middle of the night and are startled to remember that you forgot to call and help her through the process. What methods would you use to determine if the deposit had been made correctly?

_____

_____

_____

Case 2

Your bank statement has arrived in the mail and along with it is a check from a patient marked "Insufficient Funds." What does this mean, and what do you do now to get paid?

_____

_____

_____

Case 3

Your bank statement has arrived in the mail and the balance from the bank does not agree with the balance in your check register. What do you do?

_____

_____

_____

CHAPTER **19**

Organization of the Body

REVIEW

Vocabulary Review

Matching

Match the key terms in the right column with the definitions in the left column by placing the letter of each correct answer in the space provided.

_____ 1. Matter that generally contains carbon and hydrogen

_____ 2. Combination of two or more atoms from different elements

_____ 3. Chemical combination of two or more atoms

_____ 4. Segment of DNA that determines a bodily trait

_____ 5. Anything that takes up space and has weight

_____ 6. Positively and negatively charged particles

_____ 7. Simplest unit of all matter

_____ 8. Results when errors occur during DNA duplication

_____ 9. Substance that releases ions in water

_____ 10. Matter that does not contain carbon and hydrogen

_____ 11. Contains base meaning of a medical term

_____ 12. Comes at beginning of a term; alters the meaning

_____ 13. Eases pronunciation of a term; does not change the meaning

_____ 14. Comes at the end of a term; alters the meaning

_____ 15. Smallest living unit

a. gene
b. combining vowel
c. mutations
d. organic
e. inorganic
f. cell
g. ions
h. suffix
i. compound
j. matter
k. word root
l. molecule
m. atoms
n. electrolytes
o. prefix

True or False

Decide whether each statement is true or false. In the space at the left, write T for true or F for false. On the lines provided, rewrite the false statements to make them true.

_____ 16. Diffusion is an active mechanism.

_____

_____ 17. PCR is the technique used to make multiple copies of even a fragment of DNA.

_____

_____ **18.** Connective tissue covers the body and lines body cavities.

_____

_____ **19.** The ventral body cavity contains the brain and spinal cord.

_____

_____ **20.** In anatomical position, the body is erect, with the head, feet, and palms all facing anteriorly.

_____

_____ **21.** The shoulder is distal to the elbow.

_____

_____ **22.** The abdominal and pelvic cavities are separated by the diaphragm.

_____

_____ **23.** Organs are created by the combination of two or more tissue types.

_____

_____ **24.** The iliac region is also known as the inguinal region.

_____

_____ **25.** The appendix is found in the RUQ.

_____

_____ **26.** If a solution has a pH of 10, it is acidic and will turn blue litmus paper red.

_____

_____ **27.** Oxygen is the most abundant inorganic compound in the body.

_____

_____ **28.** A cell nucleus is selectively permeable.

_____

_____ **29.** A cell's energy comes from the nucleus.

_____

_____ **30.** A sagittal plane divides the body into right and left portions.

_____

Content Review

Multiple Choice

In the space provided, write the letter of the choice that best completes each statement or answers each question.

_____ **1.** The _____ cavity contains the heart, lungs, aorta, esophagus, and trachea.
   A. dorsal
   B. abdominal
   C. thoracic
   D. pelvic

_____ 2. If a characteristic is carried on the female chromosome, the disease produced is known as a(n) _____ disease.
   A. recessive
   B. X-linked
   C. dominant
   D. Y-linked
   E. mutated

_____ 3. A _____ plane divides the body into inferior and superior portions.
   A. transverse
   B. frontal
   C. sagittal
   D. midsagittal

_____ 4. Different forms of genes are called _____.
   A. traits
   B. ribosomes
   C. chromosomes
   D. DNA
   E. alleles

_____ 5. Which organelles perform the digestive function of the cell?
   A. Ribosomes
   B. Golgi apparatus
   C. Lysosomes
   D. Centrioles

_____ 6. Which type of gland secretes its product directly into the bloodstream?
   A. Endocrine
   B. Exocrine
   C. Ductal
   D. Sweat
   E. Sebaceous

_____ 7. Which one of the following terms describes organs working together?
   A. Organelles
   B. Tissues
   C. Organisms
   D. Systems

_____ 8. The ankle is _____ to the foot.
   A. distal
   B. inferior
   C. proximal
   D. lateral
   E. superficial

_____ 9. Which directional term is used to describe front to back?
   A. Mediolateral
   B. Anteroposterior
   C. Posteroanterior
   D. Anterolateral

_____ **10.** A cell carrying out its everyday function is said to be in which of the following phases?

    A. Interphase

    B. Mitosis

    C. Meiosis

    D. Cytokinesis

Sentence Completion

In the space provided, write the word or phrase that best completes each sentence.

11. _____ is defined as the relative consistency of the body's internal environment.

12. _____ is the process that utilizes pressure to separate substances in a solution.

13. The diffusion of water across a semipermeable membrane is called _____.

14. _____ is the movement of a substance to an area of low concentration from an area of higher concentration.

15. The study of matter and chemical reactions in the body is known as _____.

16. When testing pH with litmus paper, _____ will turn red litmus paper blue.

17. Blue litmus paper will turn red when testing _____ substances for pH.

18. _____ describes the overall chemical functioning of the body.

19. _____ is the study of matter composition and how it changes.

20. _____ describes the study of the body structures.

21. The study of each structure's function describes _____.

11. _____

12. _____

13. _____

14. _____

15. _____

16. _____

17. _____

18. _____

19. _____

20. _____

21. _____

Short Answer

Write the answer to each question on the lines provided.

22. Using the figure provided, label the cell organelles appropriately and also give the main function of each organelle.

Organelle	Organelle's Function
A. _____	_____
B. _____	_____
C. _____	_____
D. _____	_____
E. _____	_____
F. _____	_____
G. _____	_____

Organelle	**Organelle's Function**
H. _____	_____
I. _____	_____
J. _____	_____
K. _____	_____

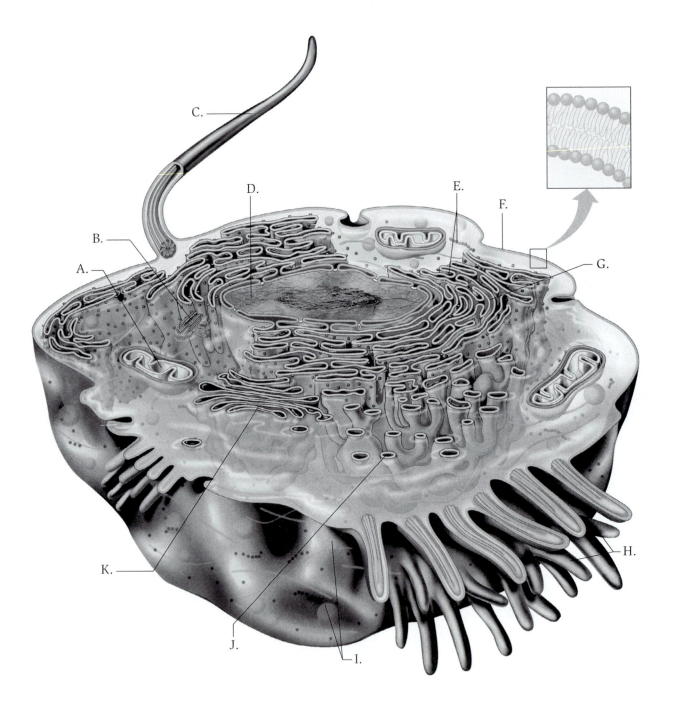

23. Using the figure below, give the terms that describe the relationship of one point of the body to another point.

    A. Point (a) in relation to point (c) _____

    B. Point (e) in relation to point (g) _____

    C. Point (l) in relation to point (k) _____

    D. Point (b) in relation to point (a) _____

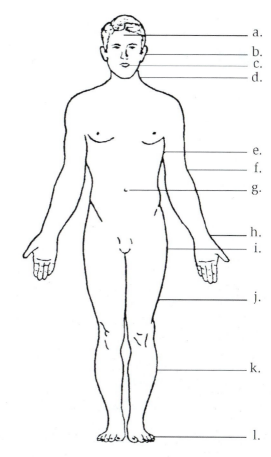

a.
b.
c.
d.
e.
f.
g.
h.
i.
j.
k.
l.

24. Using the previous figure, provide the correct anatomical term for each labeled body area.

    a. _____

    b. _____

    c. _____

    d. _____

    e. _____

    f. _____

    g. _____

    h. _____

    i. _____

    j. _____

    k. _____

    l. _____

25. What are the four most common elements in the human body?

_____

_____

_____

26. The following illustration shows the planes into which the body can be divided. Write the correct spatial terms on the blank lines in the illustration.

A. _____

B. _____

C. _____

D. _____

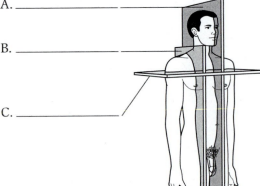
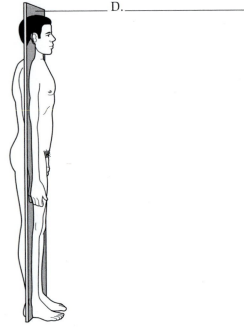

27. For each body cavity below, give its major divisions.

   A. Dorsal cavity _____

   B. Ventral cavity _____

   C. Abdominopelvic cavity _____

28. Give the locations of the following types of connective tissues.

   A. Osseous tissue _____

   B. Blood _____

   C. Cartilage _____

   D. Dense connective tissue _____

   E Adipose tissue _____

Critical Thinking

Write the answer to each question on the lines provided.

   1. Why are anatomy and physiology commonly studied together?

_____

_____

_____

2. As a medical assistant, why is it important for you to have a basic understanding of chemistry?

_____

_____

_____

3. How is mitosis different from meiosis? What is the importance of each?

_____

_____

_____

4. What are the clinical uses of PCR?

_____

_____

_____

5. If both parents have blonde hair, why can their children have brown, red, or very dark hair?

_____

_____

_____

APPLICATION

Follow the directions for each application.

Major Tissue Types

The four major tissue types in the body are epithelial, connective, muscle, and nervous. They are the components used to make organs. For each organ listed, give the probable role of each tissue type.

A. Stomach

_____

_____

_____

B. Heart

_____

_____

_____

C. Urinary bladder

_____

_____

_____

D. Biceps brachii (the muscle on the anterior surface of your arm)

_____

_____

_____

CASE STUDIES

Write your response to each case study on the lines provided.

Case 1

Sickle-cell anemia is a disease that occurs when a person inherits two recessive alleles for this disease. If a man and a woman both with sickle-cell trait conceive a child, what is the chance that the child will have the disease?

_____

_____

_____

Case 2

What are some of the signs and symptoms of Down syndrome?

_____

_____

_____

Case 3

A baby has been diagnosed with PKU. What is this disorder and how must this baby's diet be modified?

_____

_____

_____

CHAPTER **20**

The Integumentary System

REVIEW

Vocabulary Review

Matching

Match the key terms in the right column with the definitions in the left column by placing the letter of each correct answer in the space provided.

_____ 1. Also known as the subcutaneous layer

_____ 2. Epidermal cells that produce pigment

_____ 3. The term for hair loss (baldness)

_____ 4. The muscle that allows hair to stand erect

_____ 5. Cells that accumulate protein in the epidermis

_____ 6. Sudoriferous glands that produce a watery type of sweat

_____ 7. A wart

_____ 8. The skin area innervated by a nerve

_____ 9. Sweat glands commonly activated by stress or nerves

_____ 10. A fungal infection

a. alopecia
b. apocrine
c. eccrine
d. keratinocyte
e. melanocyte
f. dermatome
g. arrector pili
h. hypodermis
i. tinea
j. verruca

True or False

Decide whether each statement is true or false. In the space at the left, write T for true or F for false. On the lines provided, rewrite the false statements to make them true.

_____ 11. The integumentary system is composed of skin, hair, and nails.

_____

_____ 12. The body needs vitamin A for calcium absorption.

_____

_____ 13. The stratum germinativum is also known as stratum basale.

_____

_____ 14. The stratum corneum is the epidermal layer that contains melanin.

_____

_____ 15. The subcutaneous layer is largely made of adipose tissue.

_____

_____ **16.** All people have about the same number of melanocytes regardless of their skin color.

_____

_____ **17.** Skin rashes that cause itching are known as purpura.

_____

_____ **18.** According to the rule of nines, one entire arm equals 18% of the body surface area.

_____

_____ **19.** A partial-thickness (second-degree) burn involves the epidermis and dermis.

_____

_____ **20.** A macule is any variation in the skin's surface or appearance.

_____

Content Review

Multiple Choice

In the space provided, write the letter of the choice that best completes each statement or answers each question.

_____ **1.** Which of the following is *not* a function of skin?
  A. Vitamin C production
  B. Body temperature regulation
  C. Protection
  D. Sensation

_____ **2.** Which of the following is a pigment that traps UV radiation?
  A. Hemoglobin
  B. Keratin
  C. Melanin
  D. Carotene
  E. Melanoma

_____ **3.** A(n) _____ is a loss of the epidermis.
  A. ulcer
  B. excoriation
  C. fissure
  D. wheal
  E. cicatrix

_____ **4.** Which of the following substances is skin pigment?
  A. Melanin
  B. Hemoglobin
  C. Keratin
  D. Cyanosis

_____ **5.** Which of the following terms means blister?
  A. Pustule
  B. Papule
  C. Wheal
  D. Vesicle
  E. Ecchymosis

_____ **6.** Which of the following is a chronic skin disorder that is thought to be connected to an underlying inflammatory condition?

    A. Eczema

    B. Psoriasis

    C. Impetigo

    D. Folliculitis

    E. Purpura

_____ **7.** In addition to chickenpox, the varicella virus also causes

    A. herpes simplex.

    B. dermatitis.

    C. rosacea.

    D. herpes zoster.

_____ **8.** Which inflammatory skin disorder is caused by excess sebum production?

    A. Rosacea

    B. Folliculitis

    C. Acne vulgaris

    D. Herpes simplex

_____ **9.** The medical term for ringworm is

    A. pediculosis.

    B. tinea.

    C. herpes.

    D. verrucae.

    E. keloid.

_____ **10.** An inflamed area includes all of the following characteristics except

    A. redness.

    B. swelling.

    C. pain.

    D. scar formation.

Sentence Completion

In the space provided, write the word or phrase that best completes each sentence.

11. The _____ layer is the support layer for the skin and is composed largely of adipose tissue.

11. _____

12. Within the epidermis is the protein _____, which gives this layer of skin its protective properties.

12. _____

13. The _____ glands are most concentrated in the axillary and groin areas of the body.

13. _____

14. The topmost layer of the epidermis is the _____.

14. _____

15. The _____ is the layer of "living" skin and is composed of all major tissue types.

15. _____

16. The _____ is made up of the stratum corneum and the germinativum.

16. _____

17. The _____ glands are a type of sweat gland that responds to heat.

17. _____

18. _____ refers to the bluish tint that skin gets from cold and the illnesses that result in decreased oxygen in the tissues.

19. The _____ is the layer of the epidermis that produces new skin cells.

20. A _____ is the skin area along a central nerve pathway.

21. The half-moon-shaped area at the base of the nail is called the _____.

22. _____ gives skin and hair their coloring.

23. The hair _____ contains the blood vessel that nourishes the hair.

24. _____ glands secrete sebum or oil for the hair and skin.

25. The sweat or _____ glands are part of the body's cooling system.

18. _____

19. _____

20. _____

21. _____

22. _____

23. _____

24. _____

25. _____

Short Answer

Write the answer to each question on the lines provided.

26. The following figure shows structures and the layers of the skin. Label the figure using the following terms: hair shaft, hair follicle, arrector pili muscle, sebaceous gland, blood vessels, dermis, epidermis, hypodermis, sweat gland pore, stratum corneum, capillary, stratum germinativum, dermal papilla, basement membrane, touch receptor, sweat gland, sweat gland duct, nerve fiber, adipose tissue.

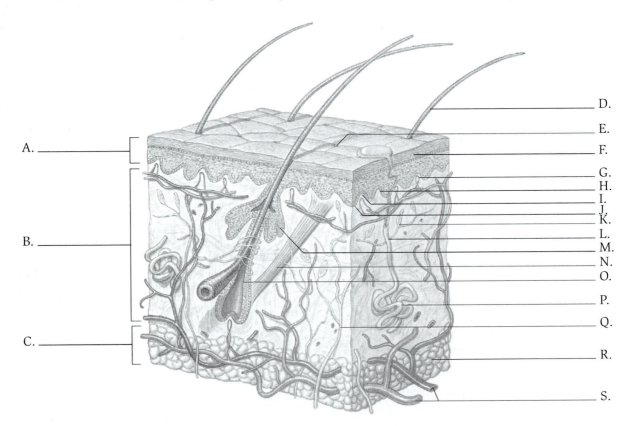

A. _____
B. _____
C. _____

D. _____
E. _____
F. _____
G. _____
H. _____
I. _____
J. _____
K. _____
L. _____
M. _____
N. _____
O. _____
P. _____
Q. _____
R. _____
S. _____

27. Describe the following stages of melanoma.

    A. Stage 0 _____

    B. Stage I _____

    C. Stage II _____

    D. Stage III _____

    E. Stage IV _____

28. Briefly describe the following skin disorders.

    A. Fissure _____

    B. Eczema _____

    C. Herpes simplex _____

    D. Wheal _____

    E. Impetigo _____

    F. Psoriasis _____

    G. Rosacea _____

    H. Scabies _____

    I. Verrucae _____

    J. Nodule _____

29. Fill in the meanings for the American Cancer Society's Cancer Warning Signs using the acronym CAUTION:

    C _____

    A _____

    U _____

    T _____

    I _____

    O _____

    N _____

Critical Thinking

Write the answer to each question on the lines provided.

1. Describe how the skin regulates body temperature.

_____

_____

_____

2. Describe the structure of the stratum corneum. How is this structure important for the function of the epidermis?

_____

_____

_____

3. Why is skin cancer more common in people with lighter skin tones?

_____

_____

_____

4. What conditions are likely to result in a person with underactive sebaceous glands?

_____

_____

_____

5. How does washing your face and hair help to prevent acne?

_____

_____

_____

APPLICATION

Follow the directions for each application.

1. Skin Cancer

Describe the appearances and treatments of the following types of skin cancer. Also name the cells that are cancerous in each type.

A. Basal cell carcinoma

B. Squamous cell carcinoma

C. Melanoma

2. Inflammation of Skin

When skin is injured, it becomes inflamed. Describe what produces each of the following signs of inflammation.

A. Redness

B. Swelling

C. Pain

CASE STUDIES

Write your response to each case study on the lines provided.

Case 1

A 35-year-old female recently had her family physician look at her moles during a routine yearly exam. The doctor asks you to explain to the patient the ABCDE rule to determine if a mole is suspected of being cancerous. How would you explain this rule?

_____

_____

_____

Case 2

Two boys are hospitalized for burns. The first boy has third-degree burns on his right hand and arm. The second boy has third-degree burns on his lower face. Why are the injuries of the second boy more life-threatening?

_____

_____

_____

Case 3

A 60-year-old diabetic woman comes to the office with a deepening sore on her left heel. It started as a blister from new shoes but is not healing. Why might this be of concern?

_____

_____

_____

Case 4

A teenager is having issues with recurrent facial breakouts due to acne. Through your physician, what can you recommend for this patient's problem?

_____

_____

_____

CHAPTER 21

The Skeletal System

REVIEW

Vocabulary Review

Matching

Match the key terms in the right column with the definitions in the left column by placing the letter of each correct answer in the space provided.

_____ 1. Attaches the finger to the hand

_____ 2. Bones of the extremities are included in this skeletal type

_____ 3. The opening for the spinal cord and brain attachment

_____ 4. Bone depression that allows for bones to join, as with the elbow

_____ 5. The baby's "soft spot"

_____ 6. The skeleton including the cranium, vertebrae, and rib cage

_____ 7. The term used to describe the finger joints

_____ 8. Nonmoveable joints, such as those within the skull

_____ 9. Large bony projection, such as at the proximal end of the femur

_____ 10. Attaches the tongue to the pharynx

_____ 11. Ridge-like bony projection

_____ 12. Cartilaginous tip of the sternum

_____ 13. The location of red bone marrow

_____ 14. A rounded bone process often found near a joint

_____ 15. A large rounded process at the end of a long bone

a. appendicular
b. axial
c. fontanel
d. foramen magnum
e. suture
f. MCP joints
g. PIP/DIP
h. hyoid
i. cancellous bone
j. xiphoid process
k. condyle
l. fossa
m. trochanter
n. head
o. crest

True or False

Decide whether each statement is true or false. In the space at the left, write T for true or F for false. On the lines provided, rewrite the false statements to make them true.

_____ 16. The femur is an example of a long bone.

_____

_____ 17. An expanded end of a long bone is called a diaphysis.

_____

_____ 18. The periosteum is a membrane that lines the medullary cavity.

_____

_____ **19.** The osteon is also known as the Haversian system.

_____

_____ **20.** Yellow bone marrow produces new blood cells.

_____

_____ **21.** The mastoid process is located on each temporal bone.

_____

_____ **22.** Ear ossicles are the smallest bones of the body.

_____

_____ **23.** The scapulae form the collar bone.

_____

_____ **24.** The first cervical vertebra is called the axis.

_____

_____ **25.** The thoracic segment of the spine includes seven vertebrae.

_____

_____ **26.** The ilium is the hip bone.

_____

_____ **27.** The humerus is the lower arm bone on the thumb (lateral) side of the arm.

_____

_____ **28.** Once growth stops, osteoclasts and osteoblasts cease their functioning.

_____

_____ **29.** Weightbearing exercises are essential for bone health.

_____

_____ **30.** A synovial joint is the most moveable of the joints.

_____

Content Review

Multiple Choice

In the space provided, write the letter of the choice that best completes each statement or answers each question.

_____ **1.** Which of the following is an example of short bones?
   A. Carpal bones
   B. Humerus
   C. Ribs
   D. Sternum
   E. Tibia

_____ **2.** The growth plate is also known as
   A. articular cartilage.
   B. diaphysis.
   C. epiphyseal plate.
   D. lamella.

_____ 3. The term for a hole or opening in a bone for blood vessels and nerves is the
     A. fossa.
     B. head.
     C. suture.
     D. process.
     E. foramen.

_____ 4. The cartilage that attaches the ribs to the sternum is called the
     A. articular cartilage.
     B. intervertebral disk.
     C. epiphyseal plate.
     D. costal cartilage.

_____ 5. Which of the following bones is located at the base of the skull?
     A. Occipital bone
     B. Parietal bone
     C. Frontal bone
     D. Temporal bone
     E. Ethmoid bones

_____ 6. Which of the following bones creates the roof of the mouth?
     A. Maxilla
     B. Vomer
     C. Palatine
     D. Sphenoid

_____ 7. The rib cage is composed of
     A. 24 ribs and the scapula.
     B. 12 ribs and the clavicle.
     C. 12 pairs of ribs and the scapula.
     D. 12 pairs of ribs and the sternum.

_____ 8. The membrane around the shaft of a long bone is the
     A. endosteum.
     B. periosteum.
     C. paraosteum.
     D. osteocyte.
     E. medullary cavity.

_____ 9. Which bone is the largest of the tarsal bones?
     A. Malleolus
     B. Femur
     C. Acetabulum
     D. Calcaneus
     E. Metatarsals

_____ 10. The coxal bones are more commonly known as the
     A. sternal bones.
     B. hip bones.
     C. hand bones.
     D. wrist bones.

Sentence Completion

In the space provided, write the word or phrase that best completes each sentence.

11. _____ are immature bone cells that create new bone.

12. _____ are cells that digest old bone in preparation for new bone growth.

13. The process of bone hardening is called _____.

14. _____ is the process of blood formation.

15. The fibrous bands that attach bone to bone are _____.

16. The _____ is commonly known as the shaft of a long bone.

17. The rounded end of the long bone is called the _____.

18. Spongy or _____ bone is where red bone marrow is located.

19. Yellow bone marrow is located in the _____.

20. The _____ is the tough fibrous membrane that covers the shaft of the long bone.

11. _____

12. _____

13. _____

14. _____

15. _____

16. _____

17. _____

18. _____

19. _____

20. _____

Short Answer

Write the answer to each question on the lines provided.

21. The figure below shows the structure of a long bone. Label the figure using the following terms: diaphysis, articular cartilage, spongy bone, compact bone, medullary cavity, yellow marrow, periosteum, epiphyseal disks, proximal epiphysis, distal epiphysis, space occupied by red marrow.

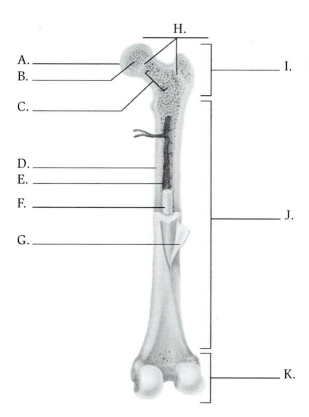

22. Label the bones of the skeleton shown below appropriately.

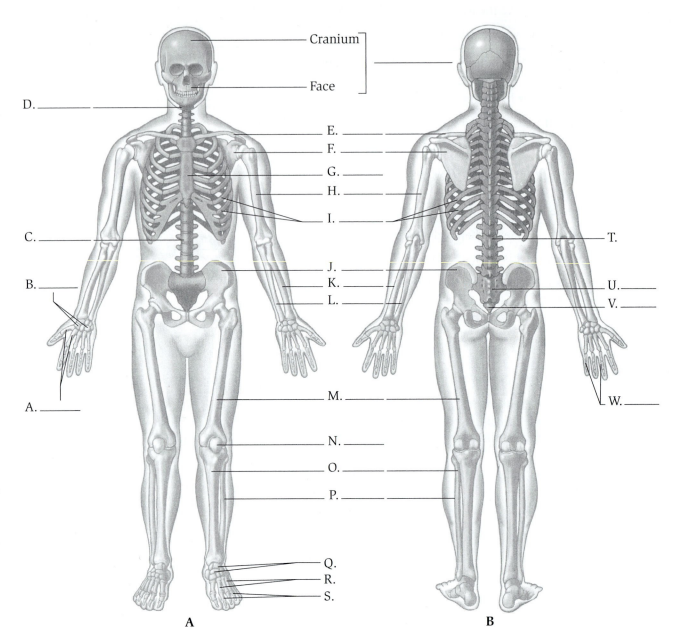

Cranium

Face

D. _____

E. _____
F. _____
G. _____
H. _____
I. _____

C. _____

B. _____

A. _____

J. _____
K. _____
L. _____

M. _____

N. _____

O. _____

P. _____

Q. _____
R. _____
S. _____

T. _____

U. _____
V. _____

W. _____

A   **B**

23. Label the bones of the skull appropriately.

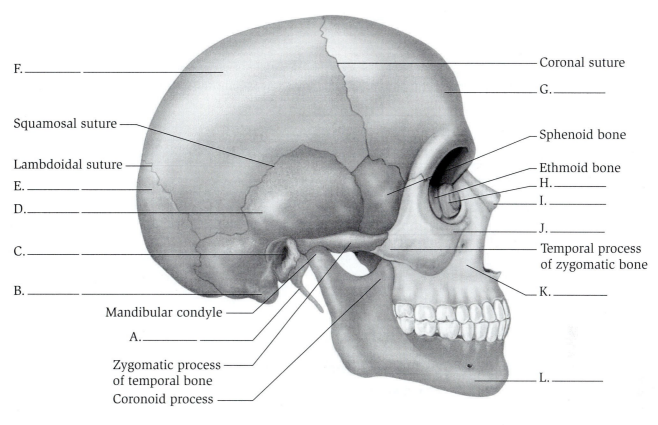

F. _____ _____

Squamosal suture

Lambdoidal suture

E. _____

D. _____

C. _____

B. _____ _____

Mandibular condyle

A. _____

Zygomatic process
of temporal bone

Coronoid process

Coronal suture

G. _____

Sphenoid bone

Ethmoid bone

H. _____

I. _____

J. _____

Temporal process
of zygomatic bone

K. _____

L. _____

24. Describe the following disorders.

A. Osteoporosis _____

B. Osteosarcoma _____

C. Carpal tunnel syndrome _____

Critical Thinking

Write the answer to each question on the lines provided.

1. What are the roles of osteoblasts and osteoclasts throughout life?

_____

_____

_____

2. Some sunlight exposure is necessary for bone growth and maintenance. What vitamin synthesis is aided by sunlight and why is it important in bone health?

_____

_____

_____

3. Explain the importance of the pectoral and pelvic girdles. What bones are included in each?

_____

_____

_____

4. Describe the three common vertebral deformities and give at least one causative factor for each.

_____

_____

_____

5. Explain the difference between compact bone and cancellous (spongy) bone.

_____

_____

_____

APPLICATION

Follow the directions for the application.

Inflammatory Diseases of Bones and Joints

Inflammation is an "enemy" of bones and joints. Explain how inflammation affects bones and joints in the following inflammatory diseases.

    a. Bursitis _____

    b. Osteoarthritis _____

    c. Rheumatoid arthritis _____

    d. Gouty arthritis _____

CASE STUDIES

Write your response to each case study on the lines provided.

Case 1

A 25-year-old woman is concerned that she may have osteoporosis because her mother has the disorder. Is the 25-year-old likely to have osteoporosis? What would you tell her about preventing the disease?

_____

_____

_____

Case 2

A young woman is pregnant and neglects to make sure that her diet has sufficient amounts of calcium. How is her diet likely to affect her bones and the bones of her fetus?

_____

_____

_____

Case 3

A 60-year-old man has just been diagnosed with gouty arthritis. What can you tell him about his condition and preventive measures he may take to prevent attacks?

_____

_____

_____

CHAPTER **22**

The Muscular System

REVIEW

Vocabulary Review

Matching

Match the key terms in the right column with the definitions in the left column by placing the letter of each correct answer in the space provided.

_____ 1. Helper muscle in skeletal muscle movement

_____ 2. A structure that covers and separates skeletal muscles

_____ 3. A condition produced by buildup of lactic acid in muscle

_____ 4. A structure that connects groups of cardiac muscle

_____ 5. Tough connective tissue that attaches muscle to bone

_____ 6. A thin covering that surrounds the entire muscle

_____ 7. The cell membrane of myocytes

_____ 8. The muscle primarily responsible for skeletal muscle movement

_____ 9. An energy-producing process for muscles that requires oxygen

_____ 10. A muscle that works in opposition to a prime mover

a. tendon
b. prime mover
c. synergist
d. agonist
e. fascia
f. aerobic respiration
g. muscle fatigue
h. epimysium
i. intercalated disc
j. sarcolemma

True or False

Decide whether each statement is true or false. In the space at the left, write T for true or F for false. On the lines provided, rewrite the false statements to make them true.

_____ 11. When muscles contract, heat is released.

_____

_____ 12. Striated muscle is found in the wall of blood vessels.

_____

_____ 13. Muscle cells are the same things as muscle fibers.

_____

_____ 14. The muscle in the iris of the eye is a voluntary muscle.

_____

_____ 15. Groups of skeletal muscle are connected to each other through intercalated discs.

_____

_____ 16. Muscle fatigue usually develops from an accumulation of hydrochloric acid.

_____

_____ 17. Epimysium surrounds an entire muscle.

_____

_____ 18. Straightening a body part is called flexion.

_____

_____ 19. Moving a body part anteriorly is called retraction.

_____

_____ 20. The orbicularis oculi muscle puckers the lips.

_____

_____ 21. The deltoid muscle acts to adduct the arm at the shoulder.

_____

_____ 22. The biceps brachii muscle extends the arm at the elbow.

_____

_____ 23. The external oblique muscle compresses the abdominal wall and flexes the vertebral column.

_____

_____ 24. The contraction of the diaphragm causes inspiration.

_____

_____ 25. The gastrocnemius acts in dorsiflexion of the foot.

_____

_____ 26. Myasthenia gravis is one of the few muscular diseases in which rest temporarily alleviates or minimizes many of its symptoms.

_____

_____ 27. An agonist works with a prime mover.

_____

_____ 28. Rotation describes the movement of a body part in a circular motion.

_____

_____ 29. Sprains involve joints, tendons, and ligaments; strains involve injuries to muscles.

_____

_____ 30. Skeletal muscle is described as being both striated and involuntary.

_____

Content Review

Multiple Choice

In the space provided, write the letter of the choice that best completes each statement or answers each question.

_____ 1. Which of the following is not a function of muscle?
A. Production of body movement
B. Stabilization of joints
C. Control of body openings
D. All of the above are functions of muscle

_____ 2. Which of the following is true about visceral muscle?
A. It is voluntary.
B. It is striated.
C. It is slow to contract and relax.
D. It is attached to bones.

_____ 3. Which of the following is a connective tissue that divides a muscle into fascicles?
A. Fascia
B. Epimysium
C. Endomysium
D. Perimysium
E. Aponeurosis

_____ 4. Which disease is commonly called lockjaw?
A. Botulism
B. Tetanus
C. Trichinosis
D. Encephalitis
E. Torticollis

_____ 5. Which disease can be caused by dented cans and undercooked or raw fish or pork?
A. Botulism
B. Tetanus
C. Trichinosis
D. Encephalitis

_____ 6. Which of the following is the action of pointing the toes up?
A. Inversion
B. Eversion
C. Plantar flexion
D. Protraction
E. Dorsiflexion

_____ 7. Which of the following is the action of moving a body part posteriorly?
A. Elevation
B. Retraction
C. Protraction
D. Depression

_____ 8. Which muscle closes the jaw?
  A. Platysma
  B. Masseter
  C. Sternocleidomastoid
  D. Orbicularis oris
  E. Mandible

_____ 9. Which of the following structures connect cardiac muscle fibers to each other?
  A. Tendons
  B. Ligaments
  C. Intracalated discs
  D. Intercalated discs

_____ 10. Which of the following terms is another name for myocyte?
  A. Muscle fiber
  B. Sarcolemma
  C. Sarcoplasm
  D. Myofibril
  E. Striation

_____ 11. Peristalsis describes the contraction of which of the following muscle types?
  A. Skeletal
  B. Visceral (smooth)
  C. Multiunit (smooth)
  D. Cardiac

_____ 12. Which of the following terms refers to the loss of a muscle's ability to contract?
  A. Oxygen debt
  B. Lactic acid production
  C. Muscle fatigue
  D. Aerobic respiration
  E. Anaerobic respiration

Sentence Completion

In the space provided, write the word or phrase that best completes each sentence.

13. _____ is the pinkish pigment of muscle that stores oxygen.

14. The attachment of muscle to the more moveable bone is known as _____.

15. The neurotransmitter _____ causes a skeletal muscle response.

16. The rhythmic movement of visceral muscle is called _____.

17. The attachment of a muscle to the least moveable bone is called the _____.

18. _____ is the enzyme responsible for skeletal muscle relaxation.

13. _____

14. _____

15. _____

16. _____

17. _____

18. _____

19. A ring of muscle known as a _____ is responsible for opening and closing body cavities and openings.

20. The _____ describes the aerobic process of creating ATP for muscle energy.

21. The byproduct of pyruvic acid conversion is _____ which occurs when muscle is low on oxygen.

22. _____ occurs during muscle fatigue, when oxygen supplies in muscles are low.

19. _____

20. _____

21. _____

22. _____

Short Answer

Write the answer to each question on the lines provided.

23. The following figure shows the muscular system. Write the names of the following muscles on the correct lines in the figure: biceps brachii, deltoid, external oblique, gastrocnemius, gluteus maximus, gluteus medius, hamstring group, latissimus dorsi, pectoralis major, quadriceps group, rectus abdominis, rectus femoris, sternocleidomastoid, trapezius, triceps brachii.

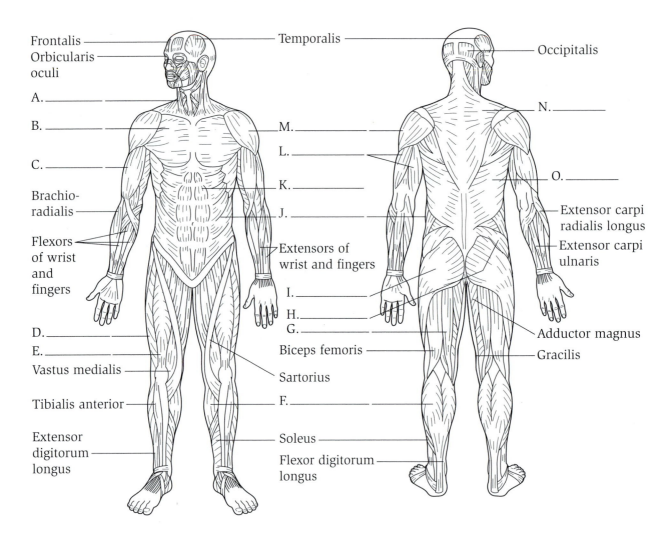

24. Briefly describe the following disorders:

A. Botulism _____

B. Fibromyalgia _____

C. Muscular dystrophy _____

D. Myasthenia gravis _____

E. Tendonitis _____

F. Trichinosis _____

G. Strains _____

H. Sprains _____

Critical Thinking

Write the answer to each question on the lines provided.

1. Norepinephrine works with the sympathetic nervous system. How does its presence in the bloodstream affect cardiac function?

_____

_____

_____

2. When a person is exercising, his breathing rate increases to ensure the adequate delivery of oxygen to skeletal muscle tissues. Why does the breathing rate stay increased for a period of time even after a person stops exercising?

_____

_____

_____

3. When a muscle is overworked, it often becomes sore. Why does massaging a muscle help reduce muscle soreness?

_____

_____

_____

4. In cooler weather, mothers often tell children to put on a sweater or "get up and move around" to warm up. Why do they think movement will warm up their children?

_____

_____

_____

5. Why do cardiac muscles have intercalated discs?

_____

_____

_____

APPLICATION

Follow the directions for the application.

Skeletal Muscle Actions

For each of the following actions, list the prime mover, at least one synergist, and the antagonist.

a. Bending the leg at the knee

_____

_____

_____

b. Raising the arm laterally at the shoulder

_____

_____

_____

c. Bending the hand at the wrist

_____

_____

_____

CASE STUDIES

Write your response to each case study on the lines provided.

Case 1

Recently a patient at your office was diagnosed with botulism. He states that he enjoys sushi at the new restaurant in town. How might this information possibly affect his diagnosis and treatment?

_____

_____

_____

Case 2

A friend calls and tells you that she thinks she has a muscle strain. You tell her that immediate RICE treatment is recommended. What does this mean?

_____

_____

_____

Case 3

A young woman arrives in the office with an increasing lateral turning of her head and neck that seems to be worsening since a motor vehicle accident in which she was rear-ended. What is her likely diagnosis and what treatment(s) should be tried?

_____

_____

_____

Case 4

A young man is hospitalized for seizures after running his first marathon. Tests reveal he has myoglobin in his blood and urine. Why does he have myoglobin in his blood and urine? How is this harmful to his kidneys?

_____

_____

_____

CHAPTER 23

The Cardiovascular System

REVIEW

Vocabulary Review

Matching

Match the key terms in the right column with the definitions in the left column by placing the letter of each correct answer in the space provided.

_____ 1. A concentration of oxygen that carries protein in red blood cells

_____ 2. The walls dividing the atria and the ventricles

_____ 3. Neutrophils, eosinophils, and basophils are this type of cell

_____ 4. Valves located between the ventricles and their arteries

_____ 5. A blood clot that is moving

_____ 6. A measure of the percentage of red blood cells in the blood

_____ 7. Monocytes and lymphocytes are this type of cell

_____ 8. A ballooned, weakened artery

_____ 9. A stationary blood clot

_____ 10. Valves located between the atria and the ventricles

a. agranulocytes
b. granulocytes
c. hematocrit
d. hemoglobin
e. bicuspid and tricuspid valves
f. semilunar valves
g. thrombus
h. embolus
i. septum
j. aneurysm

True or False

Decide whether each statement is true or false. In the space at the left, write T for true or F for false. On the lines provided, rewrite the false statements to make them true.

_____ 11. A membrane called the endocardium covers the heart.

_____

_____ 12. The myocardium is the inner layer of the wall of the heart.

_____

_____ 13. The upper chambers of the heart are called ventricles.

_____

_____ 14. The bicuspid valve is between the right atrium and right ventricle.

_____

_____ 15. *Lubb* is the first heart sound and occurs when the tricuspid and bicuspid valves snap shut.

_____

_____ **16.** The AV node is the pacemaker of the heart.

_____

_____ **17.** Venules are branches of veins.

_____

_____ **18.** Diastolic pressure is higher than systolic pressure.

_____

_____ **19.** Arteries carry blood away from the heart.

_____

_____ **20.** The phrenic artery carries blood to the intestines.

_____

_____ **21.** The radial artery carries blood to the forearm.

_____

_____ **22.** The azygous vein carries blood from the head and neck.

_____

_____ **23.** Platelets are fragments of cells that keep blood from clotting.

_____

_____ **24.** A monocyte is an example of an agranulocyte.

_____

_____ **25.** A white blood cell count above normal is termed leukocytosis.

_____

_____ **26.** The gases dissolved in plasma include oxygen, carbon dioxide, and nitrogen.

_____

_____ **27.** The bundle of His is also known as the AV node.

_____

_____ **28.** Myocardial infarction can be caused by a cerebral artery blockage.

_____

_____ **29.** Capillaries are known as exchange vessels.

_____

_____ **30.** Pernicious anemia is caused by the destruction of red blood cells.

_____

Content Review

Multiple Choice

In the space provided, write the letter of the choice that best completes each statement or answers each question.

_____ 1. The control of bleeding is called
   A. homeostasis.
   B. hemostasis.
   C. agglutination.
   D. vasospasm.
   E. deoxygenation.

_____ 2. Which antigen(s) is present on red blood cells of type A blood?
   A. Antigen A
   B. Antigen B
   C. Antigen A and antigen B
   D. Neither antigen A nor antigen B

_____ 3. Which antibody is found in the plasma of someone with blood type AB?
   A. Antigen A and antigen B
   B. No antigens
   C. Antibody A and antibody B
   D. No antibodies

_____ 4. In an ECG, what does the QRS wave represent?
   A. Atrial depolarization
   B. Ventricular depolarization
   C. Atrial repolarization
   D. Ventricular repolarization

_____ 5. Which vitamin is given to treat pernicious anemia?
   A. Iron
   B. Vitamin B_6
   C. Vitamin B_{12}
   D. Vitamin D
   E. Folate

_____ 6. Which of the following is the wall between the pumping chambers of the heart?
   A. Interventricular septum
   B. Intraventricular septum
   C. Interatrial septum
   D. Atrioventricular septum

_____ 7. Which of the following is the heart's natural pacemaker?
   A. AV septum
   B. AV node
   C. SV node
   D. SA node

_____ 8. Which of the following terms describes cell clumping?
- A. Coagulation
- B. Agglutination
- C. Thrombosis
- D. Cluster emboli
- E. Depolarization

_____ 9. Which of the following terms refers to hemoglobin when it carries carbon dioxide?
- A. Oxyhemoglobin
- B. Deoxyhemoglobin
- C. Anemia
- D. Carboxyhemoglobin

_____ 10. Which of the following conditions is hardening of the fatty plaque within arteries?
- A. Atherosclerosis
- B. Arthrosclerosis
- C. Arteriosclerosis
- D. Myocardial infarction
- E. Arrhythmia

Sentence Completion

11. When bilirubin builds up in the body tissues and skin, _____ develops.

12. _____ is defined as tissue swelling due to fluid accumulation.

13. The blood route from the venae cavae back to the left atrium is known as _____.

14. An abnormally low red blood cell count or a decrease in hemoglobin level results in a diagnosis of _____.

15. _____ is the orange-colored pigment created in bile production.

16. When an Rh-negative mom carries an Rh-positive baby, the concern for the fetus is _____.

17. An abnormal heart sound caused by faulty valve closure is _____.

18. The flow of blood from the left atrium through the body is known as _____.

19. The hormone _____ stimulates the red bone marrow to create red blood cells.

20. When a patient's blood contains the Rh antigen, she is said to have a(n) _____ blood type.

11. _____

12. _____

13. _____

14. _____

15. _____

16. _____

17. _____

18. _____

19. _____

20. _____

Short Answer

Write the answer to each question on the lines provided.

21. The illustration below shows the structure of the heart wall. Label the figure using the following terms: epicardium, myocardium, endocardium, fibrous pericardium, parietal pericardium, pericardial cavity, coronary blood vessel.

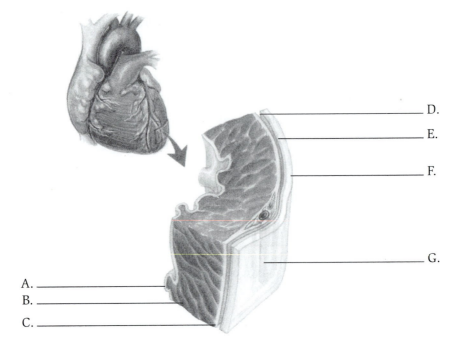

_____ D.

_____ E.

_____ F.

_____ G.

A. _____

B. _____

C. _____

22. Label the following on the illustration of the heart (below): right ventricle, left ventricle, right atrium, left atrium, superior vena cava, inferior vena cava, aorta, tricuspid valve, bicuspid valve, pulmonary semilunar valve, aortic semilunar valve, left pulmonary veins, right pulmonary veins, left pulmonary arteries, right pulmonary arteries, chordae tendinae, papillary muscles, interventricular septum, pulmonary trunk, the opening of the coronary sinus.

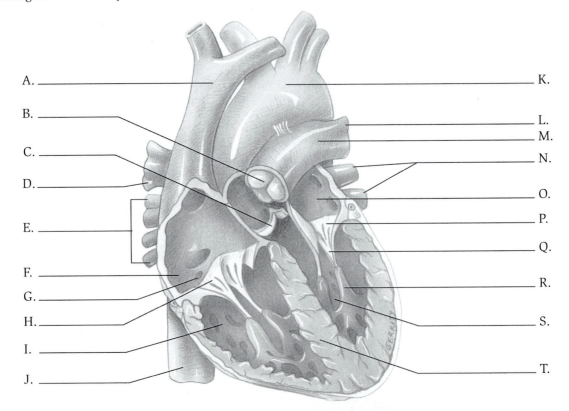

A. _____

B. _____

C. _____

D. _____

E. _____

F. _____

G. _____

H. _____

I. _____

J. _____

K. _____

L. _____

M. _____

N. _____

O. _____

P. _____

Q. _____

R. _____

S. _____

T. _____

23. The illustration below shows the flow of impulses through the cardiac conduction system. Label this figure using the following terms: interatrial septum, interventricular septum, SA node, AV node, bundle of His, Purkinje fibers, left bundle branch.

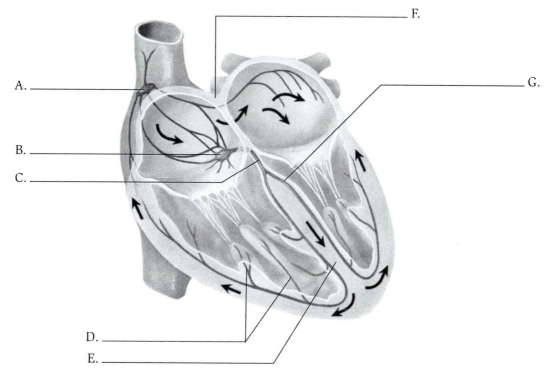

F. _____

A. _____

G. _____

B. _____

C. _____

D. _____

E. _____

24. Answer the following about chest pain.

    A. What are some cardiac causes of chest pain?

    B. What are some noncardiac causes of chest pain?

    C. What are some common tests used to determine the cause of chest pains?

    D. Angina (pectoris) is cardiac chest pain. What causes it?

Critical Thinking

Write the answer to each question on the lines provided.

    1. The left ventricular wall is more muscular than the right ventricular wall. Why do you think this is necessary?

_____

_____

_____

    2. Why is it important for tricuspid and bicuspid valves to close completely when the ventricles contract?

_____

_____

_____

3. Patients with angina pectoris are given sublingual nitroglycerin. Why is this medication helpful to them?

_____

_____

_____

APPLICATION

Follow the directions for the application.

1. Using the correct terms for the vascular system vessels of the body, trace the blood's journey as it leaves the heart to bring oxygen to the body cells and then back again. (Hint: Start with the largest artery.)

_____

_____

_____

2. Your patient's blood pressure is 126/82. What does each of these numbers represent within the cardiac cycle?

_____

_____

_____

3. Explain how the kidneys have an important role in the body's ability to create adequate red blood cells.

_____

_____

_____

4. Describe the functions of each of the following proteins found in blood plasma.

   a. albumins _____

   b. globulins _____

   c. fibrinogens _____

CASE STUDIES

Write your response to each case study on the lines provided.

Case 1

The left side of the heart in a 79-year-old patient is failing. How will the lungs of this patient be affected if the condition is not treated?

_____

_____

_____

Case 2

A 35-year-old woman thinks she is having a heart attack. She has just eaten a spicy Italian meal and her chest pains seem to get worse when she bends forward or lies down. What would you tell her?

_____

_____

_____

Case 3

A patient is being prepped for surgery, but the surgeon notices that the patient has a platelet count of 90,000 platelets per mL of blood. Is this normal? Why might the surgeon want to postpone the surgery?

_____

_____

_____

Case 4

Your 80-year-old patient states he can "see and feel" his heartbeat in his upper abdomen. The physician has ordered an abdominal ultrasound. What is the diagnosis? What should his treatment be?

_____

_____

_____

The Respiratory System

REVIEW

Vocabulary Review

Matching

Match the key terms in the right column with the definitions in the left column by placing the letter of each correct answer in the space provided.

_____ 1. Commonly referred to as the vocal cords, it is actually the space between them

_____ 2. A structure that consists of three lobes

_____ 3. The main branch from the trachea

_____ 4. Cartilaginous covering for the vocal cords

_____ 5. The voice box

_____ 6. Pulmonary parenchyma

_____ 7. A structure that consists of two lobes

_____ 8. A structure that contains the esophagus, the windpipe, and the voice box

_____ 9. The protective membrane (sac) around the lungs

_____ 10. The windpipe

a. alveoli
b. pharynx
c. larynx
d. trachea
e. bronchus
f. pleura
g. right lung
h. left lung
i. epiglottis
j. glottis

True or False

Decide whether each statement is true or false. In the space at the left, write T for true or F for false. On the lines provided, rewrite the false statements to make them true.

_____ 11. The exchange of oxygen and carbon dioxide at the cellular level is known as external respiration.

_____

_____ 12. The trachea splits into two main tubes known as bronchi.

_____

_____ 13. The medical term for the nostrils is nares.

_____

_____ 14. The more internal of the pleural membranes is the parietal pleura.

_____

_____ 15. The diaphragm relaxes during inspiration.

_____

_____ 16. The respiratory center is a group of neurons in the thalamus.

_____

_____ 17. Expiratory reserve volume is the amount of air that moves in or out of the lungs during a normal breath.

_____

_____ 18. Carboxyhemoglobin is hemoglobin carrying oxygen.

_____

_____ 19. Bronchitis is a chronic condition that damages the alveoli of the lungs.

_____

_____ 20. The most common malignant neoplasm in the United States is lung cancer.

_____

_____ 21. A pulmonary embolism is a blocked artery in the heart.

_____

_____ 22. The pharynx plays a dual role in the digestive and respiratory systems.

_____

_____ 23. Grade III snoring is heard outside of the bedroom with the door open.

_____

_____ 24. The tidal volume is the volume of air that remains in the lungs at all times.

_____

_____ 25. Pneumonia is the inflammation of the lung(s).

_____

Content Review

Multiple Choice

In the space provided, write the letter of the choice that best completes each statement or answers each question.

_____ 1. Structures that extend from the lateral walls of the nassal cavity are called
    A. nasal conchae.
    B. nasal septa.
    C. nasal sinuses.
    D. nasal microvilli.

_____ 2. Lungs are divided into sections called
    A. septa.
    B. segments.
    C. lobes.
    D. lobules.
    E. pneumons.

_____ 3. Which of the following is not a type of pneumoconiosis?

    A. Silicosis

    B. Asbestosis

    C. Anthracosis

    D. Pleuroconiosis

_____ 4. Which of the following is a volume of air moved in and out of the lungs during a respiratory cycle?

    A. Tidal volume

    B. Residual volume

    C. Vital capacity

    D. Expiratory reserve volume

_____ 5. Once oxygen gets into the bloodstream, most of it

    A. stays dissolved in plasma.

    B. reacts with water to form bicarbonate ions.

    C. binds to hemoglobin.

    D. binds to platelets.

    E. None of the above.

_____ 6. Which of the following is a condition in which the membranes covering the lungs become inflamed?

    A. Bronchitis

    B. Pericarditis

    C. Pleuritis

    D. Pneumonitis

    E. Tracheobronchitis

_____ 7. The smallest branches of the bronchial tree are the

    A. alveoli.

    B. bronchioles.

    C. bronchi.

    D. tracheoles.

_____ 8. The respiratory disease that causes abnormal dilation of the alveolar spaces is

    A. RDS.

    B. pneumoconiosis.

    C. SARS.

    D. empyema.

    E. emphysema.

_____ 9. Many respiratory conditions are linked to which of the following?

    A. Exposure to cigarette smoke

    B. Family history

    C. Obesity

    D. Alcohol abuse

    E. Pollution and other environmental factors

_____ 10. In which of the following conditions is fluid retained within the lungs?

    A. Pleural effusion

    B. Pulmonary edema

    C. Pulmonary embolism

    D. Hydrothorax

Sentence Completion

In the space provided, write the word or phrase that best completes each sentence.

11. A treatment for pneumothorax, hemothorax, or hydrothorax, a(n) _____ removes air, blood, or fluid from the chest cavity.

12. The pulmonary parenchyma are more commonly known as the _____.

13. _____ is the medical term for a collapsed lung.

14. Common in many cardiac and respiratory illnesses, _____ is excessive sweating due to illness.

15. Insertion of a chest tube or _____ is done to provide continuous drainage.

16. The inflammation of the pleural membrane is known as _____.

17. _____ describes the inflammation of the spaces within the cranium.

18. Also known as hyaline membrane disease, _____ affects mostly premature infants.

19. A symptom of TB and some respiratory neoplasms, _____ is the expectoration of blood.

20. Fluid within the thoracic cavity causes the condition of _____, which may lead to atelectasis.

11. _____

12. _____

13. _____

14. _____

15. _____

16. _____

17. _____

18. _____

19. _____

20. _____

Short Answer

Write the answer to each question on the lines provided.

21. The figure below shows the structures of the respiratory system. Label each structure using the following terms: nasal cavity, nostril, pharynx, larynx, trachea, primary bronchus, right lung, left lung, epiglottis, hard palate, soft palate, oral cavity, esophagus, paranasal sinus.

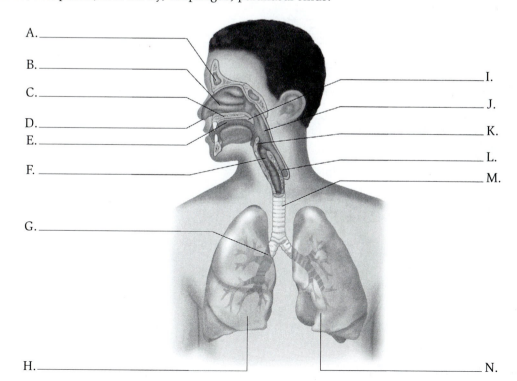

A. _____

B. _____

C. _____

D. _____

E. _____

F. _____

G. _____

H. _____

I. _____

J. _____

K. _____

L. _____

M. _____

N. _____

22. The figures below show anterior and posterior views of the larynx. Label the figures using the following terms: hyoid bone, epiglottic cartilage, thyroid cartilage, cricoid cartilage, trachea. (Hint: Each term is used twice.)

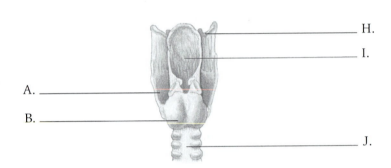

C. _____

D. _____

E. _____

F. _____

G. _____

H. _____

I. _____

A. _____

B. _____

J. _____

23. Answer the following questions about snoring.

A. What are common causes of snoring? _____

B. What is grade 4 snoring? _____

C. What are the treatments of snoring? _____

24. Briefly describe the following disorders:

A. asthma _____

B. laryngitis _____

C. SARS _____

D. COPD _____

E. tuberculosis _____

F. RDS _____

Critical Thinking

Write the answer to each question on the lines provided.

1. What causes the formation of the Adam's apple in a male? What causes the deepening of the male voice?

_____

_____

_____

2. Explain the function of the diaphragm and the intercostal muscles in the respiratory process.

_____

_____

_____

3. How do carbon dioxide levels in blood affect breathing?

_____

_____

_____

4. Why is carbon monoxide poisonous whereas carbon dioxide is not?

_____

_____

_____

5. Give an overview of the four different classifications of lung cancer and explain the meaning of the four stages of cancer.

_____

_____

_____

APPLICATION

Follow the directions for the application.

1. Respiratory Diseases

Many respiratory diseases produce similar symptoms. Give the meanings for each of the following:

a. Dyspnea

b. Orthopnea

c. Dysphonia

d. Diaphoresis

e. Pallor

f. Hemoptysis

2. Disorders of the Respiratory System

Explain why the following symptoms are produced.

a. Difficulty breathing in asthma

b. Pale skin in pulmonary edema

c. Fever in bronchitis or pneumonia

d. Fatigue in emphysema

e. Grunting in RDS

f. Barrel chest in emphysema

CASE STUDIES

Write your response to each case study on the lines provided.

Case 1

A mother brought her 5-year-old son to the doctor's office because he had had a runny nose for the past month. After several tests, it was determined that the boy had enlarged adenoids. How does this condition produce a runny nose? Recall that the adenoids (pharyngeal tonsils) sit at the back of the nasal cavity where it opens into the oral cavity.

_____

_____

_____

Case 2

A 36-year-old smoker constantly sees her doctor for the treatment of bronchitis. What other respiratory diseases is she at high risk for because she smokes?

_____

_____

_____

CHAPTER **25**

The Nervous System

REVIEW

Vocabulary Review

Matching

Match the key terms in the right column with the definitions in the left column by placing the letter of each correct answer in the space provided.

_____ 1. Governs our internal organs

_____ 2. Controls our everyday "baseline" nervous system

_____ 3. Its coating creates white matter

_____ 4. The control center for the neuron

_____ 5. The brain and spinal cord

_____ 6. Brings impulses to the cell body

_____ 7. Releases neurotransmitters to provide transmission between neurons

_____ 8. Produces the "fight-or-flight" response

_____ 9. Consists of the nerves outside of the brain and spinal cord

_____ 10. Takes impulses away from the cell body

a. CNS
b. PNS
c. ANS
d. sympathetic nervous system
e. parasympathetic nervous system
f. axon
g. dendrite
h. cell body
i. synaptic bulb
j. myelin sheath

True or False

Decide whether each statement is true or false. In the space at the left, write T for true or F for false. On the lines provided, rewrite the false statements to make them true.

_____ 11. The decision-making function of the nervous system takes place in the CNS.

_____

_____ 12. The ANS is part of the CNS.

_____

_____ 13. Motor neurons carry information from the periphery to the CNS.

_____

_____ 14. Another term for sensory neurons is afferent nerves.

_____

_____ 15. An unmyelinated axon does not conduct a nerve impulse as quickly as a myelinated axon.

_____

_____ 16. Pia mater is the layer of the meninges that contains CSF.

_____

_____ 17. The cervical enlargement of the spinal cord contains motor neurons that control muscles of
the legs.

_____

_____ 18. The cerebrum is the largest part of the brain.

_____

_____ 19. The midbrain includes the thalamus and hypothalamus.

_____

_____ 20. Oculomotor nerves carry visual information to the brain for interpretation.

_____

_____ 21. The trigeminal nerves innervate muscles of facial expression.

_____

_____ 22. The somatic nervous system consists of nerves that connect the CNS to the skin and skeletal
muscle.

_____

_____ 23. Ganglia are collections of neuron cell bodies in the CNS.

_____

_____ 24. The efferent nerves transmit impulses from the CNS to the PNS.

_____

_____ 25. The trochlear nerves are tested by asking a patient to smell various substances.

_____

Content Review

Multiple Choice

In the space provided, write the letter of the choice that best completes each statement or answers each question.

_____ 1. Which of the following neuroglial cells is a phagocyte?
   A. Oligodendrocyte
   B. Microglia
   C. Astrocyte
   D. Neurocyte
   E. Macroglia

_____ 2. Which lobe of the cerebrum contains the primary visual areas that interpret what a person
sees?
   A. Temporal
   B. Occipital
   C. Frontal
   D. Parietal

_____ **3.** Which of the following areas of the brain contains CSF?
  A. Gyri
  B. Sulci
  C. Blood-brain barrier
  D. Medulla oblongata
  E. Ventricles

_____ **4.** Which of the following is a function of the cerebellum?
  A. The interpretation of hearing
  B. The regulation of breathing
  C. The coordination of complex skeletal muscle contractions needed for body movement
  D. The secretion of hormones

_____ **5.** Which of the following acts as an "interpreter" for the two types of neurons?
  A. Interneurons
  B. Microglia
  C. Neurotransmitters
  D. Myelin
  E. Oligodendrocytes

_____ **6.** Which procedure involves the use of a needle to remove CSF from the subarachnoid space?
  A. Cerebrocentesis
  B. X-ray
  C. MRI
  D. CT scan
  E. Lumbar puncture

_____ **7.** Which cranial nerve does not control the eyes or visual functioning?
  A. II
  B. III
  C. IV
  D. V

Sentence Completion

In the space provided, write the word or phrase that best completes each sentence.

8. _____ are the neuroglial cells that anchor blood vessels to nerves.

9. The _____ is formed by a tight network of capillaries that protect the delicate tissue of the CNS.

10. The myelin sheath is created by the _____.

11. _____ wrap themselves around some axons, forming what is known as white matter.

12. Neuron cell membranes are polarized; the term for this is _____.

13. Chemicals called _____ are released from the synaptic knob.

14. Unmyelinated axons of the CNS are referred to as _____.

8. _____

9. _____

10. _____

11. _____

12. _____

13. _____

14. _____

15. The _____ tracts of the spinal cord carry sensory information to the brain.

16. A predictable automatic response to a stimulus is called a _____.

17. The cerebrum is split into four sections called _____.

18. The _____ consists of the midbrain, the pons, and the medulla oblongata.

19. The area of skin innervated by a single spinal or cranial nerve is called a(n) _____.

20. The _____ is the outermost layer of the cerebrum.

21. _____ refers to the loss of feeling in the extremities associated with neurological disorders.

22. A _____ is an x-ray of the blood vessels of the brain after an infusion of contrast media.

15. _____

16. _____

17. _____

18. _____

19. _____

20. _____

21. _____

22. _____

Short Answer

Write the answer to each question on the lines provided.

23. Use the following terms to label the illustration of a synapse (below): synaptic vesicles, neurotransmitter, axon membrane, synaptic knob, vesicle releasing neurotransmitter, postsynaptic structure, polarized membrane, depolarized membrane, synaptic cleft.

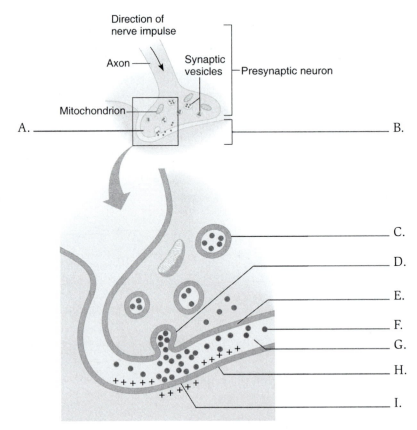

24. Use the following terms to label the illustration of a reflex arc (below): dendrite of sensory neuron, cell body of sensory neuron, axon of sensory neuron, dendrite of motor neuron, cell body of motor neuron, axon of motor neuron, spinal cord, receptor ends of sensory neuron, effector—quadriceps muscle, patella, patellar ligament.

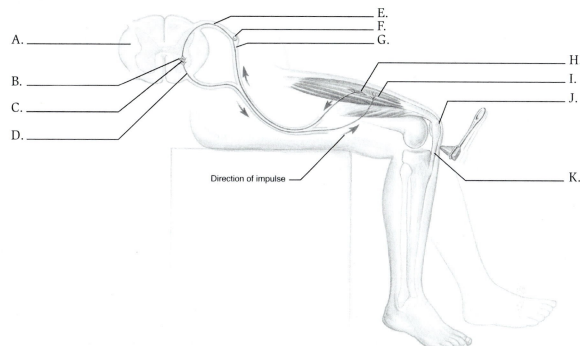

A. _____

B. _____

C. _____

D. _____

E.

F.

G.

H.

I.

J.

K.

Direction of impulse —

25. Fill in the table below with information about the following cranial nerves.

Cranial Nerve Number	Name of Cranial Nerve	Function of Cranial Nerve
II		
V		
VI		
X		
XII		

26. Give the correct number for each of the following.

A. Total number of spinal nerves _____

B. Total number of cervical spinal nerves _____

C. Total number of thoracic spinal nerves _____

D. Total number of lumbar spinal nerves _____

E. Total number of sacral spinal nerves _____

F. Total number of coccygeal spinal nerves _____

27. Briefly describe each of the following neurological disorders.

    A. Amyotrophic lateral sclerosis (ALS) _____

    B. Bell's palsy _____

    C. Migraine headaches _____

    D. Multiple sclerosis _____

Critical Thinking

Write the answer to each question on the lines provided.

    1. Explain the differences between tension and migraine headaches.

    _____

    _____

    _____

    2. Describe the roles of sodium, potassium, and negatively charged ions in creating polarized, depolarized, and repolarized states of a neuron.

    _____

    _____

    _____

    3. Explain why diseases that destroy the myelin sheath cause muscle weakness and paralysis.

    _____

    _____

    _____

    4. Explain the major differences between the somatic nervous system and autonomic nervous system.

    _____

    _____

    _____

APPLICATION

Follow the directions for each application.

    1. Nerve Plexuses

        Describe the nerves branching off each of the following plexuses.

        a. Cervical

        b. Brachial

        c. Lumbosacral

2. Evaluation of Cranial Nerves

Disorders of cranial nerves can be determined by using various tests. Name what tests might be used to evaluate the following nerves.

a. Oculomotor, trochlear, and abducens nerves

b. Trigeminal nerves

c. Hypoglossal nerves

3. Reflex Testing

Name the nerves that may be damaged if the following reflexes are abnormal.

a. Biceps reflex

b. Knee reflex

c. Abdominal reflexes

CASE STUDIES

Write your response to each case study on the lines provided.

Case 1

A patient has a bacterial infection in the brain. Why will this patient need a higher concentration of antibiotics than a patient with the same bacterial infection in the lungs?

_____

_____

_____

Case 2

Your patient shows spikes of electrical activity within the brain on an EEG. What condition may cause this finding?

_____

_____

_____

Case 3

A new mother is concerned that her 12-month-old baby has not started walking yet. The pediatrician explains that the baby's peripheral nerves are probably not yet fully myelinated. How does this explain why the baby cannot walk?

_____

_____

_____

Case 4

The spouse of your patient calls very concerned that her husband may have had a stroke during the night. His face looks lopsided and he is drooling. Strangely, he has no other symptoms. Did the patient likely have a stroke? If not, what disease or disorder might he be experiencing?

_____

_____

CHAPTER **26**

The Urinary System

REVIEW

Vocabulary Review

Matching

Match the key terms in the right column with the definitions in the left column by placing the letter of each correct answer in the space provided.

_____ 1. The working tissue of kidney that filters the blood

_____ 2. The structure that consists of the proximal convoluted tubule, the loop of Henle, and the distal convoluted tubule

_____ 3. The triangle formed by the three openings within the bladder

_____ 4. Small arteries that bring blood to the glomerulus

_____ 5. The tubes that bring urine to the bladder

_____ 6. Tightly coiled capillaries of the nephron that begin the filtration process

_____ 7. The position of the kidneys

_____ 8. Smooth muscle of the bladder wall

_____ 9. The hormone that assists with blood pressure regulation

_____ 10. Vessels that carry blood to the peritubular capillaries

_____ 11. Muscular contractions that move urine through the ureters

_____ 12. The tube leading from the bladder to the outside of the body

_____ 13. Composed of the glomerulus and the Bowman's capsule

_____ 14. The hormone that helps the body retain fluid

_____ 15. An alternate term for urination

a. afferent arteriole
b. antidiuretic hormone
c. detrusor muscle
d. efferent arteriole
e. glomerulus
f. micturition
g. nephron
h. peristalsis
i. renal corpuscle
j. renal tubule
k. renin
l. retroperitoneal
m. trigone
n. urethra
o. ureter

True or False

Decide whether each statement is true or false. In the space at the left, write T *for true or* F *for false. On the lines provided, rewrite the false statements to make them true.*

_____ 16. The kidneys lie outside the peritoneal cavity.

_____

_____ 17. Inside a kidney, the ureter expands as a renal pyramid.

_____

_____ 18. The outer portion of the kidney is called the renal medulla.

_____

_____ **19.** Erythropoietin stimulates the kidney to produce red blood cells.

_____

_____ **20.** The loop of Henle is between a distal convoluted tubule and a collecting duct.

_____

_____ **21.** The ureter enters the kidney at the hilum.

_____

_____ **22.** Glomerular filtration takes place in the renal corpuscles of nephrons.

_____

_____ **23.** In tubular secretion, substances move out of the peritubular capillaries and into the renal tubules.

_____

_____ **24.** Urine is composed mostly of urea.

_____

_____ **25.** The ureter empties the bladder to the outside.

_____

_____ **26.** The external urethral sphincter is under voluntary control.

_____

_____ **27.** Renal calculi are stones in the bladder.

_____

_____ **28.** Retention is a condition in which a person cannot control urination.

_____

_____ **29.** Pyelonephritis is considered a hereditary condition.

_____

_____ **30.** Diuretics help the body retain fluid.

_____

Content Review

Multiple Choice

In the space provided, write the letter of the choice that best completes each statement or answers each question.

_____ **1.** Which of the following are the tubes inside the kidney?
   A. Pelvis
   B. Calyces
   C. Column
   D. Ureters

_____ **2.** The triangular-shaped areas of the renal medulla are the
   A. renal pelvis.
   B. calices.
   C. renal columns.
   D. trigones.
   E. renal pyramids.

_____ 3. Which of the following is *not* a renal tubule?

   A. The glomerular capsule

   B. The distal convoluted tubule

   C. The loop of Henle

   D. The proximal convoluted tubule

_____ 4. Which of the following delivers blood to the glomerulus?

   A. The afferent arterioles

   B. The efferent arterioles

   C. The glomerulus

   D. The interlobular arteries

   E. The renal vein

_____ 5. Which of the following is responsible for tubular reabsorption?

   A. The glomerulus

   B. The ureters

   C. The collecting tubules

   D. The Bowman's capsule

   E. The proximal convoluted tubules

_____ 6. The three openings of the floor of the bladder are

   A. one opening for the ureter and two for each urethra.

   B. one opening for the urethra and two for the ureters.

   C. one opening for the urethra and two for the urinary arteries.

   D. one opening for the ureter and two for the urinary arteries.

_____ 7. The trigone refers to

   A. the proximal convoluted tubule, the loop of Henle, and the distal convoluted tubule.

   B. the two ureters and the urethra.

   C. the "jobs" of the kidney, which are filtration, reabsorption, and secretion.

   D. the area of the bladder that encompasses the ureteral and urethral openings.

   E. the shape of the renal pyramids.

_____ 8. Secretion refers to

   A. the formation and release of erythropoietin.

   B. the formation of filtrate.

   C. the removal of urine from the bladder.

   D. a substance that forms urine.

   E. a substance moving out of the peritubular capillaries and into the renal tubules.

_____ 9. The inability of kidneys to create urine is called

   A. renal failure.

   B. incontinence.

   C. retention.

   D. renal calculi.

_____ 10. The detrusor muscle is responsible for

   A. moving urine from the ureters to the bladder.

   B. retaining urine in the bladder.

   C. expelling urine from the bladder.

   D. controlling the filtration rate.

   E. sensing that the bladder is full.

Sentence Completion

In the space provided, write the word or phrase that best completes each sentence.

11. The innermost layer of the kidney is called the renal
_____.

12. A nephron consists of a renal corpuscle and a _____.

13. When more glomerular filtrate is formed, _____ urine is
ultimately formed.

14. Erythropoietin causes the formation of _____.

15. _____ is a condition in which the kidneys slowly lose
their ability to function.

16. _____ is an inflammation of the glomeruli.

17. _____ is a disorder in which the kidneys enlarge because
of the presence of many cysts within them.

18. _____ is commonly referred to as a complicated urinary
tract infection.

19. _____ is more commonly known as a bladder infection.

20. _____ describes the condition in which "stones" are
found within the kidney.

11. _____

12. _____

13. _____

14. _____

15. _____

16. _____

17. _____

18. _____

19. _____

20. _____

Short Answer

Write the answer to each question on the lines provided.

21. The figure below illustrates the organs of the urinary system. Label the illustration using the following
terms: kidney, bladder, ureter, aorta, inferior vena cava, hilum of kidney, renal artery, renal vein, urethra.

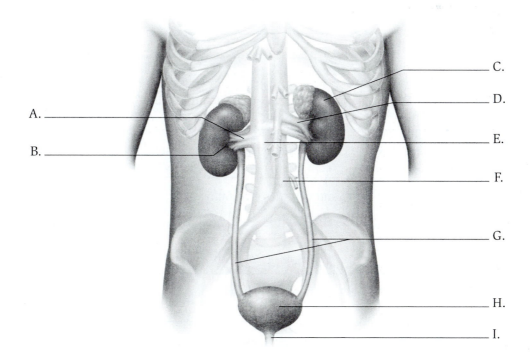

A. _____

B. _____

C. _____

D. _____

E. _____

F. _____

G. _____

H. _____

I. _____

22. The figure below illustrates a section of a kidney. Label the illustration using the following terms: renal capsule, renal pelvis, major and minor calyces, renal cortex, renal medulla, renal pyramid, renal papilla (tip of renal pyramid), ureter, renal column.

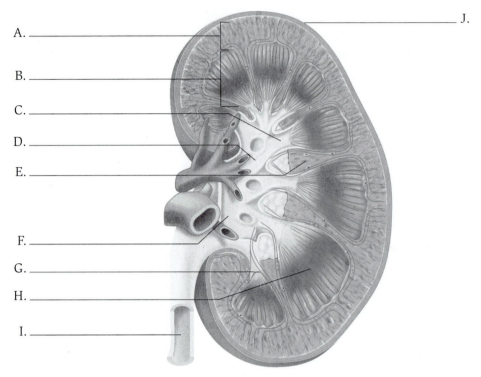

A. _____

B. _____

C. _____

D. _____

E. _____

F. _____

G. _____

H. _____

I. _____

J. _____

Critical Thinking

Write the answer to each question on the lines provided.

1. How does blood pressure affect glomerular filtration?

_____

_____

_____

2. Why do the hormones ADH and aldosterone decrease urine production?

_____

_____

_____

3. Explain the difference between acute and chronic renal failure.

_____

_____

_____

4. What is the difference between glomerulonephritis and pyelonephritis?

_____

_____

_____

5. What is the relationship between chronic renal failure and anemia?

_____

_____

_____

APPLICATION

Follow the directions for each application.

1. Kidney Hormones

Besides filtering blood and forming urine, the kidneys also release important hormones. Describe the functions of the following kidney hormones and enzyme.

a. Renin

b. Erythropoietin

c. Angiotensin II

2. Nephrons

Nephrons are functional units of kidneys. Describe the functions of the following parts of a nephron.

a. Glomerulus

b. Bowman's capsule

c. Proximal convoluted tubule

d. Loop of Henle

e. Distal convoluted tubule

CASE STUDIES

Write your response to each case study on the lines provided.

Case 1

How would you explain why females are more likely to develop urinary tract infections than males?

_____

_____

_____

Case 2

A young female patient has frequent urinary tract infections. What would you tell her to do to prevent these frequent infections?

_____

_____

_____

Case 3

How would you explain to a pregnant patient why she may develop incontinence?

_____

_____

_____

CHAPTER 27

The Reproductive Systems

REVIEW

Vocabulary Review

Matching

Match the key terms in the right column with the definitions in the left column by placing the letter of each correct answer in the space provided.

_____ 1. The area within the testes responsible for sperm production

_____ 2. Tissue responsible for male hormone production

_____ 3. The process that reduces the number of chromosomes in a cell from 46 to 23

_____ 4. A male fluid that alkalinizes the female vagina

_____ 5. The process of ovum formation

_____ 6. The monthly release of a mature ovum from an ovary

_____ 7. The neck of the uterus

_____ 8. The innermost layer of the uterus

_____ 9. The muscular layer of the uterus

_____ 10. The outermost layer of the uterus

_____ 11. The oviducts

_____ 12. The area between the vagina and the anus

_____ 13. The milk glands of the female breast

_____ 14. A cell formed by a fertilized ovum

_____ 15. The rapid mitosis of a zygote

_____ 16. The hormone released that confirms pregnancy

_____ 17. The communication organ between a pregnant woman and the developing embryo or fetus

_____ 18. The product of conception, weeks 2–8

_____ 19. Week 9 through the delivery of the neonate

_____ 20. The act of giving birth

a. prostate fluid
b. endometrium
c. embryo
d. interstitial cells
e. parturition
f. placenta
g. perimetrium
h. cleavage
i. fetus
j. seminiferous tubules
k. meiosis
l. perineum
m. fallopian tubes
n. ovulation
o. myometrium
p. HCG
q. mammary glands
r. cervix
s. zygote
t. oogenesis

True or False

Decide whether each statement is true or false. In the space at the left, write T for true or F for false. On the lines provided, rewrite the false statements to make them true.

_____ **21.** The other name for the bulbourethral glands is the Bartholin's glands.

_____

_____ **22.** The epididymis is a tube in which sperm cells mature.

_____

_____ **23.** A zygote contains 46 chromosomes.

_____

_____ **24.** In a transurethral resection of the prostate (TURP), the vas deferens are cut and tied.

_____

_____ **25.** Cryptorchidism is the term for undescended testicles.

_____

_____ **26.** FSH and LH are released by the hypothalamus.

_____

_____ **27.** The prepuce is the glans penis.

_____

_____ **28.** The fringed part of a fallopian tube is the fimbriae.

_____

_____ **29.** The cleavage is the female erectile tissue.

_____

_____ **30.** Menarche refers to the end of the menstrual period for women.

_____

_____ **31.** All fetal organs are formed by the primary germ layers.

_____

_____ **32.** The yolk sac makes new blood cells for the fetus.

_____

_____ **33.** The ovaries or testes are formed in the abdominopelvic cavity of a developing fetus.

_____

_____ **34.** The foramen ovale is a connection between the pulmonary trunk and the aorta.

_____

_____ **35.** The prenatal period is the 6-week time frame after birth.

_____

Content Review

Multiple Choice

In the space provided, write the letter of the choice that best completes each statement or answers each question.

_____ 1. The portion of a sperm cell that contains the genetic information from the biological father is the

    A. head.

    B. tail.

    C. midpiece.

    D. acrosome.

    E. flagellum.

_____ 2. Which of the following is the muscular gland at the base of the male urethra?

    A. Seminal vesicle

    B. Epididymis

    C. Seminiferous tubules

    D. Bulbourethral gland

    E. Prostate

_____ 3. The domed portion of the uterus is called the

    A. body.

    B. fundus.

    C. peristalsis.

    D. myometrium.

_____ 4. To which of the following organs does the term *effacement* apply?

    A. Uterus

    B. Ovary

    C. Vagina

    D. Cervix

_____ 5. Which of the following structures releases progesterone to increase the vascularity of the uterine lining?

    A. Follicle

    B. Oocyte

    C. Ovary

    D. Anterior pituitary

    E. Corpus luteum

_____ 6. Which of the following organ systems are the last to develop in a fetus?

    A. Reproductive and urinary

    B. Respiratory and digestive

    C. Nervous and endocrine

    D. Integumentary and muscular

    E. Cardiovascular and respiratory

_____ 7. Which of the following is not one of the openings within the fetal heart?

    A. Placenta

    B. Foramen ovale

    C. Ductus arteriosus

    D. Ductus venosus

_____ **8.** Which hormone stimulates uterine contractions for the birth process?
  A. PTH
  B. Progesterone
  C. Oxytocin
  D. Relaxin

_____ **9.** Which stage is known as *afterbirth?*
  A. Postnatal
  B. Placental
  C. Expulsion
  D. Postpartum
  E. Delivery

_____ **10.** The term *breach* refers to
  A. a fetus who is in the head-down position.
  B. a pregnancy of twins.
  C. a cesarean delivery.
  D. a fetus in the buttocks or feet-first position.

_____ **11.** Which of the following forms of contraception do not utilize hormones?
  A. Diaphragms and condoms
  B. Insertable contraceptives
  C. Implantable contraceptives
  D. Intrauterine devices
  E. Ingestable contraceptives

_____ **12.** The inability to conceive after trying for 12 consecutive months is termed
  A. impotence.
  B. conception.
  C. contraception.
  D. infection.
  E. infertility.

_____ **13.** Which of the following STDs has been implicated in cervical cancer?
  A. Gonorrhea
  B. Herpes simplex virus
  C. Human immunodeficiency virus (HIV)
  D. Human papilloma virus (HPV)
  E. Chlamydia

_____ **14.** Which of the following STDs is caused by a parasite?
  A. Gonorrhea
  B. Trichomoniasis
  C. Pediculosis pubis
  D. Genital warts

_____ **15.** Gonorrhea and chlamydia can cause infertility due to which of the following diseases?
  A. HIV
  B. PID
  C. HPV
  D. Syphilis
  E. HSV

Sentence Completion

In the space provided, write the word or phrase that best completes each sentence.

16. The _____ gland provides mucus for lubrication for the penis.

17. The process of _____ occurs when semen is forced out of the male urethra.

18. When in a nonerect state, the penis is said to be _____.

19. _____ is the malignant neoplasm (cancer) of the male sex organs.

20. The _____ are the lubricating glands of the vagina.

21. A _____ is the surgical procedure done to remove the uterus.

22. The protective sac around the developing embryo or fetus is the _____.

23. The _____ carries oxygenated blood to the developing fetus.

24. _____ of birth control include the diaphragm, condoms, and the cervical cap.

25. _____ is defined as the inability to conceive a child after 12 months of trying.

16. _____

17. _____

18. _____

19. _____

20. _____

21. _____

22. _____

23. _____

24. _____

25. _____

Short Answer

Write the answer to each question on the lines provided.

26. The figure below illustrates the male reproductive system with some structures unlabeled. Label the rest of the illustration using the following terms: scrotum, testis, penis, prostate gland, seminal vesicle, vas deferens.

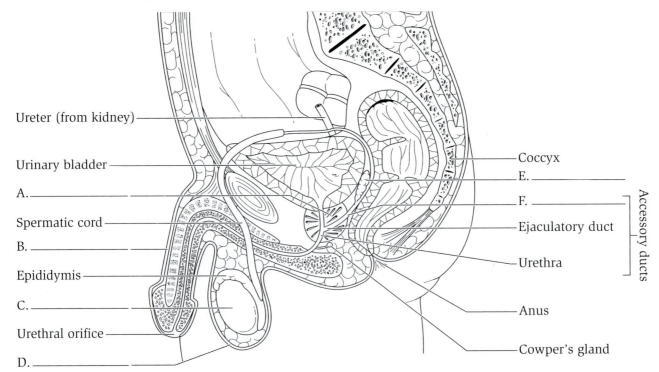

27. The figure below illustrates the female reproductive system with some structures unlabeled. Label the rest of the figure using the following terms: ovary, uterus, fallopian tube, clitoris, vagina, cervix.

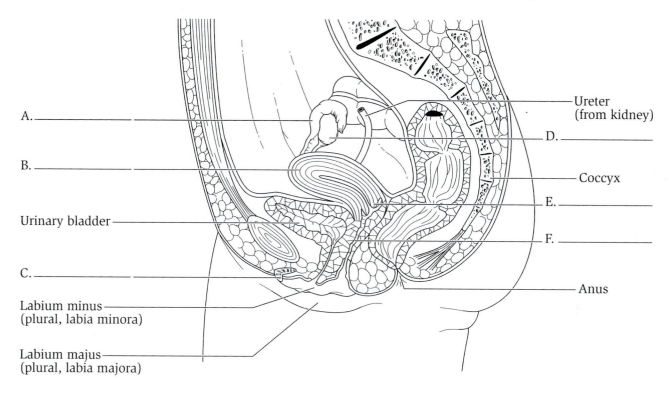

A. _____

B. _____

Urinary bladder _____

C. _____

Labium minus _____
(plural, labia minora)

Labium majus _____
(plural, labia majora)

Ureter
(from kidney)

D. _____

Coccyx

E. _____

F. _____

Anus

28. Answer the following questions about STDs.

A. Which STD has three distinct stages? _____

_____

B. Which viral STD has been found to increase the risk of cervical cancer? _____

_____

C. What three common signs or symptoms are found in a woman with an STD? _____

_____

D. What STDs are known to cause pelvic inflammatory disease? _____

_____

E. Why do both partners need to be treated for any STD, even if only one partner has symptoms? _____

_____

29. Answer the following about infertility.

A. What are common causes of infertility due to male factors? _____

_____

B. What are common causes of infertility due to female factors? _____

_____

C. What are some common tests used to diagnose infertility? _____

_____

Critical Thinking

Write the answer to each question on the lines provided.

1. Why must sperm cells and ooctyes have only 23 chromosomes instead of 46 like most body cells?

_____

_____

_____

2. Explain the differences between fetal circulation and normal circulation.

_____

_____

_____

3. Why is it possible for an egg to be fertilized in the pelvic cavity of a female instead of her reproductive tract?

_____

_____

_____

4. Explain why STDs are more readily passed from a male to a female than from a female to a male.

_____

_____

_____

5. Why can a woman not feel her fetus move before the 5th month of pregnancy?

_____

_____

_____

APPLICATION

Follow the directions for the application.

1. **Male Reproductive Organs**

   Describe the functions of the following male reproductive organs.

   a. Penis

   b. Scrotum

   c. Epididymis

   d. Prostate gland

   e. Vas deferens

2. Female Reproductive Organs

Describe the functions of the following female reproductive organs.

a. Uterus

b. Vagina

c. Fallopian tubes

d. Bartholin's glands

e. Ovaries

CASE STUDIES

Write your response to each case study on the lines provided.

Case 1

A 20-year-old man is reluctant to perform testicular self-exams. What are you going to tell him to persuade him about the importance of this exam?

_____

_____

_____

Case 2

Why is ovarian cancer harder to detect in its early stages than other types of reproductive cancers?

_____

_____

_____

Case 3

A 6-month-old baby is diagnosed with having a hole in his heart. The doctor explains that this hole is normal during fetal development but should close after the birth of the baby. How would you explain to the mother the function of this hole during fetal development?

_____

_____

_____

CHAPTER 28

The Lymphatic and Immune Systems

REVIEW

Vocabulary Review

Matching

Match the key terms in the right column with the definitions in the left column by placing the letter of each correct answer in the space provided.

_____ 1. Located in the LUQ; _____ filters blood to remove old and diseased RBCs

_____ 2. Found in mediastinum; _____ stimulates lymphocyte production

_____ 3. Areas that house macrophages and lymphocytes

_____ 4. A disease-causing substance

_____ 5. The other name for tissue fluid

_____ 6. Foreign substances in the body

_____ 7. Small foreign substances that join with proteins to trigger an immune response

_____ 8. Produced by the body in response to an antigen

_____ 9. The other term for body fluids

_____ 10. Cells that primarily target cancer cells

_____ 11. IgA, IgD, IgE, IgG, IgM

_____ 12. Occurs with the first exposure to an antigen

_____ 13. Responsible for the secondary immune response

_____ 14. A type of disease in which the body attacks itself

_____ 15. The other term for cancerous

a. interstitial fluid
b. humors
c. haptens
d. immunoglobulins
e. thymus
f. antibodies
g. NK cells
h. pathogen
i. primary immune response
j. autoimmune
k. spleen
l. memory cells
m. malignant
n. antigens
o. lymph nodes

True or False

Decide whether each statement is true or false. In the space at the left, write T for true or F for false. On the lines provided, rewrite the false statements to make them true.

_____ 16. An infection is the presence of an allergen in or on the body.

_____

_____ 17. Salt in sweat is an example of a mechanical barrier that the body uses for protection.

_____

_____ **18.** Fever causes the liver and spleen to take iron out of the bloodstream.

_____

_____ **19.** Lymphocytes are phagocytes.

_____

_____ **20.** Nonspecific defenses are called immunities.

_____

_____ **21.** Antibodies are defined as foreign substances in the body.

_____

_____ **22.** T cells respond to antigens by secreting complements.

_____

_____ **23.** T cells respond to antigens by becoming plasma cells.

_____

_____ **24.** Helper B cells make antibodies.

_____

_____ **25.** Memory cells trigger relatively slow primary immune responses.

_____

_____ **26.** IgD triggers allergic reactions.

_____

_____ **27.** Antibodies are also called immunoglobulins.

_____

_____ **28.** The spleen decreases in size as a person ages.

_____

_____ **29.** A person who receives an immunization develops an artificially acquired active immunity.

_____

_____ **30.** Epinephrine causes vasodilation to increase blood pressure.

_____

Content Review

Multiple Choice

In the space provided, write the letter of the choice that best completes each statement or answers each question.

_____ **1.** Which of the following is a nonspecific mechanism used to protect the body against pathogens?
   A. Species resistance
   B. Skin
   C. Lysozymes
   D. All of the above
   E. None of the above

_____ 2. Which of the following does *not* occur during inflammation?
   A. Blood vessels dilate
   B. More blood enters the area that is inflamed
   C. Blood vessels become leaky
   D. Fewer proteins are delivered to the areas that are inflamed

_____ 3. Which of the following cells are involved in specific defenses?
   A. B cells
   B. T cells
   C. Macrophages
   D. All of the above

_____ 4. Which of the following is not needed to activate a T cell?
   A. An eosinophil
   B. An antigen
   C. MHC proteins
   D. Macrophages
   E. An allergen

_____ 5. An activated T cell cannot become which of the following?
   A. A helper T cell
   B. A memory cell
   C. A plasma cell
   D. A cytotoxic T cell

_____ 6. Which of the following antibodies is found in breast milk, sweat, tears, saliva, and mucus?
   A. IgA
   B. IgG
   C. IgM
   D. IgD
   E. IgE

_____ 7. Exposure to a viral illness causes the formation of a(n)
   A. naturally acquired active immunity.
   B. naturally acquired passive immunity.
   C. artificially acquired active immunity.
   D. artificially acquired passive immunity.

_____ 8. Which of the following terms is used to describe an illness that occurs when the body attacks its own antigens?
   A. Immune disease
   B. Malignancy
   C. Benign growths
   D. Allergies
   E. Autoimmune disorders

_____ 9. The stage of cancer that states the malignancy has spread but is still within the primary site is
   A. stage 0.
   B. stage I.
   C. stage II.
   D. stage III.

_____ **10.** Which of the following organs takes over many functions of the spleen after a splenectomy has been performed?

    A. Thymus

    B. Pancreas

    C. Lymph nodes

    D. Gallbladder

    E. Liver

Sentence Completion

In the space provided, write the word or phrase that best completes each sentence.

11. When interstitial fluid enters lymphatic capillaries, it becomes _____.

12. Two major types of _____ are B cells and T cells.

13. Once activated, _____ divide to make plasma cells and memory cells.

14. _____ are chemicals secreted by T cells in response to antigens.

15. Some activated T cells form _____ cells to help protect the body from cancers and some viral infections.

16. A(n) _____ reaction is an immune response to a substance, such as pollen, that is not normally harmful to the body.

17. _____ is a life-threatening condition in which severe allergic reactions result from a usually harmless antigen.

18. _____ are cells that recognize, engulf, and destroy invading pathogens.

19. The uncontrolled growth of abnormal cells characterizes the disease _____.

20. _____, caused by the cytomegalovirus, is the highly contagious viral illness that is spread by saliva.

21. _____ is the blockage of lymphatic vessels, which causes tissue swelling.

22. _____ is the multisystem autoimmune disorder that may affect the integumentary, renal, and nervous systems.

11. _____

12. _____

13. _____

14. _____

15. _____

16. _____

17. _____

18. _____

19. _____

20. _____

21. _____

22. _____

Short Answer

Write the answer to each question on the lines provided.

23. Explain the differences among the following types of immunity:

    A. Naturally acquired active immunity _____

_____

    B. Artificially acquired active immunity _____

_____

    C. Naturally acquired passive immunity _____

    _____

    D. Artificially acquired passive immunity _____

    _____

24. What are three treatments used by persons with allergies?

_____

_____

_____

Critical Thinking

Write the answer to each question on the lines provided.

  1. Why is mononucleosis nicknamed "the kissing disease"?

_____

_____

  2. Penicillin is an example of a hapten. How does penicillin trigger an immune response in some people?

_____

_____

  3. Why do some allergens produce runny noses while others produce diarrhea?

_____

_____

  4. What is the difference between a cancer cell and a normal cell?

_____

_____

_____

APPLICATION

Follow the directions for each application.

  1. Nonspecific Defenses

    Explain how the following nonspecific defenses help protect the body from pathogens.

    a. Mechanical barriers

    b. Chemical barriers

    c. Fever

    d. Inflammation

2. Immune Disorders

Immune disorders develop for various reasons. Give the causes of the following conditions.

a. Chronic fatigue syndrome

b. Systemic lupus erythematosus

c. Lymphedema

d. Mononucleosis

CASE STUDIES

Write your response to each case study on the lines provided.

Case 1

A patient with cuts and scrapes is treated with antibiotic creams. Why is this treatment important?

_____

_____

_____

Case 2

A 15-month-old child received his MMR (mumps, measles, rubella) immunization yesterday. Today, his mother calls, stating he is fussy and has a runny nose and a slight temperature. Is it likely the child's symptoms are related to yesterday's immunization? Why or why not?

_____

_____

_____

Case 3

A woman has a "butterfly" rash on her face, joint pain, fatigue, and headaches. What autoimmune disease should she be tested for?

_____

_____

_____

CHAPTER 29

The Digestive System

REVIEW

Vocabulary Review

Matching

Match the key terms in the right column with the definitions in the left column by placing the letter of each correct answer in the space provided.

_____ 1. The term for the mixing of substances in the alimentary canal

_____ 2. The movement of substances throughout the alimentary canal

_____ 3. The mucus membrane flap that anchors the tongue to the floor of the mouth

_____ 4. The roof of the mouth

_____ 5. The part of the soft palate that hangs down into the throat

_____ 6. The parotid, submandibular, and sublingual glands

_____ 7. A structure that covers the opening of the larynx to prevent food from entering

_____ 8. Circular bands of muscle at the openings of many tubes

_____ 9. A substance from parietal cells; needed for vitamin B_{12} absorption

_____ 10. The term for food mixed with saliva and mucus

_____ 11. Food stuff mixed with gastric juices

_____ 12. The organ that consists of the duodenum, jejunum, and ileum

_____ 13. The organ that consists of the cecum and ascending, transverse, descending, and sigmoid colons

_____ 14. Vitamins A, D, E, and K

_____ 15. B vitamins and vitamin C

_____ 16. Mechanical digestion

_____ 17. Chemical digestion

_____ 18. The organ that filters blood and produces bile

_____ 19. The organ that stores bile

_____ 20. The organ that secretes bicarbonate ions and pancreatic juices

_____ 21. The duct that delivers bile to the duodenum

_____ 22. The structure that carries blood from the digestive organs to the liver

a. palate

b. sphincter

c. chyme

d. salivary glands

e. bolus

f. lingual frenulum

g. fat soluble vitamins

h. churning

i. small intestine

j. uvula

k. large intestine

l. water soluble vitamins

m. intrinsic factor

n. peristalsis

o. epiglottis

p. enzymes

q. liver

r. pancreas

s. hepatic portal vein

t. rugae

u. glycogen

v. gallbladder

w. microvilli

x. common bile duct

y. chewing

_____ 23. Stored sugar in the liver and skeletal muscle cells

_____ 24. The folds of the stomach lining

_____ 25. Projections that increase the surface area of the small intestine

True or False

Decide whether each statement is true or false. In the space at the left, write T for true or F for false. On the lines provided, rewrite the false statements to make them true.

_____ 26. The parietal perineum is the lining of the abdominal cavity.

_____

_____ 27. The serosa is the innermost layer of the alimentary canal and is responsible for absorbing nutrients.

_____

_____ 28. The serosa is also known as the visceral peritoneum.

_____

_____ 29. Amylase begins digestion of fats.

_____

_____ 30. The root of a tooth is covered by enamel.

_____

_____ 31. The pharynx extends from the back of the nasal cavity to the esophagus.

_____

_____ 32. The palatine tonsils also are known as the adenoids.

_____

_____ 33. The epiglottis covers the opening of the trachea.

_____

_____ 34. The main part of the stomach is called the cardiac region.

_____

_____ 35. The first portion of the small intestine is the duodenum.

_____

_____ 36. If a patient's stomach has been removed, a G tube may be placed for feeding him.

_____

_____ 37. The cardiac sphincter keeps food boluses from reentering the esophagus once inside the stomach.

_____

_____ 38. A hiatal hernia may also be called a diaphragmatic hernia.

_____

_____ 39. The liver is located in the LLQ.

_____

_____ 40. The ascending colon becomes the sigmoid colon.

_____

Content Review

Multiple Choice

In the space provided, write the letter of the choice that best completes each statement or answers each question.

_____ 1. Which of the following is *not* an organ of the alimentary canal?
   A. The mouth
   B. The stomach
   C. The liver
   D. The anal canal

_____ 2. Which layer of the alimentary canal contracts in order to move materials through the canal?
   A. The mucosa
   B. The serosa
   C. The muscular layer
   D. The submucosa
   E. The mesentery

_____ 3. Which of the following is *not* a component of saliva?
   A. Water
   B. Amylase, which digests carbohydrates
   C. Pepsin, which digests proteins
   D. Mucus

_____ 4. Which sphincter separates the stomach from the small intestine?
   A. Cardiac sphincter
   B. Esophageal sphincter
   C. Ileocecal sphincter
   D. Pyloric sphincter

_____ 5. Which of the following is the correct order of the large intestine segments?
   A. The descending colon, transverse colon, ascending colon, sigmoid colon, and the cecum
   B. The cecum and the ascending, descending, transverse, and sigmoid colons
   C. The cecum and the descending, transverse, ascending, and sigmoid colons
   D. The cecum and the ascending, transverse, descending, and sigmoid colons

_____ 6. Which of the following is *not* part of the small intestine?
   A. The ileum
   B. The cecum
   C. The duodenum
   D. The jejunum

_____ 7. Which disease occurs when normal liver tissue is replaced by scar tissue?
   A. Hepatitis
   B. Colitis
   C. Cirrhosis
   D. Jaundice

_____ 8. Which of the following is a screening test used to determine the presence of colon polyps and colon cancer?
    A. Colectomy
    B. Colonoscopy
    C. Endoscopy
    D. Colostomy

_____ 9. What common gastrointestinal disorder is also known as *GERD*?
    A. Constipation
    B. Hemorrhoids
    C. Diarrhea
    D. Hernia
    E. Heartburn

_____ 10. HBV immunizes people against one type of which of the following diseases?
    A. Hepatitis
    B. Heartburn
    C. Cirrhosis
    D. Colon cancer
    E. Hemorrhoids

Sentence Completion

In the space provided, write the word or phrase that best completes each sentence.

11. The _____ are the largest of the salivary glands.

12. If chyme moves too quickly through the small intestine, nutrients are not absorbed and _____ results.

13. The _____ is the area where the esophagus goes through the diaphragm.

14. _____ are defined as necessary food substances.

15. _____ from the parietal cells of the stomach is necessary for vitamin B_{12} absorption.

16. Vitamin _____ is needed for blood clotting.

17. Pancreatic _____ produce pancreatic juices for digestion.

18. _____ is the condition of difficult defecation.

19. Acidic chyme is neutralized in the duodenum by _____ from the pancreas.

20. The _____ is primarily responsible for most of the nutrient absorption.

11. _____

12. _____

13. _____

14. _____

15. _____

16. _____

17. _____

18. _____

19. _____

20. _____

Short Answer

Write the answer to each question on the lines provided.

21. The illustration below shows the organs of the digestive system. Label the figure using the following terms: stomach, mouth, large intestine, esophagus, small intestine, pharynx, salivary glands, liver, gallbladder, pancreas, rectum, anus.

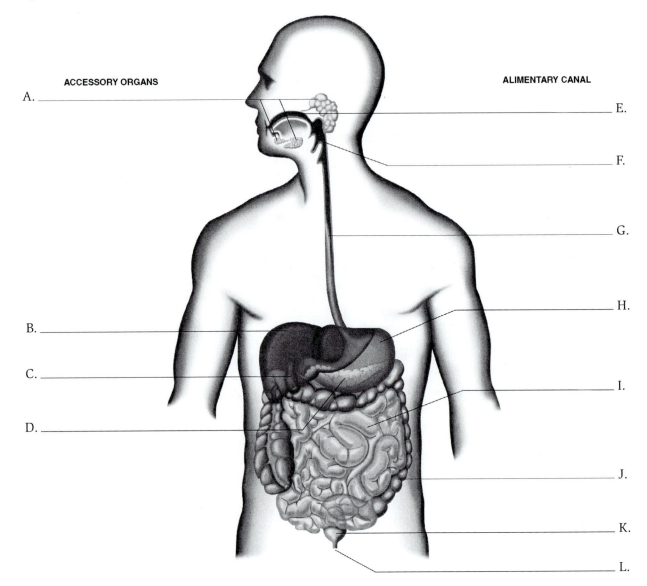

ACCESSORY ORGANS

A. _____

B. _____

C. _____

D. _____

ALIMENTARY CANAL

E. _____

F. _____

G. _____

H. _____

I. _____

J. _____

K. _____

L. _____

22. The illustration below shows the different regions of the stomach. Label the figure using the following terms: fundus, cardiac region, body, pylorus, canal in pyloric region, duodenum, pyloric sphincter, esophagus, rugae.

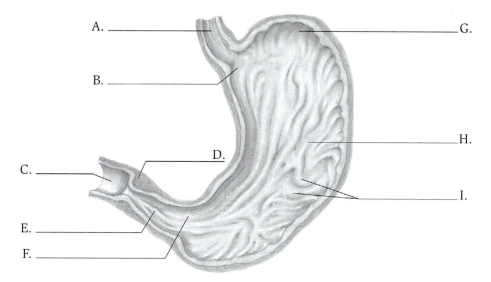

A. _____   G. _____

B. _____

D. _____   H. _____

C. _____

E. _____   I. _____

F. _____

23. The illustration below shows the various parts of the large intestine and the layers in the wall of the alimentary canal. Label the figure using the following terms: mucosa, serosa, muscular layer, vermiform appendix, cecum, ascending colon, descending colon, transverse colon, sigmoid colon, rectum, anal canal, opening of vermiform appendix, ileocecal sphincter.

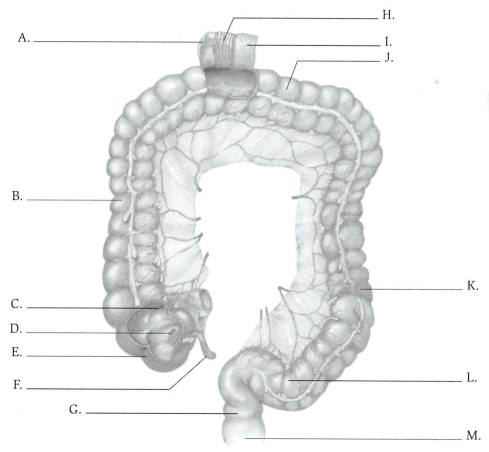

H. _____

A. _____   I. _____

J. _____

B. _____

K. _____

C. _____

D. _____

E. _____

F. _____   L. _____

G. _____

M. _____

24. Describe the importance of each of the following vitamins in the body.

    A. Vitamin A _____

    B. Riboflavin _____

    C. Vitamin C _____

    D. Vitamin B_{12} _____

    E. Folic acid _____

    F. Vitamin E _____

Critical Thinking

Write the answer to each question on the lines provided.

    1. Why is it impossible to breathe and swallow at the same time?

    _____

    _____

    _____

    2. Why are oral and dental health important in good nutrition?

    _____

    _____

    _____

    3. What sphincter must open to permit vomiting?

    _____

    _____

    _____

    4. Why would a lack of fiber (roughage) in the diet be implicated in colon diseases, including colon cancer?

    _____

    _____

    _____

    5. What is the difference between a hiatal hernia and an inguinal hernia?

    _____

    _____

    _____

APPLICATION

Follow the directions for each application.

    1. Pharynx

        The pharynx has three divisions. Describe the locations and functions of each of these divisions.

        a. Nasopharynx

        b. Oropharynx

        c. Laryngopharynx

2. Nutrients

Nutrients are necessary food substances. Tell how the body uses each of the following types of nutrients.

a. Carbohydrates

b. Proteins

c. Lipids

d. Vitamins

e. Minerals

CASE STUDIES

Write your response to each case study on the lines provided.

Case 1

A patient with cancer is having surgery to remove a portion of his small intestine. What digestive complications is this patient likely to have?

_____

_____

_____

Case 2

Why must a patient with cirrhosis or hepatitis stop alcohol consumption?

_____

_____

_____

Case 3

A young girl has a diet that lacks dairy products. What nutrients are missing from her diet, and what conditions might result?

_____

_____

_____

Case 4

If polyps are not cancerous, why should they be removed if they appear in the colon or rectum?

_____

_____

_____

CHAPTER 30

The Endocrine System

REVIEW

Vocabulary Review

Matching

Match the key terms in the right column with the definitions in the left column by placing the letter of each correct answer in the space provided.

_____ 1. A gland that secretes hormones directly into the bloodstream or target tissues

_____ 2. Chemicals secreted by cells that affect the functioning of other cells

_____ 3. Hormones that easily cross cell membranes

_____ 4. Hormones composed of amino acids or proteins

_____ 5. Tissue hormones

_____ 6. A hormone that stimulates the adrenal cortex

_____ 7. A hormone that stimulates ova or sperm production

_____ 8. A hormone that stimulates ovulation or the production of testosterone

_____ 9. A hormone that stimulates the kidneys to retain water

_____ 10. A hormone that acts as an agonist to calcitonin

_____ 11. A hormone that stimulates bone to take calcium from the blood

_____ 12. The part of the adrenal glands that stimulates the sympathetic nervous system

_____ 13. The part of the adrenal glands that is responsible for both Cushing's syndrome and Addison's disease

_____ 14. Structures within the endocrine cells of the pancreas

_____ 15. A hormone produced by the heart to help regulate blood pressure

_____ 16. A hormone that stimulates blood cell production

_____ 17. The gland also known as the hypophysis

_____ 18. The substance needed for the body to produce T_3 and T_4

_____ 19. A hormone that regulates circadian rhythms

_____ 20. An organ that has both digestive and endocrine functions

a. nonsteroidal hormones
b. FSH
c. PTH
d. atrial natriuretic peptide
e. ACTH
f. adrenal medulla
g. islets of Langerhans
h. hormones
i. calcitonin
j. pituitary
k. melatonin
l. ADH
m. endocrine gland
n. adrenal cortex
o. iodine
p. steroid hormones
q. pancreas
r. LH
s. erythropoietin
t. prostaglandins

True or False

Decide whether each statement is true or false. In the space at the left, write T for true or F for false. On the lines provided, rewrite the false statements to make them true.

_____ **21.** A hormone must target cells that have a receptor for it.

_____

_____ **22.** Steroid hormones utilize G-proteins to cross cell membranes.

_____

_____ **23.** Labor and delivery are examples of a negative feedback loop.

_____

_____ **24.** The hypothalamus produces oxytocin and ADH.

_____

_____ **25.** TSH stimulates the testes to release their hormones.

_____

_____ **26.** Osteoclasts build up bone by removing calcium from the blood.

_____

_____ **27.** The adrenal cortex secretes cortisol.

_____

_____ **28.** Insulin promotes the uptake of glucose by cells.

_____

_____ **29.** Epinephrine and norepinephrine decrease the heart rate.

_____

_____ **30.** Too much thyroid hormone produces cretinism in children.

_____

_____ **31.** Diabetes mellitus is the chronic condition of elevated blood glucose levels.

_____

_____ **32.** Diabetes insipidus is caused by hypersecretion of ADH.

_____

_____ **33.** Exophthalmos is a symptom of hypothyroidism.

_____

_____ **34.** Addison's disease is a condition caused by the adrenal medulla.

_____

_____ **35.** Somatotropin deficiency causes acromegaly.

_____

_____ **36.** A goiter is caused by a dietary iodine deficiency.

_____

Content Review

Multiple Choice

In the space provided, write the letter of the choice that best completes each statement or answers each question.

_____ 1. Which of the following is a bony structure that protects the pituitary gland?
   A. The optic chiasm
   B. The sella turcica
   C. The paranasal sinus
   D. The larynx

_____ 2. Which gland is also known as the adenohypophysis?
   A. The pineal body
   B. The posterior pituitary
   C. The pancreas
   D. The hypothalamus
   E. The anterior pituitary

_____ 3. Which of the following are small glands that are embedded within another gland?
   A. The adrenal glands
   B. The ovaries
   C. The parathyroid glands
   D. The pituitary glands

_____ 4. Which of the following is a hormone produced by a digestive organ?
   A. Gastrin
   B. Secretin
   C. Cholecystokinin
   D. All of the above

_____ 5. Which of the following is also known as hypocortisolism?
   A. Cushing's disease
   B. Graves' disease
   C. Acromegaly
   D. Dwarfism
   E. Addison's disease

_____ 6. Which cells of the islets of Langerhans secrete insulin?
   A. Alpha
   B. Beta
   C. Gastric
   D. Cortex
   E. Medulla

_____ 7. Which hormones are also known as tissue hormones?
   A. Steroidal
   B. Nonsteroidal
   C. Lipid
   D. Prostaglandins

_____ 8. Hormones from which of the following glands are responsible for T lymphocyte production?
   A. The thymus
   B. The thyroid
   C. The pancreas
   D. The parathyroid
   E. The hypothalamus

_____ 9. Which of the following diseases can result in anemia because its stimulating hormone is no longer being produced?
   A. Diabetes mellitus
   B. Diabetes insipidus
   C. Hypothyroidism
   D. Graves' disease
   E. Renal failure

_____ 10. Which of the following diseases may be congenital in nature?
   A. Myxedema
   B. Graves' disease
   C. Cretinism
   D. Addison's disease

Sentence Completion

In the space provided, write the word or phrase that best completes each sentence.

11. The target cells of a hormone are the cells that contain the _____ for the hormone.

12. A stimulus that produces a physiological change in the body is a(n) _____.

13. Glucagon is produced by the _____ cells of the pancreas.

14. Stimulating milk production in females, _____ enhances the actions of LH in males.

15. Hormone levels are controlled by _____.

16. Cretinism is caused by a _____ deficiency.

17. A "moon face" and "buffalo hump" are symptoms of _____.

18. _____ occurs when blood sugar levels rise during a woman's pregnancy.

19. _____ is extreme hypothyroidism in adults.

20. The _____ is located in the mediastinum.

11. _____

12. _____

13. _____

14. _____

15. _____

16. _____

17. _____

18. _____

19. _____

20. _____

Short Answer

Write the answer to each question on the lines provided.

21. Describe the following disorders and the signs and symptoms of each.

   A. Acromegaly _____

   _____

   B. Cushing's disease _____

   _____

   C. Graves' disease _____

   _____

   D. Myxedema _____

   _____

   E. Diabetes mellitus _____

   _____

22. Answer the following about diabetes mellitus.

   A. What is the difference between type 1 and type 2 diabetes? _____

   _____

   B. What is gestational diabetes? _____

   _____

   C. What are the causes of diabetes? _____

   _____

   D. What are some treatments of diabetes? _____

   _____

Critical Thinking

Write the answer to each question on the lines provided.

1. Why must nonsteroidal hormones have their receptors on cell surfaces and not inside cells?

_____

_____

_____

2. Why would a person have thyroid problems if his anterior pituitary gland was damaged?

_____

_____

_____

3. Given the information you know about cortisol and steroidal hormones, explain why patients taking steroids such as prednisone complain of weight gain, tiredness, and extreme hunger.

_____

_____

_____

4. How do calcitonin and parathyroid hormones work together to control calcium levels in the blood?

_____

_____

_____

5. Why is the pancreas considered both an endocrine and an exocrine gland? What other body system is affected by the exocrine function of this gland?

_____

_____

_____

APPLICATION

Follow the directions for each application.

1. Hormone Targets

Hormones do not affect all cells in the body, only their target cells. For each hormone listed below, give its target(s).

a. ACTH

b. Insulin

c. TSH

d. Calcitonin

e. FSH and LH

f. MSH

2. Endocrine Disorders

Endocrine disorders can produce too many or too few hormones. Name the disorders that may result from the following conditions.

a. Hypersecretion of GH in adults

b. Hyposecretion of GH in children

c. Hypersecretion of thyroid hormone in adults

d. Hyposecretion of thyroid hormone in adults

e. Hyposecretion of thyroid hormone in children

f. Hyposecretion of ACTH (adults or children)

CASE STUDIES

Write your response to each case study on the lines provided.

Case 1

A female patient has a diet that is totally lacking in lipids. How does her diet affect hormone production in her body?

_____

_____

_____

Case 2

A male patient wants you to explain to him how the use of steroid hormones can adversely affect his body. What would you tell him?

_____

_____

_____

Case 3

A 35-year-old woman is pregnant with her first child. Her glucose tolerance test (GTT) is elevated and she has been put on a diabetic diet. She is relieved that her diabetes is gestational and that she will return to normal blood sugar levels after her pregnancy. What information might you want to share with her?

_____

_____

_____

CHAPTER 31

Special Senses

REVIEW

Vocabulary Review

Matching

Match the key terms in the right column with the definitions in the left column by placing the letter of each correct answer in the space provided.

_____ 1. Receptors such as those found in the nose and on the tongue

_____ 2. "Bumps" on the tongue that contain taste buds

_____ 3. Fluids of the labyrinth

_____ 4. The type of hearing loss that results when sound waves are blocked

_____ 5. The type of hearing loss that results when neural tissues are damaged

_____ 6. Ringing in the ears

_____ 7. Visual receptors responsible for night vision

_____ 8. Visual receptors responsible for color vision

_____ 9. The watery fluid of the anterior chamber of the eye

_____ 10. The jelly-like fluid of the posterior chamber of the eye

_____ 11. A condition produced by increased intra-ocular pressure

_____ 12. An inner ear disease that causes bouts of vertigo, nausea, and tinnitus

_____ 13. Clouding and hardening of the lens of the eye, which causes visual disturbance

_____ 14. A condition commonly referred to as nearsightedness

_____ 15. Hearing loss due to aging

_____ 16. A visual impairment in near vision

_____ 17. The bacterial form of this condition is known as "pink eye"

_____ 18. Malleus, incus, and stapes

_____ 19. The process of the eye focusing on objects

_____ 20. A unit used to measure the relative intensity of sound

a. conductive
b. glaucoma
c. chemoreceptors
d. conjunctivitis
e. cataract
f. hyperopia
g. accommodation
h. perilymph/ endolymph
i. papillae
j. Meniere's disease
k. aqueous humor
l. sensorineural
m. presbycusis
n. rods
o. ossicles
p. myopia
q. cones
r. decibel
s. tinnitus
t. vitreous humor

True or False

Decide whether each statement is true or false. In the space at the left, write T *for true or* F *for false. On the lines provided, rewrite the false statements to make them true.*

_____ **21.** Smell receptors are located in the olfactory organ, which is in the lower part of the nasal cavity.

_____

_____ **22.** Taste cells that respond to sweet chemicals are concentrated at the back of the tongue.

_____

_____ **23.** The external ear is composed of the auricle and the external auditory canal.

_____

_____ **24.** The cornea is part of the middle layer of the eye.

_____

_____ **25.** The middle ear is connected to the pharynx by the eustachian tube.

_____

_____ **26.** The tiny bones of each eye are called ossicles.

_____

_____ **27.** The semicircular canals contain hearing receptors.

_____

_____ **28.** A cerumen impaction can cause sensorineural hearing loss.

_____

_____ **29.** In the process of seeing, the image is projected on the retina upside down.

_____

_____ **30.** The pupil is the colored part of the eye.

_____

_____ **31.** The clear covering over the iris and pupil is the sclera.

_____

_____ **32.** The optic nerves cross at the optic chiasm.

_____

_____ **33.** An M.D. who examines and treats eye diseases is the specialist called an optometrist.

_____

_____ **34.** In otosclerosis, the malleus becomes immobilized.

_____

_____ **35.** "Tubing" is done to treat otitis externa.

_____

Content Review

Multiple Choice

In the space provided, write the letter of the choice that best completes each statement or answers each question.

_____ 1. Which of the following is *not* a special sense?
  A. Smell
  B. Taste
  C. Hearing
  D. Vision
  E. Touch

_____ 2. Taste cells that respond to sour chemicals are concentrated on what part of the tongue?
  A. The tip
  B. The back
  C. The sides
  D. The bottom

_____ 3. Where is the organ of Corti located?
  A. The cochlea
  B. The vestibule
  C. The tympanic membrane
  D. The semicircular canals

_____ 4. What is the term for the physician who specializes in treating diseases and conditions of the eye?
  A. Optician
  B. Otologist
  C. Audiologist
  D. Optometrist
  E. Ophthalmologist

_____ 5. What does the abbreviation CC stand for?
  A. Vision without correction
  B. Vision with correction
  C. Hearing without correction
  D. Hearing with correction

_____ 6. The auricle begins the hearing process by collecting sound waves and channeling them to
  A. the labyrinth.
  B. the tympanic membrane.
  C. the cochlea.
  D. the pinna.
  E. the auditory nerve.

_____ 7. Physicians use tuning forks to
  A. measure air pressure in the ear.
  B. treat hearing loss.
  C. determine the extent of hearing loss.
  D. determine if the patient has hearing loss.
  E. check for cerumen impaction.

_____ 8. A myringotomy is a procedure done to treat
   A. glaucoma.
   B. conjunctivitis.
   C. otitis media.
   D. tympanic membrane rupture.

_____ 9. The most common cause for vision loss in the United States is
   A. cataracts.
   B. glaucoma.
   C. retinitis.
   D. presbyopia.
   E. macular degeneration.

_____ 10. An abnormally shaped cornea or lens causes the condition of
   A. astigmatism.
   B. amblyopia.
   C. strabismus.
   D. entropion.

Sentence Completion

In the space provided, write the word or phrase that best completes each sentence.

11. When you eat spicy foods, you are activating _____ receptors on the tongue.

12. The fifth acknowledged taste sensation is _____.

13. _____ is the medical term for crosseyes and walleyes.

14. The _____ controls the amount of light entering the eye.

15. Loss of visual acuity due to aging is called _____.

16. A(n) _____ is used to measure hearing acuity.

17. The _____ carries odor impulses to the cerebrum for interpretation.

18. _____ is an eversion of the lower eyelid.

19. The test that is done to measure fluid pressure within the eye is _____.

20. The _____ is the visual professional who fills eyeglass and contact lens prescriptions.

21. The muscles of the _____ control the shape of the lens.

22. The corneal-scleral junction is also called the _____.

23. A(n) _____ is used to visualize the internal structures of the eye.

24. Tears are produced by the _____.

25. The job of the _____ is to equalize pressure within the ears.

11. _____

12. _____

13. _____

14. _____

15. _____

16. _____

17. _____

18. _____

19. _____

20. _____

21. _____

22. _____

23. _____

24. _____

25. _____

Short Answer

Write the answer to each question on the lines provided.

26. Identify the taste associated with the darkened area on each illustration of the tongue, below.

B. _____

D. _____

A. _____

C. _____

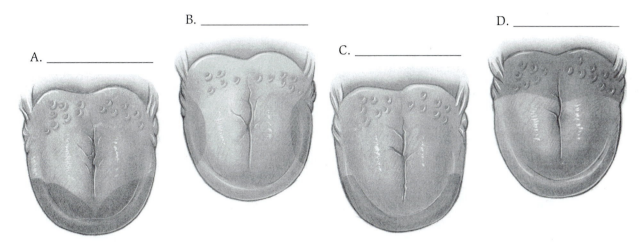

27. The illustration below shows a horizontal section of the eye. On the lines provided, label each structure.

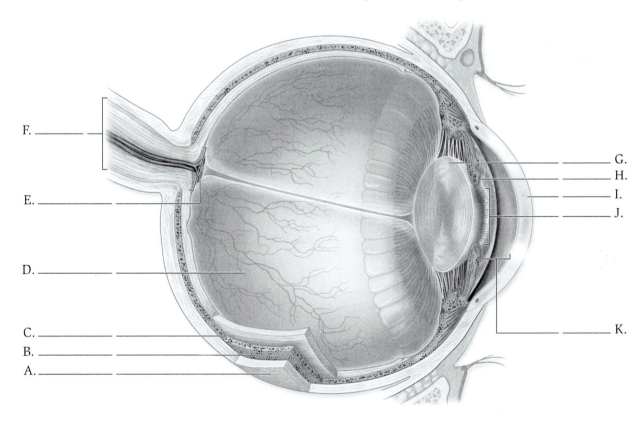

F. _____

E. _____

D. _____

C. _____

B. _____

A. _____

G. _____

H. _____

I. _____

J. _____

K. _____

28. The figure below illustrates the outer, middle, and inner ear. On the lines provided, label each structure.

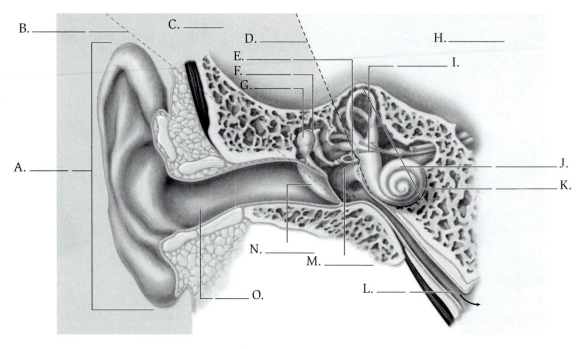

B. _____ _____   C. _____   D. _____   E. _____ _____   F. _____   G. _____   H. _____   I. _____   A. _____ _____   J. _____   K. _____   N. _____   M. _____   L. _____ _____   O. _____

29. Fill in the table for the following parts of the eye.

Part of the Eye	Function
Sclera	
Choroid	
Lens	
Retina	
Rods	
Cones	
Aqueous humor	
Vitreous humor	

30. Briefly describe the following disorders.

    A. glaucoma

    B. entropion

    C. dry eye syndrome

    D. retinal detachment

Critical Thinking

Write the answer to each question on the lines provided.

    1. If a person is on a drug that causes his nasal membranes to become dry, why might he have trouble smelling?

_____

_____

_____

2. How might a sore throat produce otitis media?

_____

_____

_____

3. Why is it important to face a person with a hearing impairment instead of speaking directly into his ear?

_____

_____

_____

4. How might the speech development of an infant with chronic otitis media be affected?

_____

_____

_____

APPLICATION

Follow the directions for each application.

1. Hearing Problems in Babies

Hearing problems in babies are not easy to recognize. For each age group listed below, give some general guidelines parents can use to identify hearing problems.

a. In babies up to 4 months old

b. In babies 4 to 8 months of age

c. In babies 8 to 12 months of age

2. Eye Safety

The overwhelming majority of eye injuries can be avoided by using eye safety practices. Name some eye safety practices for each situation.

a. At home

b. While playing sports

c. In the workplace

CASE STUDIES

Write your response to each case study on the lines provided.

Case 1

A 2-year-old is undergoing a procedure to place tubes in his ears. The doctor explains that this procedure is necessary because the toddler's auditory tubes are not functioning properly. What problems occur if auditory tubes do not function well?

_____

_____

_____

Case 2

A 79-year-old man recently suffered a stroke in his left primary visual area. Why did he lose some vision in both eyes?

_____

_____

_____

Case 3

A 65-year-old woman has been diagnosed with glaucoma. The doctor prescribes eye drops to treat the condition. However, the woman complains she does not like putting medicines in her eyes and that her eyes do not hurt. How would you convince her that she needs to use the eye drops?

_____

_____

_____

Case 4

A 52-year-old woman has noticed that when she looks at straight lines, they sometimes become wavy. She also has noticed that she cannot see details very well and that her central vision is becoming worse. What condition does she most likely have?

_____

_____

_____

CHAPTER 32

Principles of Asepsis

REVIEW

Vocabulary Review

Matching

Match the key terms in the right column with the definitions in the left column by placing the letter of each correct answer in the space provided.

_____ 1. An inanimate object that may be contaminated with infectious organisms and therefore transmit disease

_____ 2. A highly specific protein that attaches itself to a foreign substance

_____ 3. Harmless or beneficial microorganisms that have taken up residence in the body

_____ 4. An infection that occurs when there is a malfunction or abnormality in a routine body process, causing normally beneficial microorganisms to become pathogenic

_____ 5. An infection caused by introduction of a pathogen from outside the body

_____ 6. A foreign substance that invades the body

_____ 7. A simple form of life commonly made up of a single cell that can be seen only through a microscope

_____ 8. Phagocytes found in lymph nodes, liver, spleen, lungs, and bone marrow

_____ 9. The condition of being resistant to pathogens and the diseases they cause

_____ 10. A manifestation of an infection that is so slight as to be unnoticeable

a. antibody
b. antigen
c. macrophage
d. immunity
e. exogenous infection
f. resident normal flora
g. fomite
h. microorganism
i. subclinical case
j. endogenous infection

True or False

Decide whether each statement is true or false. In the space at the left, write T for true or F for false. On the lines provided, rewrite the false statements to make them true.

_____ 11. Pathogens are microorganisms that do not cause disease.

_____

_____ 12. *Mycobacterium tuberculosis* is spread through droplet transmission.

_____

_____ **13.** Monocytes are a type of T cell.

_____ **14.** Infections by microorganisms that can cause disease only when a host's resistance is low are called opportunistic infections.

_____ **15.** Another name for the disease diphtheria is whooping cough.

_____ **16.** Phagocytes are special white blood cells that engulf and digest normal flora.

_____ **17.** Macrophages are phagocytes found in the lymph nodes, liver, spleen, lungs, bone marrow, and connective tissue.

_____ **18.** A carrier is a reservoir host who is unaware of the presence of the pathogen and so spreads the disease.

_____ **19.** An endogenous infection is an infection in a reservoir host caused by the introduction of a pathogen from outside the body.

_____ **20.** A fomite is a living organism, such as an insect, that carries microorganisms from an infected person to another person.

_____ **21.** A susceptible host is a person who has little or no immunity to infection by a transmitted pathogen.

_____ **22.** The scientist who discovered how to use chemical antiseptics to control surgery-related infection by microorganisms was Hippocrates.

_____ **23.** Antigens are part of the body's natural defenses against infection.

_____ **24.** When a person receives an immunization or vaccine with killed or weakened organisms, the result is natural active immunity.

_____ **25.** B cells are a group of proteins always present in the body to help white blood cells ingest microorganisms.

_____ **26.** Viruses are the smallest known infectious agents.

Content Review

Multiple Choice

In the space provided, write the letter of the choice that best completes each statement or answers each question.

_____ **1.** The chain of infection consists of a(n)
  A. infectious agent.
  B. reservoir host.
  C. mode of transmission.
  D. portal of entry.
  E. All of the above.

_____ **2.** A microorganism's disease-producing power is called
  A. a pathogen.
  B. convalescence.
  C. immunity.
  D. virulence.
  E. resistance.

_____ **3.** Beneficial microorganisms found in the body that help create a barrier against pathogens are known as
  A. resident normal flora.
  B. carriers.
  C. endogens.
  D. fomites.

_____ **4.** A reservoir host who is unaware of the presence of a pathogen and therefore spreads disease is called
  A. transmission.
  B. a portal of exit.
  C. a portal of entry.
  D. a susceptible host.
  E. a carrier.

_____ **5.** The condition of being resistant to pathogens and the diseases they cause is called
  A. virulence.
  B. immunity.
  C. resistance.
  D. nonspecific.

_____ **6.** An animal, insect, or human whose body is capable of sustaining the growth of a pathogen is known as
  A. a reservoir host.
  B. a susceptible host.
  C. a pathogen.
  D. flora.
  E. an environmental factor.

_____ 7. An insect that carries microorganisms from one infected person to another is a
- A. fomite.
- B. pathogen.
- C. host.
- D. vector.
- E. droplet.

_____ 8. An infection in a reservoir host in which an abnormality or malfunction in routine body process has caused normally beneficial or harmless microorganisms to become pathogenic is called a(n)
- A. endogenous infection.
- B. subclinical case.
- C. exogenous infection.
- D. carrier state.

_____ 9. The process by which phagocytes destroy pathogens is known as
- A. digestion.
- B. engulfment.
- C. protection.
- D. humoral response.
- E. phagocytosis.

_____ 10. Cells that produce antibodies are called
- A. T cells.
- B. B cells.
- C. lymphocytes.
- D. antigens.
- E. phagocytes.

_____ 11. Administration of an immunization or a vaccine results in which type of immunity?
- A. Natural active
- B. Natural passive
- C. Artificial active
- D. Artificial passive

_____ 12. Exposure to a disease-causing organism results in which type of immunity?
- A. Natural active
- B. Natural passive
- C. Artificial active
- D. Artificial passive
- E. Complement

_____ 13. Which of the following are phagocytes that are formed in bone marrow and circulate throughout the blood for a short period of time?
- A. Antibodies
- B. Macrophages
- C. Neutrophils
- D. Monocytes

Short Answer

Write the answer to each question on the lines provided.

14. What are four ways in which microorganisms can damage the body?

_____

_____

_____

15. How does resident normal flora protect the body against pathogens?

_____

_____

_____

16. What is the process by which phagocytes destroy a pathogen?

_____

_____

_____

17. Describe how the body achieves active immunity to a particular disease.

_____

_____

_____

18. How does cell-mediated immunity function to protect the body?

_____

_____

_____

19. What are monocytes and how do they protect the body?

_____

_____

_____

20. What are the five means by which pathogens may be transmitted?

_____

_____

_____

21. List ways to contain tuberculosis bacteria at their source and prevent their entrance into another host.

_____

_____

_____

22. Describe the body's first lines of defense.

_____

_____

_____

23. What are the CDC's four strategies for reducing the incidence of antibiotic-resistant microorganisms?

_____

_____

_____

Critical Thinking

Write the answer to each question on the lines provided.

1. How will understanding the cycle of infection help you maintain an aseptic environment?

_____

_____

_____

2. How could a common cold be spread by shaking hands with someone?

_____

_____

_____

3. What instructions would you give a patient suspected of having tuberculosis?

_____

_____

_____

4. What information can you give a patient who is insistent he receive a prescription for antibiotics to treat his common cold?

_____

_____

_____

APPLICATION

Follow the directions for the application.

Signs and Symptoms of Diseases

Listed below are signs and symptoms of contagious diseases you may encounter as a medical assistant. Write the name of each disease on the line provided and identify its cause.

a. Patient has fluid-filled blisters that began as a rash of tiny red bumps.

b. Patient has a harsh, barking cough, with difficulty breathing, hoarseness, and a low-grade fever.

c. Patient experiences fever and an itchy rash.

d. Patient has fever and painful swelling near the back of the jaw.

e. Patient has fever, sore throat, swollen lymph nodes, and occasionally spleen and liver involvement.

f. Patient experiences the symptoms of strep throat, as well as nausea and vomiting, and has tiny, bright-red spots on his trunk, neck, face, and extremities.

CASE STUDIES

Write your response to each case study on the lines provided.

Case 1

A patient tells you she heard there was a vaccine for tuberculosis. She wants to know if she can receive the vaccine. What information about the tuberculosis vaccine will you give her?

_____

_____

_____

Case 2

You are the clinical supervisor in a pediatric office. You notice that a coworker does not wash her hands after taking a child's temperature. You know the child has chickenpox. After mentioning to the medical assistant that she did not wash her hands, she states, "I will be fine. I had the chickenpox when I was a child." Based on what you have learned about the cycle of infection, why is this statement unacceptable? What should you tell the medical assistant? What part of the cycle of infection does the patient represent? The medical assistant?

_____

_____

_____

Case 3

Imagine that you are a preformed, immune protein that has been injected into the body of a person recently exposed to a disease. What are you? What work will you do in the body? What disease or diseases are you being sent to treat?

_____

_____

_____

Case 4

Maria had measles as a child. She is now immune to the disease. What type of immunity does this represent?

_____

_____

Case 5

Sam received a tetanus booster at the time of his last physical exam. What type of immunity did Sam produce to the vaccine?

_____

_____

_____

CHAPTER 33

Infection Control Techniques

REVIEW

Vocabulary Review

True or False

Decide whether each statement is true or false. In the space at the left, write T for true or F for false. On the lines provided, rewrite the false statements to make them true.

_____ 1. The three methods of infection control are sanitization, disinfection, and sterilization.

_____

_____ 2. Sanitization is a scrubbing process used to remove the microorganisms that cause disease.

_____

_____ 3. Bleach is an effective means of immunization.

_____

_____ 4. Asepsis is the condition in which pathogens are absent or controlled.

_____

_____ 5. After sterilization, items wrapped in a sterile pack have a shelf life of 30 days.

_____

_____ 6. Sanitization involves raising the number of microorganisms on an object or a surface to a fairly safe level.

_____

_____ 7. Sterilization is the destruction of all microorganisms, including bacterial spores, by specific means.

_____

_____ 8. Hospitals now use Standard Precautions, which are a combination of Universal Precautions and rules to reduce the risk of disease transmission by means of moist body substances.

_____

_____ 9. According to OSHA guidelines, an example of a Category I task is giving mouth-to-mouth resuscitation.

_____

_____ 10. The penalty for a violation of OSHA's infectious waste disposal regulations is a fine from $5000 to $70,000.

_____

_____ 11. Preventing the spread of microorganisms in the medical environment through maintaining cleanliness is known as septic technique.

_____

_____ 12. According to OSHA requirements, all health-care workers who have occupational exposure to blood or other potentially infectious materials must be provided with the hepatitis B vaccine, a procedure that is to be billed to their insurance company.

_____

Content Review

Multiple Choice

In the space provided, write the letter of the choice that best completes each statement or answers each question.

_____ 1. The processes of sterilization include dry heat, chemicals, and
   A. sanitization.
   B. disinfection.
   C. autoclaving.
   D. scrubbing.
   E. None of the above.

_____ 2. A chemical agent that leaves an instrument clean but not sterile is a(n)
   A. cold sterilizer.
   B. antiseptic.
   C. chemical sterilizer.
   D. detergent.
   E. disinfectant.

_____ 3. Which of these methods would be the most effective in loosening debris from sharp instruments while also reducing the risk of injury?
   A. Submersion in water and detergent
   B. Ultrasound
   C. Autoclaving
   D. Chemical disinfecting

_____ 4. Sterilization tape that is used to secure autoclave wrap is also used to
   A. identify and date the contents.
   B. prove that the sterility of the items has taken place.
   C. indicate that the pack has been exposed to the autoclave process.
   D. *A* and *C* only.
   E. All of the above.

_____ 5. The proof that an instrument pack has been sterilized is achieved by using a
   A. chemical indicator strip placed under the instruments.
   B. chemical indicator strip placed in the center of the pack.
   C. chemical indicator tape around the outside of the pack.
   D. biological monitor placed next to a pack.
   E. biological monitor placed in the load with the packs.

_____ 6. The critical step of the autoclave cycle when the microorganisms are destroyed is when
  A. the greatest temperature is reached.
  B. the water is changed into pressurized steam.
  C. heat is transferred to the items in the chamber.
  D. the steam saturates items in the chamber.

_____ 7. While using an autoclave, the medical assistant must monitor
  A. temperature-pressure combinations.
  B. time-temperature combinations.
  C. pressure-time combinations.
  D. All of the above.
  E. None of the above.

_____ 8. When storing items removed from an autoclave, the major factor contributing to the integrity of the sterility is
  A. preventing dust accumulation.
  B. maintaining the temperature of the environment.
  C. the state of dryness when the pack is stored.
  D. the shelf-life expectancy.

_____ 9. The use of alcohol is an effective means of
  A. sterilization.
  B. immunization.
  C. disinfection.
  D. sanitization.
  E. All of the above.

_____ 10. Instruments that do not require sterilization can safely be prepared for their next use by
  A. washing them until they are visibly clean and free from stains and tissues.
  B. wiping them off with a paper towel.
  C. rinsing them under extremely hot water.
  D. visually inspecting them and storing them if nothing is seen on their surface.
  E. Any of the above.

_____ 11. The method that most hospitals use to reduce the risk of disease transmission by means of moist body substances is
  A. Standard Precautions.
  B. Universal Precautions.
  C. personal protective equipment.
  D. isolation.

_____ 12. The cleansing process to decrease the number of microorganisms before disinfection or sterilization is called
  A. sanitization.
  B. hand washing.
  C. asepsis.
  D. biohazardous waste.
  E. All of the above.

Short Answer

Write the answer to each question on the lines provided.

13. What are three medical instruments you can sanitize and reuse without further disinfection or sterilization?

_____

_____

_____

14. List three factors that can have an impact on the effectiveness of a disinfectant.

_____

_____

_____

15. What are the disadvantages of using acid products to disinfect instruments and equipment?

_____

_____

_____

16. What are the three leading factors that cause incomplete autoclave sterilization?

_____

_____

_____

17. What aseptic technique should be used when administering tablet or capsule medications and why?

_____

_____

_____

18. Explain how vaccines protect the body against infectious diseases.

_____

_____

_____

19. Describe possible duties and responsibilities of medical assistants in providing immunizations.

_____

_____

_____

20. Describe the process you would use to sanitize surgical instruments.

_____

_____

_____

21. When is it important to wear protective eyewear or face shields? Give an example.

_____

_____

_____

Critical Thinking

Write the answer to each question on the lines provided.

1. What should you do with a curette that a coworker says has "probably been sterilized"?

_____

_____

_____

2. Would you use transfer forceps during a procedure if you were wearing sterile gloves to handle instruments in a sterile field? Explain.

_____

_____

_____

3. Why should you know your own HIV and HBV status if you are participating in high-risk procedures?

_____

_____

_____

4. Why is informed consent important in the immunization of adults and children?

_____

_____

_____

5. How might less-invasive techniques for delivering medications help hospital patients avoid nosocomial infection?

_____

_____

_____

APPLICATION

Follow the directions for each application.

1. Sanitizing Instruments and Equipment

Work with one partner and sanitize a group of instruments. One person should sanitize the instruments and equipment. The second should act as an evaluator and should refer to the detailed description provided in the text while observing the procedure. Assume that a surgical procedure has just been completed.

a. Collect all the instruments from the procedure; place them in a sink or container filled with water and an appropriate neutral-pH detergent solution.

b. Put on utility gloves and separate the sharp instruments from all other equipment.

c. Rinse each piece of equipment in hot running water. Scrub the instruments and equipment with hot, soapy water and a plastic scrub brush. Then rinse the instruments and dry them properly.

d. Rinse and sanitize syringes following appropriate procedures for these items.

e. When the sanitizing process is complete, the observer should present a critique of the procedure, pointing out any errors in the procedure and offering suggestions for improved technique.

f. Exchange roles so that each of you has the opportunity to practice the procedure while the other observes and offers comments and suggestions.

g. When each of you has completed the sanitization procedure, follow the same process to practice and develop skill in disinfection and sterilization.

2. Making a Biohazardous Materials Checklist

Work with two partners. The chief physician wants to make sure her staff is aware of the guidelines for managing different types of biohazardous materials. She has asked your team to prepare a Biohazardous Materials Checklist.

a. As a team, decide which biohazardous materials should be included in the checklist. Have one partner make a list.

b. Each team member should choose one type of biohazardous material from the list and write guidelines for managing that particular material. Guidelines should include information about handling and disposing of the biohazardous material. Use medical journals, textbooks, or other sources as references.

c. Team members should evaluate each other's guidelines. The critique should answer these questions: Are the guidelines described in enough detail? Will the guidelines prevent potentially infectious waste materials from endangering people or the environment? Is the writing clear and concise?

d. The team should discuss the critique, noting the accuracy and completeness of the guidelines as written. Revise the guidelines as needed.

e. Members of the team should take turns choosing a different biohazardous material from the list until the checklist is complete.

f. As a team, review your Biohazardous Materials Checklist. Discuss these questions with your partners: Have all the various biohazardous materials in the medical office been accounted for? Are the guidelines as complete as they need to be?

g. Compare your Biohazardous Materials Checklist with another team's checklist. Evaluate each other's checklists. Revise your checklist to make it as complete and accurate as possible.

3. Educating Patients

Work with two partners. Have one partner play the role of a patient recovering from an infection. Have the second partner act as a medical assistant. Let the third partner act as an observer and evaluator.

a. Have the student playing the medical assistant prepare a presentation about the basic principles of hygiene and disease prevention. The aim of the presentation is to help educate patients about general ways to protect themselves from disease. It may include charts, diagrams, drawings, or other visual aids.

b. Have the medical assistant talk to the patient about ways to protect herself and her family from disease. Have the patient ask questions to clarify or expand upon the information.

c. Have the observer provide a critique of the medical assistant's patient education techniques. The critique should examine the content of the presentation as well as the medical assistant's attitude, tone, accuracy, and clarity. Comments should include both positive feedback and suggestions for improvement.

d. Exchange roles and repeat the role-playing exercise.

e. Exchange roles again so that each member of the group has an opportunity to play the role of the medical assistant in this scenario.

f. As a group, discuss the strengths and weaknesses of each group member's ability to educate a patient about hygiene and disease prevention.

CASE STUDIES

Write your response to each case study on the lines provided.

Case 1

You have been asked to check the autoclave to make sure it is sterilizing instruments. How will you accomplish this task?

_____

_____

_____

Case 2

The receptionist at your medical office arrives at work coughing and sneezing. She appears to have the signs and symptoms of a common cold. What, if anything, should you do?

_____

_____

_____

Case 3

A patient enters your reception area with a severe laceration on his arm. The blood is dripping from his arm onto the carpet and the front desk area. What actions should you take?

_____

_____

_____

Case 4

You need to take the vital signs of a patient who is suspected of having scabies. What personal protective equipment should you wear?

_____

_____

_____

Case 5

You are assisting the doctor during a minor surgical procedure. You are wearing sterile gloves and handling sterile items directly. The doctor knocks an instrument to the floor and needs a replacement. The instruments are in a supply cabinet next to you. What should you do?

_____

_____

_____

CHAPTER **34**

HIV, Hepatitis, and Other Bloodborne Pathogens

REVIEW

Vocabulary Review

True or False

Decide whether each statement is true or false. In the space at the left, write T *for true or* F *for false. On the lines provided, rewrite the false statements to make them true.*

_____ **1.** A person who is unable to react to a TB skin test because he is immunocompromised is said to be allergic.

_____

_____ **2.** HIV, hepatitis B virus, and hepatitis C virus are the bloodborne pathogens posing the greatest risks.

_____

_____ **3.** Hepatitis B is spread mainly through the fecal-oral route.

_____

_____ **4.** Shingles is caused by the reactivation of the virus that causes chickenpox.

_____

_____ **5.** A bloodborne infection that may be contracted by handling cat litter is erythema infectiosum.

_____

_____ **6.** The Federal Drug Administration (FDA) regulates the safety of health-care workers.

_____

_____ **7.** White blood cells that are a key component of the body's immune system and that work in coordination with other white blood cells to combat infection are known as helper B cells.

_____

_____ **8.** The Centers for Disease Control and Prevention (CDC) are provided with timely reports on the incidence of infectious diseases from state health departments.

_____

Content Review

Multiple Choice

In the space provided, write the letter of the choice that best completes each statement or answers each question.

_____ 1. The disease that is transmitted by handling cat feces is known as
  A. syphilis.
  B. malaria.
  C. toxoplasmosis.
  D. *Pneumocystis carinii.*
  E. hairy leukoplakia.

_____ 2. The vaccine against hepatitis B provides immunity for at least
  A. 3 years.
  B. 4 years.
  C. 5 years.
  D. 6 years.
  E. 7 years.

_____ 3. Which of the following is the only readily available method to detect evidence of HIV infection?
  A. Patient history
  B. Signs and symptoms
  C. Serologic test(s)
  D. Urinalysis

_____ 4. Hepatitis D occurs only in people who are infected with
  A. hepatitis A.
  B. hepatitis B.
  C. hepatitis C.
  D. hepatitis E.
  E. HIV.

_____ 5. Erythema infectiosum, a childhood disease, is also known as
  A. fifth disease.
  B. red measles.
  C. chickenpox.
  D. listeriosis.

_____ 6. Which of the following is a possible means of transmission of HIV?
  A. Tears
  B. Intact skin
  C. Saliva
  D. Blood

_____ 7. Hepatitis primarily affects the
  A. lungs.
  B. liver.
  C. brain.
  D. skin.
  E. intestines.

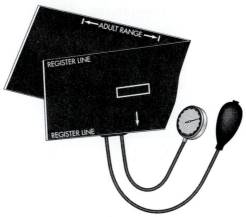

G. _____

_____

_____

H. _____

_____

_____

I. _____

_____

_____

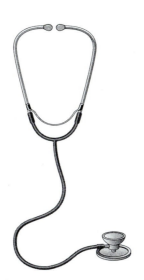

L. _____

_____

_____

J. _____

_____

_____

K. _____

_____

_____

M. _____

_____

_____

N. _____

_____

_____

19. What tasks are involved in maintaining the instruments and supplies needed in the exam room?

_____

_____

_____

20. What can you do to ensure that the floor of an exam room is physically safe?

_____

_____

_____

Critical Thinking

Write the answer to each question on the lines provided.

1. What tasks in the preparation of the exam and treatment area can influence a patient's perception of a medical practice?

_____

_____

_____

2. Why do you think OSHA regulations prohibit applying cosmetics in a room where potentially infectious materials are present?

_____

_____

_____

3. What tasks in preparing the exam and treatment area are done to aid the physician in performing his work?

_____

_____

_____

4. Why is it important to maintain proper temperature in the laboratory refrigerator? How will you accomplish this?

_____

_____

_____

5. What steps will you take to ensure the otoscope and ophthalmoscope are in good working order?

_____

_____

_____

APPLICATION

Follow the directions for each application.

1. Cleaning Instruments

Indicate the proper method of cleaning for each instrument—sanitization, disinfection, or sterilization. Then, in the space provided, give the basic guidelines for performing each cleaning method.

a. Otoscope: _____

b. Anoscope: _____

c. Sphygmomanometer: _____

d. Nasal speculum: _____

e. Syringe: _____

Guidelines

f. Sanitization: _____

_____

g. Disinfection: _____

_____

h. Sterilization: _____

_____

2. Inspecting the Medical Office

Suppose you are a health and safety inspector for your state. Describe the things you would look for, in each area listed below, when inspecting a medical office.

a. Compliance with the Americans with Disabilities Act of 1990

_____

_____

_____

b. Infection control

_____

_____

_____

c. Fire prevention

_____

_____

_____

CASE STUDIES

Write your response to each case study on the lines provided.

Case 1

While reviewing the patient list for the next day, you notice that the patient for Dr. Tejada's 10:00 AM appointment is in a wheelchair. What "reasonable accommodations" have already been made for this patient?

_____

_____

_____

Case 2

You have been asked to train Sam, a newly hired medical assistant. Sam's main responsibility will be to keep the exam rooms in proper order. What information will you give Sam?

_____

_____

_____

Case 3

At a weekly staff meeting, a coworker announces her intention of cutting overhead costs by turning thermostats down to 65°F and using only under-cabinet lights rather than overhead lights. She then asks the group for feedback on these ideas. What would you say?

_____

_____

_____

Case 4

Hearing a shout, you run into the hallway and see smoke pouring from a storage closet. Sue, a nurse, is running toward the closet with a fire extinguisher. What should you do?

_____

_____

_____

CHAPTER 36

Interviewing the Patient, Taking a History, and Documentation

REVIEW

Vocabulary Review

Matching

Match the key terms in the right column with the definitions in the left column by placing the letter of each correct answer in the space provided.

_____ 1. Stating what you think has been suggested

_____ 2. Formed as a result of deeper thought

_____ 3. Restating what is said in your own words

_____ 4. Term that describes the patient's most significant symptoms

_____ 5. Using agents in a way that is not medically approved

_____ 6. A physical or psychological dependence

_____ 7. Asking questions that provide an increase in understanding of a problem

_____ 8. Thoughts, feelings, and perceptions

_____ 9. Apparent and measurable

_____ 10. A way of organizing information so that the most recent information is featured on top

_____ 11. Repeating something back to a patient in your own words

a. addiction
b. chief complaint
c. substance abuse
d. reverse chronological
e. subjective
f. objective
g. mirroring
h. verbalizing
i. restatement
j. reflection
k. clarification

True or False

Decide whether each statement is true or false. In the space at the left, write T for true or F for false. On the lines provided, rewrite the false statements to make them true.

_____ 12. The chief complaint is the physician's diagnosis of a patient's problem.

_____

_____ 13. The Health Insurance Portability and Accountability Act (HIPAA) is part of the patient's responsibilities when receiving health care.

_____

_____ 14. Sitting back and just hearing the patient is part of active listening.

_____

_____ 15. The patient's tone of voice, facial expression, and body language are signs of nonverbal communication.

_____

_____ **16.** The statement "I think you probably just have the flu" is an example of making a diagnosis and should be said by the medical assistant.

_____

_____ **17.** A patient who has white-coat syndrome is anxious about visiting the physician.

_____

_____ **18.** If a patient is using the drug Ecstasy, you may notice an increase in her heart rate and blood pressure.

_____

Content Review

Multiple Choice

In the space provided, write the letter of the choice that best completes each statement or answers each question.

_____ **1.** During a patient interview, repeating in your own words what the patient has said is an important part of
   A. effective questioning.
   B. being aware of nonverbal clues.
   C. using a broad knowledge base.
   D. summarizing to form a general picture.
   E. effective listening.

_____ **2.** "Have you had this pain long?" is an example of a(n)
   A. hypothetical question.
   B. open-ended question.
   C. encouragement for the patient to take the lead.
   D. closed-ended question.

_____ **3.** "This pain seems to be causing you more problems than it did last week" is an example of which of the following interviewing skills?
   A. Verbalizing the implied
   B. Asking a hypothetical question
   C. Challenging the patient
   D. Asking a closed-ended question
   E. Being aware of nonverbal clues

_____ **4.** "What activities seem to make the pain worse?" is an example of which of the following interviewing skills?
   A. Asking a hypothetical question
   B. Encouraging the patient to provide more information
   C. Mirroring the patient's responses
   D. Asking a leading question

_____ **5.** Where would you look on the patient's chart for information about a previous hospitalization?
   A. Laboratory report
   B. Discharge summary
   C. Patient registration form
   D. Consent form
   E. Physician's treatment plan

_____ 6. Which of the following is an example of *subjective* data?
   A. Pain in the right arm
   B. A blood pressure reading of 138/88
   C. A height measurement of 5'6" and a weight measure of 138 lbs.
   D. A reddened rash on the left arm

_____ 7. Which of the following is an example of *objective* data?
   A. Dizziness
   B. Pain
   C. Swollen feet
   D. Weakness
   E. Tiredness

Sentence Completion

In the space provided, write the word or phrase that best completes each sentence.

8. An elderly patient who seems to be senile may actually be _____.

9. Abuse can be physical, _____, or both.

10. _____ combine SOMR and POMR and are easily accessible to health-care workers.

11. _____ are used more extensively in medical offices than any other type of medical record.

12. The _____ is the reason the patient came to the health-care facility.

13. The _____ includes information about the level of stress, exposure to hazardous substances, and heavy lifting.

14. The _____ includes information about allergies.

15. A medical assistant should obtain information about the parents, siblings, and grandparents to complete the _____.

8. _____

9. _____

10. _____

11. _____

12. _____

13. _____

14. _____

15. _____

Short Answer

Write the answer to each question on the lines provided.

16. What are the six Cs of charting?

_____

_____

_____

17. Name seven kinds of standard information that should appear in a patient's chart.

_____

_____

_____

18. To what does the acronym SOAP refer? What does each letter represent?

_____

_____

_____

19. Why might depression be called a hidden illness?

_____

_____

_____

20. What are six signs of possible physical or psychological abuse?

_____

_____

_____

Critical Thinking

Write the answer to each question on the lines provided.

1. What are important guidelines to consider when using progress notes?

_____

_____

_____

2. Why is it important to consider a patient's polypharmacy when obtaining a chief complaint or medical history?

_____

_____

_____

3. Name two general kinds of errors in taking a patient's history that could affect a physician's ability to care for the patient.

_____

_____

_____

4. Which of the following is a definite sign of depression in an adolescent patient: problems in sleeping, problems in eating, sudden mood changes, or illogical thought patterns?

_____

_____

_____

5. Name two abbreviations that have been banned by the JCAHO. Why are these abbreviations banned from patient charting?

_____

_____

_____

APPLICATION

Follow the directions for each application.

1. Conducting a Patient Interview

    a. In groups of three or four, discuss and record on index cards appropriate open-ended questions for the following chief complaints:
        1. Low back pain
        2. Diabetes follow-up
        3. Insomnia

    b. As a class, discuss the questions each group prepared. Formulate a list of interview questions for each of the patient complaints.

    c. In pairs or groups of three, role-play each scenario, interviewing and documenting the chief complaint on the progress note provided in the documentation section in the back of the workbook.

2. Charting Patient Data

    a. You have collected the following information during a client interview. Use a progress note example in the documentation section in the back of the workbook.
        A 14-year-old girl comes to the client because she has had a sore throat and fever for the past 2 days. Her vital signs are TPR 99.8-88-24, BP 110/70. She describes the pain as burning and says she has just not felt like eating lately.

    b. You have collected the following information during a client interview. Use the example encounter form in the documentation section in the back of the workbook.
        A 70-year-old male arrives at the client for a blood pressure checkup. He denies pain. His vital signs are TPR 97.4-66-20, BP 158/90, O_2 Sat 96%. He is 69¾ inches tall and 165 lbs. His previous records indicate he is allergic to "sulfa drugs." He states that he is currently taking Lipitor, 20 milligrams, one every day; Atenolol, 50 milligrams, one every day; and 81 milligrams of aspirin daily. He denies using alcohol, tobacco, and recreational drugs and does not know when he had his last tetanus shot.

CASE STUDIES

Write your response to each case study on the lines provided.

Case 1

As you interview a patient before he sees the physician, he points out a mysterious rash that developed during the night. He asks what you think it is. You explain that he needs to talk to the doctor about it. The patient insists that you know him because you were assisting the physician during his last visit. He is sure you can tell him what caused his rash. You know this patient has many allergies and probably touched something that caused his rash. What should you tell the patient?

_____

_____

_____

Case 2

A 17-year-old girl arrives alone for an appointment with the doctor. She seems tense and stiff; she avoids looking at you. When you ask why she has come to the doctor's office today, she whispers that she will tell the doctor. What should you do?

_____

_____

_____

CHAPTER 37

Obtaining Vital Signs and Measurements

REVIEW

Vocabulary Review

Matching

Match the key terms in the right column with the definitions in the left column by placing the letter of each correct answer in the space provided.

_____ 1. Difficult or painful breathing

_____ 2. An exceptionally high fever

_____ 3. A slow heart rate of less than 60 beats per minute

_____ 4. A fast heart rate of more than 100 beats per minute

_____ 5. Having a body temperature within the normal range

_____ 6. Curve in the surface of mercury in a mercury sphygmomanometer

_____ 7. Instrument that amplifies body sounds

_____ 8. A measure of blood pressure taken when the heart relaxes

_____ 9. A measure of blood pressure taken when the left ventricle contracts

_____ 10. Deep, rapid breathing

_____ 11. Pulse at the lower left corner of the heart

_____ 12. Temperature scale on which a healthy adult's temperature would be 98.6°

_____ 13. High blood pressure

_____ 14. Low blood pressure

_____ 15. To make sure an instrument is measuring correctly

_____ 16. The bend of the elbow

_____ 17. The lower left corner of the heart, where the strongest heart sounds can be heard

_____ 18. Having a body temperature above the normal range

_____ 19. A breathing pattern that includes shallow and deep breaths and apnea

_____ 20. A device used to measure the temperature on the forehead

a. Fahrenheit
b. hypotension
c. meniscus
d. diastolic pressure
e. febrile
f. systolic pressure
g. stethoscope
h. dyspnea
i. hypertension
j. apical
k. hyperpnea
l. calibrate
m. antecubital space
n. apex
o. afebrile
p. hyperpyrexia
q. Cheyne-Stokes respirations
r. temporal scanner
s. bradycardia
t. tachycardia

True or False

Decide whether each statement is true or false. In the space at the left, write T for true or F for false. On the lines provided, rewrite the false statements to make them true.

_____ 21. An adult will have his weight, head circumference, and height measured once a year.

_____

_____ **22.** A patient is febrile if her body temperature is above normal.

_____

_____ **23.** On a Fahrenheit scale, the normal oral temperature in a healthy adult is about 98.6°.

_____

_____ **24.** A patient with tachypnea breathes slowly.

_____

_____ **25.** A tympanic temperature is taken in the ear canal.

_____

_____ **26.** A tympanic thermometer measures the temperature of a patient's inner ear.

_____

_____ **27.** You should measure an adult's pulse at the radial artery.

_____

_____ **28.** The temporal artery is located at the side of the neck.

_____

_____ **29.** A sphygmomanometer is used to measure blood pressure.

_____

_____ **30.** Using the palpatory method, a medical assistant can take an estimate of a patient's systolic
blood pressure before measuring it exactly.

_____

_____ **31.** The axilla is the armpit.

_____

_____ **32.** Auscultated blood pressure is determined by palpation.

_____

_____ **33.** Hypertension is also known as low blood pressure.

_____

_____ **34.** Body temperature is affected by numerous factors including the patient's weight.

_____

Content Review

Multiple Choice

In the space provided, write the letter of the choice that best completes each statement or answers each question.

_____ **1.** A crying, fussy infant needs his respirations counted. What should you do?
- **A.** Count the respirations and report them to the physician immediately as ordered
- **B.** Attempt to quiet the infant or wait until later in the visit to count the respirations
- **C.** Do not worry about counting the respirations; the physician will need to see the infant as soon as possible
- **D.** Using an electronic sphygmomanometer, you should be able to obtain the correct respiration count
- **E.** Have the parents attempt to count the respirations while you do the other vital signs

_____ 2. An adult patient has started taking a medication for hypertension since his last visit. Which of the following would you most likely expect at this visit?

A. A blood pressure within the normal range

B. A blood pressure result higher than normal

C. A blood pressure result lower than normal

D. A blood pressure result lower than the results from the previous visit

_____ 3. Review the following vital sign results for an adult patient older than age 65 and determine which set is considered out of the normal range.

A. BP 120/80, T 98.6°F, P 98, R 20

B. BP 150/90, T 98.6°F, P 98, R 20

C. BP 108/78, T 37°C, P 88, R 18

D. BP 120/80, T 98.2°F, P 106, R 20

E. BP 120/80, T 97.2°F, P 98, R 20

_____ 4. A patient enters the facility with open lesions on his arms and hands. What *special* OSHA precautions should you take while measuring his vital signs?

A. Wear a mask and gown

B. Wear gloves and wash your hands

C. Clean the exam area before the patient arrives

D. Take a rectal temperature to ensure accurate results

_____ 5. Which of the following would most likely cause rales?

A. Congestive heart failure

B. Head injury

C. Asthma

D. Brain tumor

E. Influenza

_____ 6. What are the preferred methods for taking the temperature of a child younger than 2 years of age?

A. Oral

B. Axillary and tympanic

C. Oral, rectal, and temporal

D. Rectal, temporal, and axillary

_____ 7. Which of the following is generally *not* a health problem?

A. Apnea

B. Hypertension

C. Dyspnea

D. Hyperpnea

E. Hypotension

_____ 8. Which of the following is the best way to weigh a toddler?

A. Ask the toddler to stand very still on the scale

B. Weigh the parent and the toddler together, and then subtract the weight of the parent from the result

C. Lay the toddler on the infant scale

D. Have the toddler hold the height bar during the weighing process to encourage him to stand still

_____ 9. Which of the following is an internal factor that affects the blood pressure?

A. Papilledema

B. Blood viscosity

C. Malignant hypertension

D. Hyperpyrexis

Sentence Completion

In the space provided, write the word or phrase that best completes each sentence.

10. On the top moveable bar of the height scale, the numbers _____ as you go down the bar.

11. To ensure the proper size cuff when taking the blood pressure, the bladder inside the cuff should encircle _____ to _____ of the distance around the arm or leg being used.

12. Deep and rapid respirations associated with hysteria or excitement are called _____.

13. Abnormal changes in height or weight can indicate a disorder of a person's _____.

14. A person's axillary temperature is usually about 1° lower than her _____ temperature.

15. The eardrum was selected as a location to measure body temperature because it has the same blood supply as the _____.

16. If a patient's pulse rate is high, his _____ rate is also likely to be high.

17. Electronic sphygmomanometers are _____ likely to provide more accurate readings than other types of sphygmomanometers.

10. _____

11. _____

12. _____

13. _____

14. _____

15. _____

16. _____

17. _____

Short Answer

Write the answer to each question on the lines provided.

18. Name the five vital signs.

_____

_____

_____

19. Name and describe the parts of a stethoscope.

_____

_____

_____

20. Explain why pulse and respirations should be taken together.

_____

_____

_____

21. Name five methods for taking temperature, and discuss the circumstances under which each method might be used.

_____

_____

_____

22. How can you ensure that a tympanic temperature is accurate?

_____

_____

_____

23. Why is it necessary to hold the thermometer in place when taking a rectal temperature?

_____

_____

_____

24. When you are taking a blood pressure measurement, how do you determine that patient's proper inflation amount in mm Hg?

_____

_____

_____

25. Identify the blood pressure values on the illustration of aneroid gauges below. Write your answers on the lines in the figure.

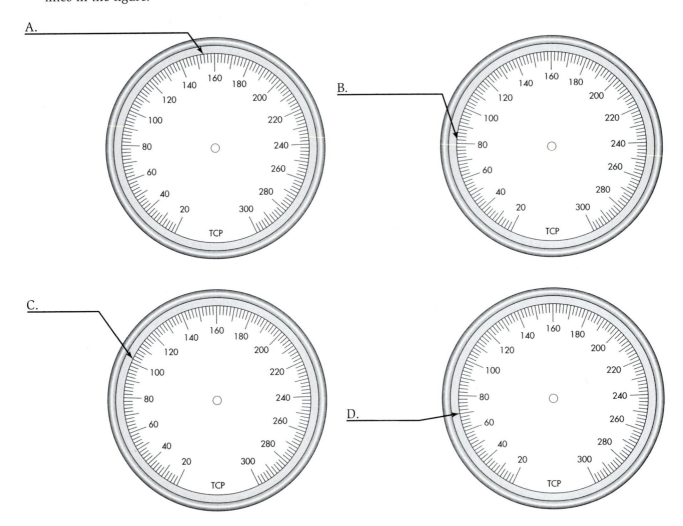

26. Explain why is it important for a physician to keep a record of how much a patient weighs.

_____

_____

_____

27. The following illustrations show sites for taking a patient's pulse rate. Identify and label the artery used for each measurement.

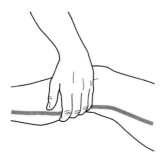 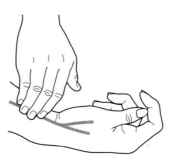 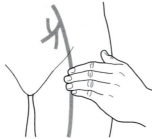 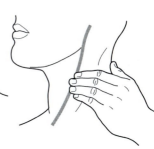

A. _____   B. _____   C. _____   D. _____

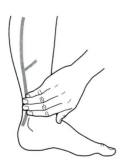 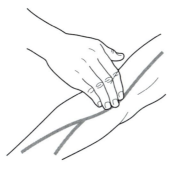 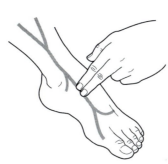 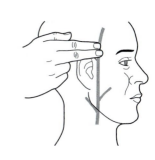

E. _____   F. _____   G. _____   H. _____

28. Name and describe the five phases of Korotkoff sounds.

_____

_____

_____

_____

_____

Critical Thinking

Write the answer to each question on the lines provided.

1. Discuss at least three ways that you can ensure accuracy when performing vital signs and measurements.

_____

_____

_____

2. When performing a head circumference on a 6-month-old infant, you note that the measurement is the same as it was when the infant was 3 months old. What should you do?

_____

_____

_____

3. Explain why you should not take a blood pressure in a patient who has lessened circulation in his or her arm.

_____

_____

_____

4. What would you do if a patient has just had a cup of coffee and you need to take his temperature?

_____

_____

_____

5. Why is the measurement of the length of a 3-month-old infant likely to be less accurate than the measurement of the height of a 3-year-old child?

_____

_____

_____

APPLICATION

1. Using Procedure Checklist 37-1, Measuring and Recording Temperature, review and practice taking temperatures. Use the following circumstances during your practice:

    a. Taking turns as the patient, role-play the sequence of taking a temperature. Be certain to use proper communication with the patient and document your results.

    b. Obtain various types of thermometers—electronic, tympanic, temporal, and disposable—and compare the results of the temperatures among them, and then document your results.

2. Using Procedure Checklist 37-2, Measuring and Recording Pulse and Respirations, review and practice taking pulse and respirations.

    Use the following circumstances during your practice:

    a. On yourself, find and count each of the pulse sites found in the figure on page 273. Determine if the results are the same.

    b. Find and count each of the pulse sites on a partner. Compare your results.

    c. Count a classmate's respirations while she is not aware that you are doing so. Then count the respirations when she is aware. Is there a difference?

    d. Obtain and record the radial pulse on five different classmates. Keep your results confidential. Once completed, compare your results with other classmates. If the difference in one person's rate is greater than 5 beats per minute, recheck the pulse of that classmate at the same time that the classmate himself does to ensure an accurate measurement.

3. Using Procedure Checklist 37-3, Taking the Blood Pressure of Adults and Older Children, review and practice taking blood pressure.

Use the following circumstances during your practice:

a. In groups of three, practice taking blood pressure readings. With one student as the patient, the other two students should take the blood pressure and record the results without telling them to the other students. Each student should have her blood pressure taken by the other two team members. Once all the blood pressure readings have been taken, compare your results. Repeat the blood pressure readings until all the results on one student are within 10 mm Hg for the systolic measure and 4 mm Hg for the diastolic measure.

4. Using Procedure Checklists 37-4, Measuring Adults and Children, and 37-5, Measuring Infants, review and practice measuring adults, children, and infants.

Use the following circumstances during your practice:

a. Obtain the height, weight, and head circumference of at least three other students. Do not disclose your results while measuring. Compare your results with other classmates who have measured the same students. If the results are different, retake the measurements until they are the same.

b. Visit a daycare center or bring infants and children to class to measure. Practice on at least one child, one toddler, and one infant. Check your results with another student.

5. Take at least one complete set of vital signs and record them correctly on the medical record example found on page 961.

6. On his first visit to your clinic, an 18-month-old male infant was 33 inches in length and weighed 33 pounds. His head circumference was 19 inches. Plot these results on the growth charts, examples on page 941, and note the percentiles for the following:

a. Length for Age _____

b. Weight for Age _____

c. Head Circumference for Age _____

d. Weight for Length _____

CASE STUDIES

Write your response to each case study on the lines provided.

Case 1

A female patient arrives at the clinic and you must take her blood pressure. During the patient interview, you discover that she has had a double mastectomy. What should you do when taking her blood pressure?

_____

_____

_____

Case 2

A parent brings her infant to the clinic for a routine checkup. You complete the infant's weight and length measurements and the parent asks you the results. When you provide her with the measurements, she says, "That can't be right!" Should you have given the parent the measurement results? What should you do now?

_____

_____

_____

Case 3

An adult patient who uses a wheelchair comes in for his annual checkup. How would you weigh him? How would you check his height?

_____

_____

_____

Case 4

An overweight 13-year-old girl comes in for an annual checkup. Her mother waits for her in the reception area. The patient seems nervous and she refuses to get on the scales when it is time to weigh her. She says she does not want anyone to know how much she weighs, not even you. You and the patient both know that another girl from her school was in the office last week and you are sure the other patient weighed much more than this patient does. The patient asks you how much the other girl weighed. Maybe telling the patient would make her feel better and she would let you weigh her. What should you do?

_____

_____

_____

CHAPTER 38

Assisting with a General Physical Examination

REVIEW

Vocabulary Review

True or False

Decide whether each statement is true or false. In the space at the left, write T *for true or* F *for false. On the lines provided, rewrite the false statements to make them true.*

_____ 1. A clinical diagnosis is based on the signs and symptoms of a disease.

_____

_____ 2. Before any laboratory or diagnostic testing is ordered, a differential diagnosis may be recorded.

_____

_____ 3. Symmetry is when one side of the body is different from the other side.

_____

_____ 4. Culture is based on a person's race.

_____

_____ 5. Nasal mucosa is the lining of the nose.

_____

_____ 6. Hyperventilation is shallow breaths caused by the loss of carbon monoxide in the blood.

_____

_____ 7. The four equal sections of the abdomen are referred to as quadrants.

_____

_____ 8. An example of a digital exam is palpating for breast lumps.

_____

_____ 9. A lateral curvature of the spine is referred to as kyphosis.

_____

_____ 10. Following the physician's orders is referred to as patient compliance.

_____

_____ 11. A drape with a special opening for easier access during an exam is called a fenestrated drape.

_____

_____ 12. The proper medical term for earwax is cerumen.

_____

_____ **13.** A prognosis is the probable course or outcome of a disease.

_____

_____ **14.** Scoliosis is a forward curvature of the spine.

_____

_____ **15.** Patients should be instructed on proper respiratory hygiene and cough etiquette.

_____

Content Review

Multiple Choice

In the space provided, write the letter of the choice that best completes each statement or answers each question.

_____ **1.** Which of the following is *not* an example of a safety measure you would take while assisting a physician with a patient's general physical exam?

    A. Performing a thorough hand washing before and after each procedure

    B. Cleaning and disinfecting the exam room after the exam

    C. Consulting the list of OSHA safety rules

    D. Wearing gloves whenever there is a possibility of contact with blood or body fluids

_____ **2.** When you prepare a patient for a physical exam, you will

    A. give the patient the opportunity to empty his bladder or bowels.

    B. explain to the patient what will occur during the exam.

    C. ask the patient to disrobe and put on an exam gown.

    D. All of the above.

    E. None of the above.

_____ **3.** One of the six methods for examining a patient during a general physical exam is

    A. palpation.

    B. supination.

    C. positioning.

    D. draping.

_____ **4.** Most physicians perform the general physical exam in the same order, starting with an exam of the patient's

    A. chest and lungs.

    B. head.

    C. overall appearance and the condition of the skin.

    D. abdomen.

    E. musculoskeletal system.

_____ **5.** Which of the following is a common problem of elderly patients that frequently goes undiagnosed?

    A. Depression

    B. Scoliosis

    C. Incontinence

    D. Lack of compliance when taking medications

_____ 6. Which of the following assists the physician in developing a prognosis?
   A. Laboratory test results
   B. An MRI report
   C. Physical therapy reports
   D. All of the above
   E. None of the above

_____ 7. In which of the following positions does the patient lie flat on his back during a procedure?
   A. Prone
   B. Sims'
   C. Trendelenburg's
   D. Fowlers
   E. Supine

_____ 8. Which of the following positions is used for gynecological exam procedures?
   A. Knee-chest
   B. Sims'
   C. Proctologic
   D. Lithotomy

_____ 9. Which of the following is the exam method in which the physician assesses characteristics such as texture, temperature, shape, and the presence of vibrations or movements by touching the skin surface and pressing against underlying tissues?
   A. Inspection
   B. Manipulation
   C. Palpation
   D. Auscultation
   E. Percussion

_____ 10. Which of the following is the exam method in which the physician is able to determine the location, size, and density of organs?
   A. Percussion
   B. Inspection
   C. Mensuration
   D. Auscultation

Sentence Completion

In the space provided, write the word or phrase that best completes each sentence.

11. One of the best positions for examining patients who are experiencing shortness of breath, _____ position has the patient on his back with his head elevated.

12. When checking a patient's general appearance, a physician looks at the patient's skin, hair, and _____.

13. By using a(n) _____, the doctor can view a patient's retinas and other internal structures of the eyes.

14. The physician uses a(n) _____, an instrument that allows her to auscultate the heart sounds.

15. You should pay special attention to educating patients about _____ for disease.

11. _____

12. _____

13. _____

14. _____

15. _____

Short Answer

Write the answer to each question on the lines provided.

16. What are the two reasons why physicians perform general physical exams?

_____

_____

_____

17. Why do physicians use six different exam methods during a general physical exam?

_____

_____

_____

18. Write the name of the exam position on the line below each illustration.

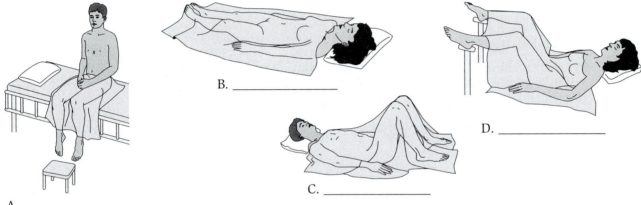

A. _____

B. _____

C. _____

D. _____

E. _____

F. _____

G. _____

H. _____

I. _____

J. _____

19. Label the instruments and supplies used for the general physical exam and identify what component of the exam each is used for.

A. _____

B. _____

C. _____

D. _____

E. _____

F. _____

G. _____

H. _____

I. _____

J. _____

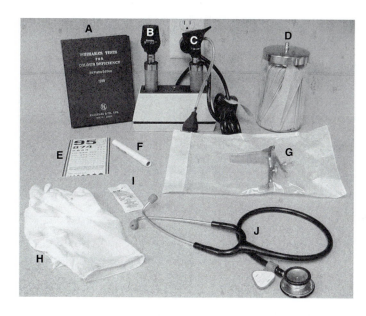

20. What are the six methods of examining a patient during a general physical exam?

_____

_____

_____

21. During an exam of the lungs, what does the stethoscope allow the physician to do?

_____

_____

_____

22. Label the nine parts of the abdomen on the illustration below.

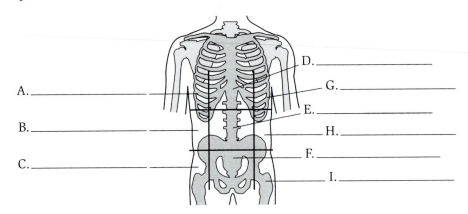

A. _____

B. _____

C. _____

D. _____

G. _____

E. _____

H. _____

F. _____

I. _____

23. What are examples of tests and procedures the doctor might order following a general physical exam?

_____

_____

_____

24. What can you do to ensure that patients understand the instructions you give them?

_____

_____

_____

25. Give three examples of patient follow-up that might be done after a physical exam.

_____

_____

_____

26. Give two behaviors that a medical assistant should observe when screening for visual acuity.

_____

_____

_____

Critical Thinking

Write the answer to each question on the lines provided.

1. Why is it particularly important to prepare children emotionally for a physical exam?

_____

_____

_____

2. Why is it important to avoid making any assumptions about patients from other cultures?

_____

_____

_____

3. Why is it necessary to assist patients into a variety of positions during a physical exam?

_____

_____

_____

4. Why is it important to help patients with disabilities during a physical exam, and what are some ways this can be accomplished?

_____

_____

_____

5. How would you prepare a patient for a diabetes follow-up? What testing may be ordered?

_____

_____

_____

APPLICATION

Follow the directions for each application.

1. Assisting During a Physical Exam

Working with two partners, role-play the procedures for assisting with the eyes, ears, nose and sinuses, and mouth and throat portions of a general physical exam. One partner should take the role of the medical assistant, one that of the patient, and the third should act as observer and evaluator. Your instructor will play the role of the doctor.

a. The medical assistant should first prepare the instruments for the exam: penlight, ophthalmoscope, vision charts, color charts, otoscope, audiometer, nasal speculum, and tongue depressor. The instruments should be organized in the order of the exam: eyes, ears, nose and sinuses, mouth and throat.

b. The assistant should wash her hands thoroughly and observe appropriate safety precautions throughout.

c. The assistant should prepare the patient emotionally and physically by explaining the procedure, what the patient will feel, and so on. She should then direct the patient to take the appropriate sitting position on the examining table.

d. The assistant should put on gloves, protective clothing, and a face mask.

e. While the doctor conducts the exam, the assistant should hand the doctor the instruments as needed as well as provide assistance to the patient.

f. After the exam, the observer should critique the medical assistant's role in the exam. Comments should concern the emotional and physical preparation given the patient, the observance of all safety precautions, aid given to the physician, and assistance given to the patient during the exam. All three students should discuss the procedure and the observer's comments.

g. Exchange roles and have the new medical assistant assist with another portion of the exam, assembling equipment and supplies, preparing and positioning the patient, and assisting the physician. Critique and discuss the exam at its conclusion.

h. Exchange roles one more time so that each partner has the opportunity to play each role during one portion of the exam.

2. Educating the Patient

Work with a partner. One partner should take the role of a medical assistant, the other the role of a patient who is at risk for breast cancer.

a. The medical assistant should review the information on the patient's chart. This patient is 42 years old. Both a sister and her mother have had breast cancer. The patient began menstruating at age 12 and has never had children. The medical assistant knows that breast cancer is the most common cancer diagnosed in women. With early detection, however, breast cancer can be successfully managed. Regular, routine screening, which includes a clinical breast exam and a mammogram, is essential for early detection and prompt treatment.

b. The medical assistant should use the foregoing information to educate the patient about breast cancer. The medical assistant should explain to the patient that she is at risk for breast cancer and why and should explain the need for regular screening. The assistant should periodically assess the patient's understanding of what is being discussed by questioning her and should then clarify misunderstandings.

c. The medical assistant should carefully explain the mammography procedure. The patient should ask questions. The medical assistant should answer all questions as fully as possible. If the assistant does not know the answer, she should tell the patient she will check with the physician and provide the information later.

d. Following the educational discussion, assess the interview with your partner. Was all pertinent information covered? Was the mammography procedure accurately and completely explained? Check the textbook for details.

3. Vision Testing of Patients with Special Needs

Two clinical situations that require special considerations when conducting vision tests are described below. In the space provided, complete each sentence.

The father of a 4-year-old boy has brought his son to your medical office for vision testing.

a. Prepare the child for testing and encourage his cooperation by _____.

b. During the testing, help the child by _____.

c. While you are using a pictorial eye chart to test the child's vision, watch for signs that he is having difficulty seeing the chart, such as _____.

d. Enlist the father's help during the testing by having him _____.

The husband of a 73-year-old woman with Alzheimer's disease has brought his wife to the office for vision testing.

e. Before the test, make the patient feel more comfortable by _____.

f. When explaining procedures to the patient, _____.

g. During testing, help the patient by _____.

h. If the patient's memory and language skills are impaired, _____.

i. If the patient seems to have trouble with one part of the exam, _____.

CASE STUDIES

Write your response to each case study on the lines provided.

Case 1

You normally place patients in the prone position to allow the physician to examine the back, feet, and musculoskeletal system. The patient being examined is extremely obese and has had some respiratory difficulties. Would you place him in this position? If not, what position(s) would you recommend?

_____

_____

_____

Case 2

A patient presents with symptoms of low back pain. What questions should you ask about the symptoms when obtaining the chief complaint? What supplies will be needed by the physician? When asking the patient to disrobe, what do you tell the patient to remove? Per the style of the practice, what testing can you perform prior to the physician's examining the patient?

_____

_____

_____

Case 3

You are performing a Snellen visual acuity exam on a patient who is being seen for an occupational physical. You notice that the patient is beginning to read the lines before you ask him to. What is the probable reason for this?

_____

_____

_____

CHAPTER 39

Assisting with Examinations in the Basic Specialties

REVIEW

Vocabulary Review

Matching

Match the key terms in the right column with the definitions in the left column by placing the letter of each correct answer in the space provided.

_____ 1. An instrument that permits the viewing of the vagina and cervix by expanding the vagina

_____ 2. A disorder that may cause a hunched-over posture

_____ 3. Of rapid onset and progress

_____ 4. An accumulation of fatty deposits along the inner walls of arteries

_____ 5. The development of secondary sexual traits and reproductive functions

_____ 6. The first day of the last menstrual period.

_____ 7. A chemical placed on a Pap smear slide to hold the cells in place until microscopic evaluation

_____ 8. Lasting a long time and recurring frequently

_____ 9. The measurement of oxygen and carbon dioxide in the blood

_____ 10. A moving blood clot

_____ 11. An exam of the vagina and cervix to identify abnormal tissue

a. acute
b. arterial blood gases
c. atherosclerosis
d. chloric
e. colposcopy
f. embolism
g. osteoporosis
h. puberty
i. speculum
j. fixative
k. LMP

Content Review

Multiple Choice

In the space provided, write the letter of the choice that best completes each statement or answers each question.

_____ 1. Which of the following is a noninvasive test used to rule out DVT?

    A. Venogram

    B. Arterial blood gas analysis

    C. Venous ultrasound

    D. Electrocardiogram

    E. Arteriogram

_____ **2.** Lyme disease is carried by
    A. ticks.
    B. fleas.
    C. mosquitoes.
    D. dogs.
    E. deer.

_____ **3.** Which of the following is a risk factor for elder abuse?
    A. Isolation of the victim from family members and friends
    B. Presence of a child in the household
    C. History of divorce in the family
    D. History of heart disease in the family

_____ **4.** What is the best thing you can do to help a patient with high cholesterol?
    A. Prescribe medication
    B. Perform a biopsy
    C. Teach about healthful eating habits
    D. Not mention the condition to the patient but inform the doctor

_____ **5.** Which of the following measures is the most effective way to prevent sexually transmitted diseases?
    A. Latex condoms
    B. Spermicide
    C. Diaphragm
    D. Abstinence
    E. Monogamy

_____ **6.** When a parent reports a child with a high fever, what should you do?
    A. Recommend aspirin
    B. Tell the doctor
    C. Take a biopsy
    D. Send the patient literature about fevers

_____ **7.** An obstetrician
    A. treats bone disorders.
    B. cares for women during pregnancy and childbirth.
    C. cares for children.
    D. treats both men and women.

_____ **8.** After the age of 2, a child should have checkups
    A. every 6 months.
    B. yearly.
    C. every 18 months.
    D. every 2 years.
    E. every 3 years.

_____ **9.** A Pap smear is used to determine
    A. pregnancy.
    B. menopause.
    C. the presence of abnormal or precancerous cells.
    D. the presence of an embolism.

_____ **10.** A digital exam is done during the gynecological exam to
    A. check the position of the internal organs.
    B. test for cancer of the cervix.
    C. obtain a smear for cytologic exam.
    D. check for abnormalities in the cervix.

_____ **11.** During her pelvic exam, you notice that Sonya seems nervous and uncomfortable. To help her relax, you suggest that she
    A. move closer to the end of the table.
    B. pull her knees together.
    C. hold her breath.
    D. take her feet out of the stirrups.
    E. take several deep breaths.

_____ **12.** Reddening of the eyes, increased heart rate, heightened appetite, and muscular weakness are signs of which of the following types of abuse?
    A. Alcohol
    B. Cocaine
    C. Marijuana
    D. Narcotics
    E. Sedatives

Sentence Completion

In the space provided, write the word or phrase that best completes each sentence.

13. Internal medicine is the specialty of an internist, who diagnoses and treats disorders and diseases of the body's _____.

14. Gout is a metabolic disease of the joints caused by over-production or retention of _____.

15. When patients are prescribed antibiotics to treat strepto-coccal infection, it is important that they _____; other-wise, the bacteria will build up a tolerance to the drug.

16. Single parenthood and financial problems are among the risk factors for _____.

17. A physician may order an AFP test to rule out _____ defects.

18. During _____, a woman may experience irregular periods, hot flashes, and vaginal dryness.

13. _____

14. _____

15. _____

16. _____

17. _____

18. _____

Short Answer

Write the answer to each question on the lines provided.

19. What are three general guidelines to offer victims of domestic violence?

_____

_____

_____

20. There are several signs of neglect of an elderly patient. Name four.

_____

_____

_____

21. Describe the symptoms of viral gastroenteritis.

_____

_____

_____

22. What signs in a child might prompt you to alert the doctor to possible child abuse?

_____

_____

_____

23. Why is viral gastroenteritis of concern in young children?

_____

_____

_____

24. What test might a doctor order to confirm a negative rapid strep test?

_____

_____

_____

25. Describe the guidelines for breast cancer screening.

_____

_____

_____

26. Genital warts are caused by which organism?

_____

_____

_____

Critical Thinking

Write the answer to each question on the lines provided.

1. In what ways would you handle readying a child for a general physical exam differently than readying an adult for this exam?

_____

_____

_____

2. Why is it important for a patient to finish the complete course of an antibiotic?

_____

_____

_____

3. Why might the isolation of an elderly person from family and friends lead to elder abuse?

_____

_____

_____

4. Which method of birth control might be controversial? Why?

_____

_____

_____

5. Two days after a cervical biopsy, a patient calls to tell you that she is experiencing some bleeding and does not know what she should do. What would you tell her?

_____

_____

_____

6. Using Nagele's rule, estimate the delivery date of a pregnant woman whose last menstrual period was July 16, 2010.

_____

_____

_____

APPLICATION

Follow the directions for each application.

Assisting with Exams and Procedures

Describe how you would prepare the patient for and assist with each of these exams and procedures.

a. A pediatric physical exam

_____

_____

_____

b. An annual gynecological exam with follow-up

_____

_____

_____

CASE STUDIES

Write your response to each case study on the lines provided.

Case 1

Austin, a 6-year-old male, is seen at the pediatrician's office today. He complains of a severe sore throat. His throat is red and he has a fever of 102.8°F. The doctor orders a rapid strep test, which is negative. Why might the doctor order a throat culture for Austin?

_____

_____

_____

Case 2

Mr. Mayer has recently been diagnosed with high cholesterol. What patient teaching would be helpful for Mr. Mayer?

_____

_____

_____

Case 3

An 18-year-old female patient has just been diagnosed with an STD. What general information should you ensure that the patient knows before she leaves the clinic? How would you go about telling her?

_____

_____

_____

Case 4

Jeanette Carson, a long-time patient at the OB/GYN practice where you work, is just past her eighth month of pregnancy. During her regular prenatal visit, Jeanette asks about classes she can take on breast-feeding. She then tells you that her sister lost her 4-month-old son to SIDS. Jeanette wants to know what she can do to avoid having the same thing happen to her baby. She wonders whether genetic factors play a role in SIDS cases. What can you tell Jeanette?

_____

_____

_____

Case 5

Megan Thomas's annual Pap smear is classified HSIL. How might the physician decide to proceed?

_____

_____

_____

CHAPTER 40

Assisting with Highly Specialized Examinations

REVIEW

Vocabulary Review

Matching

Match the key terms in the right column with the definitions in the left column by placing the letter of each correct answer in the space provided.

_____ 1. The transfer of abnormal cells to body sites far removed from an original tumor

_____ 2. A test used to diagnose contact dermatitis

_____ 3. A radiographic exam that produces a three-dimensional, cross-sectional view of the brain

_____ 4. An exam of the skin using an ultraviolet lamp

_____ 5. A technique for viewing areas inside the body without exposing patients to x-rays or surgery

_____ 6. An exam of the lower rectum

_____ 7. An x-ray exam of a blood vessel after the injection of a contrast medium

_____ 8. A metal mesh tube used to keep a vessel open

_____ 9. A test that measures a patient's response to a constant or increasing workload

_____ 10. Any procedure in which a scope is used to visually inspect a canal or cavity within the body

_____ 11. A life-threatening allergic reaction

_____ 12. A test used to detect neuromuscular disorders or nerve damage

_____ 13. A disorder characterized by an elevated level of glucose in the blood

_____ 14. A procedure in which an orthopedist examines inside a joint

a. anaphylaxis
b. angiography
c. stent
d. patch test
e. computed tomography
f. diabetes mellitus
g. arthroscopy
h. endoscopy
i. proctoscopy
j. magnetic resonance imaging
k. metastasis
l. Wood's light exam
m. stress test
n. electromyography

True or False

Decide whether each statement is true or false. In the space at the left, write T for true or F for false. On the lines provided, rewrite the false statements to make them true.

_____ 15. Another name for Holter monitoring is ambulatory cardiography.

_____

_____ **16.** An intradermal test is more sensitive than a scratch test.

_____

_____ **17.** A stress test is usually performed with the patient lying down.

_____

_____ **18.** Cardiac catheterization is a diagnostic method in which a catheter is inserted into a vein or artery in the arm or leg and passed through the blood vessels into the lungs.

_____

_____ **19.** During a whole-body skin exam, a doctor examines the visible top layer of the entire surface of the skin.

_____

_____ **20.** A macule is a small, flat, discolored spot on the skin.

_____

_____ **21.** A wheal is an elevation of the skin caused by a collection of pus.

_____

_____ **22.** Sigmoidoscopy is an exam of the S-shaped segment of the large intestine.

_____

_____ **23.** Myelography is an x-ray visualization of the spinal cord after injection of a contrast medium or air into the spinal subarachnoid space.

_____

_____ **24.** Neuromuscular disorders or nerve damage can be detected through a lumbar puncture.

_____

_____ **25.** An ophthalmoscope is a handheld instrument with a light used to view the inner ear structures.

_____

_____ **26.** An ophthalmologist uses a retinoscope or a Phoroptor to perform a refraction exam.

_____

_____ **27.** Arthroscopy enables an orthopedist to see inside a muscle.

_____

Content Review

Multiple Choice

In the space provided, write the letter of the choice that best completes each statement or answers each question.

_____ **1.** A test using sound waves to examine the structure and function of the heart is known as a(n)
   A. electrocardiogram.
   B. echocardiogram.
   C. ultrasound.
   D. angiogram.
   E. stress test.

_____ **2.** A patient with a suspected hormonal imbalance is likely to be referred to a(n)
    A. urologist.
    B. otologist.
    C. endocrinologist.
    D. gastroenterologist.

_____ **3.** An electroencephalogram can be used to detect
    A. brain injuries.
    B. bone injuries.
    C. cardiac abnormalities.
    D. neuromuscular disorders.

_____ **4.** A medical assistant in an otologist's office might
    A. perform a radioallergosorbent test.
    B. collect urine specimens.
    C. assist with electromyography.
    D. help administer tympanometry.

_____ **5.** The American Cancer Society recommends that men perform a testicular self-exam every
    A. day.
    B. week.
    C. month.
    D. year.

_____ **6.** An allergy test performed by introducing suspected allergens into the layers of skin by raising a wheal is known as a(n)
    A. patch test.
    B. scratch test.
    C. RAST test.
    D. antibody test.
    E. intradermal test.

_____ **7.** A raised or unraised brown, black, or tan spot on the skin is known as a(n)
    A. tinea.
    B. pustule.
    C. nevus.
    D. wheal.

_____ **8.** The type of diabetes that is usually diagnosed between the 24th and 28th weeks of pregnancy is known as _____ diabetes.
    A. gestational
    B. postpartum
    C. type I
    D. type II
    E. temporary

_____ **9.** Neuromuscular disorders or nerve damage can be detected through
    A. lumbar puncture.
    B. cerebral angiography.
    C. electroencephalography.
    D. electromyography.

_____ **10.** The entire area visible to the eye when the patient looks straight ahead is known as

    A. refraction.

    B. visual acuity.

    C. visual field.

    D. macular vision.

    E. peripheral vision.

_____ **11.** A diagnostic procedure that uses strong magnets and radio waves to produce images of the heart is known as

    A. PET scanning.

    B. heart CT.

    C. balloon angioplasty.

    D. heart MRI.

_____ **12.** During a scratch test, the skin should be scratched no more than how deep?

    A. 1/16 inch

    B. 1/8 inch

    C. 3/16 inch

    D. 1/4 inch

    E. 3/8 inch

_____ **13.** Two cardiology procedures often performed together are cardiac catheterization and

    A. angiography.

    B. stress test.

    C. CABG.

    D. ECG.

_____ **14.** Paralysis on one side of the body is known as

    A. paraplegia.

    B. hemiplegia.

    C. hemiparesis.

    D. quadriplegia.

    E. paraparesis.

_____ **15.** An instrument used to view inside a joint and guide surgical procedures is an

    A. arthroscope.

    B. arthrogram.

    C. arthroscopy.

    D. arthrography.

    E. arthrocentesis.

_____ **16.** The most common test ordered in a urology practice is a(n)

    A. cystogram.

    B. semen analysis.

    C. urinalysis.

    D. cystometry.

    E. pyelogram.

Sentence Completion

In the space provided, write the word or phrase that best completes each sentence.

17. Treatments for acne vulgaris can be topical or _____.

17. _____

18. Some gastrointestinal exams involve spraying the patient's throat with a(n) _____ to inhibit the gag reflex.

18. _____

19. Cataracts block the passage of _____ through the eye, resulting in a progressive loss of vision.

19. _____

20. During a needle biopsy, a surgeon removes _____ with a needle inserted through the skin and into a growth.

20. _____

Short Answer

Write the answer to each question on the lines provided.

21. List four categories of chemotherapy drugs and describe their mechanism of action.

_____

_____

_____

22. List three types of skin cancer, and identify the most dangerous type.

_____

_____

_____

23. Which specialties use imaging techniques (such as x-ray, CT scan, MRI) as diagnostic tests?

_____

_____

_____

24. What are the five categories of neurological function evaluated in a complete neurological exam?

_____

_____

_____

25. List four procedures used to detect and diagnose cancer.

_____

_____

_____

26. Describe myopia and hyperopia, and name the types of lenses that are used to correct each disorder.

_____

_____

_____

27. When might joint replacement surgery be indicated?

_____

_____

_____

28. Describe three symptoms of a ruptured eardrum. List two treatment methods an otologist might use for this condition.

_____

_____

_____

Critical Thinking

Write the answer to each question on the lines provided.

1. Why is the medical assistant's role in educating a cardiology patient about diet and exercise especially important?

_____

_____

_____

2. What advice might you give to a patient in her teens who has fair skin and hair and who is planning to work outdoors during the coming summer months?

_____

_____

_____

3. Compare and contrast an incisional biopsy and a needle biopsy.

_____

_____

_____

4. Write three questions you might ask when taking a patient's history for a urologist.

_____

_____

_____

5. How might the pretest instructions for an upper endoscopy be different from those for a colonoscopy? Why might they be different?

_____

_____

_____

6. Why are diagnostic urine and blood tests essential in endocrine exams?

_____

_____

APPLICATION

Follow the directions for each application.

1. Interviewing a Patient Before a Highly Specialized Exam

Work with two partners. While you assume the role of a medical assistant, have one partner play the role of a patient who is about to have an annual eye exam performed by an ophthalmologist. Have the second partner act as an observer and evaluator.

a. Take the patient's history, recording your questions and the patient's responses. On the basis of the responses, ask appropriate follow-up questions.

b. Explain to the patient what the doctor is likely to do and why. Allow the patient to interrupt at any time with questions, which you should answer to the best of your ability. Record your statements, the patient's questions, and your responses.

c. Have the observer present a critique of your patient interview. The critique should involve your approach and attitude as well as the appropriateness and accuracy of your questions and responses. The observer should also evaluate the order in which you took the history and its completeness.

d. You and your partners should then discuss the observer's critique, noting the strengths and weaknesses of your interview. Comments should include both positive feedback and suggestions for improvement.

e. Exchange roles and repeat the exercise with a patient who has an appointment for a general neurological, orthopedic, or urology exam. The student playing the observer chooses the specialty exam for the patient.

f. Exchange roles again so that each group member has the opportunity to play the medical assistant, the patient, and the observer once.

g. Repeat this role-playing exercise with your partners, this time with a patient who has an appointment for treatment of a specific disease or disorder. The disease or disorder may be chosen by the student who is playing the observer.

2. Educating Patients

Work with a partner to plan a health-awareness booth for a community health fair.

a. You and your partner choose one disease or disorder (such as heart disease, cancer, a thyroid gland disfunction, or a common ear disorder) to educate the public about. Brainstorm to decide what information to provide in the booth. Ask yourselves these questions: What are some important issues associated with this disease or disorder? Can these issues be organized into general categories?

b. Decide whether you will use printed materials, an oral presentation, audiovisual materials, or a combination of these. Discuss with your partner interesting and appealing ways to present the information. What resources might be available in the community to increase awareness of the causes, diagnosis, treatment, and management of this disease or disorder?

c. Outline your plan for the booth. Gather information on resources available in your community about the disease or disorder. If your plan includes posters, brochures, or flyers, make a sketch of these to demonstrate the type of information that would appear on them. If your plan includes an oral presentation, write it on paper and record it. If your plan includes audiovisual material, make or procure a videotape that demonstrates how the information would be presented.

d. You and your partner prepare your booth.

e. Present your booth to the class. Have your classmates critique your presentation. The critique should focus on the appropriateness of the content as well as its accuracy and clarity. Comments should include both positive feedback and suggestions for improvement.

f. Continue until all pairs of students have had the opportunity to present their booths to the class.

CASE STUDIES

Write your response to each case study on the lines provided.

Case 1

You are assisting a cardiologist in administering a treadmill stress test to a patient when the doctor is suddenly called out of the room. It becomes apparent that the doctor will not return for several minutes. What should you do? Why?

_____

_____

_____

Case 2

Mr. Eisner, a 78-year-old, is being seen today for post-influenza follow-up. He states that he is feeling fine. However, his wife states that he is not hearing her lately and sometimes responds to her questions in an odd way. What might be the cause of Mr. Eisner's hearing difficulty?

_____

_____

_____

Case 3

You are a medical assistant in an ophthalmologist's office. One morning you awaken to discover a crusty substance around your left eyelid. The eye is red and feels as though there is sand in it. Should you work with patients today? Why?

_____

_____

_____

Case 4

You are taking the medical history of a patient who complains of a ringing in her ears. You ask the patient about her exposure to loud noise or to toxins. What is another important question you would ask regarding this condition?

_____

_____

_____

Case 5

Marge is a patient in your office who has recently been diagnosed with type II diabetes. She asks you why it is so important for her to monitor her blood sugar and diet so carefully if she is feeling fine. What can you tell her about the long-term complications of diabetes?

_____

_____

_____

Case 6

You have just given Mr. Arturas instructions for performing a testicular self-exam. He questions you about having to do this monthly, stating that he doesn't think it is necessary to do it that often. What will you say to Mr. Arturas?

_____

_____

_____

Copyright © 2011 by The McGraw-Hill Companies, Inc.

CHAPTER 41

Assisting with Minor Surgery

REVIEW

Vocabulary Review

Matching

Match the key terms in the right column with the definitions in the left column by placing the letter of each correct answer in the space provided.

_____ 1. Applied directly to the skin

_____ 2. Initial phase of wound healing

_____ 3. During surgery

_____ 4. The removal of dead tissue

_____ 5. The elimination of all microorganisms

_____ 6. A sterile cloth with cutout section in the center

_____ 7. Suture materials

_____ 8. A collection of pus that forms as a result of infection

_____ 9. The use of extreme cold to destroy unwanted tissue

_____ 10. To bring the edges of a wound together

_____ 11. Surgical stitches used to close a wound

_____ 12. A dilute solution of formaldehyde

_____ 13. The third stage of wound healing, when scar tissue forms

_____ 14. After surgery

_____ 15. The process of removing fluid or tissue cells by aspiration with a needle and syringe

_____ 16. A jagged, open wound in the skin that can extend down into the underlying tissue

a. abscess
b. approximate
c. cryosurgery
d. debridement
e. fenestrated drape
f. formalin
g. intraoperative
h. inflammatory phase
i. laceration
j. ligature
k. maturation phase
l. needle biopsy
m. postoperative
n. surgical asepsis
o. sutures
p. topical

True or False

Decide whether each statement is true or false. In the space at the left, write T for true or F for false. On the lines provided, rewrite the false statements to make them true.

_____ 17. Surgical asepsis reduces the number of microorganisms but does not necessarily eliminate them.

_____

_____ 18. Anesthesia is a loss of sensation.

_____

_____ 19. A sterile scrub assistant assists during a procedure by handling sterile equipment.

_____

_____ 20. During the maturation phase, scar tissue forms at the wound site.

_____

_____ 21. A medical assistant may be responsible for closing a wound after a surgical procedure.

_____

_____ 22. During debridement, a doctor surgically removes healthy tissue from a wound.

_____

_____ 23. During the inflammatory phase of wound healing, bleeding is reduced by constriction of the blood vessels.

_____

_____ 24. During a surgical procedure, a sterile field is used as a work area.

_____

_____ 25. During the preoperative stage in a procedure, the surgical room is prepared for surgery.

_____

_____ 26. A doctor may use a needle biopsy to aspirate fluid or tissue cells for examination.

_____

_____ 27. A minor surgical procedure is usually performed without an anesthetic.

_____

_____ 28. Bleeding from a blood vessel can be stopped by the use of a hemostat.

_____

Content Review

Multiple Choice

In the space provided, write the letter of the choice that best completes each statement or answers each question.

_____ 1. One event that occurs during the inflammatory phase of wound healing is
   A. the formation of a scab.
   B. the clotting of the blood.
   C. the formation of scar tissue.
   D. the formation of new tissue.
   E. clot retraction.

_____ 2. When a patient's skin is prepared for surgery, how far should the prepped area extend beyond the surgical field?
   A. 1 inch
   B. 2 inches
   C. 3 inches
   D. 4 inches

_____ **3.** Lidocaine is the most commonly used
  A. anesthetic.
  B. antiseptic.
  C. disinfectant.
  D. dressing.
  E. preservative.

_____ **4.** The procedure using extreme cold to destroy tissues is known as
  A. electrocautery.
  B. laser surgery.
  C. cryosurgery.
  D. approximation.

_____ **5.** A collection of pus that forms as a result of an infection is a(n)
  A. ligature.
  B. incision.
  C. wound.
  D. debris.
  E. abscess.

_____ **6.** A surgical wound created when a doctor cuts into body tissue is a(n)
  A. laceration.
  B. incision.
  C. puncture.
  D. irrigation.
  E. biopsy.

_____ **7.** A ligature is a(n)
  A. jagged, open wound.
  B. deep layer of tissue.
  C. absorbable suture material.
  D. surgical stitch used to close a wound.
  E. type of biopsy.

_____ **8.** Using a probe or needle heated by electric current to destroy tissue is known as
  A. electrocauterization.
  B. cryosurgery.
  C. anesthesia.
  D. approximation.
  E. a needle biopsy.

_____ **9.** A dilute solution of formaldehyde used to prevent tissue changes is
  A. normal saline.
  B. lidocaine.
  C. povidone iodine.
  D. formalin.

_____ **10.** Using a needle and syringe to withdraw tissue or fluid for examination is known as a(n)

    A. debridement.

    B. needle biopsy.

    C. puncture.

    D. biopsy specimen.

    E. incision.

_____ **11.** An instrument used to hold back the sides of an incision to provide greater access and a better view is a

    A. probe.

    B. curette.

    C. hemostat.

    D. dilator.

    E. retractor.

_____ **12.** A 0.9% solution of sodium chloride is also known as

    A. zephiran chloride.

    B. normal saline.

    C. chlorhexidine gluconate.

    D. formalin.

_____ **13.** A sterile solution sometimes injected along with an anesthetic to constrict blood vessels and reduce bleeding is known as

    A. lidocaine.

    B. tetracaine.

    C. zephiran chloride.

    D. epinephrine.

    E. normal saline.

Sentence Completion

In the space provided, write the word or phrase that best completes each sentence.

14. A small wound may be approximated by using a(n) _____ or sterile strip.

15. With certain electrocautery units, a(n) _____ plate or pad will be placed somewhere on the patient's body during the procedure.

16. If a patient is allergic to _____, Hibiclens should be used as a preoperative antiseptic to swab the skin.

17. During surgery, scissors and clamps should be held by the _____ when you pass them to a surgeon.

18. Typically, suture removal takes place _____ days after minor surgery.

14. _____

15. _____

16. _____

17. _____

18. _____

Short Answer

Write the answer to each question on the lines provided.

19. The following illustration shows a variety of cutting and dissecting instruments used to perform minor surgery. Write the names of the instruments on the lines provided. Then explain the instruments' use.

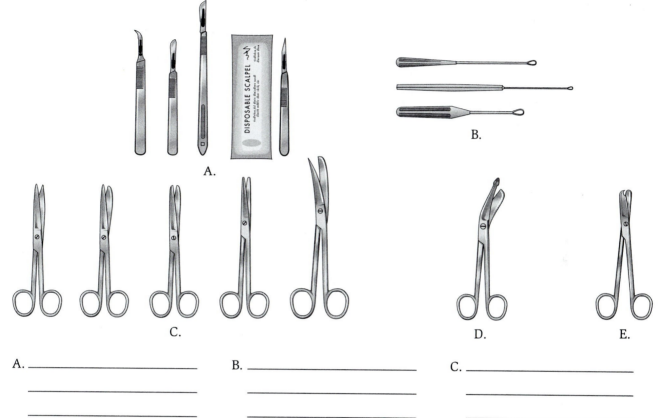

A. _____   B. _____   C. _____

_____   _____   _____

_____   _____   _____

D. _____   E. _____

_____   _____

_____   _____

20. The following illustration shows a variety of grasping and clamping instruments used to perform minor surgery. Write the names of the instruments on the lines provided.

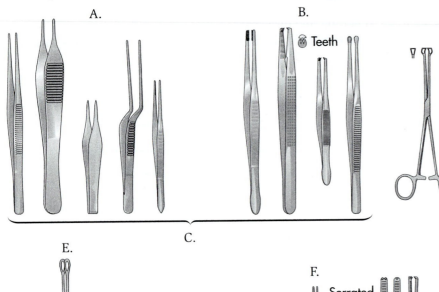

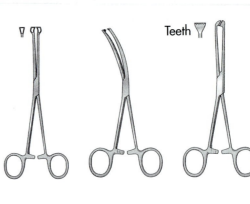

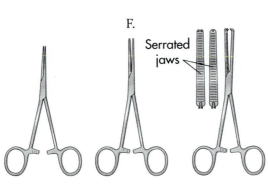

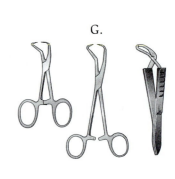

A. _____   B. _____   C. _____

D. _____   E. _____   F. _____

G. _____

21. The following illustration shows a variety of retracting, dilating, and probing instruments used to perform minor surgery. Write the names of the instruments on the lines provided. Then explain the instruments' use.

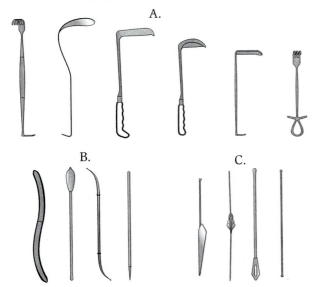

A. _____
_____
_____

B. _____
_____
_____

C. _____
_____
_____

22. The following illustration shows a variety of instruments and materials used to suture. Write the names of the instruments on the lines provided. Then explain the instruments' use.

A.

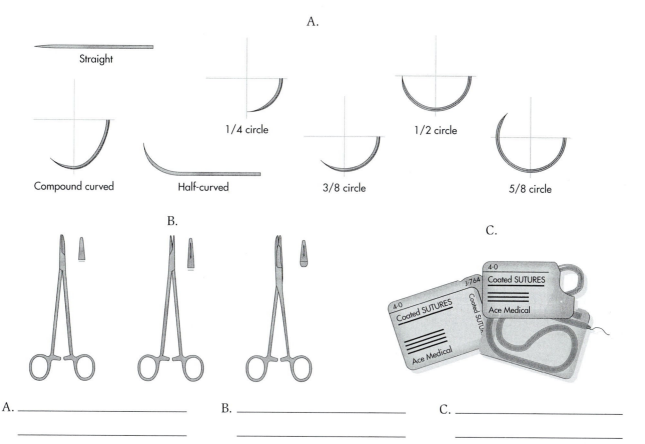

Straight

1/4 circle

1/2 circle

Compound curved   Half-curved

3/8 circle

5/8 circle

B.

C.

A. _____

_____

_____

B. _____

_____

_____

C. _____

_____

_____

23. What are some potential side effects of local anesthetics?

_____

_____

_____

24. Instruments in a surgical tray should be arranged in the order in which they will be used. The following instruments are listed in random order. On the lines provided, rewrite the names of the instruments in the order the surgeon is *most likely* to use them.

Probes   _____

Cutting instruments   _____

Needle holders   _____

Grasping instruments   _____

Suture materials   _____

Retractors   _____

25. Why is epinephrine not used in areas such as the fingers, toes, or nose?

_____

_____

_____

26. Why is it important to place biopsy specimens in a formalin solution?

_____

_____

_____

27. Describe how a nonsurgical wound should be cleaned.

_____

_____

_____

Critical Thinking

Write the answer to each question on the lines provided.

1. While opening a sterile surgical instrument pack, you notice that the sterilization indicator has not been exposed. What should you do?

_____

_____

_____

2. Following cryosurgery, a large, bloody, and painful blister often forms. Why is it important to avoid rupturing the blister?

_____

_____

_____

3. Why is a sterile field considered contaminated if you turn your back to the field?

_____

_____

_____

4. How does positioning the Mayo stand above waist height help prevent contamination?

_____

_____

_____

5. How can you avoid contaminating a sterile field when pouring liquids into a container on the field?

_____

_____

_____

6. How will you ease the fears of a patient who is about to have a minor surgical procedure?

_____

_____

_____

7. Describe how you should prepare the patient's skin before surgery.

_____

_____

_____

APPLICATION

Follow the directions for each application.

1. Interviewing Patients with Wounds

Work with two partners. One partner should assume the role of a patient with a wound. The second should play the role of a medical assistant and the third should act as an observer and evaluator. Assume the wound is an infected laceration.

a. The medical assistant should take a history, noting her questions and the patient's responses. On the basis of the responses, the medical assistant should ask appropriate follow-up questions.

b. The medical assistant should explain to the patient what the doctor is likely to do and why, allowing the patient to interrupt with questions, which the assistant should answer to the best of her ability. Again, the medical assistant should note her statements, the patient's questions, and her responses.

c. Have the observer present a critique of what the medical assistant has done. The critique should involve the assistant's attitude, or approach, as well as the appropriateness and accuracy of her questions and responses.

d. The three of you should then discuss the observer's critique, noting the strengths and weaknesses of the interview.

e. Exchange roles and reboot with a patient who has an appointment for another minor surgical procedure. The new observer should choose the procedure.

f. Exchange roles one final time so that each member of the team gets to play medical assistant, patient, and observer once.

2. Surgical Skin Preparation

You must prepare a patient's skin prior to any surgical procedure. This reduces the number of microorganisms and the risk of infection. Working with two partners, practice preparing a patient's skin prior to surgery. One student should act as the patient and one should observe and critique your performance.

a. Clean the area first with antiseptic soap and sterile water, using forceps and gauze sponges dipped in solution. Begin at the center of the site and work outward in a firm, circular motion. Discard the gauze sponge after each complete pass. Clean in concentric circles until you cover the full preparation area. Continue the process, repeating as necessary, for at least 2 minutes or the amount of time specified in the office's procedure manual. Cleaning takes more time if a wound is dirty or contains foreign materials. When procedures are performed on a hand or foot, clean the entire hand or foot.

b. Consider whether hair should be removed from the area and comment on the procedure used to remove the hair. *Do not remove the hair during this simulation.*

c. Apply antiseptic solution to the area. Swab an area 2 inches larger than the surgical field with the antiseptic solution in a circular outward motion, starting at the surgical site. For surgery on a hand or foot, swab the entire hand or foot. Allow the antiseptic to air-dry; do not pat it dry—that would remove some of the solution's antiseptic properties.

d. Cover the area with a sterile fenestrated drape, from front to back. Avoid reaching over the field. At this point, notify the physician that the patient is ready.

CASE STUDIES

Write your response to each case study on the lines provided.

Case 1

You are called away from the room while setting up a sterile surgical tray. What should you do?

_____

_____

_____

Case 2

A patient arrives at the office with a deep wound across the elbow. What type of suture should you make sure is at hand? Why?

_____

_____

_____

Case 3

You have just completed a surgical scrub and you are now donning sterile gloves. When lifting up the second glove, you think it touches the outer 1-inch margin of the sterile glove wrapper. What should you do?

_____

_____

_____

Case 4

Why is it important to use sterile solutions when irrigating a nonsurgical wound?

_____

_____

_____

CHAPTER 42

Assisting with Cold and Heat Therapy and Ambulation

REVIEW

Vocabulary Review

Matching

Match the key terms in the right column with the definitions in the left column by placing the letter of each correct answer in the space provided.

_____ 1. Applying cold to a patient's body for therapeutic reasons

_____ 2. A protractor device that measures the range of motion in degrees

_____ 3. Body position or alignment

_____ 4. Applying heat to a patient's body for therapeutic reasons

_____ 5. Redness of the skin

_____ 6. A type of heat therapy in which a machine produces high-frequency waves

_____ 7. A device designed to improve a patient's ability to move

a. cryotherapy
b. diathermy
c. erythema
d. goniometer
e. mobility aid
f. posture
g. thermotherapy

True or False

Decide whether each statement is true or false. In the space at the left, write T for true or F for false. On the lines provided, rewrite the false statements to make them true.

_____ 8. Art therapy provides treatment of musculoskeletal, nervous, and cardiovascular disorders.

_____

_____ 9. The most common form of diathermy is a hot pack.

_____

_____ 10. Cryotherapy causes blood vessels to constrict.

_____

_____ 11. Applying heat for therapeutic reasons is known as hydrotherapy.

_____

_____ 12. The degree to which a joint is able to move is known as gait.

_____

_____ 13. Posture is your body position and alignment.

_____

_____ **14.** During ROM exercises, the patient builds muscle strength.

_____

_____ **15.** Ultraviolet lamps are used to treat psoriasis.

_____

Content Review

Multiple Choice

In the space provided, write the letter of the choice that best completes each statement or answers each question.

_____ **1.** Which of the following is a mobility aid?
  A. Traction
  B. Cane
  C. ROM
  D. Diathermy

_____ **2.** Fluid accumulation in tissues is known as
  A. constriction.
  B. erythema.
  C. edema.
  D. inflammation.

_____ **3.** When using the three-point gait with crutches, the patient moves both the crutches and the affected leg forward from the tripod position and then
  A. moves the unaffected leg forward while weight is balanced on both crutches.
  B. moves the left crutch and the right foot forward at the same time.
  C. moves the right foot forward to level with the left crutch.
  D. swings both legs forward together.

_____ **4.** Redness of the skin is known as
  A. cyanosis.
  B. edema.
  C. diathermy.
  D. erythema.
  E. ROM.

_____ **5.** A treatment that uses heated wax and mineral oil is known as
  A. a paraffin bath.
  B. diathermy.
  C. fluidotherapy.
  D. a hot pack.

Sentence Completion

In the space provided, write the word or phrase that best completes each sentence.

6. Cold compresses and ice massages are types of _____ _____ applications used in cryotherapy.

6. _____

7. Static traction is also called _____ traction.

7. _____

8. _____ _____ exercises are self-directed exercises that the patient does without help.

9. During _____ traction, a physical therapist pulls gently on a patient's limb or head.

10. During _____ _____ exercises, the physical therapist moves a patient's body part.

11. _____ _____ stimulate muscles by delivering controlled amounts of low-voltage electric current to motor and sensory nerves.

8. _____

9. _____

10. _____

11. _____

Short Answer

Write the answer to each question on the lines provided.

12. What are four benefits of physical therapy?

_____

_____

_____

13. Why is it important to ask a patient how a hot pack feels?

_____

_____

_____

14. What are four beneficial results that can be achieved through cryotherapy?

_____

_____

_____

15. What is the process by which thermotherapy promotes healing?

_____

_____

_____

16. What are two types of dry heat therapy?

_____

_____

_____

17. What are two benefits of manual traction?

_____

_____

_____

18. What is the difference between active and passive mobility exercises?

_____

_____

_____

19. To make sure that crutches fit a patient properly, what conditions should you check before the patient leaves the office?

_____

_____

_____

20. What factors determine the type of mobility aid chosen for a patient?

_____

_____

_____

Critical Thinking

Write the answer to each question on the lines provided.

1. Why is it important to check a chemical cold pack for leaks before applying the pack to the patient?

_____

_____

_____

2. How might a reduction in a patient's ROM affect the type of mobility device the patient should be using?

_____

_____

_____

3. Why is it important that a patient not lie on a heating pad?

_____

_____

_____

4. Why is it important to ensure that a patient knows how to perform exercises correctly?

_____

_____

_____

5. Why might a doctor prescribe cryotherapy, thermotherapy, or some other type of therapy in addition to exercise therapy for a patient with a sports injury?

_____

_____

_____

6. What should you do if a patient who uses a walker tells you there are steps in his house?

_____

_____

_____

APPLICATION

Follow the directions for each application.

1. Teaching a Patient How to Use a Walker

Work with two partners to teach a patient how to use a mobility aid. One partner should take the role of the patient, one should take the role of a medical assistant who is teaching the patient how to use a mobility aid, and the third should serve as observer and evaluator.

a. Role-play teaching a patient to use a walker. The medical assistant should assist the patient in stepping into the walker and explain how to grip the sides of the walker. The assistant should then instruct the patient in how to position his feet and to walk securely. The patient should ask questions during the instruction. The observer should refer to the steps outlined in Procedure 42-4 while observing the teaching.

b. The medical assistant should next explain how to maneuver the walker for sitting down in a chair or on a bed.

c. The medical assistant should then teach the patient how to ascend and descend stairs.

d. Following the teaching, the observer should critique the session, pointing out any errors or omissions in the instruction. The three partners should then discuss the session and the evaluator's comments.

e. Team members should exchange roles and review the use of another mobility aid. The new observer should evaluate the session, and all three partners should discuss the session.

f. Team members should exchange roles one more time and go through the use of a third mobility aid. Each student should have the opportunity to play each role.

2. Learning Crutch Walking and Preparing an Educational Brochure

Workings in pairs, teach each other various gaits:

a. Two-point gait

b. Three-point gait

c. Four-point gait

d. Swing-to gait

e. Swing-through gait

Follow these steps:

1. First review text Figures 42-10 and 42-11 and Procedure 42-5.

2. Discuss the steps necessary to perform each type of gait. Write a list of the steps to use for each gait while performing the instruction.

3. Practice teaching and performing the various gaits.

4. Practice getting up and sitting down.

5. Practice ascending and descending stairs.

6. After you have mastered the gaits, create a patient teaching brochure for each of the types of gaits.

CASE STUDIES

Write your response to each case study on the lines provided.

Case 1

The doctor has prescribed use of a chemical ice pack for a 62-year-old patient with a sprained ankle. After the ice pack has been on the ankle for 15 minutes, the patient complains of increased pain in the ankle. What should you do?

_____

_____

_____

Case 2

While applying a moist heat pack, you notice that the patient is shivering. What should you do?

_____

_____

_____

Case 3

After a few minutes, the patient from Case 2 complains of being uncomfortably hot. What should you do?

_____

_____

_____

Case 4

A patient with paraplegia needs crutches. What type of crutches will most likely be prescribed? Why?

_____

_____

_____

Case 5

A patient who is having difficulty recovering from a leg injury sustained in an automobile accident is considering dance therapy. What will you tell her?

_____

_____

_____

CHAPTER 43

Emergency Preparedness and First Aid

REVIEW

Vocabulary Review

Matching

Match the key terms in the right column with the definitions in the left column by placing the letter of each correct answer in the space provided.

_____ **1.** A condition resulting from massive, widespread infection that affects the ability of the blood vessels to circulate blood

_____ **2.** The vomiting of blood

_____ **3.** Low blood sugar

_____ **4.** A condition that results from insufficient blood volume in the circulatory system

_____ **5.** A jarring injury to the brain

_____ **6.** A muscle injury that results from overexertion

_____ **7.** A swelling caused by blood under the skin

_____ **8.** A brain attack caused by impaired blood supply to the brain

_____ **9.** Unusually rapid, strong, or irregular pulsations of the heart

_____ **10.** A nosebleed.

a. strain
b. hematemesis
c. palpitations
d. hypoglycemia
e. epistaxis
f. hematoma
g. hypovolemic shock
h. concussion
i. septic shock
j. stroke

True or False

Decide whether each statement is true or false. In the space at the left, write T for true or F for false. On the lines provided, rewrite the false statements to make them true.

_____ **11.** A splint is used to bandage a laceration or an incision.

_____

_____ **12.** A cast is a rigid, external dressing that is molded to the contours of the body part to which it is applied.

_____

_____ **13.** The displacement of a bone end from the joint is a sprain.

_____

_____ **14.** Botulism is a life-threatening allergic reaction.

_____

_____ **15.** When caring for a person who has a poisonous snakebite, it is important to apply ice to the bite.

_____

_____ **16.** A contusion is a type of closed wound.

_____

_____ **17.** A person having a seizure should be positioned on the floor with his head turned toward the side.

_____

_____ **18.** Ventricular fibrillation is an unusually rapid, strong, or irregular pulsation of the heart.

_____

_____ **19.** The first priority for medical assistants in an emergency is a victim's airway.

_____

_____ **20.** When assisting in a disaster, you should accept an assignment that is appropriate to your age.

_____

_____ **21.** Hyperglycemia is a lack of adequate water in the body.

_____

_____ **22.** The lower extension of the breastbone is the xiphoid process.

_____

_____ **23.** Establishing a chain of custody is important in cases of rape and when testing for illicit drug use.

_____

_____ **24.** An automated external defibrillator (AED) is used during a cardiac emergency to correct abnormal rhythms such as ventricular fibrillation (VF).

_____

_____ **25.** A person is placed in the recovery position when a fracture, dislocation, sprain, or strain is suspected.

_____

_____ **26.** When treating a bee sting, use tweezers to remove the stinger.

_____

_____ **27.** Bioterrorism is the intentional release of a chemical agent with the intent to harm individuals.

_____

Content Review

Multiple Choice

In the space provided, write the letter of the choice that best completes each statement or answers each question.

_____ **1.** Dry mouth, intense thirst, muscle weakness, and blurred vision are symptoms of
   A. hypoglycemia.
   B. dehydration.
   C. hyperglycemia.
   D. hyperthermia.

_____ 2. Which of the following is the main symptom of a choking emergency?
    A. A fearful look
    B. The inability to speak
    C. Coughing
    D. Unconsciousness
    E. Pallor

_____ 3. Which of the following is a type of head injury?
    A. A contusion
    B. A dislocation
    C. Viral encephalitis
    D. Epistaxis

_____ 4. The most common abnormal rhythm that occurs during cardiac arrest is
    A. tachycardia.
    B. ventricular fibrillation.
    C. palpitations.
    D. CVA.
    E. myocardial infarction.

_____ 5. Asthma is a common disorder caused by
    A. wheezing and coughing.
    B. electrolyte imbalances.
    C. diabetes.
    D. narrowing of the bronchi.

_____ 6. An insufficient blood volume in the circulatory system causes
    A. insulin shock.
    B. ventricular fibrillation.
    C. septic shock.
    D. myocardial infarction.
    E. hypovolemic shock.

_____ 7. A series of violent and involuntary contractions of the muscles is known as
    A. epilepsy.
    B. stroke.
    C. strain.
    D. concussion.

_____ 8. A symptom specific to toxic shock syndrome is
    A. high fever.
    B. vomiting.
    C. a decreased level of consciousness.
    D. a red rash on the hands and feet.
    E. seizures.

_____ 9. A life-threatening allergic reaction is known as
    A. asthma.
    B. botulism.
    C. anaphylaxis.
    D. sepsis.

_____ **10.** Which of the following is an electrical device that shocks the heart to restore normal beating?

    A. CVA

    B. MI

    C. AED

    D. PPE

    E. EMT

Sentence Completion

In the space provided, write the word or phrase that best completes each sentence.

11. An important ally in providing emergency care is your local _____ system.

11. _____

12. A partial thickness burn produces _____.

12. _____

13. A scalp hematoma can be reduced by applying _____ immediately after the injury.

13. _____

14. If you suspect bioterrorism, your facility should first contact _____.

14. _____

15. Acute abdominal pain in the right upper quadrant may signal _____.

15. _____

16. A _____ is a rolling cart of emergency supplies and equipment.

16. _____

17. A severe condition that is the end result of severe hyperglycemia is known as _____.

17. _____

Short Answer

Write the answer to each question on the lines provided.

18. What are four ways in which first aid can benefit victims of accidents or sudden illness?

_____

_____

_____

19. How should you position a person who is having a seizure?

_____

_____

_____

20. Name and describe the types of wounds that are depicted in the following illustrations.

A. _____

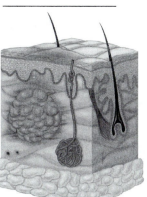

B. _____

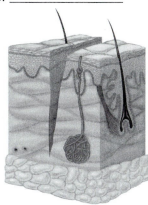

C. _____

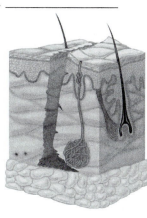

D. _____

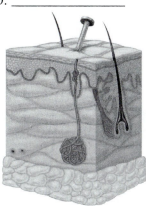

E. _____

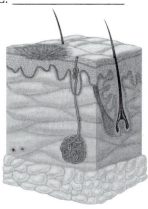

21. Describe four steps to follow when treating a patient who has swallowed poison but who is alert and not having convulsions.

_____

_____

_____

22. What are the five symptoms of dehydration?

_____

_____

_____

23. What are the symptoms of a sprain?

_____

_____

_____

24. What actions are medical personnel required to take when treating a victim of rape?

_____

_____

_____

25. Briefly describe the process of triage during a disaster.

_____

_____

_____

Critical Thinking

Write the answer to each question on the lines provided.

1. Your neighbor has been cutting down trees today. He comes to your door and says that a tree limb slid by his head and amputated his ear. What should you do?

_____

_____

_____

2. Three patients arrive in the office of a general practitioner at about the same time. One is suffering from a second-degree burn on her hand, another has been bitten by a spider, and the third is experiencing chest pain. In what order should these patients be treated? Why?

_____

_____

_____

3. Why should you look for additional symptoms when a patient complains of headache, dizziness, or vomiting?

_____

_____

_____

4. A patient arrives at your office feeling restless and confused. She has a rapid pulse; shallow respirations; hunger; profuse sweating; pale, cool, clammy skin; double vision; and tremors. She states that she took her regular does of insulin this morning but was not able to eat breakfast. What could be wrong with this patient? What should you do?

_____

_____

_____

5. When performing an emergency assessment, why should you check for a medical identification card, necklace, or bracelet?

_____

_____

_____

APPLICATION

Follow the directions for each application.

1. Performing Emergency Procedures

Each of the following descriptions of emergency procedures contains at least one error. On the lines provided, rewrite the procedures to make them correct.

a. When treating a dog bite that has caused a puncture wound, wash the area with antiseptic soap and water and use pressure to stop the bleeding.

_____

_____

b. When treating a spider bite, wash the area thoroughly with soap and water and apply a hot pack to the area to reduce swelling and pain.

_____

_____

c. When treating a first-degree burn, immerse the affected area in cold water. Then pat the area dry and apply petroleum jelly or ointment.

_____

_____

d. When treating a scalp laceration, apply indirect pressure, wash the area with soap and water, and apply a moist, sterile dressing over the area.

_____

_____

2. Choosing Personal Protective Equipment for Emergencies

For each emergency described below, list personal protective equipment that should be worn.

a. Vomiting _____

b. Childbirth _____

c. Heart attack _____

d. Eye injury _____

e. Bleeding _____

CASE STUDIES

Write your response to each case study on the lines provided.

Case 1

While eating dinner in a restaurant, you hear a commotion across the dining room. A man appears to be choking. A woman is slapping him on the back. What, if anything, should you do?

_____

_____

_____

Case 2

While walking at the local park, you see a woman stumble and fall. You notice that she catches herself with her arms extended. As you reach the victim, you notice that her right wrist looks swollen and she is complaining of severe pain in her arm. What should you do?

_____

_____

_____

Case 3

A patient who has been sitting in the waiting room comes to the reception desk and asks you for a glass of water. She seems disoriented and short of breath and her skin appears flushed. When you lean forward to ask the patient whether she is all right, you notice that her breath has a sweet odor. What might be happening, and how should you handle the situation?

_____

_____

_____

Case 4

An infant comes in your office with a high fever. While her mother is talking to you, the infant begins to have a seizure. What should you do?

_____

_____

_____

Case 5

Your neighbor, Jane Chung, has been working in her garage for most of the morning, spray-painting some patio furniture. You notice that she has had the door closed while she was working. You decide to check on her and find her sitting down, holding her chest. She says that she feels dizzy and nauseated and has a headache. What could be wrong with Jane? What should you do?

_____

_____

_____

CHAPTER 44

Complementary and Alternative Medicine

REVIEW

Vocabulary Review

Matching

Match the key terms in the right column with the definitions in the left column by placing the letter of each correct answer in the space provided.

_____ **1.** The use of essential oils extracts or essences from flowers, herbs, and trees to promote health and well-being

_____ **2.** Vitamins, minerals, herbals, and other substances taken by mouth without a prescription to promote health and well-being

_____ **3.** The practice of inserting needles into various areas of the body to restore balance

_____ **4.** A state in which the body is consciously relaxed and the mind becomes calm and focused

_____ **5.** A series of poses and breathing exercises that provide awareness of the unity of the whole being

_____ **6.** A form of medicine, originated in India, that uses herbal preparations, dietary changes, exercises, and meditation to restore health and promote well-being

_____ **7.** A therapy in which pressure is applied to zones mapped out on the feet or hands

_____ **8.** Adjustments of the spine made to relieve pressure and/or pain

_____ **9.** A system of medicine that uses remedies in an attempt to stimulate the body to recover itself

_____ **10.** A type of therapy in which an individual learns how to control involuntary body responses to promote health and treat disease

_____ **11.** A trance-like state usually induced by another person to access the subconscious mind and promote healing

_____ **12.** The use of visualization and touch to balance energy flow and bring healthy energy to affected body parts

a. reflexology
b. acupuncture
c. aroma therapy
d. Ayurveda
e. biofeedback
f. chiropractic medicine
g. dietary supplements
h. homeopathy
i. hypnosis
j. meditation
k. Reiki
l. yoga

True or False

Decide whether each statement is true or false. In the space at the left, write T for true or F for false. On the lines provided, rewrite the false statements to make them true.

_____ **13.** CAM is a set of practices and products that are considered part of conventional medicine.

_____

_____ **14.** Integrative medicine is the combination of conventional therapies and CAM therapies.

_____

_____ **15.** There are four categories of CAM according to the NCCAM.

_____

_____ **16.** Homeopathy is a biologically based therapy.

_____

_____ **17.** Homeopathic remedies are regulated by the federal government.

_____

_____ **18.** Qi regulates the person's spiritual, emotional, mental, and physical balance.

_____

_____ **19.** A chiropractor would examine the tongue of a patient for shape and color before starting treatments.

_____

_____ **20.** More than 50% of the population uses prayer as a CAM therapy.

_____

_____ **21.** In medication, calming of the conscious mind is induced by another person.

_____

_____ **22.** In most cases, it is acceptable for the medical assistant to answer questions about CAM therapy for the patients.

_____

_____ **23.** Potentization is a process that ensures the consistency and quality of each batch of medication produced.

_____

_____ **24.** Health fraud promoters target people who feel desperate about their conditions and make money off of their desperation.

_____

_____ **25.** The FDA does not approve claims made by CAM therapies.

_____

Content Review

Multiple Choice

In the space provided, write the letter of the choice that best completes each statement or answers each question.

_____ 1. Which organization supports CAM research and promotes CAM information to health-care providers and the public?
   A. Federal Trade Commission
   B. Food and Drug Administration
   C. Occupational Safety and Health Administration
   D. Health Insurance Portability and Accountability Act
   E. National Center for Complementary and Alternative Medicine

_____ 2. Which of the following is an approved health claim?
   A. Calcium may reduce the risk of the bone disease osteoporosis.
   B. Diets high in sodium reduce the risk of high blood pressure.
   C. Diets low in saturated fats increase the risk of heart disease.
   D. Diets containing foods that are a good source of potassium may increase the risk of high blood pressure and stroke.

_____ 3. If a patient is taking an anticoagulant like coumadin, which of the following dietary supplements might interact?
   A. Ginseng
   B. Valerian
   C. St. John's Wort
   D. Gingko
   E. Glucosamine chondroitin

_____ 4. Which of the following is a type of biofield therapy?
   A. Magnetic therapy
   B. Therapeutic touch
   C. Reflexology
   D. Aromatherapy

_____ 5. Which of the following supplements was taken off the market after being investigated by the FDA?
   A. Echinacea
   B. Black cohosh
   C. Gingko biloba
   D. Ephedra
   E. Milk thistle

_____ 6. Which of the following substances would have been required to provide scientific evidence of effectiveness before being marketed?
   A. Niacin
   B. Lipitor
   C. Folic acid
   D. St. John's wort

_____ 7. Biofeedback is which type of therapy?

   A. Energy therapy

   B. Mind-body therapy

   C. Biologically based therapy

   D. Alternative medical systems therapy

   E. Herbal therapy

_____ 8. Energetic forces called Tridoshas are part of which type of CAM?

   A. Ayurveda

   B. Reiki

   C. Traditional Chinese medicine

   D. Qi

_____ 9. Which of the following is a biologically based therapy?

   A. Meditation

   B. Reiki

   C. Hypnosis

   D. Yoga

   E. Dietary supplements

_____ 10. Energetic pathways are known as

   A. qi.

   B. placebos.

   C. meridians.

   D. remedies.

Sentence Completion

In the space provided, write the word or phrase that best completes each sentence.

11. Naturopathic medicine is considered _____ health care.

12. A(n) _____ inserts hollow needles under the skin to balance the flow of qi.

13. The difference between acupuncture and moxibustion involves the use of _____.

14. Everything in _____ is validated by observation, inquiry, direct exam, and knowledge derived from ancient texts.

15. Up to 35% of the therapeutic response to a medical treatment could be the result of the _____ effect.

11. _____

12. _____

13. _____

14. _____

15. _____

Short Answer

Write the answer to each question on the lines provided.

16. How are dietary supplements defined by the U.S. Congress?

_____

_____

_____

17. Describe the concept of balanced qi as it relates to traditional Chinese medicine.

_____

_____

_____

18. Name and describe the five categories of CAM as identified by NCCAM.

    1. _____

    2. _____

    3. _____

    4. _____

    5. _____

19. What are the similarities among the various types of CAM?

_____

_____

_____

20. Name at least three recommendations of the WHCCAMP regarding CAM practices and products.

_____

_____

_____

Critical Thinking

Write the answer to each question on the lines provided.

    1. What examples could you give a patient about the differences between complementary and alternative therapy?

_____

_____

_____

    2. A patient asks you a specific question about a type of CAM therapy that you have been using personally for a long time. What should you do?

_____

_____

_____

    3. An ND has been hired to work at your clinic. Is he licensed?

_____

_____

_____

4. When would a dietary supplement be taken off the market?

_____

_____

_____

5. You want to research at least three types of CAM therapies used for back pain. Name and describe the three you would choose.

_____

_____

_____

APPLICATION

Follow the directions for each application.

1. A patient is taking each of the following medications in the table below. Determine which dietary supplement he or she should not take and why by completing the table.

Medication Taken (with Classification)	Dietary Supplement That Interacts	Interaction That Can Occur
a. Coumadin (anticoagulant)		
b. Claritin-D (decongestant)		
c. Paxil (antidepressant)		
d. Valium (benzodiazepine)		

2. What are the steps you can take to determine if CAM therapies are covered by insurance?

_____

_____

_____

CASE STUDIES

Write your response to each case study on the lines provided.

Case 1

Your patient is taking three prescription medications, two megadose vitamins, and two other dietary supplements. What should you do?

_____

_____

_____

Case 2

A patient is using a new type of therapy to help her lose weight. How could you determine if the therapy is fraud?

_____

_____

_____

Case 3

A patient has refused prescription medication as treatment for blood pressure and has decided to take an herbal remedy instead. What should you do?

_____

_____

_____

CHAPTER 45

Laboratory Equipment and Safety

REVIEW

Vocabulary Review

Passage Completion

Study the key terms in the box. Use your textbook to find definitions of terms you do not understand.

biohazard symbol	focus controls	optical microscope	quality assurance program
centrifuge	hazard label	physician's office laboratory (POL)	reference laboratory
Certificate of Waiver tests	Material Safety Data Sheet (MSDS)		

In the space provided, complete the following passage, using some of the terms from the box. You may change the form of a term to fit the meaning of the sentence.

Laboratory analysis plays an important role in any medical practice. Some physicians have all laboratory tests performed by a(n) (1) _____, which is owned and operated by an organization outside the practice. Other physicians do some laboratory work in the office, in the (2) _____. This allows quick turnaround of test results.

One piece of equipment used in the laboratory is a(n) (3) _____, which spins a specimen at high speed until it separates into its component parts. The laboratory equipment that is used most often in the POL, however, is the (4) _____. There are two (5) _____ on the optical microscope, coarse and fine.

Safety is a primary concern in the laboratory. One precaution that is required by law is that all containers used to store hazardous waste products must be clearly marked with the (6) _____. For information about hazardous chemicals used in the laboratory, a medical assistant can consult the (7) _____. The shortened version of the MSDS is called a(n) (8) _____. It is permanently attached to each hazardous substance container. A(n) (9) _____ is designed to monitor the quality of patient care that a medical laboratory provides. A laboratory can gain exemption from meeting certain federal standards if it performs only (10) _____.

1. _____

2. _____

3. _____

4. _____

5. _____

6. _____

7. _____

8. _____

9. _____

10. _____

Matching

Match the key terms in the right column with the definitions in the left column by placing the letter of each correct answer in the space provided.

_____ **11.** A foreign object visible through a microscope but unrelated to the specimen

_____ **12.** A magnifying lens mounted on the nosepiece of a microscope

_____ **13.** Measures the accuracy of test results and adherence to standard operating procedures

_____ **14.** A laboratory owned and operated by an organization outside the practice

_____ **15.** A device that spins a specimen at high speed until it separates into its component parts

_____ **16.** A specimen with a known value that is used every time a patient sample is processed

_____ **17.** The eyepiece of a microscope through which an image is viewed

_____ **18.** A specimen with a known value that is used during calibration

_____ **19.** A document that shows all procedures completed during the workday

_____ **20.** Ensures accuracy in test results through careful monitoring of test procedures

a. proficiency testing program
b. centrifuge
c. artifact
d. reference laboratory
e. objective
f. standard
g. daily workload log
h. quality control program
i. control sample
j. ocular

True or False

Decide whether each statement is true or false. In the space at the left, write T for true or F for false. On the lines provided, rewrite the false statements to make them true.

_____ **21.** The steam autoclave is used to reduce the risk of fire in a laboratory.

_____

_____ **22.** Placing the end of the oil-immersion objective in oil reduces the loss of light and produces a much sharper, brighter image.

_____

_____ **23.** The Supreme Court enacted the Clinical Laboratory Improvement Amendments of 1988, which established federal regulations for laboratories.

_____

_____ **24.** Hazardous waste products include sharps and gloves.

_____

_____ **25.** Generally, positive and negative control samples are used with tests that yield a qualitative test response.

_____

Content Review

Multiple Choice

In the space provided, write the letter of the choice that best completes each statement or answers each question.

_____ 1. Objectives are mounted on a swivel base called the
   A. condenser.
   B. objective.
   C. stage.
   D. lens.
   E. nosepiece.

_____ 2. Chemicals or chemically treated substances used in testing procedures are known as
   A. controls.
   B. standards.
   C. reagents.
   D. pipettes.

_____ 3. Which of the following must an employer make available to employees so as to be in compliance with the OSHA Bloodborne Pathogens Standard?
   A. Polio vaccine
   B. Health insurance
   C. Performance ratings for handling bloodborne pathogens
   D. Hepatitis B vaccine

_____ 4. Which of the following is an instrument that measures light intensity?
   A. Artifact
   B. Hemocytometer
   C. Thermometer
   D. Photometer
   E. Pipette

_____ 5. Blood cell counts and cholesterol screening are examples of
   A. Certificate of Waiver tests.
   B. moderate-complexity tests.
   C. high-complexity tests.
   D. quality control tests.

Sentence Completion

In the space provided, write the word or phrase that best completes each sentence.

6. The iris of a microscope is used to _____ the amount of light illuminating the specimen.

7. When not in use, the microscope should be stored _____.

8. For more information about hazardous chemicals used in the laboratory, a medical assistant can consult the _____.

9. A shortened version of the MSDS found on a chemical label is a _____.

10. Tests that have been approved by the Food and Drug Administration (FDA) for use by patients at home are _____ tests.

6. _____

7. _____

8. _____

9. _____

10. _____

11. The _____ requires that employees receive training regarding workplace hazards.

12. A Materials Safety Data Sheet for a hazardous substance must include _____ for safe handling of the substance.

13. In a microscope, the _____ controls the amount of light on the specimen by opening and closing like a shutter.

14. Graduated flasks are used to measure large amounts of _____.

15. Treating patients with respect is part of the medical assistant's _____ skills.

11. _____

12. _____

13. _____

14. _____

15. _____

Short Answer

Write the answer to each question on the lines provided.

16. Where should you store caustic chemicals?

_____

_____

_____

17. Name three regulations you should be familiar with when working in a physician's office laboratory.

_____

_____

_____

18. As a medical assistant, what might your role be in the POL?

_____

_____

_____

19. Describe a biohazard symbol label.

_____

_____

_____

20. Describe four commonsense safeguards that will ensure your physical safety in the laboratory.

_____

_____

_____

21. What steps would you take to deal with a minor accident in the laboratory?

_____

_____

_____

22. How are Certificate of Waiver tests defined? Give examples.

_____

_____

_____

23. Describe the records that must be kept as part of a quality control program in addition to the quality control log, the reagent control log, and the equipment maintenance log.

_____

_____

_____

24. List six hazardous waste products.

_____

_____

_____

25. The illustration below shows the parts of a microscope. Write the name of each part on the line provided.

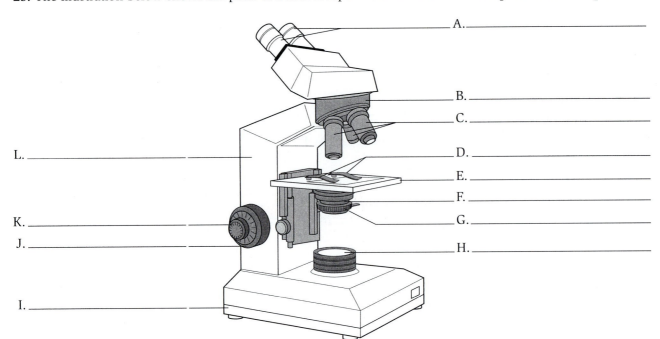

A. _____

B. _____

C. _____

L. _____

D. _____

E. _____

F. _____

K. _____

G. _____

J. _____

H. _____

I. _____

Critical Thinking

Write the answer to each question on the lines provided.

1. Why is it important to use a systematic approach when troubleshooting equipment problems?

_____

_____

_____

2. What safeguards can you use to help reduce electrical hazards?

_____

_____

_____

3. Why should you change gloves every time you move from patient to patient when collecting specimens for testing?

_____

_____

_____

4. Why do you think mouth pipetting is prohibited at all times?

_____

_____

_____

5. Explain the meaning of the motto "If it is not written down, it was not done."

_____

_____

_____

APPLICATION

Follow the directions for each application.

1. Equipping a Physician's Office Laboratory (POL)

Work with two partners. You are part of a team that is buying equipment for a new POL. Assume the POL will process routine tests involving blood and urine for a practice with two doctors.

a. You and your partners should make a preliminary list of all the laboratory equipment and supplies you think will be needed. Start with major items, such as a microscope. Then consider all the necessary support materials, such as coverslips, test tubes, dipsticks, and cotton swabs.

b. As you work with your partners, consider these questions: What tests are likely to be performed in the POL? What equipment is needed for each type of test that will be performed? What supplies are needed to run a POL? What supplies will be needed to care for and maintain the equipment in the POL? Make a list of all the possible tests the POL might perform and add the equipment needed for each procedure to your list.

c. Next, use medical supply catalogs to help you choose the laboratory equipment and supplies you would recommend for the POL.

d. Start an equipment inventory log and record your selections. Be specific about the type of equipment. Record model numbers, prices, and amounts. Use medical abbreviations as appropriate. Include illustrations as necessary.

e. Share your inventory log with another team and be prepared to justify your selections. Compare selections, prices, and amounts. Discuss items that are on one team's list but not the other. Check for completeness.

f. Then share your log with a different team.

g. On the basis of classmates' feedback, revise your inventory log to make it as complete as possible.

2. Monitoring Safety in the Laboratory

Work with a partner. You are to play the role of an OSHA representative. Your partner should play the role of a medical assistant who works in a POL. Assume that the OSHA representative is investigating a laboratory accident in which an employee's eyes were damaged when a container of caustic chemical fell from a cupboard in the POL.

a. List the questions you would ask to find out how the accident occurred. Include questions concerning OSHA requirements and office rules and policies.

b. Playing the role of the OSHA representative, ask questions of the medical assistant. Record the medical assistant's responses and ask follow-up questions.

c. Working with your partner, use your questions and answers to create a new set of accident prevention guidelines for physical safety in the laboratory.

d. Share your accident prevention guidelines with another pair of students and critique each other's guidelines. The critiques should include questions such as: Do the guidelines provide enough information? Will the guidelines help prevent accidents from occurring? Is the writing clear and concise? Offer suggestions for revisions.

e. As you and your partner discuss the critique, note the accuracy and completeness of your guidelines as written. Revise your guidelines as needed.

f. Exchange roles. Repeat the activity for this accident scenario: A medical assistant working in the laboratory is overcome by fumes from a chemical and must be rushed to the hospital. Create a new set of accident prevention guidelines for chemical safety in the laboratory.

3. Bring some items from home that you think would be interesting to view under the microscope. (Suggested items: newsprint, a feather, threads, dog or cat hair, sugar crystals) Place each item under the microscope and view them using 10X and 40X objectives. Make drawings of each item under both magnifications. Write your observations about the materials underneath each drawing.

CASE STUDIES

Write your response to each case study on the lines provided.

Case 1

Your office is planning to close the POL and send all tests to a reference laboratory. The doctors say that the complexity and expense of meeting federal regulations is forcing them to take this action. In the past, your office has performed urinalyses, pregnancy tests, and blood glucose tests. Instead of closing the POL, what other option is available?

_____

_____

_____

Case 2

You have been put in charge of the care and maintenance of the microscope in the POL. Describe the procedure you would follow at the end of the workday.

_____

_____

_____

Case 3

You have been asked to train new laboratory personnel in the housekeeping duties essential in your lab. What information should you give new employees?

_____

_____

_____

Case 4

You are a medical assistant in a physician's office laboratory that performs Level II tests. Your employer has asked for your help in designing a quality assurance program. Describe the components the program must include.

_____

_____

_____

Case 5

A patient has arrived in the office for a scheduled blood test. Describe how you will communicate with her before, during, and after the test.

_____

_____

_____

Case 6

The physician in your office suspects that one of the tests you have performed is not accurate. What action should you take?

_____

_____

_____

CHAPTER 46

Introduction to Microbiology

REVIEW

Vocabulary Review

Matching

Match the key terms in the right column with the definitions in the left column by placing the letter of each correct answer in the space provided.

_____ 1. An agent that kills or suppresses the growth of a microorganism

_____ 2. An organism that lives on or in another organism and that uses that other organism for its own nourishment or some other advantage, to the detriment of the host organism

_____ 3. A single-celled eukaryotic organism, generally much larger than bacteria and found in soil and water

_____ 4. A substance that contains all the nutrients a particular type of microorganism needs

_____ 5. A distinct group of organisms

_____ 6. The result of a Gram's stain in which the bacteria lose the purple color and pick up the red color of the safranin

_____ 7. A specimen spread thinly and evenly across a slide

_____ 8. Bacteria that appear blue after the Gram's stain procedure

_____ 9. A procedure that involves culturing a specimen and then testing the isolated bacterium's susceptibility to certain antibiotics

_____ 10. A gelatin-like substance derived from seaweed that gives a medium its consistency

_____ 11. A preparation of a specimen in a liquid that allows organisms to remain alive and mobile while they are examined under a microscope

_____ 12. Fungi that grow mainly as single-celled organisms and reproduce by budding

_____ 13. A eukaryotic organism that has a rigid cell wall at some stage in the life cycle

_____ 14. A comma-shaped bacterium

_____ 15. A staining procedure for identifying bacteria that have a waxy cell wall

_____ 16. A solution of a dye or group of dyes that imparts a color to microorganisms

_____ 17. A spiral-shaped bacterium

_____ 18. A spherical, round, or ovoid bacterium

a. antimicrobial
b. coccus
c. acid-fast stain
d. yeast
e. spirillum
f. parasite
g. agar
h. vibrio
i. fungus
j. culture and sensitivity (C&S)
k. protozoan
l. colony
m. gram-negative
n. smear
o. stain
p. wet mount
q. culture medium
r. gram-positive

True or False

Decide whether each statement is true or false. In the space at the left, write T *for true or* F *for false. On the lines provided, rewrite the false statements to make them true.*

_____ **19.** Viruses are large, prokaryotic organisms.

_____

_____ **20.** Keratin is a tough, hard protein.

_____

_____ **21.** Eukaryotic microorganisms have a simple cell structure with no nucleus and no organelles in the cytoplasm.

_____

_____ **22.** When performing a quantitative analysis of a urine specimen, incubate the plates at 20°C.

_____

_____ **23.** Gram's stain is used to differentiate bacteria according to the chemical composition of their cell walls.

_____

_____ **24.** Aerobes are bacteria that grow best in the presence of oxygen.

_____

_____ **25.** Facultative organisms grow well when oxygen is present or absent.

_____

_____ **26.** A protozoan is a multiple-celled eukaryotic organism that is generally smaller than a bacterium.

_____

_____ **27.** A mordant is a substance that can intensify or deepen the response of a specimen to a stain.

_____

_____ **28.** A parasite is an organism that lives on or in another organism and uses that other organism for its own nourishment.

_____

_____ **29.** Chlamydiae are bacteria that completely lack the rigid cell wall of other bacteria.

_____

_____ **30.** When performing a quantitative analysis of a urine specimen, mix the urine specimen well before taking the sample.

_____

_____ **31.** Trichinosis is an infection caused by *Trichinella spiralis,* a kind of virus.

_____

_____ **32.** An O&P specimen is a urine specimen that is examined for the presence of protozoans or parasites, including their eggs.

_____

_____ **33.** An etiologic agent is a living microorganism or its toxin that can cause human disease.

_____

_____ **34.** An ongoing system to evaluate the quality of medical care provided in a medical office is known as qualitative analysis.

_____

_____ **35.** A Gram's stain result is referred to as gram-positive when the bacteria appear red.

_____

Content Review

Multiple Choice

In the space provided, write the letter of the choice that best completes each statement or answers each question.

_____ **1.** A bacterium that grows best in the absence of oxygen is
  A. a protozoan.
  B. an anaerobe.
  C. an aerobe.
  D. a vibrio.

_____ **2.** A procedure to test a bacterium's susceptibility to certain antibiotics is
  A. a culture.
  B. an antimicrobial.
  C. a culture and sensitivity.
  D. a qualitative analysis.
  E. a quantitative analysis.

_____ **3.** The label on a collection specimen container should include the patient's name and identification number, source of the specimen, doctor's name, your initials, and the
  A. patient's insurance billing information.
  B. names of medications the patient is currently receiving.
  C. date and time of collection.
  D. doctor's presumptive diagnosis.

_____ **4.** A KOH mount is prepared with
  A. a 0.9% solution of sodium chloride.
  B. a 10% solution of potassium hydroxide.
  C. iodine as a mordant.
  D. alcohol as a mordant.

_____ **5.** A gelatin-like substance derived from seaweed that is used to give culture medium its consistency is known as
  A. agar.
  B. smear.
  C. safranin.
  D. gentian violet.
  E. inoculum.

Sentence Completion

In the space provided, write the word or phrase that best completes each sentence.

6. Specific microorganisms are named with two words; the first word refers to the microorganism's _____ and the second word refers to its species.

6. _____

7. _____

7. Spherical, round, or ovoid bacteria are known as _____.

8. A doctor makes a(n) _____ clinical diagnosis on the basis of a patient's vital signs, complaints, and exam.

9. To _____ a culture medium, you place a sample of a specimen in or on the medium.

10. Rod-shaped bacteria are known as _____.

11. A(n) _____ is an agent that kills microorganisms or suppresses their growth.

12. A _____ loop is a type of inoculating loop that measures a specific amount of fluid.

13. A fungus that grows mainly as a single-celled organism that reproduces by budding is referred to as a _____.

14. The most common type of culture medium used in the laboratory is _____, a nonselective medium.

15. Antimicrobial sensitivity tests are reported as sensitive (no growth), intermediate (little growth), or _____ (overgrown).

8. _____

9. _____

10. _____

11. _____

12. _____

13. _____

14. _____

15. _____

Short Answer

Write the answer to each question on the lines provided.

16. What are three ways a patient can collect a stool specimen?

_____

_____

_____

17. Compare and contrast prokaryotic and eukaryotic cells, and give examples of each.

_____

_____

_____

18. The four different bacterial shapes are shown here. On the lines provided, write the names of the bacteria that display these shapes.

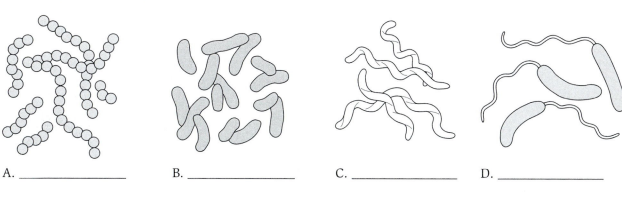

A. _____   B. _____   C. _____   D. _____

19. What are the six steps in diagnosing and treating an infection?

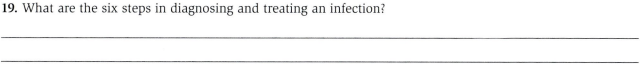

_____

_____

_____

20. Why is it important to process urine samples within 1 hour?

_____

_____

_____

21. What are the three main objectives for collecting and transporting a microbiologic specimen to an outside laboratory?

_____

_____

_____

22. What is the procedure for preparing a KOH mount?

_____

_____

_____

23. Where should you label a culture plate? Why?

_____

_____

_____

24. Describe how you would prepare a microbiological specimen for transport by the US Postal Service.

_____

_____

_____

25. What are the most common types of culture specimens?

_____

_____

_____

Critical Thinking

Write the answer to each question on the lines provided.

1. Why are cotton swabs no longer used for culture swabs?

_____

_____

_____

2. Why is it more difficult to grow and identify viruses than bacteria?

_____

_____

_____

3. Why is it important to properly collect a stool sample so that it is not contaminated by water from the toilet or urine?

_____

_____

_____

4. Why is it important to develop an up-to-date laboratory procedures manual?

_____

_____

_____

5. Why are cultures usually incubated at 35° to 37°C?

_____

_____

_____

APPLICATION

Follow the directions for the application.

Collecting a Specimen, Preparing a Specimen Smear, and Performing a Gram's Stain

Working with a partner, you are to take a throat culture from your partner, prepare a smear of the specimen for staining, and perform a Gram's stain. Your partner should serve as observer and evaluator.

a. Using a sterile swab, obtain a throat culture from your partner. Follow all safety precautions. Your partner should monitor the procedure while referring to Procedure 46-1 in the textbook and taking notes as needed for later discussion.

b. After you have obtained the specimen, prepare a specimen smear. Your partner should refer to the steps outlined in Procedure 46-3.

c. After you have prepared the smear, your partner should provide a critique of the procedure. Discuss any omissions or errors in the procedure.

d. Using the prepared smear, perform a Gram's stain. Your partner should observe your technique while referring to Procedure 46-4 in the textbook and assess your performance on completion of the stain.

e. Exchange roles and allow your partner to collect a specimen, prepare a smear, and perform a Gram's stain.

CASE STUDIES

Write your response to each case study on the lines provided.

Case 1

The doctor asks you to obtain a urine specimen from a patient. As you explain the procedure to the patient, he tells you that he is currently taking antibiotics that were prescribed by a doctor he visited for the same ailment while out of town on business. Should you have the patient collect the specimen? If not, what should you do?

_____

_____

_____

Case 2

You forgot to break the vial in the CULTURETTE before you sent it out to the lab. The lab rejected the specimen. Why?

_____

_____

_____

Case 3

While you are collecting a throat specimen, the patient gags and accidentally touches the swab with her tongue. What should you do? Why?

_____

_____

_____

Case 4

You have been asked to educate a mother about collecting a stool sample from her 1-year-old child. What tips can you give the mother about collecting the sample?

_____

_____

_____

CHAPTER **47**

Collecting, Processing, and Testing Urine Specimens

REVIEW

Vocabulary Review

Matching

Match the key terms in the right column with the definitions in the left column by placing the letter of each correct answer in the space provided.

_____ 1. Excessive nighttime urination

_____ 2. Excess protein in urine

_____ 3. Excess glucose in the urine

_____ 4. A tube used to collect specimens or instill medications

_____ 5. The presence of myoglobin in urine

_____ 6. A tube inserted in the ureter after plastic repair

_____ 7. A bile pigment formed from hemoglobin

_____ 8. An optical instrument that measures the bending of light as it passes through liquid

_____ 9. The functional unit of the kidney

_____ 10. Absence of urine production

_____ 11. A measure of the degree of acidity or alkalinity of urine

_____ 12. Insufficient production (or volume) of urine

_____ 13. Blood in the urine

_____ 14. The presence of bilirubin in urine

_____ 15. A cylinder-shaped element that forms when protein accumulates in the kidney tubules and is washed into the urine

_____ 16. A test using antigens and antibodies conjugated to an enzyme

_____ 17. A naturally produced solid of definite form that is commonly found in urine specimens

_____ 18. The liquid portion of a centrifuged urine sample

_____ 19. A genetically inherited disorder in which the body cannot properly metabolize the nutrient phenylalanine

a. drainage catheter
b. nocturia
c. supernatant
d. anuria
e. enzyme immunoassay (EIA)
f. splinting catheter
g. bilirubin
h. proteinuria
i. crystal
j. cast
k. hematuria
l. bilirubinuria
m. phenylketonuria (PKU)
n. refractometer
o. oliguria
p. glycosuria
q. myoglobinuria
r. urinary pH
s. nephron

True or False

Decide whether each statement is true or false. In the space at the left, write T for true or F for false. On the lines provided, rewrite the false statements to make them true.

_____ **20.** When a timed urine specimen is obtained, only the first specimen and the last specimen are collected during a 2- to 24-hour period.

_____

_____ **21.** The normal water content of urine is about 50%.

_____

_____ **22.** Hyaline casts form as a result of increased urine flow.

_____

_____ **23.** A clean-catch midstream urine specimen is obtained after special cleansing of the external genitalia.

_____

_____ **24.** Hemoglobinuria is a rare condition in which free hemoglobin is present in urine.

_____

_____ **25.** Glomerular filtration occurs as blood moves through a tight ball of capillaries called the tubule.

_____

_____ **26.** A first morning urine specimen contains lesser concentrations of substances that collect over time than do specimens taken during the day.

_____

_____ **27.** Hemoglobin breaks down into urea in the intestines.

_____

_____ **28.** A random urine specimen is a single urine specimen that can be taken at any time of the day.

_____

_____ **29.** With adequate fluid intake, the average daily output volume of urine is 1250 mL.

_____

_____ **30.** A 24-hour urine specimen is used to complete a quantitative and qualitative analysis of one or more substances.

_____

_____ **31.** Yeast cells are often seen in the urine of patients with diabetes.

_____

Content Review

Multiple Choice

In the space provided, write the letter of the choice that best completes each statement or answers each question.

_____ **1.** The tube that carries urine from the bladder to the outside of the body is the
   A. ureter.
   B. urethra.
   C. glomerulus.
   D. collecting tubule.

_____ **2.** A single urine specimen taken at any time of the day is
   A. a clean-catch.
   B. timed.
   C. random.
   D. 24-hour.

_____ **3.** Fresh urine specimens should be processed within
   A. 1 minute.
   B. 1 hour.
   C. 3 hours.
   D. 1 day.
   E. 1 week.

_____ **4.** The first part of the urinalysis, a visual inspection of color, volume, odor, and specific gravity, is known as what type of test?
   A. Microscopic
   B. Confirmatory
   C. Physical
   D. Chemical
   E. Metabolic

_____ **5.** The normal pH range of freshly voided urine is
   A. 0–2.9.
   B. 2.4–4.8.
   C. 3.8–6.4.
   D. 4.5–8.0.

Sentence Completion

In the space provided, write the word or phrase that best completes each sentence.

6. The presence of _____ in the urine is one of the first signs of liver disease.

7. _____ is a yellow pigment that gives urine its color.

8. A(n) _____ catheter is designed to remain in place within the bladder.

9. Ketone bodies are intermediary products of fat and _____ metabolism.

10. Leukocyte _____ is a chemical seen when leukocytes are present in urine.

11. An increase in urine specific gravity indicates that the kidneys cannot properly _____ the urine.

12. A reagent strip can be used to test for _____, which are intermediary products of fat and protein metabolism in the body.

13. The three types of cells that are found in urine are epithelial cells, white blood cells, and _____.

14. Urine pregnancy tests determine the presence of the hormone _____.

15. A(n) _____ test should be done on a urine specimen before attempting to identify crystals in the specimen.

6. _____

7. _____

8. _____

9. _____

10. _____

11. _____

12. _____

13. _____

14. _____

15. _____

Short Answer

Write the answer to each question on the lines provided.

16. What conditions can cause hematuria?

_____

_____

_____

17. What should be done to refrigerated urine specimens before processing them?

_____

_____

_____

18. Why is it necessary to clean the external genitalia when collecting a clean-catch midstream urine specimen?

_____

_____

_____

19. Why is catheterization not routinely used for collecting urine specimens instead of the clean-catch midstream method?

_____

_____

_____

20. What are the disadvantages of the nucleic acid amplification urine tests for STDs?

_____

_____

_____

21. What do changes in the color of a patient's urine generally indicate about changes in its specific gravity?

_____

_____

_____

22. What are the advantages of using a refractometer to measure urine specific gravity?

_____

_____

_____

23. Why might a doctor order the chemical testing of urine?

_____

_____

_____

24. After centrifugation, where should you pour the supernatant?

_____

_____

_____

25. What is the most common urinary parasite?

_____

_____

_____

Critical Thinking

Write the answer to each question on the lines provided.

1. During a microscopic urine exam, you find a higher than normal count of renal epithelial cells. What might this indicate?

_____

_____

_____

2. What is the purpose of taking the temperature of urine collected for a drug and alcohol analysis?

_____

_____

_____

3. Why should a glucose test be performed on a fresh urine specimen?

_____

_____

_____

4. Why is blood more commonly tested than urine for glucose?

_____

_____

_____

5. Will refrigeration cause a decrease or an increase in urine specific gravity? Explain.

_____

_____

_____

6. What is the purpose of placing a bluing agent in the toilet prior to having a patient collect a urine drug screen specimen?

_____

_____

_____

APPLICATION

Follow the directions for each application.

1. Collecting a Urine Specimen from an Elderly Patient

Working with two partners, conduct an interview with an elderly patient scheduled for a urine test. One person should play the role of the elderly patient, one should take the role of the medical assistant conducting the interview, and the third should act as an observer and evaluator. Assume that the patient is an incontinent male scheduled for a random urine specimen.

a. Take a history of the patient, noting your questions and the patient's responses. On the basis of the responses, ask appropriate follow-up questions.

b. Explain to the patient the procedure he is to follow. Allow the patient to interrupt at any time with questions, which you should answer to the best of your ability. Again, note your statements, the patient's questions, and your responses.

c. Have the observer critique the interview. The critique should include the medical assistant's attitude, or approach, as well as the appropriateness and accuracy of the questions and responses to the elderly patient. The observer also should evaluate the order in which the assistant took the history and its completeness.

d. As a team, discuss the observer's critique, noting the strengths and weaknesses of the interview.

e. Exchange roles and repeat the interview with an elderly patient (perhaps hearing-impaired) scheduled for another type of urine specimen collection. The type of collection should be chosen by the new observer.

f. Exchange roles one more time so that each team member gets to play the medical assistant, the patient, and the observer.

2. Evaluating a Urine Specimen

Indicate whether each of the following results of a urinalysis is normal or abnormal by writing *normal* or *abnormal* in the space provided.

a. Color: Red   _____

b. Turbidity: Clear   _____

c. Odor: Fruity   _____

d. Volume: 2200 mL/24 hours   _____

e. Specific gravity: 1.022   _____

f. Ketones: Negative   _____

g. pH: 5.2   _____

h. Glucose: Positive   _____

i. Red blood cells: 8/high-power field _____

j. Crystals: Negative   _____

3. Completing a Laboratory Requisition Form

a. Complete the sample reference laboratory requisition form, example found in the documentation section in the back of the book, using appropriate information from the following case.

> The physician has seen a young female patient in the office who has been complaining of vague abdominal pain, slight weight gain, fatigue, some nausea, and occasional fever. You have been asked to collect a urine specimen for this patient for a complete urinalysis and a qualitative urine pregnancy test. Your office does not perform any laboratory testing in-house.

> The patient's name is Mary Elizabeth Arnold, age 24. The physician's name is Dr. Travis Buffett; his UPIN number is 123456.

The shaded areas must be completed or the reference laboratory will reject the specimen. Remember that you must fill in the date and time of the collection even though those areas are not shaded in; use today's date and time. Do not forget to mark which tests are being requested. In addition, note the patient's unique control number, which the reference laboratory will use to track the specimen.

b. Complete the sample reference laboratory requisition form, example found in the documentation section in the back of the book, using appropriate information from the following case.

> An elderly patient by the name of William Overtell has seen the physician in the office today. The physician suspects that this patient may be entering the early phases of kidney failure based on the patient's clinical picture. A key test in diagnosing a condition of this type can be a 24-hour urine specimen.

> After measurement of the total volume of the 24-hour specimen, a small sample is prepared to forward to the reference laboratory for analysis. The physician's name is Dr. Felicia Mills and her UPIN number is 98765443. Because the patient has Medicare, the physician cannot bill the patient for the testing. The patient's Medicare number (112-33-5588B) must be provided in the appropriate block on the requisition form so that the laboratory can bill the insurance carrier directly. The total volume of the specimen was 980 mL.

Identify the test number assigned to this test on the requisition form. Also, to ensure proper collection, detail the specific instructions that should be provided to the patient prior to the collection of the specimen.

CASE STUDIES

Write your response to each case study on the lines provided.

Case 1

A patient telephones and tells you she is concerned about not having a means at home of disinfecting a jar for a urine specimen. How would you respond to the patient?

_____

_____

_____

Case 2

You notice that the lid has been left off a urine specimen container that you are supposed to test for ketone bodies. Should you perform the test? Why or why not?

_____

_____

_____

Case 3

You open a fresh container of reagent test strips 5 months before the expiration date marked on the container. You note that the test strips are not discolored. What should your next step be?

_____

_____

_____

Case 4

Elizabeth comes to the office on a very hot day. She says she has been working outside all day and hasn't had much to drink. After you perform her urinalysis, you note that she has an abnormal urine specific gravity. Would you expect the urine specific gravity to be elevated or decreased? Why?

_____

_____

_____

Copyright © 2011 by The McGraw-Hill Companies, Inc.

CHAPTER 48

Collecting, Processing, and Testing Blood Specimens

REVIEW

Vocabulary Review

True or False

Decide whether each statement is true or false. In the space at the left, write T *for true or* F *for false. On the lines provided, rewrite the false statements to make them true.*

_____ 1. The main component of erythrocytes is hemoglobin.

_____

_____ 2. The engulfing of invading bacteria is known as lymphocytosis.

_____

_____ 3. Red blood cells, or microphils, are one component of blood.

_____

_____ 4. The function of B lymphocytes is to produce antibodies that combat specific pathogens.

_____

_____ 5. A white blood cell with a solid nucleus and clear cytoplasm is an agranulocyte.

_____

_____ 6. Monocytes, large white blood cells, have oval or horseshoe-shaped nuclei.

_____

_____ 7. A small, calibrated glass tube that holds a small, precise volume of fluid is a hematocrit.

_____

_____ 8. When counting RBCs and WBCs, you use a concentrated blood sample and a hemocytometer.

_____

_____ 9. Hemoglobin is released during hemolysis, the rupturing of red blood cells.

_____

_____ 10. Capillary puncture requires a superficial puncture of the skin with a sharp point.

_____

_____ 11. Neutrophils have a light green nucleus and pale pink cytoplasm, which contains fine pink or lavender granules.

_____

_____ **12.** Through hematocrit determination, you can identify how much of the volume of a sample of blood is made up of red blood cells after the sample has been spun in a centrifuge.

_____

_____ **13.** In a tube of blood that has been spun in a centrifuge, the packed red blood cells are separated from the white blood cells by the buffy coat.

_____

_____ **14.** A complete blood count is a type of serologic test.

_____

_____ **15.** An erythrocyte sedimentation rate (ESR) test measures the rate at which red blood cells settle to the bottom of a blood sample.

_____

_____ **16.** A hematocrit is a test that measures the percentage of white blood cells in a blood sample.

_____

Matching

Match the key terms in the right column with the definitions in the left column by placing the letter of each correct answer in the space provided.

_____ **17.** The liquid part of blood in which other components are suspended

_____ **18.** The process of blood clotting

_____ **19.** The study of the shape or form of objects

_____ **20.** The portion of blood volume that includes red blood cells, white blood cells, and platelets

_____ **21.** The insertion of a needle into a vein for the purpose of withdrawing blood

_____ **22.** Granular leukocytes that capture invading bacteria and antigenantibody complexes

_____ **23.** The rupturing of blood cells

_____ **24.** A white blood cell

_____ **25.** The fever-producing substance released by a neutrophil

_____ **26.** A white blood cell with a solid nucleus and clear cytoplasm

_____ **27.** A winged infusion set

_____ **28.** Clear, yellow liquid that remains after a blood clot forms

_____ **29.** The area of a spun sample of blood that contains the white blood cells and platelets

_____ **30.** A nongranular leukocyte that regulates immunologic response

_____ **31.** The heaviest part of whole blood, which moves to one end of a microhematocrit tube after being spun in a centrifuge

_____ **32.** A blood collection device that includes a double-pointed needle, a plastic needle holder, and collection tubes

a. agranular leukocyte
b. phlebotomy
c. eosinophils
d. serum
e. morphology
f. pyrogen
g. formed elements
h. buffy coat
i. plasma
j. evacuation system
k. venipuncture
l. packed red blood cells
m. coagulation
n. butterfly system
o. leukocyte
p. T lymphocyte
q. tourniquet
r. hemolysis

_____ **33.** A flat, broad length of vinyl or rubber used during venipuncture procedures

_____ **34.** The puncture of a vein

Content Review

Multiple Choice

In the space provided, write the letter of the choice that best completes each statement or answers each question.

_____ **1.** Blood is transported throughout the body by the
   A. circulatory system.
   B. plasma.
   C. hemoglobin.
   D. transrespiratory system.

_____ **2.** Which of the following gives red blood cells their color?
   A. Hemoglobin
   B. Hemolysis
   C. Oxygen
   D. B lymphocyte

_____ **3.** The study of blood is known as
   A. morphology.
   B. cytology.
   C. histology.
   D. hematology.
   E. cardiology.

_____ **4.** Other than assembling the equipment and supplies necessary, the first step in preparing to draw blood is reviewing the
   A. patient's blood type.
   B. procedure with the patient.
   C. written request for the test.
   D. health of the patient.

_____ **5.** A small, disposable instrument with a sharp point used to puncture the skin and make a small incision is a
   A. micropipette.
   B. lancet.
   C. syringe.
   D. tourniquet.
   E. butterfly device.

_____ **6.** Fragments of megakaryocytes are known as
   A. neutrophils.
   B. basophils.
   C. red blood cells.
   D. monocytes.
   E. thrombocytes.

_____ 7. Which of the following methods of blood collection would be best to use with patients who have small or fragile veins?

  A. Evacuation system

  B. VACUTAINER system

  C. Butterfly system

  D. Venipuncture

_____ 8. Lancets are used

  A. when the amount of blood required for a procedure is not large.

  B. when the amount of blood required for a procedure is large.

  C. for infants only.

  D. for adults only.

_____ 9. A test used to monitor the health of a patient with diabetes is a

  A. complete blood count.

  B. hemoglobin A1c.

  C. creatine kinase.

  D. ESR.

  E. differential count.

Sentence Completion

In the space provided, write the word or phrase that best completes each sentence.

10. When drawing a patient's blood, you should make no more than _____ attempts.

11. Patients often fear that the more tubes of blood you require, _____.

12. Probably the greatest fear of patients undergoing blood tests is contracting _____.

13. The total volume of plasma and formed elements comprises _____.

14. _____ form a gel-like barrier between serum and the clot in a coagulated blood sample.

15. The process of clotting is called _____.

16. The normal range for a total carbon dioxide blood test is _____.

17. _____ are the first line of defense during a phlebotomy procedure.

10. _____

11. _____

12. _____

13. _____

14. _____

15. _____

16. _____

17. _____

Short Answer

Write the answer to each question on the lines provided.

18. Why might you need to wear a mask during a phlebotomy procedure?

_____

_____

_____

19. What two goals are met by wearing personal protective equipment during phlebotomy procedures?

_____

_____

_____

20. Describe three advantages of an evacuation system of blood drawing.

_____

_____

_____

21. How can you prevent infections caused by phlebotomy?

_____

_____

_____

22. Describe the biggest challenge in blood drawing that children present.

_____

_____

_____

23. Describe how you would determine the concentration of hemoglobin in a blood sample.

_____

_____

_____

24. Describe two desired characteristics of engineered safety devices.

_____

_____

_____

25. The illustration below shows several types of blood cells. On the lines provided, write the name and a brief description of each cell's function.

A. 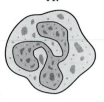 B.   C. D.

E.   F. 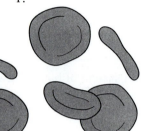  G.

A. _____

_____

_____

D. _____

_____

_____

G. _____

_____

_____

B. _____

_____

_____

E. _____

_____

_____

C. _____

_____

_____

F. _____

_____

_____

Critical Thinking

Write the answer to each question on the lines provided.

1. Why is it important to dispose of sharps promptly using approved sharps containers?

_____

_____

_____

2. What should you do if you suffer a needlestick injury?

_____

_____

_____

3. Why is it important to be absolutely sure of the meaning of any abbreviations used in laboratory work?

_____

_____

_____

4. Why is it important to identify the patient correctly before drawing blood?

_____

_____

_____

5. What are the advantages of pen-like capillary puncture devices?

_____

_____

_____

APPLICATION

Follow the directions for each application.

1. Identifying Blood Test Collection Tubes

For each test listed, name the color and additive of the collection tube used to perform the test.

a. Creatine kinase   _____

b. Bilirubin   _____

c. Leukocyte count   _____

d. Fasting glucose   _____

e. Phenylalanine   _____

f. Prothrombin   _____

g. Thyroid stimulating hormone   _____

h. Complete blood count   _____

2. Collecting Blood Specimens

Practice each technique or role-play each situation below with a partner. Critique each other by using the space provided to note pointers and suggestions that you think will help the other person perform the technique better. For situations in which you draw blood, use a mannequin arm. If a mannequin arm is not available, attach a piece of rubber tubing to a rolled piece of fabric. Then tape over a portion of the tubing to simulate skin.

a. Venipuncture with a needle and syringe

_____

_____

b. Preparing a smear slide

_____

_____

c. Capillary puncture with an automatic puncturing device

_____

_____

d. Preparing patients for blood drawing

_____

_____

e. Handling a patient who faints during blood drawing

_____

_____

3. **Completing a Laboratory Requisition Form**

a. Complete the sample reference laboratory requisition form, example on page 955, using appropriate information from the following case.

> A female patient was seen in the physician's office today. After examining the patient and reviewing her history, the physician has requested that blood be drawn for the following tests: thyroid profile II, basic chemistry, and total glycohemoglobin.
> The patient's name is Janice Jondahl, age 56. The physician's name is Dr. Rebecca Adamson; her UPIN number is 97644521.

Remember to use today's date and time for the specimen date and time and do not omit any of the shaded areas. After completing the form, name the type of specimen and tube type that are required according to the requisition form. In addition, note the test numbers assigned to each of the tests requested by the physician.

b. Complete the sample reference laboratory requisition form, example on page 955, using appropriate information from the following case.

> Charles Riffe, age 83, has seen Dr. Domingo Krishnan in the office today for a follow-up for high blood cholesterol, which has been an ongoing problem for him. The physician has placed the patient on a cholesterol-reducing medication for six weeks now and has asked that this patient return the next morning without eating to have the following blood tests drawn: lipid profile I to include a lipoprotein analysis, glucose, and a liver profile A (to rule out liver damage from the prescribed medication).
> The patient has Medicare, which means that the physician cannot bill the patient for the service. The patient's Medicare number, 678-35-0022B, must be provided to the reference laboratory in order for the laboratory to bill the insurance carrier directly.

Remember to use today's date and time for the specimen collection date and time. After completing the form, answer the following questions:

1. Why would the physician request that the patient return the next day without having eaten?

2. What are the specimen requirements for the tests requested?

3. Is there any information missing from this scenario that you must have before sending the specimen to the reference laboratory?

CASE STUDIES

Write your response to each case study on the lines provided.

Case 1

While you are preparing a patient for a blood test, she asks whether her symptoms are signs of rheumatoid arthritis. How should you respond?

_____

_____

_____

Case 2

A patient arrived in the office for a blood test. What steps should you follow, from this moment to the time you draw the blood?

_____

_____

_____

Case 3

As you are assembling the equipment for drawing blood from a patient, you notice her eyeing the needle and tubes nervously. She then asks, "Will this hurt?" As you draw the blood, the patient comments, "I guess this test is pretty common, right? I mean, do you usually need so many tubes of blood?" How should you respond to her concerns?

_____

_____

_____

Case 4

While performing a capillary puncture, you notice the patient's hands are very cold. What should you do?

_____

_____

_____

Case 5

You have been asked to prepare a blood sample for transport to an outside lab. How should you do this?

_____

_____

_____

CHAPTER **49**

Nutrition and Special Diets

REVIEW

Vocabulary Review

True or False

Decide whether each statement is true or false. In the space at the left, write T *for true or* F *for false. On the lines provided, rewrite the false statements to make them true.*

_____ 1. Antigens are chemical agents that fight cell-destroying free radicals.

_____

_____ 2. Amino acids are natural compounds found in plant and animal foods and are used by the body to create protein.

_____

_____ 3. Cholesterol is a fat-related substance that the body produces in the liver and that is also obtained from dietary sources.

_____

_____ 4. Incomplete proteins lack one or more of the essential amino acids.

_____

_____ 5. Starch is the tough, stringy part of vegetables and grains that is not absorbed by the body but aids in a variety of bodily functions.

_____

_____ 6. Proteins that contain all nine essential amino acids are complete proteins.

_____

_____ 7. Complete proteins are also known as polysaccharides.

_____

_____ 8. Lipoproteins are large molecules that are water-soluble on the inside, are fat-soluble on the outside, and carry carbohydrates through the bloodstream.

_____

_____ 9. Saturated fats are derived from animal sources, are clear and liquid at room temperature, and tend to raise blood cholesterol.

_____

_____ 10. Triglycerides are simple lipids that consist of glycerol and three fatty acids.

_____

_____ 11. Minerals are natural, inorganic substances the body needs to help build and maintain body tissues and carry on life functions.

_____

Matching

Match the key terms in the right column with the definitions in the left column by placing the letter of each correct answer in the space provided.

_____ 12. A method of feeding patients who cannot tolerate receiving supplements by way of the digestive tract

_____ 13. The phase of metabolism in which substances are changed into more complex substances and used to build body tissues

_____ 14. An eating disorder in which people starve themselves

_____ 15. The phase of metabolism when complex substances are broken down into simpler substances and converted into energy

_____ 16. A dietary system, used especially with diabetics, in which portions of foods in each of six categories are interchangeable

_____ 17. A large molecule that is fat-soluble on the inside and water-soluble on the outside

_____ 18. A procedure used to measure a person's percentage of body fat

_____ 19. When a person gets too little or loses too much water

_____ 20. Patient with this condition requires a high-fiber diet

_____ 21. A facet of weight loss or weight management that encourages people to change their eating habits

_____ 22. A standard measure for the amount of energy that a food produces in the body

_____ 23. The intolerance of the protein gluten, which causes damage to the intestines

_____ 24. A simple lipid made of glycerol and three fatty acids

_____ 25. An eating disorder in which people binge on food and then try to counter the effects through vomiting, laxatives, and/or excessive exercise

a. anabolism
b. anorexia nervosa
c. behavior modification
d. bulimia
e. calorie
f. catabolism
g. food exchange
h. lipoprotein
i. parenteral nutrition
j. skinfold test
k. triglyceride
l. dehydration
m. diverticulosis
n. celiac disease

Content Review

Multiple Choice

In the space provided, write the letter of the choice that best completes each statement or answers each question.

_____ 1. Which of the following nutrients can help prevent diverticular disease, constipation, and irritable bowel syndrome?
A. Lipids
B. Calcium
C. Fiber
D. Electrolytes
E. Complete proteins

_____ 2. An increased risk of heart disease, stroke, and peripheral vascular disease has been linked with high levels of
   A. lipoproteins and unsaturated fats.
   B. triglycerides and cholesterol.
   C. vitamins A and K.
   D. iron and fluoride.
   E. folate.

_____ 3. Which of the following is *not* a function of water in the human body?
   A. Aiding in digestion
   B. Promoting the healing of wounds
   C. Regulating body temperature
   D. Lubricating the body's moving parts

_____ 4. Which of the following statements about diet therapy is false?
   A. Diet therapy sometimes involves restricting certain foods.
   B. Diet therapy may involve changing the number of meals per day.
   C. Physicians and dietitians cooperate to determine which diet therapy is best for a patient.
   D. Diet therapy always involves lowering the daily caloric intake.

_____ 5. In terms of general nutrition, elderly patients should
   A. decrease their fiber intake.
   B. increase their caloric intake.
   C. increase their fat intake by 10% to 15%.
   D. supplement their diets with massive amounts of iron and vitamin C.
   E. decrease their caloric intake but not their protein intake.

_____ 6. Dietary guidelines that aim to lessen the risk of heart attack recommend choosing a diet that is
   A. low in saturated fats and cholesterol.
   B. low in fiber.
   C. moderate in sugars.
   D. high in salt.

_____ 7. What is the chief difference between a full-liquid diet and a clear-liquid diet?
   A. A full-liquid diet is higher in carbohydrates.
   B. A full-liquid diet includes strained cooked cereals and soups.
   C. A clear-liquid diet contains large amounts of fiber.
   D. A clear-liquid diet is higher in proteins.

_____ 8. The term *reduced cholesterol* on a food label means that the food has
   A. less than or equal to 2 mg of cholesterol per serving.
   B. less than or equal to 20 mg of cholesterol per serving.
   C. at least 25% less cholesterol per serving than the food it replaces.
   D. at least 50% less cholesterol per serving than the food it replaces.
   E. at least 75% less cholesterol per serving than the food it replaces.

_____ 9. A sign of bulimia is
   A. self-starvation.
   B. cessation of menstruation.
   C. weight gain.
   D. the buying and consuming of large quantities of food.

_____ **10.** The 2005 USDA Dietary Guidelines encourage people to do all of the following *except*

    A. get more sleep.

    B. increase physical activity.

    C. eat a well-balanced diet from all food groups.

    D. limit alcohol consumption.

    E. maintain or reduce weight.

Sentence Completion

In the space provided, write the word or phrase that best completes each sentence.

11. A(n) _____ is a health professional who designs ways for people to obtain optimal nourishment on the basis of the science of nutrition.

12. _____ fiber, found in the bran in whole wheat bread and brown rice, promotes regular bowel movements by contributing to stool bulk.

13. The Recommended Daily Allowance of vitamin C for an adult is _____.

14. The _____ on the USDA 2005 Food Guide Pyramid represents physical activity.

15. Iron deficiency can cause _____, a blood disorder that can leave a person fatigued, weak, and mentally impaired.

16. The dietary guidelines developed by the _____ encourage people to be moderate in their consumption of processed and red meats.

17. Wheat, milk, eggs, and chocolate are some of the most common food _____.

18. Patients with diabetes should not miss a meal because skipping meals disturbs the balance of _____.

19. You can learn about a packaged food's caloric, fat, and sodium content per serving by reading the _____.

20. Patient education has become increasingly important because managed care providers want to see documentation of _____ in patients' charts.

11. _____

12. _____

13. _____

14. _____

15. _____

16. _____

17. _____

18. _____

19. _____

20. _____

Short Answer

Write the answer to each question on the lines provided.

21. What are the three major ways in which the human body uses nutrients?

_____

_____

_____

22. What are RDAs? Why do you need to know about them?

_____

_____

_____

23. What is the Food Guide Pyramid? How can you use it to achieve a balanced diet?

_____

_____

_____

24. Under what circumstances might a doctor be likely to prescribe a diet to help a patient gain weight?

_____

_____

_____

25. Describe five guidelines that you can follow when discussing diets with a patient.

_____

_____

_____

26. How is the Diabetes Food Pyramid different from the USDA Food Guide Pyramid?

_____

_____

_____

27. What are the recommendations by the American Cancer Society to prevent cancer?

_____

_____

_____

28. The 2005 Food Guide Pyramid is color-coded. What are the colors and foods represented by them?

_____

_____

_____

29. List the recommended foods for each of the following patients.

    a. 1½-year-old child _____

_____

    b. 10-month-old infant _____

_____

    c. 3-month-old infant _____

_____

Critical Thinking

Write the answer to each question on the lines provided.

    1. Cities that host marathons often provide a spaghetti dinner for participants who want to "carbo-load" the night before the race. Why would marathon runners want to eat a lot of carbohydrates?

_____

_____

_____

2. What is the difference between transfat and saturated fat?

_____

_____

_____

3. Why is behavior modification generally more successful than fad dieting when it comes to long-term weight loss?

_____

_____

_____

4. Why is it important to take factors of culture and religion into account when planning a patient's diet?

_____

_____

_____

5. Explain the key recommendation within the 2005 USDA Dietary Guidelines to "maintain an adequate nutrient intake while monitoring caloric needs."

_____

_____

_____

APPLICATION

Follow the directions for each application.

1. Modifying Diets

Using the Internet, research diabetic diet exchanges and prepare a travel diet for a diabetic patient. Suggestions for research include the American Diabetes Association or American Dietetic Association.

2. Preparing Patient Education Materials

In teams of three or four, choose a disease or condition for each team to research, such as hyperlipidemia, hypertension, food allergies, or another condition. Each team should design a poster or informational booklet describing the disease and diet restrictions. Each team should present their findings to the class for discussion.

3. Educating Patients

Role-play educating a patient about his daily water requirements, food allergies, how to read food labels, and a special diet. Use the sample progress note form on page 973 to document your patient education.

CASE STUDIES

Write your response to each case study on the lines provided.

Case 1

You hear Joe, another medical assistant in your office, talking to a patient about the diet the doctor has prescribed. Joe says, "Well, if you really like red meat, go ahead and eat it. Just try to cut back your fat intake from other foods." What, if anything, has Joe done wrong?

_____

_____

_____

Case 2

"Why is the doctor telling me to cut back on beer?" complains Mr. Kowalski, who is being treated for hypertension. "I've heard that beer can be good for you!" How should you respond?

_____

_____

_____

Case 3

The doctor has just prescribed a low-cholesterol diet for Mrs. Ryan. "But how am I supposed to know how much cholesterol my food has?" she asks you. How could you help Mrs. Ryan?

_____

_____

_____

CHAPTER 50

Principles of Pharmacology

REVIEW

Vocabulary Review

Matching

Match the key terms in the right column with the definitions in the left column by placing the letter of each correct answer in the space provided.

_____ 1. A drug's official name

_____ 2. The study of what drugs do to the body

_____ 3. A drug or drug product that is categorized as potentially dangerous or addictive

_____ 4. The amount of a drug given at one time

_____ 5. The process of converting a drug from its dose form to a form the body can use

_____ 6. The process of transporting a drug from its administration site to its site of action

_____ 7. A preparation administered to a person to produce reduced sensitivity, or increased immunity, to an infectious disease

_____ 8. Pertaining to medicinal drugs

_____ 9. Produces opium-like effects

_____ 10. Absorption, distribution, metabolism, and excretion

_____ 11. Government term for opioid

_____ 12. The study of drugs

_____ 13. Also called clinical pharmacology

_____ 14. Study of the characteristics of natural drugs and their sources

_____ 15. The study of poisons or poisonous effects of drugs

_____ 16. To give a drug by any route that introduces the drug into a patient's body

_____ 17. A drug's brand or proprietary name

_____ 18. The therapeutic value of a drug

_____ 19. A physician's written order to authorize the dispensing (and, sometimes, administering) of a drug to a patient

_____ 20. The purpose or reason for using a drug

a. toxicology
b. dose
c. pharmacodynamics
d. absorption
e. indication
f. administer
g. vaccine
h. efficacy
i. opioid
j. trade name
k. controlled substance
l. generic name
m. prescription
n. distribution
o. pharmaceutical
p. pharmacokinetics
q. pharmacotherapeutics
r. pharmacognosy
s. prescribe
t. narcotic

True or False

Decide whether each statement is true or false. In the space at the left, write T *for true or* F *for false. On the lines provided, rewrite the false statements to make them true.*

_____ **21.** Pharmacology is the study of the characteristics of natural drugs and their sources.

_____

_____ **22.** The study of what the body does to drugs is known as pharmacokinesis.

_____

_____ **23.** Pharmacotherapeutics is the study of the chemical properties of drugs.

_____

_____ **24.** A doctor prescribes a drug by giving a patient a prescription to be filled by a pharmacy.

_____

_____ **25.** Drugs are eliminated from the body through absorption.

_____

_____ **26.** Labeling for a drug includes the purpose or reason for using the drug and the form of the drug.

_____

_____ **27.** A drug's dosage refers to the size of each dose.

_____

_____ **28.** Prescription drugs are medications that can be used only by order of a physician.

_____

_____ **29.** An opioid is a Schedule I substance.

_____

_____ **30.** Narcotics such as codeine, morphine, and meperidine have a lower abuse potential than Schedule IV drugs.

_____

Content Review

Multiple Choice

In the space provided, write the letter of the choice that best completes each statement or answers each question.

_____ **1.** Bacteria and fungi are simple organisms used to make
   A. antiserums and antitoxins.
   B. antibiotics.
   C. enzymes.
   D. antacids.
   E. ointments.

_____ **2.** Which of the following is the generic name for a medication that lowers cholesterol?
   A. Raloxifene
   B. Toprol XL
   C. Tramadol
   D. Atorvastatin

3. Administering morphine to reduce the accompanying pain of cancer is an example of
A. maintenance drug therapy.
B. curative drug therapy.
C. supplemental drug therapy.
D. prophylactic drug therapy.
E. palliative drug therapy.

4. The government agency that regulates the manufacture and distribution of all drugs in the United States is known as the
A. Drug Enforcement Agency.
B. Federal Drug Administration.
C. Federal Bureau of Investigation.
D. Occupational Safety and Health Administration.

5. The study of adverse reactions or drug interactions is referred to as
A. toxicology.
B. pharmacology.
C. infectious disease.
D. virology.
E. pathology.

6. Which types of drugs cannot be renewed without a written order or prescription?
A. Schedule I
B. Schedule II
C. Schedule III
D. Schedule IV

7. A doctor who needs Schedule II drugs for his or her practice must order them using
A. DEA form 214.
B. DEA form 41.
C. DEA form 222.
D. DEA form 224.
E. DEA form 41 and DEA form 224.

8. Which of the following is the generic name for a medication that controls seizures?
A. Escitalopram oxalate
B. Zolpidem
C. Celebrex
D. Gabapentin

9. According to the Controlled Substances Act of 1970, physicians are not allowed to prescribe drugs in which of the following schedules?
A. Schedule IV
B. Schedule III
C. Schedule I
D. Schedule II
E. Schedule V

_____ 10. Which of the following generic medications is used for reducing the symptoms and duration of a herpetic infection?

   A. Quinapril

   B. Valacyclovir

   C. Sildenafil citrate

   D. Concerta

_____ 11. Which of the following is one of the top 50 drugs and is given to treat asthma?

   A. Plavix

   B. Fosamax

   C. Lansoprazole

   D. Zyrtec

   E. Advair Diskus

_____ 12. What is the most likely reason someone would take the medication Zetia?

   A. to reduce blood pressure

   B. to reduce cholesterol

   C. to reduce depression

   D. to replace a hormone

Sentence Completion

In the space provided, write the word or phrase that best completes each sentence.

13. Antiserums and antitoxins for vaccines are examples of _____ substances used as drugs.

14. Tablets and capsules are absorbed through the stomach or intestines into the _____.

15. Drug metabolism usually takes place in the _____.

16. Distribution can pertain to the length of time between dosing and _____ in the bloodstream.

17. Pharmacotherapeutics is sometimes called _____.

18. A drug's trade name is selected by, is copyrighted by, and is the property of its _____.

19. A nonprescription, or _____, drug is one that the FDA has approved for use without the supervision of a licensed health-care practitioner.

20. A physician's written order that authorizes the dispensing and administering of drugs to a patient is called a(n) _____.

21. The official name of a drug is called the _____.

22. The purpose or reason for using a drug is called the _____.

23. A popular drug reference book used by physician practices is called the _____.

24. A drug that is potentially dangerous and addictive is referred to as a(n) _____.

25. A drug that is used to prevent diseases in children and adults is called _____.

13. _____

14. _____

15. _____

16. _____

17. _____

18. _____

19. _____

20. _____

21. _____

22. _____

23. _____

24. _____

25. _____

Short Answer

Write the answer to each question on the lines provided.

26. What are the regulatory functions of the Food and Drug Administration (FDA) with regard to drugs?

_____

_____

_____

27. What are the four processes of pharmacokinetics?

_____

_____

_____

28. In what ways are drugs excreted?

_____

_____

_____

29. What is out-of-labeling prescribing?

_____

_____

_____

30. What factors determine the safety of a drug?

_____

_____

_____

31. List four main sources of drug information, and describe the contents of each.

   a. _____

_____

   b. _____

_____

   c. _____

_____

   d. _____

_____

32. How does regulation of the use of an OTC drug differ from that of a prescription drug?

_____

_____

_____

33. Compare how the five schedules of drugs described in the Controlled Substances Act of 1970 differ according to degree of potential abuse or nontherapeutic effects of the drugs in each schedule.

_____

_____

_____

34. What requirements does the CSA place on doctors who administer, dispense, or prescribe any controlled substance?

_____

_____

_____

35. Explain how controlled substances are identified on their labels.

_____

_____

_____

36. How does the ordering of Schedule II drugs differ from the ordering of drugs from Schedules III, IV, and V?

_____

_____

_____

37. List in order the four parts of a prescription and explain what information is contained in each part.

a. _____

_____

b. _____

_____

c. _____

_____

d. _____

_____

38. Complete the following chart.

Action of Drug	Drug Category	Example	
		Generic Name	**Trade Name**
a. Counteracts effects of histamine and relieves allergic symptoms	_____	Cetirizine	_____
b. Dilates blood vessels, decreases blood pressure	_____	Nitroglycerin	_____
c. Increases urine output, reduces blood pressure and cardiac output	_____	Furosemide	_____
d. Kills microorganisms or inhibits or prevents their growth	_____	Azithromycin	_____
e. Normalizes heartbeat in cases of certain cardiac arrhythmias	_____	Propafenone Hydrochloride	_____
f. Prevents blood from clotting	_____	Warfarin sodium	_____
g. Prevents or relieves nausea and vomiting	_____	Prochlorperazine	_____
h. Prevents sensation of pain (generally, locally, or topically)	_____	Lidocaine HCl	_____
i. Reduces blood pressure	_____	Quinapril	_____
j. Reduces fever	_____	Acetaminophen	_____
k. Reduces inflammation	_____	Triamcinoline	_____
l. Relieves depression	_____	Escitalopram	_____
m. Relieves diarrhea	_____	Loperamide HCl	_____
n. Relieves mild to severe pain	_____	Oxycodone HCl	_____
o. Relieves or controls convulsions	_____	Divalproex	_____
p. Reduces blood sugar	_____	Metformin	_____

39. Identify the purpose of each part of the package insert pictured here.

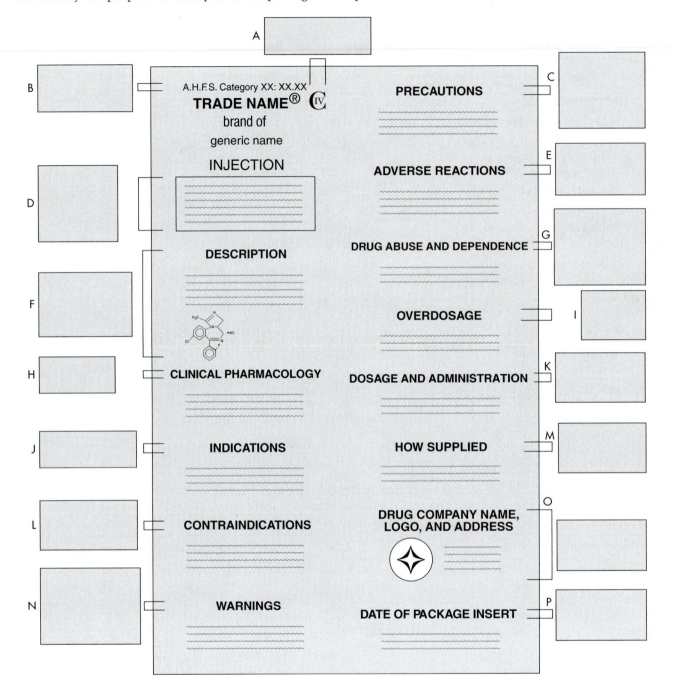

A

B

C   PRECAUTIONS

D

E   ADVERSE REACTIONS

A.H.F.S. Category XX: XX.XX

TRADE NAME® C IV

brand of

generic name

INJECTION

F

DESCRIPTION

G   DRUG ABUSE AND DEPENDENCE

H

I   OVERDOSAGE

CLINICAL PHARMACOLOGY

J   INDICATIONS

K   DOSAGE AND ADMINISTRATION

HOW SUPPLIED   M

L   CONTRAINDICATIONS

DRUG COMPANY NAME, LOGO, AND ADDRESS   O

N   WARNINGS

DATE OF PACKAGE INSERT   P

Critical Thinking

Write the answer to each question on the lines provided.

1. Why do clinical studies include both healthy individuals and patients?

_____

_____

_____

2. Why is it important that patients inform their pharmacist of all prescription and OTC drugs they are currently taking when medication is prescribed for them?

_____

_____

_____

3. What are the actions and differences of the following types of antihypertensives? Use the *PDR* or another drug reference.

   a. Calcium channel blockers

   b. ACE inhibitors

   c. Beta blockers

   d. Diuretics

_____

_____

_____

4. Why is it important that the patient chart be consulted before a prescription refill is authorized?

_____

_____

_____

5. What is the first thing a medical assistant does if a patient requests drug samples?

_____

_____

6. A pregnant patient is taking the following medications. Using a drug resource, determine the pregnancy category for each medication and discuss why it should or should not be taken by the patient.

   a. Dilantin

   b. Paracetamol

   c. Amoxicillin

   d. Accutane

   e. Codeine

_____

_____

APPLICATION

Follow the directions for each application.

1. Interpreting Prescriptions

The physician has written the following prescriptions. Interpret each prescription on the lines provided.

a. Proloprim 200 mg 10 caps

Sig l cap po daily. 10 d

_____

b. Nasalide 25 mL nasal sol

Sig ll sprays t.i.d. PRN

_____

c. Furosemide oral sol (10 mg/mL)

Sig 1 tsp po b.i.d.

_____

d. Nitro-Dur 0.3 mg transdermal nitroglycerin infusion system

Sig 1 patch daily

_____

e. Cylert 18.75 mg 14 tabs

Sig ll tabs po qam 7 d

_____

2. Conducting an Inventory of Dispensed Controlled Drugs

On a separate sheet of paper, write an office procedural plan for conducting a controlled drug inventory. The procedure should include the following information:

- How often the inventory is to be conducted
- Information you must have about each drug
- Where this information is obtained for Schedule II drugs
- Where this information is obtained for Schedules III, IV, and V drugs
- How the information for each drug is processed
- What records must be included in the inventory
- How the inventory is retained
- How long the inventory is retained

3. Charting Prescription Refills on a Progress Note

Read each of the cases below and chart the information on the progress note, example provided in the back of the workbook on page 973.

a. A patient calls in a refill for Lexapro 10 mg. She takes one tablet per day. Her pharmacy number is 216-444-0000. She states that she has no known drug allergies. She was authorized 4 refills.

b. The pharmacy calls for a refill for Mr. Smith. He would like his Ativan 1gr refilled. He has not been seen in the office in 6 months and the physician does not authorize the refill.

c. A patient calls to confirm the correct dosage and dosing schedule for her prescription of Zithromax that she received that morning.

d. A patient calls in a refill for Zocor 40 mg, one tablet per day. The physician authorized 3 refills.

CASE STUDIES

Write your response to each case study on the lines provided.

Case 1

You are interviewing a new patient who has arrived with her one-month-old child. The patient tells you that over-the-counter medication she has been taking for allergies does not seem to be working. She thinks she may need a prescription drug for her allergies. What are two important questions you should ask this patient in case the doctor prescribes medication?

_____

_____

_____

Case 2

Your workplace has been burglarized. Schedules III, IV, and V drugs were stolen. (Your workplace does not administer or dispense Schedule II drugs.) What should you do?

_____

_____

_____

Case 3

The physician has written a prescription for Achromycin, 250-mg capsules. After checking a drug reference, you find that Achromycin is a trade name for tetracycline HCl, a generic drug that is available in 250-mg capsules at a lower cost than Achromycin. Returning to the prescription, you note that the physician has failed to check the "Generic Equivalent OK" box on the prescription form. What do you do?

_____

_____

_____

CHAPTER **51**

Drug Administration

REVIEW

Vocabulary Review

Matching

Match the key terms in the right column with the definitions in the left column by placing the letter of each correct answer in the space provided.

_____ 1. Liquid used to dissolve and dilute a drug

_____ 2. Beneath the skin

_____ 3. The amount of space a drug occupies

_____ 4. A technique of IM injection that prevents a drug from leaking into the subcutaneous tissue and causing irritation

_____ 5. Between the cheek and gum

_____ 6. Within the upper layers of the skin

_____ 7. The way a drug is introduced into the body

_____ 8. Under the tongue

_____ 9. Slow drip

_____ 10. Salve

_____ 11. Through the skin

_____ 12. Vaginal irrigation

_____ 13. Within a muscle

_____ 14. A homogeneous mixture of a solid, liquid, or gaseous substance in a liquid

_____ 15. Directly into a vein

a. solution
b. intramuscular (IM)
c. Z-track method
d. buccal
e. intravenous (IV)
f. infusion
g. volume
h. intradermal (ID)
i. transdermal
j. douche
k. ointment
l. route
m. diluent
n. sublingual
o. subcutaneous (SC)

Content Review

Multiple Choice

In the space provided, write the letter of the choice that best completes each statement or answers each question.

_____ 1. A volume of 10 cubic centimeters is equal to

    A. 0.01 mL.

    B. 1.0 mL.

    C. 10 mL.

    D. 1000 mL.

    E. 0.001 mL.

2. Inhalation therapy can be administered through the nose or
   A. ear.
   B. eye.
   C. mouth.
   D. skin.

3. Which of the following forms of drugs is administered by a transdermal route?
   A. Capsule
   B. Pill
   C. Spray
   D. Patch
   E. Suppository

4. The office sharps container should be properly disposed of when it is
   A. one-third full.
   B. two-thirds full.
   C. almost full.
   D. full.

5. What information must you ask a patient every time before administering an injection?
   A. Blood pressure results
   B. Age
   C. Route preference
   D. Any known drug allergies
   E. Weight

6. What is the best site for administering an intramuscular injection for a pediatric patient?
   A. Deltoid
   B. Dorsogluteal
   C. Vastus lateralis
   D. Bicep

7. You are administering a sublingual medication. Which education statement would be correct?
   A. Place the medication between your cheek and gum until it dissolves.
   B. Place the medication under you tongue and then take a drink of water.
   C. Take a drink of water then swallow this pill with your second drink of water.
   D. Inhale the medication, holding your breath for 30 seconds after each inhalation.
   E. Place the medication under your tongue until it dissolves.

8. Why should you wear gloves during the administration of a transdermal patch?
   A. To prevent contamination of the patch
   B. To prevent the medication from getting on your skin
   C. To keep the patch sterile until it is administered
   D. To prevent infection

9. When administering eyedrops, how far should the bottle tip or dropper be away from the eye?
   A. 1 inch
   B. ¾ inch
   C. ½ inch
   D. ¼ inch
   E. It should touch the eye

_____ **10.** How should you hold a 4-year-old's ear when administering eardrops?

    A. Pull the ear upward and outward

    B. Pull the ear outward and downward

    C. Pull the ear down and back

    D. Pull the ear up and back

Sentence Completion

In the space provided, write the word or phrase that best completes each sentence.

11. Topical application is the direct application of a drug on the _____.

12. Drugs that produce systemic effects are administered by routes that allow the drugs to be absorbed and distributed in the _____ throughout the body.

13. Parenteral administration of a drug generally applies to giving drugs by _____.

14. The _____ of a needle is a measure of its inside diameter.

15. The inside diameter of a 23-gauge needle is _____ than the inside diameter of a needle with a lower gauge.

16. Skin tests are usually administered by _____ injection.

17. Physicians usually prescribe vaginal drugs to treat local bacterial or _____ infections.

18. Polypharmacy is common in _____.

11. _____

12. _____

13. _____

14. _____

15. _____

16. _____

17. _____

18. _____

Short Answer

Write the answer to each question on the lines provided.

19. To ensure accuracy, when should you read the label of a drug you are about to administer?

_____

_____

_____

20. Why do drugs that are administered buccally and sublingually produce therapeutic effects more quickly than do orally administered drugs?

_____

_____

_____

21. Why is the tip of an injection needle beveled?

_____

_____

_____

22. Why does parenteral administration of a drug pose more safety risks for patients than administration by other routes?

_____

_____

_____

23. Why do you inject aspirated air from the syringe into the vial of diluent when you are reconstituting a drug for injection?

_____

_____

_____

24. After cleansing the site of an intradermal injection with an alcohol swab, why should you let the skin dry before giving the injection?

_____

_____

_____

25. When administering a subcutaneous injection, why would you avoid an injection site that is hardened or fatty?

_____

_____

_____

26. What is the function of the small amount of air you draw into the syringe when you administer an intramuscular injection?

_____

_____

_____

27. How does a drug-drug interaction differ from the adverse effects of a drug?

_____

_____

_____

28. The illustration below shows a standard syringe. Write the name of each part of the instrument on the lines provided.

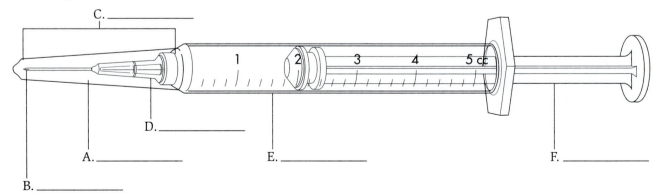

C. _____

D. _____

A. _____

B. _____

E. _____

F. _____

29. Why is it important to ask patients about drug allergies every time they come into the office?

_____

_____

_____

30. What is the purpose of a consent form when administering medications?

_____

_____

_____

31. What are some methods to ensure a smooth procedure when administering a pediatric injection?

_____

_____

_____

32. Why is the vastus lateralis the best site for administering an injection to a pediatric patient?

_____

_____

_____

33. What are some important aspects of accurate charting in a medical facility?

_____

_____

_____

34. What information is documented after giving an injection to a patient?

_____

_____

_____

35. On the figure below, label the type of injection that is being given based upon the location of the needle.

A. Intradermal (ID)

B. Subcutaneous (sub-Q) **C.** Intravenous (IV) **D.** Intramuscular (IM)

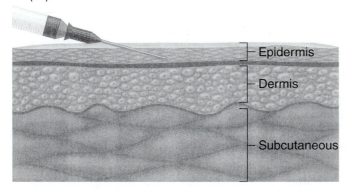

Epidermis

Dermis

Subcutaneous

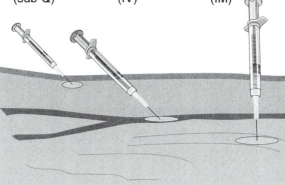

Critical Thinking

Write the answer to each question on the lines provided.

1. Why do you place a 2 × 2 gauze or cotton ball over the injection site when you withdraw the needle during an intramuscular or subcutaneous injection?

_____

_____

_____

2. The doctor has asked you to administer eye ointment and eyedrops to a patient. In what order should you administer the drugs to the patient? Why?

_____

_____

_____

3. When charting medications in the patient chart, why is it important to refrain from using statements such as "appears" or "seems like"?

_____

_____

_____

4. Why is it important to include the expiration date, lot number, and manufacturer when charting medications?

_____

_____

_____

APPLICATION

Follow the directions for each application.

1. Calculating Conversions

In the spaces provided, perform the necessary calculations for each conversion. Use a table of equivalents, if necessary.

a. 0.51 L = _____ mL

b. 75 mg = _____ g

c. 450 mL = _____ L

d. 0.205 mg = _____ µg

e. 15 gtt = _____ tsp   **f.** 500 mg = _____ g

g. 1 tsp = _____ mL   **h.** 0.125 mg = _____ mcg

2. Calculating Drug Doses

In the spaces provided, use the ratio or fraction method to calculate each of the following drug doses. For the purposes of this application, assume that the medication is being administered at the medical office on written orders from the doctor and is to be administered immediately.

a. For a patient with a urinary tract infection, the doctor orders Cotrim, 800 mg po. The stock container in your office is labeled Cotrim, sulfamethoxazole/trimethoprim, 400-mg tablets. How many tablets should you dispense to the patient?

b. The doctor orders ibuprofen, 600 mg po for a patient with back pain. The stock container of ibuprofen contains 400-mg scored tablets. How many tablets should you dispense to the patient?

c. The doctor orders dimenhydrinate liquid, 50 mg po. The stock container of the drug is labeled 12.5 mg dimenhydrinate/1 mL. What volume of the drug should you dispense to the patient?

d. The doctor orders Valium, 4 mg IM for a patient. The container label reads Valium (diazepam), 5 mg/1 mL. What volume of the drug should you prepare for the patient?

e. A patient is 5 years old and weighs 45 lb. The physician orders 225-mg Augmentin po Q8h. On hand you have Augmentin 125 mg/5 mL. The package insert states for pediatric patients ages 12 weeks and older, but less than 40 kg, the recommended dose is 40 mg/kg/day q8h.

　(i) Convert the weight to kilograms.

(ii) Determine if the dosage ordered is within the recommended amount.

(iii) If the dose is within the recommended amount, how much would you administer?

3. Demonstrating the Use of an Epinephrine Autoinjector

Work with two partners to demonstrate the use of the epinephrine autoinjector. One person can play the role of the patient, one should take the role of the medical assistant conducting the demonstration, and the third should act as an observer and evaluator.

a. The medical assistant should explain to the patient that because of his particular allergy, he might inadvertently be exposed to the allergen. Such an exposure could cause a severe allergic reaction, which is called anaphylaxis, or anaphylactic shock. Symptoms of anaphylaxis include flushing, a sharp drop in blood pressure, hives, difficulty breathing, difficulty swallowing, convulsions, vomiting, diarrhea, and abdominal cramps.

b. The medical assistant should explain that autoinjectors, which are prepackaged, deliver 0.3 mg of epinephrine (a single dose for an adult) or 0.15 mg of epinephrine (a single dose for a child).

c. The medical assistant should explain that the injector should be used if exposure to the allergen is confirmed or if exposure is suspected and signs of anaphylaxis appear.

d. The medical assistant should teach the patient to follow these steps when using the autoinjector.
  1. Remove the autoinjector from the packaging.
  2. Pull back the gray cap.
  3. Place the black tip of the injector on the outside of the upper thigh.
  4. Press firmly into the thigh and hold for 10 seconds.
  5. Remove the autoinjector and massage the injection site for a few minutes.
  6. Call the physician or go to the emergency room of a nearby hospital.

e. The patient should identify each part of the autoinjector and explain its use to the medical assistant.

f. The observer should present a critique of the medical assistant's role in the activity. The critique should involve the assistant's attitude, or approach, as well as the appropriateness and accuracy of the assistant's explanation and demonstration.

g. The medical assistant, the patient, and the observer should then discuss the observer's critique, noting the strengths and weaknesses of the assistant's explanations and demonstration.

h. Exchange roles and repeat the activity with another person perhaps acting as the caregiver of an elderly patient or a parent of a pediatric patient.

i. Exchange roles one final time so that each member of the team gets to play medical assistant, patient, and observer once.

4. Demonstrating Proper Medication Administration for Medications Given Orally, Sublingually, and Buccally

Using Procedure Checklists 51.1, Administering Oral Drugs, and 51.2, Administering Buccal or Sublingual Drugs, review and practice administering medications orally, sublingually, and buccally.

Use the following circumstances during your practice.

• Working with a partner, role-play giving the proper instructions for each type of medication.

• Chart the following medications as being administered in the sample progress note or medication flow sheet provided in the back of the workbook. Make certain your charting is complete, including the date, time, drug name, dosage, expiration date, lot number, manufacturer, route, site, significant patient reactions, and any patient education in the patient's chart. (To make the charting complete, create any information not provided below.)

- 650 mg acetaminophen PO

- Nitroglycerin gr 1/100 SL

- Methyltestosterone 10 mg buccal

5. Demonstrating Proper Medication Preparation for Medications Given by Injection

Using Procedure Checklists 51.3, Drawing a Drug from an Ampule, and 51.4, Reconstituting and Drawing a Drug for Injection, practice preparing medications for administration.

6. Demonstrating Proper Medication Administration for Medications Given by Injection

Using Procedure Checklists 51.5, Giving an Intradermal Injection; 51.6, Giving a Subcutaneous Injection; and 51.7, Giving an Intramuscular Injection, practice administering injections. Use the following circumstances during your practice.

- Working with a partner and a manikin, role-play giving the injections while providing the proper communication to the patient for each type of injection.

- Chart the following injections as being administered in the sample progress note or medication flow sheet provided. Make certain your charting is complete including the date, time, drug name, dosage, expiration date, lot number, manufacturer, route, site, significant patient reactions, and any patient education in the patient's chart. (To make the charting complete, create any information not provided below.)

- Tigan 200 milligram intramuscularly

- Humulin R 20 units subcutaneously

- Mantoux TB test intradermally

7. Demonstrating Proper Medication Administration for Medications Given by Various Routes

Using Procedure Checklists 51.8, Administering Inhalation Therapy; 51.9, Administering and Removing a Transdermal Patch and Providing Instruction; 51.10, Assisting with Administration of Urethral Drug; 51.11, Administering a Vaginal Medication; 51.12, Administering a Rectal Medication; 51.13, Administering Eye Medications; 51.14, Performing Eye Irrigation; 51.15, Administering Eardrops; and 51.16, Performing Ear Irrigation, practice administering medications of various routes. Use the following circumstances for your practice.

- Research names of medications that would be administered by the various routes using Procedures 51.8 through 51.16 or obtain medication names from your instructor.

- Working with a partner and the manikin, when necessary, role-play giving the proper instructions for each procedure performed. Take turns with a partner and review any steps in your instruction you have missed.

- Chart each medication you have researched and/or procedure performed in the sample progress note or medication flow sheet provided. Make certain your charting is complete by creating information based upon your practice session.

CASE STUDIES

Write your response to each case study on the lines provided.

Case 1

A patient received from the pharmacy a prescription for hyoscyamine sulfate tablets for buccal administration. She telephones the office and asks you if it would be all right to take the medication while having her second cup of coffee in the morning. What do you tell her? Why?

_____

_____

_____

Case 2

The physician has given a written order for the application of an ophthalmic drug for a patient. The drug is for local application and systemic absorption should be avoided. How do you prevent the systemic absorption of the drug when administering it?

_____

_____

_____

Case 3

Heparin 1.5 mL SC has been ordered for a patient. What volume syringe and needle (gauge and length) should you prepare?

_____

_____

_____

Case 4

The doctor has written an order for you to administer two 250-g tablets of Trimox (amoxicillin) to a patient who has an infection. The patient reluctantly takes the first tablet but spits out the second. What do you do?

_____

_____

_____

Case 5

You had just administered a drug to a child, and within five minutes the child vomited. Should you readminister the drug?

_____

_____

_____

Case 6

You are explaining the dosage instructions to a mother and the medication is ordered in tablet form. The mother tells you that the child has difficulty swallowing tablets. What should you do?

_____

_____

_____

CHAPTER 52

Electrocardiography and Pulmonary Function Testing

REVIEW

Vocabulary Review

Matching

Match the key terms in the right column with the definitions in the left column by placing the letter of each correct answer in the space provided.

_____ 1. The condition of having two separate poles, one of which is positive and the other negative

_____ 2. An electrical impulse that initiates a chain reaction, resulting in a contraction of the heart muscle

_____ 3. A period of electrical recovery during which polarity is restored

_____ 4. An instrument that measures and displays the electrical impulses responsible for the cardiac cycle

_____ 5. A wave recorded on an electrocardiogram that is produced by the electrical impulses responsible for the cardiac cycle

_____ 6. An erroneous mark or defect on an ECG tracing

_____ 7. An irregularity in heart rhythm

_____ 8. An instrument that measures the activity of the heart in a 24-hour period

_____ 9. The greatest volume of air that a person can expel when performing rapid, forced expiration

_____ 10. A standardized measuring instrument used to calibrate a spirometer

a. calibration syringe
b. forced vital capacity
c. Holter monitor
d. polarity
e. depolarization
f. arrhythmia
g. repolarization
h. artifact
i. electrocardiogram
j. deflection

True or False

Decide whether each statement is true or false. In the space at the left, write T for true or F for false. On the lines provided, rewrite the false statements to make them true.

_____ 11. Spirometry measures the air taken in by and expelled from the lungs.

_____

_____ 12. A spirometer or peak flow meter is used to measure breathing capacity.

_____

_____ 13. A heart attack is referred to as a myocardial infarction.

_____

_____ 14. A lead is attached to the patient's skin during electrocardiography.

_____

_____ 15. A pen-like instrument that records movement on ECG paper is called a stylus.

_____

_____ 16. An instrument that measures and displays the electrical impulses responsible for the cardiac cycle is referred to as an electrocardiography.

_____

_____ 17. An electrolyte is a substance that decreases transmission of electrical impulses.

_____

_____ 18. The atrioventricular node is a mass of specialized conducting cells located at the bottom of the right atrium that delays transmission of electrical impulses so the atria can completely contract.

_____

_____ 19. The bundle of His is an area of specialized conductive tissue in the heart that sends impulses through a series of bundle branches.

_____

_____ 20. The sequence of contraction and relaxation is referred to as a pulmonary cycle.

_____

_____ 21. A procedure that measures and evaluates a patient's lung capacity and volume is referred to as a pulmonary function test.

_____

_____ 22. The process by which a graphic pattern is created from the electrical impulses generated within the heart as it pumps is called repolarization.

_____

Content Review

Multiple Choice

In the space provided, write the letter of the choice that best completes each statement or answers each question.

_____ 1. When performing routine electrocardiography, you place electrodes on the
   A. right arm, left arm, right leg, left leg, and six on the chest.
   B. right arm, left arm, right temple, left temple, and six on the chest.
   C. right arm, right leg, and five on the chest.
   D. right arm, left arm, and one on the chest, which is moved to six different positions.

_____ 2. Augmented leads monitor
   A. bipolar leads.
   B. one electrode and a point within the heart.
   C. one limb electrode and a point midway between two other limb electrodes.
   D. electrical activity between two limb electrodes.

_____ 3. A flat line on the ECG tracing of one of the leads is typically caused by

    A. switching two of the wires.

    B. a loose or disconnected wire.

    C. a loose or disconnected patient cable.

    D. cardiac arrest.

    E. None of the above.

_____ 4. A patient who is to wear a Holter monitor should be instructed

    A. to take baths rather than showers.

    B. to avoid excessive or unusual exercise.

    C. in how to remove the electrodes before going to bed and how to replace them in the morning.

    D. to keep a written record of activities, emotional upsets, physical symptoms, and medications.

_____ 5. When administering spirometry,

    A. emergency resuscitation equipment should always be in the room.

    B. explain the procedure, but once the test begins, avoid coaching patients on their performance.

    C. position the patient with the chin slightly elevated and the neck slightly extended.

    D. position the patient with the chin bent slightly toward the chest and the back straight.

_____ 6. Electrocardiography records the transmission, _____, and duration of the various electrical impulses of the heart.

    A. heart rate

    B. magnitude

    C. amplification

    D. blood pressure

    E. Strength

_____ 7. A single-channel electrocardiograph records the electrical activity of one lead, whereas a(n) _____ electrocardiograph records more than one lead at a time.

    A. deflection

    B. pulse oximeter

    C. multichannel

    D. electronic

    E. rhythm strip

_____ 8. To ensure the conductivity of electrical impulses from the skin, you must apply _____ to each electrode before placing it on the patient's body.

    A. alcohol

    B. soap and water

    C. talcum powder

    D. lotion

    E. an electrolyte

_____ 9. On an electrocardiograph, the _____ is used to adjust the position of the stylus.

    A. sensitivity selector

    B. amplifier

    C. centering control

    D. default switch

    E. interpretative mode

_____ 10. Exercise electrocardiography typically continues until the patient reaches a(n) _____, has chest pain or fatigue, or develops complications.
   A. arrhythmia
   B. target heart rate
   C. personal best peak expiratory flow rate
   D. exhaustion rate

_____ 11. Why is it important for a medical assistant to recognize abnormal heart rhythms?
   A. To effectively triage a medical emergency
   B. To alert the physician or nurse that the patient has an irregular ECG
   C. To take control of the medical emergency
   D. Both A and B
   E. Both A and C

_____ 12. The cardiac arrhythmia that resembles a "saw tooth" is
   A. a bundle branch block.
   B. ventricular fibrillation.
   C. atrial fibrillation.
   D. bradycardia.

_____ 13. The green zone on the peak flow zone chart indicates
   A. good asthma control.
   B. that airways are beginning to narrow.
   C. that airways are constricted.
   D. low oxygen saturation.

_____ 14. Patient symptoms that include wheezing, shortness of breath, and difficulty talking and/or walking indicate patients in the _____ zone.
   A. green
   B. red
   C. yellow
   D. black
   E. safe

_____ 15. The noninvasive procedure that measures oxygen saturation in blood is
   A. peak flow.
   B. arterial blood gasses.
   C. pulse oximetry.
   D. ECG.
   E. forced vital capacity.

Short Answer

Write the answer to each question on the lines provided.

16. Briefly describe the heart's process of conduction.

_____

_____

_____

17. Examine the following ECG tracings. Then follow the directions.

   a. Circle and label the QRS complex on part A.

   b. Label the R wave on part A.

   c. Label the T wave on part A.

   d. Label the P wave on part A.

   e. On part B, draw lines and label the tracing to show when atrial relaxation occurs.

   f. On part B, draw an arrow and label the tracing to show when atrial contraction takes place.

   g. On part B, draw an arrow and label the tracing to show when repolarization takes place.

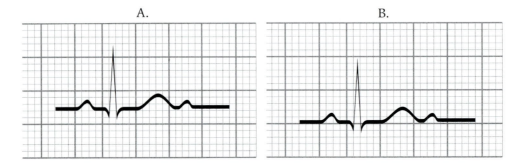

A.   B.

18. Review the abnormal ECG tracings and label each cardiac arrhythmia.

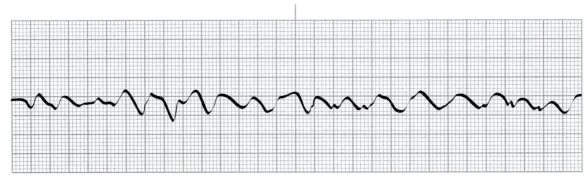

Source: From Shade, B., Wesley, K. Fast and Easy, *ECGs: A Self-Paced Learning Program,* pp. 344, Fig. 11.17.
Copyright 2007 by The McGraw-Hill Companies.

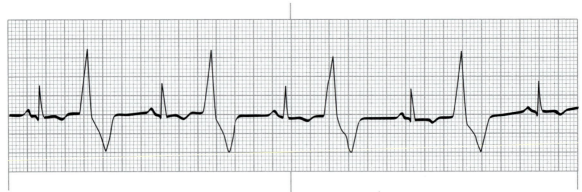

Source: From Shade, B., Wesley, K. Fast and Easy, *ECGs: A Self-Paced Learning Program,* pp. 333, Fig. 11.6a.
Copyright 2007 by The McGraw-Hill Companies.

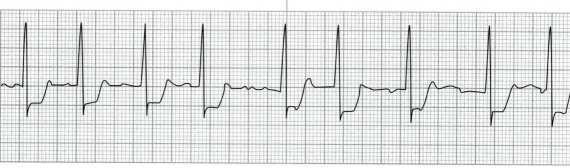

Source: From Shade, B., Wesley, K. Fast and Easy, *ECGs: A Self-Paced Learning Program*, pp. 226, Fig. 7.12. Copyright 2007 by The McGraw-Hill Companies.

19. What are four possible causes of mechanical problems that can result in a wandering baseline?

_____

_____

_____

20. How do muscles cause somatic interference that shows up as artifacts on ECG tracings?

_____

_____

_____

21. How can the heart rate be determined from an ECG?

_____

_____

_____

22. List three conditions in which a bundle branch block would appear on an ECG.

_____

_____

_____

23. What safety precautions must be taken when administering a stress test?

_____

_____

_____

24. What are four conditions and activities that can affect the outcome of a spirometry test?

_____

_____

_____

25. An acceptable maneuver on a spirometer must have what five features?

_____

_____

_____

26. Describe what occurs during a premature ventricular contraction.

_____

_____

27. Describe one treatment method that can correct ventricular defibrillation.

_____

_____

28. List three causes of atrial fibrillation.

_____

_____

29. What should a patient do if his or her peak expiratory flow is in the red zone?

_____

_____

30. What is the normal range for the peak expiratory flow rate?

_____

_____

Critical Thinking

Write the answer to each question on the lines provided.

1. What may happen if you fail to allow the electrocardiograph to warm up properly?

_____

_____

2. Why might a physician order a series of ECGs for a patient after he has changed her medication?

_____

_____

3. In what situation might it be better to position the electrodes on the upper arms and the thighs rather than lower on the arms and legs?

_____

_____

4. A patient has complained of periodic arrhythmias, but repeated ECGs have not shown any evidence of them. Why might the doctor order a Holter monitor to be used by the patient?

_____

_____

_____

5. What is the purpose of coaching the patient to improve performance during spirometry?

_____

_____

_____

6. Why is averaging the readings of the peak expiratory flow rate not recommended?

_____

_____

_____

7. While observing a pulse oximetry, you notice the reading states 89%. What should you do and why?

_____

_____

_____

APPLICATION

Follow the directions for the application.

Preparing a Patient for Electrocardiography

Working with two partners, prepare a patient for electrocardiography. One partner should play the role of the patient, one should take the role of the medical assistant preparing the patient for the procedure, and the third should act as an observer and evaluator. The patient is elderly and is anxious about the procedure.

a. The medical assistant should introduce herself and explain the procedure to the patient. The patient should ask questions and express concerns about what will happen and what he will experience. The medical assistant should answer all questions to the best of her ability and provide help in allaying the patient's anxieties.

b. The medical assistant should help the patient get into position for the procedure, helping him find the position that is most comfortable.

c. Following the preparation, the observer should critique what the medical assistant did. The critique should include the assistant's skill in communicating with the patient, the accuracy of her descriptions of the procedure, her responses to the patient's questions, how well the medical assistant succeeded in allaying the patient's concerns, and the effectiveness of the assistant's positioning of the patient.

d. As a team, discuss the observer's critique, noting the strengths and weaknesses of preparation of the patient for the procedure.

e. Exchange roles and repeat the preparation for another procedure, such as spirometry, peak flow, or providing a patient with a Holter monitor. The new observer should choose the type of procedure.

f. Exchange roles one final time so that each team member plays all three roles once.

CASE STUDIES

Write your response to each case study on the lines provided.

Case 1

After completing an ECG on a patient, you examine the tracing and find the wave peaks are very low, making it difficult to clearly read the tracing. What should you do?

_____

_____

_____

Case 2

While performing an ECG on a 55-year-old female patient, you note that all of the limb electrodes are coming off. What might cause the electrodes to come off of the patient's arms and legs? What action should you take?

_____

_____

_____

Case 3

Sam Smith is recovering from a heart attack. While you are preparing him for a stress test to determine how his heart is functioning, Mr. Smith expresses his fears. He is afraid the test will cause another heart attack. What do you tell him?

_____

_____

_____

Case 4

You are administering spirometry to a patient. She has been very cooperative but is having difficulty achieving the three acceptable maneuvers that are required. After several attempts, she complains of dizziness. You check her pulse and blood pressure and find that both are significantly elevated. What should you do?

_____

_____

_____

Case 5

You are working in an outpatient surgical clinic in the preoperative holding area. Each patient is monitored with a pulse oximeter. You check Mrs. O'Shaughnessy's fingers and notice that they are cold to the touch and have poor blood return. What should you do?

_____

_____

_____

CHAPTER 53

X-Rays and Diagnostic Radiology

REVIEW

Vocabulary Review

Matching

Match the key terms in the right column with the definitions in the left column by placing the letter of each correct answer in the space provided.

_____ 1. A type of x-ray developed with a powder toner, similar to the toner in photocopiers

_____ 2. A type of radiation therapy that allows deep penetration of tissue to treat deep tumors

_____ 3. The use of radionuclides or radioisotopes to evaluate the bone, brain, lungs, kidneys, liver, pancreas, thyroid, or spleen

_____ 4. A nuclear medicine procedure used to locate and determine the extent of brain damage from a stroke

_____ 5. An x-ray exam of the internal breast tissues

_____ 6. An x-ray of the abdomen used to assess the urinary organs, evaluate urinary system diseases or disorders, and detect kidney stones

_____ 7. A series of x-rays taken while a contrast medium travels through the kidneys, ureters, and bladder

_____ 8. A type of radiation therapy that uses radioactive implants close to or directly into cancerous tissue to treat the tumor

_____ 9. A test used to detect gallstones and other abnormalities of the gallbladder

_____ 10. An x-ray procedure in which barium sulfate is instilled through the anus into the rectum and then into the colon to help diagnose abnormalities of the colon or rectum

_____ 11. An invasive procedure that requires the insertion of a catheter, wire, or other testing device into a patient's blood vessel to obtain an image of the vessel

_____ 12. The use of x-ray technology for diagnostic purposes

_____ 13. The use of x-ray technology to identify a disease or a medical condition

a. angiography
b. barium enema
c. brachytherapy
d. cholecystography
e. diagnostic radiology
f. intravenous pyelogram
g. diagnostic radiology
h. KUB radiography
i. mammography
j. nuclear medicine
k. SPECT
l. teletherapy
m. xeroradiography

True or False

Decide whether each statement is true or false. In the space at the left, write T for true or F for false. On the lines provided, rewrite the false statements to make them true.

_____ **14.** A contrast medium makes internal organs denser and blocks the passage of x-rays to the photographic film.

_____

_____ **15.** Standard x-rays and ultrasound, which do not require inserting devices or breaking the skin, are types of invasive procedures.

_____

_____ **16.** A MUGA scan is a type of nuclear medicine test used to evaluate the condition of the heart's myocardium.

_____

_____ **17.** For patients with poor kidney function, doctors often use an IVP to evaluate the function of the ureters, bladder, and urethra.

_____

_____ **18.** Myelography is a type of fluoroscopy of the abdomen.

_____

_____ **19.** A dosimeter is a radiation exposure badge that contains a sensitized piece of film.

_____

_____ **20.** In PET, special isotopes emit positrons, which are processed by computer and viewed to diagnose brain-related conditions.

_____

_____ **21.** In ultrasound, low-frequency sound waves directed through the skin produce echoes that are converted by computer into an image on a screen.

_____

_____ **22.** 4-D ultrasound provides live-action images for observation of fetal movement.

_____

_____ **23.** Radiation therapy is used to treat cancer by promoting cellular reproduction.

_____

_____ **24.** A roentgen ray is another name for an x-ray.

_____

_____ **25.** Hysterosalpingography is a radiological exam of a vagina.

_____

Content Review

Multiple Choice

In the space provided, write the letter of the choice that best completes each statement or answers each question.

_____ 1. An x-ray is a type of electromagnetic wave that has a
  A. low energy level and an extremely long wavelength.
  B. low energy level and an extremely short wavelength.
  C. high energy level and an extremely short wavelength.
  D. high energy level and an extremely long wavelength.

_____ 2. A test that utilizes a contrast medium and fluoroscopy to help diagnose abnormalities or injuries in the cartilage, tendons, or ligaments of the joints is called
  A. arthrography.
  B. cholangiography.
  C. thermography.
  D. xeroradiography.

_____ 3. Which of the following duties in connection with diagnostic radiology are medical assistants most likely to perform?
  A. Operating x-ray equipment
  B. Assisting a radiologist with x-ray procedures
  C. Assisting a radiologic technologist with x-ray procedures
  D. Providing preprocedure and postprocedure patient care

_____ 4. Angiography requires insertion of a catheter into a patient's
  A. knee or shoulder.
  B. pancreatic duct.
  C. urethra.
  D. common bile duct.
  E. blood vessel.

_____ 5. During which of the following procedures does the patient eat a specially prepared fatty meal?
  A. Cholecystography
  B. Cholangiography
  C. A barium swallow
  D. An intravenous pyelogram
  E. MUGA scan

_____ 6. The test that uses nonionizing radiation and a strong magnetic field is known as
  A. SPECT.
  B. CT.
  C. PET.
  D. MRI.

_____ 7. Myelography is a fluoroscopic exam of the
  A. heart.
  B. spinal cord.
  C. bone marrow.
  D. gallbladder.
  E. liver.

_____ **8.** The digital storage area where digital images are sent and stored for diagnostic viewing and electronic image storage and distribution is known as

    A. DICOM.

    B. IHE.

    C. PAC.

    D. EHR.

_____ **9.** Stereotaxis is an example of

    A. magnetic resonance imaging.

    B. nuclear medicine.

    C. stereoscopy.

    D. telemedicine technology.

    E. echocardiography.

Sentence Completion

In the space provided, write the word or phrase that best completes each sentence.

10. _____ is a type of ultrasound test used to study the structure and function of the heart.

11. Before an MRI, it is important to determine whether the patient has any internal _____ materials.

12. In a double-contrast barium enema, _____ is forced into the colon to distend the tissue.

13. During an IVP, a radiologist injects a contrast medium into a patient's _____.

14. A test used to help diagnose and evaluate obstructions, ulcers, polyps, diverticulosis, tumors, or motility problems of the esophagus, stomach, duodenum, and small intestine is a _____ swallow.

15. Tumors or inflammations show up lighter on thermographic photographs because they produce more _____ than healthy tissues.

16. The _____ dense areas of an x-ray are the lightest on the film.

17. Annual mammograms are recommended for women after age _____.

10. _____

11. _____

12. _____

13. _____

14. _____

15. _____

16. _____

17. _____

Short Answer

Write the answer to each question on the lines provided.

18. What are four general duties that medical assistants may perform for patients who will undergo radiologic testing?

_____

_____

_____

19. Why are contrast media used in some diagnostic radiologic tests? List three ways that contrast media can be administered.

_____

_____

_____

20. Describe the mechanics of the diagnostic procedure fluoroscopy.

_____

_____

_____

21. Why do some radiologic diagnostic procedures require patients to be admitted to a hospital or same-day surgical facility? Give one example of such a procedure.

_____

_____

_____

22. How are conventional tomography and computed tomography similar? How are they different?

_____

_____

_____

23. Describe three ways for medical assistants to protect themselves against excessive radiation exposure.

_____

_____

_____

24. What four items of information about a patient's x-rays should be documented in the patient report card or record book?

_____

_____

_____

25. How might a cardiologist use electronic medicine to monitor a patient from afar?

_____

_____

_____

26. For what conditions do radiologists assess when performing a hysterosalpingography?

_____

_____

_____

27. What is the difference between PAC and DICOM?

_____

_____

_____

28. Define DICOM and explain how it applies to digital radiology.

_____

_____

_____

Critical Thinking

Write the answer to each question on the lines provided.

1. Why is it important to take an x-ray only within 10 days of the last menstrual period for women of childbearing age?

_____

_____

_____

2. How might a patient undergoing an invasive radiologic diagnostic procedure be at greater risk than a patient undergoing a noninvasive procedure?

_____

_____

_____

3. Why is preprocedure care especially important for patients who are scheduled to undergo an MRI?

_____

_____

_____

4. Why is it important for the patient to remain still during an x-ray exam?

_____

_____

_____

5. How could a radiologist use electronic medicine to interpret and report on a tomogram produced in another country?

_____

_____

_____

6. Why is it important to ask a patient if they have had a previous mammogram when assisting a patient with setting up an appointment for a mammogram?

_____

_____

_____

APPLICATION

Follow the directions for each application.

1. Preparing a Patient for a Radiologic Diagnostic Test

Work with two partners. One student should take the role of a patient scheduled for a radiologic diagnostic procedure in a few days. The second student should assume the role of medical assistant in a radiology facility or medical office. The third student should act as an observer and evaluator.

a. Choose one of the following procedures: arthrography, barium enema, barium swallow, cholecystography, CT scan with contrast medium, or IVP. Review the description of the chosen procedure and the preprocedure care steps.

b. The medical assistant should schedule a time for the procedure with the patient, taking into account such factors as whether the patient's digestive tract must be empty and whether the patient will want to sleep through the procedure to avoid experiencing hunger.

c. The medical assistant should describe the procedure to the patient according to the guidelines presented in the student textbook. The patient should ask questions about the procedure, which the medical assistant should answer clearly and completely.

d. The medical assistant should explain the preparation instructions. The patient should ask questions about the instructions. The medical assistant may want to have the patient repeat the instructions to ensure understanding of them.

e. After the instructions have been given and the patient's questions have been answered, the observer should provide a critique of the medical assistant's preprocedure care. Comments should include positive feedback and suggestions for improvement.

f. Change roles and repeat the exercise, using a different diagnostic test. Then change roles again so that each student has a turn at each role and all students become familiar with various procedures for different tests.

2. Develop an office policy and procedure plan for the proper storage and handling of x-ray film. Present your plan to the class.

CASE STUDIES

Write your response to each case study on the lines provided.

Case 1

A patient arrives in the office for a diagnostic test that will involve the use of a contrast medium that contains iodine. In your preprocedure interview with the patient a week ago, she reported no known allergies to iodine or shellfish. As you are preparing the patient for the procedure, she informs you that 2 days ago, after eating boiled shrimp at a party, she awoke in the middle of the night with nausea and joint pain. She says these symptoms subsided after 24 hours. You suspect the woman had a mild case of food poisoning from eating the shrimp. What should you do and why?

_____

_____

_____

Case 2

An elderly patient has just been examined by the physician, who has momentarily stepped out of the exam room. You are in the room with the patient and his son. The patient has just learned that he must undergo a barium enema in 2 days. When he asks you to explain this procedure, his son tells him that he is better off not knowing because it will only make him anxious. What, if anything, do you say to the patient?

_____

_____

_____

Case 3

A patient's mammogram indicates a small nodule in one breast. Without further testing, the physician cannot know whether the nodule is benign or malignant. He asks you to call the patient to schedule an ultrasound exam of the breast. When you call the patient to make the appointment, she tells you that she has never had an ultrasound and fears additional exposure to radiation. What can you say to the patient to reassure her?

_____

_____

_____

Case 4

You are interviewing a patient before his cholecystography procedure. When you ask if he was able to take the contrast media tablets the night before, he states that he did take them, but he thinks he might have dropped one of the pills. What should you do?

_____

_____

_____

CHAPTER 54

Medical Assisting Externships and Preparing to Find a Position

REVIEW

Vocabulary Review

Matching

Match the key terms in the right column with the definitions in the left column by placing the letter of each correct answer in the space provided.

_____	**1.** A résumé format that is used when an individual does not have relevant job experience	**a.** affiliation agreement
_____	**2.** The person who organizes and assigns your externship	**b.** chronological résumé
_____	**3.** A document that outlines the expectations of the academic institution and the medical facility	**c.** clinical coordinator
		d. constructive criticism
_____	**4.** A résumé that highlights specialty areas of accomplishments and strengths	**e.** functional résumé
		f. networking
_____	**5.** A résumé for individuals who have a strong work history	**g.** portfolio
_____	**6.** Making contacts with relatives, friends, and acquaintances that may have information about how to find a job in your field	**h.** reference
		i. targeted résumé
_____	**7.** A type of critique that is aimed at giving an individual feedback about his or her performance in order to improve	
_____	**8.** A recommendation for employment from a clinical preceptor or medical facility	
_____	**9.** A collection of an applicant's résumé, reference letter, and other documents of interest to show to a potential employer	

Content Review

Sentence Completion

In the space provided, write the word or phrase that best completes each sentence.

1. A(n) _____ is the opportunity to work within a medical facility to gain the on-the-job training that is essential for beginning your new career.

2. Educational institutions in which externships are mandatory are accredited by _____ and _____.

3. The minimum number of hours required for externship by an accredited institution is _____.

1. _____

2. _____

3. _____

4. _____ should be turned off during working hours.

5. Medical assisting extern students are expected to report to the facility _____ they are assigned.

6. Medical facilities expect the extern student to appear as a _____.

7. Accepting all assignments with enthusiasm and looking for extra work when idle is an example of showing _____.

4. _____

5. _____

6. _____

7. _____

Short Answer

Write the answer to each question on the lines provided.

8. What are three job options you might use to learn about open positions in your field?

_____

_____

_____

9. Describe how to prepare for an interview.

_____

_____

_____

10. What types of questions are you not required to answer at a job interview?

_____

_____

_____

11. What is expected of a medical assisting extern student at a medical facility?

_____

_____

_____

12. How does being an extern differ from being a medical assisting student?

_____

_____

_____

13. Name five reasons an employer would not hire a job candidate.

_____

_____

_____

14. What types of documents should be in a portfolio?

_____

_____

_____

PROCEDURE 4-1 COMMUNICATING WITH THE ANXIOUS PATIENT

Procedure Goal

To use communication and interpersonal skills to calm an anxious patient

Scoring System

To score each step, use the following scoring system:
1 = poor, 2 = fair, 3 = good, 4 = excellent

A minimum score of at least a 3 must be achieved on **each** step to achieve successful completion of the technique. Detailed instructions on the scoring system are found on page 413.

Materials

None

Procedure

Procedure Steps Total Possible Points - 44 Time Limit: 10 minutes	Practice #1	Practice #2	Practice #3	Final
1. Identify signs of anxiety in the patient.				
2. Acknowledge the patient's anxiety. (Ignoring a patient's anxiety often makes it worse.)*				
3. Identify possible sources of anxiety, such as fear of a procedure or test result, along with supportive resources available to the patient, such as family members and friends. Understanding the source of anxiety in a patient and identifying the supportive resources available can help you communicate with the patient more effectively.				
4. Do what you can to alleviate the patient's physical discomfort. For example, find a calm, quiet place for the patient to wait, a comfortable chair, a drink of water, or access to the bathroom.				
5. Allow ample personal space for conversation. Note: You would normally allow a 1½- to 4-ft distance between yourself and the patient. Adjust this space as necessary.				
6. Create a climate of warmth, acceptance, and trust. a. Recognize and control your own anxiety. Your air of calm can decrease the patient's anxiety. b. Provide reassurance by demonstrating genuine care, respect, and empathy. c. Act confidently and dependably, maintaining truthfulness and confidentiality at all times.				
7. Using the appropriate communication skills, have the patient describe the experience that is causing anxiety, her thoughts about it, and her feelings. Proceeding in this order				

(continued)

Procedure Steps Total Possible Points - 44 Time Limit: 10 minutes	Practice #1	Practice #2	Practice #3	Final
allows the patient to describe what is causing the anxiety and to clarify her thoughts and feelings about it.* a. Maintain an open posture. b. Maintain eye contact, if culturally appropriate. c. Use active listening skills. d. Listen without interrupting.				
8. Do not belittle the patient's thoughts and feelings. This can cause a breakdown in communication, increase anxiety, and make the patient feel isolated.				
9. Be empathic to the patient's concerns.				
10. Help the patient recognize and cope with the anxiety. a. Provide information to the patient. Patients are often fearful of the unknown. Helping them understand their disease or the procedure they are about to undergo will help decrease their anxiety. b. Suggest coping behaviors, such as deep breathing or other relaxation exercises.				
11. Notify the doctor of the patient's concerns.*				
Total Number of Points Achieved/Final Score				
Initials of Observer:				

Comments and Signatures

Reviewer's comments and signatures:

1. _____

2. _____

3. _____

Instructor's comments:

_____

CAAHEP Competencies Achieved

IV. C (3) Recognize communication barriers

IV. C (4) Identify techniques for overcoming communication barriers

IV. A (2) Apply listening skills

ABHES Competencies Achieved

5. (a) Define and understand abnormal behavior patterns

5. (b) Identify and respond appropriately when working/caring for patients with special needs

8. (ee) Communicate on the recipient's level of comprehension

8. (ii) Recognize and respond to verbal and non-verbal communication

PROCEDURE 4-2 IDENTIFYING COMMUNITY RESOURCES

Procedure Goal

To create a list of useful community resources for patient referrals

Scoring System

To score each step, use the following scoring system:
1 = poor, 2 = fair, 3 = good, 4 = excellent

A minimum score of at least a 3 must be achieved on **each** step to achieve successful completion of the technique. Detailed instructions on the scoring system are found on page 413.

Materials

Computer with Internet access, phone directory, printer

Procedure

Procedure Steps Total Possible Points - 24 Time Limit: 20 minutes	Practice #1	Practice #2	Practice #3	Final
1. Determine the needs of your medical office and formulate a list of community resources.*				
2. Use the Internet to research the names, addresses, and phone numbers of local resources such as Meals on Wheels, state and federal agencies, home health-care agencies, long-term nursing facilities, mental health agencies, and local charities. Use the phone directory to assist in locating local agencies as well.				
3. Contact each resource and request information such as business cards and brochures. Some agencies may send a representative to meet with you regarding their services.*				
4. Compile a list of community resources with the proper name, address, phone number, e-mail address, and contact name. Include any information that may be helpful to the office.				
5. Update and add to the information often because outdated information will only frustrate you and your patients, creating even more anxiety.				
6. Post the information in a location where it is readily available.				
Total Number of Points Achieved/Final Score				
Initials of Observer:				

(continued)

Comments and Signatures

Reviewer's comments and signatures:

1. _____

2. _____

3. _____

Instructor's comments:

_____

CAAHEP Competencies Achieved

IV. P (12) Develop and maintain a current list of community resources related to patient's health-care needs

XI. P (12) Maintain a current list of community resources for emergency preparedness

ABHES Competencies Achieved

8. (dd) Serve as a liaison between physician and others

11-a. (5) Exhibit initiative

PROCEDURE 5-1 USING A FACSIMILE (FAX) MACHINE

Procedure Goal

To correctly prepare and send a fax document while following all HIPAA guidelines to guard patient confidentiality

Scoring System

To score each step, use the following scoring system:
1 = poor, 2 = fair, 3 = good, 4 = excellent

A minimum score of at least a 3 must be achieved on **each** step to achieve successful completion of the technique. Detailed instructions on the scoring system are found on page 413.

Materials

Fax machine, fax line, cover sheet with statement of disclaimer, area code and phone number of fax recipient, document to be faxed, telephone line, and telephone

Procedure

Procedure Steps Total Possible Points - 48 Time Limit: 10 minutes	Practice #1	Practice #2	Practice #3	Final
1. Prepare a cover sheet, which provides information about the transmission. Cover sheets can vary in appearance but usually include the name, telephone number, and fax number of the sender and the receiver; the number of pages being transmitted; and the date of the transmission. Preprinted cover sheets can be used.*				
2. All cover sheets must carry a statement of disclaimer to guard the privacy of the patient. A **disclaimer** is a statement of denial of legal liability. A disclaimer should be included on the cover sheet and may read something like the following: *This fax contains confidential or proprietary information that may be legally privileged. It is intended only for the named recipient(s). If an addressing or transmission error has misdirected the fax, please notify the author by replying to this message. If you are not the named recipient, you are not authorized to use, disclose, distribute, copy, print, or rely on this fax and should immediately shred it.**				
3. Place all pages of the document, including the cover sheet, either facedown or faceup in the fax machine's sending tray, depending on the directions stamped on the sending tray.				
4. If the documents are placed facedown, write the area code and fax number on the back of the last page.				
5. Dial the telephone number of the receiving fax machine, using either the telephone attached to the fax machine or the numbers on the fax keyboard. Include the area code for long-distance calls.				

(continued)

Procedure Steps Total Possible Points - 48 Time Limit: 10 minutes	Practice #1	Practice #2	Practice #3	Final
6. When using a fax telephone, listen for a high-pitched tone. Then press the "Send" or "Start" button and hang up the telephone. This step completes the call circuit in older-model fax machines. Your fax is now being sent. Newer fax machines do not require this step.*				
7. If you use the fax keyboard, press the "Send" or "Start" button after dialing the telephone number. This button will start the call.				
8. Watch for the fax machine to make a connection. Often a green light appears as the document feeds through the machine.				
9. If the fax machine is not able to make a connection, as when the receiving fax line is busy, it may have a feature that automatically redials the number every few minutes for a specified number of attempts.				
10. When a fax has been successfully sent, most fax machines print a confirmation message. When a fax has not been sent, the machine either prints an error message or indicates on the screen that the transmission was unsuccessful.*				
11. Attach the confirmation or error message to the documents faxed. File appropriately.*				
12. The sender may call the recipient to confirm that the fax was received.				
Total Number of Points Achieved/Final Score				
Initials of Observer:				

Comments and Signatures

Reviewer's comments and signatures:

1. _____

2. _____

3. _____

Instructor's comments:

_____

CAAHEP Competency Achieved

IX. C (2) Explore issues of confidentiality as they apply to the medical assistant

ABHES Competencies Achieved

7. (b) Identify and properly utilize office machines, computerized systems and medical software

11. (3) Demonstrate professionalism by maintaining confidentiality at all times

PROCEDURE 5-2 USING A PHOTOCOPIER MACHINE

Procedure Goal

To produce copies of documents

Scoring System

To score each step, use the following scoring system:
1 = poor, 2 = fair, 3 = good, 4 = excellent

A minimum score of at least a 3 must be achieved on **each** step to achieve successful completion of the technique. Detailed instructions on the scoring system are found on page 413.

Materials

Copier machine, copy paper, documents to be copied

Procedure

Procedure Steps Total Possible Points - 28 Time Limit: 5 minutes	Practice #1	Practice #2	Practice #3	Final
1. Make sure the machine is turned on and warmed up. It will display a signal when it is ready for copying.				
2. Assemble and prepare your materials, removing paper clips, staples, and self-adhesive flags.*				
3. Place the document to be copied in the automatic feeder tray as directed, or upside down directly on the glass. The feeder tray can accommodate many pages; you may place only one page at a time on the glass. Automatic feeding is a faster process, and you should use it when you wish to collate or staple packets. Page-by-page copying is best if you need to copy a single sheet or to enlarge or reduce the image. To use any special features, such as making double-sided copies or stapling the copies, press a designated button on the machine.				
4. Set the machine for the desired paper size.*				
5. Key in the number of copies you want to make, and press the "Start" button. The copies are made automatically.				
6. Press the "Clear" or "Reset" button when your job is finished.*				
7. If the copier becomes jammed, follow the directions on the machine to locate the problem (for example, there may be multiple pieces of paper stuck inside the printer) and dislodge the jammed paper. Most copy machines will show a diagram of the printer and the location of the problem.				
Total Number of Points Achieved/Final Score				
Initials of Observer:				

(continued)

Comments and Signatures

Reviewer's comments and signatures:

1. _____

2. _____

3. _____

Instructor's comments:

_____

CAAHEP Competency Achieved

IV. P (4) Explain general office policies

ABHES Competencies Achieved

7. (b) Identify and properly utilize office machines, computerized systems and medical software

11-a. (3) Demonstrate professionalism by maintaining confidentiality at all times

PROCEDURE 5-3 USING A POSTAGE METER

Procedure Goal

To correctly apply postage to an envelope or package for mailing, according to U.S. Postal Service guidelines

Materials

Postage meter, addressed envelope or package, postal scale

Scoring System

To score each step, use the following scoring system:
1 = poor, 2 = fair, 3 = good, 4 = excellent

A minimum score of at least a 3 must be achieved on **each** step to achieve successful completion of the technique. Detailed instructions on the scoring system are found on page 413.

Procedure

Procedure Steps Total Possible Points - 40 Time Limit: 10 minutes	Practice #1	Practice #2	Practice #3	Final
1. Check that there is postage available in the postage meter.*				
2. Verify the day's date.*				
3. Check that the postage meter is plugged in and switched on before you proceed.				
4. Locate the area where the meter registers the date. Many machines have a lid that can be flipped up, with rows of numbers underneath. Months are represented numerically, with the number "1" indicating the month of January, "2" indicating February, and so on. Check that the date is correct. If it is incorrect, change the numbers to the correct date.				
5. Make sure that all materials have been included in the envelope or package. Weigh the envelope or package on a postal scale. Standard business envelopes weighing up to 1 oz require the minimum postage (the equivalent of one first-class stamp). Oversize envelopes and packages require additional postage. A postal scale will indicate the amount of postage required.				
6. Key in the postage amount on the meter and press the button that enters the amount. For amounts over $1, press the "$" sign or the "Enter" button twice.*				
7. Check that the amount you typed is the correct amount. Envelopes and packages with too little postage will be returned by the U.S. Postal Service. Sending an envelope or package with too much postage is wasteful to the practice.				

(continued)

Procedure Steps Total Possible Points - 40 Time Limit: 10 minutes	Practice #1	Practice #2	Practice #3	Final
8. While applying postage to an envelope, hold it flat and right side up (so that you can read the address). Seal the envelope (unless the meter seals it for you). Locate the plate or area where the envelope slides through. This feature is usually near the bottom of the meter. Place the envelope on the left side, and give it a gentle push toward the right. Some models hold the envelope in a stationary position. (If the meter seals the envelope for you, it is especially important that you insert it correctly to allow for sealing.) The meter will grab the envelope and pull it through quickly.				
9. For packages, create a postage label to affix to the package. Follow the same procedure for a label as for an envelope. Affix the postmarked label on the package in the upper-right corner.				
10. Check that the printed postmark has the correct date and amount and that everything written or stamped on the envelope or package is legible.				
Total Number of Points Achieved/Final Score				
Initials of Observer:				

Comments and Signatures

Reviewer's comments and signatures:

1. _____

2. _____

3. _____

Instructor's comments:

_____

CAAHEP Competency Achieved

IV. P (4) Explain general office policies

ABHES Competency Achieved

7. (b) Identify and properly utilize office machines, computerized systems and medical software

PROCEDURE 5-4 USING A DICTATION-TRANSCRIPTION MACHINE

Procedure Goal

To correctly use a dictation-transcription machine to convert verbal communication into the written word

Materials

Dictation-transcription machine, audiocassette or magnetic tape or disk with the recorded dictation, word processor or computer, and printer

Scoring System

To score each step, use the following scoring system:
1 = poor, 2 = fair, 3 = good, 4 = excellent

A minimum score of at least a 3 must be achieved on **each** step to achieve successful completion of the technique. Detailed instructions on the scoring system are found on page 413.

Procedure

Procedure Steps Total Possible Points - 40 Time Limit: 20 minutes	Practice #1	Practice #2	Practice #3	Final
1. Assemble all the necessary equipment.				
2. Select a dictation tape, cassette, or disk for transcription. Select any transcriptions marked "Urgent" first. If there are none, select the oldest-dated transcription first.*				
3. Turn on all equipment and adjust it according to personal preference.*				
4. Prepare the format and style for the selected letter or form.				
5. Insert the tape or cassette and rewind.*				
6. While listening to the transcription tape, cassette, or disk, key in the text.				
7. Adjust the speed and volume controls as needed.				
8. Proofread and spell-check final document, making any corrections.*				
9. Print the document for approval and signature.				
10. Turn off all equipment. Place the transcription tape, cassette, or disk in the proper storage area.				
Total Number of Points Achieved/Final Score				
Initials of Observer:				

(continued)

Comments and Signatures

Reviewer's comments and signatures:

1. _____

2. _____

3. _____

Instructor's comments:

_____

CAAHEP Competency Achieved

IV. A (2) Apply active listening skills

ABHES Competency Achieved

11. (hh) Receive, organize, prioritize, and transmit information expediently

PROCEDURE 5-5 USING A CHECK-WRITING MACHINE

Procedure Goal

To produce a check using a check-writing machine

Materials

Check-writing machine, blank checks, office checkbook or accounting system

Scoring System

To score each step, use the following scoring system:

1 = poor, 2 = fair, 3 = good, 4 = excellent

A minimum score of at least a 3 must be achieved on **each** step to achieve successful completion of the technique. Detailed instructions on the scoring system are found on page 413.

Procedure

Procedure Steps Total Possible Points - 40 Time Limit: 10 minutes	Practice #1	Practice #2	Practice #3	Final
1. Assemble all equipment.				
2. Turn on the check-writing machine.				
3. Place a blank check or a sheet of blank checks into the machine.				
4. Key in the date, the payee's name, and the payment amount. The check-writing machine imprints the check with this information, perforating it with the payee's name. The perforations are actual little ho les in the paper, which prevent anyone from changing the name on the check.				
5. Turn off the check-writing machine.				
6. A doctor or another authorized person then signs the check.*				
7. To complete the process, record the check in the office checkbook or accounting system.*				
Total Number of Points Achieved/Final Score				
Initials of Observer:				

(continued)

Comments and Signatures

Reviewer's comments and signatures:

1. _____

2. _____

3. _____

Instructor's comments:

_____

CAAHEP Competencies Achieved

IV. P (4) Explain general office policies

VI. C (5) Compare types of endorsements

ABHES Competency Achieved

11. (jj) Perform fundamental writing skills including correct grammar, spelling, and formatting techniques when writing prescriptions, documenting medical records, etc.

Procedure 6-1 Creating a Form Letter

Procedure Goal

To use a word processing program to create a form letter

Scoring System

To score each step, use the following scoring system:
1 = poor, 2 = fair, 3 = good, 4 = excellent

A minimum score of at least a 3 must be achieved on **each** step to achieve successful completion of the technique. Detailed instructions on the scoring system are found on page 413.

Materials

Computer equipped with a word processing program, printer, form letter to be created, 8½- by 11-inch paper.

Procedure

Procedure Steps Total Possible Points - 32 Time Limit: 10 minutes	Practice #1	Practice #2	Practice #3	Final
1. Turn on the computer. Select the word processing program.				
2. Use the keyboard to begin entering text into a new document.				
3. To edit text, press the arrow keys to move the cursor to the position at which you want to insert or delete characters, and enter the text. Either type directly or use the "Insert" mode to type over and replace existing text.				
4. To delete text, position the cursor to the left of the characters to be deleted and press the "Delete" key. Alternatively, place the cursor to the right of the characters to be deleted and press the "Backspace" key (the left-pointing arrow usually found at the top-right corner of the keyboard).				
5. If you need to move an entire block of text, you must begin by highlighting it. In most Windows-based programs, you first click the mouse at the beginning of the text to be highlighted. Then you hold down the left mouse button, drag the mouse to the end of the block of text, and release your finger from the mouse. The text should now be highlighted. Right click the mouse and choose the button or command for cutting text. Then move the cursor to the place where you want to insert the text, right click the mouse again and select the button or command for retrieving or pasting text.				
6. As you input the letter, it is important to save your work every 15 minutes or so. Some programs do this automatically. If yours does not, use the "Save" command or button to save the file. Be sure to save the file again when you have completed the letter.*				

(continued)

Procedure Steps Total Possible Points - 32 Time Limit: 10 minutes	Practice #1	Practice #2	Practice #3	Final
7. Carefully proofread the document and use the spell checker, correcting any errors in spelling or formatting.*				
8. Print the letter using the "Print" command or button.				
Total Number of Points Achieved/Final Score				
Initials of Observer:				

Comments and Signatures

Reviewer's comments and signatures:

1. _____

2. _____

3. _____

Instructor's comments:

_____

CAAHEP Competencies Achieved

IV. P (4) Explain general office policies

IV. P (10) Compose professional business letters

ABHES Competencies Achieved

8. (a) Perform basic clerical functions

8. (hh) Receive, organize, prioritize, and transmit information expediently

8. (jj) Perform fundamental writing skills including correct grammar, spelling, and formatting techniques when writing prescriptions, documenting medical records, etc.

PROCEDURE 7-1 CREATING A LETTER

Procedure Goal

To follow standard procedure for constructing a business letter

Scoring System

To score each step, use the following scoring system:
1 = poor, 2 = fair, 3 = good, 4 = excellent

A minimum score of at least a 3 must be achieved on **each** step to achieve successful completion of the technique. Detailed instructions on the scoring system are found on page 413.

Materials

Word processor or personal computer, letterhead paper, dictionaries or other sources

Procedure

Procedure Steps Total Possible Points - 60 Time Limit: 15 minutes	Practice #1	Practice #2	Practice #3	Final
1. Format the letter according to the office's standard procedure. Use the same punctuation and style throughout.*				
2. Start the dateline three lines below the last line of the printed letterhead. (Note: Depending on the length of the letter, it is acceptable to start between two and six lines below the letterhead.)*				
3. Two lines below the dateline, type in any special mailing instructions (such as REGISTERED MAIL, CERTIFIED MAIL, and so on).				
4. Three lines below any special instructions, begin the inside address. Type the addressee's courtesy title (Mr., Mrs., Ms.) and full name on the first line. If a professional title is given (M.D., RN, Ph.D.), type this title after the addressee's name instead of using a courtesy title.*				
5. Type the addressee's business title, if applicable, on the second line. Type the company name on the third line. Type the street address on the fourth line, including the apartment or suite number. Type the city, state, and zip code on the fifth line. Use the standard two-letter abbreviation for the state, followed by one space and the zip code.				
6. Two lines below the inside address, type the salutation, using the appropriate courtesy title (Mr., Mrs., Ms., Dr.) prior to typing the addressee's last name.*				
7. Two lines below the salutation, type the subject line, if applicable.				

(continued)

Procedure Steps Total Possible Points - 60 Time Limit: 15 minutes	Practice #1	Practice #2	Practice #3	Final
8. Two lines below the subject line, begin the body of the letter. Single-space between lines. Double-space between paragraphs.				
9. Two lines below the body of the letter, type the complimentary closing.				
10. Leave three blank lines (return four times) and begin the signature block. (Enough space must be left to allow for the signature.) Type the sender's name on the first line. Type the sender's title on the second line.*				
11. Two lines below the sender's title, type the identification line. Type the sender's initials in all capitals and your initials in lowercase letters, separating the two sets of initials with a colon or a forward slash.				
12. One or two lines below the identification line, type the enclosure notation, if applicable.				
13. Two lines below the enclosure notation, type the copy notation, if applicable.				
14. Edit the letter.*				
15. Proofread and spell-check the letter.*				
Total Number of Points Achieved/Final Score				
Initials of Observer:				

Comments and Signatures

Reviewer's comments and signatures:

1. _____

2. _____

3. _____

Instructor's comments:

_____

CAAHEP Competencies Achieved

IV. P (2) Report relevant information to others succinctly and accurately

IV. P (10) Compose professional business letters

ABHES Competencies Achieved

8. (a) Perform basic clerical functions

8. (jj) Perform fundamental writing skills including correct grammar, spelling, and formatting techniques when writing prescriptions, documenting medical records, etc.

PROCEDURE 7-2 SORTING AND OPENING MAIL

Procedure Goal

To follow a standard procedure for sorting, opening, and processing incoming office mail

Scoring System

To score each step, use the following scoring system:
1 = poor, 2 = fair, 3 = good, 4 = excellent

A minimum score of at least a 3 must be achieved on **each** step to achieve successful completion of the technique. Detailed instructions on the scoring system are found on page 413.

Materials

Letter opener, date and time stamp (manual or automatic), stapler, paper clips, adhesive notes

Procedure

Procedure Steps Total Possible Points - 56 Time Limit: 10 minutes	Practice #1	Practice #2	Practice #3	Final
1. Check the address on each letter or package to be sure that it has been delivered to the correct location.				
2. Sort the mail into piles according to priority and type of mail. Your system may include the following: • Top priority. This pile will contain any items that were sent by overnight mail delivery in addition to items sent by registered mail, certified mail, or special delivery. (Faxes and e-mail messages are also top priority.) • Second priority. This pile will include personal or confidential mail. • Third priority. This pile will contain all first-class mail, airmail, and Priority Mail items. These items should be divided into payments received, insurance forms, reports, and other correspondence. • Fourth priority. This pile will consist of packages. • Fifth priority. This pile will contain magazines and newspapers. • Sixth priority. This last pile will include advertisements and catalogs.				
3. Set aside all letters labeled "Personal" or "Confidential." Unless you have permission to open these letters, only the addressee should open them.				
4. Arrange all the envelopes with the flaps facing up and away from you.				
5. Tap the lower edge of the envelope to shift the contents to the bottom. This step helps to prevent cutting any of the contents when you open the envelope.				
6. Open all the envelopes.*				
7. Remove and unfold the contents, making sure that nothing remains in the envelope.				

(continued)

Procedure Steps Total Possible Points - 56 Time Limit: 10 minutes	Practice #1	Practice #2	Practice #3	Final
8. Review each document and check the sender's name and address. • If the letter has no return address, save the envelope, or cut the address off the envelope and tape it to the letter. • Check to see if the address matches the one on the envelope. If there is a difference, staple the envelope to the letter, and make a note to verify the correct address with the sender.				
9. Compare the enclosure notation on the letter with the actual enclosures to make sure that all items are included. Make a note to contact the sender if anything is missing.				
10. Clip together each letter and its enclosures.				
11. Check the date of the letter. If there is a significant delay between the date of the letter and the postmark, keep the envelope.*				
12. If all contents appear to be in order, you can discard the envelope.				
13. Review all bills and statements. • Make sure the amount enclosed is the same as the amount listed on the statement. • Make a note of any discrepancies.				
14. Stamp each piece of correspondence with the date (and sometimes the time) to record its receipt. If possible, stamp each item in the same location—such as the upper-right corner.*				
Total Number of Points Achieved/Final Score				
Initials of Observer:				

Comments and Signatures

Reviewer's comments and signatures:

1. _____

2. _____

3. _____

Instructor's comments:

_____

CAAHEP Competency Achieved

IV. P (4) Explain general office procedures

ABHES Competencies Achieved

8. (d) Apply concepts for office procedures

8. (hh) Receive, organize, prioritize, and transmit information expediently

PROCEDURE 8-1 STEP-BY-STEP OVERVIEW OF INVENTORY PROCEDURES

Procedure Goal

To set up an effective inventory program for a medical office

Scoring System

To score each step, use the following scoring system:
1 = poor, 2 = fair, 3 = good, 4 = excellent

A minimum score of at least a 3 must be achieved on **each** step to achieve successful completion of the technique. Detailed instructions on the scoring system are found on page 413.

Materials

Pen, paper, file folders, vendor catalogs, index cards or loose-leaf binder and blank pages, reorder reminder cards, vendor order forms

Procedure

Procedure Steps Total Possible Points - 60 Time Limit: 15 minutes	Practice #1	Practice #2	Practice #3	Final
1. Discuss and define with your physician/employer the extent of your responsibility in managing supplies. Know whether the physician's approval or supervision is required for certain procedures, whether any systems have already been established, and if the physician has any preference for a particular vendor or trade-name item. If your medical practice is large, determine which medical assistant is responsible for each aspect of supply management.				
2. Know what administrative and clinical supplies should be stocked in your office. Create a formal supply list of vital, incidental, and periodic items and keep a copy in the office's procedures manual.				
3. Start a file containing a list of current vendors with copies of their catalogs.				
4. Create a wish list of brands or products the office does not currently use but might like to try. Inform other staff members of the list so that they can make entries.				
5. Make a file for supply invoices and completed order forms. (Keep these documents on file for at least 3 years.)*				
6. Devise an inventory system of index cards, loose-leaf pages, or a computer spreadsheet for each item. List the following data for each item on its card: • Date and quantity of each order • Name and contact information for the vendor and sales representative • Date each shipment was received • Total cost and unit cost, or price per piece for the item				

(continued)

Procedure Steps Total Possible Points - 60 Time Limit: 15 minutes	Practice #1	Practice #2	Practice #3	Final
• Payment method used				
• Results of periodic counts of the item				
• Quantity expected to cover the office for a given period of time				
• Reorder quantity (the quantity remaining on the shelf that indicates when reorder should be made)				
7. Have a system for flagging items that need to be ordered and those that are already on order. For example, mark their cards or pages with a self-adhesive tab or note. Make or buy reorder reminder cards to put into the stock of each item at the reorder quantity level.*				
8. Establish with the physician a regular schedule for taking inventory. Every 1 to 2 weeks is usually sufficient. As a backup system for remembering to check stock and reorder, estimate the times for these activities. Mark them on your calendar or create a tickler file on your computer.*				
9. Order at the same times each week or month, after inventory is taken. However, if there is an unexpected shortage of an item, and more than a week or so remains before the regular ordering time, place the order immediately.				
10. Fill in the vendor's order form (or type a letter of request). Order by telephone, fax, e-mail, or online. Online ordering will expedite the order. Follow procedures that have been approved by the physician or office manager. When placing an order, have all the necessary information at hand, including the correct name of the item and the order and account numbers. Record the order information in the inventory file for that item. Be sure to obtain from the vendor an estimated arrival time for the order and mark that date and order number on your calendar.				
11. When ordering online, save the website to "Favorites" for easy, one-click future access. Select the website and establish an account with the company. To establish an account, you will need to give information about your office practice, including the name of the practice, contact name, the address, the phone number, an e-mail address, and a payment source. Ask about adding the practice to any special contact lists for promotional materials and discounts.				
12. When you receive the shipment, record the date and the amount received on the item's inventory card or record page. Check the shipment against the original order and the packing slip inside the package to ensure that the right items, sizes, styles, packaging, and amounts have arrived. Initial each item on the packing slip as a record that the correct item and amount was received. If there is any error, immediately call or e-mail the vendor, with the catalog page and the inventory card or record page at hand.*				

(continued)

Procedure Steps Total Possible Points - 60 Time Limit: 15 minutes	Practice #1	Practice #2	Practice #3	Final
13. Check the invoice carefully against the original order and the packing slip, making sure that the amount of the bill matches the items listed on the invoice and packing list, and to ensure that the bill has not already been paid. Sign or stamp the invoice to show that the order was received.				
14. Write a check to the vendor to be signed by the physician. (Check writing procedures are described in Chapter 18.) Be sure to show the physician the original order, packing slip, and invoice. Record the check number, date, and amount of payment on the invoice and initial it or have the physician do so. Write the invoice number on the front of the check.*				
15. Mail the check and the vendor's copy of the invoice to the vendor within 30 days and file the office copy of the invoice with the original order and packing slip.				
Total Number of Points Achieved/Final Score				
Initials of Observer:				

Comments and Signatures

Reviewer's comments and signatures:

1. _____

2. _____

3. _____

Instructor's comments:

_____

CAAHEP Competencies Achieved

V. A (2) Implement time management principles to maintain effective office function

V. P (10) Perform an office inventory

XI. P (11) Use proper body mechanics

ABHES Competencies Achieved

8. (z) Maintain inventory equipment and supplies

PROCEDURE 9-1 PREPARING A PATIENT MEDICAL RECORD/CHART

Procedure Goal

To assemble new patient record/chart

Scoring System

To score each step, use the following scoring system:
1 = poor, 2 = fair, 3 = good, 4 = excellent

A minimum score of at least a 3 must be achieved on **each** step to achieve successful completion of the technique. Detailed instructions on the scoring system are found on page 413.

Materials

File folder, labels as appropriate (alphabet, numbers, dates, insurance, allergies, etc.), forms (patient information, advance directives, physician progress notes, referrals, laboratory forms), hole punch

Procedure

Procedure Steps Total Possible Points - 24 Time Limit: 10 minutes	Practice #1	Practice #2	Practice #3	Final
1. Carefully create a chart label according to practice policy. This label may include the patient's last name followed by the first name, or it may be a medical record number for those offices that utilize numeric or alphanumeric filing.*				
2. Place the chart label on the right edge of the folder, extending the label the length of the tab on the folder.				
3. Place the date label on the top edge of the folder, updating the date according to the practice's policy. (The date is usually updated annually, provided the patient has come into the office within the last year.)*				
4. If alpha or numeric filing labels are utilized, place a patient name label on the chart according to the practice's policy.				
5. Punch holes in the appropriate forms for placement within the patient's medical record/chart.				
6. Place all the forms in appropriate sections of the patient's medical record/chart.				
Total Number of Points Achieved/Final Score				
Initials of Observer:				

(continued)

Comments and Signatures

Reviewer's comments and signatures:

1. _____

2. _____

3. _____

Instructor's comments:

_____

CAAHEP Competencies Achieved

V. C (11) Discuss principles of using electronic medical records (EMR)

V. C (12) Identify types of records common to the health-care setting

IX. P (1) Respond to issues of confidentiality

ABHES Competencies Achieved

4. (a) Document accurately

8. (b) Prepare and maintain medical records

8. (jj) Perform fundamental writing skills including correct grammar, spelling, and formatting techniques when writing prescriptions, documenting medical records, etc.

PROCEDURE 9-2 TRANSCRIBING LETTERS, REPORTS, AND NOTES

Procedure Goal

To transcribe dictation from a physician

Scoring System

To score each step, use the following scoring system:
1 = poor, 2 = fair, 3 = good, 4 = excellent

A minimum score of at least a 3 must be achieved on **each** step to achieve successful completion of the technique. Detailed instructions on the scoring system are found on page 413.

Materials

Blank paper or stationery, transcription machine or computer with foot pedal, headphones, dictation tape or file, computer/printer, medical dictionary

Procedure

Procedure Steps Total Possible Points - 28 Time Limit: 20 minutes	Practice #1	Practice #2	Practice #3	Final
1. Assemble materials. Decide what style correspondence you will choose if transcribing letters.				
2. Make sure the transcription equipment has been set up properly, and you have your headphone plugged into your computer or transcription equipment.				
3. Rewind the tape.*				
4. Type information listening to dictation. Adjust tape speed as necessary to achieve a comfortable rate of transcription.				
5. When you are transcribing, make sure you include the initials of both the person who is dictating and your initials as well.*				
6. Use spell check and proofread the information for grammar, punctuation, and style.				
7. Go back and make corrections as needed.				
8. Finally, have the physician review for accuracy and sign if there are no corrections to be made.*				
Total Number of Points Achieved/Final Score				
Initials of Observer:				

(continued)

Comments and Signatures

Reviewer's comments and signatures:

1. _____

2. _____

3. _____

Instructor's comments:

_____

CAAHEP Competencies Achieved

IV. P (10) Compose professional/business letters

IX. P (2) Perform within scope of practice

ABHES Competencies Achieved

7 a. (2) Typing medical correspondence and basic reports

7 b. (1) Efficiently maintain and understand different types of medical correspondence and medical reports

PROCEDURE 9-3 CORRECTING MEDICAL RECORDS

Procedure Goal

To follow standard procedures for correcting a medical record

Scoring System

To score each step, use the following scoring system:
1 = poor, 2 = fair, 3 = good, 4 = excellent

A minimum score of at least a 3 must be achieved on **each** step to achieve successful completion of the technique. Detailed instructions on the scoring system are found on page 413.

Materials

Patient file, other pertinent documents that contain the information to be used in making corrections (for example, transcribed notes, telephone notes, physician's comments, correspondence), good ballpoint pen

Procedure

Procedure Steps Total Possible Points - 24 Time Limit: 5 minutes	Practice #1	Practice #2	Practice #3	Final
1. Always make the correction in a way that does not suggest any intention to deceive, cover up, alter, or add information to conceal a lack of proper medical care.				
2. When deleting information, never black it out, never use correction fluid to cover it up, and never in any other way erase or obliterate the original wording. Draw a line through the original information so that it is still legible.*				
3. Write or type in the correct information above or below the original line or in the margin. The location on the chart for the new information should be clear. You may need to attach another sheet of paper or another document with the correction on it. Note in the record "See attached document A" or similar wording to indicate where the corrected information can be found.				
4. Place a note near the correction stating why it was made (for example, "error, wrong date; error, interrupted by phone call"). This indication can be a brief note in the margin or an attachment to the record. As a general rule of thumb, do not make any changes without noting the reason for them.*				
5. Enter the date and time and initial the correction.*				
6. If possible, have another staff member or the physician witness and initial the correction to the record when you make it.				
Total Number of Points Achieved/Final Score				
Initials of Observer:				

(continued)

Comments and Signatures

Reviewer's comments and signatures:

1. _____

2. _____

3. _____

Instructor's comments:

_____

CAAHEP Competencies Achieved

IV. P (2) Report relevant information to others succinctly and accurately

IV. P (8) Document patient care

IV. A (2) Apply active listening skills

ABHES Competencies Achieved

7-b. (1) Efficiently maintain and understand different types of medical correspondence and medical reports

8. (b) Prepare and maintain medical records

PROCEDURE 9-4 MAINTAINING MEDICAL RECORDS

Procedure Goal

To document continuity of care by creating a complete, accurate, timely record of the medical care provided at your facility

Scoring System

To score each step, use the following scoring system:
1 = poor, 2 = fair, 3 = good, 4 = excellent

A minimum score of at least a 3 must be achieved on **each** step to achieve successful completion of the technique. Detailed instructions on the scoring system are found on page 413.

Materials

Patient file, other pertinent documents (test results, x-rays, telephone notes, correspondence), blue ballpoint pen, notebook, keyboard, transcribing equipment

Procedure

Procedure Steps Total Possible Points - 40 Time Limit: 10 minutes	Practice #1	Practice #2	Practice #3	Final
1. Verify that you have the correct chart for the records to be filed.*				
2. Transcribe dictated doctor's notes as soon as possible and enter them into the patient record.*				
3. Spell out the names of disorders, diseases, medications, and other terms the first time you enter them into the patient record, followed by the appropriate abbreviation (for example: "congestive heart failure [CHF]"). Thereafter, you may use the abbreviation alone.*				
4. Enter only what the doctor has dictated. Do *not* add your own comments, observations, or evaluations. Use self-adhesive flags or other means to call the doctor's attention to something you have noticed that may be helpful to the patient's case. Date and initial each entry.*				
5. Follow office procedure to record routine or special laboratory test results. They may be posted in a particular section of the file or on a separate test summary form. If you use the summary form, make a note in the file that the results were received and recorded. Place the original laboratory report in the patient's file if required to do so by office policy. Date and initial each entry. Always note in the chart the date of the test and the results, whether or not test result printouts are filed in the record.				
6. Make a note in the record of all telephone calls to and from the patient. Date and initial the entries. These entries also may include the doctor's comments, observations, changes in the patient's medication, new instructions to the patient, and so on. If calls are recorded in a separate telephone log,				

(continued)

Procedure Steps Total Possible Points - 40 Time Limit: 10 minutes	Practice #1	Practice #2	Practice #3	Final
note in the patient's record the time and date of the call and refer to the log. It is particularly important to record such calls when the patient resists or refuses treatment, skips appointments, or has not made follow-up appointments.*				
7. Make notations in the medical record of any immunizations and vaccines that have been given to the patient. Notations should be posted in the patient's immunization record inside the medical chart. Input them into your state's public health database as well. Immunization records are kept indefinitely.				
8. Read over the entries for omissions or mistakes. Ask the doctor to answer any questions you have.*				
9. Make sure that you have dated and initialed each entry.				
10. Be sure that all documents are included in the file.				
11. Replace the patient's file in the filing system as soon as possible.				
Total Number of Points Achieved/Final Score				
Initials of Observer:				

Comments and Signatures

Reviewer's comments and signatures:

1. _____

2. _____

3. _____

Instructor's comments:

_____

CAAHEP Competencies Achieved

IV. P (8) Document patient care

V. C (12) Identify types of records common to health-care setting

V. A (4) File medical records

ABHES Competencies Achieved

4. (a) Document accurately

7-b. (1) Efficiently maintain and understand different types of medical correspondence and medical reports

8. (b) Prepare and maintain medical records

8. (jj) Perform fundamental writing skills including correct grammar, spelling, and formatting techniques when writing prescriptions, documenting medical records, etc.

PROCEDURE 10-1 CREATING A FILING SYSTEM FOR PATIENT RECORDS

Procedure Goal

To create a filing system that keeps related materials together in a logical order and enables office staff to store and retrieve files efficiently

Scoring System

To score each step, use the following scoring system:
1 = poor, 2 = fair, 3 = good, 4 = excellent

A minimum score of at least a 3 must be achieved on **each** step to achieve successful completion of the technique. Detailed instructions on the scoring system are found on page 413.

Materials

Vertical or horizontal filing cabinets with locks, file jackets, tabbed file folders, labels, file guides, out guides, filing sorters

Procedure

Procedure Steps Total Possible Points - 32 Time Limit: 15 minutes	Practice #1	Practice #2	Practice #3	Final
1. Evaluate which filing system is best for your office—alphabetic or numeric. Make sure the doctor approves the system you choose.*				
2. Establish a style for labeling files and make sure that all file labels are prepared in this manner. Place records for different family members in separate files.				
3. Avoid writing labels by hand. Use a keyboard, a label maker, or preprinted adhesive labels.				
4. Set up a color-coding system to distinguish the files (for example, use blue for the letters A–C, red for D–F, and so on). Create a chart, suitable to be hung in a professional file room, that indicates the color-coding system.				
5. Use file guides to divide files into sections.				
6. Use out guides as placeholders to indicate which files have been taken out of the system. Include a charge-out form to be signed and dated by the person who is taking the file.*				
7. To keep files in order and to prevent them from being misplaced, use a file sorter to hold those patient records that will be returned to the files during the day or at the end of the day.				
8. Develop a manual explaining the filing system to new staff members. Include guidelines on how to keep the system in good order.				
Total Number of Points Achieved/Final Score				
Initials of Observer:				

(continued)

Comments and Signatures

Reviewer's comments and signatures:

1. _____

2. _____

3. _____

Instructor's comments:

_____

CAAHEP Competencies Achieved

V. A (4) File medical records

V. C (7) Discuss pros and cons of various filing methods

V. C (9) Describe indexing rules

ABHES Competencies Achieved

7 b. (1) Efficiently maintain and understand different types of medical correspondence and medical reports

8. (b) Prepare and maintain medical records

8. (d) Apply concepts for office procedures

PROCEDURE 10-2 SETTING UP AN OFFICE TICKLER FILE

Procedure Goal

To create a comprehensive office tickler file designed for year-round use

Scoring System

To score each step, use the following scoring system:
1 = poor, 2 = fair, 3 = good, 4 = excellent

A minimum score of at least a 3 must be achieved on **each** step to achieve successful completion of the technique. Detailed instructions on the scoring system are found on page 413.

Materials

12 manila file folders, 12 file labels, pen or typewriter, paper

Procedure

Procedure Steps Total Possible Points - 40 Time Limit: 15 minutes	Practice #1	Practice #2	Practice #3	Final
1. Write or type 12 file labels, 1 for each month of the year. Abbreviations are acceptable. Do *not* include the current calendar year, just the month.				
2. Affix one label to the tab of each file folder.				
3. Arrange the folders so that the current month is on the top of the pile. Months should follow in chronological order.				
4. Write or type a list of upcoming responsibilities and activities. Next to each activity, indicate the date by which the activity should be completed. Leave a column after this date to indicate when the activity has been completed. Use a separate sheet of paper for each month.*				
5. File the notes by month in the appropriate folders.*				
6. Place the folders, with the current month on top, in order, in a prominent place in the office, such as in a plastic box mounted on the wall near the receptionist's desk.				
7. Check the tickler file at least once a week on a specific day, such as every Monday. Assign a backup person to check it in case you happen to be out of the office.				
8. Complete the tickler activities on the designated days, if possible. Keep notes concerning activities in progress. Be sure to note when activities are completed and by whom.*				
9. At the end of the month, place that month's file folder at the bottom of the tickler file. If there are notes remaining in that month's folder, move them to the new month's folder.*				
10. Continue to add new notes to the appropriate tickler files.*				
Total Number of Points Achieved/Final Score				
Initials of Observer:				

(continued)

Comments and Signatures

Reviewer's comments and signatures:

1. _____

2. _____

3. _____

Instructor's comments:

_____

CAAHEP Competencies Achieved

V. A (4) File medical records

V. C (7) Discuss pros and cons of various filing methods

V. C (9) Describe indexing rules

ABHES Competencies Achieved

7 b. (1) Efficiently maintain and understand different types of medical correspondence and medical reports

8. (b) Prepare and maintain medical records

8. (d) Apply concepts for office procedures

PROCEDURE 10-3 DEVELOPING A RECORDS RETENTION PROGRAM

Procedure Goal

To establish a records retention program for patient medical records that meets office needs as well as legal and government guidelines

Scoring System

To score each step, use the following scoring system:
1 = poor, 2 = fair, 3 = good, 4 = excellent

A minimum score of at least a 3 must be achieved on **each** step to achieve successful completion of the technique. Detailed instructions on the scoring system are found on page 413.

Materials

Updated guide for record retention as described by federal and state law (go to the HIPAA Advisory website), file folders, index cards, index box, paper, pen or typewriter

Procedure

Procedure Steps Total Possible Points - 48 Time Limit: 20 minutes	Practice #1	Practice #2	Practice #3	Final
1. List the types of information contained in a typical patient medical record in your office. For example, a file for an adult patient may include the patient's case history, records of hospital stays, and insurance information.				
2. Research the state and federal requirements for keeping documents. Contact your appropriate state office (such as the office of the insurance commissioner) for specific state requirements, such as rules for keeping records of insurance payments and the statute of limitations for initiating lawsuits. If your office does business in more than one state, be sure to research all applicable regulations. Consult with the attorney who represents your practice.				
3. Compile the results of your research in a chart. At the top of the chart, list the different kinds of information your office keeps in patient records. Down the left side of the chart, list the headings "Federal," "State," and "Other." Then, in each box, record the corresponding information.				
4. Compare all the legal and government requirements. Indicate which one is for the longest period of time.*				
5. Meet with the doctor to review the information. Working together with the physician, prepare a retention schedule. Determine how long different types of patient records should be kept in the office after a patient leaves the practice and how long records should be kept in storage. Although retention periods can vary based on the type of information kept in a file, it is often easiest to choose a retention period that covers all records. For example, all records				

(continued)

Procedure Steps Total Possible Points - 48 Time Limit: 20 minutes	Practice #1	Practice #2	Practice #3	Final
could be kept in the office for 1 year after a patient leaves the practice and then kept in storage for another 9 years, for a total of 10 years. Determine how files will be destroyed when they have exceeded the retention requirements. Usually, records are destroyed by paper shredding. Purchase the appropriate equipment, or contract with a shredding company as necessary.*				
6. Put the retention schedule in writing and post it prominently near the files. In addition, keep a copy of the schedule in a safe place in the office. Review it with the office staff.				
7. Develop a system for identifying files easily under the retention system. For example, for each file deemed inactive or closed, prepare an index card or create a master list containing the following information: • Patient's name and Social Security number • Contents of the file • Date the file was deemed inactive or closed and by whom • Date the file should be sent to inactive or closed file storage (the actual date will be filled in later; if more than one storage location is used, indicate the exact location to which the file was sent) • Date the file should be destroyed (the actual date will be filled in later) Have the card signed by the doctor and by the person responsible for the files. Keep the card in an index box or another safe place. This is your authorization to destroy the file at the appropriate time.				
8. Use color coding to help identify inactive and closed files. For example, all records that become inactive in 2008 could be placed in green file folders or have a green sticker with 08 placed on them and moved to a supplemental file. Then, in January 2010, all of these files could be pulled and sent to storage.				
9. One person should be responsible for checking the index cards once a month to determine which stored files should be destroyed. Before retrieving these files from storage, circulate a notice to the office staff stating which records will be destroyed. Indicate that the staff must let you know by a specific date if any of the files should be saved. You may want to keep a separate file with these notices.				
10. After the deadline has passed, retrieve the files from storage. Review each file before it is destroyed. Make sure the staff members who will destroy the files are trained to use the equipment properly. Develop a sheet of instructions for destroying files. Post it prominently with the retention schedule, near the machinery used to destroy the files.*				
11. Update the index card, giving the date the file was destroyed and by whom.				

(continued)

Procedure Steps Total Possible Points - 48 Time Limit: 20 minutes	Practice #1	Practice #2	Practice #3	Final
12. Periodically review the retention schedule. Update it with the most current legal and governmental requirements. With the staff, evaluate whether the current schedule is meeting the needs of your office or whether files are being kept too long or destroyed prematurely. With the doctor's approval, change the schedule as necessary.				
Total Number of Points Achieved/Final Score				
Initials of Observer:				

Comments and Signatures

Reviewer's comments and signatures:

1. _____

2. _____

3. _____

Instructor's comments:

_____

CAAHEP Competencies Achieved

V. C (5) Identify systems for organizing medical records

V. C (13) Identify time management principles

V. P (6) Use office hardware and software to maintain office systems

ABHES Competencies Achieved

7 b. (1) Efficiently maintain and understand different types of medical correspondence and medical reports

8. (b) Prepare and maintain medical records

8. (d) Apply concepts for office procedures

Procedure 11-1 Performing Telephone Screening

Procedure Goal

To properly screen incoming telephone calls

Scoring System

To score each step, use the following scoring system:
1 = poor, 2 = fair, 3 = good, 4 = excellent

A minimum score of at least a 3 must be achieved on **each** step to achieve successful completion of the technique. Detailed instructions on the scoring system are found on page 413.

Materials

Telephone, telephone pad, pen or pencil, appointment book or computerized scheduling software (computer)

Procedure

Procedure Steps Total Possible Points - 28 Time Limit: 10 minutes	Practice #1	Practice #2	Practice #3	Final
1. Make sure all of the materials are within reach of the telephone equipment.*				
2. Answer the telephone within two to three rings.*				
3. Identify the medical office and identify yourself. Make sure you know office procedure for answering the phone in your facility even if a telephone answering system is employed to route calls to you. For example: "Genesys Medical Practice, this is Ivy Smith."*				
4. If the caller does not identify himself, ask him to do so and the number he is calling from, writing down this information. Get an idea what the call is in reference to. Listen carefully to what the caller has to say, listening for tone and feeling. Try to decide as soon as possible if this is a call that you can handle; if so, handle it. If this is a call that needs to be transferred to someone, tell the caller to whom and where you will be transferring the call.*				
5. If you need to take a message, make sure you repeat the information that is given to you, especially the name of the person and his or her phone number.*				
6. If you have to transfer a caller, ask permission to place him on hold. Make sure you write down the caller's name and phone number in case the call is dropped. Never place a caller on hold longer than 30 seconds. Come back to the caller and let him or her know that you are still waiting for the other individual to answer. If the other staff member does not answer within a certain period or the staff member is on another line, ask the caller if he or she would like to call back, be transferred to the staff member's voice mail (if available) or would like to leave a message.*				

(continued)

Procedure Steps Total Possible Points - 28 Time Limit: 10 minutes	Practice #1	Practice #2	Practice #3	Final
7. If the caller describes a symptom that is in need of immediate care, ask questions to assess the information (ask for his or her name and telephone number). If it is indeed an emergency call and the physician or nurse is in the office, transfer the call immediately. If the doctor or nurse is not in the building, do not let the caller hang up. Have another staff member dial 911 immediately, with the name and address of the patient and his symptoms, while you stay on the phone with the patient keeping him calm and aware that help is on the way.*				
Total Number of Points Achieved/Final Score				
Initials of Observer:				

Comments and Signatures

Reviewer's comments and signatures:

1. _____

2. _____

3. _____

Instructor's comments:

_____

CAAHEP Competencies Achieved

I. A (2) Use language/verbal skills that enable patients' understanding

IV. A (2) Apply active listening skills

IV. P (7) Demonstrate telephone techniques

ABHES Competencies Achieved

8. (c) Schedule and manage appointments

8. (cc) Communicate on the recipient's level of comprehension

8. (dd) Serve as liaison between physician and others

8. (ee) Use proper telephone techniques

8. (hh) Receive, organize, prioritize, and transmit information expediently

8. (jj) Perform fundamental writing skills including correct grammar, spelling, and formatting techniques when writing prescriptions, documenting medical records, etc.

8. (ll) Apply electronic technology

PROCEDURE 11-2 HANDLING EMERGENCY CALLS

Procedure Goal

To determine whether a telephone call involves a medical emergency and to learn the steps to take if it is an emergency call

Scoring System

To score each step, use the following scoring system:
1 = poor, 2 = fair, 3 = good, 4 = excellent

A minimum score of at least a 3 must be achieved on **each** step to achieve successful completion of the technique. Detailed instructions on the scoring system are found on page 413.

Materials

Office guidelines for handling emergency calls; list of symptoms and conditions requiring immediate medical attention; telephone numbers of area emergency rooms, poison control centers, and ambulance transport services; telephone message forms or telephone message log

Procedure

Procedure Steps Total Possible Points - 32 Time Limit: 10 minutes	Practice #1	Practice #2	Practice #3	Final
1. When someone calls the office regarding a potential emergency, remain calm.*				
2. Obtain the following information, taking accurate notes: a. The caller's name b. The caller's telephone number and the address from which the call is being made* c. The caller's relationship to the patient (if it is not the patient who is calling) d. The patient's name (if the patient is not the caller) e. The patient's age f. A complete description of the patient's symptoms g. If the call is about an accident, a description of how the accident or injury occurred and any other pertinent information h. A description of how the patient is reacting to the situation i. Treatment that has been administered				
3. Read back the details of the medical problem to verify them.*				
4. If necessary, refer to the list of symptoms and conditions that require immediate medical attention to determine if the situation is indeed a medical emergency.				
If the Situation Is a Medical Emergency:				
1. Put the call through to the doctor immediately or handle the situation according to the established office procedures.*				
2. If the doctor is not in the office, follow established office procedures. They may involve one or more of the following: a. Transferring the call to the nurse practitioner or other medical personnel, as appropriate				

(continued)

Procedure Steps Total Possible Points - 32 Time Limit: 10 minutes	Practice #1	Practice #2	Practice #3	Final
b. Instructing the caller (if not the patient) to hang up and dial 911 to request an ambulance for the patient c. Instructing the patient to be driven to the nearest emergency room d. Instructing the caller to telephone the nearest poison control center for advice and supplying the caller with its telephone number e. Paging the doctor				
If the Situation Is Not a Medical Emergency: 1. Handle the call according to established office procedures.				
2. If you are in doubt about whether the situation is a medical emergency, treat it like an emergency. You must always alert the doctor immediately about an emergency call, even if the patient declines to speak with the doctor.*				
Total Number of Points Achieved/Final Score				
Initials of Observer:				

Comments and Signatures

Reviewer's comments and signatures:

1. _____

2. _____

3. _____

Instructor's comments:

_____

CAAHEP Competencies Achieved

I. A (2) Use language/verbal skills that enable patients' understanding

IV. A (2) Apply active listening skills

XI. C (13) Discuss potential role(s) of the medical assistant in emergency preparedness

ABHES Competencies Achieved

8. (aa) [Graduates] Are attentive, listen and learn

8. (cc) Communicate on the recipient's level of comprehension

8. (ee) Use proper telephone techniques

8. (hh) Receive, organize, prioritize, and transmit information expediently

8. (kk) Adapt to individualized needs

8. (ll) Apply electronic technology

PROCEDURE 11-3 RETRIEVING MESSAGES FROM AN ANSWERING SERVICE

Procedure Goal

To follow standard procedures for retrieving messages from an answering service

Scoring System

To score each step, use the following scoring system:
1 = poor, 2 = fair, 3 = good, 4 = excellent

A minimum score of at least a 3 must be achieved on **each** step to achieve successful completion of the technique. Detailed instructions on the scoring system are found on page 413.

Materials

Telephone message pad, manual telephone log, or electronic telephone log

Procedure

Procedure Steps Total Possible Points - 24 Time Limit: 10 minutes	Practice #1	Practice #2	Practice #3	Final
1. Set a regular schedule for calling the answering service to retrieve messages.*				
2. Call at the regularly scheduled time(s) to see if there are any messages.				
3. Identify yourself and state that you are calling to obtain messages for the practice.*				
4. For each message, write down all pertinent information on the telephone message pad or telephone log or key it into the electronic telephone log. Be sure to include the caller's name and telephone number, time of call, message or description of the problem, and action taken, if any.				
5. Repeat the information, confirming that you have the correct spelling of all names.*				
6. When you have retrieved all messages, route them according to the office policy.				
Total Number of Points Achieved/Final Score				
Initials of Observer:				

(continued)

Comments and Signatures

Reviewer's comments and signatures:

1. _____

2. _____

3. _____

Instructor's comments:

_____

CAAHEP Competencies Achieved

IV. P (7) Demonstrate telephone techniques

IV. A (2) Apply active listening skills

ABHES Competencies Achieved

8. (d) Apply concepts for office procedures

8. (dd) Serve as liaison between physician and others

8. (ee) Use proper telephone techniques

8. (hh) Receive, organize, prioritize, and transmit information expediently

8. (ii) Recognize and respond to verbal and non-verbal communication

8. (ll) Apply electronic technology

PROCEDURE 12-1 CREATING A CLUSTER SCHEDULE

Procedure Goal

To set up a cluster schedule; use the example in the back of the workbook, page 755.

Scoring System

To score each step, use the following scoring system:
1 = poor, 2 = fair, 3 = good, 4 = excellent

A minimum score of at least a 3 must be achieved on **each** step to achieve successful completion of the technique. Detailed instructions on the scoring system are found on page 413.

Materials

Calendar, tickler file, appointment book, colored pencils or markers (optional)

Procedure

Procedure Steps Total Possible Points - 24 Time Limit: 5 minutes	Practice #1	Practice #2	Practice #3	Final
1. Learn which categories of cases the physician would like to cluster and on what days and/or times of day.				
2. Determine the length of the average visit in each category.				
3. In the appointment book, cross out the hours in the week that the physician is typically not available.*				
4. Block out one period in midmorning and one in midafternoon for use as buffer, or reserve, times for unexpected needs.				
5. Reserve additional slots for acutely ill patients. The number of slots depends on the type of practice.*				
6. Mark the appointment times for clustered procedures. If desired, color-code the blocks of time. For example, make immunization clusters pink, blood pressure checks green, and so forth.*				
Total Number of Points Achieved/Final Score				
Initials of Observer:				

Comments and Signatures

Reviewer's comments and signatures:

1. _____

2. _____

3. _____

Instructor's comments:

_____

(continued)

CAAHEP Competencies Achieved

V. C (2) Describe scheduling guidelines

V. C (3) Recognize office policies and protocols for handling appointments

ABHES Competencies Achieved

4. (a) Document accurately

8. (c) Schedule and manage appointments

8. (d) Apply concepts for office procedures

8. (dd) Serve as liaison between physician and others

8. (ee) Use proper telephone techniques

PROCEDURE 12-2 SCHEDULING AND CONFIRMING SURGERY AT A HOSPITAL

Procedure Goal

To follow the proper procedure for scheduling and confirming surgery

Scoring System

To score each step, use the following scoring system:
1 = poor, 2 = fair, 3 = good, 4 = excellent

A minimum score of at least a 3 must be achieved on **each** step to achieve successful completion of the technique. Detailed instructions on the scoring system are found on page 413.

Materials

Calendar, telephone, notepad, pen

Procedure

Procedure Steps Total Possible Points - 24 Time Limit: 10 minutes	Practice #1	Practice #2	Practice #3	Final
1. Elective surgery is usually performed on certain days when the doctor is scheduled to be in the operating room and a room and an anesthetist are available. The patient may be given only one or two choices of days and times. (For emergency surgery the first step is to reserve the operating room.)				
2. Call the operating room secretary. Give the procedure required, the name of the surgeon, the time involved, and the preferred date and hour.				
3. Provide the patient's name (including birth name, if appropriate), address, telephone number, age, gender, Social Security number, and insurance information.*				
4. Call the admissions office (or day-stay surgery office). Arrange for the patient to be admitted on the day of surgery or the day before (depending on the surgery to be performed). Ask for a copy of the admissions form for the patient record.				
5. Some hospitals want patients to complete preadmission forms. In such cases, request a blank form for the patient. Depending on hospital policy, tell the patient to arrive for the appointment a few minutes early to complete the appropriate paperwork.				
6. Confirm the surgery and the patient's arrival time 1 business day before surgery.*				
Total Number of Points Achieved/Final Score				
Initials of Observer:				

(continued)

Comments and Signatures

Reviewer's comments and signatures:

1. _____

2. _____

3. _____

Instructor's comments:

_____

CAAHEP Competencies Achieved

IV. P (6) Prepare a patient for procedures and/or treatments

IV. P (7) Demonstrate telephone techniques

ABHES Competencies Achieved

4. (a) Document accurately

8. (c) Schedule and manage appointments

8. (d) Apply concepts for office procedures

8. (f) Schedule inpatient and outpatient admissions

8. (dd) Serve as liaison between physician and others

8. (ee) Use proper telephone techniques

PROCEDURE 13-1 CREATING A PEDIATRIC PLAYROOM

Procedure Goal

To create a play environment for children in the patient reception area of a pediatric practice

Scoring System

To score each step, use the following scoring system:
1 = poor, 2 = fair, 3 = good, 4 = excellent

A minimum score of at least a 3 must be achieved on **each** step to achieve successful completion of the technique. Detailed instructions on the scoring system are found on page 413.

Materials

Children's books and magazines, games, toys, nontoxic crayons and coloring books, television and videocassette recorder (VCR) (or DVD player), children's videotapes (or DVDs), child- and adult-size chairs, child-size table, bookshelf, boxes or shelves, decorative wall hangings or educational posters (optional)

Procedure

Procedure Steps Total Possible Points - 28 Time Limit: 15 minutes	Practice #1	Practice #2	Practice #3	Final
1. Place all adult-size chairs against the wall. Position some of the child-size chairs along the wall with the adult chairs.				
2. Place the remainder of the child-size chairs in small groupings throughout the room. In addition, put several chairs with the child-size table.				
3. Put the books, magazines, crayons, and coloring books on the bookshelf in one corner of the room near a grouping of chairs.				
4. Choose toys and games carefully. Avoid toys that encourage active play, such as balls, or toys that require a large area. Make sure that all toys meet safety guidelines. Watch for loose parts or parts that are smaller than a golf ball. Toys also should be easy to clean.*				
5. Place the activities for older children near one grouping of chairs and the games and toys for younger children near another grouping. Keep the toys and games in a toy box or on shelves designated for them. Consider labeling or color-coding boxes and shelves and the games and toys that belong there to encourage children to return the games and toys to the appropriate storage area.				
6. Place the television and VCR (or DVD player) on a high shelf, if possible, or attach it to the wall near the ceiling. Keep children's videos (or DVDs) behind the reception desk, and periodically change the video in the VCR/DVD.*				
7. To make the room more cheerful, decorate it with wall hangings or posters.				
Total Number of Points Achieved/Final Score				
Initials of Observer:				

(continued)

Comments and Signatures

Reviewer's comments and signatures:

1. _____

2. _____

3. _____

Instructor's comments:

_____

CAAHEP Competencies Achieved

II. P. (3) Maintain growth charts

XI. P. (3) Develop a personal (patient and employee) safety plan

ABHES Competencies Achieved

5. (b) Identify and respond appropriately when working/caring for patients with special needs

5. (f) Identify and discuss developmental stages of life

8. (x) Maintain medical facility

8. (bb) [Graduates] Are impartial and show empathy when dealing with patients

8. (cc) Communicate on the recipient's level of comprehension

8. (kk) Adapt to individualized needs

11 a. (5) Exhibiting initiative

PROCEDURE 13-2 CREATING A RECEPTION AREA ACCESSIBLE TO PATIENTS WITH SPECIAL NEEDS

Procedure Goal

To arrange elements in the reception area to accommodate patients with special needs

Scoring System

To score each step, use the following scoring system:
1 = poor, 2 = fair, 3 = good, 4 = excellent

A minimum score of at least a 3 must be achieved on **each** step to achieve successful completion of the technique. Detailed instructions on the scoring system are found on page 413.

Materials

Ramps (if needed), doorway floor coverings, chairs, bars or rails, adjustable-height tables, magazine rack, television/VCR or DVD player, large-type and Braille magazines

Procedure

Procedure Steps Total Possible Points - 40 Time Limit: 15 minutes	Practice #1	Practice #2	Practice #3	Final
1. Arrange chairs, leaving gaps so that substantial space is available for wheelchairs along walls and near other groups of chairs. Keep the arrangement flexible so that chairs can be removed to allow room for additional wheelchairs if needed.*				
2. Remove any obstacles that may interfere with the space needed for a wheelchair to swivel around completely. Also remove scatter rugs or any carpeting that is not attached to the floor. Such carpeting can cause patients to trip and create difficulties for wheelchair traffic.*				
3. Position coffee tables at a height and location that is accessible to people in wheelchairs.				
4. Place office reading materials, such as magazines, at a height that is accessible to people in wheelchairs (for example, on tables or in racks attached midway up the wall).				
5. Locate the television and VCR/DVD within full view of patients sitting on chairs and in wheelchairs so that they do not have to strain their necks to watch.				
6. For patients who have a vision impairment, include reading materials with large type and in Braille.				
7. For patients who have difficulty walking, make sure bars or rails are attached securely to walls 34 to 38 inches above the floor, to accommodate requirements set forth in the Americans with Disabilities Act. Make sure the bars are sturdy enough to provide balance for patients who may need it. Bars are most important in entrances and hallways, as well as in the bathroom. Consider placing a bar near the receptionist's window for added support as patients check in.*				

(continued)

Procedure Steps Total Possible Points - 40 Time Limit: 15 minutes	Practice #1	Practice #2	Practice #3	Final
8. Eliminate sills of metal or wood along the floor in doorways. Otherwise, create a smoother travel surface for wheelchairs and pedestrians with a thin rubber covering to provide a graduated slope. Be sure that the covering is attached properly and meets safety standards.*				
9. Make sure the office has ramp access.*				
10. Solicit feedback from patients with physical disabilities about the accessibility of the patient reception area. Encourage ideas for improvements. Address any additional needs.*				
Total Number of Points Achieved/Final Score				
Initials of Observer:				

Comments and Signatures

Reviewer's comments and signatures:

1. _____

2. _____

3. _____

Instructor's comments:

_____

CAAHEP Competencies Achieved

III. C. (3) Recognize communication barriers

IX. (11) Identify how the American with Disabilities Act (ADA) applies to the medical assisting professional

X. A. (3) Demonstrate awareness of diversity in providing patient care

ABHES Competencies Achieved

5. (b) Identify and respond appropriately when working/caring for patients with special needs

5. (f) Identify and discuss developmental stages of life

8. (x) Maintain medical facility

8. (bb) [Graduates] Are impartial and show empathy when dealing with patients

8. (cc) Communicate on the recipient's level of comprehension

8. (kk) Adapt to individualized needs

11 a. (5) Exhibiting initiative

PROCEDURE 14-1 DEVELOPING A PATIENT EDUCATION PLAN

Procedure Goal

To create and implement a patient teaching plan

Scoring System

To score each step, use the following scoring system:
1 = poor, 2 = fair, 3 = good, 4 = excellent

A minimum score of at least a 3 must be achieved on **each** step to achieve successful completion of the technique. Detailed instructions on the scoring system are found on page 413.

Materials

Pen, paper, various educational aids such as instructional pamphlets and brochures, and/or visual aids such as posters, videotapes, or DVDs

Procedure

Procedure Steps Total Possible Points - 32 Time Limit: 15 minutes	Practice #1	Practice #2	Practice #3	Final

1. Identify the patient's educational needs. Consider the following:
  a. The patient's current knowledge
  b. Any misconceptions the patient may have
  c. Any obstacles to learning (loss of hearing or vision, limitations of mobility, language barriers, and so on)
  d. The patient's willingness and readiness to learn (motivation)
  e. How the patient will use the information*				

2. Develop and outline a plan using the various educational aids available. Include the following areas in the outline:
  a. What you want to accomplish (your goal)
  b. How you plan to accomplish it
  c. How you will determine if the teaching was successful*				

3. Write the plan. Try to make the information interesting for the patient.				
4. Before carrying out the plan, share it with the physician to get approval and suggestions for improvement.				
5. Perform the instruction. Be sure to use more than one teaching method. For instance, if written material is being given, be sure to explain or demonstrate the material instead of simply telling the patient to read the educational materials.				
6. Document the teaching in the patient's chart.*				

7. Evaluate the effectiveness of your teaching session. Ask yourself:
  a. Did you cover all the topics in your plan?
  b. Was the information well received by the patient?
  c. Did the patient appear to learn?
  d. How would you rate your performance?				

(continued)

Procedure Steps Total Possible Points - 32 Time Limit: 15 minutes	Practice #1	Practice #2	Practice #3	Final
8. Revise your plan as necessary to make it even more effective.*				
Total Number of Points Achieved/Final Score				
Initials of Observer:				

Comments and Signatures

Reviewer's comments and signatures:

1. _____

2. _____

3. _____

Instructor's comments:

_____

CAAHEP Competencies Achieved

I. A. (2) Use language/verbal skills that enable patients' understanding

IV. C. (12) Organize technical information and summaries

ABHES Competencies Achieved

5. (b) Identify and respond appropriately when working/caring for patients with special needs

5. (e) Advocate on behalf of family/patients, having ability to deal and communicate with family

5. (g) Analyze the effect of hereditary, cultural, and environmental influences

8. (aa) [Graduates] Are attentive, listen and learn

8. (bb) [Graduates] Are impartial and show empathy when dealing with patients

8. (cc) Communicate on the recipient's level of comprehension

8. (dd) Serve as liaison between physician and others

8. (gg) Use pertinent medical terminology

8. (ii) Recognize and respond to verbal and non-verbal communication

8. (jj) Perform fundamental writing skills including correct grammar, spelling, and formatting techniques when writing prescriptions, documenting medical records, etc.

8. (kk) Adapt to individualized needs

9. (dd) Recognize and understand various treatment protocols

11 a. (6) Adapting to change

PROCEDURE 14-2 INFORMING THE PATIENT OF GUIDELINES FOR SURGERY

Procedure Goal

To inform a preoperative patient of the necessary guidelines to follow prior to surgery

Scoring System

To score each step, use the following scoring system:
1 = poor, 2 = fair, 3 = good, 4 = excellent

A minimum score of at least a 3 must be achieved on **each** step to achieve successful completion of the technique. Detailed instructions on the scoring system are found on page 413.

Materials

Patient chart, surgical guidelines

Procedure

Procedure Steps Total Possible Points - 56 Time Limit: 10 minutes	Practice #1	Practice #2	Practice #3	Final
1. Review the patient's chart to determine the type of surgery to be performed and then ask the patient what procedure is being performed.*				
2. Tell the patient that you will be providing both verbal and written instructions that should be followed prior to surgery.				
3. Inform the patient about policies regarding makeup, jewelry, contact lenses, wigs, dentures, and so on.				
4. Tell the patient to leave money and valuables at home.				
5. If applicable, suggest appropriate clothing for the patient to wear for postoperative ease and comfort.				
6. Explain the need for someone to drive the patient home following an outpatient surgical procedure.*				
7. Tell the patient the correct time to arrive at the office surgery center or hospital for the procedure.				
8. Inform the patient of dietary restrictions. Be sure to use specific, clear instructions about what may or may not be ingested and at what time the patient must abstain from eating or drinking. Also explain these points: a. The reasons for the dietary restrictions. b. The possible consequences of not following the dietary restrictions.*				
9. Ask patients who smoke to refrain from or reduce cigarette smoking during at least the 8 hours prior to the procedure. Explain to the patient that reducing smoking improves the level of oxygen in the blood during surgery.				
10. Suggest that the patient shower or bathe the morning of the procedure or the evening before.				

(continued)

Procedure Steps Total Possible Points - 56 Time Limit: 10 minutes	Practice #1	Practice #2	Practice #3	Final
11. Instruct the patient about medications to take or avoid before surgery.*				
12. If necessary, clarify any information about which the patient is unclear.				
13. Provide written surgical guidelines and suggest that the patient call the office if additional questions arise.*				
14. Document the instruction in the patient's chart.*				
Total Number of Points Achieved/Final Score				
Initials of Observer:				

Comments and Signatures

Reviewer's comments and signatures:

1. _____

2. _____

3. _____

Instructor's comments:

_____

CAAHEP Competencies Achieved

IV. P. (2) Report relevant information to other succinctly and accurately

IV. P. (9) Document patient education

IV. A. (7) Demonstrate recognition of patient's level of understanding in communications

ABHES Competencies Achieved

5. (b) Identify and respond appropriately when working/caring for patients with special needs

5. (e) Advocate on behalf of family/patients, having ability to deal and communicate with family

5. (g) Analyze the effect of hereditary, cultural, and environmental influences

8. (aa) [Graduates] Are attentive, listen and learn

8. (bb) [Graduates] Are impartial and show empathy when dealing with patients

8. (cc) Communicate on the recipient's level of comprehension

8. (dd) Serve as liaison between physician and others

(continued)

8. (gg) Use pertinent medical terminology

8. (ii) Recognize and respond to verbal and non-verbal communication

8. (jj) Perform fundamental writing skills including correct grammar, spelling, and formatting techniques when writing prescriptions, documenting medical records, etc.

8. (kk) Adapt to individualized needs

9. (d) Recognize and understand various treatment protocols

11 a. (6) Adapting to change

PROCEDURE 15-1 VERIFYING WORKERS' COMPENSATION COVERAGE

Procedure Goal

To verify workers' compensation coverage before accepting a patient

Scoring System

To score each step, use the following scoring system:
1 = poor, 2 = fair, 3 = good, 4 = excellent

A minimum score of at least a 3 must be achieved on **each** step to achieve successful completion of the technique. Detailed instructions on the scoring system are found on page 413.

Materials

Telephone, paper, pencil

Procedure

Procedure Steps Total Possible Points - 24 Time Limit: 10 minutes	Practice #1	Practice #2	Practice #3	Final
1. Call the patient's employer and verify that the accident or illness occurred on the employer's premises or at an employment-related work site.				
2. Obtain the employer's approval to provide treatment. Be sure to write down the name and title of the person giving approval, as well as his phone number.*				
3. Ask the employer for the name of its workers' compensation insurance company. (Employers are required by law to carry such insurance. It is a good policy to notify your state labor department about any employer you encounter that does not have workers' compensation insurance, although you are not required to do so.) You may wish to remind the employer to report any workplace accidents or injuries that result in a workers' compensation claim to the state labor department within 24 hours of the incident.*				
4. Contact the insurance company and verify that the employer does indeed have a policy with the company and that the policy is in good standing.*				
5. Obtain a claim number for the case from the insurance company. This claim number is used on all bills and paperwork.*				
6. At the time the patient starts treatment, create a patient record. If the patient is already one of the practice's regular patients, create separate medical and financial records for the workers' compensation case.*				
Total Number of Points Achieved/Final Score				
Initials of Observer:				

(continued)

Comments and Signatures

Reviewer's comments and signatures:

1. _____

2. _____

3. _____

Instructor's comments:

_____

CAAHEP Competencies Achieved

VII. C. (3) Discuss Workers' Compensation as it applies to patients

IX. P. (1) Respond to issues of confidentiality

IX. A. (1) Demonstrate sensitivity to patient's rights

ABHES Competencies Achieved

3. (c) Understand the various medical terminology for each specialty

3. (d) Recognize and identify acceptable medical abbreviations

4. (f) Comply with federal, state, and local health laws and regulations

8. (r) Apply third party guidelines

8. (s) Obtain managed care referrals and pre-certification

8. (dd) Serve as liaison between physician and others

8. (gg) Use pertinent medical terminology

8. (hh) Receive, organize, prioritize, and transmit information expediently

PROCEDURE 15-2 COMPLETING THE CMS-1500 CLAIM FORM

Procedure Goal

To complete the CMS-1500 claim form correctly

Scoring System

To score each step, use the following scoring system:
1 = poor, 2 = fair, 3 = good, 4 = excellent

A minimum score of at least a 3 must be achieved on **each** step to achieve successful completion of the technique. Detailed instructions on the scoring system are found on page 413.

Materials

Patient record, CMS-1500 form on page 759, typewriter or computer, patient ledger card and charge slip

Procedure

Procedure Steps Total Possible Points - 132 Time Limit: 30 minutes	Practice #1	Practice #2	Practice #3	Final
Note: The numbers below correspond to the numbered fields on the CMS-1500.				
Patient Information Section				
1. Place an *X* in the appropriate insurance box.* 1a. Enter the insured's insurance identification number as it appears on the insurance card.*				
2. Enter the patient's name in this order: last name, first name, middle initial (if any).				
3. Enter the patient's birth date using two digits each for the month and day. For example, for a patient born on February 9, 1954, enter 02-09-1954. Indicate the sex of the patient: male or female.				
4. If the insured and the patient are the same person, enter SAME. If not, enter the policyholder's name. For TRICARE claims, enter the sponsor's (service person's) full name. For Medicare, leave blank.				
5. Enter the patient's mailing address, city, state, and zip code.				
6. Enter the patient's relationship to the insured. If they are the same, mark SELF. For TRICARE, enter the patient's relationship to the sponsor. For Medicare, leave blank.				
7. Enter the insured's mailing address, city, state, zip code, and telephone number. If this address is the same as the patient's, enter SAME. For Medicare, leave blank.				
8. Indicate the patient's marital, employment, and student status by placing an *X* in the boxes.				

(continued)

Procedure Steps Total Possible Points - 132 Time Limit: 30 minutes	Practice #1	Practice #2	Practice #3	Final
9. Enter the last name, first name, and middle initial of any other insured person whose policy might cover the patient. If the claim is for Medicare and the patient has a Medigap policy, enter the patient's name again. Keep in mind that block 9 is for secondary insurance coverage; block 11 is for the patient's primary insurance plan.				
9a. Enter the policy or group number for the other insured person. If this is a Medigap policy, enter MEDIGAP before the policy number. For Medicare, leave blank.				
9b. Enter the date of birth and sex of the other insured person (field 9).				
9c. Enter the other insured's employer or school name. (Note: If this is a Medicare claim, enter the claims-processing address for the Medigap insurer from field 9. If this is a Medicaid claim and other insurance is available, note it in field 1a and in field 2, and enter the requested policy information.				
9d. Enter the other insured's insurance plan or program name. If the plan is Medigap and CMS has assigned it a nine-digit number called PAYERID, enter that number here. On an attached sheet, give the complete mailing address for all other insurance information, and enter the word ATTACHMENT in 10d.				
10. Place Xs in the appropriate YES or NO boxes in a, b, and c to indicate whether the patient's place of employment, an auto accident, or other type of accident precipitated the patient's condition. If an auto accident is responsible, for PLACE, enter the two-letter state postal abbreviation. For Medicaid claims, enter MCD and the Medicaid number at line 10d. For all other claims, enter ATTACHMENT here if there is other insurance information. Be sure the full names and addresses of the other insurers appear on the attached sheet. Also, code the insurer as follows: MSP Medicare Secondary Payer, MG Medigap, SP Supplemental Employer, MCD Medicaid.*				
11. Enter the insured's policy or group number. For Medicare claims, fill out this section only if there is other insurance primary to Medicare; otherwise, enter NONE and leave fields 11a–d blank.*				
11a. Enter the insured's date of birth and sex as in field 3, if the insured is not the patient.				
11b. Enter the employer's name or school name here. This information will determine if Medicare is the primary payer.				
11c. Enter the insurance plan or program name.				

(continued)

Procedure Steps Total Possible Points - 132 Time Limit: 30 minutes	Practice #1	Practice #2	Practice #3	Final
11d. Place an *X* to indicate YES or NO related to another health benefit plan. If YES, you must complete 9a through 9d. Failure to do so will cause the claim to be denied. *Note:* It is important to remember that section 11 is for the primary insurer and section 9 is for any secondary insurance coverage.				
12. Have the patient or an authorized representative sign and date the form here. If a representative signs, have the representative indicate the relationship to the patient. If a signature is kept on file in the office, indicate by inserting "signature on file."*				
13. Have the insured (the patient or another individual) sign here.*				
Physician Information Section				
14. Enter the date of the current illness, injury, or pregnancy, using eight digits.				
15. Enter date the patient was first seen for illness or injury. Leave it blank for Medicare.				
16. Enter the dates the patient is or was unable to work. This information could signal a workers' compensation claim.				
17. Enter the name of the referring physician, clinical laboratory, or other referring source.				
17a. If required by payer, enter the appropriate two-digit qualifier in the small space immediately to the right of 17a. Next to this, enter the appropriate provider identifier.				
17b. Enter the provider NPI number.*				
18. Enter the dates the patient was hospitalized, if at all, with the current condition.				
19. Use your payer's current instructions for this field. Some payers require you to enter the date the patient was last seen by the referring physician or other medical professional. Other payers ask for certain identifiers. If a non-NPI is used, be sure to use the appropriate non-NPI qualifier to identify the identifier used.				
20. Place an *X* in the YES box if a laboratory test was performed outside the physician's office, and enter the test price if you are billing for these tests. Ensure that field 32 carries the laboratory's exact name and address and the insurance carrier's nine-digit provider identification number (PIN). Place an X in the NO box if the test was done in the office of the physician who is billing the insurance company.				
21. Enter the multidigit *International Classification of Diseases, 9th edition, Clinical Modification* (ICD-9-CM) code				

(continued)

Procedure Steps Total Possible Points - 132 Time Limit: 30 minutes	Practice #1	Practice #2	Practice #3	Final
number diagnosis or nature of injury (see Chapter 16). Enter up to four codes in order of importance. *Note:* Some insurers are allowing up 6 or 8 diagnoses, particularly on electronic claims. Be sure to check with each carrier for its regulations.*				
22. Enter the Medicaid resubmission code and original reference number if applicable.				
23. Enter the prior authorization number if required by the payer.*				
24. The six service lines in block 24 are divided horizontally to accommodate NPI and other proprietary identifiers. The upper shaded area may also be used to provide supplemental information regarding services provided, but you must verify requirements for the use of this area with each payer prior to use. Otherwise, use the nonshaded areas.				
24A. Enter the date of each service, procedure, or supply provided. Add the number of days for each, and enter them, in chronological order, in field 24G.				
24B. Enter the two-digit place-of-service code (see Table 15-4). For example, 11 is for office, 12 is for home, and 25 is for birthing center. Your office should have a list for reference.				
24C. EMC stands for *emergency care.* Check with provider to see if this information is needed. If it is required and emergency care was provided, enter Y; if it is not required or care was not on an emergency basis, leave this field blank. For medicare, leave blank.				
24D. Enter the CPT/HCPCS codes with modifiers for the procedures, services, or supplies provided (see Chapter 16).				
24E. Enter the diagnosis code (or its reference number—1, 2, 3, or 4—depending on carrier regulations) that applies to that procedure, as listed in field 21.*				
24F. Enter the dollar amount of fee charged.				
24G. Enter the days or units on which the service was performed. If a service took 3 days or was performed 3 times, as listed in 24A, enter 3.				
24H. This field is Medicaid-specific for early periodic screening, diagnosis and treatment programs.				
24I. If required by the insurance carrier, enter the appropriate non-NPI identifier here. If not required, leave this area blank.				
24J. If a non-NPI required by the carrier, enter the PIN identified in 24I in the shaded area. Use the nonshaded area below this to enter the provider's NPI in 24I.				
25. Enter the physician's or care provider's federal tax identification number or Social Security number.				

(continued)

Procedure Steps Total Possible Points - 132 Time Limit: 30 minutes	Practice #1	Practice #2	Practice #3	Final
26. Enter the patient's account number assigned by your office, if applicable.				
27. Place an X in the YES box to indicate that the physician will accept Medicare or TRICARE assignment of benefits. The check will be sent directly to the physician.				
28. Enter the total charge for the service.				
29. Enter the amount already paid by any primary insurance company or the patient, if it pertains to his deductible. Do not enter payments by the patient if it pertains to the coinsurance amount. For primary Medicare claims, leave blank.*				
30. Enter the balance due your office (subtract field 29 from field 28 to obtain this figure). For primary Medicare claims, leave blank.				
31. Have the physician or service supplier sign and date the form here.*				
32. Enter the name and address of the organization or individual who performed the services. If performed in the patient's home, leave this field blank.				
32a. In field 32a, enter the NPI for the service facility.				
32b. Use field 32b if required by the insurance carrier. In this case, enter the appropriate two-digit qualifier immediately followed by the identification number being used. Do not place any spaces or punctuation between the qualifier and the identification number.				
33. List the billing physician's or supplier's name, address, zip code, and phone number.				
33a. In field 33a, enter the NPI of the billing provider.				
33b. If required by the insurance carrier, enter the non-NPI qualifier in field 33b immediately followed by the identification number being used.				
Total Number of Points Achieved/Final Score				
Initials of Observer:				

Comments and Signatures

Reviewer's comments and signatures:

1. _____

2. _____

3. _____

Instructor's comments:

_____

(continued)

CAAHEP Competencies Achieved

V. C. (13) Identify time management principles

VII. C (7) Describe how guidelines are used in processing an insurance claim

VII. C. (9) Describe guidelines for third-party claims

ABHES Competencies Achieved

3. (c) Understand the various medical terminology for each specialty

3. (d) Recognize and identify acceptable medical abbreviations

4. (f) Comply with federal, state, and local health laws and regulations

8. (r) Apply third party guidelines

8. (s) Obtain managed care referrals and pre-certification

8. (u) Prepare and submit insurance claims

8. (v) Use physician fee schedule

8. (dd) Serve as liaison between physician and others

8. (gg) Use pertinent medical terminology

8. (hh) Receive, organize, prioritize, and transmit information expediently

PROCEDURE 16-1 LOCATING AN ICD-9-CM CODE

Procedure Goal

To analyze diagnoses and locate the correct ICD code.

Scoring System

To score each step, use the following scoring system:
1 = poor, 2 = fair, 3 = good, 4 = excellent

A minimum score of at least a 3 must be achieved on **each** step to achieve successful completion of the technique. Detailed instructions on the scoring system are found on page 413.

Materials

Patient record, charge slip or superbill, ICD-9-CM manual

Procedure

Procedure Steps Total Possible Points - 20 Time Limit: 10 minutes	Practice #1	Practice #2	Practice #3	Final
1. Locate the patient's diagnosis. a. This information may be located on the superbill (encounter form) or elsewhere in the patient's chart. If it is on the superbill, verify documentation in the medical chart.*				
2. Find the diagnosis in the ICD's Alphabetic Index. Look for the condition first, then locate the indented subterms that make the condition more specific. Read all cross-references to check all the possibilities for a term, including its synonyms and any eponyms.*				
3. Locate the code from the Alphabetic Index in the ICD's Tabular List.*				
4. Read all information to find the code that corresponds to the patient's specific disease or condition. a. Study the list of codes and descriptions. Be sure to pick the most specific code available. Check for the symbol that shows that a four- or five-digit code is required.*				
5. Carefully record the diagnosis code(s) on the insurance claim and proofread the numbers. a. Be sure that all necessary codes are given to completely describe each diagnosis. Check for instructions stating an additional code is needed. If more than one code is needed, be sure instructions are followed and the codes are listed in the correct order.*				
Total Number of Points Achieved/Final Score				
Initials of Observer:				

(continued)

Comments and Signatures

Reviewer's comments and signatures:

1. _____

2. _____

3. _____

Instructor's comments:

_____

CAAHEP Competencies Achieved

VII. C. (2) Define up-coding and why it should be avoided

VII. C. (1) Describe how to use the most current diagnostic coding classification system

VII. P. (2) Perform diagnostic coding

ABHES Competencies Achieved

8. (b) Identify and apply the knowledge of all body systems, their structure and functions, and their common diseases, symptoms and etiologies.

8. (r) Apply third party guidelines

8. (t) Perform diagnostic and procedural coding

8. (gg) Use pertinent medical terminology

PROCEDURE 16-2 LOCATING A HCPCS CODE

Procedure Goal

To locate the proper HCPCS code for a service or piece of equipment

Scoring System

To score each step, use the following scoring system:
1 = poor, 2 = fair, 3 = good, 4 = excellent

A minimum score of at least a 3 must be achieved on **each** step to achieve successful completion of the technique. Detailed instructions on the scoring system are found on page 413.

Materials

HCPCS manual, patient record, charge slip or superbill

Procedure

Procedure Steps Total Possible Points: 20 Time Limit: 10 minutes	Practice #1	Practice #2	Practice #3	Final
1. Locate the service, supplies and equipment requiring a HCPCS code from the charge slip or from the patient's record.				
2. Use the index at the back of the manual to locate the section in which the category of codes is found.				
3. Find the code or code range by seeking first the initial letter and then the four-digit number. They are arranged alphabetically and numerically. Make sure you read the description thoroughly and determine the correct code. Do not code from the index.				
4. Make sure the code is valid for the type of insurance the patient carries.				
5. Enter the correct code(s) on the superbill or charge slip, encounter form, and if necessary the patient's computerized record so that it can be used for billing purposes.				
Total Number of Points Achieved/Final Score				
Initials of Observer:				

Comments and Signatures

Reviewer's comments and signatures:

1. _____

2. _____

3. _____

Instructor's comments:

_____

(continued)

CAAHEP Competencies Achieved

VII. (C) 7. Describe how guidelines are used in processing an insurance claims

VII. (P) 1. Perform procedural coding

IX. (C) 13. Discuss all levels of governmental legislation and regulation as they apply to medical assisting practice, including FDA and DEA regulations

ABHES Competencies Achieved

8. (r) Apply third party guidelines

8. (t) Perform diagnostic and procedural coding

8. (gg) Use pertinent medical terminology

PROCEDURE 16-3 LOCATING A CPT CODE

Procedure Goal

To locate correct CPT codes

Scoring System

To score each step, use the following scoring system:
1 = poor, 2 = fair, 3 = good, 4 = excellent

A minimum score of at least a 3 must be achieved on **each** step to achieve successful completion of the technique. Detailed instructions on the scoring system are found on page 413.

Materials

Patient record, superbill or charge slip, CPT manual

Procedure

Procedure Steps Total Possible Points - 20 Time Limit: 10 minutes	Practice #1	Practice #2	Practice #3	Final
1. Find the services listed on the superbill (if used) and in the patient's record. a. Check the patient's record to see which services were documented. For E/M procedures, look for clues as to the location of the service, extent of history, exam, and medical decision making that were involved.*				
2. Look up the procedure code(s) in the alphabetic index of the CPT manual. a. Verify the code number in the numeric index, reading all notes and guidelines for that section. b. If a code range is noted, look up the range and choose the correct code from the range given. If the correct description is not found, start the process again. Use the same process if multiple codes are given.*				
3. Determine appropriate modifiers. a. Check section guidelines and Appendix A to choose a modifier if needed to explain a situation involving the procedure being coded, such as bilateral procedure, surgical team, or a discontinued procedure.*				
4. Carefully record the procedure code(s) on the health-care claim. Usually the primary procedure, the one that is the primary reason for the encounter or visit, is listed first.*				
5. Match each procedure with its corresponding diagnosis. The primary procedure is often (but not always) matched with the primary diagnosis.*				
Total Number of Points Achieved/Final Score				
Initials of Observer:				

(continued)

Comments and Signatures

Reviewer's comments and signatures:

1. _____

2. _____

3. _____

Instructor's comments:

_____

CAAHEP Competencies Achieved

VII. C. (1) Describe how to use the most current diagnostic coding classification system

VIII. P. (1) Perform procedural coding

ABHES Competencies Achieved

8. (r) Apply third party guidelines

8. (t) Perform diagnostic and procedural coding

8. (gg) Use pertinent medical terminology

PROCEDURE 17-1 PROCESSING A CREDIT BALANCE

Procedure Goal

To process a credit balance

Scoring System

To score each step, use the following scoring system:
1 = poor, 2 = fair, 3 = good, 4 = excellent

A minimum score of at least a 3 must be achieved on **each** step to achieve successful completion of the technique. Detailed instructions on the scoring system are found on page 413.

Materials

Daily log sheet (also known as a day sheet); checks, ledger card, computer, calculator, Remittance Advice (RA), also known as an Explanation of Benefits (EOB)

Procedure (Processing a credit balance)

Procedure Steps Total Possible Points - 28 Time Limit: 10 minutes	Practice #1	Practice #2	Practice #3	Final
1. Locate patient's account in computer, or pull the patient's ledger card for paper-based systems*				
2. Review the policy manual to make sure you are following the guidelines for posting credit balances.*				
3. Review the EOB and check to be sure that the payment is being credited to the correct patient account				
4. Post the payment to the patient's account				
5. Check calculations carefully if it appears that an overpayment has been made.				
6. Review the account thoroughly in case more insurance payments are expected on the patient's account.*				
7. Adjust the credit balance off the patient's account by issuing a refund.*				
Total Number of Points Achieved/Final Score				
Initials of Observer:				

Comments and Signatures

Reviewer's comments and signatures:

1. _____

2. _____

3. _____

Instructor's comments:

_____

(continued)

CAAHEP Competencies Achieved

VI. C. (13) Discuss types of adjustments that may be made to a patient's account

VI. P. (2) (e) Process a credit balance

ABHES Competencies Achieved

8. (h) Post entries on a day sheet

8. (i) Perform billing and collection procedures

8. (k) Perform accounts receivable procedures

8. (m) Post adjustments

8. (n) Process credit balance

8. (v) Use physician fee schedule

PROCEDURE 17-2 PROCESSING REFUNDS TO PATIENTS

Procedure Goal

To process refunds to patients

Scoring System

To score each step, use the following scoring system:
1 = poor, 2 = fair, 3 = good, 4 = excellent

A minimum score of at least a 3 must be achieved on **each** step to achieve successful completion of the technique. Detailed instructions on the scoring system are found on page 413.

Materials

Payment (check), ledger card, computer, calculator, Remittance Advice (RA) also known as an Explanation of Benefits (EOB)

Procedure

Procedure Steps Total Possible Points - 20 Time Limit: 10 minutes	Practice #1	Practice #2	Practice #3	Final
1. Calculate the amount to be refunded.*				
2. Write a check to the patient for the amount to be refunded.				
3. Ask the physician or business manager to sign the check so that it can be given or mailed to the patient.*				
4. Post the refund as a negative payment (credit) to the patient's ledger card or to the account if a computerized system is being used.				
5. Make a copy of the check, retaining a copy in the patient's financial record. Give or mail the check to the patient (verify the correct address of the patient). Mail the check certified return receipt.*				
Total Number of Points Achieved/Final Score				
Initials of Observer:				

Comments and Signatures

Reviewer's comments and signatures:

1. _____

2. _____

3. _____

Instructor's comments:

_____

(continued)

CAAHEP Competencies Achieved

VI. P. (2) (f) Process refunds

VI. C. (10) Identify procedure for preparing patient accounts

ABHES Competencies Achieved

8. (h) Post entries on a day sheet

8. (i) Perform billing and collection procedures

8. (k) Perform accounts receivable procedures

8. (n) Process credit balance

8. (o) Process refunds

8. (v) Use physician fee schedule

8. (w) Use manual or computerized bookkeeping systems

PROCEDURE 17-3 HOW TO BILL WITH THE SUPERBILL

Procedure Goal

To complete a superbill accurately

Scoring System

To score each step, use the following scoring system:
1 = poor, 2 = fair, 3 = good, 4 = excellent

A minimum score of at least a 3 must be achieved on **each** step to achieve successful completion of the technique. Detailed instructions on the scoring system are found on page 413.

Materials

Superbill, patient ledger card, patient information sheet, fee schedule, insurance code list, pen

Procedure

Procedure Steps Total Possible Points - 44 Time Limit: 10 minutes	Practice #1	Practice #2	Practice #3	Final
1. From the patient ledger card and information sheet, fill in the patient data, such as name, sex, date of birth, and insurance information.*				
2. Fill in the place and date of service.				
3. Attach the superbill to the patient's medical record, and give them both to the doctor.*				
4. Accept the completed superbill from the patient after the patient sees the doctor. Make sure that the doctor has indicated the diagnosis and the procedures performed. Also make sure that an appropriate diagnosis is listed for each procedure.*				
5. If the doctor has not already recorded the charges, refer to the fee schedule for procedures that are marked. Then fill in the charges next to those procedures.*				
6. In the appropriate blanks, list the total charges for the visit and the previous balance (if any).				
7. Calculate the subtotal.				
8. Fill in the amount and type of payment (cash, check, money order, or credit card) made by the patient during this visit.*				
9. Calculate and enter the new balance.				
10. Have the patient sign the authorization-and-release section of the superbill.*				
11. Keep a copy of the superbill for the practice records. Give the original to the patient along with one copy to file with the insurer.				
Total Number of Points Achieved/Final Score				
Initials of Observer:				

(continued)

Comments and Signatures

Reviewer's comments and signatures:

1. _____

2. _____

3. _____

Instructor's comments:

_____

CAAHEP Competencies Achieved

VI. C. (9) Explain both billing and payment options

VI. P. (2) (b) Perform billing procedures

VI. P. (3) Utilize computerized office billing systems

ABHES Competencies Achieved

8. (h) Post entries on a day sheet

8. (i) Perform billing and collection procedures

8. (k) Perform accounts receivable procedures

8. (v) Use physician fee schedule

8. (w) Use manual or computerized bookkeeping systems

PROCEDURE 17-4 HOW TO CREATE AN AGE ANALYSIS RECORD

Procedure Goal

To create and examine an age analysis

Scoring System

To score each step, use the following scoring system:
1 = poor, 2 = fair, 3 = good, 4 = excellent

A minimum score of at least a 3 must be achieved on **each** step to achieve successful completion of the technique. Detailed instructions on the scoring system are found on page 413.

Materials

Computer, patient accounts, patient ledger cards (if being done by hand) accounts receivable aging record analysis form (optional); policy and procedure manual, pen

Procedure

Procedure Steps Total Possible Points - 40 Time Limit: 20 minutes	Practice #1	Practice #2	Practice #3	Final
1. Using the reporting section of your billing computer program, create an age analysis report for patients and insurance companies. This can also be done manually by pulling patient ledger cards, noting the balances due and dates of last payment. Use the ledger cards and blank Account Receivable-Age Analysis on pages 763–770.				
2. Review the accounting report. Check the report—highlight for proposed actions for each account according to your office policy.*				
3. Mark the accounts that are under 31 days as NO ACTION TO BE TAKEN AT THIS TIME				
4. Bills that are unpaid at more than 31 days should be marked as "Contact or Follow up with insurance company".*				
5. Accounts that are 31–60 days old should be marked according to your office's policy. An initial phone call may be made inquiring as to payment arrangements				
6. Accounts that are 61–90 days old should be marked according to your office's policy. Make notations such as Account Past due. A follow-up phone call and/or more insistent letter for payment may be in order.				
7. Accounts that are 91–120 days old should be marked according to your office's policy. A last phone call to attempt discussing the account and more insistent collection statement/letter should be sent.				
8. For accounts older than 120 days make sure you review the collection attempts from before. At this point, after discussion with the physician, a letter stating the account				

(continued)

Procedure Steps Total Possible Points - 40 Time Limit: 20 minutes	Practice #1	Practice #2	Practice #3	Final
will be turned over to the collection agency will take place with a specific date listed in the letter. This letter should be mailed by certified return receipt mail*				
9. Record all actions that have been taken beside each account.*				
10. Finally, write follow-up letters to patients and document any agreements that you and the patient have discussed via telephone. Be sure to keep a copy of any correspondence sent to the patient in the financial record.*				
Total Number of Points Achieved/Final Score				
Initials of Observer:				

Comments and Signatures

Reviewer's comments and signatures:

1. _____

2. _____

3. _____

Instructor's comments:

_____

CAAHEP Competencies Achieved

ABHES Competencies Achieved

8. (d) Apply concepts for office procedures

8. (i) Perform billing and collection procedures

8. (k) Perform accounts receivable procedures

8. (v) Use physician fee schedule

8. (w) Use manual or computerized bookkeeping systems

PROCEDURE 18-1 POSTING ENTRIES, ADJUSTMENTS, COLLECTION PAYMENTS

Procedure Goal

To maintain a bookkeeping system that promotes accurate record keeping for the practice

Scoring System

To score each step, use the following scoring system:
1 = poor, 2 = fair, 3 = good, 4 = excellent

A minimum score of at least a 3 must be achieved on **each** step to achieve successful completion of the technique. Detailed instructions on the scoring system are found on page 413.

Materials

Daily log sheets, patient ledger cards, and check register, or computerized bookkeeping system; summaries of charges, receipts, and disbursements

Procedure

Procedure Steps Total Possible Points - 20 Time Limit: 10 minutes	Practice #1	Practice #2	Practice #3	Final
1. Use a new log (day) sheet each day. For each patient seen that day, record the patient name, the relevant charges, and any payments received, calculating any necessary adjustments and new balances. If you're using a computerized system, enter the patient's name or account number, the relevant charges, and any payments received and adjustments made in the appropriate areas. The computer will calculate the new balances.*				
2. Create a ledger card for each new patient and maintain a ledger card for all existing patients. The ledger card should include the patient's name, address, home and work telephone numbers, and insurance company. It should also contain the name of the guarantor (if different from the patient). Update the ledger card every time the patient incurs a charge or makes a payment. Be sure to adjust the account balance after every transaction. In a computerized system, a patient record is the same as a ledger card. This record must also be maintained and updated.*				
3. Record all deposits accurately in the check register. File the deposit receipt—with a detailed listing of checks, cash and money orders deposited—for later use in reconciling the bank statement. The deposit amount should match the amount of money collected by the practice for that day.				
4. When paying bills for the practice, enter each check in the check register accurately, including the check number, date, payee, and amount before writing the check.*				

(continued)

Procedure Steps Total Possible Points - 20 Time Limit: 10 minutes	Practice #1	Practice #2	Practice #3	Final
5. Prepare and/or print a summary of charges, receipts, and disbursements every month, quarter, or year, as directed. Be sure to double-check all entries and calculations from the monthly summary before posting them to the quarterly summary. Also, double-check the entries and calculations from the quarterly summary before posting them to the yearly summary.*				
Total Number of Points Achieved/Final Score				
Initials of Observer:				

Comments and Signatures

Reviewer's comments and signatures:

1. _____

2. _____

3. _____

Instructor's comments:

_____

CAAHEP Competencies Achieved

VI. P. (2) (a) Post entries on a day sheet

VI. P. (2) (d) Post adjustments

VI. P. (2) (h) Post collection agency payments

ABHES Competencies Achieved

8. (d) Apply concepts for office procedures

8. (k) Perform accounts receivable procedures

8. (m) Post adjustments

8. (q) Post collection agency payments

8. (w) Use manual or computerized bookkeeping systems

PROCEDURE 18-2 POSTING A NON-SUFFICIENT FUNDS (NSF) CHECK

Procedure Goal

To post a Non-Sufficient Funds (NSF) Check to patient's account

Scoring System

To score each step, use the following scoring system:
1 = poor, 2 = fair, 3 = good, 4 = excellent

A minimum score of at least a 3 must be achieved on **each** step to achieve successful completion of the technique. Detailed instructions on the scoring system are found on page 413.

Materials

Computer, returned check, patient ledger sheet, calculator (optional); daily log sheet (optional)

Procedure

Procedure Steps Total Possible Points - 28 Time Limit: 10 minutes	Practice #1	Practice #2	Practice #3	Final
1. Locate the patient's account on the computer or pull the patient's ledger card for manual processes.*				
2. Use your medical facility code for NSF check or charge and create a new billing entry for the patient and post the returned check using the NSF code. On the daily log sheet, write the NSF check number and the words *check returned by bank* in the *professional services column*. In the adjustment column, place the amount of the check in parentheses to indicate that the amount is debited as an *adjustment*. Add the new charge to the old balance and enter it in the *new balance* column.				
3. Post the fees for the NSF check using the code provided by the medical facility. On the daily log sheet, post the charge for the fee in the *charge* column. Add the amount to the old balance and record in the new balance column				
4. Use your medical facility's code for an NSF check (if used), and using today's date, create a new charge log for the patient. Using the code and the description *Check returned by bank* in the description column.				
5. In the Payment column insert the amount of the NSF check in parentheses*				
6. Add the amount of the NSF check to the previous balance and insert that figure in the *Current Balance* column.*				
7. On the next line, also using today's date, add the description of *NSF Office Fee* with the office charge for NSF checks returned by the bank. Add this charge to the previous balance to obtain the new *Current Balance*				
Total Number of Points Achieved/Final Score				
Initials of Observer:				

(continued)

Comments and Signatures

Reviewer's comments and signatures:

1. _____

2. _____

3. _____

Instructor's comments:

_____

CAAHEP Competency Achieved

VI. P. (1) (g) Perform accounts receivable procedures including posting non-sufficient fund (NSF) checks.

ABHES Competency Achieved

8. (h) Post entries on a day sheet

8. (p) Post non-sufficient funds (NSF)

8. (ll) Apply electronic technology

PROCEDURE 18-3 MAKING A BANK DEPOSIT

Procedure Goal

To prepare cash and checks for deposit and to deposit them properly into a bank account

Scoring System

To score each step, use the following scoring system:
1 = poor, 2 = fair, 3 = good, 4 = excellent

A minimum score of at least a 3 must be achieved on **each** step to achieve successful completion of the technique. Detailed instructions on the scoring system are found on page 413.

Materials

Bank deposit slip and items to be deposited, such as checks, cash, and money orders

Procedure

Procedure Steps Total Possible Points - 40 Time Limit: 10 minutes	Practice #1	Practice #2	Practice #3	Final
1. Divide the bills, coins, checks, and money orders into separate piles.				
2. Sort the bills by denomination, from largest to smallest. Then, stack them, portrait side up, in the same direction. Total the amount of the bills and write this amount on the deposit slip on the line marked "Currency."*				
3. If you have enough coins to fill coin wrappers, put them in wrappers of the proper denomination. If not, count the coins and put them in the deposit bag. Total the amount of coins and write this amount on the deposit slip on the line marked "Coin."				
4. Review all checks and money orders to be sure they are properly endorsed with a restrictive endorsement. List each check on the deposit slip, including the check number and amount.				
5. List each money order on the deposit slip. Include the notation "money order" or "MO" and the name of the writer.				
6. Calculate the total deposit (total of amounts for currency, coin, checks, and money orders). Write this amount on the deposit slip on the line marked "Total." If you do not use deposit slips that record a copy for the office, photocopy the deposit slip for your office records.*				
7. Record the total amount of the deposit in the office checkbook register.*				
8. If you plan to make the deposit in person, place the currency, coins, checks, and money orders in a deposit bag. If you cannot make the deposit in person, put the checks and money orders in a special bank-by-mail envelope or put all deposit items in an envelope and send it by registered mail.*				

(continued)

Procedure Steps Total Possible Points - 40 Time Limit: 10 minutes	Practice #1	Practice #2	Practice #3	Final
9. Make the deposit in person or by mail.				
10. Obtain a deposit receipt from the bank. File it with the copy of the deposit slip in the office for later use when reconciling the bank statement.*				
Total Number of Points Achieved/Final Score				
Initials of Observer:				

Comments and Signatures

Reviewer's comments and signatures:

1. _____

2. _____

3. _____

Instructor's comments:

_____

CAAHEP Competencies Achieved

VI. C. (3) Describe banking procedures

VI. C. (4) Discuss precautions for accepting checks

VI. P. (1) Prepare a bank deposit

ABHES Competencies Achieved

8. (d) Apply concepts for office procedures

8. (g) Prepare and reconcile a bank statement and deposit record

PROCEDURE 18-4 RECONCILING A BANK STATEMENT

Procedure Goal

To ensure that the bank record of deposits, payments, and withdrawals agrees with the practice's record of deposits, payments, and withdrawals

Scoring System

To score each step, use the following scoring system:
1 = poor, 2 = fair, 3 = good, 4 = excellent

A minimum score of at least a 3 must be achieved on **each** step to achieve successful completion of the technique. Detailed instructions on the scoring system are found on page 413.

Materials

Previous bank statement, current bank statement, reconciliation worksheet (if not part of current bank statement), deposit receipts, red pencil, check stubs or checkbook register, returned checks

Procedure

Procedure Steps Total Possible Points - 40 Time Limit: 15 minutes	Practice #1	Practice #2	Practice #3	Final
1. Check the closing balance on the previous statement against the opening balance on the new statement. The balances should match. If they do not, call the bank.				
2. Record the closing balance from the new statement on the reconciliation worksheet (Figure 18-9). This worksheet usually appears on the back of the bank statement.				
3. Check each deposit receipt against the bank statement. Place a red check mark in the upper-right corner of each receipt that is recorded on the statement. Total the amount of deposits that do *not* appear on the statement. Add this amount to the closing balance on the reconciliation worksheet.*				
4. Put the redeemed checks in numerical order. (Your bank may send you several sheets consisting of photocopies of checks instead of the actual checks.)				
5. Compare each redeemed check with the bank statement, making sure that the amount on the check agrees with the amount on the statement. Place a red check mark in the upper-right corner of each redeemed check that is recorded on the statement. Also, place a check mark on the check stub or check register entry. Any checks that were written but that do not appear on the statement and were not returned as redeemed are considered "outstanding" checks. You can find these easily on the check stubs or checkbook register because they have no red check mark.				
6. List each outstanding check separately on the worksheet, including its check number and amount. Total the outstanding checks and subtract this total from the bank statement balance.*				

(continued)

Procedure Steps Total Possible Points - 40 Time Limit: 15 minutes	Practice #1	Practice #2	Practice #3	Final
7. If the statement shows that the checking account earned interest, add this amount to the checkbook balance.*				
8. If the statement lists such items as a service charge, check printing charge, or automatic payment, subtract them from the checkbook balance.*				
9. Compare the new checkbook balance with the new bank statement balance. They should match. If they do not, repeat the process, rechecking all calculations. Double-check the addition and subtraction in the checkbook register. Review the checkbook register to make sure you did not omit any items. Ensure that you carried the correct balance forward from one register page to the next. Double-check that you made the correct additions or subtractions for all interest earned and charges.				
10. If your work is correct, and the balances still do not agree, call the bank to determine if a bank error has been made. Contact the bank promptly because the bank may have a time limit for corrections. The bank may consider the bank statement correct if you do not point out an error within 2 weeks (or other period, according to bank policy).				
Total Number of Points Achieved/Final Score				
Initials of Observer:				

Comments and Signatures

Reviewer's comments and signatures:

1. _____

2. _____

3. _____

Instructor's comments:

_____

CAAHEP Competencies Achieved

VI. C. (3) Describe banking procedures

VI. C. (8) Describe common periodic financially reports

ABHES Competency Achieved

8. (g) Prepare and reconcile a bank statement and deposit record

PROCEDURE 18-5 SETTING UP THE ACCOUNTS PAYABLE SYSTEM

Procedure Goal

To set up an accounts payable system

Scoring System

To score each step, use the following scoring system:
1 = poor, 2 = fair, 3 = good, 4 = excellent

A minimum score of at least a 3 must be achieved on **each** step to achieve successful completion of the technique. Detailed instructions on the scoring system are found on page 413.

Materials

Disbursements journal, petty cash record, payroll register, pen

Procedure

Procedure Steps Total Possible Points - 48 Time Limit: 10 minutes	Practice #1	Practice #2	Practice #3	Final
Setting Up the Disbursements Journal				
1. Write in column headings for the basic information about each check: date, payee's name, check number, and check amount.				
2. Write in column headings for each type of business expense, such as rent and utilities.				
3. Write in column headings (if space is available) for deposits and the account balance.				
4. Record the data from completed checks under the appropriate column headings.				
5. Be sure to subtract payments from the balance and add deposits to it.*				
Setting Up the Petty Cash Record				
1. Write in column headings for the date, transaction number, payee, brief description, amount of transaction, and type of expense.				
2. Write in a column heading (if space is available) for the petty cash fund balance.				
3. Record the data from petty cash vouchers under the appropriate column headings.				
4. Subtract payments made from petty cash and when replenishing the fund, add the replenishment amount to the current balance.*				
Setting Up the Payroll Register				
1. Write in column headings for check number, employee name, earnings to date, hourly rate, hours worked, regular earnings, overtime hours worked, and overtime earnings.				

(continued)

Procedure Steps Total Possible Points - 48 Time Limit: 10 minutes	Practice #1	Practice #2	Practice #3	Final
2. Write in column headings for total gross earnings for the pay period and gross taxable earnings.				
3. Write in column headings for each deduction. These may include federal income tax, Federal Insurance Contributions Act (FICA) tax, state income tax, local income tax, and various voluntary deductions.				
4. Write in a column heading for net earnings.				
5. Each time you write payroll checks, record earning and deduction data under the appropriate column headings on the payroll register.				
Total Number of Points Achieved/Final Score				
Initials of Observer:				

Comments and Signatures

Reviewer's comments and signatures:

1. _____

2. _____

3. _____

Instructor's comments:

_____

CAAHEP Competencies Achieved

VI. C. (1) Explain basic bookkeeping computations

VI. C. (2) Differentiate between bookkeeping and accounting

VI. C. (6) Differentiate between accounts payable and accounts receivable

ABHES Competencies Achieved

8. (j) Perform accounts payable procedures

8. (l) Establish and maintain a petty cash fund

PROCEDURE 18-6 GENERATING PAYROLL

Procedure Goal

To handle the practice's payroll as efficiently and accurately as possible for each pay period

Scoring System

To score each step, use the following scoring system:
1 = poor, 2 = fair, 3 = good, 4 = excellent

A minimum score of at least a 3 must be achieved on **each** step to achieve successful completion of the technique. Detailed instructions on the scoring system are found on page 413.

Materials

Employees' time cards, employees' earnings records, payroll register, IRS tax tables, check register

Procedure

Procedure Steps Total Possible Points - 44 Time Limit: 15 minutes	Practice #1	Practice #2	Practice #3	Final
1. Calculate the total regular and overtime hours worked, based on the employee's time card. Enter those totals under the appropriate headings on the payroll register.*				
2. Check the pay rate on the employee earnings record. Then multiply the hours worked (including any paid vacation or paid holidays, if applicable) by the rates for regular time and overtime (time and a half or double time). This yields gross earnings.*				
3. Enter the gross earnings under the appropriate heading on the payroll register. Subtract any nontaxable benefits, such as health-care or retirement programs.				
4. Using IRS tax tables and data on the employee earnings record, determine the amount of federal income tax to withhold based on the employee's marital status and number of exemptions. Also compute the amount of FICA tax to withhold for Social Security (6.2%) and Medicare (1.45%).*				
5. Following state and local procedures, determine the amount of state and local income taxes (if any) to withhold based on the employee's marital status and number of exemptions.*				
6. Calculate the employer's contributions to FUTA and to the state unemployment fund, if any. Post these amounts to the employer's account.				
7. Enter any other required or voluntary deductions, such as health insurance or contributions to a 401(k) fund.				
8. Subtract all deductions from the gross earnings to get the employee's net earnings.				

(continued)

Procedure Steps Total Possible Points - 44 Time Limit: 15 minutes	Practice #1	Practice #2	Practice #3	Final
9. Enter the total amount withheld from all employees for FICA under the headings for Social Security and Medicare. Remember that the employer must match these amounts. Enter other employer contributions, such as for federal and state unemployment taxes, under the appropriate headings.*				
10. Fill out the check stub, including the employee's name, date, pay period, gross earnings, all deductions, and net earnings. Make out the paycheck for the net earnings.				
11. Deposit each deduction in a tax liability account.				
Total Number of Points Achieved/Final Score				
Initials of Observer:				

Comments and Signatures

Reviewer's comments and signatures:

1. _____

2. _____

3. _____

Instructor's comments:

_____

CAAHEP Competencies Achieved

II. C. (1) Demonstrate knowledge of basic math computations

VI. P. (1) Prepare a bank deposit

ABHES Competencies Achieved

8. (d) Apply concepts for office procedures

8. (j) Perform accounts payable procedures

8. (w) Use manual or computerized bookkeeping systems

PROCEDURE 33-1 ASEPTIC HAND WASHING

Procedure Goal

To remove dirt and microorganisms from under the fingernails and from the surface of the skin, hair follicles, and oil glands of the hands

Scoring System

To score each step, use the following scoring system:
1 = poor, 2 = fair, 3 = good, 4 = excellent

A minimum score of at least a 3 must be achieved on **each** step to achieve successful completion of the technique. Detailed instructions on the scoring system are found on page 413.

Materials

Liquid soap, nailbrush or orange stick, paper towels

Procedure

Procedure Steps Total Possible Points - 28 Time Limit: 10 minutes	Practice #1	Practice #2	Practice #3	Final
1. Remove all jewelry (plain wedding bands may be left on and scrubbed).				
2. Turn on the faucets using a paper towel and adjust the water temperature to moderately warm. (Sinks with knee-operated faucet controls prevent contact of the surface with the hands.)				
3. Wet your hands and apply liquid soap. Use a clean, dry paper towel to activate soap pump. Liquid soap, especially when dispensed with a foot pump, is preferable to bar soap.*				
4. Work the soap into a lather, making sure that all of both hands are lathered. Rub vigorously in a circular motion for 2 minutes. Keep your hands lower than your forearms so that dirty water flows into the sink instead of back onto your arms. Your fingertips should be pointing down. Interlace your fingers to clean between them, and use the palm of one hand to clean the back of the other. It is important that you wash every surface of your hands.*				
5. Use a nailbrush or orange stick to dislodge dirt around your nails and cuticles.*				
6. Rinse your hands well, keeping the hands lower than your forearms and not touching the sink or faucets.				
7. With the water still running, dry your hands thoroughly with clean, dry paper towels and then turn off the faucets using a clean, dry paper towel. Discard the towels.				
Total Number of Points Achieved/Final Score				
Initials of Observer:				

(continued)

Comments and Signatures

Reviewer's comments and signatures:

1. _____

2. _____

3. _____

Instructor's comments:

_____

CAAHEP Competency Achieved

III. P (4) Perform hand washing

ABHES Competency Achieved

4 (c) Apply principles of aseptic techniques and infection control

Procedure 33-2 Wrapping and Labeling Instruments for Sterilization in the Autoclave

Procedure Goal

To enclose instruments and equipment to be sterilized in appropriate wrapping materials to ensure sterilization and to protect supplies from contamination after sterilization

Scoring System

To score each step, use the following scoring system:
1 = poor, 2 = fair, 3 = good, 4 = excellent

A minimum score of at least a 3 must be achieved on **each** step to achieve successful completion of the technique. Detailed instructions on the scoring system are found on page 413.

Materials

Dry, sanitized, and disinfected instruments and equipment; wrapping material (paper, muslin, gauze, bags, envelopes); sterilization indicators; autoclave tape; labels (if wrapping does not include space for labeling); pen

Procedure

Procedure Steps Total Possible Points - 48 Time Limit: 10 minutes	Practice #1	Practice #2	Practice #3	Final
For wrapping instruments or equipment in pieces of paper or fabric: 1. Wash your hands and put on gloves before beginning to wrap the items to be sterilized.				
2. Place a square of paper or muslin on the table with one point toward you. With muslin, use a double thickness. The paper or fabric must be large enough to allow all four points to cover the instruments or equipment you will be wrapping. It also must be large enough to provide an overlap, which will be used as a handling flap.				
3. Place each item to be included in the pack in the center area of the paper or fabric "diamond." Items that will be used together should be wrapped together. Take care, however, that surfaces of the items do not touch each other inside the pack. Inspect each item to make sure it is operating correctly. Place hinged instruments in the pack in the open position. Wrap a small piece of paper, muslin, or gauze around delicate edges or points to protect against damage to other instruments or to the pack wrapping.*				
4. Place a sterilization indicator inside the pack with the instruments. Position the indicator correctly, following the manufacturer's guidelines.*				
5. Fold the bottom point of the diamond up and over the instruments in to the center. Fold back a small portion of the point.*				
6. Fold the right point of the diamond in to the center. Again, fold back a small portion of the point to be used as a handle.				

(continued)

Procedure Steps Total Possible Points - 48 Time Limit: 10 minutes	Practice #1	Practice #2	Practice #3	Final
7. Fold the left point of the diamond in to the center, folding back a small portion to form a handle. The pack should now resemble an open envelope.				
8. Grasp the covered instruments (the bottom of the envelope) and fold this portion up, toward the top point. Fold the top point down over the pack, making sure the pack is snug but not too tight.				
9. Secure the pack with autoclave tape. A "quick-opening tab" can be created by folding a small portion of the tape back onto itself. The pack must be snug enough to prevent instruments from slipping out of the wrapping or damaging each other inside the pack but loose enough to allow adequate circulation of steam through the pack.				
10. Label the pack with your initials and the date. List the contents of the pack as well. If the pack contains syringes, be sure to identify the syringe size(s).*				
11. Place the pack aside for loading into the autoclave.				
12. Remove gloves, dispose of them in the appropriate waste container, and wash your hands.				
For wrapping instruments and equipment in bags or envelopes: 1. Wash your hands and put on gloves before beginning to wrap the items to be sterilized.				
2. Insert the items into the bag or envelope as indicated by the manufacturer's directions. Hinged instruments should be opened before insertion into the package.*				
3. Close and seal the pack. Make sure the sterilization indicator is not damaged or already exposed.*				
4. Label the pack with your initials and the date. List the contents of the pack as well. The pens or pencils used to label the pack must be waterproof; otherwise, the contents of the pack and date of sterilization will be obliterated.*				
5. Place the pack aside for loading into the autoclave.				
6. Remove gloves, dispose of them in the appropriate waste container, and wash your hands.				
Total Number of Points Achieved/Final Score				
Initials of Observer:				

(continued)

Comments and Signatures

Reviewer's comments and signatures:

1. _____

2. _____

3. _____

Instructor's comments:

_____

CAAHEP Competencies Achieved

III. P (5) Prepare items for autoclaving

III. P (6) Perform sterilization procedures

ABHES Competencies Achieved

4 (o) Wrap items for autoclaving

4 (p) Perform sterilization techniques

PROCEDURE 33-3 RUNNING A LOAD THROUGH THE AUTOCLAVE

Procedure Goal

To run a load of instruments and equipment through an autoclave, ensuring sterilization of items by properly loading, drying, and unloading them

Scoring System

To score each step, use the following scoring system:
1 = poor, 2 = fair, 3 = good, 4 = excellent

A minimum score of at least a 3 must be achieved on **each** step to achieve successful completion of the technique. Detailed instructions on the scoring system are found on page 413.

Materials

Dry, sanitized, and disinfected instruments and equipment, both individual pieces and wrapped packs; oven mitts; sterile transfer forceps; storage containers for individual items

Procedure

Procedure Steps Total Possible Points - 68 Time Limit: 10 minutes	Practice #1	Practice #2	Practice #3	Final
1. Wash your hands and put on gloves before beginning to load items into the autoclave.				
2. Rest packs on their edges, and place jars and containers on their sides.				
3. Place lids for jars and containers with their sterile sides down.				
4. If the load includes plastic items, make sure no other item leans against them.*				
5. If your load is mixed—containing both wrapped packs and individual instruments—place the tray containing the instruments below the tray containing the wrapped packs.*				
6. Close the door and start the unit. For automatic autoclaves, choose the cycle based on the type of load you are running. Consult the manufacturer's recommendations before choosing the load type.				
7. For manual autoclaves, start the timer when the indicators show the recommended temperature and pressure.				
8. Right after the end of the steam cycle and just before the start of the drying cycle, open the door to the autoclave slightly (between ¼ and ½ inch).* Consult the manufacturer's recommendations regarding opening the door. Some automatic autoclaves do not require opening the door during the drying cycle.				
9. Dry according to the manufacturer's recommendations. Packs and large items may require up to 45 minutes for complete drying.				

(continued)

Procedure Steps Total Possible Points - 68 Time Limit: 10 minutes	Practice #1	Practice #2	Practice #3	Final
10. Unload the autoclave after the drying cycle is finished. Do not unload any packs or instruments with wet wrappings, or the object inside will be considered unsterile and must be processed again.*				
11. Unload each package carefully. Wear oven mitts to protect yourself from burns when removing wrapped packs. Use sterile transfer forceps to unload unwrapped individual objects.				
12. Inspect each package or item, looking for moisture on the wrapping, underexposed sterilization indicators, and tears or breaks in the wrapping. Consider the pack unsterile if any of these conditions is present.				
13. Place sterile packs aside for transfer to storage.				
14. Place individual items that are not required to be sterile in clean containers.				
15. Place items that must remain sterile in sterile containers, being sure to close the container covers tightly.				
16. As you unload items, avoid placing them in an overly cool location because the cool temperature could cause condensation on the instruments or packs.				
17. Remove gloves, dispose of them in the appropriate waste container, and wash your hands.				
Total Number of Points Achieved/Final Score				
Initials of Observer:				

Comments and Signatures

Reviewer's comments and signatures:

1. _____

2. _____

3. _____

Instructor's comments:

_____

CAAHEP Competency Achieved

III. P (5) Prepare items for autoclaving

III. P (6) Perform sterilization procedures

ABHES Competencies Achieved

4 (h) Wrap items for autoclaving

4 n. Assist physician with minor office surgical procedures o. Perform: 4) Sterilization techniques

PROCEDURE 34-1 APPLYING UNIVERSAL PRECAUTIONS

Procedure Goal

To take specific protective measures when performing tasks in which a worker may be exposed to blood, body fluids, or tissues

Scoring System

To score each step, use the following scoring system:
1 = poor, 2 = fair, 3 = good, 4 = excellent

A minimum score of at least a 3 must be achieved on **each** step to achieve successful completion of the technique. Detailed instructions on the scoring system are found on page 413.

Materials

Items needed for the specific treatment or procedure being performed

Procedure

Procedure Steps Total Possible Points - 28 Time Limit: 10 minutes	Practice #1	Practice #2	Practice #3	Final
1. Perform aseptic hand washing.				
2. Put on gloves and a gown or a laboratory coat and, if required, eye protection and a mask or a face shield.				
3. Assist with the treatment or procedure as your office policy dictates.				
4. Follow OSHA procedures to clean and decontaminate the treatment area.				
5. Place reusable instruments in appropriate containers for sanitizing, disinfecting, and sterilizing, as appropriate.				
6. Remove your gloves and all personal protective equipment. Place them in waste containers or laundry receptacles, according to OSHA guidelines.				
7. Wash your hands.				
Total Number of Points Achieved/Final Score				
Initials of Observer:				

(continued)

Comments and Signatures

Reviewer's comments and signatures:

1. _____

2. _____

3. _____

Instructor's comments:

_____

CAAHEP Competency Achieved

III. P (2) Practice Standard Precautions

ABHES Competency Achieved

4 (r) Practice Standard Precautions

PROCEDURE 34-2 NOTIFYING STATE AND COUNTY AGENCIES ABOUT REPORTABLE DISEASES

Procedure Goal

To report cases of infection with reportable disease to the proper state or county health department

Scoring System

To score each step, use the following scoring system:
1 = poor, 2 = fair, 3 = good, 4 = excellent

A minimum score of at least a 3 must be achieved on **each** step to achieve successful completion of the technique. Detailed instructions on the scoring system are found on page 413.

Materials

Communicable disease report form (see pages 777–778 for an example), pen, envelope, stamp

Procedure

Procedure Steps Total Possible Points - 16 Time Limit: 10 minutes	Practice #1	Practice #2	Practice #3	Final
1. Check to be sure you have the correct form. Some states have specific forms for each reportable infectious disease or type of disease, as well as a general form. CDC forms may also be used for reporting specific diseases.				
2. Fill in all blank areas unless they are shaded (generally for local health department use).				
3. Follow office procedures for submitting the report to a supervisor or physician before sending it out.				
4. Sign and date the form. Address the envelope, put a stamp on it, and place it in the mail.				
Total Number of Points Achieved/Final Score				
Initials of Observer:				

Comments and Signatures

Reviewer's comments and signatures:

1. _____

2. _____

3. _____

Instructor's comments:

_____

CAAHEP Competencies Achieved

IV. P (2) Report relevant information to others succinctly and accurately

IX. P (8) Apply local, state, and federal health-care legislation and regulation appropriate to the medical assisting practice setting

PROCEDURE 35-1 GUIDELINES FOR DISINFECTING EXAM ROOM SURFACES

Procedure Goal

To reduce the risk of exposure to potentially infectious microorganisms in the exam room

Scoring System

To score each step, use the following scoring system:
1 = poor, 2 = fair, 3 = good, 4 = excellent

A minimum score of at least a 3 must be achieved on **each** step to achieve successful completion of the technique. Detailed instructions on the scoring system are found on page 413.

Materials

Utility gloves, disinfectant (10% bleach solution or EPA-approved disinfecting product), paper towels, dustpan and brush, tongs, forceps, clean sponge or heavy rag

Procedure

Procedure Steps Total Possible Points - 32 Time Limit: 10 minutes	Practice #1	Practice #2	Practice #3	Final
1. Wash your hands and put on utility gloves.				
2. Remove any visible soil from exam room surfaces with disposable paper towels or a rag.*				
3. Thoroughly wipe all surfaces with the disinfectant.				
4. In the event of an accident involving a broken glass container, use tongs, a dustpan and brush, or forceps to pick up shattered glass, which may be contaminated.*				
5. Remove and replace protective coverings, such as plastic wrap or aluminum foil, on equipment if the equipment or the coverings have become contaminated. After removing the coverings, disinfect the equipment and allow it to air-dry. (Follow office procedures for the routine changing of protective coverings.)				
6. When you finish cleaning, dispose of the paper towels or rags in a biohazardous waste receptacle. (This step is especially important if you are cleaning surfaces contaminated with blood, body fluids, or tissue.)				
7. Remove the gloves and wash your hands.				
8. If you keep a container of 10% bleach solution on hand for disinfection purposes, replace the solution daily to ensure its disinfecting potency.				
Total Number of Points Achieved/Final Score				
Initials of Observer:				

(continued)

Comments and Signatures

Reviewer's comments and signatures:

1. _____

2. _____

3. _____

Instructor's comments:

_____

CAAHEP Competency Achieved

III. P (2) Practice Standard Precautions

ABHES Competencies Achieved

4 (c) Apply principles of aseptic techniques and infection control

4 (g) Prepare and maintain examination and treatment areas

PROCEDURE 35-2 MAKING THE EXAM ROOM SAFE FOR PATIENTS WITH VISUAL IMPAIRMENTS

Procedure Goal

To ensure that patients with visual impairments are safe in the exam room

Scoring System

To score each step, use the following scoring system:
1 = poor, 2 = fair, 3 = good, 4 = excellent

A minimum score of at least a 3 must be achieved on **each** step to achieve successful completion of the technique. Detailed instructions on the scoring system are found on page 413.

Materials

Reflective tape, if needed

Procedure

Procedure Steps Total Possible Points - 36 Time Limit: 10 minutes	Practice #1	Practice #2	Practice #3	Final
1. Make sure the hallway leading to the exam room is clear of obstacles.*				
2. Increase the amount of lighting in the room. Adjust the shades on windows in the room—if there are any windows—to allow for maximum natural light. Turn on all lights, especially those under cabinets, to dispel shadows.*				
3. Clear a path along which the patient can walk through the room. Make sure the chairs are out of the way. If there is a scale in the room, position it out of the path. If there is a step stool for the examining table, place it right up against the table.				
4. Make sure the floor is not slippery.				
5. Remove furniture that might be easily tipped over, such as a visitors' chair that is lightweight. If the physician will use an exam chair, push it out of the way.				
6. Provide a sturdy chair with arms and a straight back to make it easier for the patient to sit down and stand up.				
7. A wide strip of reflective tape will make the examining-table step visible for all patients. Apply it to the step's edge if tape is not there already. If your office uses a step stool instead of a step, make sure the tape on the stool is facing out.				
8. Alert the patient to protruding equipment or furnishings.				

(continued)

Procedure Steps Total Possible Points - 36 Time Limit: 10 minutes	Practice #1	Practice #2	Practice #3	Final
9. Arrange the supplies for the patient, such as gowns or drapes, with the following guideline in mind: It is easier to see light objects against dark objects or dark objects against light objects than light objects against light objects or dark objects against dark objects. If, for example, there is a dressing cubicle, lay the light-colored gown or drape against a dark bench instead of hanging the gown or drape against a light wall.*				
Total Number of Points Achieved/Final Score				
Initials of Observer:				

Comments and Signatures

Reviewer's comments and signatures:

1. _____

2. _____

3. _____

Instructor's comments:

_____

CAAHEP Competency Achieved

XI. C (2) Identify safety techniques that can be used to prevent accidents and maintain a safe work environment

ABHES Competency Achieved

9 (k) Prepare and maintain examination and treatment areas

Copyright © 2011 by The McGraw-Hill Companies, Inc.

PROCEDURE 36-1 USING CRITICAL THINKING SKILLS DURING AN INTERVIEW

Procedure Goal

To be able to use verbal and nonverbal clues and critical thinking skills to optimize the process of obtaining data for the patient's chart

Scoring System

To score each step, use the following scoring system:
1 = poor, 2 = fair, 3 = good, 4 = excellent

A minimum score of at least a 3 must be achieved on **each** step to achieve successful completion of the technique. Detailed instructions on the scoring system are found on page 413.

Materials

Patient chart, pen

Procedure

Procedure Steps Total Possible Points - 68 Time Limit: 10 minutes	Practice #1	Practice #2	Practice #3	Final
Example 1: Getting at an Underlying Meaning				
1. You are interviewing a female patient with type 2 diabetes who has recently started insulin injections. She is in the office for a follow-up visit.				
2. Use open-ended questions such as, "How are you managing your diabetes?"*				
3. The patient states that she "just can't get used to the whole idea of injections."				
4. To encourage her to verbalize her concerns more clearly, you can **mirror** her response, or restate her comments in your own words. For example, you might say, "You seem to be having some difficulty giving yourself injections."*				
5. **Verbalize** the implied, which means that you state what you think the patient is suggesting by her response.*				
6. After you determine the specific problem, you will be able to address it in the interview or note it in the patient's chart for the doctor's attention.*				
Example 2: Dealing with a Potentially Violent Patient				
1. You are interviewing a 24-year-old male patient who is new to the office. He appears agitated. You ask his reason for seeing the doctor today.				
2. The patient explains that he does not want to talk to "some assistant" about his problem. He just wants to see the doctor.				
3. You say that you respect his wish not to discuss his symptoms but explain that you need to ask him a few questions so that the doctor can provide the proper medical care.*				
4. The patient begins to yell at you, saying he wants to see the doctor and doesn't "want to answer stupid questions."				

(continued)

Procedure Steps Total Possible Points - 68 Time Limit: 10 minutes	Practice #1	Practice #2	Practice #3	Final
5. The fact that the patient appears agitated and begins to raise his voice in anger should be a warning to you that he may become violent. It would be best not to handle this patient by yourself.				
6. If you are alone with the patient, leave the room and request assistance from another staff member.				
Example 3: Gathering Symptom Information About a Child 1. A parent brings a 6-year-old boy to the office because the child is complaining about stomach pain.				

2. To gather the pertinent symptom information, ask the child various types of questions.*
  a. Can he tell you about the pain?*
  b. Can he tell you exactly where it hurts?
  c. Is there anything else that hurts?				

3. To confirm the child's answers, ask the parent to answer similar questions.				

4. You should then ask the parent additional questions. Begin with an open-ended question, as above. Follow up with specific questions such as these.
  a. How long has he had the pain?
  b. Is the pain related to any specific event (such as going to school)?				

5. Ask the child to confirm the parent's answers. He may be able to provide additional information at this time.				
Total Number of Points Achieved/Final Score				
Initials of Observer:				

Comments and Signatures

Reviewer's comments and signatures:

1. _____

2. _____

3. _____

Instructor's comments:

_____

CAAHEP Competencies Achieved

I. A (1) Apply critical thinking skills in performing patient assessment and care

IV. C (4) Identify techniques for overcoming communication barriers

ABHES Competencies Achieved

5 b. Identify and respond appropriately when working/caring for patients with special needs

5 e. Advocate on behalf of family/patients, having ability to deal and communicate with family

6 (bb) Are impartial and show empathy when dealing with patients

PROCEDURE 36-2 USING A PROGRESS NOTE

Procedure Goal

To accurately record a chief complaint on a progress note

Scoring System

To score each step, use the following scoring system:
1 = poor, 2 = fair, 3 = good, 4 = excellent

A minimum score of at least a 3 must be achieved on **each** step to achieve successful completion of the technique. Detailed instructions on the scoring system are found on page 413.

Materials

Progress note, patient chart, pen

Procedure

Procedure Steps Total Possible Points - 36 Time Limit: 5 minutes	Practice #1	Practice #2	Practice #3	Final
1. Wash your hands.				
2. Review the patient's chart notes from the patient's previous office visit. Verify that all results for any previously ordered laboratory work or diagnostics are in the chart.*				
3. Greet the patient and escort her to a private exam room.				
4. Introduce yourself and ask the patient her name.				
5. Using open-ended questions, find out why the patient is seeking medical care today.*				
6. Accurately document the chief complaint on the progress note. Document vital signs. Initial the chart entry.				
7. File the progress note in chronological order within the patient's chart.*				
8. Thank the patient and offer to answer any questions she may have. Explain that the physician will come in soon to examine her.				
9. Wash your hands.				
Total Number of Points Achieved/Final Score				
Initials of Observer:				

(continued)

Comments and Signatures

Reviewer's comments and signatures:

1. _____

2. _____

3. _____

Instructor's comments:

_____

CAAHEP Competency Achieved

IX. P (7) Document accurately in the patient record

ABHES Competencies Achieved

4 (a) Document accurately

8 (jj) Perform fundamental writing skills including correct grammar, spelling, and formatting techniques when writing prescriptions, documenting medical records, etc.

PROCEDURE 36-3 OBTAINING A MEDICAL HISTORY

Procedure Goal

To obtain a complete medical history with accuracy and professionalism

Scoring System

To score each step, use the following scoring system:

1 = poor, 2 = fair, 3 = good, 4 = excellent

A minimum score of at least a 3 must be achieved on **each** step to achieve successful completion of the technique. Detailed instructions on the scoring system are found on page 413.

Materials

Medical history form, patient chart, pen

Procedure

Procedure Steps Total Possible Points - 10 Time Limit: 10 minutes	Practice #1	Practice #2	Practice #3	Final
1. Wash your hands.				
2. Assemble the necessary materials. Review the medical history form and plan your interview.*				
3. Invite the patient to a private exam room and correctly identify the patient by introducing yourself and asking his or her name and date of birth.				
4. Explain the medical history form while maintaining eye contact. Make the patient feel at ease.				
5. Using language that the patient can understand, ask appropriate questions related to the medical history form. Use open-ended questions. Listen actively to the patient's response.				
6. Accurately document the patient's responses.				
7. Thank the patient for his or her participation in the interview. Offer to answer any questions.				
8. Sign or initial the medical history form and file it in the patient's chart.				
9. Inform the physician that you are finished with the medical history according to the physician's office policy.				
10. Wash your hands.				
Total Number of Points Achieved/Final Score				
Initials of Observer:				

(continued)

Comments and Signatures

Reviewer's comments and signatures:

1. _____

2. _____

3. _____

Instructor's comments:

_____

CAAHEP Competencies Achieved

I. P (6) Perform patient screening using established protocols

I. A (1) Apply critical thinking skills in performing patient assessment and care

I. A (2) Use language/verbal skills that enable patients' understanding

IV. C (4) Identify techniques for overcoming communication barriers

IV. C (6) Differentiate between subjective and objective information

IV. C (7) Identify resources and adaptations that are required based on individual needs, i.e., culture and environment, developmental life stage, language, and physical threats to communication

IV. P (3) Use medical terminology, pronouncing medical terms correctly, to communicate information, patient history, data, and observations

IV. A (1) Demonstrate empathy in communicating with patients, family, and staff

IV. A (2) Apply active listening skills

IV. A (3) Use appropriate body language and other nonverbal skills in communicating with patients, family, and staff

IV. A (4) Demonstrate awareness of the territorial boundaries of the person with whom communicating

IV. A (7) Demonstrate recognition of the patient's level of understanding in communications

IV. A (8) Analyze communications in providing appropriate responses/feedback

IV. A (9) Recognize and protect personal boundaries in communicating with others

IV. A (10) Demonstrate respect for individual diversity, incorporating awareness of one's own biases in areas including gender, race, religion, age, and economic status

ABHES Competencies Achieved

4 (a) Document accurately

8 (ff) Interview effectively

9 (a) Obtain chief complaint, recording patient history

PROCEDURE 37-1 MEASURING AND RECORDING TEMPERATURE

Procedure Goal

To accurately measure the temperature of patients while preventing the spread of infection

Scoring System

To score each step, use the following scoring system:
1 = poor, 2 = fair, 3 = good, 4 = excellent

A minimum score of at least a 3 must be achieved on **each** step to achieve successful completion of the technique. Detailed instructions on the scoring system are found on page 413.

Materials

Thermometer, probe cover if required by thermometer, lubricant for rectal temperature, gloves, trash receptacle, patient's chart, and recording device

Procedure

Procedure Steps Total Possible Points - 40 Time Limit: 5 minutes	Practice #1	Practice #2	Practice #3	Final
1. Gather the equipment and make sure the thermometer is in working order.				
2. Identify the patient and introduce yourself.				
3. Wash your hands and explain the procedure to the patient.				
4. Prepare the patient for the temperature. a. Oral. If the patient has had anything to eat or drink, or has been smoking, wait at least 15 minutes before measuring the temperature orally.* b. Rectal. Have the patient remove the appropriate clothing; assist as needed. Have the patient lie on his or her left side and drape for comfort.* c. Axillary. Assist the patient to expose the axilla. Provide for privacy and comfort. Pat dry the axilla.* d. Temporal or Tympanic. Remove the patient's hat if necessary.				
5. Prepare the equipment. a. Prepare an electronic thermometer by inserting the probe into the probe cover if necessary.* b. Prepare the disposable thermometer by removing the wrapper to expose the handle end. Avoid touching the part of the thermometer that goes in the mouth or on the skin.* c. Prepare the temporal scanner by removing the protective cap and making sure the lens is clean.*				

(continued)

Procedure Steps Total Possible Points - 40 Time Limit: 5 minutes	Practice #1	Practice #2	Practice #3	Final

6. Measure the temperature.
  a. Oral. Place the thermometer under the tongue in the back of the mouth on one side. Have the patient hold it in place with his or her lips and tongue. Wait for the electronic thermometer to beep or indicate completion. For a disposable thermometer, wait the required time, usually 60 seconds.
  b. Rectal. Put on gloves. Lubricate the thermometer tip. Raise the buttock to expose the anus with one hand and insert the thermometer into the anal canal, 1½ inches for adults and ½ to 1 inch for infants and children. Hold the thermometer securely in place until the indicator beeps or blinks.*
  c. Axillary. Place the thermometer into the axilla making sure the tip is in direct contact with the top of the axilla and is touching skin on all sides. Hold the arm firmly against the body until the indicator light blinks or beeps or the proper amount of time has passed.*
  d. Tympanic. Hold the outer edge of the ear (pinna) with your free hand. Gently pull the pinna up for adults and down for children. Insert the probe into the ear canal directed to the eardrum and sealing the ear canal. Press the scan button.*
  e. Temporal. Position the probe flat on the center of the exposed forehead. Press and hold the SCAN button and then slide the thermometer straight across the forehead until it beeps and the red light blinks.				

7. Remove and read the measurement in the display or on the thermometer. Discard the disposable thermometer. Eject and discard the probe cover for an electronic thermometer. Replace the cap and/or place the thermometer into the charging base.*				

8. Record the results. Chart by including the date and location where the temperature was taken.
  • Oral: 98.6
  • Rectal: 99.6 R
  • Axillary: 97.6 Ax
  • Temporal: 97.6
  • Tympanic: 97.6 Tymp.				

9. Help the patient to replace clothing as necessary. Clear the area and provide for safety and comfort for the patient.				
10. Wash your hands.				
Total Number of Points Achieved/Final Score				
Initials of Observer:				

(continued)

Comments and Signatures

Reviewer's comments and signatures:

1. _____

2. _____

3. _____

Instructor's comments:

_____

CAAHEP Competencies Achieved

I. P (1) Obtain vital signs

IV. P (2) Report relevant information to others succinctly and accurately

ABHES Competencies Achieved

9 (c) Take vital signs

9 (i) Use Standard Precautions

PROCEDURE 37-2 MEASURING AND RECORDING PULSE AND RESPIRATIONS

Procedure Goal

To accurately measure the pulse and respirations of a patient while keeping the patient unaware the respirations are being counted

Scoring System

To score each step, use the following scoring system:
1 = poor, 2 = fair, 3 = good, 4 = excellent

A minimum score of at least a 3 must be achieved on **each** step to achieve successful completion of the technique. Detailed instructions on the scoring system are found on page 413.

Materials

Watch with a second hand, patient's charts, and recording device.

Procedure

Procedure Steps Total Possible Points - 44 Time Limit: 5 minutes	Practice #1	Practice #2	Practice #3	Final
1. Gather the equipment and wash your hands.				
2. Introduce yourself and identify the patient.				
3. Explain the procedure saying, "I am going to take your vital signs. We'll start with your pulse first." Do not tell him you are counting the respirations.*				
4. Ask the patient to sit or lie in a comfortable position. Have the patient rest the arm on a table. The palm should be facing downward.				
5. Position yourself so you can observe and/or feel the chest wall movements. You may want to lay the patient's arm over the chest to feel the respiratory chest movements.				
6. Place two to three fingers on the radial pulse site. Find the radial bone on the thumb side of the wrist, then slide your fingers into the groove on the inside of the wrist to locate the pulse.				
7. Count the pulse for 15 to 30 seconds if regular. Note the rhythm and volume. If irregular, count for a full minute. Remember or note the number if necessary.*				
8. Without letting go of the wrist, observe and feel the respirations. Count for one full minute. Observe for rhythm, volume, and effort.				
9. Once you are certain of both numbers, release the wrist and record them. If the pulse was taken for less than one minute, obtain the number of beats per minute. Multiply the number of beats counted in 30 seconds by two or the number of beats counted in 15 seconds by 4.				

(continued)

Procedure Steps Total Possible Points - 44 Time Limit: 5 minutes	Practice #1	Practice #2	Practice #3	Final
10. Document results with the date and time.				
11. Report any findings that are a significant change from a previous result or outside the normal values as shown in Table 37-1 in the text.				
Total Number of Points Achieved/Final Score				
Initials of Observer:				

Comments and Signatures

Reviewer's comments and signatures:

1. _____

2. _____

3. _____

Instructor's comments:

_____

CAAHEP Competencies Achieved

I. P (1) Obtain vital signs

IV. P (2) Report relevant information to others succinctly and accurately

ABHES Competencies Achieved

9 (c) Take vital signs

9 (i) Use Standard Precautions

Procedure 37-3 Taking the Blood Pressure of Adults and Older Children

Procedure Goal

To accurately measure blood pressure in adults and older children

Scoring System

To score each step, use the following scoring system:
1 = poor, 2 = fair, 3 = good, 4 = excellent

A minimum score of at least a 3 must be achieved on **each** step to achieve successful completion of the technique. Detailed instructions on the scoring system are found on page 413.

Materials

Aneroid or mercury sphygmomanometer, stethoscope, alcohol gauze squares, patient's chart, and black pen

Procedure

Procedure Steps Total Possible Points - 96 Time Limit: 5 minutes	Practice #1	Practice #2	Practice #3	Final
1. Gather the equipment and make sure the sphygmomanometer is in working order and is correctly calibrated.*				
2. Identify the patient and introduce yourself.				
3. Wash your hands and explain the procedure to the patient.				
4. Have the patient sit in a quiet area. If she is wearing long-sleeved clothing, have her loosely roll up one sleeve. If she cannot, have her change into a gown.				
5. Have the patient rest her bared arm on a flat surface so that the midpoint of the upper arm is at the same level as the heart.*				
6. Select a cuff that is the appropriate size for the patient. The bladder inside the cuff should encircle 80% of the arm in adults and 100% of the arm in children younger than the age of 13. If you are not sure about the size, use a larger cuff.*				
7. Locate the brachial artery in the antecubital space.				
8. Position the cuff so that the midline of the bladder is above the arterial pulsation. Then wrap and secure the cuff snugly around the patient's bare upper arm. The lower edge of the cuff should be 1 inch above the antecubital space, where the head of the stethoscope is to be placed.*				
9. Place the manometer so that the center of the aneroid dial or mercury column is at eye level and easily visible and so that the tubing from the cuff is unobstructed.				
10. Close the valve of the pressure bulb until it is finger-tight.				
11. Inflate the cuff rapidly to 70 mm Hg with one hand, and increase this pressure by 10 mm Hg increments while				

(continued)

Procedure Steps Total Possible Points - 96 Time Limit: 5 minutes	Practice #1	Practice #2	Practice #3	Final
palpating the radial pulse with your other hand. Note the level of pressure at which the pulse disappears and subsequently reappears during deflation. This procedure, the **palpatory method,** provides an approximation of the systolic blood pressure to ensure an adequate level of inflation when the actual measurement is made.				
12. Open the valve to release the pressure, deflate the cuff completely, and wait 30 seconds or remove and replace the cuff.*				
13. Place the earpieces of the stethoscope in your ear canals, and adjust them to fit snugly and comfortably. When placed in the ears, they should point up or toward the nose. Switch the stethoscope head to the diaphragm position. Confirm the setting by listening as you tap the stethoscope head gently.				
14. Place the head of the stethoscope over the brachial artery pulsation, just above and medial to the antecubital space but below the lower edge of the cuff. Hold the stethoscope firmly in place between the index and middle fingers, making sure the head is in contact with the skin around its entire circumference.*				
15. Inflate the bladder rapidly and steadily to a pressure 20 to 30 mm Hg above the level previously determined by palpation. Then partially open (unscrew) the valve and deflate the bladder at 2 mm per second while you listen for the appearance of the Korotkoff sounds.				
16. As the pressure in the bladder falls, note the level of pressure on the manometer at the first appearance of repetitive sounds. This reading is the systolic pressure.				
17. Continue to deflate the cuff gradually, noting the point at which the sound changes from strong to muffled.				
18. Continue to deflate the cuff and note when the sound disappears. This reading is the diastolic pressure.				
19. Deflate the cuff completely and remove it from the patient's arm.				
20. Record the numbers, separated by slashes, in the patient's chart. Chart the date and time of the measurement, the arm on which the measurement was made, the subject's position, and the cuff size when a nonstandard size is used.*				
21. Fold the cuff and replace it in the holder.				
22. Inform the patient that you have completed the procedure.				
23. Disinfect the earpieces and diaphragm of the stethoscope with gauze squares moistened with alcohol.				
24. Properly dispose of the used gauze squares and wash your hands.				
Total Number of Points Achieved/Final Score				
Initials of Observer:				

(continued)

Comments and Signatures

Reviewer's comments and signatures:

1. _____

2. _____

3. _____

Instructor's comments:

_____

CAAHEP Competencies Achieved

I. P (1) Obtain vital signs

IV. P (2) Report relevant information to others succinctly and accurately

ABHES Competencies Achieved

9 (c) Take vital signs

9 (i) Use Standard Precautions

PROCEDURE 37-4 MEASURING ADULTS AND CHILDREN

Procedure Goal

To accurately measure weight and height of adults and children

Scoring System

To score each step, use the following scoring system:
1 = poor, 2 = fair, 3 = good, 4 = excellent

A minimum score of at least a 3 must be achieved on **each** step to achieve successful completion of the technique. Detailed instructions on the scoring system are found on page 413.

Materials

For an adult or older child, adult scale with height bar, disposable towel; for toddler, adult scale with height bar or height chart, disposable towel

Procedure

Procedure Steps Total Possible Points - 120 Time Limit: 5 minutes	Practice #1	Practice #2	Practice #3	Final
Adult or Older Child: Weight				
1. Identify the patient and introduce yourself.				
2. Wash your hands and explain the procedure to the patient.				
3. Check to see whether the scale is in balance by moving all the weights to the left side. The indicator should be level with the middle mark. If not, check the manufacturer's directions and adjust it to ensure a zero balance. If you are using a scale equipped to measure either kilograms or pounds, check to see that it is set on the desired units and that the upper and lower weights show the same units.*				
4. Place a disposable towel on the scale or have the patient leave her socks on.*				
5. Ask the patient to remove her shoes, if that is the standard office policy.*				
6. Ask the patient to step on the center of the scale, facing forward. Assist as necessary.				
7. Place the lower weight at the highest number that does not cause the balance indicator to drop to the bottom.*				
8. Move the upper weight slowly to the right until the balance bar is centered at the middle mark, adjusting as necessary.*				
9. Add the two weights together to get the patient's weight.				
10. Record the patient's weight in the chart to the nearest quarter of a pound or tenth of a kilogram.				
11. Return the weights to their starting positions on the left side.				

(continued)

Procedure Steps Total Possible Points - 120 Time Limit: 5 minutes	Practice #1	Practice #2	Practice #3	Final
Adult or Older Child: Height				
12. With the patient off the scale, raise the height bar well above the patient's head and swing out the extension.*				
13. Ask the patient to step on the center of the scale and to stand up straight and look forward.*				
14. Gently lower the height bar until the extension rests on the patient's head.				
15. Have the patient step off the scale before reading the measurement.*				
16. If the patient is fewer than 50 inches tall, read the height on the bottom part of the ruler; if the patient is more than 50 inches tall, read the height on the top movable part of the ruler at the point at which it meets the bottom part of the ruler. Note that the numbers increase on the bottom part of the bar and decrease on the top, moveable part of the bar. Read the height in the right direction.				
17. Record the patient's height.				
18. Have the patient put her shoes back on, if necessary.				
19. Properly dispose of the used towel and wash your hands.				
Toddler: Weight				
1. Identify the patient and obtain permission from the parent to weigh the toddler.				
2. Wash your hands and explain the procedure to the parent.				
3. Check to see whether the scale is in balance and place a disposable towel on the scale or have the patient wear shoes or socks, depending upon the policy of the facility.				
4. Ask the parent to hold the patient and to step on the scale. Follow the procedure for obtaining the weight of an adult.				
5. Have the parent put the child down or hand the child to another staff member.*				
6. Obtain the parent's weight.				
7. Subtract the parent's weight from the combined weight to determine the weight of the child.				
8. Record the patient's weight in the chart to the nearest quarter of a pound or tenth of a kilogram.				
Toddler: Height				
9. Measure the child's height in the same manner as you measure adult height, or have the child stand with his back against the height chart. Measure height at the crown of the head.				
10. Record the height in the patient's chart.				
11. Properly dispose of the towel (if used) and wash your hands.*				
Total Number of Points Achieved/Final Score				
Initials of Observer:				

(continued)

Comments and Signatures

Reviewer's comments and signatures:

1. _____

2. _____

3. _____

Instructor's comments:

_____

CAAHEP Competencies Achieved

II. C (7) Analyze charts, graphs, and/or tables in the interpretation of health-care results

II. P (3) Maintain growth charts

IV. P (2) Report relevant information to others succinctly and accurately

ABHES Competency Achieved

2 (c) Assist the physician with the regimen of diagnostic and treatment modalities as they relate to each body system

PROCEDURE 37-5 MEASURING INFANTS

Procedure Goal

To accurately measure weight and length of infants and infant head circumference

Scoring System

To score each step, use the following scoring system:
1 = poor, 2 = fair, 3 = good, 4 = excellent

A minimum score of at least a 3 must be achieved on **each** step to achieve successful completion of the technique. Detailed instructions on the scoring system are found on page 413.

Materials

Pediatric examining table or infant scale, cardboard, pencil, yardstick, tape measure, disposable towel

Procedure

Procedure Steps Total Possible Points - 80 Time Limit: 5 minutes	Practice #1	Practice #2	Practice #3	Final
Weight				
1. Identify the patient and obtain permission from the parent to weigh the infant.				
2. Wash your hands and explain the procedure to the parent.				
3. Ask the parent to undress the infant.*				
4. Check to see whether the infant scale is in balance and place a disposable towel on it.*				
5. Have the parent place the child face up on the scale (or on the examining table if the scale is built into it). Keep one hand over the infant at all times and hold a diaper over a male patient's penis to catch any urine the infant might void.*				
6. Place the lower weight at the highest number that does not cause the balance indicator to drop to the bottom.*				
7. Move the upper weight slowly to the right until the balance bar is centered at the middle mark, adjusting as necessary.*				
8. Add the two weights together to get the infant's weight.				
9. Record the infant's weight in the chart or on the growth chart in pounds and ounces or to the nearest tenth of a kilogram.				
10. Return the weights to their starting positions on the left side.				
Length: Scale with Length (Height) Bar				
11. If the scale has a height bar, move the infant toward the head of the scale or examining table until her head touches the bar.				
12. Have the parent hold the infant by the shoulders in this position.				

(continued)

Procedure Steps Total Possible Points - 80 Time Limit: 5 minutes	Practice #1	Practice #2	Practice #3	Final
13. Holding the infant's ankles, gently extend the legs and slide the bottom bar to touch the soles of the feet.*				
14. Note the length and release the infant's ankles.				
15. Record the length in the patient's chart or on the growth chart.				
Length: Scale or Examining Table Without Length (Height) Bar				
16. If neither the scale nor the examining table has a height bar, have the parent position the infant close to the head of the examining table and hold the infant by the shoulders in this position.				
17. Place a stiff piece of cardboard against the crown of the infant's head and mark a line on the towel or paper, or hold a yardstick against the cardboard.				
18. Holding the infant's ankles, gently extend the legs and draw a line on the towel or paper to mark the heel, or note the measure on the yardstick.*				
19. Release the infant's ankles and measure the distance between the two markings on the towel or paper using the yardstick or a tape measure.				
20. Record the length in the patient's chart or on the growth chart.				
Head Circumference				
Measurement of head circumference may be performed at the same time as weight and length, or it may be part of the general physical exam.				
21. With the infant in a sitting or supine position, place the tape measure around the infant's head at the forehead.				
22. Adjust the tape so that it surrounds the infant's head at its largest circumference.				
23. Overlap the ends of the tape and read the measure at the point of overlap.				
24. Remove the tape, and record the circumference in the patient's chart or on the growth chart.				
25. Properly dispose of the used towel and wash your hands.				
Total Number of Points Achieved/Final Score				
Initials of Observer:				

(continued)

Comments and Signatures

Reviewer's comments and signatures:

1. _____

2. _____

3. _____

Instructor's comments:

_____

CAAHEP Competencies Achieved

II. C (7) Analyze charts, graphs, and/or tables in the interpretation of health-care results

II. P (3) Maintain growth charts

IV. P (2) Report relevant information to others succinctly and accurately

ABHES Competency Achieved

2 (c) Assist the physician with the regimen of diagnostic and treatment modalities as they relate to each body system

PROCEDURE 38-1 POSITIONING THE PATIENT FOR AN EXAM

Procedure Goal

To effectively assist a patient in assuming the various positions used in a general physical exam

Scoring System

To score each step, use the following scoring system:
1 = poor, 2 = fair, 3 = good, 4 = excellent

A minimum score of at least a 3 must be achieved on **each** step to achieve successful completion of the technique. Detailed instructions on the scoring system are found on page 413.

Materials

Adjustable examining table or gynecologic table, step stool, exam gown, drape

Procedure

Procedure Steps Total Possible Points - 40 Time Limit: 10 minutes	Practice #1	Practice #2	Practice #3	Final
1. Identify the patient and introduce yourself.				
2. Wash your hands.				
3. Explain the procedure to the patient.				
4. Provide a gown or drape if the physician has requested one and instruct the patient in the proper way to wear it after disrobing. Allow the patient privacy while disrobing and assist only if the patient requests help.*				
5. Explain to the patient the necessary exam and the position required.				
6. Ask the patient to step on the stool or the pullout step of the examining table. If necessary, assist the patient onto the examining table.				
7. Assist the patient into the required position: a. Sitting. Do not use this position for patients who cannot sit unsupported. b. Supine (Recumbent). Do not use this position for patients with back injuries, low back pain, or difficulty breathing. Place a pillow or other support under the head and knees for comfort, if needed. c. Dorsal Recumbent. This position may be difficult for someone with leg disabilities. It may be used for patients when lithotomy is difficult. d. Lithotomy. This position is used to examine the female genitalia, with the patient's feet placed in stirrups. Assist as necessary. The patient's buttocks should be near the edge of the table. Drape the client with a large drape to help prevent embarrassment. e. Trendelenburg. This position is a supine position with the patient's head lower than her feet. It is used infrequently in the physician's office but may be necessary for low blood pressure or shock.				

(continued)

Procedure Steps Total Possible Points - 40 Time Limit: 10 minutes	Practice #1	Practice #2	Practice #3	Final
f. Fowler's. Adjust the head of the table to the desired angle. Help the patient move toward the head of the table until the patient's buttocks meet the point at which the head of the table begins to incline upward. g. Prone. This position is when the patient lies face down. It is not used for later stages of pregnancy, obese patients, patients with respiratory difficulty, or certain elderly patients. h. Sims'. In this position, the patient lies on her left side with her left leg slightly bent and her left arm behind her back. Her right knee is bent and raised toward her chest and her right arm is bent toward her head. This position may be difficult for patients with joint deformities. i. Knee-Chest. This position is difficult for patients to assume. The patient is face down, supporting his weight on his knees and chest or an alternative knee-elbow position. This position is used for rectal and perineal exams. Keep the patient in this position for the shortest amount of time possible. j. Proctologic. This position is also used for rectal and perineal exams. In this position, the patient bends over the examining table with his chest resting on the table.				
8. Drape the client to prevent exposure and avoid embarrassment. Place pillows for comfort as needed.*				
9. Adjust the drapes during the exam.				
10. On completion of the exam, assist the client as necessary out of the position and provide privacy as the client dresses.				
Total Number of Points Achieved/Final Score				
Initials of Observer:				

Comments and Signatures

Reviewer's comments and signatures:

1. _____

2. _____

3. _____

Instructor's comments:

_____

CAAHEP Competency Achieved

II. P (6) Prepare a patient for procedures and/or treatments

ABHES Competency Achieved

9 (l) Prepare patient for examinations and treatments

PROCEDURE 38-2 COMMUNICATING EFFECTIVELY WITH PATIENTS FROM OTHER CULTURES AND MEETING THEIR NEEDS FOR PRIVACY

Procedure Goal

To ensure effective communication with patients from other cultures while meeting their needs for privacy

Scoring System

To score each step, use the following scoring system:
1 = poor, 2 = fair, 3 = good, 4 = excellent

A minimum score of at least a 3 must be achieved on **each** step to achieve successful completion of the technique. Detailed instructions on the scoring system are found on page 413.

Materials

Exam gown, drapes

Procedure

Procedure Steps Total Possible Points - 44 Time Limit: 10 minutes	Practice #1	Practice #2	Practice #3	Final
Effective Communication				
1. When it is necessary to use a translator, direct conversation or instruction to the translator.*				
2. Direct demonstrations of what to do, such as putting on an exam gown, to the patient.				
3. Confirm with the translator that the patient has understood the instruction or demonstration.				
4. Allow the translator to be present during the exam if that is the patient's preference.				
5. If the patient understands some English, speak slowly, use simple language, and demonstrate instructions whenever possible.				
Meeting the Need for Privacy				
1. Before the procedure, thoroughly explain to the patient or translator the reason for disrobing. Indicate that you will allow the patient privacy and ample time to undress.				
2. If the patient is reluctant, reassure him that the physician respects the need for privacy and will look at only what is necessary for the exam.*				
3. Provide extra drapes if you think doing so will make the patient feel more comfortable.				
4. If the patient is still reluctant, discuss the problem with the physician; the physician may be able to negotiate a compromise with the patient.				
5. During the procedure, ensure that the patient is undraped only as much as necessary.				

(continued)

Procedure Steps Total Possible Points - 44 Time Limit: 10 minutes	Practice #1	Practice #2	Practice #3	Final
6. Whenever possible, minimize the amount of time the patient remains undraped.				
Total Number of Points Achieved/Final Score				
Initials of Observer:				

Comments and Signatures

Reviewer's comments and signatures:

1. _____

2. _____

3. _____

Instructor's comments:

_____

CAAHEP Competency Achieved

X. A (3) Demonstrate awareness of diversity in providing patient care

ABHES Competencies Achieved

5 (b) Identify and respond appropriately when working/caring for patients with special needs

9 (q) Instruct patients with special needs

PROCEDURE 38-3 TRANSFERRING A PATIENT IN A WHEELCHAIR AND PREPARING FOR AN EXAM

Procedure Goal

To assist a patient in transferring from a wheelchair to the examining table safely and efficiently

Scoring System

To score each step, use the following scoring system:
1 = poor, 2 = fair, 3 = good, 4 = excellent

A minimum score of at least a 3 must be achieved on **each** step to achieve successful completion of the technique. Detailed instructions on the scoring system are found on page 413.

Materials

Adjustable examining table or gynecologic table, step stool (optional), exam gown, drape

Procedure

Procedure Steps Total Possible Points - 68 Time Limit: 10 minutes	Practice #1	Practice #2	Practice #3	Final
Never risk injuring yourself; call for assistance when in doubt. As a rule, you should not attempt to lift more than 35% of your body weight.				
Preparation Before Transfer				
1. Identify the patient and introduce yourself.				
2. Wash your hands.				
3. Explain the procedure in detail.				
4. Position the wheelchair at a right angle to the end of the examining table. This position reduces the distance between the wheelchair and the end of the examining table across which the patient must move.				
5. Lock the wheels of the wheelchair.*				
6. Lift the patient's feet and fold back the foot and leg supports of the wheelchair.				
7. Place the patient's feet on the floor. The patient should have shoes or slippers with nonskid soles. Place your feet in front of the patient's feet.*				
8. If needed, place a step stool in front of the table and place the patient's feet flat on the stool.				
Transferring the Patient by Yourself				
9. Face the patient, spread your feet apart, align your knees with the patient's knees, and bend your knees slightly.*				
10. Have the patient hold on to your shoulders.				
11. Place your arms around the patient, under the patient's arms.				
12. Tell the patient that you will lift on the count of 3 and ask the patient to support as much of his own weight as possible (if he is able).				
13. At the count of 3, lift the patient.				

(continued)

Procedure Steps Total Possible Points - 68 Time Limit: 10 minutes	Practice #1	Practice #2	Practice #3	Final
14. Pivot the patient to bring the back of the patient's knees against the table.				
15. Gently lower the patient into a sitting position on the table. If the patient cannot sit unassisted, help him move into a supine position.				
16. Move the wheelchair out of the way.				
17. Assist the patient with disrobing as necessary, providing a gown and drape.				
Transferring the Patient with Assistance				
9. Working with your partner, both of you face the patient, spread your feet apart, position yourselves so that one of each of your knees is aligned with the patient's knees, and bend your knees slightly.*				
10. Have the patient place one hand on each of your shoulders and hold on.				
11. Each of you places your outermost arm around the patient, one under each of the patient's arms. Then interlock your wrists.				
12. Tell the patient that you will lift on the count of 3 and ask the patient to support as much of his own weight as possible (if he is able).				
13. At the count of 3, you should lift the patient together.				
14. The stronger of the two of you should pivot the patient to bring the back of the patient's knees against the table.				
15. Working together, gently lower the patient into a sitting position on the table. If the patient cannot sit unassisted, help him move into a supine position.				
16. Move the wheelchair out of the way.				
17. Assist the patient with disrobing as necessary, providing a gown and drape.				
Total Number of Points Achieved/Final Score				
Initials of Observer:				

Comments and Signatures

Reviewer's comments and signatures:

1. _____

2. _____

3. _____

Instructor's comments:

_____

CAAHEP Competency Achieved

IV. P (6) Prepare a patient for procedures and/or treatments

ABHES Competency Achieved

9 (I) Prepare patient for examinations and treatments

PROCEDURE 38-4 ASSISTING WITH A GENERAL PHYSICAL EXAM

Procedure Goal

To effectively assist the physician with a general physical exam

Scoring System

To score each step, use the following scoring system:
1 = poor, 2 = fair, 3 = good, 4 = excellent

A minimum score of at least a 3 must be achieved on **each** step to achieve successful completion of the technique. Detailed instructions on the scoring system are found on page 413.

Materials

Supplies and equipment will vary depending on the type and purpose of the exam and the physician's practice preferences. Supplies may include the following: Gown, drape, adjustable examining table, gloves, laryngeal mirror, lubricant, nasal speculum, otoscope and ophthalmoscope, pillow, reflex hammer, tuning fork, sphygmomanometer, stethoscope, tape measure, tongue depressors, penlight

Procedure

Procedure Steps Total Possible Points - 116 Time Limit: 15 minutes	Practice #1	Practice #2	Practice #3	Final
1. Wash your hands and adhere to Standard Precautions throughout the procedure.*				
2. Gather and assemble the equipment and supplies.				
3. Arrange the instruments and equipment in a logical sequence for the physician's use.				
4. Greet and properly identify the patient using at least two patient identifiers.*				
5. Review the patient's medical history with the patient if office policy requires it.				
6. Obtain vital statistics per the physician's preference.				
7. Obtain the patient's weight and height (with shoes removed).				
8. Obtain a urine specimen before the patient undresses for the exam.				
9. Explain the procedure and exam to the patient.*				
10. Obtain blood specimens or other laboratory tests per the chart or verbal order.				
11. Provide the patient with an appropriate gown and drape and explain where the opening for the gown is placed.				
12. Obtain the ECG if ordered by the physician.				
13. Assist patient to a sitting position at the end of the table with the drape placed across his or her legs.				
14. Inform the physician that the patient is ready and remain in the room to assist the physician.				
15. You may be asked to shut off the light in the exam room to allow the patient's pupils to dilate sufficiently for a retinal exam.				

(continued)

Procedure Steps Total Possible Points - 116 Time Limit: 15 minutes	Practice #1	Practice #2	Practice #3	Final
16. Hand the instruments to the physician as requested.				
17. Assist the patient to a supine position and drape him or her for an exam of the front of the body.				
18. If a gynecological exam is needed, assist and drape the patient in the lithotomy position.				
19. If a rectal exam is needed, assist and drape the patient in the Sims' position.				
20. Assist the patient to a prone position for a posterior body exam.				
21. When the exam is complete, assist the patient to a sitting position and ask the patient to sit for a brief period of time.*				
22. Ask the patient if he or she needs assistance in dressing.				
23. Dispose of contaminated materials in an appropriate container.				
24. Remove the table paper and pillow covering and dispose of them in the proper container.				
25. Disinfect and clean counters and the examining table with a disinfectant.				
26. Sanitize and sterilize the instruments, if needed.				
27. Prepare the room for the next patient by replacing the table paper, pillow case, equipment, and supplies.				
28. Document the procedure.				
Total Number of Points Achieved/Final Score				
Initials of Observer:				

Comments and Signatures

Reviewer's comments and signatures:

1. _____

2. _____

3. _____

Instructor's comments:

_____

CAAHEP Competency Achieved

I. P (10) Assist physician with patient care

ABHES Competency Achieved

9 (I) Prepare patient for examinations and treatments

PROCEDURE 38-5 PERFORMING VISION SCREENING TESTS

Objectives

To screen a patient's ability to see distant or close objects, to determine contrast sensitivity, or to detect color blindness

Scoring System

To score each step, use the following scoring system:
1 = poor, 2 = fair, 3 = good, 4 = excellent

A minimum score of at least a 3 must be achieved on **each** step to achieve successful completion of the technique. Detailed instructions on the scoring system are found on page 413.

Materials

Occluder or card; alcohol; gauze squares; appropriate vision charts to test for distance vision, near vision, and color blindness

Procedure

Procedure Steps Total Possible Points - 128 Time Limit: 10 minutes	Practice #1	Practice #2	Practice #3	Final
Distance Vision 1. Wash your hands, identify the patient, introduce yourself, and explain the procedure.				
2. Mount one of the following eye charts at eye level: Snellen letter or similar chart (for patients who can read); Snellen E, Landolt C, pictorial, or similar chart (for patients who cannot read). If using the Snellen letter chart, verify that the patient knows the letters of the alphabet. With children or nonreading adults, use demonstration cards to verify that they can identify the pictures or direction of the letters.*				
3. Make a mark on the floor 20 feet away from the chart.				
4. Have the patient stand with the heels at the 20-foot mark or sit with the back of the chair at the mark.				
5. Instruct the patient to keep both eyes open and not to squint or lean forward during the test.*				
6. Test both eyes first, then the right eye, and then the left eye. (Different offices may test in a different order. Follow your office policy.) Refer to Figure 38-13 in the text.*				
7. Have the patient read the lines on the chart (or identify the picture/direction), beginning with the 20-foot line. If the patient cannot read this line, begin with the smallest line the patient can read. (Some offices use a pointer to select one symbol at a time in random order to prevent patients from memorizing the order. It is common to start with children at the 40- or 30-foot line, or larger if low vision is suspected, and proceed to the 20-foot line.)				

(continued)

Procedure Steps Total Possible Points - 128 Time Limit: 10 minutes	Practice #1	Practice #2	Practice #3	Final
8. Note the smallest line the patient can read or identify. (When testing children, note the smallest line on which they can identify three out of four or four out of six symbols correctly.)				
9. Record the results as a fraction (for example, O.U. 20/40–1 if the patient misses one letter on a line or O.U. 20/40–2 if the patient misses two letters on a line).				
10. Show the patient how to cover the left eye with the occluder or card. Again, instruct the patient to keep both eyes open and not to squint or lean forward during the test.				
11. Have the patient read the lines on the chart.				
12. Record the results of the right eye (for example, Right Eye 20/30).				
13. Have the patient cover the right eye and read the lines on the chart.				
14. Record the results of the left eye (for example, Left Eye 20/20).				
15. If the patient wears corrective lenses, record the results using $\overline{cc}$ (if your office uses this abbreviation for "with correction") in front of the abbreviation (for example, $\overline{cc}$ both eyes 20/20).*				
16. Note and record any observations of squinting, head tilting, or excessive blinking or tearing.				
17. Ask the patient to keep both eyes open and to identify the two colored bars, and record the results in the patient's chart.				
18. Clean the occluder with a gauze square dampened with alcohol.				
19. Properly dispose of the gauze square and wash your hands.*				
Near Vision				
1. Wash your hands, identify the patient, introduce yourself, and explain the procedure.				
2. Have the patient hold one of the following at normal reading distance (approximately 14 to 16 inches): Jaeger, Richmond pocket, or similar chart or card.				
3. Ask the patient to keep both eyes open and to read or identify the letters, symbols, or paragraphs.*				
4. Record the smallest line read without error.				
5. If the card is laminated, clean it with a gauze square dampened with alcohol.				
6. Properly dispose of the gauze square and wash your hands.*				
Color Vision				
1. Wash your hands, identify the patient, introduce yourself, and explain the procedure.				
2. Hold one of the following color charts or books at the patient's normal reading distance (approximately 14 to 16 inches): Ishihara, Richmond pseudoisochromatic, or similar color-testing system.				

(continued)

Procedure Steps Total Possible Points - 128 Time Limit: 10 minutes	Practice #1	Practice #2	Practice #3	Final
3. Ask the patient to tell you the number or symbol within the colored dots on each chart or page.				
4. Proceed through all the charts or pages.				
5. Record the number correctly identified and failed with a slash between them (for example, 13 passed/1 failed).				
6. If the charts are laminated, clean them with a gauze square dampened with alcohol.				
7. Properly dispose of the gauze square and wash your hands.*				
Total Number of Points Achieved/Final Score				
Initials of Observer:				

Comments and Signatures

Reviewer's comments and signatures:

1. _____

2. _____

3. _____

Instructor's comments:

_____

CAAHEP Competency Achieved

I. P (10) Assist physician with patient care

ABHES Competency Achieved

2 (c) Assist the physician with the regimen of diagnostic and treatment modalities as they relate to each body system

PROCEDURE 38-6 MEASURING AUDITORY ACUITY

Objective

To determine how well a patient hears

Scoring System

To score each step, use the following scoring system:
1 = poor, 2 = fair, 3 = good, 4 = excellent

A minimum score of at least a 3 must be achieved on **each** step to achieve successful completion of the technique. Detailed instructions on the scoring system are found on page 413.

Materials

Audiometer, headset, graph pad (if applicable), alcohol, gauze squares

Procedure

Procedure Steps Total Possible Points - 140 Time Limit: 10 minutes	Practice #1	Practice #2	Practice #3	Final
Adults and Children 1. Wash your hands, identify the patient, introduce yourself, and explain the procedure.				
2. Clean the earpieces of the headset with a gauze square dampened with alcohol.*				
3. Have the patient sit with his back to you.				
4. Assist the patient in putting on the headset and adjust it until it is comfortable.				
5. Tell the patient he will hear tones in the right ear.				
6. Tell the patient to raise his finger or press the indicator button when he hears a tone.				
7. Set the audiometer for the right ear.				
8. Set the audiometer for the lowest range of frequencies and the first degree of loudness (usually 15 decibels). (When using automated audiometers, follow the instructions printed in the user's manual.)				
9. Press the tone button or switch and observe the patient.				
10. If the patient does not hear the first degree of loudness, raise it two or three times to greater degrees, up to 50 or 60 decibels.				
11. If the patient indicates that he has heard the tone, record the setting on the graph.				
12. Change the setting to the next frequency. Repeat steps 9, 10, and 11.				
13. Proceed to the mid-range frequencies. Repeat steps 9, 10, and 11.				
14. Proceed to the high-range frequencies. Repeat steps 9, 10, and 11.				

(continued)

Procedure Steps Total Possible Points - 140 Time Limit: 10 minutes	Practice #1	Practice #2	Practice #3	Final
15. Set the audiometer for the left ear.				
16. Tell the patient that he will hear tones in the left ear and ask him to raise his finger or press the indicator button when he hears a tone.				
17. Repeat steps 8 through 14.				
18. Set the audiometer for both ears.				
19. Ask the patient to listen with both ears and to raise his finger or press the indicator button when he hears a tone.				
20. Repeat steps 8 through 14.				
21. Have the patient remove the headset.				
22. Clean the earpieces with a gauze square dampened with alcohol.				
23. Properly dispose of the used gauze square and wash your hands.*				
Infants and Toddlers				
1. Identify the patient and introduce yourself.				
2. Wash your hands.				
3. Pick a quiet location.				
4. The patient can be sitting, lying down, or held by the parent.				
5. Instruct the parent to be silent during the procedure.				
6. Position yourself so your hands are behind the child's right ear and out of sight.*				
7. Clap your hands loudly. Observe the child's response. (Never clap directly in front of the ear because this can damage the eardrum. As an alternative to clapping, use special devices, such as rattles or clickers, which may be available in the office to generate sounds of varying loudness.)				
8. Record the child's response as positive or negative for loud noise.				
9. Position one hand behind the child's right ear, as before.				
10. Snap your fingers. Observe the child's response.				
11. Record the response as positive or negative for moderate noise.				
12. Repeat steps 6 through 11 for the left ear.				
Total Number of Points Achieved/Final Score				
Initials of Observer:				

(continued)

Comments and Signatures

Reviewer's comments and signatures:

1. _____

2. _____

3. _____

Instructor's comments:

_____

CAAHEP Competency Achieved

I. P (10) Assist physician with patient care

ABHES Competency Achieved

2 (c) Assist the physician with the regimen of diagnostic and treatment modalities as they relate to each body system

PROCEDURE 39-1 ASSISTING WITH A GYNECOLOGICAL EXAM

Procedure Goal

To assist the physician and maintain the client's comfort and privacy during a gynecological exam

Scoring System

To score each step, use the following scoring system:

1 = poor, 2 = fair, 3 = good, 4 = excellent

A minimum score of at least a 3 must be achieved on **each** step to achieve successful completion of the technique. Detailed instructions on the scoring system are found on page 413.

Materials

Gown and drape, vaginal speculum, specimen collection equipment, including cervical brush, cervical broom, and/or scraper, cotton-tipped applicator, potassium hydroxide solution (KOH), exam gloves, tissues, laboratory requisition, water-soluble lubricant, examining table with stirrups, exam light, microscopic slide(s), thin-layer collection vial, tissues, spray fixative, pen and pencil

Procedure

Procedure Steps Total Possible Points - 60 Time Limit: 10 minutes	Practice #1	Practice #2	Practice #3	Final
1. Gather equipment and make sure all items are in working order. Correctly label the slide and/or the collection vials.*				
2. Identify the patient and explain the procedure. The patient should remove all clothing, including underwear, and put the gown on with the opening in the front.				
3. Ask the patient to sit on the edge of the examining table with the drape until the physician arrives.				
4. When the physician is ready, have the patient place her feet into the stirrups and move her buttocks to the edge of the table. This is the lithotomy position.*				
5. Provide the physician with gloves and an exam lamp as she examines the genitalia by inspection and palpation.				
6. Pass the speculum to the physician. To increase patient comfort, you may place it in warm water before handing it to the physician. Water-based lubricant is not recommended prior to the Pap smear because it may interfere with the test results.				
7. For the Pap (Papanicolaou) smear, be prepared to pass a cotton-tipped applicator and cervical brush, broom, or scraper for the collection of the specimens. Have the labeled slide or vial available for the physician to place the specimen on the slide. Depending on the physician, the specimen collected, the method of collection, and the method of preparation, two or more slides or collection vials may be necessary. They may be labeled based on where the specimen was collected: endocervical E, vaginal V, and cervical C.				

(continued)

Procedure Steps Total Possible Points - 60 Time Limit: 10 minutes	Practice #1	Practice #2	Practice #3	Final
8. Once the specimen is on the slide, a cytology fixative must be applied immediately. A spray fixative is common, and it should be held 6 inches from the slide and sprayed lightly with a back and forth motion. Allow the slide to dry completely.* Cells collected for thin-layer preparation should be washed into the collection vial and transported to an outside lab for processing and analysis.				
9. After the physician removes the speculum, a digital exam is performed to check the position of the internal organs. Provide the physician with additional lubricant as needed.				
10. Upon completion of the exam, help the patient switch from the lithotomy position to a supine or sitting position.				
11. Provide tissues or moist wipes for the patient to remove the lubricant and ask the patient to get dressed. Assist as necessary or provide for privacy. Explain the procedure for communicating the laboratory results.				
12. After the patient has left, don gloves and clean the exam room and equipment. Dispose of the disposable speculum, specimen collection devices, and other contaminated waste in a biohazardous waste container.				
13. Store the supplies, straighten the room, and discard the used exam paper on the table.				
14. Prepare the laboratory requisition slip and place it and the specimen in the proper place for transport to an outside laboratory.				
15. Remove your gloves and wash your hands.				
Total Number of Points Achieved/Final Score				
Initials of Observer:				

Comments and Signatures

Reviewer's comments and signatures:

1. _____

2. _____

3. _____

Instructor's comments:

_____

CAAHEP Competencies Achieved

I. P (10) Assist physician with patient care

IV. P (6) Prepare a patient for procedures and/or treatments

ABHES Competencies Achieved

l. Prepare patient for examinations and treatments

m. Assist physician with routine and specialty examinations and treatments

Name_____ Date_____

Evaluated by_____ Score_____

PROCEDURE 39-2 ASSISTING WITH A CERVICAL BIOPSY

Procedure Goal

To assist the physician in obtaining a sample of cervical tissue for analysis

Scoring System

To score each step, use the following scoring system:
1 = poor, 2 = fair, 3 = good, 4 = excellent

A minimum score of at least a 3 must be achieved on **each** step to achieve successful completion of the technique. Detailed instructions on the scoring system are found on page 413.

Materials

Gown and drape, tray or Mayo stand, disposable cervical biopsy kit (disposable forceps, curette, and spatula in a sterile pack), transfer forceps, vaginal speculum, biopsy specimen container, clean basin, sterile cotton balls, sterile gauze squares, sanitary napkin

Procedure

Procedure Steps Total Possible Points - 60 Time Limit: 10 minutes	Practice #1	Practice #2	Practice #3	Final
1. Identify the patient and introduce yourself.				
2. Look at the patient's chart and ask the patient to confirm information or explain any changes. Specific patient information you need to ask about and note in the chart includes the following: • Date of birth and Social Security number (verify that you have the correct chart for the correct patient) • Date of last menstrual period • Method of contraception, if any • Previous gynecologic surgery • Use of hormone replacement therapy or other steroids				
3. Describe the biopsy procedure to the patient, noting that a piece of tissue will be removed to diagnose the cause of her problem. Explain that it may be painful but only for the brief moment during which tissue is taken.				
4. Give the patient a gown, if needed, and a drape. Direct her to undress from the waist down and to wrap the drape around herself. Tell her to sit at the end of the examining table.				
5. Wash your hands and put on exam gloves.				
6. Using sterile method, open the sterile pack to create a sterile field on the tray or Mayo stand and arrange the instruments with transfer forceps. Add the vaginal speculum and sterile supplies to the sterile field.*				
7. When the physician arrives in the exam room, ask the patient to lie back, place her heels in the stirrups of the table, and move her buttocks to the edge of the table.*				
8. Assist the physician by arranging the drape so that only the genitalia are exposed and place the light so that the genitalia are illuminated.				

(continued)

Procedure Steps Total Possible Points - 60 Time Limit: 10 minutes	Practice #1	Practice #2	Practice #3	Final
9. Use transfer forceps to hand instruments and supplies to the physician as he requests them. You may don sterile gloves and hand the physician supplies and instruments directly. When he is ready to obtain the biopsy, tell the patient that it may hurt. If she seems particularly fearful, instruct her to take a deep breath and let it out slowly.				
10. When the physician hands you the instrument with the tissue specimen, place the specimen in the specimen container and discard the instrument in the appropriate container.				
11. Label the specimen container with the patient's name, the date and time, cervical or endocervical (as indicated by the physician), the physician's name, and your initials.				
12. Place the container and the cytology laboratory requisition form in the envelope or bag provided by the laboratory.				
13. When the physician has removed the vaginal speculum, place it in the clean basin for later sanitization, disinfection, and sterilization. Properly dispose of used supplies and disposable instruments.				
14. Remove the gloves and wash your hands.				
15. Tell the patient that she may get dressed. Inform her that she may have some vaginal bleeding for a couple of days and provide her with a sanitary napkin. Instruct her not to take tub baths or have intercourse and not to use tampons for 2 days. Encourage her to call the office if she experiences problems or has questions.				
Total Number of Points Achieved/Final Score				
Initials of Observer:				

Comments and Signatures

Reviewer's comments and signatures:

1. _____

2. _____

3. _____

Instructor's comments:

_____

CAAHEP Competencies Achieved

I. P (10) Assist physician with patient care

IV. P (6) Prepare a patient for procedures and/or treatments

ABHES Competencies Achieved

I. Prepare patient for examinations and treatments

m. Assist physician with routine and specialty examinations and treatments

PROCEDURE 39-3 MEETING THE NEEDS OF THE PREGNANT PATIENT DURING AN EXAM

Procedure Goal

To meet the special needs of the pregnant woman during the general physical exam

Scoring System

To score each step, use the following scoring system:
1 = poor, 2 = fair, 3 = good, 4 = excellent

A minimum score of at least a 3 must be achieved on **each** step to achieve successful completion of the technique. Detailed instructions on the scoring system are found on page 413.

Materials

Patient education materials, examining table, exam gown, drape

Procedure

Procedure Steps Total Possible Points - 68 Time Limit: 10 minutes	Practice #1	Practice #2	Practice #3	Final
Providing Patient Information				
1. Identify the patient and introduce yourself.				
2. Assess the patient's need for education by asking appropriate questions and having the patient describe what she already knows about the information you are providing.				
3. Provide any appropriate instructions or materials.				
4. Ask the patient whether she has any special concerns or questions about her pregnancy that she might want to discuss with the physician.				
5. Communicate the patient's concerns or questions to the physician; include all pertinent background information on the patient.*				
Ensuring Comfort During the Exam				
1. Identify the patient and introduce yourself.				
2. Wash your hands.				
3. Explain the procedure to the patient.				
4. Provide a gown or drape and instruct the patient in the proper way to wear it after disrobing. (Allow the patient privacy while disrobing and assist only if she requests help.)				
5. Ask the patient to step on the stool or the pullout step of the examining table.				
6. Assist the patient onto the examining table.*				
7. Keeping position restrictions in mind, help the patient into the position requested by the physician.				

(continued)

Procedure Steps Total Possible Points - 68 Time Limit: 10 minutes	Practice #1	Practice #2	Practice #3	Final
8. Provide and adjust additional drapes as needed.				
9. Keep in mind any difficulties the patient may have in achieving a certain position; suggest alternative positions whenever possible.				
10. Minimize the time the patient must spend in uncomfortable positions.*				
11. If the patient appears to be uncomfortable during the procedure, ask whether she would like to reposition herself or take a break; assist as necessary.				
12. To prevent pelvic pooling of blood and subsequent dizziness or hyperventilation, allow the patient time to adjust to sitting before standing after she has been lying on the examining table.				
Total Number of Points Achieved/Final Score				
Initials of Observer:				

Comments and Signatures

Reviewer's comments and signatures:

1. _____

2. _____

3. _____

Instructor's comments:

_____

CAAHEP Competencies Achieved

    I. P (10) Assist physician with patient care

    IV. P (6) Prepare a patient for procedures and/or treatments

ABHES Competencies Achieved

    I. Prepare patient for examinations and treatments

    m. Assist physician with routine and specialty examinations and treatments

PROCEDURE 40-1 ASSISTING WITH A SCRATCH TEST EXAMINATION

Procedure Goal

To determine substances to which a patient has an allergic reaction

Scoring System

To score each step, use the following scoring system:
1 = poor, 2 = fair, 3 = good, 4 = excellent

A minimum score of at least a 3 must be achieved on **each** step to achieve successful completion of the technique. Detailed instructions on the scoring system are found on page 413.

Materials

Disposable sterile needles or lancets, allergen extracts, control solution, cotton balls, alcohol, timer, adhesive tape, ruler, cold packs or ice bag

Procedure

Procedure Steps Total Possible Points - 68 Time Limit: 10 minutes	Practice #1	Practice #2	Practice #3	Final
1. Wash your hands and assemble the necessary materials.				
2. Identify the patient and introduce yourself.				
3. Show the patient into the treatment area. Explain the procedure and discuss any concerns. Confirm whether the patient followed pretesting procedures (discontinuing antihistamines, etc.).*				
4. Put on exam gloves and assist the patient into a comfortable position.				
5. Swab the test site, usually the upper arm or back, with an alcohol prep pad.				
6. Identify the sites (if more than one) with adhesive-tape labels.*				
7. Apply small drops of the allergen extracts and control solution onto the test site at evenly spaced intervals, about 1½ to 2 inches apart.				
8. Open the package containing the first needle or lancet, making sure you do not contaminate the instrument.				
9. Assist the physician with the scratch procedure or perform the procedure if within your scope of practice. Using a new sterile needle or lancet for each site, scratch the skin beneath each drop of allergen, no more than ⅛-inch deep.				
10. Start the timer for the 20-minute reaction period.				
11. After the reaction time has passed, cleanse each site with an alcohol prep pad. (Do not remove identifying labels until the doctor has checked the patient.)				
12. Assist the physician or examine and measure the sites.				

(continued)

Procedure Steps Total Possible Points - 68 Time Limit: 10 minutes	Practice #1	Practice #2	Practice #3	Final
13. Apply cold packs or an ice bag to sites as needed to relieve itching.				
14. Record the test results in the patient's chart and initial your entries.				
15. Properly dispose of used materials and instruments.				
16. Clean and disinfect the area according to OSHA guidelines.				
17. Remove the gloves and wash your hands.				
Total Number of Points Achieved/Final Score				
Initials of Observer:				

Comments and Signatures

Reviewer's comments and signatures:

1. _____

2. _____

3. _____

Instructor's comments:

_____

CAAHEP Competencies Achieved

I. P (10) Assist physician with patient care

IV. P (6) Prepare a patient for procedures and/or treatments

ABHES Competencies Achieved

I. Prepare patient for examinations and treatments

m. Assist physician with routine and specialty examinations and treatments

PROCEDURE 40-2 ASSISTING WITH A SIGMOIDOSCOPY

Procedure Goal

To assist the doctor during the exam of the rectum, anus, and sigmoid colon using a sigmoidoscope

Scoring System

To score each step, use the following scoring system:

1 = poor, 2 = fair, 3 = good, 4 = excellent

A minimum score of at least a 3 must be achieved on **each** step to achieve successful completion of the technique. Detailed instructions on the scoring system are found on page 413.

Materials

Sigmoidoscope, suction pump, lubricating jelly, drape, patient gown, tissues

Procedure

Procedure Steps Total Possible Points - 72 Time Limit: 10 minutes	Practice #1	Practice #2	Practice #3	Final
1. Wash your hands and assemble and position materials and equipment according to the preference of the doctor.				
2. Test the suction pump.				
3. Identify the patient and introduce yourself.				
4. Show the patient into the treatment room. Explain the procedure and discuss any concerns the patient may have.				
5. Instruct the patient to empty the bladder, take off all clothing from the waist down, and put on the gown with the opening in the back.				
6. Put on exam gloves and assist the patient into the knee-chest or Sims' position. Immediately cover the patient with a drape.				
7. Use warm water to bring the sigmoidoscope to slightly above body temperature; lubricate the tip.*				
8. Assist as needed, including handing the doctor the necessary instruments and equipment.				
9. Monitor the patient's reactions during the procedure and relay any signs of pain to the doctor.				
10. Clean the anal area with tissues after the exam.				
11. Properly dispose of used materials and disposable instruments.				
12. Remove the gloves and wash your hands.				
13. Help the patient gradually assume a comfortable position.*				
14. Instruct the patient to dress.				
15. Put on clean gloves.				
16. Sanitize reusable instruments and prepare them for disinfection and/or sterilization, as necessary.				

(continued)

Procedure Steps Total Possible Points - 72 Time Limit: 10 minutes	Practice #1	Practice #2	Practice #3	Final
17. Clean and disinfect the equipment and the room according to OSHA guidelines.				
18. Remove the gloves and wash your hands.				
Total Number of Points Achieved/Final Score				
Initials of Observer:				

Comments and Signatures

Reviewer's comments and signatures:

1. _____

2. _____

3. _____

Instructor's comments:

_____

CAAHEP Competencies Achieved

I. P (10) Assist physician with patient care

IV. P (6) Prepare a patient for procedures and/or treatments

ABHES Competencies Achieved

I. Prepare patient for examinations and treatments

m. Assist physician with routine and specialty examinations and treatments

PROCEDURE 40-3 PREPARING THE OPHTHALMOSCOPE FOR USE

Procedure Goal

To ensure that the ophthalmoscope is ready for use during an eye exam

Scoring System

To score each step, use the following scoring system:
1 = poor, 2 = fair, 3 = good, 4 = excellent

A minimum score of at least a 3 must be achieved on **each** step to achieve successful completion of the technique. Detailed instructions on the scoring system are found on page 413.

Materials

Ophthalmoscope, lens, spare bulb, spare battery

Procedure

Procedure Steps Total Possible Points - 20 Time Limit: 10 minutes	Practice #1	Practice #2	Practice #3	Final
1. Wash your hands.				
2. Take the ophthalmoscope out of its battery charger. In a darkened room, turn on the ophthalmoscope light.				
3. Shine the large beam of white light on the back of your hand to check that the instrument's tiny lightbulb is providing strong enough light.				
4. Replace the bulb or battery if necessary. (The battery is located in the ophthalmoscope's handle.)				
5. Make sure the instrument's lens is screwed into the handle. If it is not, attach the lens.				
Total Number of Points Achieved/Final Score				
Initials of Observer:				

(continued)

Comments and Signatures

Reviewer's comments and signatures:

1. _____

2. _____

3. _____

Instructor's comments:

_____

CAAHEP Competency Achieved

I. P (10) Assist physician with patient care

ABHES Competencies Achieved

l. Prepare patient for examinations and treatments

m. Assist physician with routine and specialty examinations and treatments

PROCEDURE 40-4 ASSISTING WITH A NEEDLE BIOPSY

Procedure Goal

To remove tissue from a patient's body so that it can be examined in a laboratory

Scoring System

To score each step, use the following scoring system:
1 = poor, 2 = fair, 3 = good, 4 = excellent

A minimum score of at least a 3 must be achieved on **each** step to achieve successful completion of the technique. Detailed instructions on the scoring system are found on page 413.

Materials

Sterile drapes, tray or Mayo stand, antiseptic solution, cotton balls, local anesthetic, disposable sterile biopsy needle or disposable sterile syringe and needle, sterile sponges, specimen bottle with fixative solution, laboratory packaging, sterile wound-dressing materials

Procedure

Procedure Steps Total Possible Points - 56 Time Limit: 10 minutes	Practice #1	Practice #2	Practice #3	Final
1. Identify the patient and introduce yourself; instruct the patient as needed.				
2. Wash your hands and assemble the necessary materials.				
3. Prepare the sterile field and instruments.				
4. Put on exam gloves.				
5. Cleanse the biopsy site. Prepare the patient's skin.*				
6. Remove the gloves, wash your hands, and put on clean exam gloves.				
7. Assist the doctor as she injects anesthetic.				
8. During the procedure, help drape and position the patient.				
9. If you will be handing the doctor the instruments, remove the gloves, perform a surgical scrub, and put on sterile gloves.				
10. Place the sample in a properly labeled specimen bottle, complete the laboratory requisition form, and package the specimen for immediate transport to the laboratory.*				
11. Dress the patient's wound site.				
12. Properly dispose of used supplies and instruments.				
13. Clean and disinfect the room according to OSHA guidelines.				
14. Remove the gloves and wash your hands.				
Total Number of Points Achieved/Final Score				
Initials of Observer:				

(continued)

Comments and Signatures

Reviewer's comments and signatures:

1. _____

2. _____

3. _____

Instructor's comments:

_____

CAAHEP Competency Achieved

I. P (10) Assist physician with patient care

ABHES Competencies Achieved

l. Prepare patient for examinations and treatments

m. Assist physician with routine and specialty examinations and treatments

PROCEDURE 41-1 CREATING A STERILE FIELD

Procedure Goal

To create a sterile field for a minor surgical procedure

Scoring System

To score each step, use the following scoring system:
1 = poor, 2 = fair, 3 = good, 4 = excellent

A minimum score of at least a 3 must be achieved on **each** step to achieve successful completion of the technique. Detailed instructions on the scoring system are found on page 413.

Materials

Tray or Mayo stand, sterile instrument pack, sterile transfer forceps, cleaning solution, sterile drape, additionally packaged sterile items as required

Procedure

Procedure Steps Total Possible Points - 44 Time Limit: 10 minutes	Practice #1	Practice #2	Practice #3	Final
1. Clean and disinfect the tray or Mayo stand.				
2. Wash your hands and assemble the necessary materials.				
3. Check the label on the instrument pack to make sure it is the correct pack for the procedure.				
4. Check the date and sterilization indicator on the instrument pack to make sure the pack is still sterile.*				
5. Place the sterile pack on the tray or stand and unfold the outermost fold away from yourself.				
6. Unfold the sides of the pack outward, touching only the areas that will become the underside of the sterile field.*				
7. Open the final flap toward yourself, stepping back and away from the sterile field.				
8. Place additional packaged sterile items on the sterile field. • Ensure that you have the correct item or instrument and that the package is still sterile. • Stand away from the sterile field. • Grasp the package flaps and pull apart about halfway. • Bring the corners of the wrapping beneath the package, paying attention not to contaminate the inner package or item. • Hold the package over the sterile field with the opening down; with a quick movement, pull the flap completely open and snap the sterile item onto the field.				
9. Place basins and bowls near the edge of the sterile field so you can pour liquids without reaching over the field.*				

(continued)

Procedure Steps Total Possible Points - 44 Time Limit: 10 minutes	Practice #1	Practice #2	Practice #3	Final
10. Use sterile transfer forceps if necessary to add additional items to the sterile field.				
11. If necessary, don sterile gloves after a sterile scrub to arrange items on the sterile field.				
Total Number of Points Achieved/Final Score				
Initials of Observer:				

Comments and Signatures

Reviewer's comments and signatures:

1. _____

2. _____

3. _____

Instructor's comments:

_____

CAAHEP Competency Achieved

III. P (6) Perform sterilization procedures

ABHES Competency Achieved

4 (p) Perform sterilization techniques

PROCEDURE 41-2 PERFORMING A SURGICAL SCRUB

Procedure Goal

To remove dirt and microorganisms from under the fingernails and from the surface of the skin, hair follicles, and oil glands of the hands and forearms

Scoring System

To score each step, use the following scoring system:
1 = poor, 2 = fair, 3 = good, 4 = excellent

A minimum score of at least a 3 must be achieved on **each** step to achieve successful completion of the technique. Detailed instructions on the scoring system are found on page 413.

Materials

Dispenser with surgical soap, sterile surgical scrub brush or sponge, sterile towels

Procedure

Procedure Steps Total Possible Points - 36 Time Limit: 10 minutes	Practice #1	Practice #2	Practice #3	Final
1. Remove all jewelry and roll up your sleeves to above the elbow.				
2. Assemble the necessary materials.				
3. Turn on the faucet using the foot or knee pedal.				
4. Wet your hands from the fingertips to the elbows. You must keep your hands higher than your elbows.*				
5. Under running water, use a sterile brush to clean under your fingernails.				
6. Apply surgical soap and scrub your hands, fingers, areas between the fingers, wrists, and forearms with the scrub sponge, using a firm circular motion. Follow the manufacturer's recommendations to determine appropriate length of time, usually 2 to 6 minutes.*				
7. Rinse from fingers to elbows, always keeping your hands higher than your elbows.				
8. Thoroughly dry your hands and forearms with sterile towels, working from the hands to the elbows.*				
9. Turn off the faucet with the foot or knee pedal. Use a clean paper towel if a foot or knee pedal is not used.				
Total Number of Points Achieved/Final Score				
Initials of Observer:				

(continued)

Comments and Signatures

Reviewer's comments and signatures:

1. _____

2. _____

3. _____

Instructor's comments:

_____

CAAHEP Competencies Achieved

III. P (4) Perform handwashing

III. P (6) Perform sterilization procedures

ABHES Competencies Achieved

4 (c) Apply principles of aseptic techniques and infection control

4 (p) Perform sterilization techniques

Procedure 41-3 Donning Sterile Gloves

Procedure Goal

To don sterile gloves without compromising the sterility of the outer surface of the gloves

Scoring System

To score each step, use the following scoring system:
1 = poor, 2 = fair, 3 = good, 4 = excellent

A minimum score of at least a 3 must be achieved on **each** step to achieve successful completion of the technique. Detailed instructions on the scoring system are found on page 413.

Materials

Correctly sized, prepackaged, double-wrapped sterile gloves

Procedure

Procedure Steps Total Possible Points - 76 Time Limit: 10 minutes	Practice #1	Practice #2	Practice #3	Final
1. Obtain the correct size gloves.				
2. Check the package for tears and ensure that the expiration date has not passed.*				
3. Perform a surgical scrub.				
4. Peel the outer wrap from gloves and place the inner wrapper on a clean surface above waist level.				
5. Position gloves so the cuff end is closest to your body.				
6. Touch only the flaps as you open the package.*				
7. Use instructions provided on the inner package, if available.				
8. Do not reach over the sterile inside of the inner package.				
9. Follow these steps if there are no instructions: a. Open the package so the first flap is opened away from you. b. Pinch the corner and pull to one side. c. Put your fingertips under the side flaps and gently pull until the package is completely open.				
10. Use your nondominant hand to grasp the inside cuff of the opposite glove (the folded edge). Do not touch the outside of the glove. If you are right-handed, use your left hand to put on the right glove first, and vice versa.*				
11. Holding the glove at arm's length and waist level, insert the dominant hand into the glove with the palm facing up. Don't let the outside of the glove touch any other surface.				
12. With your sterile gloved hand, slip the gloved fingers into the cuff of the other glove.				
13. Pick up the other glove, touching only the outside. Don't touch any other surfaces.				

(continued)

Procedure Steps Total Possible Points - 76 Time Limit: 10 minutes	Practice #1	Practice #2	Practice #3	Final
14. Pull the glove up and onto your hand. Ensure that the sterile gloved hand does not touch skin.				
15. Adjust your fingers as necessary, touching only glove to glove.				
16. Do not adjust the cuffs because your forearms may contaminate the gloves.				
17. Keep your hands in front of you, between your shoulders and waist. If you move your hands out of this area, they are considered contaminated.				
18. If contamination or the possibility of contamination occurs, change gloves.				
19. Remove gloves the same way you remove clean gloves, by touching only the inside.*				
Total Number of Points Achieved/Final Score				
Initials of Observer:				

Comments and Signatures

Reviewer's comments and signatures:

1. _____

2. _____

3. _____

Instructor's comments:

_____

CAAHEP Competency Achieved

III. P (3) Select appropriate barrier/personal protective equipment (PPE) for potentially infectious situations

ABHES Competency Achieved

None

PROCEDURE 41-4 ASSISTING AS A FLOATER (UNSTERILE ASSISTANT) DURING MINOR SURGICAL PROCEDURES

Procedure Goal

To provide assistance to the doctor during minor surgery while maintaining clean or sterile technique as appropriate

Scoring System

To score each step, use the following scoring system:
1 = poor, 2 = fair, 3 = good, 4 = excellent

A minimum score of at least a 3 must be achieved on **each** step to achieve successful completion of the technique. Detailed instructions on the scoring system are found on page 413.

Materials

Sterile towel, tray or Mayo stand, appropriate instrument pack(s), needles and syringes, anesthetic, antiseptic, sterile water or normal saline, small sterile bowl, sterile gauze squares or cotton balls, specimen containers half-filled with preservative, suture materials, sterile dressings and tape

Procedure

Procedure Steps Total Possible Points - 28 Time Limit: 10 minutes	Practice #1	Practice #2	Practice #3	Final
1. Perform routine hand washing and put on exam gloves.				
2. Monitor the patient during the procedure; record the results in the patient's chart.				
3. During the surgery, assist as needed.				
4. Add sterile items to the tray as necessary.				
5. Pour sterile solution into a sterile bowl as needed.				

6. Assist in administering additional anesthetic.
  a. Check the medication vial two times.
  b. Clean the rubber stopper with an alcohol pad (write the date opened when using a new bottle); leave pad on top.
  c. Present the needle and syringe to the doctor.
  d. Remove the alcohol pad from the vial and show the label to the doctor.
  e. Hold the vial upside down and grasp the lower edge firmly; brace your wrist with your free hand.*
  f. Allow the doctor to fill the syringe.
  g. Check the medication vial a final time.				

7. Receive specimens for laboratory exam.
  a. Uncap the specimen container; present it to the doctor for the introduction of the specimen.
  b. Replace the cap and label the container.
  c. Treat all specimens as infectious.				

(continued)

Procedure Steps Total Possible Points - 28 Time Limit: 10 minutes	Practice #1	Practice #2	Practice #3	Final
d. Place the specimen container in a transport bag or other container. e. Complete the requisition form to send the specimen to the laboratory.				
Total Number of Points Achieved/Final Score				
Initials of Observer:				

Comments and Signatures

Reviewer's comments and signatures:

1. _____

2. _____

3. _____

Instructor's comments:

_____

CAAHEP Competencies Achieved

I. P (10) Assist physician with patient care

III. P (3) Select appropriate barrier/personal protective equipment (PPE) for potentially infectious situations

ABHES Competencies Achieved

4 (b) Prepare patients for procedures

4 (c) Apply principles of aseptic techniques and infection control

4 (h) Prepare patient for and assist physician with routine and specialty examinations and treatments and minor office surgeries

PROCEDURE 41-5 ASSISTING AS A STERILE SCRUB ASSISTANT DURING MINOR SURGICAL PROCEDURES

Procedure Goal

To provide assistance to the doctor during minor surgery while maintaining clean or sterile technique as appropriate

Scoring System

To score each step, use the following scoring system:
1 = poor, 2 = fair, 3 = good, 4 = excellent

A minimum score of at least a 3 must be achieved on **each** step to achieve successful completion of the technique. Detailed instructions on the scoring system are found on page 413.

Materials

Sterile towel, tray or Mayo stand, appropriate instrument pack(s), needles and syringes, anesthetic, antiseptic, sterile water or normal saline, small sterile bowl, sterile gauze squares or cotton balls, specimen containers half-filled with preservative, suture materials, sterile dressings and tape

Procedure

Procedure Steps Total Possible Points - 28 Time Limit: 10 minutes	Practice #1	Practice #2	Practice #3	Final
1. Perform a surgical scrub and put on sterile gloves. (Remember to remove the sterile towel covering the sterile field and instruments before gloving.)*				
2. Close and arrange the surgical instruments on the tray.*				
3. Prepare for swabbing by inserting gauze squares into the sterile dressing forceps.				
4. Pass the instruments as necessary.				
5. Swab the wound as requested.				
6. Retract the wound as requested.				
7. Cut the sutures as requested.				
Total Number of Points Achieved/Final Score				
Initials of Observer:				

Comments and Signatures

Reviewer's comments and signatures:

1. _____

2. _____

3. _____

Instructor's comments:

_____

(continued)

CAAHEP Competencies Achieved

I. P (10) Assist physician with patient care

III. P (3) Select appropriate barrier/personal protective equipment (PPE) for potentially infectious situations

ABHES Competencies Achieved

4 (b) Prepare patients for procedures

4 (c) Apply principles of aseptic techniques and infection control

4 (h) Prepare patient for and assist physician with routine and specialty examinations and treatments and minor office surgeries

PROCEDURE 41-6 ASSISTING AFTER MINOR SURGICAL PROCEDURES

Procedure Goal

To provide assistance to the doctor during minor surgery while maintaining clean or sterile technique as appropriate

Scoring System

To score each step, use the following scoring system:
1 = poor, 2 = fair, 3 = good, 4 = excellent

A minimum score of at least a 3 must be achieved on **each** step to achieve successful completion of the technique. Detailed instructions on the scoring system are found on page 413.

Materials

Examination gloves, antiseptic, tray or Mayo stand, sterile dressings and tape

Procedure

Procedure Steps Total Possible Points - 44 Time Limit: 10 minutes	Practice #1	Practice #2	Practice #3	Final
1. Monitor the patient.				
2. Put on clean exam gloves and clean the wound with antiseptic.				
3. Dress the wound.*				
4. Remove the gloves and wash your hands.				
5. Give the patient oral postoperative instructions in addition to the release packet.*				
6. Discharge the patient.				
7. Put on clean exam gloves.				
8. Properly dispose of used materials and disposable instruments.				
9. Sanitize reusable instruments and prepare them for disinfection and/or sterilization as needed.				
10. Clean equipment and the exam room according to OSHA guidelines.				
11. Remove the gloves and wash your hands.				
Total Number of Points Achieved/Final Score				
Initials of Observer:				

(continued)

Comments and Signatures

Reviewer's comments and signatures:

1. _____

2. _____

3. _____

Instructor's comments:

_____

CAAHEP Competencies Achieved

I. P (10) Assist physician with patient care

III. P (3) Select appropriate barrier/personal protective equipment (PPE) for potentially infectious situations

ABHES Competencies Achieved

4 (b) Prepare patients for procedures

4 (c) Apply principles of aseptic techniques and infection control

4 (h) Prepare patient for and assist physician with routine and specialty examinations and treatments and minor office surgeries

PROCEDURE 42-2 ADMINISTERING THERMOTHERAPY

Procedure Goal

To administer thermotherapy safely and effectively

Scoring System

To score each step, use the following scoring system:
1 = poor, 2 = fair, 3 = good, 4 = excellent

A minimum score of at least a 3 must be achieved on **each** step to achieve successful completion of the technique. Detailed instructions on the scoring system are found on page 413.

Materials

Gloves, towels, blanket, heat application materials required for order: chemical hot pack, heating pad, hot-water bottle, heat lamp, container and medication for hot soak, container and gauze for hot compress

Procedure

Procedure Steps Total Possible Points - 68 Time Limit: 10 minutes	Practice #1	Practice #2	Practice #3	Final
1. Double-check the physician's order. Be sure you know where to apply therapy, the proper temperature for the application, and how long it should remain in place.				
2. Identify the patient and explain the procedure and its purpose. Ask if the patient has any questions.				
3. Have the patient undress and put on a gown, if required; provide privacy or assistance as needed.				
4. Wash your hands and put on gloves.				
5. Position the patient comfortably and drape appropriately.*				
6. If the patient has a dressing, check the dressing for blood and change as necessary. Alert the physician and ask if treatment should continue.*				
7. Check the temperature by touch and look for the presence of adverse skin conditions (excessive redness, blistering, or irritation) on all applications before and during the treatment.*				
8. As necessary, reheat devices or solutions to provide therapeutic temperatures and then reapply them.				

9. Prepare the therapy as ordered.
 • Chemical hot pack
   a. Check the pack for leaks.*
   b. Activate the pack. (Check manufacturer's directions.)*
   c. Cover the pack with a towel.
 • Heating pad
   a. Turn the heating pad on, selecting the appropriate temperature setting.
   b. Cover the pad with a towel or pillowcase.
   c. Make sure the patient's skin is dry and do not allow the patient to lie on top of the heating pad.*				

(continued)

Procedure Steps Total Possible Points - 68 Time Limit: 10 minutes	Practice #1	Practice #2	Practice #3	Final

• Hot-water bottle
  a. Fill the bottle one-half full with hot water of the correct temperature—usually 110°F to 115°F. Use a thermometer. The physician can provide information on the ideal water temperature that should be used, which will depend on the area being treated.
  b. Expel the air and close the bottle.*
  c. Cover the bottle with a towel or pillowcase.*
• Heat lamp
  a. Place the lamp 2 feet to 4 feet away from the treatment area. (Check manufacturer's directions.)
  b. Follow the treatment time as ordered.
• Hot soak
  a. Select a container of the appropriate size for the area to be treated.
  b. Fill the container with hot water that is no more than 110°F. Use a thermometer. Add medication to the container if ordered.
• Hot compress
  a. Soak a washcloth or gauze in hot water. Wring it out.
  b. Frequently rewarm the compress to maintain the temperature.				

10. Place the device on the patient's affected body part or place the affected body part in the container. If you are using a compress, place a hot-water bottle on top, if desired, to keep it warm longer.				
11. Ask the patient how the device feels. During any heat therapy, remember that dilated blood vessels cause heat loss from the skin and that this heat loss may make the patient feel chilled. Be prepared to cover the patient with sheets or blankets.				
12. Leave the device in place for the length of time ordered by the physician. Periodically check the skin for redness, blistering, or irritation. If the area becomes excessively red or develops blisters, remove the patient from the heat source and have the physician examine the area.				
13. Remove the application and observe the area for inflammation and swelling. Replace the patient's dressing if necessary.				
14. Help the patient dress, if needed.				
15. Remove equipment and supplies, properly discarding used disposable materials, and sanitize, disinfect, and/or sterilize reusable equipment and materials as needed.				
16. Remove the gloves and wash your hands.				
17. Document the treatment and your observation in the patient's chart. If you teach the patient or the patient's family how to use the device, document your instructions.				
Total Number of Points Achieved/Final Score				
Initials of Observer:				

(continued)

Comments and Signatures

Reviewer's comments and signatures:

1. _____

2. _____

3. _____

Instructor's comments:

_____

CAAHEP Competencies Achieved

IV. P. (6) Prepare a patient for procedures and/or treatments

IV. P. (8) Document patient care

IV. P. (9) Document patient education

ABHES Competency Achieved

2. c. Assist the physician with the regimen of diagnostic and treatment modalities as they relate to each body system

PROCEDURE 42-3 TEACHING A PATIENT HOW TO USE A CANE

Procedure Goal

To teach a patient how to use a cane safely

Scoring System

To score each step, use the following scoring system:
1 = poor, 2 = fair, 3 = good, 4 = excellent

A minimum score of at least a 3 must be achieved on **each** step to achieve successful completion of the technique. Detailed instructions on the scoring system are found on page 413.

Materials

Cane suited to the patient's needs

Procedure

Procedure Steps Total Possible Points - 64 Time Limit: 15 minutes	Practice #1	Practice #2	Practice #3	Final
Standing from a Sitting Position				
1. Instruct the patient to slide his buttocks to the edge of the chair.				
2. Tell the patient to place his right foot slightly behind and inside the right front leg of the chair and his left foot slightly behind and inside the left front leg of the chair. (This provides him with a wide, stable stance.)				
3. Instruct the patient to lean forward and use the armrests or seat of the chair to push upward. Caution the patient not to lean on the cane.				
4. Have the patient position the cane for support on the uninjured or strong side of his body as indicated.				
Walking				
1. Teach the patient to hold the cane on the uninjured or strong side of her body with the tip(s) of the cane 4 to 6 inches from the side and in front of her strong foot. Remind the patient to make sure the tip is flat on the ground.*				
2. Have the patient move the cane forward approximately 8 inches and then move her affected foot forward, parallel to the cane.				
3. Next have the patient move her strong leg forward past the cane and her weak leg.				
4. Observe as the patient repeats this process.				
Ascending Stairs				
1. Instruct the patient to always start with his uninjured or strong leg when going up stairs.				

(continued)

Procedure Steps Total Possible Points - 64 Time Limit: 15 minutes	Practice #1	Practice #2	Practice #3	Final
2. Advise the patient to keep the cane on the uninjured or strong side of his body and to use the wall or rail, if available, for support on the weak side. If a rail is not available, the patient may need assistance for safety.				
3. After the patient steps on the strong leg, instruct him to bring up his weak leg and then the cane.				
4. Remind the patient not to rush.				
Descending Stairs				
1. Instruct the patient to always start with her weak leg when going down stairs.				
2. Advise the patient to keep the cane on the uninjured or strong side of her body and to use the wall or rail, if available, for support on the weak side. If a rail is not available, the patient may need assistance for safety.				
3. Have the patient use the uninjured or strong leg and wall or rail to support her body, put the cane on the next step, and bend the strong leg as she lowers the weak leg to the next step.				
4. Instruct the patient to step down with the strong leg.				
Walking on Snow or Ice				
Suggest that the patient try a metal ice-gripping cane or a ski pole. These can be dug into the snow or ice to prevent slipping. Instruct the patient to avoid walking on ice unless absolutely necessary.				
Total Number of Points Achieved/Final Score				
Initials of Observer:				

Comments and Signatures

Reviewer's comments and signatures:

1. _____

2. _____

3. _____

Instructor's comments:

_____

CAAHEP Competencies Achieved

IV. P. (**6**) Prepare a patient for procedures and/or treatments

IV. P. (**8**) Document patient care

IV. P (**9**) Document patient education

ABHES Competencies Achieved

5. b. Identify and respond appropriately when working/caring for patients with special needs

9. q. Instruct patients with special needs

PROCEDURE 42-4 TEACHING A PATIENT HOW TO USE A WALKER

Procedure Goal

To teach a patient how to use a walker safely

Scoring System

To score each step, use the following scoring system:
1 = poor, 2 = fair, 3 = good, 4 = excellent

A minimum score of at least a 3 must be achieved on **each** step to achieve successful completion of the technique. Detailed instructions on the scoring system are found on page 413.

Materials

Walker suited to the patient's needs

Procedure

Procedure Steps Total Possible Points - 44 Time Limit: 10 minutes	Practice #1	Practice #2	Practice #3	Final
Walking				
1. Instruct the patient to step into the walker.				
2. Tell the patient to place her hands on the handgrips on the sides of the walker.				
3. Make sure the patient's feet are far enough apart so that she feels balanced.*				
4. Instruct the patient to pick up the walker and move it forward about 6 inches.				
5. Have the patient move one foot forward and then the other foot.				
6. Instruct the patient to pick up the walker again and move it forward. If the patient is strong enough, explain that she may advance the walker after moving each leg rather than waiting until she has moved both legs.				
Sitting				
1. Teach the patient to turn his back to the chair or bed.				
2. Instruct the patient to take small, careful steps and to back up until he feels the chair or bed at the back of his legs.				
3. Instruct the patient to keep the walker in front of himself, let go of the walker, and place both his hands on the arms or seat of the chair or on the bed.				
4. Teach the patient to balance himself on his arms while lowering himself slowly to the chair or bed.				
5. If the patient has an injured or affected leg, he should keep it forward while bending his unaffected leg and lowering his body to the chair or bed.				

(continued)

Procedure Steps Total Possible Points - 44 Time Limit: 10 minutes	Practice #1	Practice #2	Practice #3	Final
Ascending and Descending Stairs				
If a patient needs to use a walker on stairs, refer him to a physical therapist for additional training.				
Total Number of Points Achieved/Final Score				
Initials of Observer:				

Comments and Signatures

Reviewer's comments and signatures:

1. _____

2. _____

3. _____

Instructor's comments:

_____

CAAHEP Competencies Achieved

IV. P. (**6**) Prepare a patient for procedures and/or treatments

IV. P. (**8**) Document patient care

IV. P. (**9**) Document patient education

ABHES Competencies Achieved

5. b. Identify and respond appropriately when working/caring for patients with special needs

9. q. Instruct patients with special needs

PROCEDURE 42-5 TEACHING A PATIENT HOW TO USE CRUTCHES

Procedure Goal

To teach a patient how to use crutches safely

Scoring System

To score each step, use the following scoring system:
1 = poor, 2 = fair, 3 = good, 4 = excellent

A minimum score of at least a 3 must be achieved on **each** step to achieve successful completion of the technique. Detailed instructions on the scoring system are found on page 413.

Materials

Crutches suited to the patient's needs

Procedure

Procedure Steps Total Possible Points - 44 Time Limit: 15 minutes	Practice #1	Practice #2	Practice #3	Final
1. Verify the physician's order for the type of crutches and gait to be used.				
2. Wash your hands, identify the patient, and explain the procedure.				
3. Elderly patients or patients with muscle weakness should be taught muscle strength exercises for their arms.				
4. Have the patient stand erect and look straight ahead.				
5. Tell the patient to place the crutch tips 2 to 4 inches in front of and 4 to 6 inches to the side of each foot.				
6. When instructing a patient to use an axillary crutch, make sure the patient has a 2-inch gap between the axilla and the axillary bar and that each elbow is flexed 25 degrees to 30 degrees.*				
7. Teach the patient how to get up from a chair: a. Instruct the patient to hold both crutches on his affected or weaker side. b. Have the patient slide to the edge of the chair. c. Tell the patient to push down on the arm or seat of the chair on his stronger side and use his strong leg to push up. If indicated, keep the affected leg forward. d. Advise the patient to put the crutches under his arms and press down on the hand grips with his hands.				
8. Teach the patient the required gait. Which gait the patient will use depends on the muscle strength and coordination of the patient. It also depends on the type of crutches, the injury, and the patient's condition. Check the physician's orders, and see Figures 42-10 and 42-11 in the text for examples.				

(continued)

Procedure Steps Total Possible Points - 44 Time Limit: 15 minutes	Practice #1	Practice #2	Practice #3	Final

9. Teach the patient how to ascend stairs:
  a. Start the patient close to the bottom step and tell her to push down with her hands.
  b. Instruct the patient to step up on the first step with her good foot.
  c. Tell the patient to lift the crutches to the same step and then lift her other foot. Advise the patient to keep her crutches with her affected limb.
  d. Remind the patient to check her balance before she proceeds to the next step.				

10. Teach the patient how to descend stairs:
  a. Have the patient start at the edge of the steps.
  b. Instruct the patient to bring his crutches and then the affected foot down first. Advise the patient to bend at the hips and knees to prevent leaning forward, which could cause him to fall.
  c. Tell the patient to bring his unaffected foot to the same step.
  d. Remind the patient to check his balance before he proceeds. In some cases, a handrail may be easier and can be used with both crutches in one hand.				

11. Give the patient the following general information related to the use of crutches:
  a. Do not lean on crutches.
  b. Report to the physician any tingling or numbness in the arms, hands, or shoulders.
  c. Support body weight with the hands.
  d. Always stand erect to prevent muscle strain.
  e. Look straight ahead when walking.
  f. Generally, move the crutches not more than 6 inches at a time to maintain good balance.
  g. Check the crutch tips regularly for wear; replace the tips as needed.
  h. Check the crutch tips for wetness; dry the tips if they are wet.
  i. Check all wing nuts and bolts for tightness.
  j. Wear flat, well-fitting, nonskid shoes.
  k. Remove throw rugs and other unsecured articles from traffic areas.
  l. Report any unusual pain in the affected leg.				

Total Number of Points Achieved/Final Score				
Initials of Observer:				

(continued)

Comments and Signatures

Reviewer's comments and signatures:

1. _____

2. _____

3. _____

Instructor's comments:

_____

CAAHEP Competencies Achieved

IV. P. **(6)** Prepare a patient for procedures and/or treatments

IV. P. **(8)** Document patient care

IV. P. **(9)** Document patient education

ABHES Competencies Achieved

5. b. Identify and respond appropriately when working/caring for patients with special needs

9. q. Instruct patients with special needs

PROCEDURE 43-1 STOCKING THE CRASH CART

Procedure Goal

To ensure that the crash cart includes all appropriate drugs, supplies, and equipment needed for emergencies

Scoring System

To score each step, use the following scoring system:
1 = poor, 2 = fair, 3 = good, 4 = excellent

A minimum score of at least a 3 must be achieved on **each** step to achieve successful completion of the technique. Detailed instructions on the scoring system are found on page 413.

Materials

Protocol for or list of crash cart items, crash cart

Procedure

Procedure Steps Total Possible Points - 20 Time Limit: 10 minutes	Practice #1	Practice #2	Practice #3	Final
1. Review the office protocol for or list of items that should be on the crash cart.				
2. Verify each drug on the crash cart and check the amount against the office protocol or list. Restock those that were used and replace those that have passed their expiration date.* Some typical crash cart drugs are listed here: • Activated charcoal • Atropine • Dextrose 50% • Diazepam (Valium) • Digoxin (Lanoxin) • Diphenhydramine hydrochloride (Benadryl) • Epinephrine, injectable • Furosemide (Lasix) • Glucagon • Glucose paste or tablets • Insulin (regular or a variety) • Intravenous dextrose in saline and intravenous dextrose in water • Isoproterenol hydrochloride (Isuprel), aerosol inhaler and injectable • Lactated Ringer's solution • Lidocaine (Xylocaine), injectable • Methylprednisolone tablets • Nitroglycerin tablets • Phenobarbital, injectable • Phenytoin (Dilantin) • Saline solution, isotonic (0.9%) • Sodium bicarbonate, injectable • Sterile water for injection				

(continued)

Procedure Steps Total Possible Points - 20 Time Limit: 10 minutes	Practice #1	Practice #2	Practice #3	Final
3. Check the supplies on the crash cart against the list. Restock items that were used and make sure the packaging of supplies on the cart has not been opened.* Some typical crash cart supplies are listed here: • Adhesive tape • Constricting band or tourniquet • Dressing supplies (alcohol wipes, rolls of gauze, bandage strips, bandage scissors) • Intravenous tubing, venipuncture devices, and butterfly needles • Personal protective equipment • Syringes and needles in various sizes				
4. Check the equipment on the crash cart against the list and examine it to make sure that it is in working order. Restock equipment that is missing or broken.* Some typical crash cart equipment is listed here: • Airways in assorted sizes • Ambu-bag, a trademark for a breathing bag used to assist respiratory ventilation • **Automated external defibrillator** (electrical device that shocks the heart to restore normal beating) • Endotracheal tubes in various sizes • Oxygen tank with oxygen mask and cannula				
5. Check miscellaneous items on the crash cart against the list and restock as needed. Some typical miscellaneous crash cart items are listed here: • Orange juice • Sugar packets				
Total Number of Points Achieved/Final Score				
Initials of Observer:				

Comments and Signatures

Reviewer's comments and signatures:

1. _____

2. _____

3. _____

Instructor's comments:

_____

CAAHEP Competency Achieved

XI. P. (3) Develop a personal (patient and employee) safety plan.

ABHES Competency Achieved

9. k. Prepare and maintain examination and treatment area

PROCEDURE 43-2 PERFORMING AN EMERGENCY ASSESSMENT

Procedure Goal

To assess a medical emergency quickly and accurately

Scoring System

To score each step, use the following scoring system:
1 = poor, 2 = fair, 3 = good, 4 = excellent

A minimum score of at least a 3 must be achieved on **each** step to achieve successful completion of the technique. Detailed instructions on the scoring system are found on page 413.

Materials

Patient's chart, pen, gloves

Procedure

Procedure Steps Total Possible Points - 52 Time Limit: 5 minutes	Practice #1	Practice #2	Practice #3	Final
1. Put on gloves.				
2. Form a general impression of the patient, including his level of responsiveness, level of distress, facial expressions, age, ability to talk, and skin color.				
3. If the patient can communicate clearly, ask what happened. If not, ask someone who observed the accident or injury.				
4. Assess an unresponsive patient by tapping on his shoulder and asking, "Are you OK?" If there is no response, proceed to the next step.*				
5. Assess the patient's airway. If necessary, open the airway by using the head tilt–chin lift maneuver. Give two breaths of 1 second each.				
6. Assess the patient's breathing. If the patient is not breathing, then perform rescue breathing.				
7. Assess the patient's circulation. Determine if the patient has a pulse. Is there any serious external bleeding? Perform CPR as needed (Procedure 43-8). Control any significant bleeding (Procedure 43-5).				
8. If all life-threatening problems have been identified and treated, perform a focused exam. Start at the head and perform the following steps rapidly, taking about 90 seconds. a. Head: Check for deformities, bruises, open wounds, tenderness, depressions, and swelling. Check the ears, nose, and mouth for fluid, blood, or foreign bodies. b. Eyes: Open the eyes and compare the pupils. They should be the same size. c. Neck: Look and feel for deformities, bruises, depressions, open wounds, tenderness, and swelling. Check for a medical alert bracelet or necklace.				

(continued)

Procedure Steps Total Possible Points - 52 Time Limit: 5 minutes	Practice #1	Practice #2	Practice #3	Final
d. Chest: Look and feel for deformities, bruises, open wounds, tenderness, depressions, and swelling. e. Abdomen: Look and feel for deformities, bruises, open wounds, tenderness, depressions, and swelling. f. Pelvis: Look and feel for deformities, bruises, open wounds, tenderness, depressions, and swelling. g. Arms: Look and feel for deformities, bruises, open wounds, depressions, tenderness, and swelling. Compare the arms for any differences in size, color, or temperature. h. Legs: Look and feel for deformities, bruises, open wounds, depressions, tenderness, and swelling. Compare the legs for any differences in size, color, or temperature. i. Back: Look and feel for deformities, bruises, open wounds, depressions, tenderness, and swelling. Feel under the patient for pools of blood.*				
9. Check vital signs and observe the patient for pallor (paleness) or cyanosis (a bluish tint). If the patient is dark-skinned, observe for pallor or cyanosis on the inside of the lips and mouth.*				
10. Document your findings and report them to the doctor or emergency medical technician (EMT).				
11. Assist the doctor or EMT as requested.				
12. Dispose of biohazardous waste according to OSHA guidelines.				
13. Remove your gloves and wash your hands.				
Total Number of Points Achieved/Final Score				
Initials of Observer:				

Comments and Signatures

Reviewer's comments and signatures:

1. _____

2. _____

3. _____

Instructor's comments:

_____

CAAHEP Competency Achieved

XI. P. (10) Perform first aid procedures

ABHES Competencies Achieved

9. e. Recognize emergencies and treatments and minor office surgical procedures

9. o. 5) First aid and CPR

PROCEDURE 43-3 FOREIGN BODY AIRWAY OBSTRUCTION IN A RESPONSIVE ADULT OR CHILD

Procedure Goal

To correctly relieve a foreign body from the airway of an adult or child

Scoring System

To score each step, use the following scoring system:

1 = poor, 2 = fair, 3 = good, 4 = excellent

A minimum score of at least a 3 must be achieved on **each** step to achieve successful completion of the technique. Detailed instructions on the scoring system are found on page 413.

Materials

Choking adult or child patient

Caution: Never perform this procedure on someone who is not choking.

Procedure

Procedure Steps Total Possible Points - 32 Time Limit: 5 minutes	Practice #1	Practice #2	Practice #3	Final
1. Ask, "Are you choking?" If the answer is "Yes," indicated by a nod of the head or some other sign, ask, "Can you speak?" If the answer is "No," tell the patient that you can help. A choking person cannot speak, cough, or breathe and exhibits the universal sign of choking. If the patient is coughing, observe him closely to see if he clears the object. If he is not coughing or stops coughing, use abdominal thrusts.				
2. Position yourself behind the patient. Place your fist against the abdomen just above the navel and below the xiphoid process.				
3. Grasp your fist with your other hand and provide quick inward and upward thrusts into the patient's abdomen.* Note: If a pregnant or obese person is choking, you will need to place your arms around the chest and perform thrusts over the center of the breastbone.				
4. Continue the thrusts until the object is expelled or the patient becomes unresponsive.				
5. If the patient becomes unresponsive, call EMS and position the patient on his back.*				
6. Use the head tilt–chin lift to open the patient's airway.				
7. Look into the mouth. If you see the foreign body, remove it using your index finger. Do not perform any blind finger sweeps on a child.				

(continued)

Procedure Steps Total Possible Points - 32 Time Limit: 5 minutes	Practice #1	Practice #2	Practice #3	Final
8. Open the airway and look, listen, and feel for breathing. If the patient is not breathing, attempt a rescue breath. Observe the chest. If it does not rise with the breath, reposition the airway and administer another rescue breath. If the chest does not rise after the second attempt, assume that the airway is still blocked and begin CPR (Procedure 43-8).				
Total Number of Points Achieved/Final Score				
Initials of Observer:				

Comments and Signatures

Reviewer's comments and signatures:

1. _____

2. _____

3. _____

Instructor's comments:

_____

CAAHEP Competencies Achieved

XI. P. (9) Maintain provider/professional level CPR certification.

XI. P. (10) Perform first aid procedures

ABHES Competencies Achieved

9. e. Recognize emergencies and treatments and minor office surgical procedures

9. o. 5) First aid and CPR

PROCEDURE 43-4 FOREIGN BODY AIRWAY OBSTRUCTION IN A RESPONSIVE INFANT

Procedure Goal

To correctly relieve a foreign body from the airway of an infant

Scoring System

To score each step, use the following scoring system:
1 = poor, 2 = fair, 3 = good, 4 = excellent

A minimum score of at least a 3 must be achieved on **each** step to achieve successful completion of the technique. Detailed instructions on the scoring system are found on page 413.

Materials

Choking infant

Caution: Never perform this procedure on an infant who is not choking.

Procedure

Procedure Steps Total Possible Points - 44 Time Limit: 5 minutes	Practice #1	Practice #2	Practice #3	Final
1. Assess the infant for signs of severe or complete airway obstruction, which include: a. Sudden onset of difficulty in breathing. b. Inability to speak, make sounds, or cry. c. A high-pitched, noisy, wheezing sound, or no sounds while inhaling. d. Weak, ineffective coughs. e. Blue lips or skin.				
2. Hold the infant with his head down, supporting the body with your forearm. His legs should straddle your forearm and you should support his jaw and head with your hand and fingers. This is best done in a sitting or kneeling position.				
3. Give up to five back blows with the heel of your free hand. Strike the infant's back forcefully between the shoulder blades. At any point, if the object is expelled, discontinue the back blows.*				
4. If the obstruction is not cleared, turn the infant over as a unit, supporting the head with your hands and the body between your forearms.				
5. Keep the head lower than the chest and perform five chest thrusts.* Place two fingers over the breastbone (sternum), above the xiphoid. Give five quick chest thrusts about ½ to 1 inch deep. Stop the compressions if the object is expelled.				
6. Alternate five back blows and five chest thrusts until the object is expelled or until the infant becomes unconscious. If the infant becomes unconscious, call EMS or have someone do it for you.				

(continued)

Procedure Steps Total Possible Points - 44 Time Limit: 5 minutes	Practice #1	Practice #2	Practice #3	Final
7. Open the infant's mouth by grasping both the tongue and the lower jaw between the thumb and fingers and pull up the lower jawbone. **If you see the object, remove it using your smallest finger. Do not use blind finger sweeps on an infant.***				
8. Open the airway and attempt to provide rescue breaths. If the chest does not rise, reposition the airway (both head and chin) and try to provide another rescue breath.				
9. If the rescue breaths are unsuccessful, begin CPR. Hold the infant, supporting her body with your forearm and her head with your hand and fingers. Deliver 30 chest compressions about ½ to 1 inch deep.				
10. Open the infant's mouth and look for the foreign object. If you see an object, remove it with your smallest finger.				
11. Open the airway and attempt to provide rescue breaths. If the chest does not rise, continue CPR until the doctor or EMS arrives.				
Total Number of Points Achieved/Final Score				
Initials of Observer:				

Comments and Signatures

Reviewer's comments and signatures:

1. _____

2. _____

3. _____

Instructor's comments:

_____

CAAHEP Competencies Achieved

XI. P. (9) Maintain provider/professional level CPR certification.

XI. P. (10) Perform first aid procedures

ABHES Competencies Achieved

9. e. Recognize emergencies and treatments and minor office surgical procedures

9. o. 5) First aid and CPR

PROCEDURE 43-5 CONTROLLING BLEEDING

Procedure Goal

To control bleeding and minimize blood loss

Scoring System

To score each step, use the following scoring system:
1 = poor, 2 = fair, 3 = good, 4 = excellent

A minimum score of at least a 3 must be achieved on **each** step to achieve successful completion of the technique. Detailed instructions on the scoring system are found on page 413.

Materials

Clean or sterile dressings

Procedure

Procedure Steps Total Possible Points - 36 Time Limit: 10 minutes	Practice #1	Practice #2	Practice #3	Final
1. If you have time, wash your hands and put on exam gloves, face protection, and a gown.*				
2. Using a clean or sterile dressing, apply direct pressure over the wound.				
3. If blood soaks through the dressing, do not remove it. Apply an additional dressing over the original one.*				
4. If possible, elevate the body part that is bleeding.				
5. If direct pressure and elevation do not stop the bleeding, apply pressure over the nearest pressure point between the bleeding and the heart. For example, if the wound is on the lower arm, apply pressure on the brachial artery. For a lower-leg wound, apply pressure on the femoral artery in the groin.				
6. When the doctor or EMT arrives, assist as requested.				
7. After the patient has been transferred to a hospital, properly dispose of contaminated materials.				
8. Remove the gloves and wash your hands.				
9. Document your care in the patient's chart.				
Total Number of Points Achieved/Final Score				
Initials of Observer:				

(continued)

Comments and Signatures

Reviewer's comments and signatures:

1. _____

2. _____

3. _____

Instructor's comments:

_____

CAAHEP Competency Achieved

XI. P. (10) Perform first aid procedures

ABHES Competencies Achieved

9. e. Recognize emergencies and treatments and minor office surgical procedures

9. o. 5) First aid and CPR

PROCEDURE 43-6 CLEANING MINOR WOUNDS

Procedure Goal

To clean and dress minor wounds

Scoring System

To score each step, use the following scoring system:
1 = poor, 2 = fair, 3 = good, 4 = excellent

A minimum score of at least a 3 must be achieved on **each** step to achieve successful completion of the technique. Detailed instructions on the scoring system are found on page 413.

Materials

Sterile gauze squares, basin, antiseptic soap, warm water, sterile dressing

Procedure

Procedure Steps Total Possible Points - 44 Time Limit: 10 minutes	Practice #1	Practice #2	Practice #3	Final
1. Wash your hands and put on exam gloves.				
2. Dip several gauze squares in a basin of warm, soapy water.				
3. Wash the wound from the center outward.* Use a new gauze square for each cleansing motion.				
4. As you wash, remove debris that could cause infection.				
5. Rinse the area thoroughly, preferably by placing the wound under warm, running water.*				
6. Pat the wound dry with sterile gauze squares.				
7. Cover the wound with a dry, sterile dressing. Bandage the dressing in place.				
8. Properly dispose of contaminated materials.				
9. Remove the gloves and wash your hands.				
10. Instruct the patient on wound care.				
11. Record the procedure in the patient's chart.				
Total Number of Points Achieved/Final Score				
Initials of Observer:				

(continued)

Comments and Signatures

Reviewer's comments and signatures:

1. _____

2. _____

3. _____

Instructor's comments:

_____

CAAHEP Competencies Achieved

III. P. (3) Select appropriate barrier/personal protective equipment (PPE) for potentially infectious situations

IV. P. (6) Prepare a patient for procedures and/or treatments

XI. P. (10) Perform first aid procedures

ABHES Competencies Achieved

9. e. Recognize emergencies and treatments and minor office surgical procedures

9. o. 5) First aid and CPR

PROCEDURE 43-7 CARING FOR A PATIENT WHO IS VOMITING

Procedure Goal

To increase comfort and minimize complications, such as aspiration, for a patient who is vomiting

Scoring System

To score each step, use the following scoring system:
1 = poor, 2 = fair, 3 = good, 4 = excellent

A minimum score of at least a 3 must be achieved on **each** step to achieve successful completion of the technique. Detailed instructions on the scoring system are found on page 413.

Materials

Emesis basin, cool compress, cup of cool water, paper tissues or a towel, and (if ordered) intravenous fluids and electrolytes and an antinausea drug

Procedure

Procedure Steps Total Possible Points - 32 Time Limit: 10 minutes	Practice #1	Practice #2	Practice #3	Final
1. Wash your hands and put on exam gloves and other PPE.				
2. Ask the patient when and how the vomiting started and how frequently it occurs. Find out whether she is nauseated or in pain.				
3. Give the patient an emesis basin to collect vomit. Observe and document its amount, color, odor, and consistency. Particularly note blood, bile, undigested food, or feces in the vomit.				
4. Place a cool compress on the patient's forehead to make her more comfortable. Offer water and paper tissues or a towel to clean her mouth.				
5. Monitor for signs of dehydration, such as confusion, irritability, and flushed, dry skin. Also monitor for signs of electrolyte imbalances, such as leg cramps or an irregular pulse.				
6. If requested, assist by laying out supplies and equipment for the physician to use in administering intravenous fluids and electrolytes. Administer an antinausea drug if prescribed.				
7. Prepare the patient for diagnostic tests if instructed.				
8. Remove the gloves and wash your hands.				
Total Number of Points Achieved/Final Score				
Initials of Observer:				

(continued)

Comments and Signatures

Reviewer's comments and signatures:

1. _____

2. _____

3. _____

Instructor's comments:

_____

CAAHEP Competencies Achieved

III. P. (3) Select appropriate barrier/personal protective equipment (PPE) for potentially infectious situations

IV.P. (6) Prepare a patient for procedures and/or treatments

XI. P. (10) Perform first aid procedures

ABHES Competencies Achieved

9. e. Recognize emergencies and treatments and minor office surgical procedures

9. o. 5) First aid and CPR

9. q. Instruct patients with special needs

PROCEDURE 43-8 PERFORMING CARDIOPULMONARY RESUSCITATION (CPR)

Procedure Goal

To provide ventilation and blood circulation for a patient who shows none

Scoring System

To score each step, use the following scoring system:

1 = poor, 2 = fair, 3 = good, 4 = excellent

A minimum score of at least a 3 must be achieved on **each** step to achieve successful completion of the technique. Detailed instructions on the scoring system are found on page 413.

Materials

Mouth shield, or if not in the office, a piece of plastic with a hole for the mouth

Procedure

Procedure Steps Total Possible Points - 32 Time Limit: 10 minutes	Practice #1	Practice #2	Practice #3	Final
1. Check responsiveness. • Tap shoulder. • Ask, "Are you OK?"				
2. If patient is unresponsive, call 911 or the local emergency number or have someone place the call for you.*				
3. Open the patient's airway. • Tilt the patient's head back, using the head tilt–chin lift maneuver.*				
4. Check for breathing. • Place your ear next to the patient's mouth, turn your head, and watch the chest. • Look for the chest to rise and fall, listen for sounds coming out of the mouth or nose, and feel for air movement. • If the patient is breathing and you do not suspect a spinal injury, place him in the **recovery position:** • Kneel beside the patient and place the arm closest to you straight out from the body. Position the far arm with the back of the hand against the patient's near cheek. • Grab and bend the patient's far knee. • Protecting the patient's head with one hand, gently roll him toward you by pulling the opposite knee over and to the ground. • Position the top leg to balance the patient onto his side. • Tilt his head up slightly so that the airway is open. Make sure that his hand is under his cheek. Place a blanket or coat over the person and stay close until help arrives.				

(continued)

Procedure Steps Total Possible Points - 32 Time Limit: 10 minutes	Practice #1	Practice #2	Practice #3	Final
• If the patient is not breathing or has inadequate breathing, position the patient on his back and give two rescue breaths, each one second long. Each breath should cause the chest to rise. When giving rescue breaths, use one of three methods: a. Mouth-to-mouth or mouth-to-nose rescue breathing: • Place your mouth around the patient's mouth and pinch the nose, or close the patient's mouth and place your mouth around the patient's nose. • Deliver two slow breaths. Use a face shield. b. Mouth-to-mask device. c. Bag-mask ventilation. Ensure the adequate rise and fall of the patient's chest. If his chest does not rise, reposition the airway and try again. If on the second attempt the chest does not rise, your patient may have an airway obstruction. See Procedure 43-3.				
5. Place the heel of one hand on the patient's sternum between the nipples. Place your other hand over the first, interlacing your fingers.				
6. Give 30 chest compressions 1½ to 2 inches deep. You should compress the chest hard and fast (100 compressions per minute).* Give two breaths.				
7. Continue cycles of 30:2 until the patient begins to move, an AED is available, qualified help arrives, or you are too exhausted to continue.				
8. If the patient starts moving, check for breathing. If the patient is breathing adequately, put him in the recovery position and monitor him until the doctor or EMS arrives.				
Total Number of Points Achieved/Final Score				
Initials of Observer:				

(continued)

Comments and Signatures

Reviewer's comments and signatures:

1. _____

2. _____

3. _____

Instructor's comments:

_____

CAAHEP Competencies Achieved

XI. P. (9) Maintain provider/professional level CPR certification.

XI. P. (10) Perform first aid procedures

ABHES Competencies Achieved

9. e. Recognize emergencies and treatments and minor office surgical procedures

9. o. 5) First aid and CPR

PROCEDURE 43-9 ASSISTING WITH EMERGENCY CHILDBIRTH

Procedure Goal

To assist in performing an emergency childbirth

Scoring System

To score each step, use the following scoring system:

1 = poor, 2 = fair, 3 = good, 4 = excellent

A minimum score of at least a 3 must be achieved on **each** step to achieve successful completion of the technique. Detailed instructions on the scoring system are found on page 413.

Materials

Clean cloths, sterile or clean sheets or towels, two sterile clamps or two pieces of string boiled in water for at least 10 minutes, sterile scissors, plastic bag, soft blankets or towels

Procedure

Procedure Steps Total Possible Points - 84 Time Limit: 10 minutes	Practice #1	Practice #2	Practice #3	Final
1. Ask the woman her name and age, how far apart her contractions are (about two per minute signals that the birth is near), if her water has broken, and if she feels straining or pressure as if the baby is coming. Alert the doctor or call the EMS system.				
2. Help remove the woman's lower clothing.				
3. Explain that you are about to do a visual inspection to see if the baby's head is in position. Ask the woman to lie on her back with her thighs spread, her knees flexed, and her feet flat. Examine her to see if there is crowning (a bulging at the vaginal opening from the baby's head).				
4. If the head is crowning, childbirth is imminent. Place clean cloths under the woman's buttocks and use sterile sheets or towels (if they are available) to cover her legs and stomach.				
5. Wash your hands thoroughly and put on exam gloves. If other PPE is available, put it on now.				
6. At this point the physician would begin to take steps to deliver the baby, and you would position yourself at the woman's head to provide emotional support and help in case she vomited. If no physician is available, position yourself at the woman's side so that you have a constant view of the vaginal opening.				
7. Talk to the woman and encourage her to relax between contractions while allowing the delivery to proceed naturally.				
8. Position your gloved hands at the woman's vaginal opening when the baby's head starts to appear.* Do not touch her skin.				

(continued)

Procedure Steps Total Possible Points - 84 Time Limit: 10 minutes	Practice #1	Practice #2	Practice #3	Final
9. Place one hand below the baby's head as it is delivered. Spread your fingers evenly around the baby's head.* Use your other hand to help cradle the baby's head. Never pull on the baby.				
10. If the umbilical cord is wrapped around the baby's neck, gently loosen the cord and slide it over the baby's head.				
11. If the amniotic sac has not broken by the time the baby's head is delivered, use your finger to puncture the membrane. Then pull the membranes away from the baby's mouth and nose.*				
12. Wipe blood or mucus from the baby's mouth with a clean cloth.				
13. Continue to support the baby's head as the shoulders emerge. The upper shoulder will deliver first, followed quickly by the lower shoulder.				
14. After the feet are delivered, lay the baby on his side with the head slightly lower than the body. Keep the baby at the same level as the mother until you cut the umbilical cord.				
15. If the baby is not breathing, lower the head, raise the lower part of the body, and tap the soles of the feet. If the baby is still not breathing, begin rescue breathing and CPR.				
16. To cut the cord, wait several minutes, until pulsations stop. Use the clamps or pieces of string to tie the cord in two places.				
17. Use sterilized scissors to cut the cord in between the placement of the two clamps or pieces of string.				
18. Within 10 minutes of the baby's birth, the placenta will begin to expel. Save it in a plastic bag for further examination.				
19. Keep the mother and baby warm by wrapping them in towels or blankets. Do not touch the baby any more than necessary.				
20. Massage the mother's abdomen just below the navel every few minutes to control internal bleeding.				
21. Arrange for transport of the mother and baby to the hospital.				
Total Number of Points Achieved/Final Score				
Initials of Observer:				

(continued)

Comments and Signatures

Reviewer's comments and signatures:

1. _____

2. _____

3. _____

Instructor's comments:

_____

CAAHEP Competency Achieved

XI. P. (10) Perform first aid procedures

ABHES Competencies Achieved

9. e. Recognize emergencies and treatments and minor office surgical procedures

9. o. 5) First aid and CPR

9. q. Instruct patients with special needs

PROCEDURE 43-10 PERFORMING TRIAGE IN A DISASTER

Procedure Goal

To prioritize disaster victims

Scoring System

To score each step, use the following scoring system:
1 = poor, 2 = fair, 3 = good, 4 = excellent

A minimum score of at least a 3 must be achieved on **each** step to achieve successful completion of the technique. Detailed instructions on the scoring system are found on page 413.

Materials

Disaster tag and pen

Procedure

Procedure Steps Total Possible Points - 28 Time Limit: 10 minutes	Practice #1	Practice #2	Practice #3	Final
1. Wash your hands and put on exam gloves and other PPE if available.				
2. Quickly assess each victim.				
3. Sort victims by type of injury and need for care, classifying them as emergent, urgent, nonurgent, or dead.*				
4. Label the emergent patients no. 1 and send them to appropriate treatment stations immediately. Emergent patients, such as those who are in shock or who are hemorrhaging, need immediate care.				
5. Label the urgent patients no. 2 and send them to basic first-aid stations. Urgent patients need care within the next several hours. Such patients may have lacerations that can be dressed quickly to stop the bleeding but can wait for suturing.				
6. Label nonurgent patients no. 3 and send them to volunteers who will be empathic and provide refreshments. Nonurgent patients are those for whom timing of treatment is not critical, such as patients who have no physical injuries but who are emotionally upset.				
7. Label patients who are dead no. 4. Ensure that the bodies are moved to an area where they will be safe until they can be identified and proper action can be taken.				
Total Number of Points Achieved/Final Score				
Initials of Observer:				

(continued)

Comments and Signatures

Reviewer's comments and signatures:

1. _____

2. _____

3. _____

Instructor's comments:

_____

CAAHEP Competency Achieved

XI. P. (6) Participate in a mock environmental exposure event with documentation of steps taken.

ABHES Competencies Achieved

2. c. Assist the physician with the regimen of diagnostic and treatment modalities as they relate to each body system

9. e. Recognize emergencies and treatments and minor office surgical procedures

PROCEDURE 45-1 USING A MICROSCOPE

Procedure Goal

To correctly focus the microscope using each of the three objectives for examination of a prepared specimen slide

Scoring System

To score each step, use the following scoring system:
1 = poor, 2 = fair, 3 = good, 4 = excellent

A minimum score of at least a 3 must be achieved on **each** step to achieve successful completion of the technique. Detailed instructions on the scoring system are found on page 413.

Materials

Microscope, lens paper, lens cleaner, prepared specimen slide, immersion oil, tissues

Procedure

Procedure Steps Total Possible Points - 92 Time Limit: 10 minutes	Practice #1	Practice #2	Practice #3	Final
1. Wash your hands and put on exam gloves.				
2. Remove the protective cover from the microscope. Examine the microscope to make sure that it is clean and that all parts are intact.				
3. Plug in the microscope and make sure the light is working. If you need to replace the bulb, refer to the manufacturer's guidelines. (Be sure to note bulb replacements in the maintenance log for the microscope.) Turn the light off before cleaning the lenses.				
4. Clean the lenses and oculars with lens paper. Avoid touching the lenses with anything except lens paper. Pay careful attention to the oculars. They are easily dirtied by dust and eye makeup. If a lens is particularly dirty, use a small amount of lens cleaner. Oil-immersion lenses are prone to oil buildup if not cleaned properly. Too much lens cleaner, however, can loosen the cement that holds the lens in place.*				
5. Place the specimen slide on the stage. Slide the edges of the slide under the slide clips to secure the slide to the stage.				
6. Adjust the distance between the oculars to a position of comfort.				
7. Adjust the objectives so that the low-power (10X) objective points directly at the specimen slide, as shown in Figure 45-4 in the text. Before swiveling the objective assembly, be sure you have sufficient space for the objective. Recheck the distance between the oculars, making sure the field you see through the eyepieces is a merged field, not separate left and right fields. Raise the body tube by using the coarse adjustment control and lower the stage as needed.*				

(continued)

Procedure Steps Total Possible Points - 92 Time Limit: 10 minutes	Practice #1	Practice #2	Practice #3	Final
8. Turn on the light and, using the iris controls, adjust the amount of light illuminating the specimen so that the light fills the field but does not wash out the image. (At this point you are not examining the specimen image for focus but adjusting the overall light level.)				
9. Observe the microscope from one side and slowly lower the body tube to move the objective closer to the stage and specimen slide. This adjustment is shown in Figure 45-5 in the text. If you used the stage controls to lower the stage away from the objectives, you may also need to adjust those controls. Again, take care not to strike the stage with the objective. The objective should almost meet the specimen slide but not touch it.				
10. Look through the oculars and use the coarse focus control to slowly adjust the image. If necessary, adjust the amount of light coming through the iris.				
11. Continue using the fine focus control to adjust the image. When the image is correctly focused, the specimen will be clearly visible and the field illumination will be bright enough to show details but not so bright that it is uncomfortable to view or washed out.				
12. Switch to the high-power (40X) objective. Use the fine focus controls to view the specimen clearly.*				
13. Rotate the objective assembly so that no objective points directly at the stage and specimen slide. You will now have enough room to apply a drop of immersion oil to the slide. (Only dry slides, without coverslips, are used with the oil-immersion objective.)				
14. Apply a small drop of immersion oil to the specimen slide, as shown in Figure 45-6 in the text.				
15. Gently swing the oil-immersion (100X) objective over the stage and specimen slide so that it is surrounded by the immersion oil.				
16. Examine the image and adjust the amount of light and focus as needed. Only use the fine focus adjustment with this objective. To eliminate air bubbles in the immersion oil, gently move the stage left and right.				
17. After you have examined the specimen as required by the testing procedure, lower the stage and raise the objectives.				
18. Remove the slide. Dispose of it or store it as required by the testing procedure. If you must dispose of the slide, be sure to use the appropriate biohazardous waste container. If you must store the slide, remove the immersion oil with a tissue.				
19. Turn off the light. Unplug the microscope if that is your laboratory's standard operating procedure.				

(continued)

Procedure Steps Total Possible Points - 92 Time Limit: 10 minutes	Practice #1	Practice #2	Practice #3	Final
20. Clean the microscope stage, ocular lenses, and objectives. Be careful to remove all traces of immersion oil from the stage and oil-immersion objective.				
21. Rotate the objective assembly so that the low-power objective points toward the stage. Lower the objective so that it comes close to but does not rest on the stage.				
22. Cover the microscope with its protective cover. Check the work area to be sure you have cleaned everything correctly and disposed of all waste material.				
23. Remove the gloves and wash your hands.				
Total Number of Points Achieved/Final Score				
Initials of Observer:				

Comments and Signatures

Reviewer's comments and signatures:

1. _____

2. _____

3. _____

Instructor's comments:

_____

CAAHEP Competency Achieved

III. P. (2) Practice Standard Precautions

ABHES Competencies Achieved

9. b. Apply principles of aseptic techniques and infection control

10. a. Practice quality control

10. c. Dispose of Biohazardous materials

PROCEDURE 45-2 DISPOSING OF BIOHAZARDOUS WASTE

Procedure Goal

To correctly dispose of contaminated waste products, including sharps and contaminated cleaning and paper products

Scoring System

To score each step, use the following scoring system:
1 = poor, 2 = fair, 3 = good, 4 = excellent

A minimum score of at least a 3 must be achieved on **each** step to achieve successful completion of the technique. Detailed instructions on the scoring system are found on page 413.

Materials

Biohazardous waste containers, gloves, waste materials

Procedure

Procedure Steps Total Possible Points - 36 Time Limit: 5 minutes	Practice #1	Practice #2	Practice #3	Final
To dispose of sharps or other materials that pose a danger of cutting, slicing, or puncturing the skin:				
1. While wearing gloves, hold the article by the unpointed or blunt end.				
2. Drop the object directly into an approved container. (If you are using an evacuation system, do not unscrew the needle. Drop the entire system with the needle attached and the safety device engaged into the receptacle.) The container should be puncture-proof, with rigid sides and a tight-fitting lid.*				
3. If you are disposing of a needle, do not bend, break, or attempt to recap the needle before disposal. If the needle is equipped with a safety device, activate the device immediately and drop the entire assembly into the sharps container.*				
4. When the container is two-thirds full, replace it with an empty container.*				
5. Depending on your office's procedures, the container and its contents may be sterilized before further disposal, or they may be collected by an authorized waste management agency.				
6. Remove the gloves and wash your hands.				
To dispose of contaminated paper waste:				
1. While wearing gloves, deposit the materials in a properly marked biohazardous waste container. A standard biohazardous waste container has an inner plastic liner, either red or orange and marked with the biohazard symbol, and a puncture-proof outer shell, also marked with the biohazard symbol.				

(continued)

Procedure Steps Total Possible Points - 36 Time Limit: 5 minutes	Practice #1	Practice #2	Practice #3	Final
2. If the container is full, secure the inner liner and place it in the appropriate area for biohazardous waste.*				
3. Remove the gloves and wash your hands.				
Total Number of Points Achieved/Final Score				
Initials of Observer:				

Comments and Signatures

Reviewer's comments and signatures:

1. _____

2. _____

3. _____

Instructor's comments:

_____

CAAHEP Competencies Achieved

III. P. (2) Practice Standard Precautions

XI. P. (2) Evaluate the work environment to identify safe vs. unsafe working conditions.

ABHES Competencies Achieved

9. b. Apply principles of aseptic techniques and infection control

10. c. Dispose of Biohazardous materials

PROCEDURE 46-1 OBTAINING A THROAT CULTURE SPECIMEN

Procedure Goal

To isolate a pathogenic microorganism from the throat or to rule out strep throat

Scoring System

To score each step, use the following scoring system:
1 = poor, 2 = fair, 3 = good, 4 = excellent

A minimum score of at least a 3 must be achieved on **each** step to achieve successful completion of the technique. Detailed instructions on the scoring system are found on page 413.

Materials

Tongue depressor, sterile collection system or sterile swab plus blood agar culture plate

Procedure

Procedure Steps Total Possible Points - 64 Time Limit: 10 minutes	Practice #1	Practice #2	Practice #3	Final
1. Identify the patient, introduce yourself, and explain the procedure.				
2. Assemble the necessary supplies; label the culture plate if used.				
3. Wash your hands and put on exam gloves and goggles and a mask or a face shield.*				
4. Have the patient assume a sitting position. (Having a small child lie down rather than sit may make the process easier. If the child refuses to open the mouth, gently squeeze the nostrils shut. The child will eventually open the mouth to breathe. Enlist the help of the parent to restrain the child's hands if necessary.)				
5. Open the collection system or sterile swab package by peeling the wrapper halfway down; remove the swab with your dominant hand.				
6. Ask the patient to tilt back her head and open her mouth as wide as possible.				
7. With your other hand, depress the patient's tongue with the tongue depressor.				
8. Ask the patient to say "Ah."				
9. Insert the swab and quickly swab the back of the throat in the area of the tonsils, twirling the swab over representative areas on both sides of the throat. Avoid touching the uvula, the soft tissue hanging from the roof of the mouth; the cheeks; or the tongue.*				

(continued)

Procedure Steps Total Possible Points - 64 Time Limit: 10 minutes	Practice #1	Practice #2	Practice #3	Final
10. Remove the swab and then the tongue depressor from the patient's mouth.				
11. Discard the tongue depressor in a biohazardous waste container.				
To transport the specimen to a reference laboratory:				
12. Immediately insert the swab back into the plastic sleeve, being careful not to touch the outside of the sleeve with the swab.				
13. Crush the vial of transport medium to moisten the tip of the swab.*				
14. Label the collection system and arrange for transport to the laboratory.				
To prepare the specimen for evaluation in the physician's office laboratory:				
12. Immediately inoculate the culture plate with the swab, using a back-and-forth motion.				
13. Discard the swab in a biohazardous waste container.				
14. Place the culture plate in the incubator.				
To use the specimen for a quick strep screening test:				
12. Collect a throat culture specimen using the swab provided in the quick strep test kit.				
13. Follow manufacturer's instructions in the test kit. Confirm that the controls worked as expected.				
14. Dispose of biohazardous materials according to OSHA guidelines.				
When finished with all specimens:				
15. Remove the gloves and wash your hands.				
16. Document the procedure in the patient's chart.				
Total Number of Points Achieved/Final Score				
Initials of Observer:				

Comments and Signatures

Reviewer's comments and signatures:

1. _____

2. _____

3. _____

Instructor's comments:

_____

(continued)

CAAHEP Competencies Achieved

III. P. (7) Obtain specimens for microbiological testing

III. P. (8) Perform CLIA-waived microbiology testing

ABHES Competencies Achieved

9. b. Apply principles of aseptic techniques and infection control

10. b. Perform selected CLIA-waived tests that assist with diagnosis and treatment
5) Microbiology testing

10. c. Dispose of Biohazardous materials

PROCEDURE 46-2 PREPARING MICROBIOLOGIC SPECIMENS FOR TRANSPORT TO AN OUTSIDE LABORATORY

Procedure Goal

To properly prepare a microbiologic specimen for transport to an outside laboratory

Scoring System

To score each step, use the following scoring system:
1 = poor, 2 = fair, 3 = good, 4 = excellent

A minimum score of at least a 3 must be achieved on **each** step to achieve successful completion of the technique. Detailed instructions on the scoring system are found on page 413.

Materials

Specimen-collection device, requisition form, secondary container or zipper-type plastic bag

Procedure

Procedure Steps Total Possible Points - 44 Time Limit: 10 minutes	Practice #1	Practice #2	Practice #3	Final
1. Wash your hands and put on exam gloves (and goggles and a mask or a face shield if you are collecting a microbiologic throat culture specimen).				
2. Obtain the microbiologic culture specimen. a. Use the collection system specified by the outside laboratory for the test requested. b. Label the microbiologic specimen-collection device at the time of collection. c. Collect the microbiologic specimen according to the guidelines provided by the laboratory and office procedure.*				
3. Remove the gloves and wash your hands.				
4. Complete the test requisition form.				
5. Place the microbiologic specimen container in a secondary container or zipper-type plastic bag.*				
6. Attach the test requisition form to the outside of the secondary container or bag, per laboratory policy.				
7. Log the microbiologic specimen in the list of outgoing specimens.*				
8. Store the microbiologic specimen according to guidelines provided by the laboratory for that type of specimen (for example, refrigerated, frozen, or 37°C).				
9. Call the laboratory for pickup of the microbiologic specimen, or hold it until the next scheduled pickup.				

(continued)

Procedure Steps Total Possible Points - 44 Time Limit: 10 minutes	Practice #1	Practice #2	Practice #3	Final
10. At the time of pickup ensure that the carrier takes all microbiologic specimens that are logged and scheduled to be picked up.				
11. If you are ever unsure about collection or transportation details, call the laboratory.				
Total Number of Points Achieved/Final Score				
Initials of Observer:				

Comments and Signatures

Reviewer's comments and signatures:

1. _____

2. _____

3. _____

Instructor's comments:

_____

CAAHEP Competency Achieved

III. P. (7) Obtain specimens for microbiological testing

ABHES Competencies Achieved

9. b. Apply principles of aseptic techniques and infection control

10. b. Perform selected CLIA-waived tests that assist with diagnosis and treatment
    5) Microbiology testing

PROCEDURE 46-3 PREPARING A MICROBIOLOGIC SPECIMEN SMEAR

Procedure Goal

To prepare a smear of a microbiologic specimen for staining

Scoring System

To score each step, use the following scoring system:
1 = poor, 2 = fair, 3 = good, 4 = excellent

A minimum score of at least a 3 must be achieved on **each** step to achieve successful completion of the technique. Detailed instructions on the scoring system are found on page 413.

Materials

Glass slide with frosted end, pencil, specimen swab, Bunsen burner, forceps

Procedure

Procedure Steps Total Possible Points - 40 Time Limit: 10 minutes	Practice #1	Practice #2	Practice #3	Final
1. Wash your hands and put on exam gloves.				
2. Assemble all the necessary items.				
3. Use a pencil to label the frosted end of the slide with the patient's name.				
4. Roll the specimen swab evenly over the smooth part of the slide, making sure that all areas of the swab touch the slide.*				
5. Discard the swab in a biohazardous waste container. (Retain the microbiologic specimen for culture as necessary or according to office policy.)				
6. Allow the smear to air-dry. Do not wave the slide to dry it.*				
7. Heat-fix the slide by holding the frosted end with forceps and passing the clear part of the slide, with the smear side up, through the flame of a Bunsen burner three or four times. (Your office may use an alternate procedure for fixing the slide, such as flooding the smear with alcohol, allowing it to sit for a few minutes, and either pouring off the remaining liquid or allowing the smear to air-dry. Chlamydia slides come with their own fixative.)*				
8. Allow the slide to cool before the smear is stained.				
9. Return the materials to their proper location.				
10. Remove the gloves and wash your hands.				
Total Number of Points Achieved/Final Score				
Initials of Observer:				

(continued)

Comments and Signatures

Reviewer's comments and signatures:

1. _____

2. _____

3. _____

Instructor's comments:

_____

CAAHEP Competency Achieved

III. P. (7) Obtain specimens for microbiological testing

ABHES Competencies Achieved

9. b. Apply principles of aseptic techniques and infection control

10. b. Perform selected CLIA-waived tests that assist with diagnosis and treatment
     5) Microbiology testing

10. c. Dispose of Biohazardous materials

Procedure 46-4 Performing a Gram's Stain

Procedure Goal

To make bacteria present in a specimen smear visible for microscopic identification

Scoring System

To score each step, use the following scoring system:
1 = poor, 2 = fair, 3 = good, 4 = excellent

A minimum score of at least a 3 must be achieved on **each** step to achieve successful completion of the technique. Detailed instructions on the scoring system are found on page 413.

Materials

Heat-fixed smear, slide staining rack and tray, crystal violet dye, iodine solution, alcohol or acetone-alcohol decolorizer, safranin dye, wash bottle filled with water, forceps, blotting paper or paper towels (optional)

Procedure

Procedure Steps Total Possible Points - 68 Time Limit: 10 minutes	Practice #1	Practice #2	Practice #3	Final
1. Assemble all the necessary supplies.				
2. Wash your hands and put on examination gloves.				
3. Place the heat-fixed smear on a level staining rack and tray, with the smear side up.				
4. Completely cover the specimen area of the slide with the crystal violet stain. (Many commercially available Gram's stain solutions have flip-up bottle caps that allow you to dispense stain by the drop. If the stain bottle you are using does not have an attached dropper cap, use an eyedropper.)				
5. Allow the stain to sit for 1 minute; wash the slide thoroughly with water from the wash bottle.*				
6. Use the forceps to hold the slide at the frosted end, tilting the slide to remove excess water.				
7. Place the slide flat on the rack again and completely cover the specimen area with iodine solution.				
8. Allow the iodine to remain for 1 minute; wash the slide thoroughly with water.*				
9. Use the forceps to hold and tilt the slide to remove excess water.				
10. While still tilting the slide, apply the alcohol or decolorizer drop by drop until no more purple color washes off. (This step usually takes 10 to 30 seconds.)*				
11. Wash the slide thoroughly with water; use the forceps to hold and tip the slide to remove excess water.				
12. Completely cover the specimen with safranin dye.				

(continued)

Procedure Steps Total Possible Points - 68 Time Limit: 10 minutes	Practice #1	Practice #2	Practice #3	Final
13. Allow the safranin to remain for 1 minute; wash the slide thoroughly with water.*				
14. Use the forceps to hold the stained smear by the frosted end, and carefully wipe the back of the slide to remove excess stain.				
15. Place the smear in a vertical position and allow it to air-dry. (The smear may be blotted lightly between blotting paper or paper towels to hasten drying. Take care not to rub the slide or the specimen may be damaged.)				
16. Sanitize and disinfect the work area.				
17. Remove the gloves and wash your hands.				
Total Number of Points Achieved/Final Score				
Initials of Observer:				

Comments and Signatures

Reviewer's comments and signatures:

1. _____

2. _____

3. _____

Instructor's comments:

_____

CAAHEP Competency Achieved

III. P. (7) Obtain specimens for microbiological testing

ABHES Competencies Achieved

9. b. Apply principles of aseptic techniques and infection control

10. a. Practice quality control

10. b. Perform selected CLIA-waived tests that assist with diagnosis and treatment
5) Microbiology testing

10. c. Dispose of Biohazardous materials

Copyright © 2011 by The McGraw-Hill Companies, Inc.

PROCEDURE 47-1 COLLECTING A CLEAN-CATCH MIDSTREAM URINE SPECIMEN

Procedure Goal

To collect a urine specimen that is free from contamination

Scoring System

To score each step, use the following scoring system:
1 = poor, 2 = fair, 3 = good, 4 = excellent

A minimum score of at least a 3 must be achieved on **each** step to achieve successful completion of the technique. Detailed instructions on the scoring system are found on page 413.

Materials

Dry, sterile urine container with lid; label; written instructions (if the patient is to perform procedure independently); antiseptic towelettes

Procedure

Procedure Steps Total Possible Points - 48 Time Limit: 10 minutes	Practice #1	Practice #2	Practice #3	Final
1. Confirm the patient's identity and be sure all forms are correctly completed.				
2. Label the sterile urine specimen container with the patient's name, ID number, date of birth, the physician's name, the date and time of collection, and the initials of the person collecting the specimen.				
When the patient will be completing the procedure independently: 3. Explain the procedure in detail. Provide the patient with written instructions, antiseptic towelettes, and the labeled sterile specimen container.				
4. Confirm that the patient understands the instructions, especially not to touch the inside of the specimen container and to refrigerate the specimen until bringing it to the physician's office.*				
When you are assisting a patient: 3. Explain the procedure and how you will be assisting in the collection.				
4. Wash your hands and put on exam gloves.				
5. Remove the lid from the specimen container and place the lid upside down on a flat surface.				
6. Use three antiseptic towelettes to clean the perineal area by spreading the labia and wiping from front to back. Wipe with the first towelette on one side and discard it. Wipe with the second towelette on the other side and discard it. Wipe with the third towelette down the middle and discard it. To remove soap residue that could cause a higher pH and affect chemical test results, rinse the area once from front to back with water.*				

(continued)

Procedure Steps Total Possible Points - 48 Time Limit: 10 minutes	Practice #1	Practice #2	Practice #3	Final
7. Keeping the patient's labia spread to avoid contamination, tell her to urinate into the toilet. After she has expressed a small amount of urine, instruct her to stop the flow.*				
8. Position the specimen container close to but not touching the patient.				
9. Tell the patient to start urinating again. Collect the necessary amount of urine in the container. (If the patient cannot stop her urine flow, move the container into the urine flow and collect the specimen anyway.)				
10. Allow the patient to finish urinating. Place the lid back on the collection container.				
11. Remove the gloves and wash your hands.				
12. Complete the test request slip and record the collection in the patient's chart.				
When you are assisting in the collection for male patients: 5. Remove the lid from the specimen container and place the lid upside down on a flat surface.				
6. If the patient is circumcised, use an antiseptic towelette to clean the head of the penis. Wipe with a second towelette directly across the urethral opening. If the patient is uncircumcised, retract the foreskin before cleaning the penis. To remove soap residue that could cause a higher pH and affect chemical test results, rinse the area once from front to back with water.*				
7. Keeping an uncircumcised patient's foreskin retracted, tell the patient to urinate into the toilet. After he has expressed a small amount of urine, instruct him to stop the flow.*				
8. Position the specimen container close to but not touching the patient.				
9. Tell the patient to start urinating again. Collect the necessary amount of urine in the container. (If the patient cannot stop his urine flow, move the container into the urine flow and collect the specimen anyway.)				
10. Allow the patient to finish urinating. Place the lid back on the collection container.				
11. Remove the gloves and wash your hands.				
12. Complete the laboratory request form and record the collection in the patient's chart.				
Total Number of Points Achieved/Final Score				
Initials of Observer:				

(continued)

PROCEDURE 47-3 ESTABLISHING CHAIN OF CUSTODY FOR A URINE SPECIMEN

Procedure Goal

To collect a urine specimen for drug testing, maintaining a chain of custody

Scoring System

To score each step, use the following scoring system:
1 = poor, 2 = fair, 3 = good, 4 = excellent

A minimum score of at least a 3 must be achieved on **each** step to achieve successful completion of the technique. Detailed instructions on the scoring system are found on page 413.

Materials

Dry, sterile urine container with lid; chain of custody form (CCF); two additional specimen containers

Procedure

Procedure Steps Total Possible Points - 64 Time Limit: 10 minutes	Practice #1	Practice #2	Practice #3	Final
1. Positively identify the patient. (Complete the top part of CCF with the name and address of the drug testing laboratory, the name and address of the requesting company, and the Social Security number of the patient. Make a note on the form if the patient refuses to give her Social Security number.) Ensure that the number on the printed label matches the number at the top of the form.				
2. Ensure that the patient removes any outer clothing and empties her pockets, displaying all items.*				
3. Instruct the patient to wash and dry her hands.				
4. Instruct the patient that no water is to be running while the specimen is being collected. Tape the faucet handles in the *off* position and add bluing agent to the toilet.*				
5. Instruct the patient to provide the specimen as soon as it is collected so that you may record the temperature of the specimen.				
6. Remain by the door of the restroom.				
7. Measure and record the temperature of the urine specimen within 4 minutes of collection. Make a note if its temperature is out of acceptable range.*				
8. Examine the specimen for signs of adulteration (unusual color or odor).				
9. *In the presence of the patient,* check the "single specimen" or "split specimen" box. The patient should witness you transferring the specimen into the transport specimen bottle(s), capping the bottle(s), and affixing the label on the bottle(s).*				

(continued)

Procedure Steps Total Possible Points - 64 Time Limit: 10 minutes	Practice #1	Practice #2	Practice #3	Final
10. The patient should initial the specimen bottle label(s) *after* it is placed on the bottle(s).*				
11. Complete any additional information requested on the form, including the authorization for drug screening. This information will include • Patient's daytime telephone number • Patient's evening telephone number • Test requested • Patient's name • Patient's signature • Date				
12. Sign the CCF; print your full name and note the date and time of the collection and the name of the courier service.				
13. Give the patient a copy of the CCF.				
14. Place the specimen in a leakproof bag with the appropriate copy of the form.				
15. Release the specimen to the courier service.				
16. Distribute additional copies as required.				
Total Number of Points Achieved/Final Score				
Initials of Observer:				

Comments and Signatures

Reviewer's comments and signatures:

1. _____

2. _____

3. _____

Instructor's comments:

_____

CAAHEP Competencies Achieved

IX. P. (7) Document accurately in the patient record

IX. P. (8) Apply local, state, and federal health care legislation and regulation appropriate to the medical assisting practice

ABHES Competencies Achieved

3. d. Recognize and identify acceptable medical abbreviations

9. f. Screen and follow up patient test results

9. q. Instruct patients with special needs

10. e. Instruct patients in the collection of a clean-catch mid-stream urine specimen

PROCEDURE 47-4 MEASURING SPECIFIC GRAVITY WITH A REFRACTOMETER

Procedure Goal

To measure the specific gravity of a urine specimen with a refractometer

Scoring System

To score each step, use the following scoring system:
1 = poor, 2 = fair, 3 = good, 4 = excellent

A minimum score of at least a 3 must be achieved on **each** step to achieve successful completion of the technique. Detailed instructions on the scoring system are found on page 413.

Materials

Urine specimen, refractometer, dropper, laboratory report form

Procedure

Procedure Steps Total Possible Points - 60 Time Limit: 10 minutes	Practice #1	Practice #2	Practice #3	Final
1. Wash your hands and put on exam gloves.				
2. Check the specimen for proper labeling and examine it to make sure that there is no visible contamination and that no more than 1 hour has passed since collection (or since the specimen has been removed from the refrigerator and brought back to room temperature).				
3. Swirl the specimen.*				
4. Confirm that the refractometer has been calibrated that day. If not, you must calibrate it with distilled water. You also must use two standard solutions as controls to check the accuracy of the refractometer. Follow steps 6 through 11, using each of the three samples in place of the specimen. Clean the refractometer and the dropper after each use and record the calibration values in the quality control log.*				
5. Open the hinged lid of the refractometer.				
6. Draw up a small amount of the specimen into the dropper.				
7. Place one drop of the specimen under the cover.				
8. Close the lid.				
9. Turn on the light and look into the eyepiece of the refractometer. As the light passes through the specimen, the refractometer measures the refraction of the light and displays the refractive index on a scale on the right with corresponding specific gravity values on the left.				
10. Read the specific gravity value at the line where light and dark meet.				
11. Record the value on the laboratory report form.				

(continued)

Procedure Steps Total Possible Points - 60 Time Limit: 10 minutes	Practice #1	Practice #2	Practice #3	Final
12. Sanitize and disinfect the refractometer and the dropper. Put them away when they are dry.				
13. Clean and disinfect the work area.				
14. Remove the gloves and wash your hands.				
15. Record the value in the patient's chart.				
Total Number of Points Achieved/Final Score				
Initials of Observer:				

Comments and Signatures

Reviewer's comments and signatures:

1. _____

2. _____

3. _____

Instructor's comments:

_____

CAAHEP Competencies Achieved

I. P. (14) Perform CLIA-waived urinalysis

I. P. (16) Screen test results

ABHES Competencies Achieved

9. f. Screen and follow up patient test results

10. a. Practice quality control

10. b. Perform selected CLIA-waived tests that assist with diagnosis and treatment
1) Urinalysis

PROCEDURE 47-5 PERFORMING A REAGENT STRIP TEST

Procedure Goal

To perform chemical testing on urine specimens (This test is used to screen for the presence of leukocytes, nitrite, urobilinogen, protein, pH, blood, specific gravity, ketones, bilirubin, and glucose.)

Scoring System

To score each step, use the following scoring system:
1 = poor, 2 = fair, 3 = good, 4 = excellent

A minimum score of at least a 3 must be achieved on **each** step to achieve successful completion of the technique. Detailed instructions on the scoring system are found on page 413.

Materials

Urine specimen, laboratory report form, reagent strips, paper towel, timer

Procedure

Procedure Steps Total Possible Points - 44 Time Limit: 10 minutes	Practice #1	Practice #2	Practice #3	Final
1. Wash your hands and put on personal protective equipment.				
2. Check the specimen for proper labeling and examine it to make sure that there is no visible contamination. Perform the test as soon as possible after collection. Refrigerate the specimen if testing will take place more than 1 hour later. Bring the refrigerated specimen back to room temperature prior to testing.				
3. Check the expiration date on the reagent strip container and check the strip for damaged or discolored pads.*				
4. Swirl the specimen.*				
5. Dip a urine strip into the specimen, making sure each pad is completely covered. Briefly tap the strip sideways on a paper towel. *Do not blot* the test pads.*				
6. Read each test pad against the chart on the bottle at the designated time. Note: It is important to read each pad at the appropriate time. Most reagent strip results are invalid after 2 minutes.*				
7. Record the values on the laboratory report form.				
8. Discard the used disposable supplies.				
9. Clean and disinfect the work area.				
10. Remove your gloves and wash your hands.				
11. Record the result in the patient's chart.				
Total Number of Points Achieved/Final Score				
Initials of Observer:				

(continued)

Comments and Signatures

Reviewer's comments and signatures:

1. _____

2. _____

3. _____

Instructor's comments:

_____

CAAHEP Competencies Achieved

I. P. (14) Perform CLIA-waived urinalysis

I. P. (16) Screen test results

ABHES Competencies Achieved

3. d. Recognize and identify acceptable medical abbreviations

9. f. Screen and follow up patient test results

10. a. Practice quality control

10. b. Perform selected CLIA-waived tests that assist with diagnosis and treatment
    1) Urinalysis
    6) Kit testing
        c) Dip sticks

10. c. Dispose of Biohazardous materials

PROCEDURE 47-6 PREGNANCY TESTING USING THE EIA METHOD

Procedure Goal

To perform the enzyme immunoassay in order to detect HCG in the urine (or serum) and to interpret results as positive or negative

Scoring System

To score each step, use the following scoring system:
1 = poor, 2 = fair, 3 = good, 4 = excellent

A minimum score of at least a 3 must be achieved on **each** step to achieve successful completion of the technique. Detailed instructions on the scoring system are found on page 413.

Materials

Gloves, urine specimen, timing device, surface disinfectant, pregnancy control solutions, pregnancy test kits

Procedure

Procedure Steps Total Possible Points - 40 Time Limit: 10 minutes	Practice #1	Practice #2	Practice #3	Final
1. Wash your hands and put on exam gloves.				
2. Gather the necessary supplies and equipment.				
3. If materials have been refrigerated, allow all materials to reach room temperature prior to conducting the testing.				
4. Label the test chamber with the patient's name or identification number; label one test chamber for a negative and positive control.				
5. Apply the urine (or serum) to the test chamber per the manufacturer's instructions.*				
6. At the appropriate time, read and interpret the results.*				
7. Document the patient's results in the chart; document the quality control results in the appropriate log book.				
8. Dispose of used reagents in a biohazard container.				
9. Clean the work area with a disinfectant solution.				
10. Wash your hands.				
Total Number of Points Achieved/Final Score				
Initials of Observer:				

(continued)

Comments and Signatures

Reviewer's comments and signatures:

1. _____

2. _____

3. _____

Instructor's comments:

_____

CAAHEP Competencies Achieved

I. P. (6) Perform patient screening using established protocols

I. P. (13) Perform chemistry testing

ABHES Competencies Achieved

9. f. Screen and follow up patient test results

10. a. Practice quality control

10. b. Perform selected CLIA-waived tests that assist with diagnosis and treatment
6) Kit testing
a) Pregnancy

10. c. Dispose of Biohazardous materials

PROCEDURE 47-7 PROCESSING A URINE SPECIMEN FOR MICROSCOPIC EXAMINATION OF SEDIMENT

Objective

To prepare a slide for microscopic examination of urine sediment

Scoring System

To score each step, use the following scoring system:
1 = poor, 2 = fair, 3 = good, 4 = excellent

A minimum score of at least a 3 must be achieved on **each** step to achieve successful completion of the technique. Detailed instructions on the scoring system are found on page 413.

Materials

Fresh urine specimen, two glass or plastic test tubes, water, centrifuge, tapered pipette, glass slide with coverslip, microscope with light source, laboratory report form

Procedure

Procedure Steps Total Possible Points - 80 Time Limit: 15 minutes	Practice #1	Practice #2	Practice #3	Final
1. Wash your hands and put on exam gloves.				
2. Check the specimen for proper labeling and examine it to make sure that there is no visible contamination and that no more than 1 hour has passed since collection (or since the specimen has been removed from the refrigerator and brought back to room temperature).				
3. Swirl the urine specimen.*				
4. Pour approximately 10 mL of urine into one test tube and 10 mL of plain water into the balance tube.				
5. Balance the centrifuge by placing the test tubes on either side.*				
6. Make sure the lid is secure and set the centrifuge timer for 5 to 10 minutes.*				
7. Set the speed as prescribed by your office's protocol (usually 1500 to 2000 revolutions per minute) and start the centrifuge.				
8. After the centrifuge stops, lift out the tube containing the urine and carefully pour most of the liquid portion—called the **supernatant**—down the drain in the sink.				
9. A few drops of urine should remain in the bottom of the test tube with any sediment. Mix the urine and sediment together by gently tapping the bottom of the tube on the palm of your hand.*				
10. Use the tapered pipette to obtain a drop or two of urine sediment. Place the drops in the center of a clean glass slide.				
11. Place the coverslip over the specimen, allow it to settle, and place it on the stage of the microscope.				
12. Correctly focus the microscope as directed in Procedure 45-1. *Note:* Most medical assistants are trained to perform this procedure only up to this point. After this, the physician usually				

(continued)

Procedure Steps Total Possible Points - 80 Time Limit: 15 minutes	Practice #1	Practice #2	Practice #3	Final
examines the specimen. You may, however, be asked to clean the items after the examination is completed. The remaining steps are provided for your information.				
13. Use a dim light and view the slide under the low-power objective. Observe the slide for casts (found mainly around the edges of the coverslip) and count the casts viewed.				
14. Switch to the high-power objective. Identify the casts. Identify any epithelial cells, mucus, protozoa, yeasts, and crystals. Adjust the slide position so that you can view and count the cells, protozoa, yeasts, and crystals from at least 10 different fields. Turn off the light after the examination is completed.				
15. Record the observations on the laboratory report form.				
16. Properly dispose of used disposable materials.				
17. Sanitize and disinfect nondisposable items; put them away when they are dry.				
18. Clean and disinfect the work area.				
19. Remove the gloves and wash your hands.				
20. Record the observations in the patient's chart.				
Total Number of Points Achieved/Final Score				
Initials of Observer:				

Comments and Signatures

Reviewer's comments and signatures:

1. _____

2. _____

3. _____

Instructor's comments:

_____

CAAHEP Competencies Achieved

I.P. (14) Perform CLIA-waived urinalysis

I. P. (16) Screen test results

ABHES Competencies Achieved

3. d. Recognize and identify acceptable medical abbreviations

9. f. Screen and follow up patient test results

10. a. Practice quality control

10. b. Perform selected CLIA-waived tests that assist with diagnosis and treatment
    1) Urinalysis

10. c. Dispose of Biohazardous materials

PROCEDURE 48-1 QUALITY CONTROL PROCEDURES FOR BLOOD SPECIMEN COLLECTION

Procedure Goal

To follow proper quality control procedures when taking a blood specimen

Scoring System

To score each step, use the following scoring system:
1 = poor, 2 = fair, 3 = good, 4 = excellent

A minimum score of at least a 3 must be achieved on **each** step to achieve successful completion of the technique. Detailed instructions on the scoring system are found on page 413.

Materials

Necessary sterile equipment, specimen-collection container, paperwork related to the type of blood test the specimen is being drawn for, requisition form, marker, proper packing materials for transport

Procedure

Procedure Steps Total Possible Points - 36 Time Limit: 10 minutes	Practice #1	Practice #2	Practice #3	Final
1. Review the request form for the test ordered, verify the procedure, prepare the necessary equipment and paperwork, and prepare the work area.				
2. Identify the patient and explain the procedure. Confirm the patient's identification. Ask the patient to spell her name. Make sure the patient understands the procedure that is to be performed, even if she has had it done before.				
3. Confirm that the patient has followed any pretest preparation requirements such as fasting, taking any necessary medication, or stopping a medication. For example, if a fasting specimen is being taken, the patient should not have eaten anything after midnight of the day before. Some doctors' offices will let the patient drink water or black coffee, however. It often depends on the type of specimen being taken.*				
4. Collect the specimen properly. Collect it at the right time intervals if that applies. Use sterile equipment and proper technique.				
5. Use the correct specimen-collection containers and the right preservatives, if required. For example, blood collected into a test tube with additives should be mixed immediately.*				
6. Immediately label the specimens. The label should include the patient's name, the date and time of collection, the test's name, and the name of the person collecting the specimen. Do not label the containers before collecting the specimen.*				

(continued)

Procedure Steps Total Possible Points - 36 Time Limit: 10 minutes	Practice #1	Practice #2	Practice #3	Final
7. Follow correct procedures for disposing of hazardous specimen waste and decontaminating the work area. Used needles, for instance, should immediately be placed in a biohazard sharps container.				
8. Thank the patient. Keep the patient in the office if any follow-up observation is necessary.				
9. If the specimen is to be transported to an outside laboratory, prepare it for transport in the proper container for that type of specimen, according to OSHA regulations. Place the container in a clear plastic bag with a zip closure and dual pockets with the international biohazard label imprinted in red or orange. The requisition form should be placed in the outside pocket of the bag. This ensures protection from contamination if the specimen leaks. Have a courier pick up the specimen and place it in an appropriate carrier (such as an insulated cooler) with the biohazard label. Place specimens to be sent by mail in appropriate plastic containers and then place the containers inside a heavy-duty plastic container with a screw-down, nonleaking lid. Then place this container in either a heavy-duty cardboard box or nylon bag. The words *Human Specimen* or *Body Fluids* should be imprinted on the box or bag. Seal with a strong tape strip.*				
Total Number of Points Achieved/Final Score				
Initials of Observer:				

Comments and Signatures

Reviewer's comments and signatures:

1. _____

2. _____

3. _____

Instructor's comments:

_____

CAAHEP Competency Achieved

I. P. (11) Perform quality control measures

ABHES Competencies Achieved

10. a. Practice quality control

10. c. Dispose of Biohazardous materials

10. d. Collect, label, and process specimens
    1) Perform venipuncture
    2) Perform capillary puncture

PROCEDURE 48-2 PERFORMING VENIPUNCTURE USING AN EVACUATION SYSTEM

Procedure Goal

To collect a venous blood sample using an evacuation system

Scoring System

To score each step, use the following scoring system:
1 = poor, 2 = fair, 3 = good, 4 = excellent

A minimum score of at least a 3 must be achieved on **each** step to achieve successful completion of the technique. Detailed instructions on the scoring system are found on page 413.

Materials

VACUTAINER components (safety needle, needle holder/adapter, collection tubes), antiseptic and cotton balls or antiseptic wipes, tourniquet, sterile gauze squares, sterile adhesive bandages

Procedure

Procedure Steps Total Possible Points - 88 Time Limit: 10 minutes	Practice #1	Practice #2	Practice #3	Final
1. Review the laboratory request form and make sure you have the necessary supplies.				
2. Greet the patient, confirm the patient's identity, and introduce yourself.				
3. Explain the purpose of the procedure and confirm that the patient has followed the pretest instructions.*				
4. Make sure the patient is sitting in a venipuncture chair or is lying down.				
5. Wash your hands. Put on exam gloves.				
6. Prepare the safety needle holder/adapter assembly by inserting the threaded side of the needle into the adapter and twisting the adapter in a clockwise direction. Push the first collection tube into the other end of the needle holder/adapter until the outer edge of the collection tube stopper meets the guideline.*				
7. Ask the patient whether one arm is better than the other for the venipuncture. The chosen arm should be positioned slightly downward.				
8. Apply the tourniquet to the patient's upper arm midway between the elbow and the shoulder. Wrap the tourniquet around the patient's arm and cross the ends. Holding one end of the tourniquet against the patient's arm, stretch the other end to apply pressure against the patient's skin. Pull a loop of the stretched end under the end held tightly against the patient's skin, as shown in Figure 48-7 in the text. The				

(continued)

Copyright © 2011 by The McGraw-Hill Companies, Inc.

Procedure Steps Total Possible Points - 88 Time Limit: 10 minutes	Practice #1	Practice #2	Practice #3	Final
tourniquet should be tight enough to cause the veins to stand out but should not stop the flow of blood. You should still be able to feel the patient's radial pulse.*				
9. Palpate the proposed site and use your index finger to locate the vein, as shown in Figure 48-8 in the text. The vein will feel like a small tube with some elasticity. If you feel a pulsing beat, you have located an artery. Do not draw blood from an artery. If you cannot locate the vein within 1 minute, release the tourniquet and allow blood to flow freely for 1 to 2 minutes. Then reapply the tourniquet and try again to locate the vein.				
10. After locating the vein, clean the area with a cotton ball moistened with antiseptic or an antiseptic wipe. Use a circular motion to clean the area, starting at the center and working outward. Allow the site to air-dry.*				
11. Remove the plastic cap from the outer point of the needle cover and ask the patient to tighten the fist. Hold the patient's skin taut below the insertion site.*				
12. With a steady and quick motion, insert the needle—held at a 15-degree angle, bevel side up, and aligned parallel to the vein—into the vein. You will feel a slight resistance as the needle tip penetrates the vein wall. Penetrate to a depth of ¼ to ½ inch. Grasp the holder/adapter between your index and great (middle) fingers. Using your thumb, seat the collection tube firmly into place over the needle point, puncturing the rubber stopper. Blood will begin to flow into the collection tube.				
13. Fill each tube until the blood stops running to ensure the correct proportion of blood to additives. Switch tubes as needed by pulling one tube out of the adapter and inserting the next in a smooth and steady motion. (The soft plastic cover on the inner point of the needle retracts as each tube is inserted and recovers the needle point as each tube is removed.)				
14. Once blood is flowing steadily, ask the patient to release the fist and untie the tourniquet by pulling the end of the tucked-in loop. The tourniquet should, in general, be left on no longer than 1 minute.* You must remove the tourniquet before you withdraw the needle from the vein.*				
15. As you withdraw the needle in a smooth and steady motion, place a sterile gauze square over the insertion site. Immediately activate the safety device on the needle if it is not self-activating. Properly dispose of the needle immediately. Instruct the patient to hold the gauze pad in place with slight pressure. The patient should keep the arm straight and slightly elevated for several minutes.*				
16. If the collection tubes contain additives, you will need to invert them slowly several times.*				

(continued)

Procedure Steps Total Possible Points - 88 Time Limit: 10 minutes	Practice #1	Practice #2	Practice #3	Final
17. Label specimens and complete the paperwork.				
18. Check the patient's condition and the puncture site for bleeding. Replace the sterile gauze square with a sterile adhesive bandage.				
19. Properly dispose of used supplies and disposable instruments and disinfect the work area.				
20. Remove the gloves and wash your hands.				
21. Instruct the patient about care of the puncture site.				
22. Document the procedure in the patient's chart.				
Total Number of Points Achieved/Final Score				
Initials of Observer:				

Comments and Signatures

Reviewer's comments and signatures:

1. _____

2. _____

3. _____

Instructor's comments:

_____

CAAHEP Competency Achieved

I. P. (2) Perform venipuncture

ABHES Competencies Achieved

3. d. Recognize and identify acceptable medical abbreviations

9. f. Screen and follow up patient test results

10. c. Dispose of Biohazardous materials

10. d. Collect, label, and process specimens
   1) Perform venipuncture

PROCEDURE 48-3 PERFORMING CAPILLARY PUNCTURE

Procedure Goal

To collect a capillary blood sample using the finger puncture method

Scoring System

To score each step, use the following scoring system:
1 = poor, 2 = fair, 3 = good, 4 = excellent

A minimum score of at least a 3 must be achieved on **each** step to achieve successful completion of the technique. Detailed instructions on the scoring system are found on page 413.

Materials

Capillary puncture device (safety lancet or automatic puncture device such as Autolet or Glucolet), antiseptic and cotton balls or antiseptic wipes, sterile gauze squares, sterile adhesive bandages, reagent strips, micropipettes, smear slides

Procedure

Procedure Steps Total Possible Points - 72 Time Limit: 10 minutes	Practice #1	Practice #2	Practice #3	Final
1. Review the laboratory request form and make sure you have the necessary supplies.				
2. Greet the patient, confirm the patient's identity, and introduce yourself.				
3. Explain the purpose of the procedure and confirm that the patient has followed the pretest instructions, if indicated.*				
4. Make sure the patient is sitting in the venipuncture chair or is lying down.				
5. Wash your hands. Put on exam gloves.				
6. Examine the patient's hands to determine which finger to use for the procedure. Avoid fingers that are swollen, bruised, scarred, or calloused. Generally, the ring and great (middle) fingers are the best choices. If you notice that the patient's hands are cold, you may want to warm them between your own, have the patient put them in a warm basin of water or under warm running water, or wrap them in a warm cloth.*				
7. Prepare the patient's finger with a gentle "massaging" or rubbing motion toward the fingertip. Keep the patient's hand below heart level so that gravity helps the blood flow.				
8. Clean the area with a cotton ball moistened with antiseptic or an antiseptic wipe. Allow the site to air-dry.*				

(continued)

Procedure Steps Total Possible Points - 72 Time Limit: 10 minutes	Practice #1	Practice #2	Practice #3	Final
9. Hold the patient's finger between your thumb and forefinger. Hold the safety lancet or automatic puncture device at a right angle to the patient's fingerprint, as shown in Figure 48-14 in the text. Puncture the skin on the pad of the fingertip with a quick, sharp motion. The depth to which you puncture the skin is generally determined by the length of the lancet point. Most automatic puncturing devices are designed to penetrate to the correct depth.				
10. Allow a drop of blood to form at the end of the patient's finger. If the blood droplet is slow in forming, apply steady pressure. Avoid milking the patient's finger.*				
11. Wipe away the first droplet of blood. (This droplet is usually contaminated with tissue fluids released when the skin is punctured.) Then fill the collection devices, as described. *Micropipettes:* Hold the tip of the tube just to the edge of the blood droplet. The tube will fill through capillary action. If you are preparing microhematocrit tubes, you need to seal one end of each tube with clay sealant. *Reagent strips:* With some reagent strips (dipsticks), you must touch the strip to the blood drop but not smear it; with other strips, you must smear it. Follow the manufacturer's guidelines. *Smear slides:* Gently touch the blood droplet to the smear slide and process the slide as described in Procedure 48-4.				
12. After you have collected the required samples, dispose of the lancet immediately. Then wipe the patient's finger with a sterile gauze square. Instruct the patient to apply pressure to stop the bleeding.				
13. Label specimens and complete the paperwork. Some tests, such as glucose monitoring, must be completed immediately.				
14. Check the puncture site for bleeding. If necessary, replace the sterile gauze square with a sterile adhesive bandage.				
15. Properly dispose of used supplies and disposable instruments and disinfect the work area.				
16. Remove the gloves and wash your hands.				
17. Instruct the patient about care of the puncture site.				
18. Document the procedure in the patient's chart. (If the test has been completed, include the results.)				
Total Number of Points Achieved/Final Score				
Initials of Observer:				

(continued)

Comments and Signatures

Reviewer's comments and signatures:

1. _____

2. _____

3. _____

Instructor's comments:

_____

CAAHEP Competency Achieved

I. P. (2) Perform capillary puncture

ABHES Competencies Achieved

3. d. Recognize and identify acceptable medical abbreviations

10. c. Dispose of Biohazardous materials

10. d. Collect, label, and process specimens
     2) Perform capillary puncture

PROCEDURE 48-4 PREPARING A BLOOD SMEAR SLIDE

Procedure Goal

To prepare a blood specimen to be used in a morphologic or other study

Scoring System

To score each step, use the following scoring system:
1 = poor, 2 = fair, 3 = good, 4 = excellent

A minimum score of at least a 3 must be achieved on **each** step to achieve successful completion of the technique. Detailed instructions on the scoring system are found on page 413.

Materials

Blood specimen (either from a capillary puncture or a specimen tube containing anticoagulated blood), capillary tubes, sterile gauze squares, slide with frosted end, wooden applicator sticks

Procedure

Procedure Steps Total Possible Points - 48 Time Limit: 10 minutes	Practice #1	Practice #2	Practice #3	Final
1. Wash your hands and put on exam gloves.				
2. If you will be using blood from a capillary puncture, follow the steps in Procedure 48-3 to express a drop of blood from the patient's finger. If you will be using a venous sample, check the specimen for proper labeling, carefully uncap the specimen tube, and use wooden applicator sticks to remove any coagulated blood from the inside rim of the tube. You may use a special safety transfer device if available.*				
3. Touch the tip of the capillary tube to the blood specimen either from the patient's finger or the specimen tube. The tube will take up the correct amount through capillary action.				
4. Pull the capillary tube away from the sample, holding it carefully to prevent spillage. Wipe the outside of the capillary tube with a sterile gauze square.*				
5. With the slide on the work surface, hold the capillary tube in one hand and the frosted end of the slide against the work surface with the other.				
6. Apply a drop of blood to the slide, about ¾ inch from the frosted end, as shown in Figure 48-20 in the text. Place the capillary tube in the sharps container.				
7. Pick up the spreader slide with your dominant hand. Hold the slide at approximately a 30- to 35-degree angle. Place the edge of the spreader slide on the smear slide close to the unfrosted end. Pull the spreader slide toward the frosted end until the spreader slide touches the blood drop. Capillary action will spread the droplet along the edge of the spreader slide.*				

(continued)

Procedure Steps Total Possible Points - 48 Time Limit: 10 minutes	Practice #1	Practice #2	Practice #3	Final
8. As soon as the drop spreads out to cover most of the spreader slide edge, push the spreader slide back toward the unfrosted end of the smear slide, pulling the sample across the slide behind it, as shown in Figure 48-22 in the text. Maintain the 30- to 35-degree angle.				
9. Continue pushing the spreader until you come off the end, still maintaining the angle, as shown in Figure 48-23 in the text. The resulting smear should be approximately 1½ inches long, preferably with a margin of empty slide on all sides. The smear should be thicker on the frosted end of the slide.				
10. Properly label the slide, allow it to dry, and follow the manufacturer's directions for staining it for the required tests.				
11. Properly dispose of used supplies and disinfect the work area.				
12. Remove the gloves and wash your hands.				
Total Number of Points Achieved/Final Score				
Initials of Observer:				

Comments and Signatures

Reviewer's comments and signatures:

1. _____

2. _____

3. _____

Instructor's comments:

_____

CAAHEP Competency Achieved

I. P. (12) Perform CLIA-waived hematology testing

ABHES Competencies Achieved

10. c. Dispose of Biohazardous materials

10. d. Collect, label, and process specimens

PROCEDURE 48-5 MEASURING HEMATOCRIT PERCENTAGE AFTER CENTRIFUGE

Procedure Goal

To identify the percentage of a blood specimen represented by RBCs after the sample has been spun in a centrifuge

Scoring System

To score each step, use the following scoring system:
1 = poor, 2 = fair, 3 = good, 4 = excellent

A minimum score of at least a 3 must be achieved on **each** step to achieve successful completion of the technique. Detailed instructions on the scoring system are found on page 413.

Materials

Blood specimen (either from a capillary puncture or a specimen tube containing anticoagulated blood), microhematocrit tube, sealant tray containing sealing clay, centrifuge, hematocrit gauge, wooden applicator sticks, gauze squares

Procedure

Procedure Steps Total Possible Points - 60 Time Limit: 10 minutes	Practice #1	Practice #2	Practice #3	Final
1. Wash your hands and put on exam gloves.				
2. If you will be using blood from a capillary puncture, follow the steps in Procedure 48-3 to express a drop of blood from the patient's finger. If you will be using a venous blood sample, check the specimen for proper labeling, carefully uncap the specimen tube, and use wooden applicator sticks to remove any coagulated blood from the inside rim of the tube. Alternately, use a special safety transfer device if available.*				
3. Touch the tip of one of the microhematocrit tubes to the blood sample, as shown in Figure 48-25 in the text. The tube will take up the correct amount through capillary action.				
4. Pull the microhematocrit tube away from the sample, holding it carefully to prevent spillage. Wipe the outside of the microhematocrit tube with a gauze square.*				
5. Hold the microhematocrit tube in one hand with a gloved finger over one end to prevent leakage and press the other end of the tube gently into the clay in the sealant tray. The clay plug must completely seal the end of the tube.*				
6. Repeat the process to fill another microhematocrit tube. Tubes must be processed in pairs.*				
7. Place the tubes in the centrifuge, with the sealed ends pointing outward. If you are processing more than one sample, record the position identification number in the patient's chart to track the sample.				
8. Seal the centrifuge chamber.				

(continued)

Procedure Steps Total Possible Points - 60 Time Limit: 10 minutes	Practice #1	Practice #2	Practice #3	Final
9. Run the centrifuge for the required time, usually between 3 and 5 minutes. Allow the centrifuge to come to a complete stop before unsealing it.				
10. Determine the hematocrit percentage by comparing the column of packed RBCs in the microhematocrit tubes with the hematocrit gauge, as shown in Figure 48-28 in the text. Position each tube so that the boundary between sealing clay and RBCs is at zero on the gauge. Some centrifuges are equipped with gauges, but others require separate handheld gauges.				
11. Record the percentage value on the gauge that corresponds to the top of the column of RBCs for each tube. Compare the two results. They should not vary by more than 2%. If you record a greater variance, at least one of the tubes was filled incorrectly, and you must repeat the test.				
12. Calculate the average result by adding the two tube figures and dividing that number by 2.				
13. Properly dispose of used supplies and clean and disinfect the equipment and the area.				
14. Remove the gloves and wash your hands.				
15. Record the test result in the patient's chart. Be sure to identify abnormal results.				
Total Number of Points Achieved/Final Score				
Initials of Observer:				

Comments and Signatures

Reviewer's comments and signatures:

1. _____

2. _____

3. _____

Instructor's comments:

_____

CAAHEP Competency Achieved

I. P. (12) Perform CLIA-waived hematology testing

ABHES Competencies Achieved

3. d. Recognize and identify acceptable medical abbreviations

9. f. Screen and follow up patient test results

10. b. Perform selected CLIA-waived tests that assist with diagnosis and treatment
   2) Hematology testing

10. c. Dispose of Biohazardous materials

10. d. Collect, label, and process specimens

Procedure 48-6 Measuring Blood Glucose Using A Handheld Glucometer

Procedure Goal

To measure the amount of glucose present in a blood sample.

Scoring System

To score each step, use the following scoring system:
1 = poor, 2 = fair, 3 = good, 4 = excellent

A minimum score of at least a 3 must be achieved on **each** step to achieve successful completion of the technique. Detailed instructions on the scoring system are found on page 413.

Materials

Safety engineered capillary puncture device (automatic puncture device or other safety lancet), antiseptic and cotton balls or antiseptic wipes, sterile gauze squares, sterile adhesive bandages, handheld glucometer, reagent strips appropriate for the device.

Procedure

Procedure Steps Total Possible Points - 56 Time Limit: 10 minutes	Practice #1	Practice #2	Practice #3	Final
1. Wash your hands and put on exam gloves.				
2. Review the manufacturer's instructions for the specific device used.				
3. Check the expiration date on the reagent strips.*				
4. Code the meter to the reagent strips if required.*				
5. Turn the device on according to the manufacturer's instructions.				
6. Perform the required quality control procedures.*				
7. Perform a capillary puncture following the steps outlined in Procedure 48-3.				
8. Touch the drop of blood to the reagent strip, allowing it to be taken up by the strip.				
9. Read the digital result after the required amount of time.				
10. Record the time of the test and result on the laboratory slip.				
11. Discard the reagent strip and used supplies according to OSHA standards.				
12. Disinfect the equipment and area.				
13. Remove the gloves and wash your hands.				
14. Document the test results in the patient's chart. Record the quality control tests in the laboratory control log.				
Total Number of Points Achieved/Final Score				
Initials of Observer:				

(continued)

Comments and Signatures

Reviewer's comments and signatures:

1. _____

2. _____

3. _____

Instructor's comments:

_____

CAAHEP Competency Achieved

I. P. (12) Perform CLIA-waived chemistry testing

ABHES Competencies Achieved

9. f. Screen and follow up patient test results

10. a. Practice quality control

10. b. Perform selected CLIA-waived tests that assist with diagnosis and treatment
   3) Chemistry testing

10. c. Dispose of Biohazardous materials

10. d. Collect, label, and process specimens

PROCEDURE 49-1 EDUCATING ADULT PATIENTS ABOUT DAILY WATER REQUIREMENTS

Procedure Goal

To teach patients how much water their bodies need to maintain health

Scoring System

To score each step, use the following scoring system:
1 = poor, 2 = fair, 3 = good, 4 = excellent

A minimum score of at least a 3 must be achieved on **each** step to achieve successful completion of the technique. Detailed instructions on the scoring system are found on page 413.

Materials

Patient education literature, patient's chart, pen

Procedure

Procedure Steps Total Possible Points - 28 Time Limit: 15 minutes	Practice #1	Practice #2	Practice #3	Final
1. Explain to patients the importance of water to the body. Point out the water content of the body and the many functions of water in the body: maintaining the body's fluid balance, lubricating the body's moving parts, transporting nutrients and secretions.				
2. Add any comments applicable to an individual patient's health status—for example, issues related to medication use, physical activity, pregnancy, fluid limitation, or increased fluid needs.*				
3. Explain that people obtain water by drinking water and other fluids and by eating water-containing foods. On average, an adult should drink six to eight glasses of water a day to maintain a healthy water balance in which intake equals excretion. People's daily need for water varies with size and age, the temperatures to which they are exposed, degree of physical exertion, and the water content of foods eaten. Make sure you reinforce the physician's or dietitian's recommendations for a particular patient's water needs.				
4. Caution patients that soft drinks, coffee, and tea are not good substitutes for water and that it would be wise to filter out any harmful chemicals contained in the local tap water or to drink bottled water, if possible.				
5. Provide patients with tips about reminders to drink the requisite amount of water. Some patients may benefit from using a water bottle of a particular size, so they know they have to drink, say, three full bottles of water each day. Another helpful tip is to make a habit of drinking a glass of water at certain points in the daily routine, such as first thing in the morning and before lunch.				

(continued)

Procedure Steps Total Possible Points - 28 Time Limit: 15 minutes	Practice #1	Practice #2	Practice #3	Final
6. Remind patients that you and the physician are available to discuss any problems or questions.				
7. Document any formal patient education sessions or significant exchanges with a patient in the patient's chart, noting whether the patient understood the information presented. Then initial the entry.*				
Total Number of Points Achieved/Final Score				
Initials of Observer:				

Comments and Signatures

Reviewer's comments and signatures:

1. _____

2. _____

3. _____

Instructor's comments:

_____

CAAHEP Competency Achieved

IV. P. (5) Instruct patients according to their needs to promote health maintenance and disease prevention

ABHES Competency Achieved

9 (r). Teach patients methods of health promotion and disease prevention

PROCEDURE 49-2 TEACHING PATIENTS HOW TO READ FOOD LABELS

Procedure Goal

To explain how patients can use food labels to plan or follow a diet

Scoring System

To score each step, use the following scoring system:
1 = poor, 2 = fair, 3 = good, 4 = excellent

A minimum score of at least a 3 must be achieved on **each** step to achieve successful completion of the technique. Detailed instructions on the scoring system are found on page 413.

Materials

Food labels from products

Procedure

Procedure Steps Total Possible Points - 28 Time Limit: 15 minutes	Practice #1	Practice #2	Practice #3	Final
1. Identify the patient and introduce yourself.				
2. Explain that food labels can be used as a valuable source of information when planning or implementing a prescribed diet.				
3. Using a label from a food package, such as the ice-cream label shown in Figure 49-16 in the text, point out the Nutrition Facts section.				
4. Describe the various elements on the label—in this case the ice-cream label. • Serving size is the basis for the nutrition information provided. One serving of the ice cream is ½ cup. There are 14 servings in the package of ice cream.* • Calories and calories from fat show the proportion of fat calories in the product. One serving of the ice cream contains 180 calories; more than 41% of the calories come from fat. • The % Daily Value section shows how many grams (g) or milligrams (mg) of a variety of nutrients are contained in one serving. Then the label shows the percentage (%) of the recommended daily intake of each given nutrient (assuming a diet of 2000 calories a day). The ice cream contains 28% of a person's recommended daily saturated fat intake and no dietary fiber. • Recommendations for total amounts of various nutrients for both a 2000-calorie and a 2500-calorie diet are shown in chart form near the bottom of the label. These numbers provide the basis for the daily value percentages. • Ingredients are listed in order from largest quantity to smallest quantity. In this half-gallon of ice cream, skim milk, cream, and cookie dough are the most abundant ingredients.				

(continued)

Procedure Steps Total Possible Points - 28 Time Limit: 15 minutes	Practice #1	Practice #2	Practice #3	Final
5. Inform the patient that a variety of similar products with significantly different nutritional values are often available. Explain that patients can use nutrition labels, such as those shown in Figures 49-16 and 49-17 in the text, to evaluate and compare such similar products. Patients must consider what a product contributes to their diets, not simply what it lacks. To do this, patients must read the entire label. Compared with the regular ice cream, the "light, no sugar added" ice cream contains less fat, fewer carbohydrates, and two grams of dietary fiber, but it contributes an additional 25 milligrams of sodium and contains sugar alcohol, which is an artificial sweetner.				
6. Ask the patient to compare two other similar products and determine which would fit in better as part of a healthy, nutritious diet that meets that patient's individual needs.				
7. Document the patient education session in the patient's chart, indicate the patient's understanding, and initial the entry.*				
Total Number of Points Achieved/Final Score				
Initials of Observer:				

Comments and Signatures

Reviewer's comments and signatures:

1. _____

2. _____

3. _____

Instructor's comments:

_____

CAAHEP Competency Achieved

IV. P. (5) Instruct patients according to their needs to promote health maintenance and disease prevention

ABHES Competency Achieved

9 (r). Teach patients methods of health promotion and disease prevention

PROCEDURE 49-3 ALERTING PATIENTS WITH FOOD ALLERGIES TO THE DANGERS OF COMMON FOODS

Procedure Goal

To explain how patients can eliminate allergy-causing foods from their diets

Scoring System

To score each step, use the following scoring system:
1 = poor, 2 = fair, 3 = good, 4 = excellent

A minimum score of at least a 3 must be achieved on **each** step to achieve successful completion of the technique. Detailed instructions on the scoring system are found on page 413.

Materials

Results of the patient's allergy tests, patient's chart, pen, patient education materials

Procedure

Procedure Steps Total Possible Points - 36 Time Limit: 15 minutes	Practice #1	Practice #2	Practice #3	Final
1. Identify the patient and introduce yourself.				
2. Discuss the results of the patient's allergy tests (if available), reinforcing the physician's instructions. Provide the patient with a checklist of the foods that the patient has been found to be allergic to and review this list with the patient.				
3. Discuss with the patient the possible allergic reactions those foods can cause.*				
4. Discuss with the patient the need to avoid or eliminate those foods from the diet. Point out that the patient needs to be alert to avoid the allergy-causing foods not only in their basic forms but also as ingredients in prepared dishes and packaged foods. (Patients allergic to peanuts, for example, should avoid products containing peanut oil as well as peanuts.)				
5. Tell the patient to read labels carefully and to inquire at restaurants about the use of those ingredients in dishes listed on the menu.				
6. With the physician's or dietitian's consent, talk with the patient about the possibility of finding adequate substitutes for the foods if they are among the patient's favorites. Also discuss, if necessary, how the patient can obtain the nutrients in those foods from other sources (for example, the need for extra calcium sources if the patient is allergic to dairy products). Provide these explanations to the patient in writing, if appropriate, along with supplementary materials such as recipe pamphlets, a list of resources for obtaining food substitutes, and so on.				
7. Discuss with the patient the procedures to follow if the allergy-causing foods are accidentally ingested.*				

(continued)

Procedure Steps Total Possible Points - 36 Time Limit: 15 minutes	Practice #1	Practice #2	Practice #3	Final
8. Answer the patient's questions and remind the patient that you and the rest of the medical team are available if any questions or problems arise later on.				
9. Document the patient education session or interchange in the patient's chart, indicate the patient's understanding, and initial the entry.*				
Total Number of Points Achieved/Final Score				
Initials of Observer:				

Comments and Signatures

Reviewer's comments and signatures:

1. _____

2. _____

3. _____

Instructor's comments:

_____

CAAHEP Competency Achieved

IV. P. (5) Instruct patients according to their needs to promote health maintenance and disease prevention

ABHES Competency Achieved

9 (r). Teach patients methods of health promotion and disease prevention

PROCEDURE 50-1 HELPING THE PHYSICIAN COMPLY WITH THE CONTROLLED SUBSTANCES ACT OF 1970

Procedure Goal

To comply with the Controlled Substances Act of 1970

Scoring System

To score each step, use the following scoring system:
1 = poor, 2 = fair, 3 = good, 4 = excellent

A minimum score of at least a 3 must be achieved on **each** step to achieve successful completion of the technique. Detailed instructions on the scoring system are found on page 413.

Materials

DEA Form 224, DEA Form 222, DEA Form 41, pen

Procedure

Procedure Steps Total Possible Points - 28 Time Limit: 10 minutes	Practice #1	Practice #2	Practice #3	Final
1. Use DEA Form 224 to register the physician with the Drug Enforcement Administration. Be sure to register each office location at which the physician administers or dispenses drugs covered under Schedules II through V. Renew all registrations every 3 years using DEA Form 224a. Form 224 can be printed from the U.S. Department of Justice website. Renewal applications (Form 224a) can be completed through registration at this site.				
2. Order Schedule II drugs using DEA Form 222, shown in Figure 50-8 in the text, as instructed by the physician. (Stocks of these drugs should be kept to a minimum.)*				
3. Include the physician's DEA registration number on every prescription for a drug in Schedules II through V.*				
4. Complete an inventory of all drugs in Schedules II through V every 2 years (as permitted in your state; this task may be reserved to other health-care professionals).				
5. Store all drugs in Schedules II through V in a secure, locked safe or cabinet (as permitted in your state).*				
6. Keep accurate dispensing and inventory records for at least 2 years.				
7. Dispose of expired or unused drugs according to the DEA regulations. Always complete DEA Form 41 when disposing of controlled drugs.				
Total Number of Points Achieved/Final Score				
Initials of Observer:				

(continued)

Comments and Signatures

Reviewer's comments and signatures:

1. _____

2. _____

3. _____

Instructor's comments:

_____

CAAHEP Competency Achieved

IX. C. (13) Discuss all levels of governmental legislation and regulation as they apply to medical assisting practice, including FDA and DEA regulations

ABHES Competency Achieved

6 (e) Comply with federal, state, and local health laws and regulations

PROCEDURE 50-2 RENEWING THE PHYSICIAN'S DEA REGISTRATION

Procedure Goal

To accurately complete DEA Form 224a to renew the physician's DEA registration on time

Scoring System

To score each step, use the following scoring system:
1 = poor, 2 = fair, 3 = good, 4 = excellent

A minimum score of at least a 3 must be achieved on **each** step to achieve successful completion of the technique. Detailed instructions on the scoring system are found on page 413.

Materials

Calendar, tickler file (optional), pen, DEA Form 224a or Internet connection for electronic renewal

Procedure

Procedure Steps Total Possible Points - 24 Time Limit: 10 minutes	Practice #1	Practice #2	Practice #3	Final
1. Calculate a period of 3 years from the date of the original registration or the most recent renewal. Note that date as the expiration date of the physician's DEA registration.				
2. Subtract 45 days from the expiration date and mark this date on the calendar or create a reminder in your electronic calendar program. You also might put a reminder to submit renewal forms in the physician's tickler file for that date.*				
3. If you receive registration renewal paperwork (DEA Form 224a) from the DEA well before the submission date, put it in a safe place until you can complete it and have the physician sign it.				
4. Before the expiration deadline, complete DEA Form 224a as instructed on the form and have the physician sign it. Prepare or request a check for the fee.				
5. Submit the original and one copy of the completed form with the appropriate fee to the DEA so that it will arrive before the deadline. Keep one copy for the office records.				
6. Applicants are encouraged to use the online forms system for electronic renewal. Search the Internet for DEA Form 224A. Note: The DEA form website is for renewals only and Internet renewals should not be done if you have already sent a paper renewal. Update and complete the areas of the form including Personal Information, Activity, State License(s), Background Information, Payment, and Confirmation. You will be able to print copies of the form once completed.*				
Total Number of Points Achieved/Final Score				
Initials of Observer:				

(continued)

Comments and Signatures

Reviewer's comments and signatures:

1. _____

2. _____

3. _____

Instructor's comments:

_____

CAAHEP Competency Achieved

IX. C. (13) Discuss all levels of governmental legislation and regulation as they apply to medical assisting practice, including FDA and DEA regulations

ABHES Competency Achieved

6 (e) Comply with federal, state, and local health laws and regulations

Procedure 50-3 Renewing a Prescription by Telephone

Procedure Goal

To ensure a complete and accurate prescription is received by the patient

Scoring System

To score each step, use the following scoring system:
1 = poor, 2 = fair, 3 = good, 4 = excellent

A minimum score of at least a 3 must be achieved on **each** step to achieve successful completion of the technique. Detailed instructions on the scoring system are found on page 413.

Materials

Telephone, appropriate phone numbers, message pad or prescription refill request form, pen and patient chart with prescription order

Procedure

Procedure Steps Total Possible Points - 52 Time Limit: 10 minutes	Practice #1	Practice #2	Practice #3	Final
1. Take the message from the call or the message system. For the prescription to be complete, you must obtain the patient's name, date of birth, phone number, pharmacy name and/or phone number, medication, and dosage.				
2. Follow your facility policy regarding prescription renewals. Typically, the prescription is usually called into the pharmacy the day it is requested. An example policy may be posted at the facility and may state, "Nonemergency prescription refill requests must be made during regular business hours. Please allow 24 hours for processing."				
3. Communicate the policy to the patient. You should know the policy and the time when the refills will be reviewed. For example, you might state, "Dr. Alexander will review the prescription between patients and it will be telephoned within one hour to the pharmacy. I will call you back if there is a problem."*				
4. Obtain the patient's chart or reference the electronic chart to verify you have the correct patient and that the patient is currently taking the medication. Check the patient's list of medications, which are usually part of the chart.				
5. Give the prescription refill request and the chart to the physician or prescriber. Do not give a prescription refill request to the physician without the chart or chart access information. Wait for an authorization from the physician before you proceed.*				
6. Once the physician authorizes the prescription, prepare to call the pharmacy with the renewal information. You cannot call in Schedule II or III medications. However, renewals can be called in for Schedule IV and V medications. Be				

(continued)

Procedure Steps Total Possible Points - 52 Time Limit: 10 minutes	Practice #1	Practice #2	Practice #3	Final
certain to have the physician order, the patient's chart, and the refill request in front of you when you make the call. The request should include the name of the drug, the drug dosage, the frequency and mode of administration, the number of refills authorized, and the name and phone number of the pharmacy.				
7. Telephone the pharmacy. Identify yourself by name, the practice name, and the doctor's name.*				
8. State the purpose of the call. (Example: "I am calling to request a prescription refill for a patient.")				
9. Identify the patient. Include the patient's name, date of birth, address, and phone number.*				
10. Identify the drug (spelling the name when necessary), the dosage, the frequency and mode of administration, and any other special instructions or changes for administration (such as "take at bedtime").*				
11. State the number of refills authorized.				
12. If leaving a message on a pharmacy voicemail system set up for physicians, state your name, the name of the doctor you represent, and your phone number before you hang up.*				
13. Document the prescription renewal in the chart after the medication has been called into the pharmacy. Include the date, the time, the name of pharmacy, and the person taking your call. Also include the medication, dose, amount, directions, and number of refills. Sign your first initial, last name, and title.				
Total Number of Points Achieved/Final Score				
Initials of Observer:				

Comments and Signatures

Reviewer's comments and signatures:

1. _____

2. _____

3. _____

Instructor's comments:

_____

CAAHEP Competency Achieved

IV. P. (7) Demonstrate telephone techniques

ABHES Competency Achieved

8 (ee) Use proper telephone techniques

PROCEDURE 51-1 ADMINISTERING ORAL DRUGS

Procedure Goal

To safely administer an oral drug to a patient

Scoring System

To score each step, use the following scoring system:
1 = poor, 2 = fair, 3 = good, 4 = excellent

A minimum score of at least a 3 must be achieved on **each** step to achieve successful completion of the technique. Detailed instructions on the scoring system are found on page 413.

Materials

Drug order (in patient chart), container of oral drug, small paper cup (for tablets, capsules, or caplets) or plastic calibrated medicine cup (for liquids), glass of water or juice, straw (optional), package insert or drug information sheet

Procedure

Procedure Steps Total Possible Points - 52 Time Limit: 10 minutes	Practice #1	Practice #2	Practice #3	Final
1. Identify the patient and wash your hands.				
2. Select the ordered drug (tablet, capsule, or liquid).				
3. Check the rights, comparing information against the drug order.*				
4. If you are unfamiliar with the drug, check the *PDR* or other drug reference, read the package insert, or speak with the physician. Determine whether the drug may be taken with or followed by water or juice.				
5. Ask the patient about any drug or food allergies. If the patient is not allergic to the ordered drug or other ingredients used to prepare it, proceed.*				
6. Perform any calculations needed to provide the prescribed dose. If you are unsure of your calculations, check them with a coworker or the physician.				
If You Are Giving Tablets or Capsules				
7. Open the container and tap the correct number into the cap. Do not touch the inside of the cap because it is sterile. If you pour out too many tablets or capsules and you have not touched them, tap the excess back into the container.				
8. Tap the tablets or capsules from the cap into the paper cup.				
9. Recap the container immediately.*				
10. Give the patient the cup along with a glass of water or juice. If the patient finds it easier to drink with a straw, unwrap the straw and place it in the fluid. If patients have difficulty swallowing pills, have them drink some water or juice before putting the pills in the mouth.*				

(continued)

Procedure Steps Total Possible Points - 52 Time Limit: 10 minutes	Practice #1	Practice #2	Practice #3	Final
If You Are Giving a Liquid Drug				
11. If the liquid is a suspension, shake it well.				
12. Locate the mark on the medicine cup for the prescribed dose. Keeping your thumbnail on the mark, hold the cup at eye level and pour the correct amount of the drug. Keep the label side of the bottle on top as you pour, or put your palm over it.*				
13. After pouring the drug, place the cup on a flat surface and check the drug level again. At eye level the base of the meniscus (the crescent-shaped form at the top of the liquid) should align with the mark that indicates the prescribed dose. If you poured out too much, discard it.*				
14. Give the medicine cup to the patient with instructions to drink the liquid. If appropriate, offer a glass of water or juice to wash down the drug.				
After You Have Given an Oral Drug				
15. Wash your hands.				
16. Give the patient an information sheet about the drug. Discuss the information with the patient and answer any questions she may have. If the patient has questions you cannot answer, refer her to the physician.				
17. Document the drug administration with the date, time, drug name, dosage, expiration date, lot number, manufacturer, route, site, significant patient reactions, and any patient education in the patient's chart.				
Total Number of Points Achieved/Final Score				
Initials of Observer:				

Comments and Signatures

Reviewer's comments and signatures:

1. _____

2. _____

3. _____

Instructor's comments:

_____

CAAHEP Competencies Achieved

I. P. (8) Administer oral medications

II. P. (1) Prepare proper dosages of medication for administration

II. A. (1) Verify ordered doses/dosages prior to administration

ABHES Competency Achieved

9 (j) Prepare and administer oral and parenteral medications as directed by physicians

PROCEDURE 51-2 ADMINISTERING BUCCAL OR SUBLINGUAL DRUGS

Procedure Goal

To safely administer a buccal or sublingual drug to a patient

Scoring System

To score each step, use the following scoring system:
1 = poor, 2 = fair, 3 = good, 4 = excellent

A minimum score of at least a 3 must be achieved on **each** step to achieve successful completion of the technique. Detailed instructions on the scoring system are found on page 413.

Materials

Drug order (in patient chart), container of buccal or sublingual drug, small paper cup, package insert or drug information sheet

Procedure

Procedure Steps Total Possible Points - 56 Time Limit: 10 minutes	Practice #1	Practice #2	Practice #3	Final
1. Identify the patient and wash your hands.				
2. Select the ordered drug.				
3. Check the rights, comparing information against the drug order.*				
4. If you are unfamiliar with the drug, check the *PDR* or other drug reference, read the package insert, or speak with the physician.				
5. Ask the patient about any drug or food allergies. If the patient is not allergic to the ordered drug or other ingredients used to prepare it, proceed.*				
6. Perform any calculations needed to provide the prescribed dose. If you are unsure of your calculations, check them with a coworker or the physician.				
7. Open the container and tap the correct number into the cap. Do not touch the inside of the cap because it is sterile. If you pour out too many tablets or capsules and you have not touched them, tap the excess back into the container.				
8. Tap the tablets or capsules from the cap into the paper cup.				
9. Recap the container immediately.*				
If You Are Giving Buccal Medication				
10. Provide patient instruction, including • Tell the patient not to chew or swallow the tablet. • Place the medication between the cheek and gum until it dissolves.* • Instruct the patient not to eat, drink, or smoke until the tablet is completely dissolved.*				

(continued)

Procedure Steps Total Possible Points - 56 Time Limit: 10 minutes	Practice #1	Practice #2	Practice #3	Final
If You Are Giving a Sublingual Drug				
10. Provide patient instruction, including • Tell the patient not to chew or swallow the tablet. • Place the medication under the tongue until it dissolves.* • Instruct the patient not to eat, drink, or smoke until the tablet is completely dissolved.*				
After You Have Given a Buccal or Sublingual Medication				
11. Remain with patients until their tablet dissolves to monitor for possible adverse reaction and to ensure that patients have allowed the tablet to dissolve in the mouth instead of chewing or swallowing it.				
12. Wash your hands.				
13. Give the patient an information sheet about the drug. Discuss the information with the patient and answer any questions she may have. If the patient has questions you cannot answer, refer her to the physician.				
14. Document the drug administration with the date, time, drug name, dosage, expiration date, lot number, manufacturer, route, site, significant patient reactions, and any patient education in the patient's chart.				
Total Number of Points Achieved/Final Score				
Initials of Observer:				

Comments and Signatures

Reviewer's comments and signatures:

1. _____

2. _____

3. _____

Instructor's comments:

_____

CAAHEP Competencies Achieved

I. P. (7) Select proper sites for administering parenteral medication

I. P. (9) Administer parenteral (excluding IV) medications

II. P. (1) Prepare proper dosages of medication for administration

II. A. (1) Verify ordered doses/dosages prior to administration

ABHES Competency Achieved

9 (j) Prepare and administer oral and parenteral medications as directed by physicians

PROCEDURE 51-3 DRAWING A DRUG FROM AN AMPULE

Procedure Goal

To safely open an ampule and draw a drug, using sterile technique

Scoring System

To score each step, use the following scoring system:
1 = poor, 2 = fair, 3 = good, 4 = excellent

A minimum score of at least a 3 must be achieved on **each** step to achieve successful completion of the technique. Detailed instructions on the scoring system are found on page 413.

Materials

Ampule of drug, alcohol swab, 2-by-2-inch gauze square, small file (provided by the drug manufacturer), sterile filtered needle, sterile needle, and a syringe of the appropriate size

Procedure

Procedure Steps Total Possible Points - 28 Time Limit: 10 minutes	Practice #1	Practice #2	Practice #3	Final
1. Wash your hands and put on exam gloves.				
2. Gently tap the top of the ampule with your forefinger to settle the liquid to the bottom of the ampule.				
3. Wipe the ampule's neck with an alcohol swab.				
4. Wrap the 2-by-2-inch gauze square around the ampule's neck. Then snap the neck away from you. If it does not snap easily, score the neck with the small file and snap it again.				
5. Insert the filtered needle into the ampule without touching the side of the ampule.*				
6. Pull back on the plunger to aspirate (remove by vacuum or suction) the liquid completely into the syringe.				
7. Replace with the regular needle and push the plunger on the syringe until the medication just reaches the tip of the needle. The drug is now ready for injection.				
Total Number of Points Achieved/Final Score				
Initials of Observer:				

Comments and Signatures

Reviewer's comments and signatures:

1. _____

2. _____

3. _____

Instructor's comments:

_____

(continued)

CAAHEP Competencies Achieved

II. P. (1) Prepare proper dosages of medication for administration

II. A. (1) Verify ordered doses/dosages prior to administration

ABHES Competency Achieved

9 (j) Prepare and administer oral and parenteral medications as directed by physicians

Procedure 51-4 Reconstituting and Drawing a Drug for Injection

Procedure Goal

To reconstitute and draw a drug for injection, using sterile technique

Scoring System

To score each step, use the following scoring system:
1 = poor, 2 = fair, 3 = good, 4 = excellent

A minimum score of at least a 3 must be achieved on **each** step to achieve successful completion of the technique. Detailed instructions on the scoring system are found on page 413.

Materials

Vial of drug, vial of diluent, alcohol swabs, two disposable sterile needle and syringe sets of appropriate size, sharps container

Procedure

Procedure Steps Total Possible Points - 40 Time Limit: 15 minutes	Practice #1	Practice #2	Practice #3	Final
1. Wash your hands and put on exam gloves.				
2. Place the drug vial and diluent vial on the countertop. Wipe the rubber diaphragm of each with an alcohol swab.				
3. Remove the cap from the needle and the guard from the syringe. Pull the plunger back to the mark that equals the amount of diluent needed to reconstitute the drug ordered.*				
4. Puncture the diaphragm of the vial of diluent with the needle and inject the air into the diluent.*				
5. Invert the vial and aspirate the diluent.				
6. Remove the needle from the diluent vial, inject the diluent into the drug vial, and withdraw the needle. Properly dispose of this needle and syringe.				
7. Roll the vial between your hands to mix the drug and diluent thoroughly. Do not shake the vial unless so directed on the drug label. When completely mixed, the solution in the vial should have no flakes. The solution will be clear or cloudy when completely mixed (depending on the drug).				
8. Remove the cap and guard from the second needle and syringe.				
9. Pull back the plunger to the mark that reflects the amount of drug ordered. Inject the air into the drug vial.				
10. Invert the vial and aspirate the proper amount of the drug into the syringe. The drug is now ready for injection.				
Total Number of Points Achieved/Final Score				
Initials of Observer:				

(continued)

Comments and Signatures

Reviewer's comments and signatures:

1. _____

2. _____

3. _____

Instructor's comments:

_____

CAAHEP Competencies Achieved

II. P. (1) Prepare proper dosages of medication for administration

II. A. (1) Verify ordered doses/dosages prior to administration

ABHES Competency Achieved

9 (j) Prepare and administer oral and parenteral medications as directed by physicians

PROCEDURE 51-5 GIVING AN INTRADERMAL INJECTION

Procedure Goal

To administer an intradermal injection safely and effectively, using sterile technique

Scoring System

To score each step, use the following scoring system:
1 = poor, 2 = fair, 3 = good, 4 = excellent

A minimum score of at least a 3 must be achieved on **each** step to achieve successful completion of the technique. Detailed instructions on the scoring system are found on page 413.

Materials

Drug order (in patient's chart), alcohol swab, disposable needle and syringe of the appropriate size filled with the ordered dose of drug, sharps container

Procedure

Procedure Steps Total Possible Points - 48 Time Limit: 15 minutes	Practice #1	Practice #2	Practice #3	Final
1. Identify the patient. Wash your hands and put on exam gloves.				
2. Check the rights, comparing information against the drug order.*				
3. Identify the injection site on the patient's forearm. To do so, rest the patient's arm on a table with the palm up. Measure two to three finger-widths below the antecubital space and a hand-width above the wrist. The space between is available for the injection.				
4. Prepare the skin with the alcohol swab, moving in a circle from the center out.				
5. Let the skin dry before giving the injection.*				
6. Hold the patient's forearm and stretch the skin taut with one hand.				
7. With the other hand, place the needle—bevel up—almost flat against the patient's skin. Press the needle against the skin and insert it.				
8. Inject the drug slowly and gently. You should see the needle through the skin and feel resistance. As the drug enters the upper layer of skin, a wheal (raised area of the skin) will form.				
9. After the full dose of the drug has been injected, withdraw the needle. Properly dispose of used materials and the needle and syringe immediately.				
10. Remove the gloves and wash your hands.				
11. Stay with the patient to monitor for unexpected reactions.				
12. Document the injection with the date, time, drug name, dosage, expiration date, lot number, manufacturer, route, site, significant patient reactions, and any patient education in the patient's chart.				

(continued)

Procedure Steps Total Possible Points - 48 Time Limit: 15 minutes	Practice #1	Practice #2	Practice #3	Final
Total Number of Points Achieved/Final Score				
Initials of Observer:				

Comments and Signatures

Reviewer's comments and signatures:

1. _____

2. _____

3. _____

Instructor's comments:

_____

CAAHEP Competencies Achieved

I. P. (7) Select proper sites for administering parenteral medication

I. P. (9) Administer parenteral (excluding IV) medications

II. P. (1) Prepare proper dosages of medication for administration

II. A. (1) Verify ordered doses/dosages prior to administration

ABHES Competency Achieved

9 (j) Prepare and administer oral and parenteral medications as directed by physicians

PROCEDURE 51-8 ADMINISTERING INHALATION THERAPY

Procedure Goal

To administer inhalation therapy safely and effectively

Scoring System

To score each step, use the following scoring system:
1 = poor, 2 = fair, 3 = good, 4 = excellent

A minimum score of at least a 3 must be achieved on **each** step to achieve successful completion of the technique. Detailed instructions on the scoring system are found on page 413.

Materials

Drug order (in patient's chart), container of the ordered drug, tissues, package insert or patient education sheet about medication

Procedure

Procedure Steps Total Possible Points - 40 Time Limit: 20 minutes	Practice #1	Practice #2	Practice #3	Final
1. Identify the patient. Wash your hands.				
2. Check the rights, comparing information against the drug order. Make sure you have the correct type of inhaler based upon the order (oral or nasal).*				
3. Prepare the container of medication as directed. Use the package insert and show the directions to the patient.				
4. Shake the container as directed and stress this step to the patient.*				
For a Nasal Inhaler 5. Instruct the patient to complete the following steps: • Have the patient blow the nose to clear the nostrils. • Tilt the head back, and with one hand, place the inhaler tip about ½ inch into the nostril. • Point the tip straight up toward the inner corner of the eye.* • Use the opposite hand to block the other nostril. • Inhale gently while quickly and firmly squeezing the inhaler. • Remove the inhaler tip and exhale through the mouth. • Shake the inhaler and repeat the process in the other nostril. • If indicated in the package insert, instruct patients to keep the head tilted back and not to blow their nose for several minutes.				
For an Oral Inhaler 5. Instruct the patient to complete the following steps: • Warm the canister by rolling it between the palms of your hands. • Uncap the mouthpiece and assemble the inhaler as directed on the package insert. • Hold the mouth open and place the canister in the mouth or about 1 inch from the mouth.				

(continued)

Procedure Steps Total Possible Points - 40 Time Limit: 20 minutes	Practice #1	Practice #2	Practice #3	Final
• Check the package insert for the proper placement. • Exhale normally and inhale through the canister as he or she depresses it. The medication must be inhaled. • Breathe in until the lungs are full and hold the breath for 10 seconds. • Breathe out normally.				
After You Have Given an Inhalation Medication				
6. Remain with the patient to monitor for changes and possible adverse reaction.				
7. Recap and secure the medication container. Instruct the patient in this procedure.				
8. Wash your hands.				
9. Give the patient an information sheet about the drug. Discuss the information with the patient and answer any questions she may have. If the patient has questions you cannot answer, refer her to the physician.				
10. Document the drug administration with the date, time, drug name, dosage, expiration date, lot number, manufacturer, route, site, significant patient reactions, and any patient education in the patient's chart.				
Total Number of Points Achieved/Final Score				
Initials of Observer:				

Comments and Signatures

Reviewer's comments and signatures:

1. _____

2. _____

3. _____

Instructor's comments:

_____

CAAHEP Competencies Achieved

I. P. (7) Select proper sites for administering parenteral medication

I. P. (9) Administer parenteral (excluding IV) medications

II. P. (1) Prepare proper dosages of medication for administration

II. A. (1) Verify ordered doses/dosages prior to administration

ABHES Competency Achieved

9 (j) Prepare and administer oral and parenteral medications as directed by physicians

PROCEDURE 51-9 ADMINISTERING AND REMOVING A TRANSDERMAL PATCH AND PROVIDING PATIENT INSTRUCTION

Procedure Goal

To safely administer and remove a transdermal patch drug to a patient

Scoring System

To score each step, use the following scoring system:
1 = poor, 2 = fair, 3 = good, 4 = excellent

A minimum score of at least a 3 must be achieved on **each** step to achieve successful completion of the technique. Detailed instructions on the scoring system are found on page 413.

Materials

Drug order (in patient chart), transdermal patch medication, gloves, package insert or drug information sheet, patient chart

Procedure

Procedure Steps Total Possible Points - 76 Time Limit: 10 minutes	Practice #1	Practice #2	Practice #3	Final
1. Identify the patient, wash your hands, and put on gloves.*				
2. Select the ordered transdermal patch and check the rights, comparing information against the drug order.*				
3. Ask the patient about any drug or food allergies. If the patient is not allergic to the ordered drug or other ingredients used to prepare it, proceed.*				
4. If you are unfamiliar with the drug, check the *PDR* or other drug reference, read the package insert, or speak with the physician. The package insert is extremely detailed for transdermal medications and should be used when applying the medication and/or doing patient teaching.				
5. Perform any calculations needed to provide the prescribed dose. If you are unsure of your calculations, check them with a coworker or the physician.				
Applying the Transdermal Medication				
6. Remove the patch from its pouch. The plastic backing is easily peeled off once the patch is removed from the pouch. For patches without a protective pouch, bend the sides of the transdermal unit back and forth until the clear plastic backing snaps down the middle.				
7. For either type of patch, demonstrate how to peel off the clear plastic backing to expose the sticky side of the patch.				
8. Apply the patch to a reasonably hair-free site, such as the abdomen. Note that estrogen patches are usually placed on the hip.				

(continued)

Procedure Steps Total Possible Points - 76 Time Limit: 10 minutes	Practice #1	Practice #2	Practice #3	Final
9. Instruct the patient how to apply the patch. Advise the patient to avoid using the extremities below the knee or elbow, skin folds, scar tissue, or burned or irritated areas.*				
Removing the Transdermal Patch				
6. Gently lift and slowly peel the patch back from the skin. Wash the area with soap and dry it with a towel. Instruct the patient on this technique.				
7. Explain to the patient that the skin may appear red and warm, which is normal. Reassure the patient that the redness will disappear. In some cases, lotion may be applied to the skin if it feels dry.				
8. Instruct the patient to notify the doctor if the redness does not disappear in several days or if a rash develops.				
9. *Never* apply a new patch to the site just used. It is best to allow each site to rest between applications. Some transdermal systems call for waiting 7 days before using a site again. Be sure to check the package directions regarding site rotation.				
After You Have Applied and/or Removed the Transdermal Patch				
10. Wash your hands and instruct the patient they should do the same after applying or removing a transdermal system at home.				
11. Give the patient an information sheet about the drug. Discuss the information with the patient and answer any questions she may have. If the patient has questions you cannot answer, refer her to the physician.				
12. Document the drug administration with the date, time, drug name, dosage, expiration date, lot number, manufacturer, route, site, significant patient reactions, and any patient education in the patient's chart.				
Total Number of Points Achieved/Final Score				
Initials of Observer:				

Comments and Signatures

Reviewer's comments and signatures:

1. _____

2. _____

3. _____

Instructor's comments:

_____

CAAHEP Competencies Achieved

I. P. (7) Select proper sites for administering parenteral medication

I. P. (9) Administer parenteral (excluding IV) medications

II. P. (1) Prepare proper dosages of medication for administration

II. A. (1) Verify ordered doses/dosages prior to administration

ABHES Competency Achieved

9 (j) Prepare and administer oral and parenteral medications as directed by physicians

PROCEDURE 51-10 ASSISTING WITH ADMINISTRATION OF A URETHRAL DRUG

Procedure Goal

To assist with a urethral administration

Scoring System

To score each step, use the following scoring system:
1 = poor, 2 = fair, 3 = good, 4 = excellent

A minimum score of at least a 3 must be achieved on **each** step to achieve successful completion of the technique. Detailed instructions on the scoring system are found on page 413.

Materials

Urinary catheter kit, either a syringe without a needle or tubing and a bag (depending on the amount of drug to be administered), sterile gloves, the prescribed drug, a drape, and a bedsaver pad

Procedure

Procedure Steps Total Possible Points - 48 Time Limit: 10 minutes	Practice #1	Practice #2	Practice #3	Final
1. Wash your hands and use sterile technique to assemble the equipment.				
2. Check the rights, comparing information against the drug order, and explain the procedure and the drug order to the patient.*				
3. Assist the patient into the lithotomy position and drape her to preserve her modesty while exposing the vulva.				
4. Place a bedsaver pad under the buttocks.				
5. Open the catheter kit.				
6. Put on sterile gloves.				
7. Cleanse the vulva as you would to perform catheterization, using the materials in the kit. As you sweep down with the antiseptic swab, watch for the urethral opening to "wink."*				
8. The physician or nurse will insert the lubricated catheter. Tell the patient that she should feel pressure, not pain, and that the physician or nurse is going to attach the syringe to the catheter and insert the drug (or attach the tubing and bag to the catheter and let the drug run in by gravity).				
9. After instilling the drug, the physician or nurse will clamp the catheter and leave the drug in place for the ordered amount of time.				
10. Stay with the patient not only to ensure that she remains still but also to reassure her that the full feeling in the bladder is normal. She also may say she feels the need to urinate. Advise her that this feeling, too, is normal and is caused by the catheter.				

(continued)

Procedure Steps Total Possible Points - 48 Time Limit: 10 minutes	Practice #1	Practice #2	Practice #3	Final
11. When the time is up, unclamp the catheter, gently remove it, and allow the patient to urinate. Assist the patient as needed.				
12. While the patient is dressing, immediately document the drug instillation with date, time, drug, dose, route, and any significant patient reactions.				
Total Number of Points Achieved/Final Score				
Initials of Observer:				

Comments and Signatures

Reviewer's comments and signatures:

1. _____

2. _____

3. _____

Instructor's comments:

_____

CAAHEP Competencies Achieved

I. P. (7) Select proper sites for administering parenteral medication

I. P. (9) Administer parenteral (excluding IV) medications

II. P. (1) Prepare proper dosages of medication for administration

II. A. (1) Verify ordered doses/dosages prior to administration

ABHES Competency Achieved

9 (j) Prepare and administer oral and parenteral medications as directed by physicians

Procedure 51-11 Administering a Vaginal Medication

Procedure Goal

To safely administer a vaginal medication with patient instruction

Scoring System

To score each step, use the following scoring system:
1 = poor, 2 = fair, 3 = good, 4 = excellent

A minimum score of at least a 3 must be achieved on **each** step to achieve successful completion of the technique. Detailed instructions on the scoring system are found on page 413.

Materials

Prescription or drug order in the patient's chart, a cloth or paper drape, a bedsaver pad, gloves, cotton balls, water-soluble lubricant, and the prescribed drug

Procedure

Procedure Steps Total Possible Points - 52 Time Limit: 15 minutes	Practice #1	Practice #2	Practice #3	Final
1. Wash your hands.				
2. Check the rights, comparing information against the drug order, and explain the procedure and the drug order to the patient.*				
3. Give the patient the opportunity to empty her bladder before beginning.				
4. Assist the patient into the lithotomy position and drape her.*				
5. Place a bedsaver pad under the buttocks.				
6. Put on gloves.				
7. Cleanse the perineum with soap and water, using one cotton ball per stroke, and cleanse the center last, while spreading the labia.*				
8. Lubricate the vaginal suppository applicator in lubricant spread on a paper towel. For vaginal drugs in the forms of creams, ointments, gels, and tablets, use the appropriate applicator, preparing it according to the package insert.				
9. While spreading the labia with one hand, insert the applicator with the other (the applicator should be about 2 inches into the vagina and angled toward the sacrum).				
10. Release the labia and push the applicator's plunger to release the suppository into the vagina.				
11. Remove the applicator and wipe any excess lubricant off the patient.				
12. Help her to a sitting position and assist with dressing if needed.				

(continued)

Procedure Steps Total Possible Points - 52 Time Limit: 15 minutes	Practice #1	Practice #2	Practice #3	Final
13. Document the administration with date, time, drug, dose, route, and any significant patient reactions.				
Total Number of Points Achieved/Final Score				
Initials of Observer:				

Comments and Signatures

Reviewer's comments and signatures:

1. _____

2. _____

3. _____

Instructor's comments:

_____

CAAHEP Competencies Achieved

I. P. (7) Select proper sites for administering parenteral medication

I. P. (9) Administer parenteral (excluding IV) medications

II. P. (1) Prepare proper dosages of medication for administration

II. A. (1) Verify ordered doses/dosages prior to administration

ABHES Competency Achieved

9 (j) Prepare and administer oral and parenteral medications as directed by physicians

PROCEDURE 51-12 ADMINISTERING A RECTAL MEDICATION

Procedure Goal

To safely administer a rectal medication

Scoring System

To score each step, use the following scoring system:
1 = poor, 2 = fair, 3 = good, 4 = excellent

A minimum score of at least a 3 must be achieved on **each** step to achieve successful completion of the technique. Detailed instructions on the scoring system are found on page 413.

Materials

Prescription or drug order in the patient's chart, a cloth or paper drape, a bedsaver pad, gloves, water-soluble lubricant, and the prescribed drug

Procedure

Procedure Steps Total Possible Points - 52 Time Limit: 15 minutes	Practice #1	Practice #2	Practice #3	Final
1. Check the rights, comparing information against the drug order.*				
2. Explain the procedure and the drug order to the patient.				
3. Give the patient the opportunity to empty the bladder before beginning.				
4. Help the patient into Sims' position. Place a bedsaver pad under the patient.				
5. Lift the patient's gown to expose the anus.				
6. Put on gloves and prepare the medication.				
When Administering a Suppository				
7. Lubricate the tapered end of the suppository with about 1 tsp of lubricant.				
8. While spreading the patient's buttocks with one hand, insert the suppository—tapered end first—into the anus with the other hand.				
9. Gently advance the suppository past the sphincter with your index finger. Before it passes the sphincter, the suppository may feel as if it is being pushed back out the anus. When it passes the sphincter, it seems to disappear.				
10. Use tissues to remove excess lubricant from the area.				
11. Remove your gloves and ask the patient to lie quietly and retain the suppository for at least 20 minutes. When the treatment is completed, help the patient to a sitting, then standing, position.*				
When Administering a Retention Enema				
7. Place the tip of a syringe into a rectal tube. Let a little rectal solution flow through the syringe and tube. While holding the tip up, clamp the tubing.				

(continued)

Procedure Steps Total Possible Points - 52 Time Limit: 15 minutes	Practice #1	Practice #2	Practice #3	Final
8. Lubricate the end of the tube, spread the patient's buttocks, and slide the tube into the rectum about 4 inches.				
9. Slowly pour the rectal solution into the syringe, release the clamp, and let gravity move the solution into the patient. When you have administered the ordered amount of solution, clamp the tube and then remove it.				
10. Using tissues, apply pressure over the anus for 20 seconds to stifle the patient's urge to defecate and then wipe any excess lubricant or solution from the area. Encourage the patient to retain the enema for the time ordered.*				
11. When the time has passed, help the patient use a bedpan or direct the patient to a toilet to expel the solution.				
After the Administration Is Complete				
12. Remove your gloves and wash your hands.				
13. Immediately document the drug administration with date, time, drug, dose, route, and any significant patient reactions.				
Total Number of Points Achieved/Final Score				
Initials of Observer:				

Comments and Signatures

Reviewer's comments and signatures:

1. _____

2. _____

3. _____

Instructor's comments:

_____

CAAHEP Competencies Achieved

I. P. (7) Select proper sites for administering parenteral medication

I. P. (9) Administer parenteral (excluding IV) medications

II. P. (1) Prepare proper dosages of medication for administration

II. A. (1) Verify ordered doses/dosages prior to administration

ABHES Competency Achieved

9 (j) Prepare and administer oral and parenteral medications as directed by physicians

PROCEDURE 51-13 ADMINISTERING EYE MEDICATIONS

Procedure Goal

To instill medication into the eye for treatment of certain eye disorders

Scoring System

To score each step, use the following scoring system:
1 = poor, 2 = fair, 3 = good, 4 = excellent

A minimum score of at least a 3 must be achieved on **each** step to achieve successful completion of the technique. Detailed instructions on the scoring system are found on page 413.

Materials

Medication (drops, cream, or ointment), tissues, eye patch (if applicable)

Procedure

Procedure Steps Total Possible Points - 96 Time Limit: 15 minutes	Practice #1	Practice #2	Practice #3	Final
1. Identify the patient, introduce yourself, and explain the procedure.				
2. Review the doctor's medication order. This should include the patient's name, drug name, concentration, number of drops (if a liquid), into which eye(s) the medication is to be administered, and the frequency of administration.*				
3. Compare the drug with the medication order three times, checking the rights of medication administration.*				
4. Ask whether the patient has any known allergies to substances contained in the medication.				
5. Wash your hands and put on gloves.				
6. Assemble the supplies.				
7. Ask the patient to lie down or to sit back in a chair with the head tilted back.				
8. Give the patient a tissue to blot excess medication as needed.				
9. Remove an eye patch, if present.				
10. Ask the patient to look at the ceiling. Instruct the patient to keep both eyes open during the procedure.				
11. With a tissue, gently pull the lower eyelid down by pressing downward on the patient's cheekbone just below the eyelid with your nondominant hand. This pressure will open a pocket of space between the eyelid and the eye.				
Eyedrops 12. Resting your dominant hand on the patient's forehead, hold the filled eyedropper or bottle approximately ½ inch from the conjunctiva.*				

(continued)

Copyright © 2011 by The McGraw-Hill Companies, Inc.

Procedure Steps Total Possible Points - 96 Time Limit: 15 minutes	Practice #1	Practice #2	Practice #3	Final
13. Drop the prescribed number of drops into the pocket. If any drops land outside the eye, repeat instilling the drops that missed the eye.				
Creams or Ointments				
12. Rest your dominant hand on the patient's forehead and hold the tube or applicator above the conjunctiva.				
13. Without touching the eyelid or conjunctiva with the applicator, evenly apply a thin ribbon of cream or ointment along the inside edge of the lower eyelid on the conjunctiva, working from the medial (inner) to the lateral (outer) side.*				
All Medications				
14. Release the lower lid and instruct the patient to gently close the eyes.				
15. Repeat the procedure for the other eye as necessary.				
16. Remove any excess medication by wiping each eyelid gently with a fresh tissue from the medial to the lateral side.				
17. Apply a clean eye patch to cover the entire eye as necessary.				
18. Ask whether the patient felt any discomfort and observe for any adverse reactions. Notify the doctor as necessary.				
19. Instruct the patient on self-administration of medication and patch application as necessary.				
20. Ask the patient to repeat the instructions.				
21. Provide written instructions.				
22. Properly dispose of used disposable materials.				
23. Remove gloves and wash your hands.				
24. Document administration in the patient's chart. Include the drug, concentration, the number of drops, the time of administration, and the eye(s) that received the medication.				
Total Number of Points Achieved/Final Score				
Initials of Observer:				

Comments and Signatures

Reviewer's comments and signatures:

1. _____

2. _____

3. _____

Instructor's comments:

_____

CAAHEP Competencies Achieved

I. P. (7) Select proper sites for administering parenteral medication

I. P. (9) Administer parenteral (excluding IV) medications

II. P. (1) Prepare proper dosages of medication for administration

II. A. (1) Verify ordered doses/dosages prior to administration

ABHES Competency Achieved

9 (j) Prepare and administer oral and parenteral medications as directed by physicians

PROCEDURE 51-14 PERFORMING EYE IRRIGATION

Procedure Goal

To flush the eye to remove foreign particles or relieve eye irritation

Scoring System

To score each step, use the following scoring system:
1 = poor, 2 = fair, 3 = good, 4 = excellent

A minimum score of at least a 3 must be achieved on **each** step to achieve successful completion of the technique. Detailed instructions on the scoring system are found on page 413.

Materials

Sterile irrigating solution, sterile basin, sterile irrigating syringe and kidney-shaped basin, tissues

Procedure

Procedure Steps Total Possible Points - 68 Time Limit: 20 minutes	Practice #1	Practice #2	Practice #3	Final
1. Identify the patient, introduce yourself, and explain the procedure.				
2. Review the physician's order. This should include the patient's name, the irrigating solution, the volume of solution, and for which eye(s) the irrigation is to be performed.				
3. Compare the solution with the instructions three times, checking the rights of medication administration.*				
4. Wash your hands and put on gloves, a gown, and a face shield.*				
5. Assemble supplies.				
6. Ask the patient to lie down or to sit with the head tilted back and to the side that is being irrigated. The solution should not spill over into the other eye.*				
7. Place a towel over the patient's shoulder (or under the head and shoulder, if the patient is lying down). Have the patient hold the kidney-shaped basin at the side of the head next to the eye to be irrigated.				
8. Pour the solution into the sterile basin.				
9. Fill the irrigating syringe with solution (approximately 50 mL).				
10. Hold a tissue on the patient's cheekbone below the lower eyelid with your nondominant hand, and press downward to expose the eye socket.				
11. Holding the tip of the syringe ½ inch away from the eye, direct the solution onto the lower conjunctiva from the inner to the outer aspect of the eye. (Avoid directing the solution against the cornea because it is sensitive; do not use excessive force.)*				

(continued)

Procedure Steps Total Possible Points - 68 Time Limit: 20 minutes	Practice #1	Practice #2	Practice #3	Final
12. Refill the syringe and continue irrigation until the prescribed volume of solution is used or until the solution is used up.				
13. Dry the area around the eye with tissues.				
14. Properly dispose of used disposable materials.				
15. Remove your gloves, gown, and face shield and wash your hands.				
16. Record in the patient's chart the procedure, the amount of solution used, the time of administration, and the eye(s) irrigated.				
17. Put on gloves and clean the equipment and room according to OSHA guidelines.				
Total Number of Points Achieved/Final Score				
Initials of Observer:				

Comments and Signatures

Reviewer's comments and signatures:

1. _____

2. _____

3. _____

Instructor's comments:

_____

CAAHEP Competencies Achieved

I. P. (7) Select proper sites for administering parenteral medication

I. P. (9) Administer parenteral (excluding IV) medications

II. P. (1) Prepare proper dosages of medication for administration

II. A. (1) Verify ordered doses/dosages prior to administration

ABHES Competency Achieved

9 (j) Prepare and administer oral and parenteral medications as directed by physicians

PROCEDURE 51-15 ADMINISTERING EARDROPS

Procedure Goal

To instill medication into the ear to treat certain ear disorders

Scoring System

To score each step, use the following scoring system:
1 = poor, 2 = fair, 3 = good, 4 = excellent

A minimum score of at least a 3 must be achieved on **each** step to achieve successful completion of the technique. Detailed instructions on the scoring system are found on page 413.

Materials

Liquid medication, cotton balls

Procedure

Procedure Steps Total Possible Points - 88 Time Limit: 6 minutes	Practice #1	Practice #2	Practice #3	Final
1. Identify the patient, introduce yourself, and explain the procedure.				
2. Check the physician's medication order. It should include the patient's name, drug name, concentration, the number of drops, into which ear(s) the medication is to be administered, and the frequency of administration.				
3. Compare the drug with the instructions three times, checking the rights of medication administration.*				
4. Ask whether the patient has any allergies to ear medications.				
5. Wash your hands and put on gloves.				
6. Assemble supplies.				
7. If the medication is cold, warm it to room temperature with your hands or by placing the bottle in a pan of warm water.*				
8. Have the patient lie on the side with the ear to be treated facing up.				
9. Straighten the ear canal by pulling the auricle upward and outward for adults, down and back for infants and children.*				
10. Hold the dropper ½ inch above the ear canal.*				
11. Gently squeeze the bottle or dropper bulb to administer the correct number of drops.				
12. Have the patient remain in this position for 10 minutes.				
13. If ordered, loosely place a small wad of cotton in the outermost part of the ear canal.				
14. Note any adverse reaction, notifying the physician as necessary.				
15. Repeat the procedure for the other ear if ordered.				
16. Instruct the patient on how to administer the drops at home.				
17. Ask the patient to repeat the instructions.*				

(continued)

Procedure Steps Total Possible Points - 88 Time Limit: 6 minutes	Practice #1	Practice #2	Practice #3	Final
18. Provide written instructions.				
19. Remove the cotton after 15 minutes.				
20. Properly dispose of used disposable materials.				
21. Remove gloves and wash your hands.				
22. Record in the patient's chart the medication, concentration, the number of drops, the time of administration, and which ear(s) received the medication.				
Total Number of Points Achieved/Final Score				
Initials of Observer:				

Comments and Signatures

Reviewer's comments and signatures:

1. _____

2. _____

3. _____

Instructor's comments:

_____

CAAHEP Competencies Achieved

I. P. (7) Select proper sites for administering parenteral medication

I. P. (9) Administer parenteral (excluding IV) medications

II. P. (1) Prepare proper dosages of medication for administration

II. A. (1) Verify ordered doses/dosages prior to administration

ABHES Competency Achieved

9 (j) Prepare and administer oral and parenteral medications as directed by physicians

PROCEDURE 51-16 PERFORMING EAR IRRIGATION

Procedure Goal

To wash out the ear canal to remove impacted cerumen, relieve inflammation, or remove a foreign body

Scoring System

To score each step, use the following scoring system:
1 = poor, 2 = fair, 3 = good, 4 = excellent

A minimum score of at least a 3 must be achieved on **each** step to achieve successful completion of the technique. Detailed instructions on the scoring system are found on page 413.

Materials

Fresh irrigating solution, clean basin, clean irrigating syringe, towel or absorbent pad, kidney-shaped basin, cotton balls

Procedure

Procedure Steps Total Possible Points - 84 Time Limit: 15 minutes	Practice #1	Practice #2	Practice #3	Final
1. Identify the patient, introduce yourself, and explain the procedure.				
2. Check the doctor's order. It should include the patient's name, the irrigating solution, the volume of solution, and for which ear(s) the irrigation is to be performed. If the doctor has not specified the volume of solution, use the amount needed to remove the wax.				
3. Compare the solution with the instructions three times, checking the rights of medication administration.*				
4. Wash your hands and put on gloves, a gown, and a face shield.*				
5. Look into the patient's ear to identify if cerumen or a foreign body needs to be removed. You will know when you have completed the irrigation when the cerumen or foreign body is removed.				
6. Assemble the supplies.				
7. If the solution is cold, warm it to room temperature by placing the bottle in a pan of warm water.*				
8. Have the patient sit or lie on her back with the ear to be treated facing you.				
9. Place a towel over the patient's shoulder (or under the head and shoulder if she is lying down) and have her hold the kidney-shaped basin under her ear.				
10. Pour the solution into the other basin.				
11. If necessary, gently clean the external ear with cotton moistened with the solution.				
12. Fill the irrigating syringe with solution (approximately 50 mL).				

(continued)

Procedure Steps Total Possible Points - 84 Time Limit: 15 minutes	Practice #1	Practice #2	Practice #3	Final
13. Straighten the ear canal by pulling the auricle upward and outward for adults, down and back for infants and children.*				
14. Holding the tip of the syringe ½ inch above the opening of the ear, slowly instill the solution into the ear. Allow the fluid to drain out during the process.*				
15. Refill the syringe and continue irrigation until the canal is cleaned or the solution is used up.				
16. Dry the external ear with a cotton ball and leave a clean cotton ball loosely in place for 5–10 minutes.				
17. If the patient becomes dizzy or nauseated, allow her time to regain balance before standing up. Assist her as needed.				
18. Properly dispose of used disposable materials.				
19. Remove your gloves, gown, and face shield and wash your hands.				
20. Record in the patient's chart the procedure and result, the amount of solution used, the time of administration, and the ear(s) irrigated.				
21. Put on gloves and clean the equipment and room according to OSHA guidelines.				
Total Number of Points Achieved/Final Score				
Initials of Observer:				

Comments and Signatures

Reviewer's comments and signatures:

1. _____

2. _____

3. _____

Instructor's comments:

_____

CAAHEP Competencies Achieved

I. P. (7) Select proper sites for administering parenteral medication

I. P. (9) Administer parenteral (excluding IV) medications

II. P. (1) Prepare proper dosages of medication for administration

II. A. (1) Verify ordered doses/dosages prior to administration

ABHES Competency Achieved

9 (j) Prepare and administer oral and parenteral medications as directed by physicians

PROCEDURE 52-1 OBTAINING AN ECG

Procedure Goal

To obtain a graphic representation of the electrical activity of a patient's heart

Scoring System

To score each step, use the following scoring system:
1 = poor, 2 = fair, 3 = good, 4 = excellent

A minimum score of at least a 3 must be achieved on **each** step to achieve successful completion of the technique. Detailed instructions on the scoring system are found on page 413.

Materials

Electrocardiograph, ECG paper, electrodes, electrolyte preparation, wires, patient gown, drape, blanket, pillows, gauze pads, alcohol, moist towel, small scissors for trimming hair (if needed)

Procedure

Procedure Steps Total Possible Points - 108 Time Limit: 15 minutes	Practice #1	Practice #2	Practice #3	Final
1. Turn on the electrocardiograph and, if necessary, allow the stylus to heat up.				
2. Identify the patient, introduce yourself, and explain the procedure.				
3. Wash your hands.				
4. Ask the patient to disrobe from the waist up and remove jewelry, socks or stockings, bra, and shoes. If the electrodes will be placed on the patient's legs, have the patient roll up his or her pant legs. Sometimes the electrodes are placed on the sides of the lower abdomen—check the manufacturer's instructions. Provide a gown if the patient is female and instruct her to wear the gown with the opening in front.*				
5. Assist the patient onto the table and into a supine position. Cover the patient with a drape (and a blanket if the room is cool). If the patient experiences difficulty breathing or cannot tolerate lying flat, use a Fowler's or semi-Fowler's position, adjusting with pillows under the head and knees for comfort if needed.				
6. Tell the patient to rest quietly and breathe normally. Explain the importance of lying still to prevent false readings.				
7. Wash the patient's skin, using gauze pads moistened with alcohol. Then rub it vigorously with dry gauze pads to promote better contact of the electrodes.*				
8. If the patient's leg or chest hair is dense, use a small pair of scissors to closely trim the hair where you will attach the electrode.				

(continued)

Procedure Steps Total Possible Points - 108 Time Limit: 15 minutes	Practice #1	Practice #2	Practice #3	Final
9. Apply electrodes to fleshy portions of the limbs, making sure that the electrodes on one arm and leg are placed similarly to those on the other arm and leg. Attach electrodes to areas that are not bony or muscular. The arm lead tabs on the electrode point downward and the electrode tabs for the leg leads point upward. Peel off the backings of the disposable electrodes and press them into place.*				
10. Apply the precordial electrodes at specified locations on the chest. Precordial electrode tabs point downward.				
11. Attach wires and cables, making sure all wire tips follow the patient's body contours.				
12. Check all electrodes and wires for proper placement and connection; drape wires over the patient to avoid creating tension on the electrodes that could result in artifacts.				
13. Enter the patient data into the electrocardiograph. Press the on, run, or record button. Standardize the machine, if necessary, by following these steps: a. Set the paper speed to 25 mm per second or as instructed. b. Set the sensitivity setting to 1 or as instructed. c. Turn the lead selector to standardization mode. d. Adjust the stylus so the baseline is centered. e. Press the standardization button. The stylus should move upward above the baseline 10 mm (two large squares).				
14. Run the ECG. a. If the machine has an automatic feature, set the lead selector to automatic. b. For manual tracings, turn the lead selector to standby mode. Select the first lead (I) and record the tracing. Switch the machine to standby and then repeat the procedure for all 12 leads.				
15. Check tracings for artifacts.				
16. Correct problems and repeat any tracings that are not clear.				
17. Disconnect the patient from the machine.				
18. Remove the tracing from the machine and label it with the patient's name, the date, and your initials.				
19. Disconnect the wires from the electrodes and remove the electrodes from the patient.				
20. Clean the patient's skin with a moist towel.				
21. Assist the patient into a sitting position.				
22. Allow a moment for rest and then assist the patient from the table.*				
23. Assist the patient in dressing if necessary, or allow the patient privacy to dress.				
24. Wash your hands.				
25. Record the procedure in the patient's chart.				

Procedure Steps Total Possible Points - 108 Time Limit: 15 minutes	Practice #1	Practice #2	Practice #3	Final
26. Properly dispose of used materials and disposable electrodes.				
27. Clean and disinfect the equipment and the room according to OSHA guidelines.				
Total Number of Points Achieved/Final Score				
Initials of Observer:				

Comments and Signatures

Reviewer's comments and signatures:

1. _____

2. _____

3. _____

Instructor's comments:

_____

CAAHEP Competency Achieved

I. P. (5) Perform electrocardiography

ABHES Competencies Achieved

2 (c) Assist the physician with the regimen of diagnostic and treatment modalities as they relate to each body system

9 (o) Perform: 1) Electrocardiograms

Procedure 52-2 Holter Monitoring

Procedure Goal

To monitor the electrical activity of a patient's heart over a 24-hour period to detect cardiac abnormalities that may go undetected during routine electrocardiography or stress testing

Scoring System

To score each step, use the following scoring system:
1 = poor, 2 = fair, 3 = good, 4 = excellent

A minimum score of at least a 3 must be achieved on **each** step to achieve successful completion of the technique. Detailed instructions on the scoring system are found on page 413.

Materials

Holter monitor, battery, cassette tape, patient diary or log, alcohol, gauze pads, small scissors for trimming hair, disposable electrodes, hypoallergenic tape, drape, electrocardiograph

Procedure

Procedure Steps Total Possible Points - 72 Time Limit: 15 minutes	Practice #1	Practice #2	Practice #3	Final
1. Identify the patient, introduce yourself, and explain the procedure.				
2. Ask the patient to remove clothing from the waist up; provide a drape if necessary.				
3. Wash your hands and assemble the equipment.				
4. Assist the patient into a comfortable position (sitting or supine).				
5. If the patient's body hair is particularly dense, put on exam gloves and trim the areas where the electrodes will be attached.*				
6. Clean the electrode sites with alcohol and gauze.				
7. Rub each electrode site vigorously with a dry gauze square.*				
8. Attach wires to the electrodes and peel off the paper backing on the electrodes. Apply as indicated, pressing firmly to ensure that each electrode is securely attached and is making good contact with the skin.*				
9. Attach the patient cable.				
10. Insert a fresh battery and position the unit.				
11. Tape wires, cable, and electrodes as necessary to avoid tension on the wires as the patient moves.				
12. Insert the cassette tape and turn on the unit.				
13. Confirm that the cassette tape is actually running. Indicate the start time in the patient's chart.*				
14. Instruct the patient on proper use of the monitor and how to enter information in the diary. Caution the patient not to alter any diary entries; it is crucial to know what the patient is doing at all times.				

(continued)

Procedure Steps Total Possible Points - 72 Time Limit: 15 minutes	Practice #1	Practice #2	Practice #3	Final
15. Schedule the patient's return visit for the same time on the following day.				
16. On the following day, remove the electrodes, discard them, and clean the electrode sites.				
17. Wash your hands.				
18. Remove the cassette and obtain a printout of the tracing according to office procedure. Document all parts of the procedure.				
Total Number of Points Achieved/Final Score				
Initials of Observer:				

Comments and Signatures

Reviewer's comments and signatures:

1. _____

2. _____

3. _____

Instructor's comments:

_____

CAAHEP Competency Achieved

I. P. (5) Perform electrocardiography

ABHES Competencies Achieved

2 (c) Assist the physician with the regimen of diagnostic and treatment modalities as they relate to each body system

9 (o) Perform: 1) Electrocardiograms

PROCEDURE 52-3 MEASURING FORCED VITAL CAPACITY USING SPIROMETRY

Procedure Goal

To determine a patient's forced vital capacity using a volume-displacing spirometer

Scoring System

To score each step, use the following scoring system:
1 = poor, 2 = fair, 3 = good, 4 = excellent

A minimum score of at least a 3 must be achieved on **each** step to achieve successful completion of the technique. Detailed instructions on the scoring system are found on page 413.

Materials

Adult scale with height bar, spirometer, patient tubing (tubing that runs from the mouthpiece to the machine), mouthpiece, nose clip, disinfectant

Procedure

Procedure Steps Total Possible Points - 84 Time Limit: 10 minutes	Practice #1	Practice #2	Practice #3	Final
1. Prepare the equipment. Ensure that the paper supply in the machine is adequate.				
2. Calibrate the machine as necessary.				
3. Identify the patient and introduce yourself.				
4. Check the patient's chart to see whether there are special instructions to follow.				
5. Ask whether the patient has followed instructions.				
6. Wash your hands and put on exam gloves.				
7. Measure and record the patient's height and weight.				
8. Explain the proper positioning.				
9. Explain the procedure.				
10. Demonstrate the procedure.*				
11. Turn on the spirometer and enter applicable patient data and the number of tests to be performed.				
12. Ensure that the patient has loosened any tight clothing, is comfortable, and is in the proper position. Apply the nose clip.				
13. Have the patient perform the first maneuver, coaching when necessary.				
14. Determine whether the maneuver is acceptable.				
15. Offer feedback to the patient and recommendations for improvement if necessary.				
16. Have the patient perform additional maneuvers until three acceptable maneuvers are obtained.				

(continued)

Procedure Steps Total Possible Points - 84 Time Limit: 10 minutes	Practice #1	Practice #2	Practice #3	Final
17. Record the procedure in the patient's chart and place the chart and the test results on the physician's desk for interpretation.				
18. Ask the patient to remain until the physician reviews the results.*				
19. Properly dispose of used materials and disposable instruments.				
20. Sanitize and disinfect patient tubing and reusable mouthpiece and nose clip.				
21. Clean and disinfect the equipment and room according to OSHA guidelines.				
Total Number of Points Achieved/Final Score				
Initials of Observer:				

Comments and Signatures

Reviewer's comments and signatures:

1. _____

2. _____

3. _____

Instructor's comments:

_____

CAAHEP Competency Achieved

I. P. (4) Perform pulmonary function testing

ABHES Competencies Achieved

2 (c) Assist the physician with the regimen of diagnostic and treatment modalities as they relate to each body system

9 (o) Perform: 2) Respiratory testing

PROCEDURE 52-4 OBTAINING A PEAK EXPIRATORY FLOW RATE

Procedure Goal

To determine a patient's peak expiratory flow rate

Scoring System

To score each step, use the following scoring system:
1 = poor, 2 = fair, 3 = good, 4 = excellent

A minimum score of at least a 3 must be achieved on **each** step to achieve successful completion of the technique. Detailed instructions on the scoring system are found on page 413.

Materials

Peak flow meter, disposable mouthpiece

Procedure

Procedure Steps Total Possible Points - 64 Time Limit: 10 minutes	Practice #1	Practice #2	Practice #3	Final
1. Assemble all necessary equipment and supplies for the test.				
2. Wash your hands and identify the patient.				
3. Explain and demonstrate the procedure to the patient.*				
4. Position the patient in a sitting or standing position with good posture. Make sure that any chewing gum or food is removed from the patient's mouth.				
5. Set the indicator to zero.*				
6. Ensure that the disposable mouthpiece is securely placed onto the peak flow meter.				
7. Hold the peak flow meter with the gauge uppermost and ensure that your fingers are away from the gauge.				
8. Instruct patient to take as deep a breath as possible.				
9. Instruct the patient to place the mouthpiece into her mouth and close her lips tightly around the mouthpiece, sealing her lips around the mouthpiece.				
10. Instruct the patient to blow out as fast and as hard as possible.*				
11. Observe the reading where the arrowhead is on the indicator.				
12. Reset the indicator to zero and repeat the procedure two times, for a total of three readings. You will know the technique is correct if the reading results are close. If coughing occurs during the procedures, repeat the step.				
13. Document the readings into the patient's chart. The highest reading will be peak flow rate.*				

(continued)

Procedure Steps Total Possible Points - 64 Time Limit: 10 minutes	Practice #1	Practice #2	Practice #3	Final
14. Dispose of mouthpiece in a biohazardous waste container.				
15. Disinfect or dispose of the peak flow meter per office policy.				
16. Wash your hands.				
Total Number of Points Achieved/Final Score				
Initials of Observer:				

Comments and Signatures

Reviewer's comments and signatures:

1. _____

2. _____

3. _____

Instructor's comments:

_____

CAAHEP Competency Achieved

I. P. (4) Perform pulmonary function testing

ABHES Competencies Achieved

2 (c) Assist the physician with the regimen of diagnostic and treatment modalities as they relate to each body system

9 (o) Perform: 2) Respiratory testing

PROCEDURE 52-5 OBTAINING A PULSE OXIMETRY READING

Procedure Goal
To obtain a pulse oximetry reading

Scoring System
To score each step, use the following scoring system:
1 = poor, 2 = fair, 3 = good, 4 = excellent

A minimum score of at least a 3 must be achieved on **each** step to achieve successful completion of the technique. Detailed instructions on the scoring system are found on page 413.

Materials
Pulse oximeter

Procedure

Procedure Steps Total Possible Points - 44 Time Limit: 5 minutes	Practice #1	Practice #2	Practice #3	Final
1. Assemble all the necessary equipment and supplies.				
2. Wash your hands and correctly identify the patient.				
3. Select the appropriate site to apply the sensor to by assessing capillary refill in the patient's toe or finger.*				
4. Prepare the selected site, removing nail polish or earrings if necessary. Wipe the selected site with alcohol and allow it to air-dry.*				
5. Attach the sensor to the site (if a finger is used, placed in the clip).				
6. Instruct the patient to breathe normally.				
7. Attach the sensor cable to the oximeter. Turn on the oximeter and listen to the tone.				
8. Set the alarm limits for high and low oxygen saturations and high and low pulse rates as directed by the physician's order.				
9. Read the saturation level and document it in the patient's chart. Report to the physician readings that are less than 95%. Manually check the patient's pulse and compare it to the pulse oximeter. Document all the readings and the application site in the patient's medical chart.				
10. Wash your hands.				
11. Rotate the patient's finger sites every four hours if using a pulse oximeter long-term.				
Total Number of Points Achieved/Final Score				
Initials of Observer:				

(continued)

Comments and Signatures

Reviewer's comments and signatures:

1. _____

2. _____

3. _____

Instructor's comments:

_____

CAAHEP Competencies Achieved

I. P. (4) Perform pulmonary function testing

I. P. (1) Obtain Vital Signs

ABHES Competencies Achieved

2 (c) Assist the physician with the regimen of diagnostic and treatment modalities as they relate to each body system

9 (o) Perform: 2) Respiratory testing

PROCEDURE 53-1 ASSISTING WITH AN X-RAY EXAM

Procedure Goal

To assist with a radiologic procedure under the supervision of a radiologic technologist

Scoring System

To score each step, use the following scoring system:
1 = poor, 2 = fair, 3 = good, 4 = excellent

A minimum score of at least a 3 must be achieved on **each** step to achieve successful completion of the technique. Detailed instructions on the scoring system are found on page 413.

Materials

X-ray exam order, x-ray machine, x-ray film and holder, x-ray film developer, drape, patient shield

Procedure

Procedure Steps Total Possible Points - 60 Time Limit: 10 minutes	Practice #1	Practice #2	Practice #3	Final
1. Check the x-ray exam order and equipment needed.				
2. Identify the patient and introduce yourself.				
3. Determine whether the patient has complied with the preprocedure instructions. Do not depend on the patient to inform you, but ask the patient if and how he prepped for the procedure.*				
4. Explain the procedure and the purpose of the exam to the patient.				
5. Instruct the patient to remove clothing and all metals (including jewelry) as needed, according to body area to be examined, and to put on a gown. Explain that metals may interfere with the image. Ask whether the patient has any surgical metal or a pacemaker and report this information to the radiologic technologist. Leave the room to ensure patient privacy.				
Note: Steps 6 through 11 are nearly always performed by a radiologic technologist.				
6. Position the patient according to the x-ray view ordered.				
7. Drape the patient and place the patient shield appropriately.				
8. Instruct the patient about the need to remain still and to hold his breath when requested.				
9. Leave the room or stand behind a lead shield during the exposure.				
10. Ask the patient to assume a comfortable position while the films are developed. Explain that x-rays sometimes must be repeated.				
11. Develop the films.				
12. Determine if the x-ray films are satisfactory by allowing the radiologist to review the films.*				

(continued)

Procedure Steps Total Possible Points - 60 Time Limit: 10 minutes	Practice #1	Practice #2	Practice #3	Final
13. Instruct the patient to dress and tell the patient when to contact the physician's office for the results.				
14. Label the dry, finished x-ray films; place them in a properly labeled envelope; and file them according to the policies of your office.				
15. Record the x-ray exam, along with the final written findings, in the patient's chart.				
Total Number of Points Achieved/Final Score				
Initials of Observer:				

Comments and Signatures

Reviewer's comments and signatures:

1. _____

2. _____

3. _____

Instructor's comments:

_____

CAAHEP Competencies Achieved

IV. P. (6) Prepare a patient for procedures and/or treatments

III. A. (2) Explain the rationale for performance of a procedure to the patient

III. A (3) Show awareness of patient's concerns regarding their perceptions related to the procedure being performed

ABHES Competencies Achieved

2 (c) Assist the physician with the regimen of diagnostic and treatment modalities as they relate to each body system

9 (m) Assist physician with routine and specialty examinations and treatments

PROCEDURE 53-2 DOCUMENTATION AND FILING TECHNIQUES FOR X-RAYS

Procedure Goal

To document x-ray information and file x-ray films properly

Scoring System

To score each step, use the following scoring system:

1 = poor, 2 = fair, 3 = good, 4 = excellent

A minimum score of at least a 3 must be achieved on **each** step to achieve successful completion of the technique. Detailed instructions on the scoring system are found on page 413.

Materials

X-ray film(s), patient x-ray record card or book, label, film-filing envelopes, film-filing cabinet, inserts, marking pen

Procedure

Procedure Steps Total Possible Points - 16 Time Limit: 10 minutes	Practice #1	Practice #2	Practice #3	Final
1. Document the patient's x-ray information on the patient record card or in the record book. Include the patient's name, the date, the type of x-ray, and the number of x-rays taken.				
2. Verify that the film is properly labeled with the referring doctor's name, the date, and the patient's name. To note corrections or unusual positions or to identify a film that does not include labeling, attach the appropriate label and complete the necessary information. Some facilities also record the name of the radiologist who interpreted the x-ray.*				
3. Place the processed film in a film-filing envelope. File the envelope alphabetically or chronologically (or according to your office's protocol) in the filing cabinet.				
4. If you remove an envelope for any reason, put an insert or an "out card" in its place until it is returned to the cabinet.*				
Total Number of Points Achieved/Final Score				
Initials of Observer:				

(continued)

Comments and Signatures

Reviewer's comments and signatures:

1. _____

2. _____

3. _____

Instructor's comments:

_____

CAAHEP Competencies Achieved

IV. P. (3) Use medical terminology, pronouncing medical terms correctly, to communicate information, patient history, data, and observation

IV. P. (8) Document Patient Care

ABHES Competencies Achieved

8 (jj) Perform fundamental writing skills including correct grammar, spelling, and formatting techniques when writing prescriptions, documenting medical records, etc.

8. ll. Apply electronic technology

PROCEDURE 54-1 RÉSUMÉ WRITING

Objective

To write a résumé that reflects a defined career objective and highlights your skills

Scoring System

To score each step, use the following scoring system:
1 = poor, 2 = fair, 3 = good, 4 = excellent

A minimum score of at least a 3 must be achieved on **each** step to achieve successful completion of the technique. Detailed instructions on the scoring system are found on page 413.

Materials

Paper; pen; dictionary; thesaurus; computer

Procedure

Procedure Steps Total Possible Points - 32 Time Limit: 20 minutes	Practice #1	Practice #2	Practice #3	Final
1. Write your full name, address (temporary and permanent, if you have both), telephone number with area code, and e-mail address (if you have one).				
2. List your general career objective. You also may choose to summarize your skills. If you want to phrase your objective to fit a specific position, you should include that information in a cover letter to accompany the résumé.				
3. List the highest level of education or the most recently obtained degree first. Include the school name, degree earned, and date of graduation. Be sure to list any special projects, courses, or participation in overseas study programs.				
4. Summarize your work experience. List your most recent or most relevant employment first. Describe your responsibilities and list job titles, company names, and dates of employment. Summer employment, volunteer work, and student externships also may be included. Use short sentences with strong action words such as *directed, designed, developed*, and *organized*. For example, condense a responsibility into "Handled insurance and billing" or "Drafted correspondence as requested."*				
5. List any memberships and affiliations with professional organizations. List them alphabetically or by order of importance.				
6. Do not list references on your résumé.*				
7. Do not list the salary you wish to receive in a medical assisting position. Salary requirements should not be discussed until a job offer is received. If the ad you are answering requests that you include a required salary, it is best to state a range (no broader than $5,000 from lowest to highest point in the range for an annual salary).				

(continued)

Procedure Steps Total Possible Points - 32 Time Limit: 20 minutes	Practice #1	Practice #2	Practice #3	Final
8. Print your résumé on an 8½- by 11-inch sheet of high-quality white, off-white, or pastel bond paper. Carefully check your résumé for spelling, punctuation, and grammatical errors. Have someone else double-check your résumé whenever possible.*				
Total Number of Points Achieved/Final Score				
Initials of Observer:				

Comments and Signatures

Reviewer's comments and signatures:

1. _____

2. _____

3. _____

Instructor's comments:

_____

CAAHEP Competencies Achieved

IV. C. (8) Recognize elements of fundamental writing skills

IV. P. (10) Compose professional/business letters

ABHES Competency Achieved

11 (a) Perform the essential requirements for employment such as résumé writing, effective interviewing, dressing professionally, and following up appropriately

PROCEDURE 54-2 WRITING THANK-YOU NOTES

Objective

To write an appropriate, professional thank-you note after an interview or externship

Scoring System

To score each step, use the following scoring system:
1 = poor, 2 = fair, 3 = good, 4 = excellent

A minimum score of at least a 3 must be achieved on **each** step to achieve successful completion of the technique. Detailed instructions on the scoring system are found on page 413.

Materials

Paper; pen; dictionary; thesaurus; computer; #10 business envelope

Procedure

Procedure Steps Total Possible Points - 32 Time Limit: 10 minutes	Practice #1	Practice #2	Practice #3	Final
1. Complete the letter within 2 days of the interview or completion of the externship. Begin by typing the date at the top of the letter.*				
2. Type the name of the person who interviewed you (or who was your mentor in the externship). Include credentials and title, such as Dr. or Director of Client Services. Include the complete address of the office or organization.				
3. Start the letter with "Dear Dr., Mr., Mrs., Miss, or Ms. _____:"				
4. In the first paragraph, thank the interviewer for his time and for granting the interview. Discuss some specific impressions, for example, "I found the interview and tour of the facilities an enjoyable experience. I would welcome the opportunity to work in such a state-of-the-art medical setting." If you are writing to thank your mentor for her time during your externship and for allowing you to perform your externship at her office, practice, or clinic, discuss the knowledge and experience you gained during the externship.				
5. In the second paragraph, mention the aspects of the job or externship that you found most interesting or challenging. For a job interview thank-you note, state how your skills and qualifications will make you an asset to the staff. When preparing an externship thank-you letter, mention interest in any future positions.				
6. In the last paragraph, thank the interviewer for considering you for the position. Ask to be contacted at his earliest convenience regarding his employment decision.				
7. Close the letter with "Sincerely" and type your name. Leave enough space above your typewritten name to sign your name.				

(continued)

Procedure Steps Total Possible Points - 32 Time Limit: 10 minutes	Practice #1	Practice #2	Practice #3	Final
8. Type your return address in the upper-left corner of the #10 business envelope. Then type the interviewer's name and address in the envelope's center, apply the proper postage, and mail the letter. You also can e-mail your thank-you letter. Proper letter format and professional tone and appearance still apply. Send the thank-you letter as an attachment.				
Total Number of Points Achieved/Final Score				
Initials of Observer:				

Comments and Signatures

Reviewer's comments and signatures:

1. _____

2. _____

3. _____

Instructor's comments:

_____

CAAHEP Competencies Achieved

IV. C. (8) Recognize elements of fundamental writing skills

IV. P. (10) Compose professional/business letters

ABHES Competency Achieved

11 (a) Perform the essential requirements for employment such as resume writing, effective interviewing, dressing professionally, and following up appropriately

Work Product Documentation/Forms

Use these forms while performing procedures that include a work product icon.

WORK // PRODUCT PROCEDURE WORK PRODUCT FORMS

PROCEDURE 8-1 STEP-BY-STEP OVERVIEW OF INVENTORY PROCEDURES

Name _____ Class _____ Date _____

Comprehensive Medical Practice								
Inventory Sheet								
Date:	Item	Qty.	Cost Per Unit	Total Cost	Pymt. Method	Vendor Info.	Date Shipment Received	Received By:
9/17/XX	paper	Two reams	7.00	14.00	check	Office Pak 133 Shield St. Arburs, NM 45908	9/22/XX	SMR, RMA(AMT)

PROCEDURE 12-1 CREATING A CLUSTER SCHEDULE

Name _____ Class _____ Date _____

APPOINTMENT RECORD

		DOCTOR		
12 November Tuesday			**13** November Wednesday	
Dr. Torrance	Dr. Hilbert		Dr. Torrance	Dr. Hilbert
		AM		
Surgery (8:00–9:45)		**8** 00/15/30/45	Surgery (8:00–9:45)	
		9 00/15/30/45		
		10 00/15/30/45		
		11 00/15/30/45		
	Lunch	**12** 00/15/30/45		
		PM		
		1 00/15/30/45		
		2 00/15/30/45		
		3 00/15/30/45		
Staff Meeting at Mercy General		**4** 00/15/30/45		Conference
		5 00/15/30/45		

REMARKS & NOTES _____

Procedure 15-1 Verifying Worker's Compensation Coverage

Workers' Compensation Verification

Date:_____

Patient's Name:_____

Employer:_____

Address:_____

Phone:_____ Fax:_____

Employer Contact Name:_____

Date of Accident/Illness:_____

Accident/Illness verified as employment-related: _____Yes   _____No

W/C Insurance Carrier:_____

Address:_____

Phone:_____ First Report of Incident Filed? ____Yes _____No

(If no, remind employer they have 24 hours to report such incidences to state labor department)

W/C Insurance Carrier verified coverage? _____Yes   _____No

Name of Person providing verification:_____

Claim Number from W/C (for incident):_____

Treating Physician:_____

Verification completed by:_____

1500

HEALTH INSURANCE CLAIM FORM

APPROVED BY NATIONAL UNIFORM CLAIM COMMITTEE 08/05

CARRIER

| | PICA | | | | | PICA | |

1. MEDICARE (Medicare #)   MEDICAID (Medicaid #)   TRICARE CHAMPUS (Sponsor's SSN)   CHAMPVA (Member ID#)   GROUP HEALTH PLAN (SSN or ID)   FECA BLK LUNG (SSN)   OTHER (ID)

1a. INSURED'S I.D. NUMBER (For Program in Item 1)

2. PATIENT'S NAME (Last Name, First Name, Middle Initial)

3. PATIENT'S BIRTH DATE MM DD YY   SEX M   F

4. INSURED'S NAME (Last Name, First Name, Middle Initial)

5. PATIENT'S ADDRESS (No., Street)

6. PATIENT RELATIONSHIP TO INSURED   Self   Spouse   Child   Other

7. INSURED'S ADDRESS (No., Street)

CITY   STATE

8. PATIENT STATUS   Single   Married   Other

CITY   STATE

ZIP CODE   TELEPHONE (Include Area Code) ( )

Employed   Full-Time Student   Part-Time Student

ZIP CODE   TELEPHONE (Include Area Code) ( )

9. OTHER INSURED'S NAME (Last Name, First Name, Middle Initial)

10. IS PATIENT'S CONDITION RELATED TO:

11. INSURED'S POLICY GROUP OR FECA NUMBER

a. OTHER INSURED'S POLICY OR GROUP NUMBER

a. EMPLOYMENT? (Current or Previous)   YES   NO

a. INSURED'S DATE OF BIRTH MM DD YY   SEX M   F

b. OTHER INSURED'S DATE OF BIRTH MM DD YY   SEX M   F

b. AUTO ACCIDENT?   PLACE (State)   YES   NO

b. EMPLOYER'S NAME OR SCHOOL NAME

c. EMPLOYER'S NAME OR SCHOOL NAME

c. OTHER ACCIDENT?   YES   NO

c. INSURANCE PLAN NAME OR PROGRAM NAME

d. INSURANCE PLAN NAME OR PROGRAM NAME

10d. RESERVED FOR LOCAL USE

d. IS THERE ANOTHER HEALTH BENEFIT PLAN?   YES   NO   *If yes*, return to and complete item 9 a-d.

READ BACK OF FORM BEFORE COMPLETING & SIGNING THIS FORM.

12. PATIENT'S OR AUTHORIZED PERSON'S SIGNATURE I authorize the release of any medical or other information necessary to process this claim. I also request payment of government benefits either to myself or to the party who accepts assignment below.

SIGNED _____

13. INSURED'S OR AUTHORIZED PERSON'S SIGNATURE I authorize payment of medical benefits to the undersigned physician or supplier for services described below.

SIGNED _____

> **17a. 2-digit qualifier in small shaded box.**
> **1B=Blue Shield**
> **PIN of referring, ordering, or supervising provider**

14. DATE OF CURRENT: MM DD YY   ◄ ILLNESS (First symptom) OR INJURY (Accident) OR PREGNANCY(LMP)

15. IF PATIENT HAS HAD SAME OR SIMILAR ILLNESS. GIVE FIRST DATE

16. DATES PATIENT UNABLE TO WORK IN CURRENT OCCUPATION MM DD YY FROM   MM DD YY TO

17. NAME OF REFERRING PROVIDER OR OTHER SOURCE

17a. 1B   BCBSND PIN #

17b. NPI   NPI #

> **17b. NPI of referring, ordering, or supervising provider**

18. HOSPITALIZATION DATES RELATED TO CURRENT SERVICES MM DD YY FROM   MM DD YY TO

19. RESERVED FOR LOCAL USE

20. OUTSIDE LAB?   YES   NO $ CHARGES

21. DIAGNOSIS OR NATURE OF ILLNESS OR INJURY (Relate Items 1, 2, 3 or 4 to Item 24E by Line)

1. ____ . ____   3. ____ . ____

2. ____ . ____   4. ____ . ____

22. MEDICAID RESUBMISSION CODE   ORIGINAL REF.

23. PRIOR AUTHORIZATION NUMBER

> **24J. Enter first three letters of last name and PIN in shaded area**
> **Example: WAH1974**

24. A. DATE(S) OF SERVICE From MM DD YY To MM DD YY	B. PLACE OF SERVICE	C. EMG	D. PROCEDURES, SERVICES, OR SUPPLIES (Explain Unusual Circumstances) CPT/HCPCS MODIFIER	E. DIAGNOSIS POINTER	F. $ CHARGES	G. DAYS OR UNITS	H. EPSDT Family Plan	I. ID. QUAL.	J. RENDERING PROVIDER ID. #
1	Supplemental information inserted in shaded area. See example below.							1B	BCBSND PIN #
								NPI	Provider's NPI #
2	Amevive								
	03 10 07 03 10 07	23		J3490					
3								NPI	
4								NPI	
5								NPI	
6								NPI	

> **24. 1-6**
> **Shaded area is to be used for supplemental information.**
> **White area is for line item detail such as date, modifier etc...**

> **24J. Enter the NPI # of the Individual providing services**

25. FEDERAL TAX I.D. NUMBER   SSN   EIN

26. PATIENT'S ACCOUNT NO.

27. ACCEPT ASSIGNMENT? (For govt. claims, see back)   YES   NO

28. TOTAL CHARGE $

29. AMOUNT PAID $

30. BALANCE DUE $

31. SIGNATURE OF PHYSICIAN OR SUPPLIER INCLUDING DEGREES OR CREDENTIALS (I certify that the statements on the reverse apply to this bill and are made a part thereof.)

SIGNED _____ DATE _____

32. SERVICE FACILITY LOCATION INFORMATION

a. Service facility NPI#   b. 1B 4578

33. BILLING PROVIDER INFO & PH # ( )

a. Billing provider NPI#   b. 1B 47894

NUCC Instruction Manual available at: www.nucc.org

APPROVED OMB-0938-0999 FORM CMS-1500 (08/05)

> **Two digit qualifier identifying the non-NPI #**
> **1A=Blue Cross**
> **1B=Blue Shield**
> **See examples below**

PATIENT AND INSURED INFORMATION

PHYSICIAN OR SUPPLIER INFORMATION

Copyright © 2011 by The McGraw-Hill Companies, Inc.

PROCEDURE 17-3 HOW TO BILL WITH THE SUPERBILL

Name _____ Class _____ Date _____

ENCOUNTER FORM

Tel: (404) 466-0000	Kim Whitley, MD	EIN: 33-0980987
Fax: (404) 466-008	Ivy Smith, MD	

Family Practice
456 Boyard Ct.
Tyrone, Georgia 34450

Office Visits	New	Fee	Est.	Fee	OFFICE PROCEDURES			INJECTIONS		
☐Level I	99201	75.00	99211	55.00	☐EKG with interpretation	93000	125.00	☐ Influenza virus vaccine		90565
☐Level II	99202	85.00	99212	75.00	☐Oximetry with interpret.	94760	145.00	☐Admin of influenza vaccine		G0008
☐Level III	99203	95.00	99213	85.00	**LABORATORY TESTS**			☐Pneumococcal vaccine		90732
☐Level IV	99204	110.00	99214	95.00	☐ Blood, occult (feces)	82270	45.00	☐Adm. of Pneumococcal vaccine		G0009
☐Level V	99205	125.00	99215	110.00	☐ Skin test Tb, intradermal (PPD) 86580 75.00			☐Hepatitis B vaccine		90746
OFFICE CONSULTS (NEW or EST)					☐			☐Adm. of Hepatitis B vaccine		G0010
☐Level I	99214	65.00			☐			☐Tetanus toxoid vaccine		90703
☐Level II	99242	75.00			☐			☐Immunization admin.		90471
☐Level III	99243	85.00			☐			☐		
☐Level IV	99244	95.00			☐			☐		
☐Level V	99245	110.00			☐			☐		

DIAGNOSIS

☐ Abnormal heart sounds	785.3	☐Chronic ischemic heart disease	414.9	☐Hypertension	401.9
☐ Abnormal pain	789.0__	☐Chronic obstructive lung disease	496	☐Hormone replacement	V07.4
☐ Abnormal feces	787.7	☐Congestive heart failure	428.0	☐Hyperlipidemia	272.4
☐ Allergic rhinitis	477.9	☐Cough	786.2	☐Hyperthyroidism	242.9__
☐ Anemia, pernicious	281.0	☐Depressive disorder	311	☐Influenza	487.1
☐ Anxiety	300.0__	☐Diabetes mellitus	250.__	☐Loss of weight	783.21
☐ Asthma	493.9__	☐Diarrhea	787.91	☐Nausea	787.02
☐ Atrophy, cerebral	331.0	☐Dizziness	780.4	☐Nausea with vomiting	787.01
☐ B-12 deficiency	281.1	☐Emphysema	492.8	☐Pneumonia	486
☐ Back pain	724.5	☐Fatigue and malaise	780.79	☐Sore throat	462
☐ Bronchitis	490.0	☐Fever	780.6	☐Vaccine, hepatitis B	V05.3
☐ Cardiovascular disease	429.2__	☐Gastritis, atrophic	535.1__	☐Vaccine, Influenza	V04.81
☐ Cervicalgia	723.1	☐Heartburn	787.1	☐Vaccine, pneumococcus	V03.82
☐ Chest pain	786.5__	☐Hematuria	599.7	☐Vaccine, tetanus toxoid	V03.7
☐	_____	☐	_____	☐	_____

PATIENT IDENTIFICATION		FINANCIAL TRANSACTION DATA	
Patient Name:		Invoice No.	
Patient #:		Account No.	
Date of Birth:		Total for Service:	$
ENCOUNTER DATE		Amount Received:	$
Date of Service: ____/____/____		Paid by:	☐ Cash
RETURN VISIT DATE			☐ Check
Date of Return Visit: ____/____/____			☐ Credit Cart
Cashier's Initials:			

NOTE: All Injections are $45.00, and the administrations of injections are $15.00

PROCEDURE 17-4 PREPARING AN AGE ANALYSIS

Name _____ Class _____ Date _____

Ledger Card # 1

Patient's Name   Brendan Whelan

Home Phone   555-222-5678   **Work Phone** 555-424-0001

Social Security No.   999-88-7777

Employer   US Government

Insurance   Federal BC/BS

Policy #   805268975

Person Responsible for Charges (if Different from Patient) _____

Brendan Whelan
2 Outward Bound
Anywhere, US 00000

Date	Reference	Description	Charge	Credits		Current Balance
				Payments	Adj.	
		Balance Forward ⟶				
01-02	99202		100 00			100 00
	81000		25 00			125 00
	85652		45 00			160 00
01-04	Submit to BC/BS					160 00
03-02	ROA BC/BS; Bal to Pt			85 00		75 00
04-12	ROA Pt			25 00		50 00

Please Pay Last Amount in This Column ▲

OV—Office Visit   C—Consultation   EX—Examination
X—X-ray   NC—No Charge   INS—Insurance
ROA—Received on Account   MA—Missed Appointment

Name _____ Class _____ Date _____

Ledger Card # 2

Patient's Name   Matthew Starks

Home Phone   555-333-5324   **Work Phone** 555-232-1141

Social Security No.   888-22-3343

Employer   Meditech

Insurance   Aetna

Policy #   A52678901

Person Responsible for Charges (if Different from Patient) _____

Matthew Starks
16 Roberts Road
Anytown, US 00000

Date	Reference	Description	Charge	Credits Payments	Credits Adj.	Current Balance
			Balance Forward ⟶			
10-30	99281		375 00			375 00
12-07	Submit to Aetna					375 00
01-09	Respond to Aetna inquiry					375 00
02-12	Aetna Denial; Bill Pt					375 00
02-20	ROA Pt			50 00		325 00
03-10	ROA Pt			50 00		275 00

Please Pay Last Amount in This Column ▲

OV—Office Visit   C—Consultation   EX—Examination
X—X-ray   NC—No Charge   INS—Insurance
ROA—Received on Account   MA—Missed Appointment

Name _____ Class _____ Date _____

Ledger Card # 3

Patient's Name	Eleanora Ward
Home Phone	555-628-0723
Social Security No.	111-22-3333
Employer	Retired
Insurance	Medicare/Medex
Policy #	111-22-3333A 87629451

Work Phone None

Person Responsible for Charges (if Different from Patient) _____

Eleanora Ward
P.O. Box 315
Anytown, US 00000

Date	Reference	Description	Charge	Credits		Current Balance
				Payments	Adj.	
			Balance Forward ⟶			
02-14	99212		60 : 00			60 : 00
02-15	Submit to MCR					60 : 00
03-25	ROA MCR			25 : 00		35 : 00
04-02	ROA Medex			10 : 00		25 : 00
04-12	Bill Pt	(deductible)				25 : 00
05-25	ROA Pt			10 : 00		15 : 00

Please Pay Last Amount in This Column ▲

OV—Office Visit	C—Consultation	EX—Examination
X—X-ray	NC—No Charge	INS—Insurance
ROA—Received on Account	MA—Missed Appointment	

Name _____ Class _____ Date _____

Ledger Card # 4

Patient's Name   Gerald Atwood

Home Phone   555-111-4211   **Work Phone**   666-140-5432

Social Security No.   555-66-7778

Employer   Atwood Trucking

Insurance   Metropolitan

Policy #   667752452

Person Responsible for Charges (if Different from Patient) _____

Gerald Atwood
32 Maple Street
Anywhere, US 00000

Date	Reference	Description	Charge		Payments		Adj.		Current Balance	
			Balance Forward ⟶							
06-05	99205		200	00					200	00
	93000		125	00					325	00
	36415		25	00					350	00
06-08	Submit to Metropolitan								350	00
08-10	ROA Metropolitan				210	00			140	00
11-30	ROA Pt				25	00			115	00
03-23	ROA Pt				25	00			95	00

Please Pay Last Amount in This Column ▲

OV—Office Visit   C—Consultation   EX—Examination
X—X-ray   NC—No Charge   INS—Insurance
ROA—Received on Account   MA—Missed Appointment

Name _____ Class _____ Date _____

Ledger Card # 5

Patient's Name	Emmie Wyneman
Home Phone	555-232-6886

Work Phone None

Social Security No.	999-78-6543
Employer	Student
Insurance	Prudential
Policy #	46789521

Person Responsible for Charges (if Different from Patient) Dale (father)

Dale Wyneman
RE: Emily Weiman
2 Old Stagecoach Rd
Anytown, MA 00000

Date	Reference	Description	Charge	Credits		Current Balance
				Payments	Adj.	
		Balance Forward →				
03-06	99211		50 00			50 00
03-08	Submit to Prudential					50 00
04-09	Apply to deductible					50 00
04-10	Bill Pt					50 00
06-01	ROA Pt			25 00		25 00

Please Pay Last Amount in This Column ▲

OV—Office Visit	C—Consultation	EX—Examination
X—X-ray	NC—No Charge	INS—Insurance
ROA—Received on Account	MA—Missed Appointment	

Name _____ Class _____ Date _____

ACCOUNTS RECEIVABLE–AGE ANALYSIS

Date: _____

Patient	Balance	Date of Charges	Most Recent Payment	30 days	60 days	90 days	120 days	Remarks

PROCEDURE 18-3 RECONCILING A BANK STATEMENT

Name _____ Class _____ Date _____

HOW TO BALANCE YOUR CHECKING ACCOUNT

1. Subtract any service charges that appear on this statement from your checkbook balance.
2. Add any interest paid on your checking account to your checkbook balance.
3. Check off (✔) in your checkbook register all checks and pre-authorized transactions listed on your statement.
4. Use the worksheet to list checks you have written, ATM withdrawals, and Point of Sale transactions which are not listed on your statement.

5. Enter the closing balance on the statement.	$	.
6. Add any deposits not shown on the statement.	+	.
7. Subtotal	$	.
8. Subtract total transactions outstanding (from worksheet on right).	−	.
9. Account balance (should match balance in your checkbook register).	$	.

IF YOUR ACCOUNT DOES NOT BALANCE

a. Check your addition and subtraction first on this form and then in your checkbook.
b. Be sure the deposit amounts on your statement are the same as those in your checkbook.
c. Be sure all the check amounts on your statement agree with the amounts entered in your checkbook register.
d. Be sure all checks written prior to this reconcilement period but not listed on the statement are listed on the worksheet.
e. Verify that all MAC® ATM, Point of Sale, and other pre-authorized transactions have been recorded in your checkbook register.
f. Review last month's statement to be certain any corrections were entered into your checkbook.

WORKSHEET
Transactions Outstanding

Number or Date	Amount
TOTAL	

Name _____ Class _____ Date _____

| Genysis Family Medicine |
| Cash Disbursements Journal |

Month _____

General Ledger Number _____

DATE	CHECK #	BUSINESS EXPENSE	PAYABLE TO	ACCOUNT #
5/23/xx	567	RENT	SESSION MORTGAGE	A1234

Name _____ Class _____ Date _____

Dr. James Wilson, MD
Family Practice
Petty Cash Journal

Reporting Period

From _____ To _____ Balance _____

Date	Voucher #	Purpose	Account #	Payee	Approved By	Total	Balance
3/19/xx	12234	Gifts for staff	653	Dr. Wilson	*smw*, Manager	100.00	275.00

Audited By: __smw__

Approved By __Dr. Wilson__

Total Voucher Amount	100.00	
Total Receipts	1	
Prior Cash on Hand	375.00	
Petty Cash Reimbursement	100.00	
Balance Forward	275.00	

Name _____ Class _____ Date _____

Using the payroll register below, calculate and complete the rest of the employees' net pay for the month. The first employee has been completed for you.

GENESYS FAMILY MEDICINE
Payroll Register

Period Ending: 2/1/20XX

Employee ID	Employee Name	Hours Worked	Hourly Rate	Regular Pay	Overtime Pay	No. of Exempts	Gross Pay	Taxes and Deductions	Other Deduction	Net Pay
1	Jay Christopher	160	17.50	2800	78.00	1-S	$2,878.00	$325.00	$20.00	$2,533.00
2	Grace Ososona	168	13.00	2184	56.00	2-M		$139.78	$0.00	
3	Vanessa Vaughn	160	12.00	1920	0.00	3-M		$267.50	$38.00	
4	Jessica Jules	132	16.50	2178	23.00	2-S		$312.00	$150.00	
5	Kent Harrell	168	13.50	2268	78.00	1-M		$156.89	$20.00	
6	Henrietta Gbanga	160	14.00	2240	0.00	1-M		$389.67	$35.00	
7	Sheila Ferguson	168	11.00	1848	96.00	4-M		$116.00	$25.00	
8							$0.00	$0.00		$0.00
9							$0.00	$0.00		$0.00
10							$0.00	$0.00		$0.00
11							$0.00	$0.00		$0.00
12							$0.00	$0.00		$0.00
13							$0.00	$0.00		$0.00
14							$0.00	$0.00		$0.00

PROCEDURE 34-2 NOTIFYING STATE AND COUNTY AGENCIES ABOUT REPORTABLE DISEASES

Name _____ Class _____ Date _____

MICHIGAN DEPARTMENT OF PUBLIC HEALTH
Division of Disease Surveillance

ENTERIC ILLNESS CASE INVESTIGATION
(Please check appropriate illness)

_____Shigellosis   _____Giardiasis
_____Non-typhoid Salmonellosis   _____Amebiasis
_____Campylobacter enteritis

CASE INFORMATION

Name: _____ Age or Birthdate: _____ Sex: _____ Race: _____

Address: _____ Phone: _____
　　　　　(Street)　　　　　　　　　　　(City)　　(County)　　(Zip)

Occupation: _____ *High Risk:　Y　N
　　　　　　　(What)　　　　　　　　　　　(Where)
　　　(If infant or student list school, nursery or day care center)

Attending　　　　　　　　Address or　　　　　　　　Was the patient
Physician: _____ Phone: _____ hospitalized:　Y　N

Hospital: _____ Dates: _____
　　　　　　　　　　　　　　　　　　　　(Admission)　　　　　　　(Discharge)

Onset: _____ Date recovered: _____ Symptom Summary: _____

_____

_____

Suspected Causative Agent: _____
(include species or serotype if known)

HOUSEHOLD CONTACTS INFORMATION

Name	Age	Family Relationship	Occupation	*High Risk Y　N	Provide date of onset for all household members with concurrent similar illness
1)					
2)					
3)					
4)					
5)					
6)					
7)					
8)					
9)					
10)					

*"High Risk" = occupation as food handler, direct patient care worker, day care center worker or person attending day care <u>or</u> who is institutionalized. Stool specimens should be obtained on "high risk" cases and "high risk" household contacts as appropriate for the illness. Results may be recorded in <u>Laboratory Information Section</u> of this form (see over).

Name of the person who completed this form: _____ County: _____

Information obtained from: _____ Date: _____

Telephone Interview: _____ Home Visit: _____ Outbreak Investigation: _____

C-30 Rev. 10/83　　AUTH: Act 368, P.A. 1978

PROCEDURE 34-2 NOTIFYING STATE AND COUNTY AGENCIES ABOUT REPORTABLE DISEASES (*concluded*)

Name _____ Class _____ Date _____

NON-HOUSEHOLD CONTACTS WITH A CONCURRENT SIMILAR ILLNESS

Name	Approximate date of onset of symptoms	Address and/or Phone	Relationship to case (Nature of contact)
1)			
2)			
3)			
4)			
5)			

ADDITIONAL EXPOSURES OR COMMENTS

Home Sewage System: Municipal   Septic Tank   Other_____

Home drinking Water Type: Municipal   Private Well   Other_____

As appropriate for the illness, ask about meals eaten away from home, stores where groceries bought, brand of poultry, meat, dairy products consumed, overnight travel, recent foreign travel, group functions, exposure to raw milk, untreated water, animals, etc. within one incubation period before onset.

(shigellosis to 7 days, salmonellosis - up to 3 days, Campylobacter enteritis - up to 10 days)

Be specific, provide place name(s) and date(s).

FOLLOW-UP FECAL CULTURE RESULTS FOR "HIGH RISK" CASE AND/OR CONTACTS.

Name or Initials	Date(s) Obtained and Findings
1)	
2)	
3)	
4)	
5)	

ARIZONA DEPARTMENT OF HEALTH SERVICES COMMUNICABLE DISEASE REPORT Important Instructions on Reverse Side PLEASE PRINT OR TYPE		County/IHS ID Number/Chapter		State ID Number	
PATIENT'S NAME (Last) (First)		DATE OF BIRTH	SEX ☐ Male ☐ Female	ETHNICITY ☐ Hispanic ☐ Non-Hispanic	
STREET ADDRESS		CENSUS TRACT	CITY	RACE ☐ White ☐ Am. Indian ☐ Asian	
COUNTY	STATE	ZIP CODE	PHONE NO.	☐ Black ☐ Other ☐ Unknown	
DIAGNOSIS OR SUSPECT REPORTABLE CONDITION				COUNTY USE ONLY: LAB CONFIRMATION DATE:_____	
DATE ONSET	DATE OF DIAGNOSIS	LAB RESULTS		☐ Negative ☐ Positive	
PATIENT OCCUPATION OR SCHOOL				☐ Not Done ☐ Unknown	
PHYSICIAN OR OTHER REPORTING SOURCE		PHONE NUMBER		COUNTY USE ONLY: ☐ Confirmed case ☐ Probable case	
STREET ADDRESS		CITY	STATE ZIP CODE	☐ Outbreak Associated ☐ Ruled Out	

Original and 1st copy to County Health Department   ☐ CHECK IF ADDITIONAL FORMS ARE NEEDED (Quantity)_____

PROCEDURE 36-2 USING A PROGRESS NOTE

Total Care Clinic
Progress Notes

Name: _____ Chart #: _____

DATE	

Name _____ Class _____ Date _____

Name _____ DOB _____ Date _____

ALLERGIES: _____

Note

Review of Systems

Systems	NL	Note	Systems	NL	Note
Constitutional			Musculoskeletal		
Eyes			Skin/breasts		
ENT/mouth			Neurologic		
Cardiovascular			Psychiatric		
Respiratory			Endocrine		
GI			Hem/lymph		
GU			Allergy/immun		

Current Medicines	Date	Current Diagnosis

H: _____   W: _____   T: _____   P: _____   R: _____

B/P Sitting _____ or Standing _____ Supine _____

Last Tetanus _____   Social Habits   Yes   No

L.M.P. _____   Tobacco ____ ____

                              Alcohol ____ ____

O2 Sat: _____ Pain Scale: _____   Rec. Drugs ____ ____

CC:

HPI:

PROCEDURE 36-3 OBTAINING A MEDICAL HISTORY

Name _____ Class _____ Date _____

Total Care Clinic
Medical History Form

Name _____ Date _____

Age _____ Date of birth _____ Sex _____ Marital status _____

Place of birth _____ Occupation _____ Blood type _____

Reason for visit _____

Are you seeing another doctor, health practitioner or therapist? If yes, Who? _____

Medications _____

Allergies to medications _____

Supplements _____

Surgeries _____

Injuries _____

Have you ever had the following problems? When?

Weight loss	Headaches/Migraines	Kidney disease
Weight gain	Hair loss	Frequent urination
Fevers	Bladder infections	Chills
Arthritis	Rheumatic fever	Muscle cramps
Blurred vision	Hearing loss	Dizziness
Ringing in the ears	Swollen glands	Thyroid disease
Pneumonia	Difficulty breathing	Chest pain
Heart attack	Ankle swelling	HIV positive
Sinusitis	Peptic ulcers	Gall bladder disease
Pancreatitis	Hepatitis type?	Diverticulitis
Food allergies	Diabetes	Back pain
Varicose veins	Insomnia	Depression
Anxiety	Numbness	Fibromyalgia
Fatigue	Anemia	Tuberculosis
Epstein Barr	Yeast infections	Mononucleosis
Hypertension	Memory loss	Hemorrhoids

Social Habits:

Do you smoke cigarettes? _____ How many per day? _____ How long? _____

Do you drink caffeinated beverages? _____ How many per day? _____

Do you drink alcohol? _____ How often? _____ What type? _____

Do you use recreational drugs? _____ How often? _____ What type? _____

How many sexual partners? _____ Have you had unprotected sex? _____

Do you exercise? _____ What type? _____ How often? _____

Do you have any dietary restrictions? _____

Family History:

Age of mother _____ Age of father _____ Siblings _____

If deceased mark age of death _____

Has any of your family had the following diseases (please mark who)

Cancer _____ Arthritis _____ High blood pressure _____

Heart disease _____ Stroke _____ Diabetes _____

Allergies/Asthma _____ Emphysema _____

Mental disorders _____ Tuberculosis _____

Other _____

Preventative Health

Mammogram _____

Pap smear _____

Blood chemistry _____ Chest X-ray _____

Hemmocult _____ Sigmoid/Colonoscopy _____

Tetanus _____ TB _____ Pneumovax _____

Flu shot _____ Other immunizations _____

For Women Only

Age of onset of first menses _____ Are your periods regular? _____

Length of time between cycles? _____ How many days? _____

No. of pregnancies _____ Miscarriages? _____ No. of living children? _____

What form of birth control do you use? _____ Have you had an abnormal pap? _____

If yes, describe type of problem and treatment _____

For Men Only

Have you ever had prostate problems? _____

Have you had any of the symptoms listed below? _____

Frequent urination _____

Waking more than once at night to urinate _____

Decrease in urine flow or dribbling _____

Burning or discharge from the penis _____

Testicular swelling or lumps _____

Sexual problems _____

Have you had a PSA? _____ Was it normal? _____

Patient Signature _____

Date _____

Name _____ Class _____ Date _____

HEALTH HISTORY
(Confidential)

Name _____
Age _____ Birthdate _____ Date of last physical examination _____ Today's Date _____
What is your reason for visit? _____

SYMPTOMS Check (✓) symptoms you currently have or have had in the past year.

GENERAL
- ☐ Chills
- ☐ Depression
- ☐ Dizziness
- ☐ Fainting
- ☐ Fever
- ☐ Forgetfulness
- ☐ Headache
- ☐ Loss of sleep
- ☐ Loss of weight
- ☐ Nervousness
- ☐ Numbness
- ☐ Sweats

MUSCLE/JOINT/BONE
Pain, weakness, numbness in:
- ☐ Arms ☐ Hips
- ☐ Back ☐ Legs
- ☐ Feet ☐ Neck
- ☐ Hands ☐ Shoulders

GENITO-URINARY
- ☐ Blood in urine
- ☐ Frequent urination
- ☐ Lack of bladder control
- ☐ Painful urination

GASTROINTESTINAL
- ☐ Appetite poor
- ☐ Bloating
- ☐ Bowel changes
- ☐ Constipation
- ☐ Diarrhea
- ☐ Excessive hunger
- ☐ Excessive thirst
- ☐ Gas
- ☐ Hemorrhoids
- ☐ Indigestion
- ☐ Nausea
- ☐ Rectal bleeding
- ☐ Stomach pain
- ☐ Vomiting
- ☐ Vomiting blood

CARDIOVASCULAR
- ☐ Chest pain
- ☐ High blood pressure
- ☐ Irregular heart beat
- ☐ Low blood pressure
- ☐ Poor circulation
- ☐ Rapid heart beat
- ☐ Swelling of ankles
- ☐ Varicose veins

EYE, EAR, NOSE, THROAT
- ☐ Bleeding gums
- ☐ Blurred vision
- ☐ Crossed eyes
- ☐ Difficulty swallowing
- ☐ Double vision
- ☐ Earache
- ☐ Ear discharge
- ☐ Hay fever
- ☐ Hoarseness
- ☐ Loss of hearing
- ☐ Nosebleeds
- ☐ Persistent cough
- ☐ Ringing in ears
- ☐ Sinus problems
- ☐ Vision – Flashes
- ☐ Vision – Halos

SKIN
- ☐ Bruise easily
- ☐ Hives
- ☐ Itching
- ☐ Change in moles
- ☐ Rash
- ☐ Scars
- ☐ Sore that won't heal

MEN only
- ☐ Breast lump
- ☐ Erection difficulties
- ☐ Lump in testicles
- ☐ Penis discharge
- ☐ Sore on penis
- ☐ Other

WOMEN only
- ☐ Abnormal Pap smear
- ☐ Bleeding between periods
- ☐ Breast lump
- ☐ Extreme menstrual pain
- ☐ Hot flashes
- ☐ Nipple discharge
- ☐ Painful intercourse
- ☐ Vaginal discharge
- ☐ Other
- Date of last menstrual period _____
- Date of last Pap smear _____
- Have you had a mammogram? _____
- Are you pregnant? _____
- Number of children _____

CONDITIONS Check (✓) conditions you have or have had in the past.
- ☐ AIDS
- ☐ Alcoholism
- ☐ Anemia
- ☐ Anorexia
- ☐ Appendicitis
- ☐ Arthritis
- ☐ Asthma
- ☐ Bleeding Disorders
- ☐ Breast Lump
- ☐ Bronchitis
- ☐ Bulimia
- ☐ Cancer
- ☐ Cataracts
- ☐ Chemical Dependency
- ☐ Chicken Pox
- ☐ Diabetes
- ☐ Emphysema
- ☐ Epilepsy
- ☐ Glaucoma
- ☐ Goiter
- ☐ Gonorrhea
- ☐ Gout
- ☐ Heart Disease
- ☐ Hepatitis
- ☐ Hernia
- ☐ Herpes
- ☐ High Cholesterol
- ☐ HIV Positive
- ☐ Kidney Disease
- ☐ Liver Disease
- ☐ Measles
- ☐ Migraine Headaches
- ☐ Miscarriage
- ☐ Mononucleosis
- ☐ Multiple Sclerosis
- ☐ Mumps
- ☐ Pacemaker
- ☐ Pneumonia
- ☐ Polio
- ☐ Prostate Problem
- ☐ Psychiatric Care
- ☐ Rheumatic Fever
- ☐ Scarlet Fever
- ☐ Stroke
- ☐ Suicide Attempt
- ☐ Thyroid Problems
- ☐ Tonsillitis
- ☐ Tuberculosis
- ☐ Typhoid Fever
- ☐ Ulcers
- ☐ Vaginal Infections
- ☐ Venereal Disease

ALLERGIES To medications or substances
_____
_____
_____

MEDICATIONS List medications you are currently taking
_____
Pharmacy Name _____ Phone _____

(All information is strictly confidential)

FAMILY HISTORY Fill in health information about your family.

Relation	Age	State of Health	Age at Death	Cause of Death
Father				
Mother				
Brothers				
Sisters				

Check (✓) if your blood relatives had any of the following:

Disease		Relationship to you
Arthritis, Gout		
Asthma, Hay Fever		
Cancer		
Chemical Dependency		
Diabetes		
Heart Disease, Strokes		
High Blood Pressure		
Kidney Disease		
Tuberculosis		
Other		

HOSPITALIZATIONS

Year	Hospital	Reason for Hospitalization and Outcome

Have you ever had a blood transfusion? ☐ Yes ☐ No
If yes, please give approximate dates. _____

SERIOUS ILLNESS/INJURIES

	DATE	OUTCOME

PREGNANCY HISTORY

Year of Birth	Sex of Birth	Complications if any

HEALTH HABITS Check (✓) which substances you use and describe how much you use.
- ☐ Caffeine
- ☐ Tobacco
- ☐ Drugs
- ☐ Other

OCCUPATIONAL CONCERNS Check (✓) if your work exposes you to the following:
- ☐ Stress
- ☐ Hazardous Substances
- ☐ Heavy Lifting
- ☐ Other
- Your occupation: _____

I certify that the above information is correct to the best of my knowledge. I will not hold my doctor or any members of his/her staff responsible for any errors or omissions that I may have made in the completion of this form.

Signature _____ Date _____

Reviewed By _____ Date _____

PROCEDURE 37-1 MEASURING AND RECORDING TEMPERATURE

Name _____ Class _____ Date _____

TOTAL CARE CLINIC

Facility _____

DATE	TIME	T	P	R	BP		DATE	TIME	T	P	R	BP	

Patient Name:	Last:	First:	Middle:	Physician:

VITAL SIGN CHART # _____

PROCEDURE 37-2 MEASURING AND RECORDING PULSE AND RESPIRATIONS

Name _____ Class _____ Date _____

TOTAL CARE CLINIC

Facility _____

DATE	TIME	T	P	R	BP		DATE	TIME	T	P	R	BP	

Patient Name:	Last:	First:	Middle:	Physician:

VITAL SIGN CHART # _____

PROCEDURE 37-3 TAKING THE BLOOD PRESSURE OF ADULTS AND OLDER CHILDREN

Name _____ Class _____ Date _____

TOTAL CARE CLINIC
Facility _____

DATE	TIME	T	P	R	BP		DATE	TIME	T	P	R	BP	

Patient Name:	Last:	First:	Middle:	Physician:

VITAL SIGN CHART # _____

PROCEDURE 37-4 MEASURING ADULTS AND CHILDREN

Name _____ Class _____ Date _____

TOTAL CARE CLINIC

Facility _____

MONTH: _____ YEAR: _____

DATE	WEIGHT	HEIGHT

MONTH: _____ YEAR: _____

DATE	WEIGHT	HEIGHT

MONTH: _____ YEAR: _____

DATE	WEIGHT	HEIGHT

MONTH: _____ YEAR: _____

DATE	WEIGHT	HEIGHT

MONTH: _____ YEAR: _____

DATE	WEIGHT	HEIGHT

MONTH: _____ YEAR: _____

DATE	WEIGHT	HEIGHT

MONTH: _____ YEAR: _____

DATE	WEIGHT	HEIGHT

MONTH: _____ YEAR: _____

DATE	WEIGHT	HEIGHT

MONTH: _____ YEAR: _____

DATE	WEIGHT	HEIGHT

MONTH: _____ YEAR: _____

DATE	WEIGHT	HEIGHT

MONTH: _____ YEAR: _____

DATE	WEIGHT	HEIGHT

MONTH: _____ YEAR: _____

DATE	WEIGHT	HEIGHT

Patient Name:	Last:	First:	Middle:	Admin. Number:
Physician:				

WEIGHT RECORD

Name _____ Class _____ Date _____

2 to 20 years: Boys
Body mass index-for-age percentiles

NAME _____

RECORD # _____

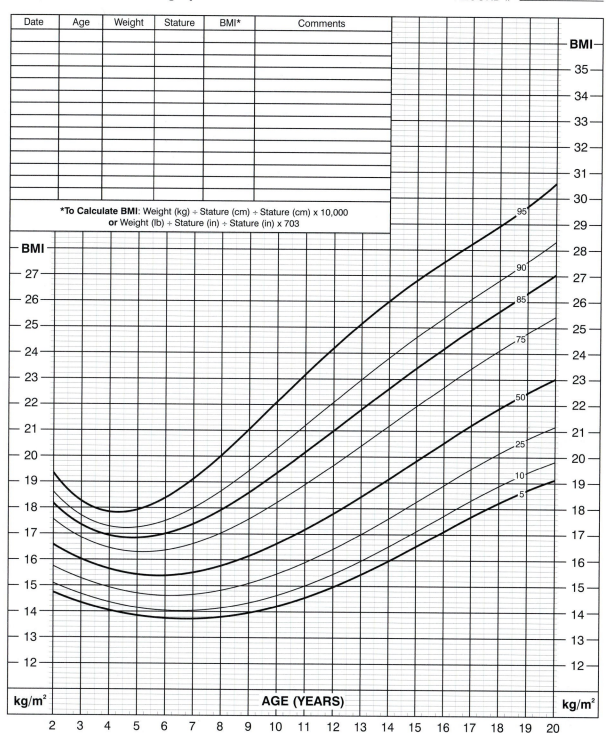

*To Calculate BMI: Weight (kg) ÷ Stature (cm) ÷ Stature (cm) x 10,000
or Weight (lb) ÷ Stature (in) ÷ Stature (in) x 703

AGE (YEARS)

Published May 30, 2000 (modified 10/16/00).
SOURCE: Developed by the National Center for Health Statistics in collaboration with
the National Center for Chronic Disease Prevention and Health Promotion (2000).
http://www.cdc.gov/growthcharts

SAFER · HEALTHIER · PEOPLE™

Name _____ Class _____ Date _____

2 to 20 years: Girls
Body mass index-for-age percentiles

NAME _____

RECORD # _____

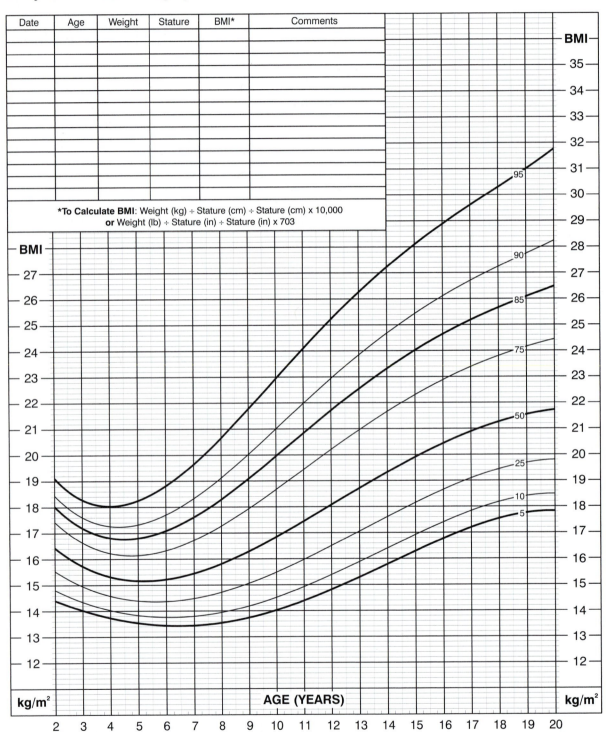

Date	Age	Weight	Stature	BMI*	Comments

*To Calculate BMI: Weight (kg) ÷ Stature (cm) ÷ Stature (cm) x 10,000
or Weight (lb) ÷ Stature (in) ÷ Stature (in) x 703

AGE (YEARS)

kg/m²

Published May 30, 2000 (modified 10/16/00).
SOURCE: Developed by the National Center for Health Statistics in collaboration with
the National Center for Chronic Disease Prevention and Health Promotion (2000).
http://www.cdc.gov/growthcharts

SAFER · HEALTHIER · PEOPLE™

Name _____ Class _____ Date _____

2 to 20 years: Boys
Stature-for-age and Weight-for-age percentiles

NAME _____

RECORD # _____

Mother's Stature _____ Father's Stature _____

Date	Age	Weight	Stature	BMI*

*To Calculate BMI: Weight (kg) ÷ Stature (cm) ÷ Stature (cm) x 10,000
or Weight (lb) ÷ Stature (in) ÷ Stature (in) x 703

Published May 30, 2000 (modified 11/21/00).

SOURCE: Developed by the National Center for Health Statistics in collaboration with
the National Center for Chronic Disease Prevention and Health Promotion (2000).
http://www.cdc.gov/growthcharts

CDC

SAFER・HEALTHIER・PEOPLE™

Name _____ Class _____ Date _____

2 to 20 years: Girls
Stature-for-age and Weight-for-age percentiles

NAME _____

RECORD # _____

Mother's Stature _____		Father's Stature _____		
Date	Age	Weight	Stature	BMI*

*To Calculate BMI: Weight (kg) ÷ Stature (cm) ÷ Stature (cm) x 10,000
or Weight (lb) ÷ Stature (in) ÷ Stature (in) x 703

AGE (YEARS)

STATURE

WEIGHT

AGE (YEARS)

Published May 30, 2000 (modified 11/21/00).
SOURCE: Developed by the National Center for Health Statistics in collaboration with
the National Center for Chronic Disease Prevention and Health Promotion (2000).
http://www.cdc.gov/growthcharts

SAFER · HEALTHIER · PEOPLE™

PROCEDURE 37-5 MEASURING INFANTS

Name _____ Class _____ Date _____

TOTAL CARE CLINIC

Facility _____

MONTH: _____ YEAR: _____

DATE	WEIGHT	HEIGHT

MONTH: _____ YEAR: _____

DATE	WEIGHT	HEIGHT

MONTH: _____ YEAR: _____

DATE	WEIGHT	HEIGHT

MONTH: _____ YEAR: _____

DATE	WEIGHT	HEIGHT

MONTH: _____ YEAR: _____

DATE	WEIGHT	HEIGHT

MONTH: _____ YEAR: _____

DATE	WEIGHT	HEIGHT

MONTH: _____ YEAR: _____

DATE	WEIGHT	HEIGHT

MONTH: _____ YEAR: _____

DATE	WEIGHT	HEIGHT

MONTH: _____ YEAR: _____

DATE	WEIGHT	HEIGHT

MONTH: _____ YEAR: _____

DATE	WEIGHT	HEIGHT

MONTH: _____ YEAR: _____

DATE	WEIGHT	HEIGHT

MONTH: _____ YEAR: _____

DATE	WEIGHT	HEIGHT

Patient Name:	Last:	First:	Middle:	Admin. Number:
Physician:				

WEIGHT RECORD

Name _____ Class _____ Date _____

Birth to 36 months: Girls
Head circumference-for-age and
Weight-for-length percentiles

NAME _____

RECORD # _____

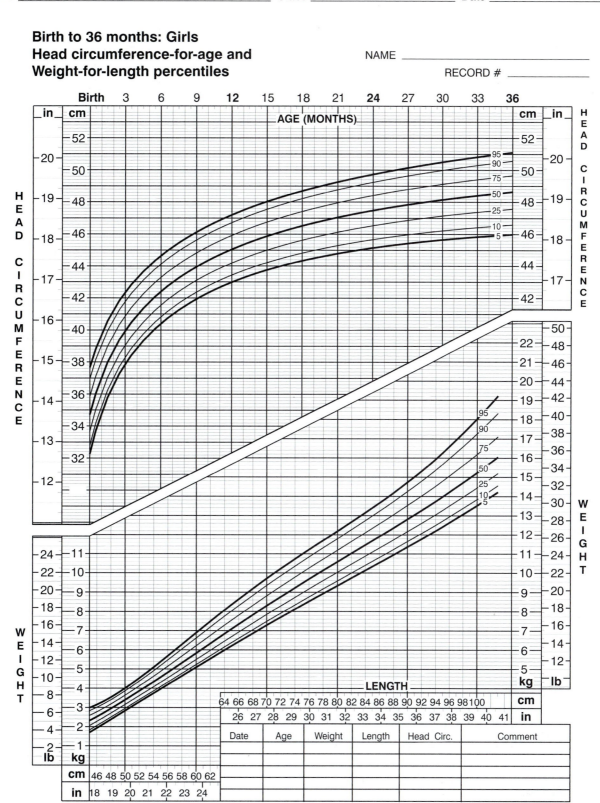

Published May 30, 2000 (modified 10/16/00).
SOURCE: Developed by the National Center for Health Statistics in collaboration with
the National Center for Chronic Disease Prevention and Health Promotion (2000).
http://www.cdc.gov/growthcharts

SAFER · HEALTHIER · PEOPLE™

Name _____ Class _____ Date _____

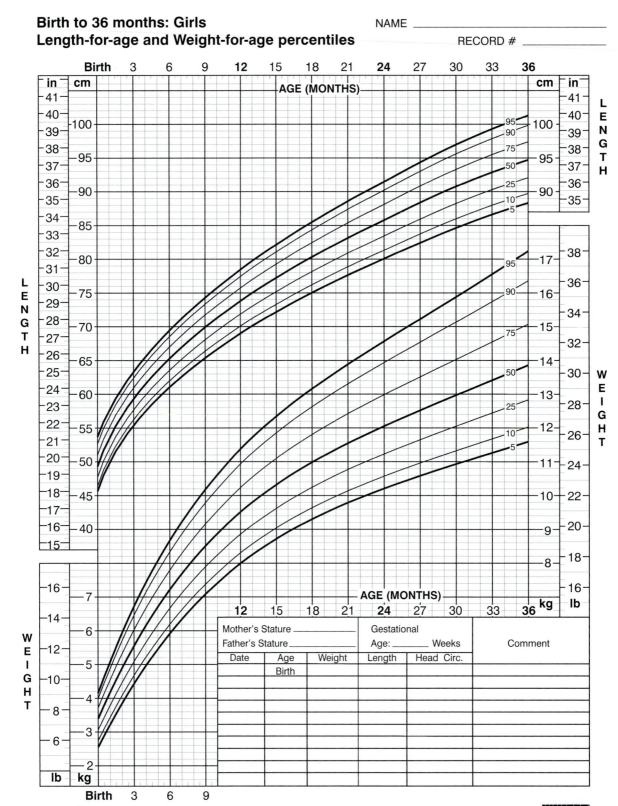

Birth to 36 months: Girls
Length-for-age and Weight-for-age percentiles

NAME _____

RECORD # _____

Published May 30, 2000 (modified 4/20/01).
SOURCE: Developed by the National Center for Health Statistics in collaboration with
the National Center for Chronic Disease Prevention and Health Promotion (2000).
http://www.cdc.gov/growthcharts

CDC

SAFER · HEALTHIER · PEOPLE™

Name _____ Class _____ Date _____

Birth to 36 months: Boys
Head circumference-for-age and
Weight-for-length percentiles

NAME _____

RECORD # _____

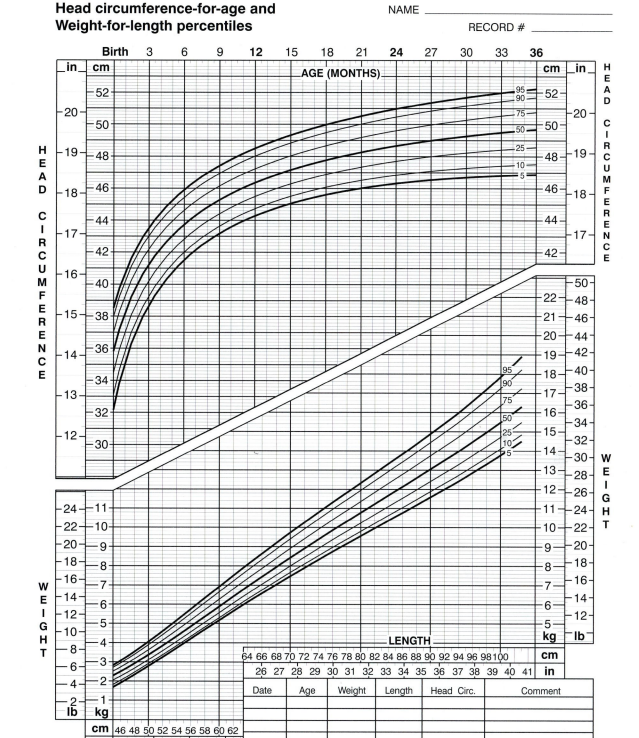

Published May 30, 2000 (modified 10/16/00).
SOURCE: Developed by the National Center for Health Statistics in collaboration with
the National Center for Chronic Disease Prevention and Health Promotion (2000).
http://www.cdc.gov/growthcharts

SAFER · HEALTHIER · PEOPLE™

Name _____ Class _____ Date _____

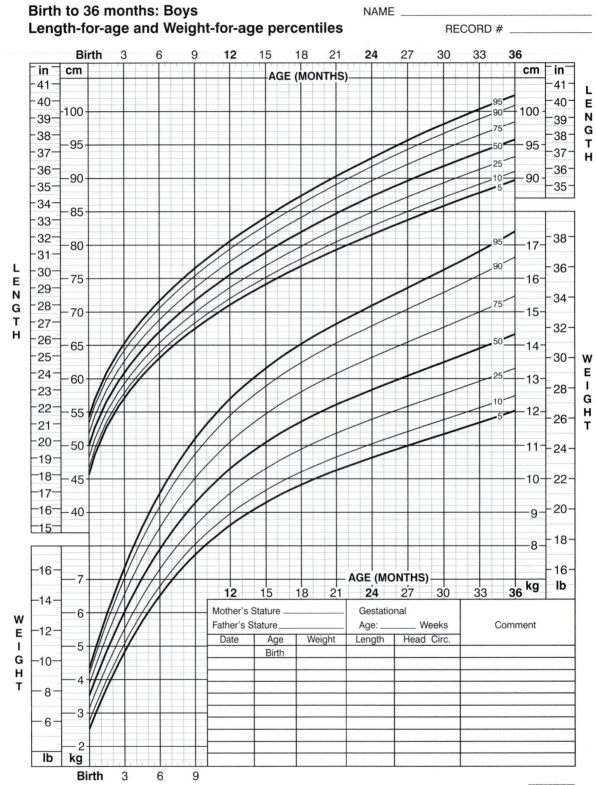

Birth to 36 months: Boys
Length-for-age and Weight-for-age percentiles

NAME _____

RECORD # _____

Mother's Stature _____	Gestational	
Father's Stature _____	Age: _____ Weeks	Comment

Date	Age	Weight	Length	Head Circ.	
	Birth				

Published May 30, 2000 (modified 4/20/01).
SOURCE: Developed by the National Center for Health Statistics in collaboration with
the National Center for Chronic Disease Prevention and Health Promotion (2000).
http://www.cdc.gov/growthcharts

SAFER · HEALTHIER · PEOPLE™

Name _____ Class _____ Date _____

Total Care Clinic
Progress Notes

Name: _____ Chart #: _____

DATE	

PROCEDURE 38-6 MEASURING AUDITORY ACTIVITY

Name _____ Class _____ Date _____

Total Care Clinic
Progress Notes

Name: _____ Chart #: _____

DATE	

PROCEDURE 40-1 ASSISTING WITH A SCRATCH TEST EXAMINATION

Name _____ Class _____ Date _____

	Total Care Clinic Progress Notes

Name: _____ Chart #: _____

DATE	

Procedure 41-4 Assisting as a Floater (Unsterile Assistant) During Minor Surgical Procedures

Name _____ Class _____ Date _____

70Y

Significant Clinical Information

_____ Fasting   _____ Non-Fasting

CHEMISTRY REQUEST

(EMBOSSING AREA)

Submit Separate Specimens (Not Request Forms) for each Frozen Test Requested.

Account No.

Specimen Date Mo Day Yr	Specimen Time Hr Min	Patient Name (Last)	(First, MI)	Sex	Date of Birth Mo Day Yr	Age Yrs Mos

50 8649 9000 4

* I certify that I have read the informed consent on the back and understand its content.

Patient I.D. #	Physician I.D.	Patient/Resp. Party's Phone #
Responsible Party or Insured's Name (Last, First)		Patient's SS #

Patient's Signature

Address	City	State	Zip Code

Resp. Party's Employer	Medicaid Number/HMO #	Medicare #

Physician Name	UPIN #	Physician's Signature	Provider #

Diagnosis Code (ICD-9)	Insurance Code or Company Name and Address	Insurance I.D. #	Workers Comp. Yes No

Group # or Name	Relationship to Insured (Circle One) 1-Self 2-Spouse 3-Other

Urine Random   † Ⓤ Total 24hr. Vol. _____ Ht. _____ Wt. _____

✳ = EDTA Plasma	Ⓢ = Serum	Ⓡ = Red	Ⓖ = Gray	Ⓑ = Light Blue
ⒶⒻ = Amniotic Fluid	Ⓕ = Frozen Specimen	Ⓛ = Lavender	ⒼⓃ = Green	ⓇⒷ = Royal Blue

Apply Labels to Patient Specimens Only Patient Control No.

50 8649 9000 4

50 8649 9000 4   50 8649 9000 4   50 8649 9000 4

CHEMISTRY REQUEST

Code	Test		Code	Test		Code	Test	
58867	☐ Basic Chemistry	Ⓢ	1693	☐ Glycohemoglobin, Total	Ⓛ	4465	☐ Prolactin	Ⓢ
1396	☐ Amylase, Serum	Ⓢ	4416	☐ HCG, Beta Chain, Quant	Ⓢ	4747	☐ Prostatic Acid Phosphatase (EIA)	Ⓢ
6254	☐ Antinuclear Antibody (ANA), Qnt.	Ⓢ	1453	☐ Hemoglobin A1C	Ⓛ	10322	☐ Prostate-Specific Antigen (PSA)	Ⓢ
1040	☐ BUN	Ⓢ	6510	☐ Hepatitis B Surf Antigen (HBsAg)	Ⓢ	5199	☐ Prothrombin Time	Ⓑ
7419	☐ Carbamazepine (Tegretol)	Ⓢ	6395	☐ Hepatitis B Surf Antibody (Anti HBs)	Ⓢ	6502	☐ Ra Latex Screen	Ⓢ
5009	☐ CBC With Differential	Ⓛ	58560	☐ Hepatitis Profile I (Diagnostic)	Ⓢ	5215	☐ Sedimentation Rate	Ⓛ
2139	☐ CEA-EIA Roche	△ ✳	46938	☐ Hepatitis Profile II (Follow up)	Ⓢ	6072	☐ STS	Ⓢ
98012	☐ Chlamydia by DNA Probe	△	58552	☐ Hepatitis Profile VII (A and B)	Ⓢ	1149	☐ T₄ (Thyroxine)	Ⓢ
96479	☐ Chlamydia/GC, DNA Probe	△	83824	☐ HIV-1 ABS-EIA	Ⓢ	7336	☐ Theophylline (Theo-Dur)	Ⓢ
1065	☐ Cholesterol, Total	Ⓢ	7625	☐ Lead, Blood	ⓇⒷ	620	☐ Thyroid Profile I	Ⓢ
1370	☐ Creatinine, Serum	Ⓢ	235002	☐ Lipid Profile I (Lipoprotein Analysis)	Ⓢ	27011	☐ Thyroid Profile II	Ⓢ
7385	☐ Digoxin (Lanoxin)	Ⓢ	235028	☐ Lipid Profile III (incl Apolipoproteins)	Ⓢ	4259	☐ TSH, 3rd Generation	Ⓢ
604	☐ Electrolytes (Na, K, Cl)	Ⓢ	7708	☐ Lithium	Ⓢ	810	☐ Vitamin B-12 and Folate	Ⓢ
4598	☐ Ferritin	Ⓢ	505	☐ Liver Profile A				
4309	☐ Follicle Stim. Hormone (FSH)	Ⓢ	7401	☐ Phenytoin (Dilantin)	Ⓢ		**URINE CHEMISTRY**	
1818	☐ Glucose	Ⓖ	1180	☐ Potassium	Ⓢ	3038	☐ Urinalysis (Microscopic if indicated)	Ⓤ
	☐ Glucose Tolerance	Ⓖ	4556	☐ Pregnancy, Serum, Ql.	Ⓢ	3772	☐ Urinalysis, Complete	Ⓤ
	Indicate No. Of Tubes _____		53520	☐ Prenatal Profile B with HBsAG	②-Ⓛ Ⓡ			

ADDITIONAL TESTS

Test #	Name
☐ 1375	24 Hr Urine for Protein Ⓤ
☐ 4550	Pregnancy, Urine, Qul Ⓤ

Procedure 41-7 Suture Removal

Name _____ Class _____ Date _____

Total Care Clinic
Progress Notes

Name: _____ Chart #:_____

DATE	

Name _____ Class _____ Date _____

Total Care Clinic
Progress Notes

Name: _____ Chart #: _____

DATE	

PROCEDURE 42-2 ADMINISTERING THERMOTHERAPY

Name _____ Class _____ Date _____

Total Care Clinic
Progress Notes

Name: _____ Chart #: _____

DATE	

PROCEDURE 43-5 CONTROLLING BLEEDING

Name _____ Class _____ Date _____

Total Care Clinic
Progress Notes

Name: _____ Chart #: _____

DATE	

PROCEDURE 43-6 CLEANING MINOR WOUNDS

Name _____ Class _____ Date _____

Total Care Clinic
Progress Notes

Name: _____ Chart #: _____

DATE	

PROCEDURE 46-1 OBTAINING A THROAT CULTURE SPECIMEN

Name _____ Class _____ Date _____

<table>
<tr><td colspan="2" align="center">Total Care Clinic
Progress Notes</td></tr>
<tr><td colspan="2">Name: _____ Chart #: _____</td></tr>
<tr><td>DATE</td><td></td></tr>
<tr><td></td><td></td></tr>
<tr><td></td><td></td></tr>
<tr><td></td><td></td></tr>
<tr><td></td><td></td></tr>
<tr><td></td><td></td></tr>
<tr><td></td><td></td></tr>
<tr><td></td><td></td></tr>
<tr><td></td><td></td></tr>
<tr><td></td><td></td></tr>
<tr><td></td><td></td></tr>
<tr><td></td><td></td></tr>
<tr><td></td><td></td></tr>
<tr><td></td><td></td></tr>
<tr><td></td><td></td></tr>
<tr><td></td><td></td></tr>
<tr><td></td><td></td></tr>
<tr><td></td><td></td></tr>
</table>

PROCEDURE 46-2 PREPARING MICROBIOLOGICAL SPECIMENS FOR TRANSPORT TO AN OUTPATIENT LABORATORY

Name _____ Class _____ Date _____

‖‖‖‖‖‖‖‖‖‖‖
70Y

Significant Clinical Information

_____ Fasting   _____ Non-Fasting

CHEMISTRY REQUEST

(EMBOSSING AREA)

Submit Separate Specimens (Not Request Forms) for each Frozen Test Requested.

Account No.

Specimen Date Mo Day Yr	Specimen Time Hr Min	Patient Name (Last)	(First, MI)	Sex	Date of Birth Mo Day Yr	Age Yrs Mos

50   8649   9000   4

Patient I.D. #	Physician I.D.	Patient/Resp. Party's Phone #

* I certify that I have read the informed consent on the back and understand its content.

Responsible Party or Insured's Name (Last, First)	Patient's SS #

Patient's Signature

Address	City	State	Zip Code

Resp. Party's Employer

Medicaid Number/HMO #	Medicare #

Physician Name	UPIN #	Physician's Signature	Provider #

Diagnosis Code (ICD-9)	Insurance Code or Company Name and Address	Insurance I.D. #	Workers Comp. Yes No

Group # or Name	Relationship to Insured (Circle One) 1-Self 2-Spouse 3-Other

REV. 6/95

| Urine Random | † ⓤ Total 24hr. Vol. _____ Ht. _____ Wt. _____ |

✸ = EDTA Plasma	Ⓢ = Serum	Ⓡ = Red	Ⓖ = Gray	Ⓑ = Light Blue
AF = Amniotic Fluid	Ⓕ = Frozen Specimen	Ⓛ = Lavender	GN = Green	RB = Royal Blue

Apply Labels to Patient Specimens Only
Patient Control No.

50 8649 9000 4

50 8649 9000 4   50 8649 9000 4   50 8649 9000 4
50 8649 9000 4   50 8649 9000 4   50 8649 9000 4

CHEMISTRY REQUEST

#	Test		#	Test		#	Test	
58867	☐ Basic Chemistry	Ⓢ	1693	☐ Glycohemoglobin, Total	Ⓛ	4465	☐ Prolactin	Ⓢ
1396	☐ Amylase, Serum	Ⓢ	4416	☐ HCG, Beta Chain, Quant	Ⓢ	4747	☐ Prostatic Acid Phosphatase (EIA)	Ⓢ
6254	☐ Antinuclear Antibody (ANA), Qnt.	Ⓢ	1453	☐ Hemoglobin A1C	Ⓛ	10322	☐ Prostate-Specific Antigen (PSA)	Ⓢ
1040	☐ BUN	Ⓢ	6510	☐ Hepatitis B Surf Antigen (HBsAg)	Ⓢ	5199	☐ Prothrombin Time	Ⓑ
7419	☐ Carbamazepine (Tegretol)	Ⓢ	6395	☐ Hepatitis B Surf Antibody (Anti HBs)	Ⓢ	6502	☐ Ra Latex Screen	Ⓢ
5009	☐ CBC With Differential	Ⓛ	58560	☐ Hepatitis Profile I (Diagnostic)	Ⓢ	5215	☐ Sedimentation Rate	Ⓛ
2139	☐ CEA-EIA Roche	△ ✸	46938	☐ Hepatitis Profile II (Follow up)	Ⓢ	6072	☐ STS	Ⓢ
98012	☐ Chlamydia by DNA Probe	△	58552	☐ Hepatitis Profile VII (A and B)	Ⓢ	1149	☐ T₄ (Thyroxine)	Ⓢ
96479	☐ Chlamydia/GC, DNA Probe	△	83824	☐ HIV-1 ABS-EIA	Ⓢ	7336	☐ Theophylline (Theo-Dur)	Ⓢ
1065	☐ Cholesterol, Total	Ⓢ	7625	☐ Lead, Blood	RB	620	☐ Thyroid Profile I	Ⓢ
1370	☐ Creatinine, Serum	Ⓢ	235002	☐ Lipid Profile I (Lipoprotein Analysis)	Ⓢ	27011	☐ Thyroid Profile II	Ⓢ
7385	☐ Digoxin (Lanoxin)	Ⓢ	235028	☐ Lipid Profile III (incl Apolipoproteins)	Ⓢ	4259	☐ TSH, 3rd Generation	Ⓢ
604	☐ Electrolytes (Na, K, Cl)	Ⓢ	7708	☐ Lithium	Ⓢ	810	☐ Vitamin B-12 and Folate	Ⓢ
4598	☐ Ferritin	Ⓢ	505	☐ Liver Profile A	Ⓢ			
4309	☐ Follicle Stim. Hormone (FSH)	Ⓢ	7401	☐ Phenytoin (Dilantin)	Ⓢ		**URINE CHEMISTRY**	
1818	☐ Glucose	Ⓖ	1180	☐ Potassium	Ⓢ	3038	☐ Urinalysis (Microscopic if indicated)	ⓤ
	☐ Glucose Tolerance	Ⓖ	4556	☐ Pregnancy, Serum, Ql.	Ⓢ	3772	☐ Urinalysis, Complete	ⓤ
	Indicate No. Of Tubes ____		53520	☐ Prenatal Profile B with HBsAG	2-L Ⓡ			

ADDITIONAL TESTS

Test #	Name
☐ 1375	24 Hr Urine for Protein ⓤ
☐ 4550	Pregnancy, Urine, Qul ⓤ

Copyright © 2011 by The McGraw-Hill Companies, Inc.

Procedure 47-1 Collecting a Clean-Catch Midstream Urine Specimen

Name _____ Class _____ Date _____

70Y

Significant Clinical Information

_____ Fasting   _____ Non-Fasting

CHEMISTRY REQUEST

(EMBOSSING AREA)

Submit Separate Specimens (Not Request Forms) for each Frozen Test Requested.

Account No.

Specimen Date Mo Day Yr	Specimen Time Hr Min	Patient Name (Last)	(First, MI)	Sex	Date of Birth Mo Day Yr	Age Yrs Mos

50   8649   9000   4

	Patient I.D. #	Physician I.D.	Patient/Resp. Party's Phone #

* I certify that I have read the informed consent on the back and understand its content.

Responsible Party or Insured's Name (Last, First)	Patient's SS #

_____
Patient's Signature

Address	City	State	Zip Code

REV. 6/95

Resp. Party's Employer	Medicaid Number/HMO #	Medicare #

Physician Name	UPIN #	Physician's Signature	Provider #

Diagnosis Code (ICD-9)	Insurance Code or Company Name and Address	Insurance I.D. #	Workers Comp. Yes No

Group # or Name	Relationship to Insured (Circle One) 1-Self 2-Spouse 3-Other

---

Urine Random	† Ⓤ Total 24hr. Vol. _____ Ht. _____ Wt. _____

✷ = EDTA Plasma	Ⓢ = Serum	Ⓡ = Red	Ⓖ = Gray	Ⓑ = Light Blue
AF = Amniotic Fluid	Ⓕ = Frozen Specimen	Ⓛ = Lavender	GN = Green	RB = Royal Blue

Apply Labels to Patient Specimens Only Patient Control No. ➡

50 8649 9000 4

50 8649 9000 4   50 8649 9000 4   50 8649 9000 4

50 8649 9000 4   50 8649 9000 4   50 8649 9000 4

CHEMISTRY REQUEST

Code	Test		Code	Test		Code	Test	
58867	☐ Basic Chemistry	Ⓢ	1693	☐ Glycohemoglobin, Total	Ⓛ	4465	☐ Prolactin	Ⓢ
1396	☐ Amylase, Serum	Ⓢ	4416	☐ HCG, Beta Chain, Quant	Ⓢ	4747	☐ Prostatic Acid Phosphatase (EIA)	Ⓢ
6254	☐ Antinuclear Antibody (ANA), Qnt.	Ⓢ	1453	☐ Hemoglobin A1C	Ⓛ	10322	☐ Prostate-Specific Antigen (PSA)	Ⓢ
1040	☐ BUN	Ⓢ	6510	☐ Hepatitis B Surf Antigen (HBsAg)	Ⓢ	5199	☐ Prothrombin Time	Ⓑ
7419	☐ Carbamazepine (Tegretol)	Ⓢ	6395	☐ Hepatitis B Surf Antibody (Anti HBs)	Ⓢ	6502	☐ Ra Latex Screen	Ⓢ
5009	☐ CBC With Differential	Ⓛ	58560	☐ Hepatitis Profile I (Diagnostic)	Ⓢ	5215	☐ Sedimentation Rate	Ⓛ
2139	☐ CEA-EIA Roche	△ ✷	46938	☐ Hepatitis Profile II (Follow up)	Ⓢ	6072	☐ STS	Ⓢ
98012	☐ Chlamydia by DNA Probe	△	58552	☐ Hepatitis Profile VII (A and B)	Ⓢ	1149	☐ T₄ (Thyroxine)	Ⓢ
96479	☐ Chlamydia/GC, DNA Probe	△	83824	☐ HIV-1 ABS-EIA	Ⓢ	7336	☐ Theophylline (Theo-Dur)	Ⓢ
1065	☐ Cholesterol, Total	Ⓢ	7625	☐ Lead, Blood	RB	620	☐ Thyroid Profile I	Ⓢ
1370	☐ Creatinine, Serum	Ⓢ	235002	☐ Lipid Profile I (Lipoprotein Analysis)	Ⓢ	27011	☐ Thyroid Profile II	Ⓢ
7385	☐ Digoxin (Lanoxin)	Ⓢ	235028	☐ Lipid Profile III (incl Apolipoproteins)	Ⓢ	4259	☐ TSH, 3rd Generation	Ⓢ
604	☐ Electrolytes (Na, K, Cl)	Ⓢ	7708	☐ Lithium	Ⓢ	810	☐ Vitamin B-12 and Folate	Ⓢ
4598	☐ Ferritin	Ⓢ	505	☐ Liver Profile A	Ⓢ			
4309	☐ Follicle Stim. Hormone (FSH)	Ⓢ	7401	☐ Phenytoin (Dilantin)	Ⓢ			
1818	☐ Glucose	Ⓖ	1180	☐ Potassium	Ⓢ			
	☐ Glucose Tolerance	Ⓖ	4556	☐ Pregnancy, Serum, Ql.	Ⓢ			
	Indicate No. Of Tubes _____		53520	☐ Prenatal Profile B with HBsAG	2-L Ⓡ			

ADDITIONAL TESTS

Test # | Name

☐ 1375 24 Hr Urine for Protein Ⓤ

☐ 4550 Pregnancy, Urine, Qul Ⓤ

URINE CHEMISTRY

3038	☐ Urinalysis (Microscopic if indicated)	Ⓤ
3772	☐ Urinalysis, Complete	Ⓤ

PROCEDURE 47-2 COLLECTING A URINE SPECIMEN FROM A PEDIATRIC PATIENT

Name _____ Class _____ Date _____

<table>
<tr><td colspan="2" align="center">**Total Care Clinic**
Progress Notes</td></tr>
<tr><td colspan="2">Name: _____ Chart #: _____</td></tr>
<tr><td>DATE</td><td></td></tr>
<tr><td></td><td></td></tr>
<tr><td></td><td></td></tr>
<tr><td></td><td></td></tr>
<tr><td></td><td></td></tr>
<tr><td></td><td></td></tr>
<tr><td></td><td></td></tr>
<tr><td></td><td></td></tr>
<tr><td></td><td></td></tr>
<tr><td></td><td></td></tr>
<tr><td></td><td></td></tr>
<tr><td></td><td></td></tr>
<tr><td></td><td></td></tr>
<tr><td></td><td></td></tr>
<tr><td></td><td></td></tr>
<tr><td></td><td></td></tr>
<tr><td></td><td></td></tr>
<tr><td></td><td></td></tr>
<tr><td></td><td></td></tr>
</table>

Copyright © 2011 by The McGraw-Hill Companies, Inc.

PROCEDURE 47-3 ESTABLISHING A CHAIN OF CUSTODY FOR A URINE SPECIMEN

Name _____ Class _____ Date _____

Total Care Clinic
Newfield, New Jersey 07655-3213
201-555-4000

Drug Screen Consent Form

A urine drug test is required by_____ as part of your pre-employment screening. Please provide us with a list of all medications that you are presently taking.

_____

_____

_____

_____

_____

I understand that my prospective or continued employment is contingent on a successful screening.

Date: _____ Signature:_____

Witness: _____

Name _____ Class _____ Date _____

Total Care Clinic
Progress Notes

Name: _____ Chart #: _____

DATE	

PROCEDURE 47-3 ESTABLISHING A CHAIN OF CUSTODY FOR A URINE SPECIMEN *(concluded)*

Name _____ Class _____ Date _____

CHAIN OF CUSTODY FORM

TOTAL CARE LABORATORY

542 East Park Boulevard
Funton, XY 12345-6789
(521) 234-0001

SPECIMEN I.D. NO: _____

STEP 1—TO BE COMPLETED BY COLLECTOR OR EMPLOYER REPRESENTATIVE.

Employer Name, Address, and I.D. No.:　　OR　　Medical Review Officer Name and Address:

_____　　_____

_____　　_____

_____　　_____

Donor Social Security No. or Employee I.D. No.: _____

Donor I.D. verified:　❐ Photo I.D.　❐ Employer Representative _____
Signature

Reason for test: (check one)　❐ Preemployment　❐ Random　❐ Postaccident
　　　　　　　　　　　　　　❐ Periodic　❐ Reasonable suspicion/cause
　　　　　　　　　　　　　　❐ Return to duty　❐ Other (specify)

Test(s) to be performed: _____　Total tests ordered: ☐

Type of specimen obtained:　❐ Urine　❐ Blood　❐ Semen　❐ Other (specify)

Submit only one specimen with each requisition.

STEP 2—TO BE COMPLETED BY COLLECTOR.

For urine specimens, read temperature within 4 minutes of collection.
Check here if specimen temperature is within range.　❐ Yes, 90°–100°F/32°–38°C
Or record actual temperature here: _____

STEP 3—TO BE COMPLETED BY COLLECTOR.

Collection site: _____　Address _____
City _____　State _____　Zip _____　Phone _____
Collection date: _____　Time: _____　❐ a.m.　❐ p.m.

I certify that the specimen identified on this form is the specimen presented to me by the donor identified in step 1 above, and that it was collected, labeled, and sealed in the donor's presence.

Collector's name: _____　Signature of collector _____

STEP 4—TO BE INITIATED BY DONOR AND COMPLETED AS NECESSARY THEREAFTER.

Purpose of change	Released by Signature	Received by Signature	Date
A. Provide specimen for testing			
B. Shipment to Laboratory			
C.			

Comments:

STEP 5—TO BE COMPLETED BY THE LABORATORY:

Specimen package seal(s) intact when received in lab?　❐ Yes　❐ No. If no, explain.
Laboratory receiver's initials _____

Copy 1 - Original - Must accompany specimen to laboratory.

PROCEDURE 47-4 MESURING SPECIFIC GRAVITY WITH A REFRACTOMETER

Name _____ Class _____ Date _____

Total Care Clinic
Laboratory Report Form

Patient Name _____ Medical Record # _____ Age _____ Sex _____

Address _____ Phone _____

Referring Physician _____

Laboratory Findings:

Date	Blood Test	Patient Result	Normal Value/Range

Date	Urinalysis	Patient Result	Normal Value/Range

Test completed by: _____   _____
(Print name)   (Signature)

PROCEDURE 47-5 PERFORMING A REAGENT STRIP TEST

Name _____ Class _____ Date _____

Total Care Clinic
Laboratory Report Form

Patient Name _____ Medical Record # _____ Age _____ Sex_____

Address _____ Phone _____

Referring Physician _____

Laboratory Findings:

Date	Blood Test	Patient Result	Normal Value/Range

Date	Urinalysis	Patient Result	Normal Value/Range

Test completed by: _____ _____
                (Print name)   (Signature)

PROCEDURE 47-6 PREGNANCY TESTING USING THE EIA METHOD

Name _____ Class _____ Date _____

Total Care Clinic
Progress Notes

Name: _____ Chart #: _____

DATE	

Name _____ Class _____ Date _____

Quality Control Daily Log

Name of Unit	Glucose Control Solution	Strip Lot No./ Exp. Date	Low Control Value 35–65 mg/dL	High Control Value 175–235 mg/dL	Analyzed By	Date	Remedial Action Taken If Control Values Abnormal	Retest After Remedial Action Taken

Procedure 47-7 Processing a Urine Specimen for Microscopic Examination of Sediment

Name _____ Class _____ Date _____

Total Care Clinic
Laboratory Report Form

Patient Name _____Medical Record # _____ Age _____ Sex_____

Address _____ Phone _____

Referring Physician _____

Laboratory Findings:

Date	Blood Test	Patient Result	Normal Value/Range

Date	Urinalysis	Patient Result	Normal Value/Range

Test completed by: _____ _____
                          (Print name)   (Signature)

Name _____ Class _____ Date _____

Total Care Clinic
Progress Notes

Name: _____ Chart #: _____

DATE	

PROCEDURE 48-1 QUALITY CONTROL PROCEDURES FOR BLOOD SPECIMEN COLLECTION

Name _____ Class _____ Date _____

	70Y		Significant Clinical Information

Significant Clinical Information

_____ Fasting   _____ Non-Fasting

CHEMISTRY REQUEST

(EMBOSSING AREA)

Submit Separate Specimens (Not Request Forms) for each Frozen Test Requested.

Account No.

Specimen Date Mo Day Yr	Specimen Time Hr Min	Patient Name (Last)	(First, MI)	Sex	Date of Birth Mo Day Yr	Age Yrs Mos

50   8649   9000   4

Patient I.D. #	Physician I.D.	Patient/Resp. Party's Phone #

* I certify that I have read the informed consent on the back and understand its content.

Responsible Party or Insured's Name (Last, First)	Patient's SS #

Patient's Signature

Address	City	State	Zip Code

REV. 6/95

Resp. Party's Employer	Medicaid Number/HMO #	Medicare #

Physician Name	UPIN #	Physician's Signature	Provider #

Diagnosis Code (ICD-9)	Insurance Code or Company Name and Address	Insurance I.D. #	Workers Comp. Yes No

Group # or Name	Relationship to Insured (Circle One) 1-Self 2-Spouse 3-Other

---

Urine Random	† Ⓤ Total 24hr. Vol. _____ Ht. _____ Wt. _____

✱ = EDTA Plasma	Ⓢ = Serum	Ⓡ = Red	Ⓖ = Gray	Ⓑ = Light Blue
ⒶⒻ = Amniotic Fluid	Ⓕ = Frozen Specimen	Ⓛ = Lavender	ⒼⓃ = Green	ⓇⒷ = Royal Blue

Apply Labels to Patient Specimens Only
Patient Control No. ➔

50 8649 9000 4

50 8649 9000 4	50 8649 9000 4	50 8649 9000 4

CHEMISTRY REQUEST

58867	☐ Basic Chemistry	Ⓢ	1693	☐ Glycohemoglobin, Total	Ⓛ	4465	☐ Prolactin	Ⓢ
1396	☐ Amylase, Serum	Ⓢ	4416	☐ HCG, Beta Chain, Quant	Ⓢ	4747	☐ Prostatic Acid Phosphatase (EIA)	Ⓢ
6254	☐ Antinuclear Antibody (ANA), Qnt.	Ⓢ	1453	☐ Hemoglobin A1C	Ⓛ	10322	☐ Prostate-Specific Antigen (PSA)	Ⓢ
1040	☐ BUN	Ⓢ	6510	☐ Hepatitis B Surf Antigen (HBsAg)	Ⓢ	5199	☐ Prothrombin Time	Ⓑ
7419	☐ Carbamazepine (Tegretol)	Ⓢ	6395	☐ Hepatitis B Surf Antibody (Anti HBs)	Ⓢ	6502	☐ Ra Latex Screen	Ⓢ
5009	☐ CBC With Differential	Ⓛ	58560	☐ Hepatitis Profile I (Diagnostic)	Ⓢ	5215	☐ Sedimentation Rate	Ⓛ
2139	☐ CEA-EIA Roche	△ ✱	46938	☐ Hepatitis Profile II (Follow up)	Ⓢ	6072	☐ STS	Ⓢ
98012	☐ Chlamydia by DNA Probe	△	58552	☐ Hepatitis Profile VII (A and B)	Ⓢ	1149	☐ T₄ (Thyroxine)	Ⓢ
96479	☐ Chlamydia/GC, DNA Probe	△	83824	☐ HIV-1 ABS-EIA	Ⓢ	7336	☐ Theophylline (Theo-Dur)	Ⓢ
1065	☐ Cholesterol, Total	Ⓢ	7625	☐ Lead, Blood	ⓇⒷ	620	☐ Thyroid Profile I	Ⓢ
1370	☐ Creatinine, Serum	Ⓢ	235002	☐ Lipid Profile I (Lipoprotein Analysis)	Ⓢ	27011	☐ Thyroid Profile II	Ⓢ
7385	☐ Digoxin (Lanoxin)	Ⓢ	235028	☐ Lipid Profile III (incl Apolipoproteins)	Ⓢ	4259	☐ TSH, 3rd Generation	Ⓢ
604	☐ Electrolytes (Na, K, Cl)	Ⓢ	7708	☐ Lithium	Ⓢ	810	☐ Vitamin B-12 and Folate	Ⓢ
4598	☐ Ferritin	Ⓢ	505	☐ Liver Profile A	Ⓢ			
4309	☐ Follicle Stim. Hormone (FSH)	Ⓢ	7401	☐ Phenytoin (Dilantin)	Ⓢ		**URINE CHEMISTRY**	
1818	☐ Glucose	Ⓖ	1180	☐ Potassium	Ⓢ	3038	☐ Urinalysis (Microscopic if indicated)	Ⓤ
	☐ Glucose Tolerance	Ⓖ	4556	☐ Pregnancy, Serum, Ql.	Ⓢ	3772	☐ Urinalysis, Complete	Ⓤ
	Indicate No. Of Tubes _____		53520	☐ Prenatal Profile B with HBsAG	2-L Ⓡ			

ADDITIONAL TESTS

Test #		Name
☐ 1375	24 Hr Urine for Protein	Ⓤ
☐ 4550	Pregnancy, Urine, Qul	Ⓤ

Name _____ Class _____ Date _____

Total Care Clinic
Progress Notes

Name: _____ Chart #: _____

DATE	

Name _____ Class _____ Date _____

70Y

Submit Separate Specimens (Not Request Forms) for each Frozen Test Requested.

Account No.

Specimen Date Mo Day Yr	Specimen Time Hr Min	Patient Name (Last)	(First, MI)	Sex	Date of Birth Mo Day Yr	Age Yrs Mos

REV. 6/95

50 8649 9000 4

* I certify that I have read the informed consent on the back and understand its content.

Patient's Signature

Patient I.D. #	Physician I.D.	Patient/Resp. Party's Phone #
Responsible Party or Insured's Name (Last, First)		Patient's SS #
Address	City	State Zip Code

Resp. Party's Employer | Medicaid Number/HMO # | Medicare #

Physician Name	UPIN #	Physician's Signature	Provider #

Diagnosis Code (ICD-9)	Insurance Code or Company Name and Address	Insurance I.D. #	Workers Comp. Yes No

Group # or Name	Relationship to Insured (Circle One) 1-Self 2-Spouse 3-Other

Urine Random   † (U) Total 24hr. Vol. _____ Ht. _____ Wt. _____

| ✱ = EDTA Plasma | (S) = Serum | (R) = Red | (G) = Gray | (B) = Light Blue |
| (AF) = Amniotic Fluid | (F) = Frozen Specimen | (L) = Lavender | (GN) = Green | (RB) = Royal Blue |

Apply Labels to Patient Specimens Only Patient Control No. ➔

50 8649 9000 4

50 8649 9000 4 | 50 8649 9000 4 | 50 8649 9000 4 | 50 8649 9000 4

50 8649 9000 4 | 50 8649 9000 4 | 50 8649 9000 4

CHEMISTRY REQUEST

#	Test		#	Test		#	Test	
58867	☐ Basic Chemistry	(S)	1693	☐ Glycohemoglobin, Total	(L)	4465	☐ Prolactin	(S)
1396	☐ Amylase, Serum	(S)	4416	☐ HCG, Beta Chain, Quant	(S)	4747	☐ Prostatic Acid Phosphatase (EIA)	(S)
6254	☐ Antinuclear Antibody (ANA), Qnt.	(S)	1453	☐ Hemoglobin A1C	(L)	10322	☐ Prostate-Specific Antigen (PSA)	(S)
1040	☐ BUN	(S)	6510	☐ Hepatitis B Surf Antigen (HBsAg)	(S)	5199	☐ Prothrombin Time	(B)
7419	☐ Carbamazepine (Tegretol)	(S)	6395	☐ Hepatitis B Surf Antibody (Anti HBs)	(S)	6502	☐ Ra Latex Screen	(S)
5009	☐ CBC With Differential	(L)	58560	☐ Hepatitis Profile I (Diagnostic)	(S)	5215	☐ Sedimentation Rate	(L)
2139	☐ CEA-EIA Roche	△ ✱	46938	☐ Hepatitis Profile II (Follow up)	(S)	6072	☐ STS	(S)
98012	☐ Chlamydia by DNA Probe	△	58552	☐ Hepatitis Profile VII (A and B)	(S)	1149	☐ T4 (Thyroxine)	(S)
96479	☐ Chlamydia/GC, DNA Probe	△	83824	☐ HIV-1 ABS-EIA	(S)	7336	☐ Theophylline (Theo-Dur)	(S)
1065	☐ Cholesterol, Total	(S)	7625	☐ Lead, Blood	(RB)	620	☐ Thyroid Profile I	(S)
1370	☐ Creatinine, Serum	(S)	235002	☐ Lipid Profile I (Lipoprotein Analysis)	(S)	27011	☐ Thyroid Profile II	(S)
7385	☐ Digoxin (Lanoxin)	(S)	235028	☐ Lipid Profile III (incl Apolipoproteins)	(S)	4259	☐ TSH, 3rd Generation	(S)
604	☐ Electrolytes (Na, K, Cl)	(S)	7708	☐ Lithium	(S)	810	☐ Vitamin B-12 and Folate	(S)
4598	☐ Ferritin	(S)	505	☐ Liver Profile A	(S)			
4309	☐ Follicle Stim. Hormone (FSH)	(S)	7401	☐ Phenytoin (Dilantin)	(S)		**URINE CHEMISTRY**	
1818	☐ Glucose	(G)	1180	☐ Potassium	(S)	3038	☐ Urinalysis (Microscopic if indicated)	(U)
	☐ Glucose Tolerance	(G)	4556	☐ Pregnancy, Serum, Ql.	(S)	3772	☐ Urinalysis, Complete	(U)
	Indicate No. Of Tubes _____		53520	☐ Prenatal Profile B with HBsAG	(2-L) (R)			

ADDITIONAL TESTS

Test # | Name

☐ 1375 24 Hr Urine for Protein (U)

☐ 4550 Pregnancy, Urine, Qul (U)

Procedure 48-2 Performing Venipuncture Using an Evacuation System *(concluded)*

Name _____ Class _____ Date _____

Total Care Clinic
Laboratory Report Form

Patient Name _____ Medical Record # _____ Age _____ Sex_____

Address _____ Phone _____

Referring Physician _____

Laboratory Findings:

Date	Blood Test	Patient Result	Normal Value/Range

Date	Urinalysis	Patient Result	Normal Value/Range

Test completed by: _____ _____
                          (Print name)   (Signature)

PROCEDURE 48-3 PERFORMING CAPILLARY PUNCTURE

Name _____ Class _____ Date _____

Total Care Clinic
Progress Notes

Name: _____ Chart #: _____

DATE	

Name _____ Class _____ Date _____

‖‖‖‖‖‖‖‖‖‖‖‖
70Y

Significant Clinical Information

_____ Fasting   _____ Non-Fasting

CHEMISTRY REQUEST

(EMBOSSING AREA)

Account No.

REV. 6/95

Specimen Date Mo Day Yr	Specimen Time Hr Min	Patient Name (Last)	(First, MI)	Sex	Date of Birth Mo Day Yr	Age Yrs Mos

50 8649 9000 4

Patient I.D. #	Physician I.D.	Patient/Resp. Party's Phone #

* I certify that I have read the informed consent on the back and understand its content.

Responsible Party or Insured's Name (Last, First)	Patient's SS #

Patient's Signature

Address	City	State	Zip Code

Resp. Party's Employer

Medicaid Number/HMO #	Medicare #

Physician Name	UPIN #	Physician's Signature	Provider #

Diagnosis Code (ICD-9)	Insurance Code or Company Name and Address	Insurance I.D. #	Workers Comp. Yes No

Group # or Name	Relationship to Insured (Circle One) 1-Self 2-Spouse 3-Other

---

Urine Random   † Ⓤ Total 24hr. Vol. _____ Ht. _____ Wt. _____

✹ = EDTA Plasma	Ⓢ = Serum	Ⓡ = Red	Ⓖ = Gray	Ⓑ = Light Blue
AF = Amniotic Fluid	Ⓕ = Frozen Specimen	Ⓛ = Lavender	GN = Green	RB = Royal Blue

Apply Labels to Patient Specimens Only
Patient Control No. →

50 8649 9000 4

50 8649 9000 4

50 8649 9000 4

50 8649 9000 4

50 8649 9000 4

CHEMISTRY REQUEST

Code	Test		Code	Test		Code	Test	
58867	☐ Basic Chemistry	Ⓢ	1693	☐ Glycohemoglobin, Total	Ⓛ	4465	☐ Prolactin	Ⓢ
1396	☐ Amylase, Serum	Ⓢ	4416	☐ HCG, Beta Chain, Quant	Ⓢ	4747	☐ Prostatic Acid Phosphatase (EIA)	Ⓢ
6254	☐ Antinuclear Antibody (ANA), Qnt.	Ⓢ	1453	☐ Hemoglobin A1C	Ⓛ	10322	☐ Prostate-Specific Antigen (PSA)	Ⓢ
1040	☐ BUN	Ⓢ	6510	☐ Hepatitis B Surf Antigen (HBsAg)	Ⓢ	5199	☐ Prothrombin Time	Ⓑ
7419	☐ Carbamazepine (Tegretol)	Ⓢ	6395	☐ Hepatitis B Surf Antibody (Anti HBs)	Ⓢ	6502	☐ Ra Latex Screen	Ⓢ
5009	☐ CBC With Differential	Ⓛ	58560	☐ Hepatitis Profile I (Diagnostic)	Ⓢ	5215	☐ Sedimentation Rate	Ⓛ
2139	☐ CEA-EIA Roche	△ ✹	46938	☐ Hepatitis Profile II (Follow up)	Ⓢ	6072	☐ STS	Ⓢ
98012	☐ Chlamydia by DNA Probe	△	58552	☐ Hepatitis Profile VII (A and B)	Ⓢ	1149	☐ T₄ (Thyroxine)	Ⓢ
96479	☐ Chlamydia/GC, DNA Probe	△	83824	☐ HIV-1 ABS-EIA	Ⓢ	7336	☐ Theophylline (Theo-Dur)	Ⓢ
1065	☐ Cholesterol, Total	Ⓢ	7625	☐ Lead, Blood	RB	620	☐ Thyroid Profile I	Ⓢ
1370	☐ Creatinine, Serum	Ⓢ	235002	☐ Lipid Profile I (Lipoprotein Analysis)	Ⓢ	27011	☐ Thyroid Profile II	Ⓢ
7385	☐ Digoxin (Lanoxin)	Ⓢ	235028	☐ Lipid Profile III (incl Apolipoproteins)	Ⓢ	4259	☐ TSH, 3rd Generation	Ⓢ
604	☐ Electrolytes (Na, K, Cl)	Ⓢ	7708	☐ Lithium	Ⓢ	810	☐ Vitamin B-12 and Folate	Ⓢ
4598	☐ Ferritin	Ⓢ	505	☐ Liver Profile A	Ⓢ			
4309	☐ Follicle Stim. Hormone (FSH)	Ⓢ	7401	☐ Phenytoin (Dilantin)	Ⓢ		**URINE CHEMISTRY**	
1818	☐ Glucose	Ⓖ	1180	☐ Potassium	Ⓢ	3038	☐ Urinalysis (Microscopic if indicated)	Ⓤ
	☐ Glucose Tolerance	Ⓖ	4556	☐ Pregnancy, Serum, Ql.	Ⓢ	3772	☐ Urinalysis, Complete	Ⓤ
	Indicate No. Of Tubes _____		53520	☐ Prenatal Profile B with HBsAG	(2-L) Ⓡ			

ADDITIONAL TESTS

Test #	Name
☐ 1375	24 Hr Urine for Protein Ⓤ
☐ 4550	Pregnancy, Urine, Qul Ⓤ

PROCEDURE 48-5 MEASURING HEMATOCRIT PERCENTAGE AFTER CENTRIFUGE

Name _____ Class _____ Date _____

Total Care Clinic
Laboratory Report Form

Patient Name _____ Medical Record # _____ Age _____ Sex_____

Address _____ Phone _____

Referring Physician _____

Laboratory Findings:

Date	Blood Test	Patient Result	Normal Value/Range

Date	Urinalysis	Patient Result	Normal Value/Range

Test completed by: _____ _____
                  (Print name)   (Signature)

PROCEDURE 48-6 MEASURING BLOOD GLUCOSE USING A HANDHELD GLUCOMETER

Name _____ Class _____ Date _____

Total Care Clinic
Laboratory Report Form

Patient Name _____Medical Record # _____ Age _____ Sex_____

Address _____ Phone _____

Referring Physician _____

Laboratory Findings:

Date	Blood Test	Patient Result	Normal Value/Range

Date	Urinalysis	Patient Result	Normal Value/Range

Test completed by: _____ _____
                         (Print name)   (Signature)

Name _____ Class _____ Date _____

Quality Control Daily Log

Name of Unit	Glucose Control Solution	Strip Lot No./ Exp. Date	Low Control Value 35–65 mg/dL	High Control Value 175–235 mg/dL	Analyzed By	Date	Remedial Action Taken If Control Values Abnormal	Retest After Remedial Action Taken

PROCEDURE 49-1 EDUCATING PATIENTS ABOUT DAILY WATER REQUIREMENTS

Name _____ Class _____ Date _____

Total Care Clinic
Progress Notes

Name: _____ Chart #:_____

DATE	

PROCEDURE 49-2 TEACHING PATIENTS HOW TO READ FOOD LABELS

Name _____ Class _____ Date _____

<table>
<tr><td colspan="2" style="text-align:center">Total Care Clinic
Progress Notes</td></tr>
<tr><td colspan="2">Name: _____ Chart #: _____</td></tr>
<tr><td>DATE</td><td></td></tr>
<tr><td></td><td></td></tr>
<tr><td></td><td></td></tr>
<tr><td></td><td></td></tr>
<tr><td></td><td></td></tr>
<tr><td></td><td></td></tr>
<tr><td></td><td></td></tr>
<tr><td></td><td></td></tr>
<tr><td></td><td></td></tr>
<tr><td></td><td></td></tr>
<tr><td></td><td></td></tr>
<tr><td></td><td></td></tr>
<tr><td></td><td></td></tr>
<tr><td></td><td></td></tr>
<tr><td></td><td></td></tr>
<tr><td></td><td></td></tr>
<tr><td></td><td></td></tr>
<tr><td></td><td></td></tr>
<tr><td></td><td></td></tr>
</table>

Procedure 49-3 Alerting Patients with Food Allergies to the Dangers or Common Foods

Name _____ Class _____ Date _____

Total Care Clinic
Progress Notes

Name: _____ Chart #: _____

DATE	

PROCEDURE 50-1 HELPING THE PHYSICIAN COMPLY WITH THE CONTROLLED SUBSTANCES ACT OF 1970

Name _____ Class _____ Date _____

Sample Only

Form-224	APPLICATION FOR REGISTRATION Under the Controlled Substances Act	APPROVED OMB NO 1117-0014 FORM DEA-224 (10-06) Previous editions are obsolete

---

INSTRUCTIONS

Save time—apply on-line at www.deadiversion.usdoj.gov

1. To apply by mail complete this application. Keep a copy for your records.
2. Print clearly, using black or blue ink, or use a typewriter.
3. Mail this form to the address provided in Section 7 or use enclosed envelope.
4. Include the correct payment amount. FEE IS NON-REFUNDABLE.
5. If you have any questions call 800-882-9539 prior to submitting your application.

IMPORTANT: DO NOT SEND THIS APPLICATION AND APPLY ON-LINE.

DEA OFFICIAL USE:

Do you have other DEA registration numbers?
☐ NO   ☐ YES

MAIL-TO ADDRESS   Please print mailing address changes to the right of the address in this box.

FEE FOR THREE (3) YEARS IS $551
FEE IS NON-REFUNDABLE

SECTION 1   APPLICANT IDENTIFICATION   ☐ Individual Registration   ☐ Business Registration

Name 1   (Last Name of individual -OR- Business or Facility Name)

Name 2   (First Name and Middle Name of individual -OR- Continuation of business name)

Street Address Line 1 (if applying for fee exemption, this must be address of the fee exempt institution)

Address Line 2

City   **State**   **Zip Code**

Business Phone Number   **Point of Contact**

Business Fax Number   **Email Address**

DEBT COLLECTION INFORMATION

Mandatory pursuant to Debt Collection Improvements Act

Social Security Number (if registration is for individual)

Provide **SSN** or **TIN**.
See additional information note #3 on page 4.

Tax Identification Number (if registration is for business)

FOR Practitioner or MLP ONLY:

Professional Degree: *select from list only*

Professional School:

Year of Graduation:

National Provider Identification:

Date of Birth (*MM-DD-YYYY*):

SECTION 2
BUSINESS ACTIVITY

Check one business activity box only

☐ Central Fill Pharmacy
☐ Retail Pharmacy
☐ Nursing Home
☐ Automated Dispensing System

☐ Practitioner (DDS, DMD, DO, DPM, DVM, MD or PHD)
☐ Practitioner Military (DDS, DMD, DO, DPM, DVM, MD or PHD)
☐ Mid-level Practitioner (MLP) (DOM, HMD, MP, ND, NP, OD, PA, or RPH)
☐ Euthanasia Technician

☐ Ambulance Service
☐ Animal Shelter
☐ Hospital/Clinic
☐ Teaching Institution

FOR Automated Dispensing System (ADS) ONLY:

DEA Registration # of Retail Pharmacy for this ADS

An ADS is automatically fee-exempt.
Skip Section 6 and Section 7 on page 2.
You must attach a notorized affidavit.

SECTION 3
DRUG SCHEDULES

Check all that apply

☐ Schedule II Narcotic
☐ Schedule II Non-Narcotic

☐ Schedule III Narcotic
☐ Schedule III Non-Narcotic

☐ Schedule IV
☐ Schedule V

Name _____ Class _____ Date _____

Sample Only

SECTION 4
STATE LICENSE(S)

Be sure to include both state license numbers if applicable

You MUST be currently authorized to prescribe, distribute, dispense, conduct research, or otherwise handle the controlled substances in the schedules for which you are applying under the laws of the **state** or jurisdiction in which you are operating or propose to operate.

State License Number (required)

What state was this license issued in? _____

Expiration Date (required)   /   /
MM - DD - YYYY

State Controlled Substance License Number (if required)

What state was this license issued in? _____

Expiration Date   /   /
MM - DD - YYYY

SECTION 5
LIABILITY

IMPORTANT

All questions in this section must be answered.

1. Has the applicant ever been **convicted of a crime** in connection with controlled substance(s) under state or federal law, or is any such action pending?
   YES ☐   NO ☐

   Date(s) of incident MM-DD-YYYY: ☐☐–☐☐–☐☐☐☐

2. Has the applicant ever surrendered (for cause) or had a **federal** controlled substance registration revoked, suspended, restricted, or denied, or is any such action pending?
   YES ☐   NO ☐

   Date(s) of incident MM-DD-YYYY: ☐☐–☐☐–☐☐☐☐

3. Has the applicant ever surrendered (for cause) or had a **state** professional license or controlled substance registration revoked, suspended, denied, restricted, or placed on probation, or is any such action pending?
   YES ☐   NO ☐

   Date(s) of incident MM-DD-YYYY: ☐☐–☐☐–☐☐☐☐

4. If the applicant is a **corporation** (other than a corporation whose stock is owned and traded by the public), association, partnership, or pharmacy, has any officer, partner, stockholder, or proprietor been **convicted of a crime** in connection with controlled substance(s) under state or federal law, or ever surrendered, for cause, or had a **federal** controlled substance registration revoked, suspended, restricted, denied, or ever had a **state** professional license or controlled substance registration revoked, suspended, denied, restricted or placed on probation, or is any such action pending?
   YES ☐   NO ☐

   Date(s) of incident MM-DD-YYYY: ☐☐–☐☐–☐☐☐☐

   Note: If question 4 does not apply to you, be sure to mark 'NO'. It will slow down processing of your application if you leave it blank.

EXPLANATION OF "YES" ANSWERS

Applicants who have answered "YES" to any of the four questions above **must provide a statement to explain each "YES" answer.**

Use this space or attach a separate sheet and return with application

Liability question # _____

Location(s) of incident: _____

Nature of incident:

Disposition of incident:

SECTION 6   EXEMPTION FROM APPLICATION FEE

☐ Check this box if the applicant is a federal, state, or local government official or institution. Does not apply to contractor-operated institutions.

Business or Facility Name of Fee Exempt Institution. **Be sure to enter the address of this exempt institution in Section 1.**

The undersigned hereby certifies that the applicant named hereon is a federal, state or local government official or institution, and is exempt from payment of the application fee.

FEE EXEMPT CERTIFIER

Provide the name and phone number of the certifying official

Signature of certifying official (other than applicant)   Date

Print or type name and title of certifying official   Telephone No. (required for verification)

SECTION 7
METHOD OF PAYMENT

Check one form of payment only

Sign if paying by credit card

☐ Check   Make check payable to: **Drug Enforcement Administration**
See page 4 of instructions for important information.

☐ American Express   ☐ Discover   ☐ Master Card   ☐ Visa

Credit Card Number   Expiration Date

Signature of Card Holder

Printed Name of Card Holder

Mail this form with payment to:

U.S. Department of Justice
Drug Enforcement Administration
P.O. Box 28083
Washington, DC 20038-8083

FEE IS NON-REFUNDABLE

SECTION 8
APPLICANTS SIGNATURE

Sign in ink

I certify that the foregoing information furnished on this application is true and correct.

Signature of applicant (sign in ink)   Date

Print or type name and title of applicant

WARNING: Section 843(a)(4)(A) of Title 21, United States Code states that any person who knowingly or intentionally furnishes false or fraudulent information in this application is subject to imprisonment for not more than four years, a fine of not more than $30,000,00 or both.

Name _____ Class _____ Date _____

Sample Only

DEA Form-222 **(Oct. 1992)**	**U.S. OFFICIAL ORDER FORMS - SCHEDULES I & II** Drug Enforcement Administration **SUPPLIER'S Copy 1**

See Reverse of PURCHASER'S Copy for Instructions	No order form may be issued for Schedule I and II substances unless a completed application form has been received. (21 CFR 1305.04).	**OMB APPROVAL No. 1117-0010**

To: (Name of Supplier)

Street Address

Address

City   State

Date (MM-DD-YYYY)   Suppliers DEA Registration No.

To Be Filled in By PURCHASER

To Be Filled in By SUPPLIER

Line No.	No. of Packages	Size of Package	Name of Item	National Drug Code	Packages Shipped	Date Shipped
1						
2						
3						
4						
5						
6						
7						
8						
9						
10						

◄ **LAST LINE COMPLETED**   *(MUST BE 10 OR LESS)*

Signature of **PURCHASER** or Attorney or Agent

Date Issued

DEA Registration No.

Schedules

Name and Address of Registrant

Registered As a

No. of This Order Form

Name _____ Class _____ Date _____

Sample Only

OMB Approval No. 1117-0007	U.S. Department of Justice/Drug Enforcement Administration **REGISTRANTS INVENTORY OF DRUGS SURRENDERED**	PACKAGE NO.

The following schedule is an inventory of controlled substances which is hereby surrendered to you for proper disposition.

FROM: *(Include Name, Street, City, State and ZIP Code in space provided below.)*

Signature of applicant or authorized agent

Registrant's DEA Number

Registrant's Telephone Number

NOTE: CERTIFIED MAIL (Return Receipt Requested) IS REQUIRED FOR SHIPMENTS OF DRUGS VIA U.S. POSTAL SERVICE. See instructions on reverse (page 2) of form.

NAME OF DRUG OR PREPARATION (Registrants will fill in Columns 1, 2, 3, and 4 ONLY.)	Number of Containers	CONTENTS (Number of grams, tablets, ounces or other units per container)	Controlled Substance Content, (Each Unit)	FOR DEA USE ONLY DISPOSITION	QUANTITY GMS.	QUANTITY MGS.
1	2	3	4	5	6	7
1						
2						
3						
4						
5						
6						
23						
24						

The controlled substances surrendered in accordance with Title 21 of the Code of Federal Regulations, Section 1307.21, have been received in _____ packages purporting to contain the drugs listed on this inventory and have been: **(1) Forwarded tape-sealed without opening; (2) Destroyed as indicated and the remainder forwarded tape-sealed after verifying contents; (3) Forwarded tape-sealed after verifying contents.

DATE _____   DESTROYED BY: _____

**Strike out lines not applicable.   WITNESSED BY: _____

INSTRUCTIONS

1. List the name of the drug in column 1, the number of containers in column 2, the size of each container in column 3, and in column 4 the controlled substance content of each unit described in column 3; e.g., morphine sulfate tabs., 3 pkgs., 100 tabs., 1/4 gr. (16 mg.) or morphine sulfate tabs., 1 pkg., 83 tabs., 1/2 gr. (32 mg.), etc.

2. All packages included on a single line should be identical in name, content and controlled substance strength.

3. Prepare this form in quadruplicate. Mail two (2) copies of this form to the Special Agent in Charge, under separate cover. Enclose one additional copy in the shipment with the drugs. Retain one copy for your records. One copy will be returned to you as a receipt. No further receipt will be furnished to you unless specifically requested. Any further inquiries concerning these drugs should be addressed to the DEA District Office which serves your area.

4. There is no provision for payment for drugs surrendered. This is merely a service rendered to registrants enabling them to clear their stocks and records of unwanted items.

5. Drugs should be shipped tape-sealed via prepaid express or certified mail (**return receipt requested**) to Special Agent in Charge, Drug Enforcement Administration, of the DEA District Office which serves your area.

PRIVACY ACT INFORMATION

AUTHORITY: Section 307 of the Controlled Substances Act of 1970 (PL 91-513).
PURPOSE: To document the surrender of controlled substances which have been forwarded by registrants to DEA for disposal.
ROUTINE USES: This form is required by Federal Regulations for the surrender of unwanted Controlled Substances. Disclosures of information from this system are made to the following categories of users for the purposes stated.
  A. Other Federal law enforcement and regulatory agencies for law enforcement and regulatory purposes.
  B. State and local law enforcement and regulatory agencies for law enforcement and regulatory purposes.
EFFECT: Failure to document the surrender of unwanted Controlled Substances may result in prosecution for violation of the Controlled Substances Act.

Under the Paperwork Reduction Act, a person is not required to respond to a collection of information unless it displays a currently valid OMB control number. Public reporting burden for this collection of information is estimated to average 30 minutes per response, including the time for reviewing instructions, searching existing data sources, gathering and maintaining the data needed, and completing and reviewing the collection of information. Send comments regarding this burden estimate or any other aspect of this collection of information, including suggestions for reducing this burden, to the Drug Enforcement Administration, FOI and Records Management Section, Washington, D.C. 20537; and to the Office of Management and Budget, Paperwork Reduction Project no. 1117-0007, Washington, D.C. 20503.

Procedure 50-2 Renewing the Physician's DEA Registration

Name _____ Class _____ Date _____

Sample Only

Completed Internet Form - NOT FOR SUBMISSION
DEA/Control Number -
Submission Date:

APPLICATION FOR REGISTRATION
UNDER CONTROLLED SUBSTANCES ACT OF 1970

Form DEA 224A

NAME: APPLICANT OR BUSINESS (LAST)

(First, MI)

TAX IDENTIFYING NUMBER   AND/OR

SOCIAL SECURITY NUMBER

THE DEBT COLLECTION IMPROVEMENT ACT OF 1996 (PL 104-134) REQUIRES THAT YOU FURNISH YOUR FEDERAL TAXPAYER IDENTIFYING NUMBER TO DEA. THIS NUMBER IS REQUIRED FOR DEBT COLLECTION PROCEDURES SHOULD YOUR FEE BECOME UNCOLLECTABLE. IF YOU DO NOT HAVE A FEDERAL TAXPAYER IDENTIFYING NUMBER, USE YOUR SOCIAL SECURITY NUMBER.

PROPOSED BUSINESS ADDRESS. (WHEN ENTERING A P.O. BOX, YOU ARE REQUIRED TO ENTER A STREET ADDRESS)

CITY

STATE   ZIP CODE

APPLICANT'S BUSINESS PHONE NUMBER

APPLICANT'S FAX NUMBER

REGISTRATION CLASSIFICATION

1. BUSINESS ACTIVITY:		2. INDICATE HERE IF YOU REQUIRE ORDER FORM BOOKS. ☐

3. Drug Schedules. (Fill in all circles that apply)

☑ Schedule II Narcotic   ☑ Schedule II Non Narcotic   ☑ Schedule III Narcotic   ☑ Schedule III Non Narcotic   ☑ Schedule IV   ☑ Schedule V

Practitioner Details

National Provider ID

* Degree

* Birthdate

* Graduation Year

* Professional School

4. All Applicants must answer the following:

Are you currently authorized to prescribe, distribute, dispense, conduct research, or otherwise handle the controlled substances in the schedules for which you are applying under the laws of the state or jurisdiction in which you are operating or propose to operate?

State License No. _____ State: PA
Expire Date:

State Controlled Substance Lic. No. _____ State:
Expire Date: --

1. Has the applicant ever been **convicted of a crime** in connection with controlled substance(s) under state or federal law, or is any such action pending?

2. Has the applicant ever surrendered or had a **federal** controlled substance registration revoked, suspended, restricted or denied, or is any such action pending?

3. Has the applicant ever had a **state** professional license or controlled substance registration revoked, suspended, denied, restricted, or placed on probation, or is any such action pending?

4. If the applicant is a **corporation** (other than a corporation whose stock is owned or traded by the public), association, partnership, or pharmacy, has any officer, partner, stockholder or proprietor been **convicted of a crime** in connection with controlled substances under state or federal law, or ever surrendered, for cause, or had a **federal** controlled substance registration revoked, suspended, restricted or denied, or ever had a **state** professional license or controlled substance registration revoked, suspended, denied, restricted, or placed on probation, or is any such action pending?

PROCEDURE 50-3 RENEWING A PRESCRIPTION BY TELEPHONE

Name _____ Class _____ Date _____

Total Care Clinic
Progress Notes

Name: _____ Chart #: _____

DATE	

Procedure 51-1 Administering Oral Drugs

Name _____ Class _____ Date _____

MEDICATION FLOWSHEET		
Patient Name		**Allergies**
DATE	**MEDICATION**	**REFILLS**
Start / Stop	Dosage/Direction/Amount	Date/Amount/Initials

PROCEDURE 51-2 ADMINISTERING BUCCAL OR SUBLINGUAL DRUGS

Name _____ Class _____ Date _____

MEDICATION FLOWSHEET		
Patient Name		Allergies

DATE	MEDICATION	REFILLS
Start / Stop	Dosage/Direction/Amount	Date/Amount/Initials

PROCEDURE 51-5 GIVING AN INTRADERMAL INJECTION

Name _____ Class _____ Date _____

MEDICATION FLOWSHEET		
Patient Name		Allergies

DATE	MEDICATION	REFILLS			
Start / Stop	Dosage/Direction/Amount	Date/Amount/Initials			

PROCEDURE 51-6 GIVING A SUBCUTANEOUS (SUB-Q) INJECTION

Name _____ Class _____ Date _____

MEDICATION FLOWSHEET						
Patient Name			**Allergies**			
DATE	**MEDICATION**		**REFILLS**			
Start / Stop	Dosage/Direction/Amount		Date/Amount/Initials			

PROCEDURE 51-7 GIVING AN INTRAMUSCULAR INJECTION

Name _____ Class _____ Date _____

MEDICATION FLOWSHEET						
Patient Name			Allergies			
DATE	**MEDICATION**		**REFILLS**			
Start / Stop	Dosage/Direction/Amount		Date/Amount/Initials			

PROCEDURE 51-8 ADMINISTERING INHALATION THERAPY

Name _____ Class _____ Date _____

MEDICATION FLOWSHEET		
Patient Name		**Allergies**
DATE	**MEDICATION**	**REFILLS**
Start / Stop	Dosage/Direction/Amount	Date/Amount/Initials

PROCEDURE 51-9 ADMINISTERING AND REMOVING A TRANSDERMAL PATCH AND PROVIDING PATIENT INSTRUCTION

Name _____ Class _____ Date _____

MEDICATION FLOWSHEET						
Patient Name			Allergies			
DATE	**MEDICATION**		**REFILLS**			
Start / Stop	Dosage/Direction/Amount		Date/Amount/Initials			

Procedure 51-10 Assisting with Administration of an Urethral Drug

Name _____ Class _____ Date _____

MEDICATION FLOWSHEET					
Patient Name			Allergies		
DATE	**MEDICATION**		**REFILLS**		
Start ⟋ Stop	Dosage/Direction/Amount		Date/Amount/Initials		

PROCEDURE 51-11 ADMINISTERING A VAGINAL MEDICATION

Name _____ Class _____ Date _____

MEDICATION FLOWSHEET		
Patient Name		Allergies

DATE	MEDICATION	REFILLS			
Start / Stop	Dosage/Direction/Amount	Date/Amount/Initials			

Procedure 51-12 Administering a Rectal Medication

Name _____ Class _____ Date _____

MEDICATION FLOWSHEET						
Patient Name			**Allergies**			
DATE		**MEDICATION**	**REFILLS**			
Start	Stop	Dosage/Direction/Amount	Date/Amount/Initials			

Procedure 51-13 Administering Eye Medication

Name _____ Class _____ Date _____

MEDICATION FLOWSHEET		
Patient Name		**Allergies**

DATE	MEDICATION	REFILLS			
Start / Stop	Dosage/Direction/Amount	Date/Amount/Initials			

Copyright © 2011 by The McGraw-Hill Companies, Inc.

PROCEDURE 51-14 PERFORMING EYE IRRIGATION

Name _____ Class _____ Date _____

MEDICATION FLOWSHEET						
Patient Name			Allergies			
DATE	**MEDICATION**		**REFILLS**			
Start Stop	Dosage/Direction/Amount		Date/Amount/Initials			

Name _____ Class _____ Date _____

MEDICATION FLOWSHEET		
Patient Name		Allergies

DATE	MEDICATION	REFILLS			
Start / Stop	Dosage/Direction/Amount	Date/Amount/Initials			

PROCEDURE 51-16 PERFORMING EAR IRRIGATION

Name _____ Class _____ Date _____

MEDICATION FLOWSHEET		
Patient Name		Allergies

DATE	MEDICATION	REFILLS
Start / Stop	Dosage/Direction/Amount	Date/Amount/Initials

PROCEDURE 52-1 OBTAINING AN ECG

Name _____ Class _____ Date _____

Total Care Clinic
Progress Notes

Name: _____ Chart #: _____

DATE	

PROCEDURE 52-2 HOLTER MONITORING

Name _____ Class _____ Date _____

Total Care Clinic
Progress Notes

Name: _____ Chart #: _____

DATE	

PROCEDURE 52-3 MEASURING FORCED VITAL CAPACITY USING SPIROMETRY

Name _____ Class _____ Date _____

Total Care Clinic
Progress Notes

Name: _____ Chart #:_____

DATE	

Name _____ Class _____ Date _____

Total Care Clinic
Progress Notes

Name: _____ Chart #: _____

DATE	

PROCEDURE 52-5 OBTAINING A PULSE OXIMETRY READING

Name _____ Class _____ Date _____

Name _____ DOB _____ Date _____

ALLERGIES: _____

Note

Review of Systems

Systems	NL	Note	Systems	NL	Note
Constitutional			Musculoskeletal		
Eyes			Skin/breasts		
ENT/mouth			Neurologic		
Cardiovascular			Psychiatric		
Respiratory			Endocrine		
GI			Hem/lymph		
GU			Allergy/immun		

Current Medicines		Date	Current Diagnosis

H: _____ W: _____ T: _____ P: _____ R: _____

B/P Sitting _____ or Standing _____ Supine _____

Last Tetanus _____

L.M.P. _____

O2 Sat: _____ Pain Scale: _____

Social Habits Yes No

Tobacco ___ ___

Alcohol ___ ___

Rec. Drugs ___ ___

CC:

HPI:

Name _____ DOB _____ Date _____

ALLERGIES: _____

Note

Review of Systems

Systems	NL	Note	Systems	NL	Note
Constitutional			Musculoskeletal		
Eyes			Skin/breasts		
ENT/mouth			Neurologic		
Cardiovascular			Psychiatric		
Respiratory			Endocrine		
GI			Hem/lymph		
GU			Allergy/immun		

Current Medicines		Date	Current Diagnosis

H: _____ W: _____ T: _____ P: _____ R: _____

B/P Sitting _____ or Standing _____ Supine _____

Last Tetanus _____

L.M.P. _____

O2 Sat: _____ Pain Scale: _____

Social Habits Yes No

Tobacco ___ ___

Alcohol ___ ___

Rec. Drugs ___ ___

CC:

HPI:

PROCEDURE 53-1 ASSISTING WITH AN X-RAY EXAMINATION

Name _____ Class _____ Date _____

Total Care Clinic
Progress Notes

Name: _____ Chart #: _____

DATE	

PROCEDURE 53-2 DOCUMENTATION AND FILING TECHNIQUES FOR X-RAYS

Name _____ Class _____ Date _____

X-RAY EXAMINATIONS RECORD

Patient	Date	Type X-Ray	No. Taken	Referring Doctor	Comments

Work Product Documentation/Forms

Use these forms to complete application activities from the textbook or the workbook. Make additional copies for extra practice.

APPOINTMENT RECORD (MULTIPLE PHYSICIANS)

APPOINTMENT RECORD

12 November Tuesday			**13** November Wednesday	
Dr. Torrance	Dr. Hilbert	DOCTOR	Dr. Torrance	Dr. Hilbert
		AM		
Surgery (X)		8 — 00/15/30/45	Surgery (X)	
		9 — 00/15/30/45		
		10 — 00/15/30/45		
		11 — 00/15/30/45		
	Lunch (X)	12 — 00/15/30/45		
		PM		
		1 — 00/15/30/45		
		2 — 00/15/30/45		
		3 — 00/15/30/45		
Staff Meeting at Mercy General (X)		4 — 00/15/30/45		Conference (X)
		5 — 00/15/30/45		

REMARKS & NOTES _____

APPOINTMENT RECORD

12 November Tuesday

Dr. Torrance					
		AM			
		8	00		
			15		
			30		
			45		
		9	00		
			15		
			30		
			45		
		10	00		
			15		
			30		
			45		
		11	00		
			15		
			30		
			45		
		12	00		
			15		
			30		
			45		
		PM			
		1	00		
			15		
			30		
			45		
		2	00		
			15		
			30		
			45		
		3	00		
			15		
			30		
			45		
		4	00		
			15		
			30		
			45		
		5	00		
			15		
			30		
			45		

REMARKS & NOTES _____

BANK STATEMENT RECONCILIATION

<table>
<tr><td colspan="2">

HOW TO BALANCE YOUR CHECKING ACCOUNT

1. Subtract any service charges that appear on this statement from your checkbook balance.
2. Add any interest paid on your checking account to your checkbook balance.
3. Check off (✔) in your checkbook register all checks and pre-authorized transactions listed on your statement.
4. Use the worksheet to list checks you have written, ATM withdrawals, and Point of Sale transactions which are not listed on your statement.

</td></tr>
</table>

5. Enter the closing balance on the statement.	$	.
6. Add any deposits not shown on the statement.	+	.
7. Subtotal	$	.
8. Subtract total transactions outstanding (from worksheet on right).	−	.
9. Account balance (should match balance in your checkbook register).	$	.

IF YOUR ACCOUNT DOES NOT BALANCE

a. Check your addition and subtraction first on this form and then in your checkbook.
b. Be sure the deposit amounts on your statement are the same as those in your checkbook.
c. Be sure all the check amounts on your statement agree with the amounts entered in your checkbook register.
d. Be sure all checks written prior to this reconcilement period but not listed on the statement are listed on the worksheet.
e. Verify that all MAC® ATM, Point of Sale, and other pre-authorized transactions have been recorded in your checkbook register.
f. Review last month's statement to be certain any corrections were entered into your checkbook.

WORKSHEET
Transactions Outstanding

Number or Date	Amount
TOTAL	

BUDGET EXAMPLE

Example:

Expense	Monthly Amount	Annual
Rent	500.00	6000.00
Car payment and insurance	300.00	3600.00
Food	200.00	2400.00
Utilities	200.00	2400.00
Student loan	80.00	960.00
Credit cards	100.00	1200.00
Clothing	100.00	1200.00
Child care	400.00	4800.00
Other	100.00	1200.00
TOTAL	1980.00	23,760.00

Your budget:

Expense	Monthly Amount	Annual
Rent or mortgage		
Car payment and insurance		
Food		
Utilities		
Student loan		
Credit cards		
Clothing		
Child care		
Other		
TOTAL		

CHARTING FORM

Name of Patient: _____   Date: _____

Physician: _____

DAILY LOG

Dr. _____   Date _____

Hour	Patient	Service Provided	Charge	Paid
1				
2				
3				
4				
5				
6				
7				
8				
9				
10				
11				
12				
13				
14				
15				
16				
		Totals		

DEPOSIT TICKET

DEPOSIT TICKET

THOMAS SHEEHAN, M.D.

P.O. BOX 810654
CLINTON, NJ 07472

DATE _____ **20** _____
DEPOSITS MAY NOT BE AVAILABLE FOR IMMEDIATE WITHDRAWAL

_____

CASH	CURRENCY		
	COIN		
LIST CHECKS SINGLY			
TOTAL			
LESS CASH RECEIVED			
NET DEPOSIT			

89-852
622

BE SURE EACH ITEM IS
PROPERLY ENDORSED

FIRST NATIONAL BANK

CLINTON BRANCH

⑆062208525⑆ 526 6612 1‖ 0789

CHECKS AND OTHER ITEMS ARE RECEIVED FOR DEPOSIT SUBJECT TO THE PROVISIONS OF THE UNIFORM COMMERCIAL CODE OR ANY APPLICABLE COLLECTION AGREEMENT

CHECKS LIST SINGLY	DOLLARS	CENTS
1		
2		
3		
4		
5		
6		
7		
8		
9		
10		
11		
12		
13		
14		
15		
TOTAL		

ENTER TOTAL ON THE FRONT SIDE OF THIS TICKET

DISBURSEMENT JOURNAL

Total Care Clinic
Disbursements Journal

Month _____

General Ledger Number _____

DATE	CHECK #	BUSINESS EXPENSE	PAYABLE TO	ACCOUNT #

Copyright © 2011 by The McGraw-Hill Companies, Inc.

EARNINGS RECORD FORM

Name_____ Soc. Sec. No. _____ Dependents _____ Year _____

Address_____ Birth Date _____ Deductions _____

Job Title _____

Employed on _____ Pay Rate _____

Spouse_____ Terminated on _____ Record of Changes

Phone Reason

| Check Number | Period Number | Earnings | | | Deductions | | | | | Net Pay | Cumulative FICA |
		Regular	OT	Total	FICA	Fed. Tax	State	SUI	SDI		
1st Quarter Total											
2d Quarter Total											
3d Quarter Total											
4th Quarter Total											

Record of Changes

Date	Rate

EMERGENCY PREPAREDNESS WORKSHEET
PREPARING FOR AN EMERGENCY – HAZARD ANALYSIS AND PLAN

1. What types of emergency situations have occurred in your community during the last five years?

2. Did any of these situations result in an emergency or disaster declaration? If you do not know, contact your local emergency management office or Red Cross. If a disaster declaration has occurred, describe briefly.

3. Select the five most likely hazards that your community has the highest probability of facing now and in the future.

Natural	Technological	Intentional
Floods	HazMat Spill	Terrorism
Winds	Power Grid Failure	Civil Distrubance
Wild Land Fires	Explosives	WMD (weapons of mass destruction)
Lightning Fires	Chemical Fire	Strikes
Tsunami	Pipeline	Riots
Tornado	Utility Services Failure	Nuclear Attack
Earthquake	Poisons	Nuclear Attack Fallout
Volcanic Eruptions	Radioactive Materials	
Pandemics	Chemical Waste	

4. For each of the five hazards you selected describe what your role as a Medical Assistant will be if the hazard/emergency occurs in your community.

5. Create a list of local community resources that would be utilized if a hazard or emergency occurred in your area.

ENCOUNTER FORM

ENCOUNTER FORM

Tel: (404) 466-0000
Fax: (404) 466-008

Kim Whitley, MD
Ivy Smith, MD
Family Practice
456 Boyard Ct.
Tyrone, Georgia 34450

EIN: 33-0980987

Office Visits	New	Fee	Est.	Fee
☐Level I	99201	75.00	99211	55.00
☐Level II	99202	85.00	99212	75.00
☐Level III	99203	95.00	99213	85.00
☐Level IV	99204	110.00	99214	95.00
☐Level V	99205	125.00	99215	110.00

OFFICE CONSULTS (NEW or EST)

☐Level I	99214	65.00
☐Level II	99242	75.00
☐Level III	99243	85.00
☐Level IV	99244	95.00
☐Level V	99245	110.00

OFFICE PROCEDURES		
☐EKG with interpretation	93000	125.00
☐Oximetry with interpret.	94760	145.00
LABORATORY TESTS		
☐ Blood, occult (feces)	82270	45.00
☐ Skin test Tb, intradermal (PPD) 86580 75.00		
☐		
☐		
☐		
☐		
☐		
☐		

INJECTIONS	
☐ Influenza virus vaccine	90565
☐Admin of influenza vaccine	G0008
☐Pneumococcal vaccine	90732
☐Adm. of Pneumococcal vaccine	G0009
☐Hepatitis B vaccine	90746
☐Adm. of Hepatitis B vaccine	G0010
☐Tetanus toxoid vaccine	90703
☐Immunization admin.	90471
☐	
☐	

DIAGNOSIS

☐ Abnormal heart sounds	785.3	☐Chronic ischemic heart disease	414.9	☐Hypertension	401.9
☐ Abnormal pain	789.0__	☐Chronic obstructive lung disease	496	☐Hormone replacement	V07.4
☐ Abnormal feces	787.7	☐Congestive heart failure	428.0	☐Hyperlipidemia	272.4
☐ Allergic rhinitis	477.9	☐Cough	786.2	☐Hyperthyroidism	242.9__
☐ Anemia, pernicious	281.0	☐Depressive disorder	311	☐Influenza	487.1
☐ Anxiety	300.0__	☐Diabetes mellitus	250.__	☐Loss of weight	783.21
☐ Asthma	493.9__	☐Diarrhea	787.91	☐Nausea	787.02
☐ Atrophy, cerebral	331.0	☐Dizziness	780.4	☐Nausea with vomiting	787.01
☐ B-12 deficiency	281.1	☐Emphysema	492.8	☐Pneumonia	486
☐ Back pain	724.5	☐Fatigue and malaise	780.79	☐Sore throat	462
☐ Bronchitis	490.0	☐Fever	780.6	☐Vaccine, hepatitis B	V05.3
☐ Cardiovascular disease	429.2__	☐Gastritis, atrophic	535.1__	☐Vaccine, Influenza	V04.81
☐ Cervicalgia	723.1	☐Heartburn	787.1	☐Vaccine, pneumococcus	V03.82
☐ Chest pain	786.5__	☐Hematuria	599.7	☐Vaccine, tetanus toxoid	V03.7
☐	_____	☐	_____	☐	_____

PATIENT IDENTIFICATION		FINANCIAL TRANSACTION DATA	
Patient Name:		Invoice No.	
Patient #:		Account No.	
Date of Birth:		Total for Service:	$
ENCOUNTER DATE		Amount Received:	$
Date of Service: ____/____/____		Paid by:	☐ Cash
RETURN VISIT DATE			☐ Check
Date of Return Visit: ____/____/____			☐ Credit Cart
Cashier's Initials:			

NOTE: All Injections are $45.00, and the administrations of injections are $15.00

EQUIPMENT CHECKLIST

Equipment Description	Shannon Photocopier	Model No. 123A9
Serial Number: 56AC90-001L		
Date:	**Action/Comments**	**Initials**
9/17/XX	Machine checked	SM, CMA (AAMA)

FEE SCHEDULE

John Q. Davis, MD

Adult and Pediatric Urology-Infertility

SERVICE RENDERED	CPT	FEE	SERVICE RENDERED	CPT	FEE
Initial OV	99204	$100.00	Condyloma Treatment	54050	$40.00
Follow-up Visit	99214	$65.00	Cystoscopy	52000	$300.00
Fertility Consultation	99243	$140.00	Catheterization	93975	$45.00
Office Consultation	99244	$140.00	Vasectomy	55250	$775.00
Hospital Admission	99223	$150.00	Ultrasonic Guide Needle Biopsy	76942	$395.00
Hospital Consultation	99254	$150.00			
ER Visit	99284	$75.00–$150.00	Prostate Biopsy	55700	$325.00
			Biopsy Gun	A9270	$45.00
Hospital Visit	99232	$55.00	Uroflowmeter	51741	$80.00
Urinalysis w/ Micro	81000	$14.00	Renal Ultrasound	76775	$295.00
Culture	87086	$45.00	Scrotal Ultrasound	76870	$295.00
Stone Analysis	32360	$60.00	Acidic Acid	99070	$20.00
Venipuncture	36415	$10.00	Foley Catheter Starter Set	A4329	$35.00

GROWTH CHART (2–20 YEARS BOYS)

2 to 20 years: Boys
Stature-for-age and Weight-for-age percentiles

NAME _____

RECORD # _____

Mother's Stature _____		Father's Stature _____		
Date	Age	Weight	Stature	BMI*

*To Calculate BMI: Weight (kg) ÷ Stature (cm) ÷ Stature (cm) x 10,000
or Weight (lb) ÷ Stature (in) ÷ Stature (in) x 703

AGE (YEARS)

12 13 14 15 16 17 18 19 20

STATURE

WEIGHT

AGE (YEARS)

2 3 4 5 6 7 8 9 10 11 12 13 14 15 16 17 18 19 20

Published May 30, 2000 (modified 11/21/00).
SOURCE: Developed by the National Center for Health Statistics in collaboration with
the National Center for Chronic Disease Prevention and Health Promotion (2000).
http://www.cdc.gov/growthcharts

CDC
SAFER · HEALTHIER · PEOPLE™

GROWTH CHART (2–20 YEARS GIRLS)

2 to 20 years: Girls
Stature-for-age and Weight-for-age percentiles

NAME _____

RECORD # _____

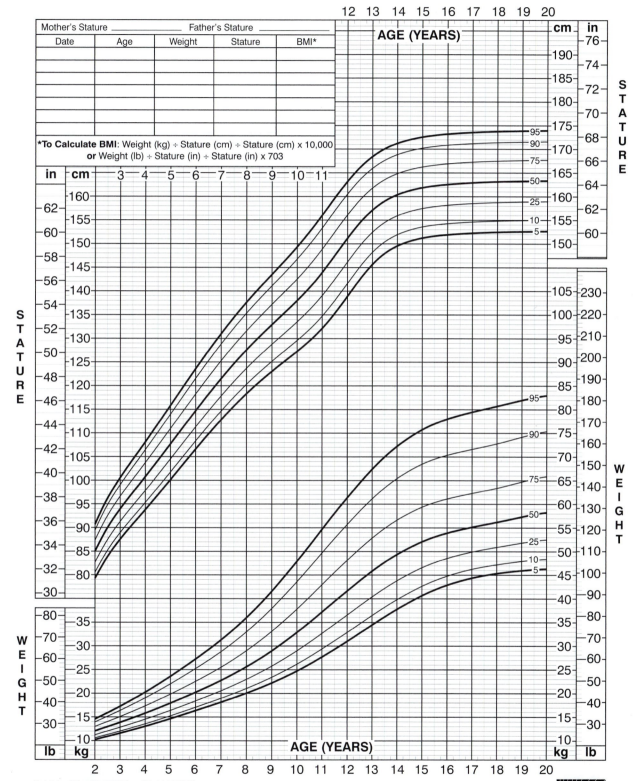

Mother's Stature _____		Father's Stature _____		
Date	Age	Weight	Stature	BMI*

***To Calculate BMI:** Weight (kg) ÷ Stature (cm) ÷ Stature (cm) x 10,000
or Weight (lb) ÷ Stature (in) ÷ Stature (in) x 703

AGE (YEARS)

STATURE

WEIGHT

Published May 30, 2000 (modified 11/21/00).
SOURCE: Developed by the National Center for Health Statistics in collaboration with
the National Center for Chronic Disease Prevention and Health Promotion (2000).
http://www.cdc.gov/growthcharts

CDC
SAFER · HEALTHIER · PEOPLE™

GROWTH CHART (BIRTH–36 MONTHS BOYS)

Birth to 36 months: Boys
Length-for-age and Weight-for-age percentiles

NAME _____

RECORD # _____

Published May 30, 2000 (modified 4/20/01).
SOURCE: Developed by the National Center for Health Statistics in collaboration with
the National Center for Chronic Disease Prevention and Health Promotion (2000).
http://www.cdc.gov/growthcharts

Copyright © 2011 by The McGraw-Hill Companies, Inc.

GROWTH CHART (BIRTH–36 MONTHS GIRLS)

Birth to 36 months: Girls
Length-for-age and Weight-for-age percentiles

NAME _____

RECORD # _____

Published May 30, 2000 (modified 4/20/01).
SOURCE: Developed by the National Center for Health Statistics in collaboration with
the National Center for Chronic Disease Prevention and Health Promotion (2000).
http://www.cdc.gov/growthcharts

Copyright © 2011 by The McGraw-Hill Companies, Inc.

SAFER · HEALTHIER · PEOPLE™

HEALTH HISTORY FORM

HEALTH HISTORY
(Confidential)

Name_____ Today's Date_____

Age_____ Birthdate_____ Date of last physical examination_____

What is your reason for visit?_____

SYMPTOMS Check (✓) symptoms you currently have or have had in the past year.

GENERAL
- ☐ Chills
- ☐ Depression
- ☐ Dizziness
- ☐ Fainting
- ☐ Fever
- ☐ Forgetfulness
- ☐ Headache
- ☐ Loss of sleep
- ☐ Loss of weight
- ☐ Nervousness
- ☐ Numbness
- ☐ Sweats

MUSCLE/JOINT/BONE
Pain, weakness, numbness in:
- ☐ Arms
- ☐ Hips
- ☐ Back
- ☐ Legs
- ☐ Feet
- ☐ Neck
- ☐ Hands
- ☐ Shoulders

GENITO-URINARY
- ☐ Blood in urine
- ☐ Frequent urination
- ☐ Lack of bladder control
- ☐ Painful urination

GASTROINTESTINAL
- ☐ Appetite poor
- ☐ Bloating
- ☐ Bowel changes
- ☐ Constipation
- ☐ Diarrhea
- ☐ Excessive hunger
- ☐ Excessive thirst
- ☐ Gas
- ☐ Hemorrhoids
- ☐ Indigestion
- ☐ Nausea
- ☐ Rectal bleeding
- ☐ Stomach pain
- ☐ Vomiting
- ☐ Vomiting blood

CARDIOVASCULAR
- ☐ Chest pain
- ☐ High blood pressure
- ☐ Irregular heart beat
- ☐ Low blood pressure
- ☐ Poor circulation
- ☐ Rapid heart beat
- ☐ Swelling of ankles
- ☐ Varicose veins

EYE, EAR, NOSE, THROAT
- ☐ Bleeding gums
- ☐ Blurred vision
- ☐ Crossed eyes
- ☐ Difficulty swallowing
- ☐ Double vision
- ☐ Earache
- ☐ Ear discharge
- ☐ Hay fever
- ☐ Hoarseness
- ☐ Loss of hearing
- ☐ Nosebleeds
- ☐ Persistent cough
- ☐ Ringing in ears
- ☐ Sinus problems
- ☐ Vision – Flashes
- ☐ Vision – Halos

SKIN
- ☐ Bruise easily
- ☐ Hives
- ☐ Itching
- ☐ Change in moles
- ☐ Rash
- ☐ Scars
- ☐ Sore that won't heal

MEN only
- ☐ Breast lump
- ☐ Erection difficulties
- ☐ Lump in testicles
- ☐ Penis discharge
- ☐ Sore on penis
- ☐ Other

WOMEN only
- ☐ Abnormal Pap smear
- ☐ Bleeding between periods
- ☐ Breast lump
- ☐ Extreme menstrual pain
- ☐ Hot flashes
- ☐ Nipple discharge
- ☐ Painful intercourse
- ☐ Vaginal discharge
- ☐ Other

Date of last menstrual period_____

Date of last Pap smear_____

Have you had a mammogram?_____

Are you pregnant?_____

Number of children_____

CONDITIONS Check (✓) conditions you have or have had in the past.

- ☐ AIDS
- ☐ Alcoholism
- ☐ Anemia
- ☐ Anorexia
- ☐ Appendicitis
- ☐ Arthritis
- ☐ Asthma
- ☐ Bleeding Disorders
- ☐ Breast Lump
- ☐ Bronchitis
- ☐ Bulimia
- ☐ Cancer
- ☐ Cataracts

- ☐ Chemical Dependency
- ☐ Chicken Pox
- ☐ Diabetes
- ☐ Emphysema
- ☐ Epilepsy
- ☐ Glaucoma
- ☐ Goiter
- ☐ Gonorrhea
- ☐ Gout
- ☐ Heart Disease
- ☐ Hepatitis
- ☐ Hernia
- ☐ Herpes

- ☐ High Cholesterol
- ☐ HIV Positive
- ☐ Kidney Disease
- ☐ Liver Disease
- ☐ Measles
- ☐ Migraine Headaches
- ☐ Miscarriage
- ☐ Mononucleosis
- ☐ Multiple Sclerosis
- ☐ Mumps
- ☐ Pacemaker
- ☐ Pneumonia
- ☐ Polio

- ☐ Prostate Problem
- ☐ Psychiatric Care
- ☐ Rheumatic Fever
- ☐ Scarlet Fever
- ☐ Stroke
- ☐ Suicide Attempt
- ☐ Thyroid Problems
- ☐ Tonsillitis
- ☐ Tuberculosis
- ☐ Typhoid Fever
- ☐ Ulcers
- ☐ Vaginal Infections
- ☐ Venereal Disease

MEDICATIONS List medications you are currently taking

ALLERGIES To medications or substances

Pharmacy Name_____ Phone_____

HEALTH HISTORY FORM *(continued)*

(All information is strictly confidential)

FAMILY HISTORY Fill in health information about your family.

Relation	Age	State of Health	Age at Death	Cause of Death	Check (✓) if your blood relatives had any of the following: Disease	Relationship to you
Father					Arthritis, Gout	
Mother					Asthma, Hay Fever	
Brothers					Cancer	
					Chemical Dependency	
					Diabetes	
					Heart Disease, Strokes	
Sisters					High Blood Pressure	
					Kidney Disease	
					Tuberculosis	
					Other	

HOSPITALIZATIONS

Year	Hospital	Reason for Hospitalization and Outcome

PREGNANCY HISTORY

Year of Birth	Sex of Birth	Complications if any

HEALTH HABITS Check (✓) which substances you use and describe how much you use.

Caffeine	
Tobacco	
Drugs	
Other	

Have you ever had a blood transfusion? ☐ Yes ☐ No
If yes, please give approximate dates. _____

SERIOUS ILLNESS/INJURIES	DATE	OUTCOME

OCCUPATIONAL CONCERNS
Check (✓) if your work exposes you to the following:

Stress	
Hazardous Substances	
Heavy Lifting	
Other	

Your occupation: _____

I certify that the above information is correct to the best of my knowledge. I will not hold my doctor or any members of his/her staff responsible for any errors or omissions that I may have made in the completion of this form.

_____   _____
Signature   Date

_____   _____
Reviewed By   Date

HEALTH INSURANCE CLAIM FORM

1500

HEALTH INSURANCE CLAIM FORM

APPROVED BY NATIONAL UNIFORM CLAIM COMMITTEE 08/05

| | | PICA | | | | | | | PICA | | |

1. MEDICARE   MEDICAID   TRICARE CHAMPUS   CHAMPVA   GROUP HEALTH PLAN   FECA BLK LUNG   OTHER
(Medicare #)   (Medicaid #)   (Sponsor's SSN)   (Member ID#)   (SSN or ID)   (SSN)   (ID)

1a. INSURED'S I.D. NUMBER   (For Program in Item 1)

2. PATIENT'S NAME (Last Name, First Name, Middle Initial)

3. PATIENT'S BIRTH DATE MM | DD | YY   SEX   M ☐   F ☐

4. INSURED'S NAME (Last Name, First Name, Middle Initial)

5. PATIENT'S ADDRESS (No., Street)

6. PATIENT RELATIONSHIP TO INSURED
Self ☐   Spouse ☐   Child ☐   Other ☐

7. INSURED'S ADDRESS (No., Street)

CITY   STATE

8. PATIENT STATUS
Single ☐   Married ☐   Other ☐
Employed ☐   Full-Time Student ☐   Part-Time Student ☐

CITY   STATE

ZIP CODE   TELEPHONE (Include Area Code)   ( )

ZIP CODE   TELEPHONE (Include Area Code)   ( )

9. OTHER INSURED'S NAME (Last Name, First Name, Middle Initial)

10. IS PATIENT'S CONDITION RELATED TO:

11. INSURED'S POLICY GROUP OR FECA NUMBER

a. OTHER INSURED'S POLICY OR GROUP NUMBER

a. EMPLOYMENT? (Current or Previous)
YES ☐   NO ☐

a. INSURED'S DATE OF BIRTH MM | DD | YY   SEX   M ☐   F ☐

b. OTHER INSURED'S DATE OF BIRTH MM | DD | YY   SEX   M ☐   F ☐

b. AUTO ACCIDENT?   PLACE (State)
YES ☐   NO ☐

b. EMPLOYER'S NAME OR SCHOOL NAME

c. EMPLOYER'S NAME OR SCHOOL NAME

c. OTHER ACCIDENT?
YES ☐   NO ☐

c. INSURANCE PLAN NAME OR PROGRAM NAME

d. INSURANCE PLAN NAME OR PROGRAM NAME

10d. RESERVED FOR LOCAL USE

d. IS THERE ANOTHER HEALTH BENEFIT PLAN?
YES ☐   NO ☐   *If yes*, return to and complete item 9 a-d.

READ BACK OF FORM BEFORE COMPLETING & SIGNING THIS FORM.

12. PATIENT'S OR AUTHORIZED PERSON'S SIGNATURE I authorize the release of any medical or other information necessary to process this claim. I also request payment of government benefits either to myself or to the party who accepts assignment below.

SIGNED _____ DATE _____

13. INSURED'S OR AUTHORIZED PERSON'S SIGNATURE I authorize payment of medical benefits to the undersigned physician or supplier for services described below.

SIGNED _____

14. DATE OF CURRENT: MM | DD | YY   ILLNESS (First symptom) OR INJURY (Accident) OR PREGNANCY(LMP)

15. IF PATIENT HAS HAD SAME OR SIMILAR ILLNESS. GIVE FIRST DATE MM | DD | YY

16. DATES PATIENT UNABLE TO WORK IN CURRENT OCCUPATION MM | DD | YY   FROM   MM | DD | YY   TO

17. NAME OF REFERRING PROVIDER OR OTHER SOURCE

17a.   17b. NPI

18. HOSPITALIZATION DATES RELATED TO CURRENT SERVICES MM | DD | YY   FROM   MM | DD | YY   TO

19. RESERVED FOR LOCAL USE

20. OUTSIDE LAB? $ CHARGES
YES ☐   NO ☐

21. DIAGNOSIS OR NATURE OF ILLNESS OR INJURY (Relate Items 1, 2, 3 or 4 to Item 24E by Line)
1. └─── . ───   3. └─── . ───
2. └─── . ───   4. └─── . ───

22. MEDICAID RESUBMISSION CODE   ORIGINAL REF. NO.

23. PRIOR AUTHORIZATION NUMBER

24. A. DATE(S) OF SERVICE						B. PLACE OF SERVICE	C. EMG	D. PROCEDURES, SERVICES, OR SUPPLIES (Explain Unusual Circumstances)		E. DIAGNOSIS POINTER	F. $ CHARGES	G. DAYS OR UNITS	H. EPSDT Family Plan	I. ID. QUAL.	J. RENDERING PROVIDER ID. #
From MM	DD	YY	To MM	DD	YY			CPT/HCPCS	MODIFIER						
1														NPI	
2														NPI	
3														NPI	
4														NPI	
5														NPI	
6														NPI	

25. FEDERAL TAX I.D. NUMBER   SSN ☐ EIN ☐

26. PATIENT'S ACCOUNT NO.

27. ACCEPT ASSIGNMENT? (For govt. claims, see back)
YES ☐   NO ☐

28. TOTAL CHARGE $

29. AMOUNT PAID $

30. BALANCE DUE $

31. SIGNATURE OF PHYSICIAN OR SUPPLIER INCLUDING DEGREES OR CREDENTIALS (I certify that the statements on the reverse apply to this bill and are made a part thereof.)

SIGNED _____ DATE _____

32. SERVICE FACILITY LOCATION INFORMATION

a. NPI   b.

33. BILLING PROVIDER INFO & PH # ( )

a. NPI   b.

NUCC Instruction Manual available at: www.nucc.org

APPROVED OMB-0938-0999 FORM CMS-1500 (08/05)

INSURANCE CLAIM REGISTER

Patient's Name	Insurance Company	Claim Filed		Payment Received		Difference (owed by patient)
		Date	Amount	Date	Amount	

INVENTORY WORKSHEET

Medical Office Supply Inventory

Description	Quantity	On-Hand	Needed	Notes
Batteries	4	0	2	*Check expiration dates*

LABORATORY REPORT FORM

Total Care Clinic
Laboratory Report Form

Patient Name _____Medical Record # _____ Age _____ Sex_____

Address _____ Phone _____

Referring Physician _____

Laboratory Findings:

Date	Blood Test	Patient Result	Normal Value/Range

Date	Urinalysis	Patient Result	Normal Value/Range

Test completed by: _____ _____
                         (Print name)   (Signature)

LABORATORY REQUISITION FORM

Name _____ Class _____ Date _____

70Y

Significant Clinical Information

_____ Fasting   _____ Non-Fasting

CHEMISTRY REQUEST

(EMBOSSING AREA)

Submit Separate Specimens (Not Request Forms) for each Frozen Test Requested.

Account No.

Specimen Date Mo Day Yr	Specimen Time Hr Min	Patient Name (Last)	(First, MI)	Sex	Date of Birth Mo Day Yr	Age Yrs Mos

50 8649 9000 4

Patient I.D. #	Physician I.D.	Patient/Resp. Party's Phone #

* I certify that I have read the informed consent on the back and understand its content.

Responsible Party or Insured's Name (Last, First)	Patient's SS #

_____
Patient's Signature

Address	City	State	Zip Code

Resp. Party's Employer | Medicaid Number/HMO # | Medicare #

Physician Name | UPIN # | Physician's Signature | Provider #

Diagnosis Code (ICD-9) | Insurance Code or Company Name and Address | Insurance I.D. # | Workers Comp. Yes No

Group # or Name | Relationship to Insured (Circle One) 1-Self 2-Spouse 3-Other

---

Urine Random   † Ⓤ Total 24hr. Vol. _____ Ht. _____ Wt. _____

✱ = EDTA Plasma	Ⓢ = Serum	Ⓡ = Red	Ⓖ = Gray	Ⓑ = Light Blue
AF = Amniotic Fluid	Ⓕ = Frozen Specimen	Ⓛ = Lavender	GN = Green	RB = Royal Blue

Apply Labels to Patient Specimens Only
Patient Control No.

50 8649 9000 4

50 8649 9000 4   50 8649 9000 4   50 8649 9000 4
50 8649 9000 4   50 8649 9000 4   50 8649 9000 4

CHEMISTRY REQUEST

Code	Test		Code	Test		Code	Test	
58867	☐ Basic Chemistry	Ⓢ	1693	☐ Glycohemoglobin, Total	Ⓛ	4465	☐ Prolactin	Ⓢ
1396	☐ Amylase, Serum	Ⓢ	4416	☐ HCG, Beta Chain, Quant	Ⓢ	4747	☐ Prostatic Acid Phosphatase (EIA)	Ⓢ
6254	☐ Antinuclear Antibody (ANA), Qnt.	Ⓢ	1453	☐ Hemoglobin A1C	Ⓛ	10322	☐ Prostate-Specific Antigen (PSA)	Ⓢ
1040	☐ BUN	Ⓢ	6510	☐ Hepatitis B Surf Antigen (HBsAg)	Ⓢ	5199	☐ Prothrombin Time	Ⓑ
7419	☐ Carbamazepine (Tegretol)	Ⓢ	6395	☐ Hepatitis B Surf Antibody (Anti HBs)	Ⓢ	6502	☐ Ra Latex Screen	Ⓢ
5009	☐ CBC With Differential	Ⓛ	58560	☐ Hepatitis Profile I (Diagnostic)	Ⓢ	5215	☐ Sedimentation Rate	Ⓛ
2139	☐ CEA-EIA Roche △ ✱		46938	☐ Hepatitis Profile II (Follow up)	Ⓢ	6072	☐ STS	Ⓢ
98012	☐ Chlamydia by DNA Probe △		58552	☐ Hepatitis Profile VII (A and B)	Ⓢ	1149	☐ T₄ (Thyroxine)	Ⓢ
96479	☐ Chlamydia/GC, DNA Probe △		83824	☐ HIV-1 ABS-EIA	Ⓢ	7336	☐ Theophylline (Theo-Dur)	Ⓢ
1065	☐ Cholesterol, Total	Ⓢ	7625	☐ Lead, Blood	RB	620	☐ Thyroid Profile I	Ⓢ
1370	☐ Creatinine, Serum	Ⓢ	235002	☐ Lipid Profile I (Lipoprotein Analysis)	Ⓢ	27011	☐ Thyroid Profile II	Ⓢ
7385	☐ Digoxin (Lanoxin)	Ⓢ	235028	☐ Lipid Profile III (incl Apolipoproteins)	Ⓢ	4259	☐ TSH, 3rd Generation	Ⓢ
604	☐ Electrolytes (Na, K, Cl)	Ⓢ	7708	☐ Lithium	Ⓢ	810	☐ Vitamin B-12 and Folate	Ⓢ
4598	☐ Ferritin	Ⓢ	505	☐ Liver Profile A	Ⓢ			
4309	☐ Follicle Stim. Hormone (FSH)	Ⓢ	7401	☐ Phenytoin (Dilantin)	Ⓢ		**URINE CHEMISTRY**	
1818	☐ Glucose	Ⓖ	1180	☐ Potassium	Ⓢ	3038	☐ Urinalysis (Microscopic if indicated)	Ⓤ
	☐ Glucose Tolerance	Ⓖ	4556	☐ Pregnancy, Serum, Ql.	Ⓢ	3772	☐ Urinalysis, Complete	Ⓤ
	Indicate No. Of Tubes		53520	☐ Prenatal Profile B with HBsAG	2-L Ⓡ			

ADDITIONAL TESTS

Test #		Name
☐	1375	24 Hr Urine for Protein Ⓤ
☐	4550	Pregnancy, Urine, Qul Ⓤ

LETTERHEAD EXAMPLE

Comprehensive Medical Associates

2345 Peachtree-Wimberly Place
Ste. 234
Atlanta, Georgia 30303
(404) 223-0987

MEDICAL HISTORY FORM

Total Care Clinic
Medical History

Name _____ Age _____ Sex _____ S M W D
Address _____ Phone _____ Date _____

Occupation _____ Ref. by _____
Chief Complaint _____

Present Illness _____
_____
_____
_____

History —Military _____
—Social _____
—Family _____
—Marital _____
—Menstrual _____ Menarche _____ Para. _____ LMP _____
—Illness Measles ___ Pert. ___ Var. ___ Pneu. ___ Pleur. ___ Typh. ___ Mal. ___ Rh. Fev. ___ Sc. Fev. ___ Diphth. ___ Other ___
—Surgery _____
—Allergies _____
—Current Medications _____

Physical Examination

Temp. _____ Pulse _____ Resp. _____ BP _____ Ht. _____ Wt. _____
General Appearance _____ Skin _____ Mucous Membrane _____
Eyes: _____ Vision _____ Pupil _____ Fundus _____
Ears: _____
Nose: _____
Throat: _____ Pharynx _____ Tonsils _____
Chest: _____ Breasts _____
Heart: _____
Lungs: _____
Abdomen: _____
Genitalia: _____
Rectum: _____
Pelvic: _____
Extremities: _____ Pulses: _____
Lymph Nodes: _____ Neck _____ Axilla _____ Inguinal _____ Abdominal _____
Neurological: _____
Diagnosis: _____
_____
_____

Treatment: _____
_____
_____

Laboratory Findings:
Date _____ Blood _____
_____
_____

Date _____ Urine _____
_____
_____
_____
_____
_____
_____

MEDICAL RECORD (VITAL SIGNS)

TOTAL CARE CLINIC

Facility _____

DATE	TIME	T	P	R	BP		DATE	TIME	T	P	R	BP	

Patient Name:	Last:	First:	Middle:	Physician:

VITAL SIGN CHART # _____

MEDICAL RECORD (HEIGHT AND WEIGHT)

TOTAL CARE CLINIC

Facility _____

MONTH: _____ YEAR: _____

DATE	WEIGHT	HEIGHT

MONTH: _____ YEAR: _____

DATE	WEIGHT	HEIGHT

MONTH: _____ YEAR: _____

DATE	WEIGHT	HEIGHT

MONTH: _____ YEAR: _____

DATE	WEIGHT	HEIGHT

MONTH: _____ YEAR: _____

DATE	WEIGHT	HEIGHT

MONTH: _____ YEAR: _____

DATE	WEIGHT	HEIGHT

MONTH: _____ YEAR: _____

DATE	WEIGHT	HEIGHT

MONTH: _____ YEAR: _____

DATE	WEIGHT	HEIGHT

MONTH: _____ YEAR: _____

DATE	WEIGHT	HEIGHT

MONTH: _____ YEAR: _____

DATE	WEIGHT	HEIGHT

MONTH: _____ YEAR: _____

DATE	WEIGHT	HEIGHT

MONTH: _____ YEAR: _____

DATE	WEIGHT	HEIGHT

Patient Name:	Last:	First:	Middle:	Admin. Number:
Physician:				

WEIGHT RECORD

MEDICATION FLOWSHEET

MEDICATION FLOWSHEET						
Patient Name			Allergies			
DATE	**MEDICATION**		**REFILLS**			
Start / Stop	Dosage/Direction/Amount		Date/Amount/Initials			

PATIENT LEDGER CARD

Patient's Name _____

Home Phone _____ Work Phone _____

Social Security No. _____

Employer _____

Insurance _____

Policy # _____

Person Responsible for Charges (if Different from Patient) _____

| Date | Reference | Description | Charge | Credits | | Current Balance |
				Payments	Adj.	
		Balance Forward ⟶				

Please Pay Last Amount in This Column ▲

OV—Office Visit
X—X-ray
ROA—Received on Account

C—Consultation
NC—No Charge
MA—Missed Appointment

EX—Examination
INS—Insurance

PATIENT REGISTRATION FORM

Community Health Center • 6508 South Street • Kokomo, IN 46902
(317) 555-1234 • Fax: (317) 555-1245

Patient Registration
Patient Information

Name: _____ Today's Date: _____

Address: _____

City: _____ State: _____ Zip Code: _____

Telephone (Home): _____ (Work): _____ (Cell): _____

Birthdate: _____ Age: _____ Sex: M F No. of Children _____ Marital Status: M S W D

Social Security Number: _____ Employer: _____ Occupation: _____

Primary Physician: _____

Referred by: _____

Person to Contact in Emergency: _____

Emergency Telephone: _____

Special Needs: _____

Responsible Party

Party Responsible for Payment: Self   Spouse   Parent   Other

Name (If Other Than Self): _____

Address: _____

City: _____ State: _____ Zip Code: _____

Primary Insurance

Primary Medical Insurance: _____

Insured party: Self   Spouse   Parent   Other

ID#/Social Security No.: _____ Group/Plan No.: _____

Name (If Other Than Self): _____

Address: _____

City: _____ State: _____ Zip Code: _____

Secondary Insurance

Secondary Medical Insurance: _____

Insured party: Self   Spouse   Parent   Other

ID#/Social Security No.: _____ Group/Plan No.: _____

Name (If Other Than Self): _____

Address: _____

City: _____ State: _____ Zip Code: _____

PAYROLL REGISTER

GENESYS FAMILY MEDICINE
Payroll Register

Period Ending: 2/1/20XX

Employee ID	Employee Name	Hours Worked	Hourly Rate	Regular Pay	Overtime Pay	No. of Exempts	Gross Pay	Taxes and Deductions	Other Deduction	Net Pay
1	Jay Christopher	160	17.50	2800	78.00	1-S	$2,878.00	$325.00	$20.00	$2,533.00
2	Grace Ososona	168	13.00	2184	56.00	2-M		$139.78	$0.00	
3	Vanessa Vaughn	160	12.00	1920	0.00	3-M		$267.50	$38.00	
4	Jessica Jules	132	16.50	2178	23.00	2-S		$312.00	$150.00	
5	Kent Harrell	168	13.50	2268	78.00	1-M		$156.89	$20.00	
6	Henrietta Gbanga	160	14.00	2240	0.00	1-M		$389.67	$35.00	
7	Sheila Ferguson	168	11.00	1848	96.00	4-M		$116.00	$25.00	
8							$0.00	$0.00		$0.00
9							$0.00	$0.00		$0.00
10							$0.00	$0.00		$0.00
11							$0.00	$0.00		$0.00
12							$0.00	$0.00		$0.00
13							$0.00	$0.00		$0.00
14							$0.00	$0.00		$0.00

Using the payroll register above, calculate and complete the rest of the employees' net pay for the month. The first employee has been completed for you.

PROGRESS NOTES

Total Care Clinic
Progress Notes

Name: _____   Chart #: _____

DATE	

PURCHASE ORDER

PURCHASE ORDER #2532

Submitted by: _____

Order Number: _____

Date Ordered: _____

Date Required: _____

SHIP TO: Dr. Carlotta Montoni
201 Oak Walk, Suite 32
Gilead, PA 19034

PHONE: 215-610-4120

	ITEM	DESCRIPTION/MODEL	COLOR	SIZE	QUANTITY	PRICE EACH	TOTAL
1.							
2.							
3.							
4.							
5.							
6.							
7.							
8.							
						TOTAL	

Approved: _____   Date: _____

RECONCILING BANK STATEMENT

HANNIFIELD BANK & TRUST

P. O. Box 4560912
Orlando, FL 34567-0912

To change your address, please call 1-800-426-6434. Business clients call 1-800-786-6789.

Complete this section to balance this statement to your transaction register.

MONTH _____ YEAR_____

Bank Balance Shown on Statement	$ **1326.00**

Add (+) $_____
Deposits not shown on this
statement (if any).   _____
                                                                     _____
                                                                     _____

                 Total (+) $_____

Subtract (-)
Check and other items outstanding but not paid on this statement
(if any).

                                    $_____

                                    _____

                                    _____

                                    _____

Total (-)	$ _____
Balance	$ _____

Your Transaction Register Balance $ **1807.00**

Add (+) $_____
Other credits shown on this
statement but not in transaction   _____
register.   _____
                                                     _____

Add (+) $_____
Interest paid (for use in balancing interest-bearing
accounts only).
Total (+) $_____

Subtract (-) other debits shown on this statement
but not in transaction register.

Service Fees (if any) $ **18.00**

                               _____ **60.00**

                               _____

Total (-)	$ _____
Balance	$ _____ **1885.00**

These balances should agree

In case of errors or questions about electronic transfers, telephone us at the number listed shown on the statement, or write us at the address shown on the statement within 60 days of the statement on which the problem first appeared. Please give us your name and account number, describe the transaction and explain your concern.

SUPERBILL

Lakeridge Medical Group
262 East Pine Street, Suite 100
Santa Cruz, CA 95062

☐ PRIVATE ☐ BLUECROSS ☐ IND. ☐ MEDICARE ☐ MEDI-CAL ☐ HMO ☐ PPO

PATIENT'S LAST NAME	FIRST	ACCOUNT #	BIRTHDATE / /	SEX ☐ MALE ☐ FEMALE	TODAY'S DATE / /
INSURANCE COMPANY	SUBSCRIBER		PLAN #	SUB. #	GROUP

ASSIGNMENT: I hereby assign my insurance benefits to be paid directly to the undersigned physician. I am financially responsible for non-covered services.
SIGNED: (Patient, or Parent, if Minor)
DATE: / /

RELEASE: I hereby authorize the physician to release to my insurance carrers any information required to process this claim.
SIGNED: (Patient, or Parent, if Minor)
DATE: / /

✔	DESCRIPTION	M/Care	CPT/Mod	DxRe	FEE	✔	DESCRIPTION	M/Care	CPT/Mod	DxRe	FEE	✔	DESCRIPTION	M/Care	CPT/Mod	DxRe	FEE
	OFFICE CARE						PROCEDURES						INJECTIONS/IMMUNIZATIONS				
	NEW PATIENT						Tread Mill (In Office)		93015				Tetanus		90718		
	Brief		99201				24 Hour Holter		93224				Hypertet	J1670	90782		
	Limited		99202				If Medicare (Set up Fee)		93225				Pneumococcal		90732		
	Intermediate		99203				Physician Interpret		93227				Influenza		90724		
	Extended		99204				EKG w/Interpretation		93000				TB Skin Test (PPD)		86585		
	Comprehensive		99205				EKG (Medicare)		93005				Antigen Injection-Single		95115		
							Sigmoidoscopy		45300				Multiple		95117		
	ESTABLISHED PATIENT						Sigmoidoscopy, Flexible		45330				B12 Injection	J3420	90782		
	Minimal		99211				Sigmoidos. , Flex. w/Bx.		45331				Injection, IM		90782		
	Brief		99212				Spirometry, FEV/FVC		94010				Compazine	J0780	90782		
	Limited		99213				Spirometry, Post-Dilator		94060				Demerol	J2175	90782		
	Intermediate		99214										Vistaril	J3410	90782		
	Extended		99215				LABORATORY						Susphrine	J0170	90782		
	Comprehensive		99215				Blood Draw Fee		36415				Decadron	J0890	90782		
							Urinalysis, Chemical		81005				Estradiol	J1000	90782		
	CONSULTATION-OFFICE						Throat Culture		87081				Testosterone	J1080	90782		
	Focused		99241				Occult Blood		82270				Lidocaine	J2000	90782		
	Expanded		99242				Pap Handling Charge		99000				Solumedrol	J2920	90782		
	Detailed		99243				Pap Life Guard		88150-90				Solucortef	J1720	90782		
	Comprehensive 1		99244				Gram Stain		87205				Hydeltra	J1690	90782		
	Comprehensive 2		99245				Hanging Drop		87210				Pen Procaine	J2510	90788		
	Dr.						Urine Drug Screen		99000								
	Case Management		98900										INJECTIONS - JOINT/BURSA				
													Small Joints		20600		
	Post-op Exam		99024										Intermediate		20605		
							SUPPLIES						Large Joints		20610		
													Trigger Point		20550		
													MISCELLANEOUS				

DIAGNOSIS:

		ICD-9														
	Abdominal Pain	789.0		Gout	274.0		C.V.A. - Acute	436.		Electrolyte Dis.	276.9		Herpes Simplex	054.9
	Abscess (Site)	682.9		Asthma	493.90		Cere. Vas. Accid. (Old)	438		Fatigue	780.7		Herpes Zoster	053.9
	Adverse Drug Rx	995.2		Asthmatic Bronchitis	493.90		Cerumen	380.4		Fibrocys. Br. Dis	610.1		Hydrocele	603.9
	Alcohol Detox	291.8		Atrial Fib.	427.31		Chestwall Pain	786.59		Fracture (Site)	829.0		Hyperlipidemia	272.4
	Alcoholism	303.90		Atrial Tachi.	427.0		Cholecystitis	575.0		Open/Close			Hypertension	401.9
	Allergic Rhinitis	477		Bowel Obstruct.	560.9		Cholelithiasis	574.00		Fungal Infect. (Site)	110.8		Hyperthyroidism	242.9
	Allergy	995.3		Breast Mass	611.72		COPD	492.8		Gastric Ulcer	531.90		Hypothyroidism	244.9
	Alzheimer's Dis.	290.1		Bronchitis	490		Cirrhosis	571.5		Gastritis	535.0		Labyrinthitis	386.30
	Anemia	285.9		Bursitis	727.3		Cong. Heart Fail.	428.9		Gastroenteritis	558.9		Lipoma (Site)	214.9
	Anemia - Pernicious	281.0		Cancer, Breast (Site)	174.9		Conjunctivitis	372.30		G.I. Bleeding	578.9		Lymphoma	202.8
	Angina	413.9		Metastatic (Site)	199.1		Contusion (Site)	924.9		Glomerulonephritis	583.9		Mit. Valve Prolapse	424.0
	Anxiety Synd.	300.00		Colon	153.9		Costochondritis	733.99		Headache	784.0		Myocard. Infarction (Area)	410.9
	Appendicitis	541		Cancer, Rectal	154.1		Depression	311.		Headache, Tension	307.81		M.I., Old	412
	Arterioscl. H.D.	414.0		Lung (Site)	162.9		Dermatitis	692.9		Migraine (Type)	346.9		Myositis	729.1
	Arthritis, Osteo.	715.90		Skin (Site)	173.9		Diabetes Mellitus	250.00		Hemorrhoids	455.6		Nausea/Vomiting	787.0
	Rheumatoid	714.0		Card. Arrhythmia (Type)	427.9		Diabetic Ketosis	250.1		Hernia, Hiatal	553.3		Neuralgia	729.2
	Lupus	710.0		Cardiomyopathy	425.4		Diverticulitis	562.11		Inguinal	550.9		Nevus (Site)	216.9
				Cellulitis (Site)	682.9		Diverticulosis	562.10		Hepatitis	573.3		Obesity	278.0

DIAGNOSIS: (IF NOT CHECKED ABOVE)

SERVICES PERFORMED AT: ☐ Office ☐ E.R. ☐ ☐ CLAIM CONTAINS NO ORDERED REFERRING SERVICE

REFERRING PHYSICIAN & I.D. NUMBER

RETURN APPOINTMENT INFORMATION:
5 - 10 - 15 - 20 - 30 - 40 - 60
[DAYS] [WKS.] [MOS.] [PRN]

NEXT APPOINTMENT
M - T - W - TH - F - S
DATE / / TIME:
AM
PM

ACCEPT ASSIGNMENT?
☐ YES
☐ NO

DOCTOR'S SIGNATURE

INSTRUCTIONS TO PATIENT FOR FILING INSURANCE CLAIMS:		
1. Complete upper portion of this form, sign and date. 2. Attach this form to your own insurance company's form for direct reimbursement. **MEDICARE PATIENTS - DO NOT SEND THIS TO MEDICARE. WE WILL SUBMIT THE CLAIM FOR YOU.**	☐ CASH ☐ CHECK # ___ ☐ VISA ☐ MC ☐ CO-PAY	TOTAL TODAY'S FEE
		OLD BALANCE
		TOTAL DUE
		AMOUNT REC'D. TODAY

GAYLORD